D1000108

Hoover Institution Publications

NATO in Quest of Cohesion

This work is based on a conference held at The Center for Strategic Studies, Georgetown University

NATO in Quest of Cohesion

A Confrontation of Viewpoints at

THE CENTER FOR STRATEGIC STUDIES
GEORGETOWN UNIVERSITY

Edited by

Karl H. Cerny *and* Henry W. Briefs

Foreword by

General Lauris Norstad

Published for the

HOOVER INSTITUTION ON WAR, REVOLUTION, AND PEACE

by

FREDERICK A. PRAEGER, *Publishers*

New York • Washington • London

341.1
C41n

h.h.

The Hoover Institution on War, Revolution, and Peace, founded at Stanford University in 1919 by Herbert Hoover, is a center for advanced study and research on public and international affairs in the twentieth century. The views expressed in its publications are entirely those of the authors and do not necessarily reflect the views of the Hoover Institution.

FREDERICK A. PRAEGER, *Publishers*
111 Fourth Avenue, New York, N.Y. 10003, U.S.A.
77-79 Charlotte Street, London W.1, England

Published in the United States of America in 1965
by Frederick A. Praeger, Inc., Publishers

All rights reserved

© 1965 by the Board of Trustees of
the Leland Stanford Junior University

Library of Congress Catalog Card Number: 65-20045

Printed in the United States of America

Foreword

There is no more important order of business for the Atlantic Community than NATO's quest for cohesion. Unfortunately, the relationship among allies has deteriorated over the years. As it continues to weaken, fears arise that this erosion of one of the very pillars of our policy, if not checked and rebuilt, will destroy the Western alliance.

I, for one, am confident that this will not happen. But the climate of solid trust and confidence must be restored to its previous high. Only a unified West can hope to achieve our goals of peace and freedom and turn the subtleties of the current Soviet strategy to our advantage. It seems to me that the threat remains although it becomes somewhat shadowy as the Kremlin substitutes less flamboyant pressures for the nuclear blackmail of the 1950's in its effort to divide and erode the free world. Under these circumstances, Western unity becomes more elusive; the danger of lapsing into euphoria increases.

Such a climate could undermine NATO. Most of U. S. foreign policy—whether directed toward the Soviet Union, toward Europe, toward the Far East or Southeast Asia—is based upon the assumption that the fifteen nations of NATO remain firmly united against serious threat, external or internal. That this assumption is indeed well founded in the case of dramatic and clearly defined threats is evidenced by the strong and unanimous support given the United States during the Cuban crisis of 1962, and the prompt action taken in late 1964 to meet Britain's monetary crisis.

JUL 22 '66

THE HUNT LIBRARY
CARNEGIE INSTITUTE OF TECHNOLOGY

The problem facing our policymakers is one of how best to contribute to the restoration of unity among the fifteen members of the alliance. I think it is apparent both from the views expressed in this volume and from public statements by our allies that many of those allies have developed a resistance, even a resentment, to the type of "hard sell" that has sometimes been used by the United States—for example, in the case of our MLF proposal. Hence, I think it was vastly reassuring when, toward the end of 1964, President Johnson made it clear that his would be a new approach:

> We want to work out with all nations the best solution possible. We are not going to be adamant in our attitudes. We are going to try to be cooperative and helpful, and we hope that we can obtain a meeting of the minds of all of our allies.

The Cuban crisis in 1962 and the action taken to meet the recent British monetary problem add weight to already overwhelming evidence that there are many problems involving our vital interests, the vital interests of the free world, with which no one country, however powerful, can deal by itself. In this category are found almost all the major matters of foreign policy, of finance and economy, of defense. It is clearly indicated that greater-than-national means are needed to deal with these broader-than-national questions, and this has led many good people on both sides of the ocean to consider the idea of establishing a true Atlantic Community. President Kennedy made a very strong case for this when on the 4th of July, 1962, he declared the willingness of the United States to join with its allies in signing a declaration of interdependence. He said:

> Acting on our own by ourselves, we cannot establish justice throughout the world. We cannot insure its domestic tranquility, or provide for its common defense, or promote its general welfare, or secure the blessings of liberty to ourselves and our posterity. But joined with other free nations we can do all this and more. We can assist the developing nations to throw off the yoke of poverty. We can balance our worldwide trade and payments at the highest possible level of growth. We can mount a deterrent powerful enough to deter any aggression and ultimately we can help achieve a world of law and free choice, banishing the world of war and coercion.

Earlier President Eisenhower sent a message to the NATO Council in which he said essentially the same thing:

> Together we must build a Community which will best safeguard the individual freedom and national values of our various peoples and at the same time provide effective means of dealing with problems with which none of us, alone, can now deal effectively.

And now President Johnson in speaking on this subject has said:

> There are no problems which we cannot solve together, and there are very few which any of us can settle by himself. The United States sees no safe future for ourselves and none for any other Atlantic nation in a policy of narrow national self-interest.

These are not American views alone; they are shared by leaders on the other side of the Atlantic as well. Support for Atlantic unity is almost unanimous, but the precise relationship we are seeking is not clear. Among those who have shown particular interest in this subject one finds the widest range of views as to the proper political form—views extending from "union now" on the one hand, to the other end of the spectrum which calls simply for strengthening existing institutions and achieving a more or less permanent basis for greater cooperation. These various viewpoints are well aired in this volume.

But certainly most people feel that some progress should be made—some initial step taken at this time. In fact, action is long overdue.

Establishing new and important relationships between governments, between peoples except under the lash of necessity, under the threat of attack, always involves difficulties. It is for this reason, I am sure, that this government and the other NATO governments have not yet taken any action to study formally and officially this question of the Atlantic Community—the appointment of a special governmental commission for this purpose, for example.

But it is *because* of the difficulties, *because* of the differences, because we are losing so much of our momentum that I feel strongly that action should be taken now. We should remember that the things that unite us are greater, stronger, and more important than the problems that remain unresolved, that seem to divide us. Some difficulties are perhaps inevitable under any circumstance, but a number of the present differences between the allies, by their very existence, give evidence that we have not yet found the right answers, we have not yet found the machinery for dealing effectively, collectively, with the great pressing problems with which none of our governments can deal effectively alone. This, I believe, is another proper and useful field for initiative by our government—and again in this volume are found a number of proposals to this end.

It is for these reasons that I believe The Center for Strategic Studies at Georgetown University was indeed wise to bring this broad subject into focus in a single volume and to develop it on the basis of its three aspects—political, military, and economic. This volume includes, in the essays and in the debate, the contributions of eminent experts of both practical and scholarly backgrounds in these three areas.

This volume, the final product of the effort of distinguished experts, began with their study papers. In May of 1964 these experts debated the points in their papers before an equally distinguished group of over 250 persons from the executive and legislative branches of our government, from the research and university community, and from the Atlantic Council. Those in the audience had an opportunity to make their comments. The viewpoints varied, as indeed the participants had been invited with the idea that no synthetic consensus, no array of diluted recommendations, was sought. Rather, the search was for a definition of the real problems in NATO's quest for cohesion, for an exchange of views that would provide for better understanding of all the views. This forum for debate, afforded by Georgetown University in our Nation's Capital, may be a help in the restoration and strengthening of the alliance to which we may hope our government will now rededicate its efforts. Therefore these essays and debates become increasingly important, not just for the student and the informed public, but also for our policymakers.

LAURIS NORSTAD

Acknowledgments

We wish to acknowledge our debt to all who made this book possible. To the contributors, we express our admiration for their unfailing co-operation in resolving the inevitable questions and points editors feel it necessary to raise. We are also grateful to David M. Abshire and Richard V. Allen of The Center for Strategic Studies for their steady advice and counsel. But our special thanks belong to Mary Catherine McCarthy of the Center's staff. Her expert preparation of the manuscript for publication, with its great burden of attention to every sort of detail, amounted to more than a technical contribution.

K.H.C.
H.W.B.

CONTENTS

Foreword	*Lauris Norstad*	v

I. THE ISSUES

Karl H. Cerny and Henry W. Briefs	The Issues in Perspective	3
George W. Ball	U.S. Policy Toward NATO	11

II. THE DIALOGUE

The Nuclear Question	23
Economic Problems	65
The Political Dimension	99

III. AMERICAN AND EUROPEAN ESSAYS

Hans J. Morgenthau	The Crisis of the Alliance	125
Robert Strausz-Hupé	The Crisis of Political Leadership	135
Klaus Knorr	Perspective on Nuclear Policy	149
James E. Moore	The Military Effectiveness of NATO	161
W. Randolph Burgess	Practical Considerations About Cooperation	177
Friedrich Ruge	The Need for a Common Nuclear Strategy	199

André Beaufre | Nuclear Deterrence and World Strategy | 215

Stefan T. Possony | The Problem of the Nuclear Trigger | 225

Sir John Slessor | The Case for a Multinational Nuclear Strike Force | 239

Philip E. Mosely | Requirements for a European Deterrent in the 1970's | 257

Kurt Birrenbach | European Integration and Atlantic Partnership | 271

John W. Holmes | The Advantages of Diversity in NATO | 289

Lawrence B. Krause | Economic Problems of the Alliance | 303

Stanislaw Wasowski | The Trend Toward Economic Cooperation | 321

Karl Brandt | An Economic Strategy for NATO | 327

Pierre Uri | Economic Dimensions of Atlantic Partnership | 345

Maurice Allais | Toward an Integrated Atlantic Community | 359

Hendrik Brugmans | Toward Constructive World Leadership | 387

Milorad Drachkovitch | NATO and East-Central Europe | 405

Robert Kleiman | Background for Atlantic Partnership | 431

Notes on Contributors 461

Index 467

NATO in Quest of Cohesion

I

The Issues

The Issues in Perspective

—THE EDITORS

Ever since the establishment of NATO in 1949, commentators have invariably balanced their discussion of NATO's accomplishments with warnings about the problems and dangers which lie ahead. During this fifteenth year of NATO's existence, the pattern of commentary on the Atlantic alliance has changed. Current preoccupation is focused almost exclusively on the threats to the future of the alliance. Against the background of disputes over the role of France in NATO, over the Cyprus issue, and over trade policy toward the Sino-Soviet bloc, the most persistent theme has been the lack of cohesion within the alliance, Erosion of the alliance, if not its actual dissolution, no longer seem to be remote possibilities; increasingly they have become topics of serious discussion.

An assessment of the present crisis in NATO relations requires a knowledge both of the difficulties which beset the alliance and of the prospects for their resolution on a mutually beneficial basis. This book is designed to serve as a guide for such an assessment. In the Dialogue, the confrontation of conflicting views held by American and European experts yields a well-defined picture of the basic issues relevant to an appraisal of NATO. The fuller development of the various positions is found in the essays that follow. Despite differences in emphasis and coverage, they provide a full examination of the strategic, economic, and political dimensions of the problem of alliance cohesion. Together, the

Dialogue and the essays register agreement or disagreement not only on a range of issues but also on likely solutions to major problems facing the alliance. In this way, the present book gives some indication of the prospects for NATO's quest for cohesion.

Quite clearly, the views of the experts point to the need for something other than minor adjustments within the NATO alliance. The proliferation of nuclear weapons, the changing nature of the Soviet threat, the economic and political resurgence of Europe—these developments have undermined the foundations of the NATO that was established in 1949.

Although still the predominant member of the alliance, the United States is no longer accepted—openly or tacitly—as the unquestioned leader. Significantly, the merits of specific United States policies are not the only points at issue. Equally if not more important are the ways in which the policies have been formulated. The testimony of the experts is itself indicative. Seldom do they explore the substance of such controversial policy issues as disarmament or Cyprus. And when they do explore issues such as coordination and control of nuclear weapons or trade policy toward the Sino-Soviet bloc, their interest goes beyond the substance of particular policy questions. They are just as interested in the role that will be allotted to NATO's partners in the making of key decisions. On the evidence of this book's contributors, therefore, NATO's quest for cohesion must include above all an adequate solution to the demand of our partners in NATO for a meaningful share in the formulation of alliance policy.

But in which policy areas should there be an "alliance" policy? How far should shared control in such areas extend? Within this framework, how best can the sharing of control be effected?

Military Policy

Predictably, since today as in the past NATO is chiefly a defensive military alliance, the contributors to this volume look upon military policy as the key field for an "alliance" policy. None of the participants suggests that NATO may be outliving its military usefulness. None speculates about the advantages of deemphasizing NATO through, for example, the signing of a nonaggression treaty with the Warsaw Pact countries. On the contrary, the implicit agreement is that NATO still performs an important military function. Explicitly, moreover, the contributors agree that the basic need is for some modification of the United States nuclear monopoly. What divides them sharply is the determination of the extent and the means of modifying the United States monopoly.

To a substantial degree these differences come to light in the statements of support for, or opposition to, the United States-sponsored Multilateral Force (MLF) proposal. Those who support MLF view the effort to create a mixed-manned surface fleet equipped with Polaris weapons as a desirable alternative to the proliferation of national nuclear deterrents and as a significant United States initiative to provide Europeans with a greater voice in nuclear strategy. Those who oppose MLF—and they are a majority of the contributors to this volume—criticize the proposal because of the limited role accorded to the Europeans and the misplaced emphasis on such matters as mixed-manning and the dangers of national nuclear deterrents.

Not all of the opponents of the MLF, however, agree with all of these criticisms nor do they agree on the desirable alternative. Some call for more effective coordination of existing national nuclear capabilities. Specific proposals range from a wider application of the techniques of Berlin contingency planning to the use of electronic computers for pre-programming allied responses to certain potential moves of the enemy. Other opponents of MLF speak of the need to create a multinational nuclear strike force under NATO. Since the major purpose of such a force would be the direct defense of Europe, it should have the capability of long-range interdiction. Finally, still other opponents of MLF point to the desirability of first creating an integrated European nuclear deterrent and then coordinating the European and United States deterrents under the aegis of NATO.

Although the MLF controversy is an important index to the causes of division within NATO, exclusive focus upon the differences between MFL proponents and opponents can result in the neglect of important areas of agreement and in a failure to discriminate between fundamental and more easily surmountable differences. For example, whatever their views on MLF, the contributors to this volume agree that the basic problem is the prior planning of strategy and tactics in peacetime, not the actual use of nuclear weapons in wartime. Again, when the experts speak of consultation and coordination of the purposes of planning, they are in agreement that such consultation and coordination should imply something more than the mere exchange of information. America's allies must in some way be given an active and meaningful role in the making of the decisions affecting strategic and tactical planning.

If account is taken of these basic areas of agreement, some of the differences expressed in the MLF controversy are not as sharp as at first glance they may appear to be. For example, those who support MLF and those who offer the alternatives of a European deterrent or a multinational nuclear strike force have more in common than appears on the surface. Both sides advance their proposals with the hope of avoiding the risks of the proliferation of national nuclear deterrents. Furthermore, the United States-sponsored MLF does not prevent evolution into either one of the suggested alternatives. The United States Government has stated on numerous occasions that MLF is only a first step, and that it would welcome initiatives toward a more integrated European military effort. On this showing, the differences are not necessarily differences about objectives. They may well be differences about timing—whether to concentrate on the first step toward a larger objective or attempt to gain the larger objective all at once. At this level of the analysis, if there are any serious differences of view they are not so much between supporters and opponents of MLF as between supporters of an integrated European deterrent and supporters of a multinational nuclear strike force. Between them, the central issue is the degree of European integration they desire or believe possible.

As the Dialogue record indicates, the experts do not actually pursue the explosive issue of the kind of integration that should take place in Europe and the way in which an integrated Europe should be coordinated with the United States under the NATO alliance. Instead, they explore the fundamental issue that in a more immediate way affects the vital interests of the United States. As we have seen, there is agreement on the need for meaningful consultation and coordination of nuclear strategic and tactical planning. But just how much control over the making of decisions is the United States prepared to concede to its allies? MLF is indeed a step in the direction of sharing control. Yet the actual political control of the European participants is left undefined; moreover, even if defined, such control will be limited largely to the level of nuclear tactical planning. Admittedly, the possibility of wider control over strategic planning is not denied, but it is left vague by making it dependent upon the outcome of the MLF experience.

Can this United States offer suffice to hold NATO together as an effective alliance? Those who support MLF argue that it is the best available alternative in the present circumstances. Worried about nuclear proliferation, they support the limited objectives of MLF as a practical first step. Conversely, those who oppose MLF fail to see in the proposal any significant and meaningful concession to European desires for a greater voice in nuclear strategy decisions. Not only is the problem of political control left undefined, but MLF appears more as a device for preventing the development of national nuclear deterrents than one designed to share nuclear control. More prepared to accept the national nuclear deterrents of the United Kingdom and France, the opponents of MLF are also more prepared to support proposals for coordinating NATO military policy so as to give the European allies a much greater share in strategic and tactical nuclear planning.

In short, the MLF debate reveals a cluster of interrelated, although quite separable, issues. There is the issue of how best to deal with national nuclear deterrents. There is also the issue of determining the kind of Europe that should share control with the United States. Finally, there is the issue of the degree of control that the United States is prepared to concede to its allies. Given this complexity, it should not be surprising that current discussion of MLF has become so heated. It is entirely possible that discussion proceeds at cross purposes, since the issues are not always properly joined, or the priorities in terms of which they should be solved are not always agreed upon.

Serious as the current dissension within the alliance may be, there is the additional risk that preoccupation with the MLF debate will cause us to overlook promising long-term developments. As one participant has observed, it may well be that, quite apart from the acceptance or rejection of MLF, a partial solution of NATO's military problem is already emerging in the growing acceptance of the idea of a small inner directorate of NATO members. Whether limited to the existing nuclear powers or expanded to insure representation of other NATO members, such a directorate would have as its function the formulation of guidelines for allied nuclear strategy and the determination of allied contingency planning.

Economic Policy

With respect to alliance problems arising from economic circumstances, the record shows agreement on three points. First, everyone quite obviously accepts the proposition that severe unemployment, inflation, balance of payments difficulties, trade discrimination and the like —in short, serious economic disorganization—would undermine the cohesion and effectiveness of NATO. Second, the consensus is that great efforts must be made to facilitate economic advance in underdeveloped areas through such concerted policy actions as trade liberalization. Third, there is agreement that the internal tensions and fissures in the Soviet bloc are serious and that they afford substantial opportunities for economic policy initiatives. No one questions the premise that the allies can, if they choose, take advantage of moral, economic, and political weaknesses in the Communist camp and that such a policy has reasonable prospects for gains in freedom and security.

Despite these areas of agreement, the participants differ sharply on the policy implications that are to be drawn. To a considerable extent, discussion is dominated by disagreement about which policies are appropriate to deal with the various economic problems that adversely affect the alliance, or may threaten to do so in the future. In this context, debate is joined on whether a certain amount of trade discrimination on the part of the developing countries of the Third World should be permitted or rejected; whether international commodity agreements are a success and should be used more extensively; whether any new measures to boost international liquidity are needed; and whether the difficulties encountered in the Geneva tariff negotiations threaten cooperation among NATO countries in other spheres.

Unlike the disagreements over nuclear policy, where there is a common conviction that nuclear planning must be shared, the disagreements about economic policy reflect a lack of consensus regarding a basic approach. Most of the contributors to this volume take the view that NATO should remain primarily a military alliance, and that various other international organizations should serve as vehicles for whatever coordination of economic policies is deemed useful. The other contributors, although arguing for a common approach, differ on its character. According to one view, the effort should be to work toward a wider acceptance of economic organization based on the market process and on market efficiency. A second view calls rather for supranational organizations in which plans can be agreed to that would overcome obstacles in the way of meaningful economic improvement arising from conflicts of interest between nations and groups within nations. Still a third view rests on the belief that the basic problems of the alliance and more generally of the modern world call for joint action by Western countries, solidly rooted in a basic minimum of common political institutions and based on true Western ideals.

With respect to East-West trade, the difference of opinion is not so fundamental. Although there is some question as to the merits of a more liberal and differentiated trade policy toward various Communist countries, all participants favor restrictions on the export of "strategic" items. That term, however, is not sharply defined and seems to hide different conceptions of "strategic" items as well as different estimates of the impact of greater East-West trade. Some participants view the sale of wheat to the Soviet Union as an unfortunate precedent; they refuse to accept the proposition that the selective removal of restrictions on the sale of nonstrategic items will weaken the Communist camp and strengthen Western influence. Conversely, many participants believe that increased trade in key items with the Soviet Union and other Communist countries can be used to help limit and moderate the aggressive nature of these regimes. In offering to engage in such trade, the aim would be not only to contain Communist regimes, but also to press for more humane treatment of the peoples living under these regimes.

Understandably, East-West trade is the one economic area for which a NATO alliance policy is favored. Viewed chiefly as a weapon in the relations between NATO members and the Communist camp, East-West trade seems an appropriate subject area for a military alliance. Yet here, quite apart from differences over the kind of trade policy that should be pursued, another issue is occasionally raised, though seldom explored; that is, whether trade is to be liberalized or narrowly restricted, it will in either case require the concerted efforts of the NATO members. Accordingly, some participants call for a NATO board of economic warfare or a NATO general economic staff to deal with the problem. Other participants doubt that the will to organize for such a concerted effort exists at the present time. In this brief discussion the participants only touch upon the important issue of the extent to which control over alliance economic policy is to be shared among the NATO members. Yet in their argumentation about the substance of East-West trade policy, the contributors to this volume also raise the wider issue alluded to above. In criticizing the feasibility of rigid restrictions or of more liberal trade policies which require Communist concessions, and by pointing out that NATO members are not likely to cooperate, they give evidence, indirectly at least, of the lack of cohesion within the alliance. The separate and diverse interests of the individual allies appear to take precedence over the common interest as this interest has presently been elaborated.

Foreign Policy

Is the chief need, therefore, to establish more effective political institutions for making collective decisions? Insofar as this question is discussed, it arises mainly in relation to military and foreign policy. In the case of military policy, the stress is on meaningful consultation and coordination; and the discussion returns to the same theme upon examination of the merits of securing a much greater degree of foreign policy coordination than has existed until now.

Once again a fundamental issue is the degree of control, the degree of sovereignty, that is to be shared among the NATO allies. A vigorous debate takes place between proponents of improved consultation and coordination within the existing nation-state system and proponents of a more formal union involving the surrender of some national sovereignty and the establishment of supranational institutions. At the same time, some participants advance imaginative proposals that may serve to bridge the gap between the two opposing sides. For example, based on the experience with consultation in the institutionalized framework of the European Economic Community, the view is advanced that a comparable form of consultation within NATO will lead to far greater coordination without posing the issue of a surrender of sovereignty so sharply. Still another proposal is to establish a "partnership" between the United States and Canada on the one hand and an integrated Europe on the other.

This discussion about sharing sovereignty, however, is not solely an extension of the discussion about sharing control in the military field. The fact is that a consideration of coordinating the foreign policies of NATO countries raises the additional issue confronted when the coordination of economic policy was considered: namely, to what extent should there be an "alliance" policy in the field of foreign affairs? Those who advocate and those who oppose some form of "federal" or "supranational" framework are concerned not only with the feasibility but likewise with the desirability of such an arrangement.

How much unity of foreign policy is desirable? A telling case for the negative is based on the view that so long as there is basic agreement on Western security policy, the advantages are all on the side of permitting a variety of foreign policy initiatives in attacking the many problems confronting the alliance. Although in appearance, and to an extent also in fact, the unity of NATO is thereby disturbed, the more important result is that opportunities are provided for new and more finely graduated policy options in the political sphere. Those who oppose this conception believe that renewed and improved cohesion within NATO requires stronger and more extensive coordination among the allies. And as a means of achieving anything very substantial along these lines, they urge the creation of new supranational institutions.

In the foreign policy field as in the economic field, therefore, the issues are not so much the extent and means of sharing control, but rather the prior issue of determining whether there should be an "alliance" policy for which control is to be shared. That there is no agreement on this prior issue should not be surprising. Ever since NATO was established, the effort to broaden the scope of the alliance to include such policy fields as economics, foreign policy, and cultural affairs has been inconclusive. If the testimony of the present volume suggests that the effort still faces major difficulties, it also suggests that disagreement on these matters is not a major cause for current preoccupation with NATO's lack of cohesion. The major cause is rather disagreement among the NATO allies on the extent of sharing control in the making of decisions regarding military (and especially nuclear) strategy and tactics. The allies disagree on their respective roles in achieving the basic purpose for which the NATO alliance was originally founded.

That such disagreement is potentially serious can hardly be denied. The current controversy over military policy raises issues of such magnitude that continued disagreement among the political leaders of the NATO countries can indeed lead to decisions that would disrupt the alliance. On the other hand, if the testimony of the contributors to this volume is any guide, the cleavage of opinions is not irreconcilable. As this brief review of the basic issues dividing the experts has indicated, there are important areas of agreement underlying the current controversy. To have defined these areas is fully as significant as to have defined the areas of disagreement. The dimensions of the problem are thereby placed in proper perspective and the avenues of possible reconciliation come into sharper focus.

Georgetown University
January 1965

Karl H. Cerny
Henry W. Briefs

U. S. Policy Toward NATO*

—*THE HONORABLE GEORGE W. BALL*

Alliances have rarely had a good reputation. As an institution they need the services of a dilligent press agent. Napoleon's rude remarks on the weakness of alliances are a part of his legend. Bismarck's comments were less quotable but equally scornful.

But contempt for alliances was not invented in the Nineteenth Century. Pericles said it all—and said it better—long before, when, according to Thucydides, he observed that within the classical alliance

> the great wish of some is to avenge themselves on some particular enemy, the great wish of others to save their own pocket. Slow in assembling, they devote a very small fraction of the time to the consideration of any public object, most of it to the prosecution of their own objects. Meanwhile each fancies that no harm will come of his neglect, and that it is the business of somebody else to look after this or that for him; and so, by the same notion being entertained by all separately, the common cause imperceptibly decays.

Pericles' prediction as to the inevitability of decay of the classical alliance is not applicable to NATO, since NATO is not—or, at least, not merely—a classical alliance. We should never forget that it is something more—something quite different.

And so I should like to recall some elemental facts about this Atlantic institution—an institution with a name that, in Prime Minister Pearson's words, sounds like a new breakfast food, but an institution

* This is Under Secretary Ball's address to the conference, May 1964.

that has nevertheless served us well as the central structural framework for the defense of the free world.

NATO was born in a time of crisis. It developed its present shape and form during a sustained period of tension. Today the fact—or at least the appearance—of relaxation between East and West is subjecting it to a new strain and test.

In today's relaxed environment there is danger that NATO may gradually lose some of its vitality through apathy and a kind of international wishful thinking. The present generally good state of economic health on both sides of the ocean has produced a pervasive sense of well-being, almost of euphoria. The Atlantic world feels increasingly strong and confident of the future. There is danger that, if this happy state persists for long, some may be tempted to regard the obligations of a massive enterprise such as NATO as unnecessarily heavy and some of our European friends—out of a sense of new-found confidence—may be led to consider NATO as too much an American show. There is already an apparent trend that way.

No human institution is ever perfect, and over time we should continue to improve further the present NATO alliance. But at the same time we must be extremely wary of any suggestion that the alliance is, of course, a good thing but that the NATO structure is a bad idea. Such a suggestion, if seriously regarded, could do great harm. For it might reduce NATO to the status of a classical alliance—an alliance inactive in peace and impotent in war.

An Unprecedented Alliance

Let me recall certain obvious facts about the character and meaning of NATO—facts that we sometimes overlook but which we can never afford to take for granted.

The first relates to the nature of NATO as we now know it. If NATO is not just a classical alliance, what is it?

I suppose it can be accurately described as a full-fledged collective defense arrangement of an unprecedented kind. Obviously, the foundation stone of NATO is the common commitment of the member states that an armed attack against one shall be considered an armed attack against all. But NATO rests on far more than that basic assurance.

NATO expresses the indivisible nature of Western defense. Within its structure the member states have created a unified force of great power and dimensions operating under a unified command. This command, in turn, is subject to a Council of Permanent Representatives that serves as a conduit for political guidance from the member states.

This is NATO today, but we sometimes forget that it was not born full-armed. As first established in 1949, it was little more than the Council and a collection of committees. In fact, there was a saying in those days that "before we established NATO the Russians could march to the Pyrenees in a fortnight. It will take them much longer now; they will have to walk through all those committees."

Stalin was the author of NATO's present structure. It was only after the Korean invasion, when the West first fully comprehended the magnitude of the Communist danger, that the member nations created a Supreme High Command under General Eisenhower and revamped NATO to make it an effective instrument for collective defense.

The road by which the Western world arrived at this point was long and bloody.

Any illusions as to the virtues of an old-fashioned alliance will be dispelled if one recalls the early years of the first World War. We must never forget the events of 1914 to 1918—nor will be permitted to do so if one can judge by the spate of books presently being written about that period.

The story of those years is a tragic chronicle of unnecessary slaughter. In 1914, 1915, 1916, and even 1917 the two principal allies—France and Great Britain—worked largely at cross purposes. There was little joint preparation and management. Planning was only haphazardly coordinated. Strategies, more often than not, were divergent and self-defeating. In fact, it was not until April of 1918—and then only through the efforts of a great French statesman, Georges Clemenceau—that the Entente powers finally pooled their resources under the strategic command of General Foch, as Commander-in-Chief of the Allied Armies in France. Soon thereafter—out of disarray—came unity and victory.

Thanks to Sir John Slessor, I need not point out that in the second World War the same Allies once again went into battle without adequate coordination. In his stimulating essay he describes quite vividly the lack of contact between the British and French staff that prevailed up to six months before the outbreak of the war. Again there was no common policy and no combined strategic planning.

But we have profited—and with good sense we can continue to profit—from all that. Today we have achieved what has never before been possible in peacetime—an effective unified command. This we must cherish and preserve. It is an invaluable resource of the free world. Let us not assess it too cheaply. For if the lack of a unified command proved tragic in 1914, it would be even more catastrophic today. This nuclear age would permit no war of attrition but only of destruction, and we would not have four years—or even four days—to organize a unified command.

It is not enough, however, merely to safeguard what we have. Like any living organism, NATO must grow and change in order to

THE HUNT LIBRARY
CARNEGIE INSTITUTE OF TECHNOLOGY

survive. Several of the essays considered by this group emphasize two major pieces of unfinished business:

First, we must develop ways and means for managing the nuclear deterrent power of the West in a manner that will take account of the aspirations for participation by member states not now possessing atomic weapons. At the same time we must avoid the manifest dangers of proliferation.

Second, we must continue to perfect NATO as an instrument by which the member nations can concert policies with respect to problems that arise not merely within the NATO area but elsewhere in the world.

Each of these pieces of unfinished business is, in my view, complicated by the same central difficulty—that most of the nation states which form the membership of NATO are not large enough by themselves to play roles commensurate with the requirements of the present age.

Managing the Nuclear Deterrent

Clearly this is true with regard to atomic weapons. The defense of the West requires not merely that an individual nation have the ability to mobilize vast resources of men, money, material, industrial plant, and technology, but also that there be unity of control of the life or death decision of nuclear destruction.

I am sure that no one here favors nuclear proliferation as an objective of policy. Its dangers are manifest. For first one country, then another, to develop a national nuclear system could not help but heighten feelings of distrust within the Western alliance, while at the same time increasing tensions between the free world and the Communist bloc. The multiplication of national deterrents would increase the danger that a nuclear holocaust might be triggered through accident or miscalculation. At the same time it would multiply the chance that—at some point—nuclear weapons might fall under the control of an irresponsible individual or government. And finally, it would render progressively more difficult the achievement of an ultimate agreement to control or limit nuclear armament.

But the road toward proliferation has no logical ending—and as we start down that road there are no logical stopping points other than the limits which nations impose on themselves or the limits imposed by the availability of resources or technology.

The renunciation of proliferation as a general principle is clearly not good enough. Such a solemn pronouncement is unlikely to influence the decisions of individual governments. Unless we can produce workable alternatives, proliferation will almost certainly occur whether we like it or not.

Here is where the political organization of Europe becomes relevant. If Europe were sufficiently far advanced toward political unity that it could by itself manage and control an atomic deterrent, we could hopefully look forward to an effective and integrated Atlantic defense founded on a true nuclear partnership. But this is not the case today nor is it likely to be for some time. Effective nuclear control means the delegation to a central executive of the power of life or death involved in the use of atomic weapons. Obviously this presupposes a very high degree of political unity—a degree that far transcends anything immediately in contemplation.

Meanwhile, time will not stand still. Whatever the situation today —and the evidence on the point is confusing—we would delude ourselves if we assumed that the gifted and vigorous people in several of the countries of Western Europe would not sooner or later insist on playing an effective role in their own nuclear defense. If we provide no opportunity for even partial fulfillment of this quite natural desire, the consequences are easily foreseeable. Political pressures for the multiplication of national nuclear deterrents will accumulate—and governments will yield to them. The process moreover will feed on itself; the decision of one country to build a nuclear deterrent will almost certainly increase pressures for similar decisions in others.

The dilemma we face cannot, therefore, be safely brushed aside. If we regard the proliferation of national deterrent systems as undesirable and if we consider that the present exclusion of a large part of the members of the Western alliance from nuclear management is not likely to last, what other options do we have?

It is our attempt to answer this question that led us in 1960 to propose the creation of a multilateral nuclear force. I recognize that this force has become a subject of some controversy not merely among you *cognoscenti* in this dialogue but in similar discussions elsewhere. Yet, as I see it, those who challenge the wisdom or effectiveness of such a force are yet to suggest an adequate alternative.

The multilateral force we are proposing would be organized within the framework of the Western alliance. To constitute a truly international force, we have felt that it should meet four conditions:

First, it should be assigned to NATO by all countries participating in the force. To meet this condition, we propose that it be collectively owned by the participants and that all participating nations share in the costs of creating, maintaining, and operating it.

Second, it should not be predominantly based on the soil of any one nation. To meet this condition, we are proposing a sea-based force consisting of Polaris-type missiles mounted on surface warships. This force, deployed on the high seas, would operate outside the national limits of any state.

Third, it should be managed and operated by nationals of all participating countries under such conditions that it could not be withdrawn from the alliance to serve the national uses of any participating government. To meet this requirement, we propose that the ships themselves be manned by mixed crews of nationals of the participating nations.

The United States Joint Chiefs of Staff and the Secretary of Defense have concluded that an efficient first-class force can be created in this fashion. SACEUR has stated he would welcome the force as a significant addition to NATO's deterrent forces.

Fourth, the decision to fire the Polaris weapons should be a collective decision of the participating nations. One proposal is that political control be exercised through an executive body representing the participating nations. Obviously this control question is the heart of the matter. We are confident it can be solved.

In an ideal world we could no doubt devise less elaborate means for managing nuclear weapons. But we must work within the limitations of existing political arrangements. Those limitations arise from the fact that Western political institutions have not evolved in pace with the march of our technology. Until the West has achieved a far greater political unity than it possesses today, we believe that the development of a multilateral force is the best available course to pursue.

Not only does it offer the most effective means of dealing with the nuclear problem in the present political framework, it can also make possible a gradual and constructive evolution within that framework. The multilateral force would provide a new opportunity for working toward a greater unity in Europe and a closer partnership between the two sides of the Atlantic.

For the striking progress that has been achieved toward these goals in the past decade and a half has, to a considerable extent, come about from necessity—from the fact that governments have been compelled to cope with specific and immediate problems in Europe and the Atlantic area. And, as we seek to cope with the problem of nuclear management, I have no doubt that we shall—of necessity—make further strides toward a greater political unity in the years ahead.

Over the long pull, it will not be abstract principle but importunate necessity—the urgent need to get hard things done in order that we may survive and flourish—that will move us toward the attainment of the ultimate objective of unity and partnership.

Toward Effective Political Consultation

If the lack of political unity in Europe complicates the management of nuclear weapons systems within the NATO alliance, it also limits the development of NATO as an instrument for effective political consultation.

This question of consultation has been a favorite subject for discussions in dialogues such as you have been having here at The Center for Strategic Studies. A strong case can be made—and is frequently made—for greater consultation among NATO members—particularly with regard to world problems that lie outside the scope of the alliance.

The logic of this is clear enough. The member nations of NATO represent 90 per cent of the industrial strength of the free world. They are, in Dean Acheson's words, "the central power which will support—if it is to be supported at all—a non-Communist world system."

I do not mean to suggest that, in the modern decentralized world, it would make sense to reserve the management of world affairs to an exclusive board of directors drawn solely from the NATO nations. Such a proposal would be an affront to friendly nations the world over that are playing responsible roles in their own areas. The United States, for example, has military alliances with twenty-eight countries in addition to its NATO partners.

At the same time it is clear that unity of policy among the members of NATO is an essential component of free-world power. To quote Mr. Acheson again: "If the center is not solid, relations with the periphery will not provide strength."

Unity of policy should presumably be hammered out through consultation. But consultation—essential though it be—can be fruitful only if all powers concerned are determined to make it so. It can produce little, for example, in the face of rigid philosophical differences such as those we have encountered in attempting to develop a common economic policy toward Cuba. It will also produce little when the consulting parties hold widely differing concepts of responsibility for world problems.

It is this latter point that imposes the most severe limit on the efficacy of consultation today.

Until the second World War the metropolitan nations of Europe spread their dominance over vast areas of the world through colonial arrangements. But, with the crumbling of the great colonial systems and the emergence in their stead of half a hundred new states during the turbulent years since the war, world power relationships have had to be vastly revised.

During this period the world interests of European states have greatly altered; at the same time America has had to devise new concepts of world responsibility.

I mention this dichotomy between interests and responsibility for it is, I think, fundamental to the question of consultation. We Americans have few national interests—in the narrow sense—outside our own territory, but we have assumed vast world responsibility.

The result is an unequal allocation among the Atlantic nations, both of responsibility and of the burden of decision that goes with it. This imbalance derives from the imperatives of history—not from deliberate American choice. We are aware that policy and responsibility must not be divorced. We recognize that no nation can be expected to share one without the other.

The United States today is quite prepared to share both with its NATO partners.

So far, however, such sharing has been severely limited by differences of attitude within the NATO alliance. The willingness to accept world responsibility—as distinct from the preservation of national interests—is, in our observation and experience, not universal among the NATO membership.

Hopefully this is a passing phenomenon. For the past decade and a half most European nations have been preoccupied with pressing postwar business—the liquidation of colonial arrangements and the building of strong domestic economies. Now this business is largely finished.

Yet this alone will not solve the problem. The problem will never be fully solved until Europe gets on further with the achievement of its own unity—until it organizes itself on a scale commensurate with the requirements of the age.

There are quite obvious reasons for this. The undertaking of world responsibility requires a world view. The discharge of such responsibility under post-colonial conditions must be based on the command of vast resources for defense and foreign aid—and on the will to use them. Western Europe collectively has more than enough resources, but a fragmented Europe cannot efficiently mobilize them in support of a common effort and a common view.

The existing structure of Europe, therefore, sets limits to the effective sharing both of responsibility and decision. But this does not mean that—within the limits thus imposed—we should not continue to improve the present imperfect allocation.

In fact, the United States is quite ready to go forward in sharing its responsibilities around the world wherever there is a will on the part of its European partners to share—and this includes a willingness to provide resources to make that sharing effective.

It was this thought which underlay President Johnson's comment in a speech to the Associated Press in New York when he said, in speaking of our Atlantic relations:

> We also welcome agreed new mechanisms for political consultation on mutual interests throughout the world with whatever

changes in organization are necessary to make such consultation rapid and effective.

I approach the end of my observations with three general conclusions:

The *first* is that NATO as it exists today—an Atlantic alliance with a unified force in being under a unified command—is an extraordinary peacetime achievement—a platform of accomplishment on which we should continue to build. And we should be wary, indeed, of any actions that might reduce its full effectiveness.

The *second* is that we cannot safely ignore the problem of widening participation in the management of our atomic defense—complicated as it may be by the fragmented structure of Western Europe. And unless you gentlemen are able, out of the collected wisdom represented here, to come up with a better solution than the multilateral force, I strongly urge your support for that proposal.

Finally, if NATO is to fulfill its purpose as the central arrangement for the defense of the free world, it must gradually extend its concern to the larger questions of free-world policy. Here again the limitations that obtain are not hard to isolate. They do not derive from any fault in the institutional structure of NATO but rather from the limited sense of world responsibility—as distinct from national interests—felt by many of our NATO partners.

These then are some of the problems for which we must find solutions over the coming months and years. Effective solutions will not be achieved merely by tinkering with the NATO structure but rather by progress in achieving a greater cohesion in relations among the member nations. This, it seems to me, is already in process. It has already produced substantial results but there is much more to be done.

NATO, therefore, should not be regarded as an end in itself. It should be thought of as one of the pillars in a more comprehensive Atlantic relationship—an Atlantic relationship we must achieve in due course if we are to gain that ultimate goal of which Woodrow Wilson spoke with such prophetic passion—the "universal dominion of right, by such a concert of free peoples as shall bring peace and safety to all nations and make the world itself at last free."

II

The Dialogue

The Nuclear Question

Cerny: As a framework for this dialogue, we propose the following broad outline of topic headings:

Security within the Alliance: Changing Perspectives
European Defense Capabilities
The Role of National Nuclear Deterrents
Coordination and Control of Nuclear Weapons

Security within the Alliance: Changing Perspectives

During the past few years we have been witnessing on both sides of the Atlantic considerable reassessment of the security requirements of the NATO allies. Mr. Morgenthau, for example, has argued that the NATO alliance, as presently constituted, is obsolescent and does not satisfy the security requirements either of the United States or of its allies. To lead into our discussion of this problem, we have selected a statement from Mr. Morgenthau's essay that presents part of his point of view in particularly striking form.

> Proliferation combined with traditional alliance commitments turns the obsolescence of the Western alliance, as presently constituted, against the survival of the United States. Allies of the United States armed with nuclear weapons could virtually decide whether the United States shall live or die.
>
> Hans J. Morgenthau*

* This and subsequent quotations found in the Dialogue were taken from the advance study papers to serve as points of departure for the debate and discussion by the conference participants. The method used was to project the quotations on large screens in the conference hall.

Morgenthau: There is in my opinion a fundamental difference between a conventional alliance and an alliance in the nuclear age. In a conventional alliance, Nation *A* can commit itself to support the interests of Nation *B*, even though its interests are not always completely and directly involved, because the risks Nation *A* takes are generally limited. At worst, Nation *A* can lose a war; it can lose some of its territory; it can incur great political disadvantages. In the nuclear age, however, when Nation *A* commits its support to the interests of Nation *B*, even though its interests may not be completely or directly involved, it thereby puts its very existence at stake.

It is this fundamental difference to which President de Gaulle has called attention. While General de Gaulle has had a rather bad press in this country, I think that he has put forward a profound truth. Perhaps he has done so in a way which was not calculated to win friends and influence people on this side of the Atlantic; but the manner of presentation, in my opinion, does not detract from the truth. The difference between a nation's commitment to a nuclear and a conventional alliance has nothing to do with the reliability of promises of a particular government or a particular administration. The difference is rather the outgrowth of an objective assessment; namely, that it is no longer possible to rely completely on the promise of a nuclear ally to forfeit its very existence on behalf of another nation.

To be specific: when the Soviet Union declares that it will unleash a nuclear war in defense of Cuba against the United States, it may or may not do so. In any event, this promise cannot be taken as completely plausible, as completely convincing. Similarly, when the United States declares that it will risk its own existence for the defense of the Western alliance—in West Berlin, for example—this promise may or may not be fulfilled when the chips are down. There is a difference in quality between a promise implying the risk of physical destruction of the promising nation and a promise made in the pre-nuclear age.

We have here an entirely new situation which requires new instrumentalities, new modes of thought and action, adapted to new circumstances. It seems to me that the crisis of NATO resides exactly in the fact that it tries to meet the requirements of the nuclear age with conventional and largely obsolescent modes of organization and institutions.

Knorr: According to Mr. Morgenthau's statement, if of several allies some or all of them possess independent nuclear forces, each one of them has it in his power to decide on the life or death of his fellow allies. Now, I think that there is a great deal of truth in this statement. It is one of the new facts of the nuclear age that we all should recognize. At the same time this particular risk of a "catalytic" war—

that one particular country triggers off the nuclear war in which his ally becomes involved—perhaps should not be put as strongly as Mr. Morgenthau has put it here.

It very much looks as if our allies, to the extent that they will have or do now have independent nuclear forces, will have rather modest forces compared with those of the United States or of the Soviet Union. I would not think that they will be very eager to precipitate a nuclear war. In fact, one of my great difficulties about the utility of these forces is that I cannot easily think of situations in which they would take such an initiative.

But even if they should do so, it seems to me there is a great deal that the fellow ally can do in order to minimize the catalytic risk. I am quite sure that as more of our allies possess independent nuclear forces which are not integrated into a system of central control, we will take very important steps in order to minimize the risk. We can do a great deal, for example, by telling the Soviet Union either in a crisis or even before crises occur, that we will not necessarily be involved in a nuclear war initiated without our approval by one of our allies.

Furthermore—and here is where the real risk lies—it isn't so much that an ally possessing nuclear weapons will deliberately initiate a nuclear war. This I think is extraordinarily unlikely. But what is not impossible is that such an ally may adopt courses of action which are risky in terms of foreign and military policy and may lead to serious crises. Insofar as the ally brings about such crises as a result of independent courses of action, a limited conflict may come about that will confront his fellow allies as well as himself with a need to decide on the use of nuclear weapons. It is in this subtle and more indirect way that the risk of the "catalytic" war really resides.

Burgess: I think that Mr. Morgenthau has raised a very important question of European psychology. Although far be it from me to think I know how to interpret it, the question deals with the ambiguity of the American defense commitment to Europe.

I would have thought that that commitment was most unambiguous, and that the American position had been firmly established. But admittedly, the question is how Europe thinks about the American commitment. What real evidence have we on this? We have the French position. We have a great many learned dissertations about it.

I wonder if the greater danger of the alliance is not that Europe is relying too much on the unambiguous quality of the United States position. My supporting evidence is that, during my years in serving in NATO, there was increasing difficulty in getting the European nations to spend any increased amount on defense. In my view, there is a growing feeling in Europe that war is impossible. Because the balance of power between the two great powers is so fixed and determined, the European nations don't have to worry.

I would like to hear from our European friends as to how deep this sense of ambiguity runs—how deep this doubt runs. Does it run to the real feeling of these countries? Or is it rather this other danger that they are just too confident of their position?

Brugmans: I agree with Mr. Morgenthau that President de Gaulle's intervention in the debate over nuclear defense has on the whole been useful, that he has put the right question, although perhaps he has not given the right answer.

But there is one point which is fairly weak in his position. If you really think that you can't expect any nation in the nuclear age to make final decisions, except when its own existence is at stake, then the same thing holds true for France as for the United States. If you can't expect the American position to be without ambiguity, the same is true as well for France. Why should the non-French Europeans rely on a French striking force?

No doubt there would be very obvious cases where either the United States, or France for that matter, would be obliged to go to war. But the real problem is over occasions where it would *not* be clear. Then the basic ambiguity Mr. Morgenthau referred to is not eliminated by the fact that there is a proliferation of nuclear weapons on both sides of the ocean. Rather the opposite.

As far as I understand the French position, it was thought that the Franco-German friendship treaty would at least solve parts of the problem by bringing Germany into alliance with France. Well, after more than a year of this treaty, we can say that it has not solved the problem at all. Each time a political decision has had to be taken, the French and German positions have been in conflict.

To sum up, I would say that a dogmatic anti-proliferation policy is no longer realistic. Proliferation cannot be stopped; we can't put the clock back. Conversely, I don't think that proliferation by itself is a solution either. It will not give *all* allies that feeling of security that they have been looking for in the alliance.

Cerny: To what extent have recent developments in American strategic doctrine helped bring a new awareness among Europeans of their own strategic situation? For purposes of discussion, we have selected two statements, one by Mr. Kurt Birrenbach[1] and one by Mr. Kissinger.

> The implication of this evolution was not immediately understood. It was only when the Kennedy Administration promulgated the McNamara doctrine . . . that the European nations were aware of their new strategic situation.

[1] Unfortunately Mr. Birrenbach was unable to participate in the dialogue.

> This weakened the decisive component within the alliance system, the fact of United States leadership, while, on the other hand, the claims of a number of the member states to sovereignty were more strongly emphasized. This is a development which would be even more evident if there were European development toward political unity.
>
> Kurt Birrenbach

> The real problem is not that the Europeans fail to understand our quest for multiple options. Their opposition derives from their rejection of it for their particular situation. When the issue is Asia or Latin America, Europeans favor an even more flexible response than we do. With respect to the defense of Europe, the European attitude is more rigid. As long as the United States retains ultimate control over nuclear weapons, the European incentive is bound to be exactly the opposite of ours.
>
> Henry A. Kissinger

Kissinger: One of the difficulties in our dialogue with the Europeans is the fact that we are not necessarily talking about the same problem. I would like to suggest that there is a difference of perspective, and the difference in perspective arises in part from the geographic location of the Europeans. I think it is in part true that there is, as Ambassador Burgess has said, an unambiguous American commitment, and that the Europeans have not made a sufficient effort. In part they have been reluctant to make an adequate effort because they did not want to give us any other choice except nuclear retaliation. If this control of nuclear strategy is in the hands of one ally, then it is to the interest of the protected countries to limit the range of choices which this ally has.

When we speak of the desirability of having a "pause" so that wider risks can be assessed, it is inevitable that Europeans will ask themselves what that assessment will involve. While a "pause" may seem desirable to those who know that whenever the difficulty becomes too great they can resort to nuclear weapons, the "pause" does not become desirable to those about whom that decision will be made and who have no direct control over it.

I suggest that the Europeans understand the problem of multiple options very well. If we ask the Europeans about the kind of strategy to pursue in Latin America or in Southeast Asia they can think of options that haven't even occurred to us. It is when the options are to be applied to Europe that their reluctance arises. As long as we control the nuclear weapons, NATO strategy has to restrain the European tendency to trigger our nuclear arsenal as soon as possible.

Ambassador Burgess' remarks have great psychological significance. The Europeans have never looked on their conventional forces until 1961 as anything else than the price of admission to the American nuclear guarantee. They wanted them large enough to make sure that we would keep some American forces on the Continent but not so large as to give us another option. They wanted American forces on the Continent for the same reason that was given by a French marshal when he was asked before World War I how many British soldiers he wanted. He was reported to have said: "I want one, and I will make sure that he gets killed on the first day of the war." In the nuclear age the price of a nuclear guarantee has risen to something like five divisions.

There is then an inevitable difference of perspective between those who know that when things get difficult they can press the button and those who know that when things get difficult somebody else has to press the button. I believe that it is in the long term impossible to have a strategy of multiple options and central American control of nuclear weapons. If we want to retain central control over nuclear weapons, the Europeans will try to turn the "shield" forces into a trigger for the American nuclear forces.[2]

Mosely: Up to now our European allies have felt that the entire United States nuclear deterrent was for one purpose: to protect Western Europe. Our NATO allies are extremely reluctant even to consider any other possible uses for it. Yet if we consider the military plans of Communist China—in terms of their militant statements about driving the

[2] During question-time from the floor, Dr. William V. O'Brien of the Department of Government, Georgetown University, stimulated further discussion of the McNamara doctrine by directing this question to Mr. Kissinger:

"How can the objective of the McNamara doctrine, namely, the avoidance of countercity warfare, be attained if the U.S. does not retain ultimate control over the West's nuclear retaliatory power, or if a European, NATO, French, or other retaliatory power does not have the invulnerability and capacity for discrimination that the U.S. now possesses?"

Mr. Kissinger replied: "I do not think that this question of the countercity doctrine or the counterforce doctrine should become the crucial consideration. I believe that it is an excessively sophisticated way of looking at alliance policy and that it does not go to the heart of the problem. The heart of the problem is whether we can achieve common war plans and a common diplomacy during peacetime. If we can do so (as we have for over a decade with the British who possess an autonomous nuclear force), then I believe the various forces within the alliance can be successfully coordinated. If we cannot, then the question of a countercity or counterforce strategy is still unanswered. If I had to choose between Atlantic cohesion and the capacity to conduct the kind of strategy which Secretary McNamara has described, I would choose Atlantic cohesion."

Mr. Possony added: "If the Europeans are to carry out this sort of counterforce strategy, or participate with us in this strategy, or not adopt an opposite strategy, they obviously have to have equipment for carrying out the war plans assigned to them. This implication casts a new light on the question of Europeans sharing in the preparation of our war plans. It also highlights the very important point that you cannot have an alliance and maintain nuclear forces in various countries when the capabilities are so desperately unequal as they are today."

Finally, *Mr. Morgenthau* argued: "I do not believe for a moment that a counterforce strategy is possible, given the extreme disparity of weapons systems between ourselves and the Soviet Union and also the disparity of available targets for us and for the Soviet Union. I have always believed that a counterforce strategy is one of the necessarily futile attempts to transform nuclear war into some variation of conventional war, to make nuclear war something acceptable, something manageable. In the nature of things, this attempt is impossible."

"imperialists" from Asia, although not yet their actions—and consider that they are likely with great travail to go on developing their strength, which has already made them the strongest power on land in Asia, we may have a whole range of problems to face outside Europe anywhere from five to ten years from now. It will be very difficult for the United States to cope with these problems without being able to use its nuclear power. Yet our European allies not only want to invoke our military power only for their own defense, they also want to dissuade us from the use of this power or the threat of its use anywhere except for the defense of Europe.

The Cuban missile crisis of October 1962 did lead to strong backing by our allies after the United States had already made the basic decision. It also increased the pressures among and by European policy-makers to make sure that no similar decisions would be made by the United States in the future without prior and substantive consultations with them. From their point of view, this pressure is quite logical, indeed, inevitable.

It seems to me that, looking ahead ten years from now we ought to try to help Europe provide its own nuclear deterrent. Europe will not be strongly unified in its own defense until it feels sovereign in its own defense. That means possessing the ability, with or without the United States, to deter the use of Soviet nuclear forces or of Soviet nuclear threats against itself. That means provided there is a politically integrated Europe, perhaps ten years from now, with its own nuclear deterrent. This, in turn, would release the U. S. deterrent from its sole commitment to Europe and would make it available for political use elsewhere in the world.

Strausz-Hupe: I agree with Mr. Kissinger that the problem of the European relationship to the American nuclear deterrent is largely a psychological one, that is, the feeling of people about whom—and despite whom—the button might be pressed toward the people who have the power to press the button. However, I think it is also perhaps a more rational calculation. Today, nuclear technology—what we in this country call "nucleonics"—holds approximately the same position of eminence as the metallurgical industry did in the Nineteenth Century. If you really want to be ahead in things, if you want to be able to compete internationally, if you want to have a vital economy, you must be able to develop these truly twentieth-century devices.

This technology is very complex and very sophisticated. It stands to reason that the Europeans whose brains are as good as ours, who have developed many technologies before, would like to be in on that development. I think that there is great pressure in Europe to participate in these new developments—not only from the politicians and the military, but also from the industrialists and many other sectors of the economy.

Here the two tendencies join and I think that this explains very largely the appeal of General de Gaulle in France. Some people would like to go into these developments because they believe that Europe must have its own options, its own choices. Others want to go into it because they feel that the United States should not retain a strategic monopoly which also signifies an economic monopoly.

It is not only the question of lowering tariffs in certain commodities and thus maximizing Atlantic trade. The question is also: how can we maximize the joint technological and scientific resources of the Atlantic Community as a whole, so that as a whole it will grow more rapidly economically? At this point the strategic and economic problems are very closely interrelated.

European Defense Capabilities

Cerny: Taking a cue from what Mr. Strausz-Hupé has just said, I suggest that we move to the next topic of our discussion outline. To what extent are Europeans capable of playing a greater role in providing for their own security—particularly a nuclear role? The following two statements by Mr. Knorr and Mr. Mosely suggest that European capabilities are indeed great.

> In order to reach a realistic appraisal of the security problem faced by the United States and by the West European nations, we must recognize that it is possible for the Western European countries, within the next five or ten years, to provide for their military security without *formal* alignment with the United States, and, at the same time, to gain freedom of action uncurbed by such ties.
>
> I must stress two important qualifications implied in my statement. First, even if NATO were abandoned, or, though formally continued, became looser and less cohesive, Western Europe would not necessarily forfeit a degree of military protection by the United States. . . . My second qualification is that although it is *possible* for our NATO allies in due time to provide for their military security without formal ties with the United States, it is not certain that they *can* and it is not certain that they *will,* even if they can.
>
> Klaus Knorr

> Over the next five to ten years, if Western Europe chooses to do so, it will be able, economically and financially, to organize a much larger body of military power, a power that it can then bring to bear either for its own defense against Soviet pressure, or to extend its own influence in world affairs, or for both purposes.
>
> Philip E. Mosely

Knorr: It is often assumed in this country and perhaps more surprisingly it is often held in European countries, that the Western European countries are not really in a position—even in the foreseeable future—to take care of their own national security requirements. It seems to me that this is not necessarily true. Furthermore, the possibility that Western Europe might exploit the opportunity to make a much greater effort in order to meet its own national security would not be altogether bad.

There is something unhealthy about a group of nations as resourceful and as wealthy as the Western European countries to remain as dependent militarily on an ally several thousand miles across the ocean. As President de Gaulle suggests, it is perhaps not entirely honorable that a rich community of nations should remain so militarily dependent.

Obviously, if this degree of dependence could be lessened, this would be a great boon to the Western Europeans. After all, they pay for this dependency in terms of constraints upon their policies in various ways. I would also suggest that it would be to the interest of the United States if the Western Europeans would assume a larger burden in meeting their own security requirements. The alliance has placed constraints on United States policies fully as much as on European policies. And these constraints may well increase as the United States position of dominance decreases within the alliance.

What I have said is not a prediction. I have said that if one surveys European resources, one sees very considerable possibilities of the Europeans' providing for their own defense. The two main qualifications that I have made in this statement are, first of all, that even if the Europeans do more for their own security requirements than they have been doing, they do not necessarily have to provide for them completely independently of what the United States can do within the alliance. Even if the Europeans would do more for themselves, the American interest in keeping Western Europe free would still give the United States an enormous incentive to come to their assistance to help protect this area both by means of deterrents and by means of defense. After all, this country has come to the aid of Western European countries twice within a relatively small number of decades without having been formally in alliance with them.

The other qualification is that even though the resources and resourcefulness are present, there are a number of restraints that the Europeans will have to overcome. Economically, the restraints involve the ability of France, England, or Western Germany to allocate the very large resources that would be required for example if Europe went into building its own nuclear force. There are also technological restraints. Unless the United States would assist in overcoming them, there would be delay and much more expense in achieving the greater means of military self-sufficiency. Finally, and above all, there are political restraints; that is, do these nations *want* to make these allocations, to make these sacrifices to translate potentiality into reality?

Mosely: To build a nuclear force will be a very great cost, but this cost will be much less to Europe than the original creation of it in the United States. The very large expenses for research and development do not need to be duplicated in order to have a second nuclear deterrent organized on a regional basis, with strong political control, for the protection of Western Europe. And as Mr. Knorr has intimated, the Soviet leadership would continue to expect that the United States would not stand by and let Europe be destroyed.

Moreover, five or ten years from now, the United States may face a series of problems in other parts of the world from which Europeans may wish to remain aloof. Thus the question of whether the two deterrents could be used in tandem or separately would have different implications for different parts of the world. For Europe, the European deterrent would be reinforced by the United States' basic interest. In other parts of the world the United States would have an ability to use or threaten to use the kind of force necessary to protect the interests of the free world. Accordingly, we should look not only at the costs to Europe of building a separate nuclear force but also at the costs to the United States in the next ten to twenty years of relying solely on its own nuclear deterrent to protect both European and worldwide interests.

Possony: I want to make three points in connection with the present discussion. First of all, the fact that the United States has come to the aid of Europe twice does not dispel European doubts regarding United States intentions. These doubts rest not necessarily on American experience but on European experience. The American experience has indeed been that America has come to the aid of Europe. But the Europeans have not evaluated this experience in quite the same way.

In 1917, when the United States entered the war, the war had been going on for three years and effective American intervention in the war occurred only in September of 1918. Furthermore, American participation in World War I followed the destruction of Russia, which was a main ally of the West. The whole train of subsequent political events was the outcome of belated American intervention.

In World War II the United States did not intervene voluntarily. The United States was attacked by Japan in December 1941, after the war had been going on for something over two years. The European continent was occupied; there was no way really for Britain and the Soviet Union to defeat Nazi Germany. At that time, the United States, while engaged in a program of rearmament, was hardly giving the impression that it was "raring" to go.

So the facts of life are that although the United States did get into the war in both instances, I do not think that the Europeans can rightfully be expected to desire a repetition of the experiences of those two World Wars.

My second point deals with the ability of the Europeans to provide for their own defense. The ability is certainly there—especially in terms of technological and economic potential. But I think that there are a few other hurdles to be overcome before we have a full-fledged European military power. For one thing, the technology which the United States has today cannot be easily duplicated in Europe. It will require more than five to ten years to catch up with what we have. For another thing, the word "Europe" is a very vague expression for something which does not really exist. When we talk about European military power, we are talking about France, Britain and Germany; on a lower level there are a few small powers, notably the Low Countries.

My third point is that it is a grave mistake to look at the problem as though it is just a question of the nuclear deterrent. This mistake is twofold. First, it is more than a nuclear question. It is a question both of the fireball and of the more difficult and costly means of delivery and defense. The second mistake is that we are only talking about the deterrent. "Deterrence" is a very nice term and we hope it is a very significant term inasmuch as war may be deterred. But you can't develop a strategy in the hope that war won't come. The war may come despite all deterrents. The question is, how do you fight the non-deterred war, and if you fight it, how do you win it? As long as we persist in saying that nuclear war is unthinkable—that everybody is going to be dead as soon as the first bomb explodes—as long as we persist in this sort of mental paralysis, the problem cannot be solved.

The problem should be approached in a more constructive manner. When we look at the question of what Europe or the United States can do or cannot do, I think it is often overlooked that the United States with its present substantial military outlay of some fifty billion dollars is in no position to support, on its own, a military program sufficient to achieve a superior capability, not only to deter but also to fight and win a war. Since the United States has trouble meeting the challenge, and since the Europeans experience even greater difficulty, I think the proper approach is for the United States and Europe to combine their resources, exchange their technical and scientific knowledge, avoid duplication, and develop a truly integrated NATO alliance. In such a way, and only in such a way, can the alliance really achieve a very vast superiority of power, that is, assured deterrence.

Uri: What do we really mean by calling for an increased European military effort? I wonder if we really know. Do we mean that a greater percentage of the European national product should be allocated for military expenditures? But how much greater? At least two of the major

European powers, Britain and France, spend on defense just about the same percentage of the national product as the United States—or at any rate, not much less. Now it may be true that other European countries do not reach this level. But even if they did, European military power would be much below the military power of the Soviet Union. The combined national product of Europe is just about equal to the national product of the Soviet Union. And the Soviet Union is spending a much larger percentage of its national product on defense so that its expenditure is presumably of the same order of magnitude as the American defense expenditure.

Do we mean then that Europe should spend as great a percentage of its national product as the Soviet Union? In this case, the military effort of Europe could obviously be similar to the Soviet military effort. But I wonder what would remain of the free economy. Europe would be on a permanent wartime economy and this situation is not exactly what we are striving for.

The call for an increased European effort can perhaps mean something else. The problem may be that the total level of military expenditure is not really too low but rather that it is not very effectively spent. There may be great truth in this version of the problem. It is quite possible that Europe is trying to do too many things at the same time. But in this case, we have a completely different version of what we mean by an increased European military effort.

Finally, do we perhaps mean that the Europeans should direct their expenditures in support of a particular type of military effort? If so, I think it would be wise not to be too dogmatic. The trouble with this version of the problem is that every solution may turn out to be unsatisfactory. It has already been noted that complete dependence on an ally in the nuclear age may not be considered fully safe. The other solution—each country fighting for itself—is not satisfactory either. The will may be there but the reprisals are much more formidable. So one might think of a third solution which is the creation of a nuclear force for a group of countries which feel close enough together so that they are really like one nation.

The trouble with this idea of a European force is that we cannot yet assume that this degree of integration in Europe is already a fact. We have gone a long way toward economic integration, but we do not know yet what political union means, and we certainly do not have the institutions to work it. Thus we have to ask whether the coordination of nuclear forces among different countries is at all possible. If this question can be answered, then we may after all arrive at a solution. If we cannot, then I am afraid that we are left with my rather negative conclusion that of the formulas which are currently being considered—complete monopoly and full reliance on one power, national deterrents, or European forces—each is going to fail.

Slessor: I would like to say how very strongly I agree with everything that Mr. Possony said. To me it is an article of faith that as far as the United Kingdom is concerned, the only defense policy that makes any sense at all in the second half of the Twentieth Century is an Atlantic defense policy.

I do not believe that it is possible, as Mr. Knorr has stated, for the Western European countries within the next five or ten years to provide for their military security. I just do not believe that is so. Or perhaps I should say that it may be possible but that there is a sharp difference between what is possible and what is practicable. When it comes to actually spending more money on military defense, there are individual problems in the European countries which are different from those in America. For example, I remember after one of the early meetings of NATO, we in the British Chief of Staff thought that, if there were an autopsy, they would find engraved on our hearts the words, "the metal-using industries." At the time we were not told that the money was unavailable. Rather we were repeatedly told that Britain lives on her export trade and that her ability to contribute to the alliance depends on her exports. If we were going to use the products of the metal-using industries, we would not be able to export in order to live and in order to contribute to the alliance.

It is perhaps an overstatement when Mr. Uri said that Britain was spending the same proportion of her gross national product on defense as the United States. We are not quite. But Britain is indeed spending a pretty considerable proportion of it. What Britain ought to be doing is not spending a larger proportion of her national product on defense. Rather she ought to be spending on the forms of defense which contribute more to the Atlantic Community, to the Atlantic alliance.

Ruge: I fully agree with Sir John that Western defense can only be Atlantic defense. From the point of view of military strategy, NATO Europe is far too narrow a strip of land to be defended by its own means. It must have the sea and the American continent behind it. And the military service of my country hasn't the slightest doubt that the United States will come to the support of Europe.

Uniform Atlantic defense, however, means cooperation, avoidance of duplication in the conventional and nuclear fields, division of labor, and most particularly, standardization. If we could standardize our conventional weapons, we would save considerable money for the purchase of nuclear and other arms. For example, I think NATO started with three types of jets; now there are twelve types of jets. From a military point of view, this development does not make any sense.

Knorr: I would like to answer some of the critical remarks that have been made by the preceding speakers. First of all, to comment on Mr. Possony's observations, I was aware of the fact that the United States did get into the last two World Wars belatedly and perhaps reluctantly. However, I thought it would be understood that the posture of the United States now is quite different in all relevant respects from what it was at those two times.

Then the United States had assumed the posture of neutrality which it has not now. Then the United States was militarily unprepared, which it is not now. And then also, the United States was not nearly as clear and didn't have to be as clear about her own interest in protecting the security of Western Europe as is the case now. Because in these three essential respects the situation is quite different from what it was then, I do think that it was not altogether unrealistic for me to have cited the experience of America's coming to the aid of Europe in two world wars. If she did so then, there is much more reason to believe that she will do so in the future.

I have also been misunderstood with respect to Western Europe's defense capabilities. I am not against the alliance although I do think we have to prepare to adjust it in several respects. Again, I did not mean to predict that Western Europe could—even if she wanted to—take care of her own security problems without the support of the United States. I agree with Sir John Slessor that Europe could not do so within any foreseeable future. However, with the backing that the United States will provide, I think that Europe can do a great deal more than she has done in the past to provide for her security. This is a very important qualification.

Now, with respect to Europe's ability to do more, I would also like to say that Mr. Uri's remarks about the percentage of the national income devoted to defense in the alliance are perhaps not quite right. Even now, the United States still spends an appreciably higher percentage than does either Britain or France. If the Europeans really want to do more for their national security, they could no doubt afford a larger proportion than they are affording now for this particular purpose. Whether they will is an entirely different question. I myself think that Europe will in some ways—and the record will be different for different countries—do more than has been done in the past. But because of political constraints, Europe probably will not in fact do as much as is necessary to secure even a pseudo-independence from the United States.

Possony: As an economic exercise, calculating defense effort in terms of gross national product may be very useful. But militarily, the problem that you must calculate is: what do you need in order to pose a certain threat? Now, the alliance operates on the doctrine of the second strike and, for a variety of reasons, a second strike strategy is more expensive than a first strike strategy. It is therefore necessary to have a military establishment which, if you want to put it in broad economic terms, would have to be about twice as large as the force that the Soviet Union can use for its first surprise attack.

However, the heart of the problem is not the size of the effort quite as much as the types of expenditure. In this respect, "cost-effectiveness" analysis can be a very useful device. Unfortunately, the United States does not apply "cost-effectiveness" analysis across the board. Were it to do so, it would become very clear that all forces have to be equipped with nuclear arms, including, of course, the European forces.

This point leads to the question of United States support for European efforts. I have no doubt, as Mr. Knorr said, that the United States will back European efforts. But how will we back Europe? Specifically, are we going to enable Europeans to obtain nuclear weapons? For example, we have on the books an amendment to the Atomic Energy Act which in essence would now allow France to buy nuclear weapons—or "components"—from this country. Admittedly, this amendment was very carefully written several years ago to prevent us from selling nuclear devices to France. Couched in very strange language, the amendment restricts the sale of United States weapons to those nations that already possess the necessary nuclear capability. Specifically written in this way to help Britain, the Act now clearly should apply to France as well. Yet the application has not been made. The U. S. Government has not "determined" that France has become a nuclear power. In my view, here is a specific example of how we can become serious: if we want to be supporting European efforts, let us support the nuclear program of France—let us start a genuinely cooperative effort.

The Role of National Nuclear Deterrents

Cerny: In turning to the third topic of our discussion outline, we have selected statements by General Beaufre, Sir John Slessor, and Mr. Mosely. In his paper, General Beaufre advances a closely reasoned argument on behalf of the positive advantage to the NATO alliance of having more than one nuclear power in the NATO camp pursuing a strategy of nuclear deterrence. Sir John Slessor questions the military value of a claim to nuclear independence and suggests that there may be other motivations behind such a claim. Finally, Mr. Mosely, although doubting the desirability of proliferation, raises the prospect of the United States' promoting the emergence of a directorate of nuclear powers.

> A multipolar nuclear system, uniting the initiative of the allies, thanks to a common concept, could achieve a deterrent more complete and more stable than a strictly bipolar system. Some organizational schemes seem to be achievable. Besides, a more intensive analysis would show that there

> exists only a difference of degree, but not of kind, between the coordination which prevailed on the conventional level (with regard to Berlin, for example) and that which it would be necessary to achieve on the nuclear level.
>
> General André Beaufre

> If [independence] means anything [it] must mean that the nation owning the nuclear force concerned must be politically and militarily capable in the last resort of *using* it independently, singlehandedly and, if necessary, against the wishes of their allies, to carry nuclear devastation into the heart of an enemy country. . . .
> The French attitude to nuclear independence has, to me, an air of almost total unreality, and I doubt whether more than a very few people outside the Elysée really believe in it. I wonder whether the truth is not that General de Gaulle does not believe in the possibility of war as long as the United States retains her nuclear capacity, but regards his theoretical independence as a political symbol of the greatness of France and of her influence in world affairs.
>
> Sir John Slessor

> Proliferation of nuclear weapons is certainly not desirable in itself, but over the next ten to twenty years it is a highly probable trend. The question is, then, whether U. S. policy should resist this trend, probably without permanent success, or whether it should attempt to guide it in an orderly way so as to promote the emergence, within the non-Communist world, of a "directorate" of nuclear powers.
>
> Philip E. Mosely

Beaufre: My basic point is not contrary to, but slightly different from, what Mr. Possony has previously stated. I have the strong belief that the function of nuclear weapons is deterrence and not use. I do not mean that they shouldn't be used, but rather I mean that it is not their function. They are very powerful as deterrents; they are very cumbersome to use.

Because we think that the function of nuclear weapons is to achieve the best deterrence, we also think—and here I would supplement what has been said by Mr. Kissinger—that Europe in general looks much more to deterrence than to defense. This is not because we think that it is a very agreeable way to get away from war, but just because we think that, if war would come in Europe, the situation would be very very dangerous. That is why in our military policy we emphasize the need for the best deterrence we can achieve instead of a policy which would leave some room for a kind of limited war. Here is the basic difference between the whole European position and the one that has been taken in the United States during the last few years. And it leads to the conclusion that the function of a national European deterrent is not at all to trigger American nuclear power. Those who state this view just do not understand the problem. The function of a national European deterrent is not to trigger, but to reinforce, the deterrent.

Nobody in Europe, or probably very few of us, hope to achieve a military system that is completely independent from the United States or from the allies. This is certainly not the aim. I think that the aim is to achieve a better balance in the alliance. Up to now nuclear policy has been completely in American hands. For several reasons which you all know, it is impossible now to continue in this situation. We have to achieve a better balance in the alliance in this field of nuclear policy as well as in the other fields.

The way to a better balance is coordination of our military policies. Such coordination is not coordination to press the button. Because our aim is deterrence, we do not primarily seek coordination in times of war. We want to have coordination in the deterrent phase—that is before any button has been pushed. Here is the area where effective coordination can and should be made.

Slessor: Although General Beaufre has said that the function of a nuclear force is deterrence and not use, the force cannot be a deterrent unless the enemy is at least exceedingly uncertain about its use or nonuse. For this reason, I don't believe that these so-called independent deterrents are really independent or deterrents.

I feel that you must have—and General de Gaulle himself has accepted this point in his press conference of January 1963—something like comparative and not relative damage. If the enemy can completely obliterate Great Britain or France, and Great Britain or France on their part can inflict at most very heavy damage on the enemy, it does seem to be a one-sided affair. It is often overlooked that this deterrent business is a two-way street. I can never make out why it should be assumed that Britain would not be deterred from using her nuclear force by the inevitability of complete obliteration of the United Kingdom, but that Russia would be deterred by a far less cataclysmic degree of damage. The credibility of an independent nuclear deterrent requires the capability of inflicting comparative, not relative, damage on the enemy.

Mosely: When I speak of proliferation, I do not speak of national proliferation. I speak of a development that the United States has thus far not chosen to foster: a European regional deterrent which would in turn require a very high degree of political unification, of ability to establish a common defense and foreign policy for Western Europe.

In times of tension and crisis, a common political strategy is extremely difficult to achieve among a number of national deterrents. On the other hand, a European regional deterrent backed by political integration would be a source of great stability and would bring about something approaching equality in the alliance. The alliance would also be stronger between the United States and a regionally integrated Western Europe. Admittedly this goal is something for the future. Yet Europeans must come to feel that there is a possibility of providing more vigorously for their own defense.

The most promising solution would be participation in common decisions on a one-to-one basis between the United States and Canada on the one side and Western Europe on the other. Moreover, I think we can have a better and firmer coordination of decision-making if Western Europe has a nuclear deterrent of its own. However complicated it may be to work out the necessary arrangements, it is still more feasible to work out political integration within Europe than to secure agreement on the complicated decision-making process that would be required in a completely unified Atlantic deterrent.

If we are going to try to arrive at some redivision of nuclear deterrent responsibilities ten years from now, we have to begin thinking about it now. We must begin to plan policies that will be compatible with that goal rather than cling to a unilateral deterrent. Europe is going to be able to provide its own deterrent and is, I think, going to do it in cooperation with the United States, if we can think of ways of helping to bring it about in an orderly and reasonable way.

Possony: In my view, some of the difficulties of the NATO alliance arise from the dubious assumption that the only way a country can fight a nuclear war is to pay with its national existence and that deterrence can be achieved through willingness to commit suicide. Fortunately, technology does not stop. We have to move forward so that it is no longer feasible, say five or ten years from now, for Sir John Slessor to say that Britain would be completely obliterated if there were a nuclear war. The practical problem of achieving this technological breakthrough can be solved best —or only—through cooperation within the alliance, cooperation bearing not only on old weapons but much more important, on new and future weapons.

Moore: When we concentrate on the merits of promoting a European regional deterrent, we are compounding the troubles that presently confront us. The prospect of establishing an integrated European political institution to handle the control of nuclear weapons is such a distant vision that I doubt it will ever materialize. In the meantime, in spite of Sir John Slessor's protests, his government is going to have a so-called independent nuclear deterrent, and so is the French government. We might as well recognize this fact. Neither of these deterrents is going to be militarily independent in the sense that the United States deterrent is. But both are going to be independent in that the political authorities of these two countries will determine when and how they will be used.

Yet if either the United Kingdom or France, or both of them, wish to use their nuclear forces, they will certainly make sure that the United States is going to be in on the act, to finish it, if necessary, preferably to start it. By the same token, I cannot believe that the United States would ever entertain any idea of independent nuclear action without at least consulting with these allies. As our experience in Berlin has demonstrated, every time we have been confronted with a crisis the three countries have stuck together. The tougher it was, the quicker they got together.

I am sure therefore that, if we were confronted with a situation where the use of atomic weapons was contemplated, there is no doubt that there would be consultation between these three nations. I would suggest, however, that the Secretary General of NATO be included in such consultations in order to represent the nations that are not nuclear powers and that are not members of the Standing Group of nations.[3] In other words, I think that if we are going to have a "hot line" to Moscow we ought to have a "hot line" to our allies and at least to the Secretary General of NATO.

One might argue that this policy promotes proliferation. One might argue further that we should take on more nations—Western Germany, for example. But the three nations who are the three occupying powers in Berlin are the ones who are going to be the nuclear powers. Since such is the case, I agree with Mr. Possony that the United States ought to give France a lift and get some modern weapons in there, instead of France going through the long, tedious process of developing her own nuclear force. Perhaps with the funds saved we can get some conventional forces from France up to Germany.[4]

---

[3] The Standing Group is composed of the Permanent Military Representatives of the United States, Great Britain, and France. An executive arm of the Military Committee (composed of the Chiefs of Staff of each NATO member country other than Ireland), the Standing Group meets in Washington and is in actual charge of directing the NATO military command structure.

[4] Although the problem of conventional forces within the NATO alliance was not a specific topic for discussion, both General Moore and Admiral Ruge commented on the need to establish reserve militia forces as a supplement to the regular conventional forces of NATO.

Moore: In focusing attention on the use of nuclear weapons in the more exotic forms of warfare, we run the risk of playing down the idea that we could have a conventional war in Europe. We may come to feel that if we deter nuclear war, we deter all forms of warfare. Yet there are obviously many situations where only conventional forces are required and very logically will be used. For example, in connection with the approaches to Berlin or perhaps an uprising in East Germany. We also face the possibility of a limited attack in order to confront us with a *fait accompli*. The resulting political situation can be embarrassing unless we are able to respond promptly with strong conventional forces.

Such forces are an essential military requirement, but we are not getting the thirty divisions that estimates have indicated are necessary to deal with the various situations that might arise. I have therefore suggested that even if we are going to fight a truly mobile type of war (which I think is the type that is indicated), we still must look out for the areas that have to be protected. Every

Ruge: Having talked with two Ministers of Defense and quite a number of other people in the German Federal Republic, I have never met any-

---

commander who is confronted with the situation of defending a city is faced with the choice of tying down part of his troops or having someone operating in his rear.

An additional problem is that our allies are too dependent upon the United States for combat and service support units. If they cannot create these units out of forces which they feel they can put on a regular M-day status, then the units must be made up of reserve forces.

For these reasons I think that the Germans and others can do a great deal more to provide for their own conventional defense. The type of forces that would be particularly useful are service forces plus those to defend cities in which they live. From World War II, I am conversant with the fact that the so-called German stomach battalions put up a rugged defense of their homeland. If we were to organize comparable units now, we would considerably improve NATO's conventional forces and over-all defense posture.

Ruge: The number of army divisions necessary for the defense of Europe has never been reached. In 1950 at New York, the military goal was fifty divisions; in 1952 at Lisbon, the goal was ninety divisions with forty-three divisions earmarked for the central European front. Today, according to most experts, there should be a minimum of thirty fully equipped divisions. But at the present time there are at most only twenty-five divisions under the command of SACEUR.

Even at full strength, however, NATO's forces should have the support of territorial forces who are ready for rapid action and who are capable of occupying the terrain between and behind the NATO forces. These territorial forces should be composed chiefly of young, not older, reservists. They should be organized so that they can do more than merely guard bridges and other installations. They should likewise be trained and armed well enough to fight air-borne troops, vanguards of armored units, and motorized infantry. Organized in the right way, such territorial forces would increase NATO's capability for deterrence.

Western Germany has just started building up a territorial reserve for men who have served in the Bundeswehr. In my view, this move is vitally necessary since in case of war, our entire country will be a battle zone in which the regular armed forces will need the support of territorial forces. We now have about one-half million reservists. In a few years there will be some two million trained civilians. Only slowly have we tried to do something about organizing them. As a first step, a voluntary association was formed a few years ago of which I am currently the president. Then, with minimal subsidization from the government, a small organization was built up by some 160 active officers and sergeants, who have given training and lectures to about 50,000 to 60,000 volunteers. Finally, the government has now announced its plan for a territorial reserve to be composed of 10,000 men this year and 50,000 within three years.

In my opinion, the government's efforts have thus far been excessively focused on problems of top-level organization. We should rather begin from the point of view of the men who volunteer, who want to take part in the reserve. This desire to serve voluntarily should spread throughout the population. I am trying to convince government officials that we should start as simply as possible—from the squad, to the platoon, and then to the company. The first priority is to find adequate leaders of these small groups. Initially, I would not form specialized battalions of engineers, communication specialists, and so on. I would train the men around their own villages and towns; their units should bear the names of these towns. In this way the interest and support of the general public would be facilitated. Having properly organized the base, I would then turn to developing the larger units and specialized units.

If our territorial reserve is adequately prepared, I am convinced that it will be a good contribution to the deterrent. We know that the Russians are afraid of these types of troops because they have had their own experience with guerrillas. If they can reasonably expect this kind of resistance throughout all of Western Germany, they will in all probability not attempt a surprise attack.

body who has advocated that we should make our own nuclear weapons—contrary to what the newspapers have said about it. What we do desire is that nuclear weapons be made available to our NATO forces, because without such weapons they would be at a great disadvantage in case of an attack. We would welcome a European nuclear force but this will take time. We would also welcome more political unity but this will take time, too.

For the immediate future, we would like to share in the common responsibility of nuclear weapons planning. This is not so much a military problem as it is largely a psychological problem that requires political leadership for its solution. As far as the military are concerned, they have demonstrated the possibility of combined planning. It has been constantly shown by the work of the integrated staffs.

Allais: There is an important point which has not yet been raised concerning French atomic policy. Many people think that this policy would change substantially if General de Gaulle were no longer in power in France.

Certainly it is difficult in practice for the United States to renounce any part of her final control of the use of her atomic weapons.

But where the vital interests of Western Europe are at issue, it is also absolutely impossible for Europeans to accept that the final decision of peace or war could be taken only by the United States.

From this point of view, my conviction is that French atomic policy would not change very much if General de Gaulle were no longer in power.

In any case, I think that the present situation cannot be maintained. Major changes are called for.

Kissinger: I do not think that the issue of nuclear weapons in Europe should be put in terms of either complete dependence of the Europeans of the United States or complete independence of the Europeans from the United States. In any foreseeable situation, we will have no choice in the case of a massive attack on Europe except to support the Europeans—whatever military strategy they adopt. Equally, I agree with Sir John Slessor that a war started by Europeans without American support is the most remote possibility and the one for which European forces are ill suited. In any event, I know no responsible Europeans who would argue that the Europeans should fight a nuclear war all by themselves. They look at nuclear weapons rightly or wrongly in the terms outlined by General Beaufre.

The fundamental question we have to ask ourselves about the Europeans and their role in nuclear weapons is not the technical capabilities of their weapons systems but what kind of Europe we want to deal with. We have become too obsessed with de Gaulle. We are overlooking the strong possibility that ten years from now we may be facing not a Europe that wants to assert itself successfully but a Europe that is perfectly willing to turn over all responsibilities to the United States. In such a case we will have central commanding control of everything and we will have to ask ourselves whether that is the kind of world we wanted to live in.

I would suggest therefore that the issue of what specific nuclear forces can or cannot do is not as crucial as the kind of political and psychological milieu within which any force has to operate. Before I give up on the possibility of cooperating with different nuclear forces in the alliance, I really believe that we should address ourselves to General Beaufre's question. I do not know why it is impossible for autonomous nuclear forces to be coordinated according to different plans. I do not see why the major thrust of American policy has to be an attempt to break up the establishment of different national nuclear forces within the alliance.

Finally, from a purely military point of view, I would like to underline a point of Mr. Mosely which he has been making about the problem of third area conflict. If one projects American involvement over the next fifteen years, one has reasonably to assume that we will be heavily engaged in Asia, Latin America, perhaps Africa. In these conditions we have to ask ourselves whether it is healthy for Europe to be in a position of being blackmailed by the Soviets while our attention is diverted elsewhere, or whether there is some utility in having some European autonomy, if only from the point of view of its impact on Soviet calculations.

Coordination and Control of Nuclear Weapons

Cerny: As the comments so far have already made quite clear, it is difficult to discuss particular aspects of the nuclear problem in the NATO alliance without raising at the same time the aspect of coordination and control of nuclear weapons. In his address to us,[5] Secretary Ball pinpointed this aspect as one of the major pieces of unfinished business in the NATO alliance. To give some indication of the wide spectrum of views here represented on this vital issue, we have chosen statements from Ambassador Burgess, General Beaufre, and Mr. Morgenthau. Participants in this exchange of views will doubtless wish to comment as well on the address of Secretary Ball. For not only did the Secretary present a forthright defense of the current United States proposal for the creation of a multilateral nuclear force (MLF) but he also challenged critics of this proposal to offer a more practical and effective alternative.

---

[5] See p. 11.

On this topic it is most desirable to set the record straight. All through current discussion one finds the statement that the United States has reserved for itself a monopoly of nuclear weapons. This is a dangerous half-truth.

Each NATO country already has the opportunity to become a direct partner with the United States in nuclear armaments, and such participation involves sharing in the development of strategic concepts and plans.

W. Randolph Burgess

Because of failure to adopt a joint strategic policy . . . an attempt has been made at a system of consultation within the framework of NATO which has not really worked, and which, moreover, could hardly have practical results since within NATO, interest in extra-European questions is very different between the nations. Thus, we have returned to a policy of disunity. . . .

The only logical solution . . . is a return to consultation on common strategy among nations having worldwide interests, subsequently discussing the original application of that strategy with other allied nations concerned.

General André Beaufre

Since proliferation appears to be inevitable and political "Atlantic Union" unattainable, a European nuclear deterrent controlled by a European political authority is the best attainable alternative. Such support implies a radical change in our present policies which, by trying to isolate France, render the political unification of Europe impossible and seek in vain to restore the Atlantic alliance on foundations which no longer exist.

Hans J. Morgenthau

(Since the panel members so frequently referred to Secretary Ball's address, the relevant portions are hereby reproduced.)

The dilemma we face cannot, therefore, be safely brushed aside. If we regard the proliferation of national deterrent systems as undesirable and if we consider that the present exclusion of a large part of the members of the Western alliance from nuclear management is not likely to last, what other options do we have?

It is our attempt to answer this question that led us in 1960 to propose the creation of a multilateral nuclear force. I recognize that this force has become a subject of some controversy not merely among you *cognoscenti* in this dialogue but in similar discussions elsewhere. Yet, as I see it, those who challenge the wisdom or effectiveness of such a force are yet to suggest an adequate alternative.

The multilateral force we are proposing would be organized within the framework of the Western alliance. To constitute a truly international force, we have felt that it should meet four conditions:

First, it should be assigned to NATO by all countries participating in the force. To meet this condition, we propose that all participating nations share in the costs of creating, maintaining, and operating it.

Second, it should not be predominantly based on the soil of any one nation. To meet this condition, we are proposing a sea-based force consisting of Polaris-type missiles mounted on surface warships. This force, deployed on the high seas, would operate outside the national limits of any state.

Third, it should be managed and operated by nationals of all participating countries under such conditions that it could not be withdrawn from the alliance to serve the national uses of any participating government. To meet this requirement, we propose that the ships themselves be manned by mixed crews of nationals of the participating nations.

The United States Joint Chiefs of Staff and the Secretary of Defense have concluded that an efficient first-class force can be created in this fashion. SACEUR[6] has stated he would welcome the force as a significant addition to NATO's deterrent forces.

Fourth, the decision to fire the Polaris weapons should be a collective decision of the participating nations. One proposal is that political control be exercised through an executive body representing the participating nations. Obviously this control question is the heart of the matter. We are confident it can be solved.

In an ideal world we could no doubt devise less elaborate means for managing nuclear weapons. But we must work within the limitations of existing political arrangements.

Those limitations arise from the fact that Western political institutions have not evolved in pace with the march of our technology. Until the West has achieved a far greater political unity than it possesses today, we believe that the development of a multilateral force is the best available course to pursue.

Not only does it offer the most effective means of dealing with the nuclear problem in the present political framework, it can also make possible a gradual and constructive evolution

---

[6] Supreme Allied Commander Europe.

within that framework. The multilateral force would provide a new opportunity for working toward a greater unity in Europe and a closer partnership between the two sides of the Atlantic.

For the striking progress that has been achieved toward these goals in the past decade and a half has, to a considerable extent, come about from necessity—from the fact that governments have been compelled to cope with specific and immediate problems in Europe and the Atlantic area. And, as we seek to cope with the problem of nuclear management, I have no doubt that we shall—of necessity—make further strides toward a greater political unity in the years ahead.

Over the long pull, it will not be abstract principle but importunate necessity—the urgent need to get hard things done in order that we may survive and flourish—that will move us toward the attainment of the ultimate objective of unity and partnership.

George W. Ball

Burgess: I thought that George Ball gave us an extremely useful and valuable exposition of the MLF. Although I agree with a great part of his address, there is one footnote that I would have added and that is suggested by the statements selected from my essay. The "new" United States policy to which the Secretary alluded did not originate in 1960. Certainly since 1957 the United States has been struggling with this problem of the control of nuclear weapons. Moreover, over a period of years our country has moved in a very substantial way towards sharing political and military control of nuclear weapons.

In some of the essays by my fellow panelists, the claim is repeatedly made that the United States has preserved sole control over nuclear weapons. I do not believe that this claim is valid. With respect to actual military control, a great many weapons are now posted in Europe which, under the two-key system, can only be fired with the consent of an ally and the United States. With respect to the far more important issue of political control, the NATO Council has to a substantial extent undertaken joint analysis of basic problems, objectives, strategy, and deployment. During the period that I was United States Permanent Ambassador to NATO (1957-1961), we spent a good deal of time in the NATO Council and in committees, reviewing this whole question of the relation of the alliance to nuclear weapons. Further steps were made after I left, including the establishment of an allied committee in Omaha, and the organization under European command at SHAPE [Supreme Headquarters Allied Powers Europe] of a more formalized staff to plan nuclear weapons strategy. Moreover, for many years, the targeting of NATO's nuclear equipment has been done by an inter-allied staff. (In my day it was headed by a Canadian.) It is certainly not true therefore to claim that the allies have had no participation in the general philosophy and control—political control—of nuclear weapons.

But if I were to underline a part of George Ball's address, it is the need for carrying this joint political control still further. The heart of the problem is not who finally pulls the trigger. At that point there will be no time for consultation. The heart of the problem is to improve consultation on the determination of the broad policies that will guide any use or potential use of nuclear weapons.

I can't refrain from expressing my full disagreement with those of my colleagues here who advocate that the United States should offer to our European allies control over nuclear weapons. Our government representatives certainly have no such power or authority because American policy against the proliferation of nuclear weapons is written very clearly into the law. Not only do I see no prospect that Congress will change the law, but furthermore, if I were called as a witness, I certainly would not recommend any change.

I think that the arguments made by George Ball are very conclusive as to the extreme unwisdom of our spraying more nuclear knowledge about the world. Even among our own allies, political parties do change in Europe; somebody may come to power whose policies are not fully reliable. Let me illustrate by one political point. Some day the satellites are going to kick up their heels again. What will be the policy of Western Germany, for example, with respect to a new rebellion in East Germany? If Western Germany had an independent nuclear deterrent as a result of our having broken down the barrier of non-proliferation, we would face, in my view, an extremely dangerous situation for world peace.

I conclude by emphasizing once again the importance of further consultation, of securing wider political agreements. I think that one of the strongest arguments for the MLF—which I favor not necessarily in every detail, but in principle—is that it will lead to further pressure for political consultation and further desire on the part of the participant countries to engage actively in such consultation.

Beaufre: I have been somewhat less than encouraged by the remarks of Ambassador Burgess. As I am optimistic, however, I would say that his remarks have the necessary components for achieving something useful; that is, the acknowledgement that we need some kind of better consultation—whatever the opinions we might have on the aims of such consultation. If I say that I have been somewhat less than encouraged by what Ambassador Burgess has said, it is because I know very well what the Standing Group is or has been, just as he knows very well what the NATO Council is or has been. And I know that there has not been—and I state this very firmly—any consultation on strategic nuclear matters at the Standing Group level. Of course, there have been discussions on details and applications, but not on basic principles.

The lack of meaningful consultation has been the major cause of European discontent with American nuclear strategy within the alliance. It is not simply that American strategy has been constantly changing; the important point is that it has been unilaterally changing. If Americans had elaborated their changing strategic ideas about joint consideration and deliberation with their allies, I am sure that the strategic conclusions would probably have been similar. And the necessity for changing alliance strategy would probably have been met about the same time.

It is quite true that Europeans have different interests and different points of view. Where such interests and views have been overlooked in American strategic thinking, then proper consultation would insure that they be incorporated into the assumptions of the strategic deliberations. And I am sure that the resulting strategy would be much better because of such incorporation. However, here too, European discontent with American nuclear strategy is caused not only by neglect of their different interests and views, but also because Europeans have not had the opportunity to study the problems as well as the Americans. Americans have devoted considerable time and skill to the study of nuclear matters. Europeans have not. If we had studied such matters together, then we probably would have reached the same conclusions.

I think therefore that the only way to cure the present difficulties of NATO is to devise a better means of working in common, of elaborating strategy in common. Here is the only way to create a joint appreciation of what our common interests—if we have any—really are. During World War II, I remember that certain decisions were taken by the British which at the time seemed very hard to us Frenchmen. But on the whole these decisions were in the common interest to win the war. It is the common, the joint over-all, interest that we must come to appreciate and understand.

I am also reminded of an old saying of Marshal Foch when he became Allied Commander-in-Chief during the first World War: "Now I no longer give orders. I have only to convince." Based on my many years of experience at different levels in NATO, I agree with Marshal Foch that the only way of commanding an alliance is to convince. If there is any American leadership, and I think there is, it rests on its ability to convince. And to convince means to speak together, to explore new problems together, to arrive at answers together. In these ways, common understanding can probably be reached. To do otherwise is to have a repetition of the events of the past few years: the unilateral enunciation of successive decisions and strategies which fail to secure agreement and instead increase the difficulties of the alliance.

Morgenthau: Secretary Ball's challenge to those of us who have been critical of MLF contains an element of sophistry. I am reminded of a story which is told about the earthquake of Lisbon in 1755. After the quake, somebody walked through the streets of Lisbon hawking anti-earthquake pills. When he was approached and asked about the value of the pills, he replied, "What would you put in their place?" I don't share the assumptions that there is a gimmick against earthquakes which you can swallow. I don't have any alternative pill to prescribe, but I think I have an answer to the question which was implicit in the challenge of Secretary Ball's address.

The problem which we are facing today has stared us in the face, without our acknowledging it, for a full decade. When an atomic stalemate developed between East and West, it became obvious to some of us, and it should have become obvious to the Government of the United States, that one of the very foundation stones of the Atlantic alliance was in the process of eroding. I would say again that in spite of his unpopularity, it is to President de Gaulle's credit to have made this fundamental fact obvious. In politics, as in life in general, facts unfortunately do not go away by not being recognized. I agree fully therefore with the criticism which has been expressed about the lack of policies on the part of our government, about the lack of awareness of those facts which were obvious to others and should have been obvious to our Government. In a sense, this criticism is water over the dam. But if one wants to solve the present problem, it is still important to recognize what the present problem is and where we have gone astray.

The first conclusion I would reach is that it is impossible to preserve or to restore the status quo of January 14, 1963. You cannot restore the Atlantic alliance on a foundation which in good measure no longer exists. The question before us, then, is how to build a new foundation appropriate to changed circumstances. In my view, proliferation is an evil, and bipolarity is greatly to be preferred to proliferation. Unfortunately we are faced here once again with a fact, not a theory. While nobody can say how far proliferation will go, it is developing. It is idle, therefore, to think in terms of restoring bipolarity or preserving some semblance of it. The real question is: how can you live with proliferation? What kind of political institutions, what kind of political policy can you pursue in order to minimize the obvious dangers and risks inherent in proliferation?

So stated, the problem is not one of military technicalities; it is a political problem. For the problem would not exist if the United States and its European allies saw eye to eye on the basic interests and policies that might call for the use or the threat of the use of nuclear weapons. The real problem then is a problem of creative statesmanship. Out of the inchoate political issues which face us today and which on the surface evoke different policies, statesmen must literally create the common interest which underlies the surface differences. For my part, I am firmly convinced that such a common interest exists and that it has exerted a very profound influence, tying the United States to the nations of Western Europe.

I am not convinced, however, that consultation is the whole answer to this quest for a common interest. Consultation among people who disagree can perhaps best be described as a kind of social exercise which makes everybody feel better afterwards but which does not solve the fundamental problem. In the case of NATO, the fundamental problem is really the problem of sovereignty, of the ultimate decision upon which the life and death of nations depend. And as Alexander Hamilton noted in the Constitutional Convention, sovereignty cannot rest in two places; it must be either here or there.

From this vantage point, the great and fundamental criticism that I have against the MLF is that it sidesteps this fundamental issue concerning the ultimate decision on the use of nuclear weapons. Terms such as "partnership," "interdependence," or "consultation" merely gloss over the issue, rather than face it squarely. Short of such remote objectives as a confederation or a real Atlantic Community, there is no solution to our problem other than the continuous application of creative statesmanship. On a piecemeal day-by-day basis, such statesmanship must create a true community of interests out of apparent divergences of interests. In this way, whenever the problem of the use, or the threat of use, of nuclear weapons arises, the nations concerned will see eye to eye and proceed to use or threaten to use the weapons for the same interests.

Brugmans: I do agree that simple consultation among sovereign nations is not enough. For "consultation" means that if nations can agree, all is well; if they cannot, it is just too bad. But is there some mid-point between sheer consultation and a full-fledged federation? I think that there is and that it works tolerably well in the European communities. The purists will probably discuss whether this is "pre-federal," "federalistic," "confederal," "supranational," or "supranationalistic." Let's say it is "communitarian"—if there is such a word. In any event, the reality is much *more* than consultation, and much *less* than the building of a federal state. It is rather the formation of a group of peoples, around a kind of strong international secretariat or "commission" who are deeply rooted in their own national identities and who still must, as part of their official function, go beyond their separate national interests to search for the interests of the community. As long as the political will to achieve such a common denominator is there, the technical solution of establishing such a secretariat is quite manageable. On the other hand, of course, if the political will is lacking, then to call for a well-equipped international secretariat or "commission" is not a formula able in itself to achieve practical results.

Moore: I know that the consultations that go on in the NATO Council now are much more extensive than most of us around this table seem to think. Ambassador Burgess has verified that members of the Council just do not sit around twiddling their thumbs all day. They are responsible people with jobs to do, and they address themselves to these problems constantly.

Furthermore, I believe that these consultations on NATO strategy have been very useful. For one thing, no military man wants the politicians to get off the hook on determining when nuclear weapons are to be used. It is their responsibility. For another thing, to explore various situations, such as the NATO Council has done at considerable length with Berlin contingency planning, yields indirect benefits. I doubt that any one of the plans which have been developed will ever be used exactly as written. When the time comes to act, conditions are always different from previous planning; at least that has been my experience. Indirectly, however, the consultations with the NATO Council convey to the military a feeling of what the political people are thinking, how the different nations react, and just how far they want to go. Thus when a crisis suddenly develops—usually about two o'clock on a Sunday morning—and when there is no time to contact anybody, a General Norstad or a General Lemnitzer has some understanding of what the political sense of the NATO Council may be. Because of this, past military decisions have been politically sound.

Strausz-Hupé: In accepting Secretary Ball's challenge to come up with a better alternative than MLF, I should like to refer to an idea of General Gallois, an idea which he advanced some four or five years ago. General Gallois distinguished between what he calls strategy *tout court* and a strategy of means. With respect to the first kind of strategy—strategy in the conventional meaning of the word—he suggested that each member of the alliance should pursue his own strategy (an observation with which I do not agree). With respect to a strategy of means, he suggested that the allies should cooperate closely on matters of procurement and logistics.

In keeping with General Gallois' strategy of means, I suggest that the United States institute a nucleonics procurement program in which our European allies would be cut in. That is, we would farm out to our European allies some of the contractual work for our missilery, our command and control electronics systems. To my mind, this program would be a far more valuable and a much cheaper education in the mysteries of nuclear warfare than the multilateral force. It would be of mutual benefit and unlike the multilateral force, it would actually advance the state of the arts. It would enlist the imagination and inventiveness of our European allies.

My second suggestion takes up a point that was made in Secretary Ball's address. If I understood him rightly, he expressed his assent to the creation of a true European nuclear force with Britain in it. Now, if this is an approach which we approve of, then why not take it forthrightly? Why not say to our European allies, that if they agree to create such a united nuclear force, then we will give them support? If we can't give them nuclear warheads under the McMahon Act, then most certainly we will give them the missilery and the electronic know-how. In short we will help them as rapidly as possible to create this European nuclear deterrent—provided they meet our conditions.

Our conditions may well be tough. But let us make a clear proposal and, if you will, a proposal that does commit us to the idea of transferring under certain circumstances the political control of that nuclear force to Europe. This is precisely what the MLF does not do. You can produce a very entertaining production of Hamlet without the Danish Prince; but it is not Hamlet. The same point applies to the MLF. It is a European collective nuclear force, and yet it is not a European collective force, for the simple reason that the all-important problem of political control (as incidentally Secretary Ball himself conceded) is left in suspense.

It can of course be argued that our European allies will not accept our proposal for a united nuclear force, and that de Gaulle will sabotage it. Let us however put our proposal on the table. Let us see what our European friends do and let us see whether European public opinion, including French public opinion, will not find such a proposal acceptable. I think it will. It can be argued that if we make such a proposal, the Soviets will be angry. Yet they are angry at MLF now. How much angrier is the Soviet leadership going to get? It is also true that if we make such a proposal we will perhaps damage the prospects for disarmament and arms control in Europe. But this argument reveals our major difficulty in the alliance. We have been trying to work both sides of the street. We have to make up our minds as to which goal comes first: Atlantic unity? or arms control and the détente with the Soviet Union? I think that it would be a tragedy if for the sake of the myth of a Soviet-United States nuclear community of interests, for the sake of preventing "war by inadvertence"—incidentally, one of the most celebrated myths—we would postpone taking the steps that must now be taken to keep the Atlantic alliance alive.

Knorr: I recognize that the MLF proposal has very definite weaknesses, the greatest of which is that very few of our allies are really interested in it. Whatever other advantages the MLF proposal may have, this weakness is crucial. I myself therefore am very much interested in alternatives that may be found more acceptable by our allies. It seems to me, however, that Mr. Strausz-Hupé's alternative to the MLF bears a very close resemblance to what is actually the United States proposal. If I understand him rightly, he is talking about a multinational force and not just about independent nuclear forces in Western Europe. Furthermore, he is suggesting that within such a force the United States must be ready not to exercise a special veto over the employment of strategic forces. I think that we ought to be aware of the fact that United States official policy about the MLF does envisage the possible relinquishment of the United States veto. It is a definite direction in which the MLF may evolve. Mr. Strausz-Hupé also said that if the United States proposes such a multinational force, we may want to attach very tough conditions. I can very easily see why we might want to. But he did not spell out what these conditions might be. Until I know more about them, I question how different Mr. Strausz-Hupé's alternative really is.

Kissinger: I would like to make one brief methodological point about which I feel very strongly. According to Secretary Ball's address, it is necessary to have an alternative to something that is proposed in order to be able to criticize it. Yet if one accepts the assumptions in terms of which the proposal is made, then the proposal becomes unanswerable. If one assumes that proliferation is undesirable and that it would be best to end the British and French nuclear programs, and if one assumes that there is a great German desire—indeed, an Italian, a Greek, a Turkish desire—to be brought into the nuclear business, then of course one is bound to come up with answers very similar to those that are now advanced by the United States Government. It is the assumptions which are in question and not a particular technical gimmick which is advanced in terms of a particular set of assumptions.

The United States had two choices in Europe. The first choice was to try to build on the existing nuclear programs in Europe; namely, those of Britain and France. The second choice was to create something new with the stated advantages of blocking the two existing programs and bringing all the European non-nuclear countries into a new program. I believe that the first choice would have been by far the wiser course. Moreover, I am impressed by the fact that if we once make up our minds which way we want to go, the technical solutions can be found. If we had put as much thought on the first choice as on the second, we might have an available alternative today.

Possony: I do not agree with the effort to divorce psycho-political from technological considerations of the nuclear problem. If I were to believe some of my colleagues here, politics and psychology are the means to solve difficult technical and military problems. But to solve technological problems is not a matter of mere gimmickry. To be sure, all strategic decisions are political and therefore reflect psychological considerations. Nevertheless I should have thought that by 1964 we had progressed to a realization that technological and psycho-political factors are interrelated.

As I see it, the main problem of the alliance is to solve the trigger problem. I agree that the trigger problem is a question of sovereignty; but it is really more significantly a question of timing. In the nuclear era, the new fact is that when the warning signal of a possible attack is received, there are only some five to ten minutes trans-Atlantic time to make a decision. European warning times are even shorter, as are warning times against submarine attacks on the United States. Under these conditions, traditional methods of consultation and decision-making are no longer feasible.

To deal with this question of timing, I have suggested (and the proposal is discussed at greater length in my essay) the utilization of electronic computers for the purpose of pre-planning and pre-programming entire ranges of NATO responses to potential aggressive moves by the enemy. My proposal is hardly revolutionary. If the man who has the finger on the trigger today, namely the President of the United States, does not pre-program what he will do in case of attack, he will not do anything and we—and NATO—will be defeated very rapidly. Preplanning is therefore a fact of life. Moreover, it has the distinct advantage of minimizing the dangers of last-minute panic decisions which may be either very defeatist or overly aggressive.

From the point of view of the NATO alliance, the principle of preplanning and pre-programming can enable the allies not only to consult beforehand, but also to make important decisions on the nature and extent of the NATO response. There is simply no reason why we need to continue the old-fashioned type of consultation where people sit together and in some rather vague and nebulous way discuss problems without ever coming to grips with details. It is all very well to suggest that details are unimportant; yet it is the details that count. Under preprogramming it will soon become evident that there is a need for integrating intelligence. Estimates will have to be made jointly, not just by intelligence chiefs but certainly from time to time by the chiefs of government as well. These estimates may have to be revised as situations change. Without a common base of estimating the actual threats, there is simply no common basis for making decisions. And there is no reason in the world why there should be a divergence of views as to whether a particular threat is conventional or unconventional in nature, whether it is composed of 300 missiles or two divisions, whether there is a military threat at all. Agreement on these matters is perfectly feasible—given the same base of facts and data.

Of course, agreement depends upon objective fact-finding—objectivity on all pertinent facts. Still, it is possible—indeed it is necessary—to go much further. For example, I think one of the high priority items that should be decided is the treatment of the medium-range ballistic missile threat against Europe. This problem can neither be ignored nor glossed over by some statement to the effect that it can be handled from the United States continent.

A more important example involves the problem of nuclear weapons development, for it highlights the complete disparity between American policy and European interests. The United States has a whole stable of nuclear weapons to cover all conceivable military needs. Yet these weapons are not always well adapted to the needs of Europe. If I were a European chief of staff, I would insist on two specifications for nuclear weaponry: (a) the weapons must be clean because Europe has densely populated areas to defend; and (b) the delivery means have to be of the utmost accuracy so that we can reduce nuclear yields.

To achieve these specifications is perfectly feasible—*if* the development of nuclear technology were to be unfettered. But we in the United States just cannot make the decisions alone and only for ourselves; we must take into account the specific interests of our allies. (For that matter, I would like to stress that I do not believe clean weapons and accurate delivery systems are contrary to the national interests of the United States.) With proper pre-planning and pre-programming, "consultation" can become something more than a catch-all, something more than merely sending polite and perhaps misleading notes on matters of disagreement.

These general considerations lead me to the currently much debated question of establishing an international force within the NATO alliance. What precisely is intended by proposing such an international force? Is the essential purpose that national forces are to be coordinated, as I have suggested, through proper pre-programming under a NATO-wide system of control command communications? Or is the essential purpose to achieve mixed manning of weapons systems? If the latter, the feasibility and utility of the scheme are highly limited. Perhaps mixed manning is feasible on naval vessels; but I don't think it has any real value. In any event, the present MLF proposal if implemented would set up only a fraction of the force needed to protect the alliance in Europe. In addition to ship-based missiles, land-based missiles and aircraft are just as necessary. A composite force is required. Not only the types, but likewise the size of such a composite military force would complicate the task of mixed manning. Assume, for purposes of illustration, a force of 1,000 missiles and 500 aircraft. To establish such a force, the military personnel of the United States, Great Britain, France, and the German Federal Republic can be mixed up in various ways. But surely the point is that whatever the particular solution to manning, the real challenge is to coordinate decision-making at the top echelons. No matter what it may be called, the process still amounts to placing national forces under a coordinated international command structure. We are fooling ourselves if we think there is any way to avoid the "integration" of national units under international command.

I also think that we are tilting at windmills when we struggle against "proliferation." There is no such thing as "proliferation" because there cannot be. At most some two dozen nations are capable of producing adequate supplies of nuclear weapons; at least this will be true for a long time to come. Of these nations, probably no more than six nations are capable of producing the whole range of offensive and defensive weapons systems that are necessary to fight a modern war. Today many more nations can produce aircraft that can produce nuclear weapons. Yet how many nations actually do produce good and modern aircraft? How many do so even for their own security needs? If the task is to produce the whole range of weapons systems, the number of capable nations is bound to be—and to remain—very small. In short, if the dangers of "proliferation" refer to the number of nations that may become "nuclear powers," those dangers are largely fictional.

On the other hand, if the dangers of "proliferation" refer to the example raised by Ambassador Burgess, then I believe that we are still conjuring up unrealistic dangers. Admittedly the Germans have a problem; some action would be required in the case of an uprising in East Germany. But surely such a crisis presents precisely the kind of contingency for which there should be a NATO-wide policy, a policy that must be pre-programmed and that should represent a joint policy. Even if the policy were to break down and the Germans were able to shift for themselves, it is highly unlikely that they would decide unilaterally to use offensive military force to aid the East Germans. In the first place, they have no offensive capability. Second, the German Army is under the NATO commander. Third, it would be suicidal for a nation to fight a war with the Soviets when it has at most one-fourth of the Soviet Union's population and when it lacks the strength even to defend itself.

It is time, therefore, that we stop deluding ourselves with false fears and false expectations. The real problems which we face are sufficiently formidable; their solution will not come by wishful thinking, nor will it be helped by diversionary preoccupations. I suggest that we start by tackling the trigger problem along the lines of pre-planning and pre-programming and then move on to the joint research and development of adequate weapon systems, of the types of weapons that will be best for NATO as a whole.

Brugmans: I wish to reinforce what Mr. Possony has said concerning German reunification. I think that if there is no basic agreement within the NATO alliance on the necessity of bringing more liberty to Eastern Europe as a whole and East Germany in particular, I do not see what the whole alliance is about. We should refrain from thinking that the East German problem is specifically a German affair or that the Germans might toy with the idea of going it alone militarily. Neither of these propositions is realistic, although it may well be true that another East German uprising would find West Germans reacting more emotionally and demanding top priority for some kind of allied policy response.

Ruge: We West Germans are not as emotional as we are sometimes made to appear, and we would definitely not start a war on our own for reunification. What we ask from our allies is help to keep the prospect of reunification alive. Among the seventy million people who have been forced into colonial status in Eastern Europe, the case of Eastern Germany is particularly bad. On this matter the Soviets have a very bad conscience, and they will have to change in the course of time. We can facilitate this change by firmness, close cooperation, and the clarification of our common aims within the alliance.

With respect to the MLF, it is in our opinion an entirely feasible proposal; mixed manning presents no difficulties. We do not look upon the MLF, however, as a substitute for Polaris submarines. It is rather a substitute for mobile MRBM's [medium-range ballistic missiles] within the Federal Republic. Although the problem has not been studied very extensively, we are so cramped for room in the Federal Republic, that mobile MRBM's are not a very good military solution. Admittedly, it is quite clear that the MLF does not solve the political problem of sharing control. Yet Western Germany is quite reconciled to this drawback and it will also agree to bear the financial burdens. In any event, whatever the drawbacks of the MLF proposal, one strong point in its favor is that the Soviets are greatly worried about its establishment.

Slessor: In accepting Secretary Ball's challenge to produce a viable alternative to the MLF, I am not scoffing at the American proposal. It is rather that the MLF does not serve very well to satisfy what in my view are two essential requirements of any alternative proposal.

The first of these requirements is political. I agree with Ambassador Burgess and Mr. Knorr that tremendous progress has been made toward decision-sharing and that the MLF is a genuine American move toward furthering this process of sharing common responsibilities and authority. Still, the MLF does not serve this political purpose very well because control continues to rest ultimately with the United States. To "mix-man" the means of delivery is completely irrelevant. We should not confuse the issue by questioning the feasibility of mixed manning. Of course it is feasible. But we don't want to "mix-man" the means of delivery; we want to "mix-man" the method of control. It is also perfectly true that all the allies must share financial burdens if they are going to feel that they really have a share in the common responsibility. Yet practically all the allies already have a share in the ownership and financial burdens of the means of delivery of nuclear weapons. What they lack is strategic capacity and ownership of warheads. These don't matter too much if we are really an alliance and provided that we have a reasonable system of control and shared responsibility for command.

The second requirement of any alternative proposal is that it will not waste enormous resources—and mind you, this MLF is going to be darned expensive—at the cost of real military needs. From the European point of view, these needs are twofold: to increase our capacity for the direct defense of Europe by strengthening the equipment of our land forces and supporting air forces; and to improve our position for meeting threats to Western interests elsewhere in the world. The MLF does not serve these needs very well. It is a single-shot weapon which has only one use in one exceedingly unique contingency.

My alternative proposal is that we go back to the Nassau conception of a multinational force composed of national contingents under an international command.[7] All nuclear weapons other than pure battlefield weapons like Davy Crocketts would be placed under a SHAPE-type command. I would like to go further and see that the headquarters of the national contingents also contain international elements. The job of this NATO nuclear strike force should be the direct defense of Europe against invasion. And for this part of the deterrent to be credible, it must include provision for long-range interdiction.

In my view, two common criticisms against this type of multinational force are unrealistic. To those who argue that a multilateral force is less easily unscrambled than a multinational force, I would answer that we can't base a policy on the assumption that one ally is going to go crazy at the last minute and try to pull out. To those who argue that the United States will still retain a veto in a multinational force, I would answer that this veto is one of the unavoidable facts of life. Whether we Europeans like it or not, this veto exists and perhaps we do harm to the alliance by spelling out too much this ultimate responsibility. In any event, let's not assume that if the United States refuses to go to war in any particular crisis the English or the French are ever going to take on a bilateral nuclear exchange with Russia. Such an assumption is nonsense. Conversely, let's not assume that if the United States decides to go to war, we Europeans are going to be able to sit back and keep our fingers crossed while a bilateral exchange between the two colossi goes on over our heads. This assumption is also absolute nonsense.

Where I do agree with the critics of a multinational force is that the present methods of consultation must be vastly improved. Although

[7] In December 1962, President Kennedy and Prime Minister Macmillan met at Nassau, the Bahamas, and agreed to a plan whereby the United States would furnish Polaris missiles to British-owned submarines which would be assigned within five years to a multinational NATO submarine force. The British retained the right "in the supreme national interest" to withdraw their contingents. A similar offer was made to France.

organization is not the answer to everything, it is sometimes very important psychologically. On this point, I differ with Mr. Possony because I rate the psychological factor somewhat more highly than he does and find myself a bit frightened by his emphasis on the use of electronic computers for pre-programming. To my mind, a matter of great psychological and political importance is the present two-key system of controlling nuclear weapons. Europeans will not feel that they really have a share in making decisions as long as a junior American officer holds the second key in every unit having nuclear capacity. Control at this level ought to be transferred to a NATO agency; it should not be held exclusively by American officers but by a specially recruited corps of NATO officers responsible to the NATO Council.

To sum up, I believe that my alternative of a multinational force under the command of SACEUR would be better than the MLF. Capable of being introduced in a matter of a few months instead of five or six years, it would give the allies some measure of real control—not just over a few hundred Polaris weapons floating in ships in the Atlantic but over the total nuclear arsenal on both sides of the Atlantic. It would not lead to any further proliferation. It would mean financing no more weapons or units other than those which already exist. It would not, I am afraid, meet with the approval of General de Gaulle. But I would like to see us go along without him and I feel sure that in due course the French would come to see NATO as the means of protecting their own best interests.

Radford: [8] I get the general impression that in the minds of most of the panel participants, a nuclear weapon is a nuclear weapon. In other words, if any nuclear weapon is used at all, it is going to be the beginning of the nuclear exchange on a large scale. I don't feel that way. I feel that we are going to have occasions when there will be an exchange of nuclear weapons and the so-called holocaust of World War III will not take place. I don't know where this is going to take place first, whether it is going to be in Southeast Asia or the Middle East, but I feel there will be exchanges of small nuclear weapons.

In the last ten years, we have made a great deal of progress in the development of tactical nuclear weapons. I feel that tactical nuclear weapons are going to be used quickly in the event of hostilities. There are going to be antiaircraft weapons fired with nuclear warheads. There will probably be exchanges of small tactical weapons from artillery pieces or something similar. And these weapons are going to be used offensively and defensively. They are going to be used by the

[8] Admiral Arthur W. Radford, USN (Ret.), former Chairman of the Joint Chiefs of Staff (1953-1957), is a member of the Advisory Board of The Center for Strategic Studies. These remarks were made in response to a question regarding his views on the subject under discussion.

man on the scene at the time. In any basic war planning I do not see how any other conclusion can be reached.

I feel that the solution to the control of nuclear weapons within NATO is the organization of a force under NATO command that would have control over defensive tactical weapons that are on the front lines. Since I have not been consulted by the Navy or the Defense Department about the MLF proposal, I feel perfectly free in giving my opinion. In my view, the MLF is a waste of money. I think that at this time it is not needed. It is not really a solution to the basic problem of control nor will it ever be.

Moore: I cannot agree with Admiral Radford's comments that the use of tactical nuclear weapons is just employment of another weapon with a little bit bigger bang. I think it is considerably more than that. In my view it is next to the last blue chip going in on the table; the final one is all-out nuclear war. Therefore, I feel it is important that we try and devise some method by which we place the potential use of these tactical weapons within the framework of the control mechanism, the political control mechanism, that should be operating in NATO. I also believe that the three Standing Group nations, the United States, Great Britain, and France, have a peculiar position here in the determination of what the next step should be.

In devising an adequate control procedure for the use of tactical nuclear weapons, the really critical problem to be faced is the method of dealing with the kind of attack that does not invite an automatic nuclear response and yet poses a very serious threat if we were to rely solely on our conventional forces. In such a situation some one has to make the determination that our conventional forces are really unable to cope with the attack. I suggest that the chap to make that decision is, in the first instance, the commander of the region where the attack is taking place. If he feels that he must use tactical nuclear weapons, he should first have the consent of the country in which they are going to be used—Germany for example. This request should be relayed to SACEUR, who should put his endorsement on it one way or another. If there are any additional forces that could be used to help out in the situation, SACEUR should have control over them. He might determine that instead of using tactical nuclear weapons at this stage of the game, he will reinforce the regional commander with additional air support. On the other hand, if SACEUR feels that the situation calls for the use of nuclear weapons, his estimate should be referred promptly to the heads of the three Standing Group nations plus the Secretary General of NATO. Operating under guidelines that would have been laid down by the NATO Council, they should make the determination as to whether or not the use of tactical nuclear weapons is authorized.

The reason I believe that the three Standing Group countries should make the final determination is because these are the three that will be in on the next act of an all-out nuclear war in the event that the use of tactical nuclear weapons does not suffice. This escalation might follow in a matter of minutes or hours, so strategic forces must be ready. In any case, under the general guidelines that would have been previously laid down, it is the Standing Group countries—with the Secretary General representing the remaining NATO nations in a non-voting capacity—that should make the final determination.

Kleiman: General Beaufre's view that nuclear coordination is needed for purposes of deterrence rather than for defense—a view which is not shared completely by the French chiefs of staff—reflects, I believe, General de Gaulle's personal conviction that nuclear war is highly improbable if not impossible.

General de Gaulle, it should be noted, has been offered coordination of nuclear forces since June 1962, when Secretary Rusk came to Paris for the purpose. The offer has not yet been accepted. What President de Gaulle really wants is the kind of political and military contingency planning that worked so well for Berlin. He would like this applied elsewhere in the world and to other problems, particularly to the question of the nuclear deterrent. Among other things, and I am going here on the private remarks of several of his ministers, he wants to see the American war plans and to have a share in shaping them.

I am reminded of a story about Ambassador Finletter, after President Truman appointed him Chairman of the Air Policy Committee back in 1946 or 1947. He and his Committee—this was just before Mr. Finletter became Secretary of the Air Force—called on the Joint Chiefs of Staff. Among other things, they asked to see the American war plans. The Joint Chiefs were agreeable and promised to produce them for the next meeting. At the next meeting, the war plans were still not produced. Mr. Finletter began to believe that he was getting the run-around. So he went to President Truman, who issued a very stern directive. The Air Policy Committee then went back and met with the Joint Chiefs of Staff. But the war plans were still not produced. After the meeting was over, General Eisenhower, Chief of Staff of the Army at the time, took Mr. Finletter by the elbow and said: "I think you have been treated shamefully, and I want to tell you what is really up. . . . There are no war plans."

This is a true story. I do not know whether there were any war plans in 1946 or 1947. But I do know that, since 1958, General de Gaulle has been trying to get a look at America's war plans, and he has not succeeded. This highlights the critical problem in NATO as far as the nuclear question is concerned. The issue does not primarily involve the making of decisions on the use of nuclear weapons. President de Gaulle does not seem to be asking any longer for a veto over the use of nuclear weapons anywhere in the world.[9] What he is primarily interested in, I believe, is the idea of a small nuclear directorate in NATO and also a tripartite U.S.-British-French body that would help the three chiefs of government shape a world strategy for the West in foreign policy and defense.

The issue of a small directorate, I think, is more alive now than it has ever been because it has been taken up by other people. For example, both the Conservative and Labour Parties of Great Britain are demanding a greater role for Great Britain in the preparation of American war plans. That is the chief device through which they hope to share in the making of nuclear decisions. They seem content to leave the actual decision on use in American hands. I don't know whether the British agree with General de Gaulle that such a final decision will never be made. But they think that the important aspect of the problem is the preparation of the war plans. In their scheme, in other words, the United States would be the executive agent for a joint policy.

The case of General Norstad is another good example of how far the concept of a small nuclear directorate has moved since de Gaulle first proposed it in 1958. Initially, as many of you know, General Norstad very strongly opposed the concept of a directorate. He believed that NATO had to be run by the fifteen nations and all decisions had to be made by the fifteen nations. Yet interestingly enough, in his last months in Paris, he changed his mind. Shortly after he returned to this country in 1963, he spoke of the possibility of a group of three, four, five, even possibly six, nations forming an inner directorate for nuclear matters. More recently, however, he has come to the conclusion that a tripartite United States-British-French group should be established; the Germans would have a special status but they would not be members of this inner group. This change of position by General Norstad is most extraordinary and highly significant. There is probably no individual who has studied the question more closely and who is more familiar with all its political, psychological, and military aspects.

Still another interesting development is that the United States Government, in proposing the multilateral force, has also come around to the restricted-directorate concept. Actually this position is not entirely new to Kennedy-Johnson Administration thinking but it had never been endorsed formally and, in effect, publicly. The secret Acheson report

---

[9] In response to a question from the audience as to whether the French intended to have a veto in 1958 over United States use of nuclear weapons, General Beaufre replied, "In short, the answer is no." Mr. Kleiman later responded: "I am afraid I must disagree with General Beaufre. General de Gaulle's 1958 memorandum may not have stated this with precision; but by early 1959, he and several of his Cabinet Ministers made the French position clear in private discussions. And General de Gaulle, in a speech in Grenoble in October 1960, finally stated publicly: "France intends that if unhappily atomic bombs should be launched in the world, none be launched by the free world without her having agreed."

on NATO made to President Kennedy in the spring of 1961 proposed something in the nature of a nuclear war council of five, including the Germans and the Italians. In the multilateral force (MLF) proposal, the small group is not defined except to say that the major participants —normally considered to be those who contribute more than ten per cent—would be represented on an executive council or committee.

To conclude, it is quite obvious, in my view, that the United States is not going to show its war plans to fifteen NATO countries. I do not think that it is even going to show its Strategic Air Command target plans to fifteen NATO countries. It refuses, as yet, to show them even to the British and the French. British, French, German, and Italian officers are now or shortly will be represented both in SHAPE in Paris and at Omaha in special nuclear planning groups. But they are concerned only with targeting that is in SACEUR's area in Europe; they are not involved in the remainder of SAC target planning.

Clearly, if American war plans are ever shown to others, they are going to be shown to as few people as possible. A single partner would be the best solution, if there were the possibility of a European force including the British that would be controlled by a European political union. President Kennedy himself indicated that he would be delighted at the ability to have a "hot line" to the president of Europe in order to reach a joint decision with him. Such a development, however, is a long way off, even if it is, as I believe, the ultimate direction in which things are moving. I rather suspect therefore that we will have to move fairly soon toward some kind of a small nuclear directorate along the lines of the Norstad or British proposals. In this respect, one of the values in the MLF proposal is that the MLF executive would provide experience in this field and might even become the embryo out of which a true NATO directorate would evolve.

Economic Problems

Briefs: NATO's problems also have economic roots. And although the loss of cohesion that may be developing because of them is probably of second rank compared with disagreements due to nuclear issues, economic policy differences are important determinants of the future of the alliance. These differences are discussed under three headings:

Economic Policy Differences as Source of NATO Disarray.
A NATO Policy of Trade and Aid Toward the "Third World"?
East-West Trade as NATO Problem.

Economic Difficulties as Source of NATO Disarray

Economic developments and the policies designed to guide them can undermine the relation between allies. The statements that follow serve to introduce a discussion of this danger for the NATO alliance.

> If the [Kennedy Round of tariff] negotiations get[s] scuttled . . . , it will only be because there is no will for success. It is not clear that all countries do want the Kennedy Round to succeed. . . . If this is true, then one must contemplate what failure might mean. The fragmentation of the West into trading blocks would take on added meaning in . . . [that] it would sharpen the split, partly because of the disappointment of expectations and partly because of the drift toward protectionism that might well occur in the absence of a major step in the other direction.
>
> Lawrence B. Krause

> Inflation tends also to deteriorate a country's balance of payments. If the shrinkage of the gold and foreign exchange reserves of the currency goes far enough in corroding the residual confidence in its stability, it leads to a crisis. . . . Unless the crisis is solved by the surgery of changing the relation of the currency unit to gold, it is usually countered by a variety of measures which control the foreign exchange of goods, services, and money by quantitative import restrictions. . . . The worst one is the rationing of foreign exchange by licenses. . . .
>
> This sorry sequence of events led in the past, in the period from 1928 to 1933 and the following years, to the progressive deterioration of cooperation among the former Allies of World War I, with disastrous results for foreign trade, entrenchment in depression, and default in joint efforts to prevent World War II.
>
> Karl Brandt

> Other than an undesirable but widely accepted price-raising policy abroad, particularly in Europe, there exist only two means for remedying the deficit in the American balance of payments: a devaluation of the dollar . . . , or a lowering of the tariff barriers of the countries friendly to the United States. . . .
>
> The countries friendly to the United States are in a position today to help the United States substantially. Besides, for Europe it is only a question today of discharging a debt of gratitude.
>
> Maurice Allais

> There is probably no other economic issue on which the basic interests of the Western countries correspond so closely as with the desire to improve the international monetary mechanism. . . . The interests of the countries while close are not identical. If agreement cannot be reached on this issue, then it is a very bad omen for the unity of the West. On the other hand, the spirit of cooperation that could be kindled from a successful attack on this problem could carry over into other areas.
>
> Lawrence B. Krause

Krause: We should note, first of all, that the particular group of countries that make up NATO is not a natural economic grouping. It is neither geographically homogeneous nor does it combine, say, all of the developed countries to the exclusion of underdeveloped countries. For us in the United States, this implies that our economic ties cut across and go beyond NATO ties. In this sense, therefore, our economic relationships with NATO countries enter by the back door, and where inconsistencies develop between these sets of relations, diplomatic and economic problems vis-à-vis our NATO allies may arise.

The Kennedy Round—the sixth round of negotiations under GATT [10]—brings these and other aspects of this situation sharply into focus.

A lot of hope has been attached to these negotiations. They represent the first promise of movement toward a true, freer trading system. It was not intended that the sixth was to be the last round. Quite the contrary, it was to be the first of a new series that would look toward a real dismantling of trade restrictions among the free-world countries, thereby allowing economic growth to proceed in line with the ideal of comparative advantage.

In addition, it was hoped that as a result of these negotiations some substance would also be given to the idea of an Atlantic Community. This was and is an important consideration because, except in the economic sphere, the Atlantic Community is largely an empty shell. With the United States among those most reluctant to give up sovereignty in any respect, we are still very far from any meaningful political concept of a community, such as the concept toward which the European Economic Community [11] might lead. Progress in the military sphere is also unpromising. The Atlantic Community cannot be something in this respect that goes beyond what NATO could develop. On the contrary, our military ties could be jeopardized by a breakdown of agreement on economic policy.

With stakes of this magnitude riding on the GATT negotiations at Geneva, we need to take stock of the situation and see what the chances of success are. I think the chances are very good, technically speaking; the basis for significant progress is there, assuming all participants want the round to succeed.

Some of the bargainers at Geneva, however, seem to be reluctant, and it takes only one large country to prevent a full agreement. Under standing GATT rules, if a tariff is reduced, it is reduced on the "most favored nation" basis: any such tariff reduction is extended to all countries, regardless of whether or not they in turn reduce their own tariff. Under these circumstances, a large country can, in effect, veto agreement by refusing to participate in the tariff reductions. We should contemplate what might happen if that veto were used.

Obviously, we would forgo the gains of greater economic growth as a result of reduced tariffs. But, more important than that, failure at Geneva would certainly destroy the hope for a movement toward an

[10] The General Agreement on Tariffs and Trade. Some seventy countries are signatories to the Agreement or participate under some type of arrangement.
[11] The European Economic Community (EEC) includes West Germany, France, Italy, The Netherlands, Belgium, and Luxembourg.

Atlantic Community. On the contrary, it might make the division of Europe much more striking than it is today. Unless the split between the two trading groups, the European Free Trade Association [12] and the European Economic Community, is moderated by a reduction of tariffs through the GATT round, the mutual market access restrictions which it implies could lead to considerable economic distress in some of these countries. In turn, this could lead to abandonment of the multilateral approach of the "most favored nation" principle. Instead the aim would be to limit tariff reductions to those countries that agree on a reciprocal basis; those that do not agree would be excluded. And once the major trading nations start down this road, one should expect economic discrimination and an embittering of relations that would surely carry over into the diplomatic and into the military sphere.

Brandt: The trouble in NATO is much less one of military arrangements and military power than it is one of making basic economic and political decisions. Nations still persist in deciding major issues, foreign and domestic, on the basis of national political forces. It almost seems as if we cannot make up our mind as nations where our major common ends lie—what the real hard interests of each country are and where these interests are so closely aligned that coordination of purpose and a common approach are a necessity.

The negotiations going on at Geneva point up our seeming helplessness—despite all of the military power we possess—when it comes to deciding on common objectives and coordinated means for achieving them in the political and economic area. The countries under GATT have begun negotiations to free international trade in accordance with the principle of comparative advantage. But weeks before these negotiations began, a United Nations Conference on Tariffs and Trade with over 150 delegates started in Geneva and urged the expansion of world trade through a reorganization of the world trading system on the basis of commodity cartels, trade blocks, and protective discrimination in favor of underdeveloped countries. Why? Because, so the argument of underdeveloped countries goes, in industrial countries trade unions increase wage and price levels with the result that raw materials-exporting countries are forced to exchange their output for industrial imports on such unfavorable terms of trade that their development is stunted. I consider the approach to trade expansion urged at the UN Conference an invitation to worldwide depression. Experience has shown that the approach favored by many UN delegates from less developed countries simply does not work.

---

[12] The European Free Trade Association (EFTA) includes Austria, Denmark, Norway, Portugal, Sweden, Switzerland, the United Kingdom, and an associate member, Finland.

The point I made about the disruptive effects of inflation in the statement above is one that should be considered very carefully. Inflation raises problems both among the leading industrial countries, most of which are NATO powers, and between advanced and underdeveloped countries of the world. Inflationary policy makes proper contracting fraudulent and disorganizes economic procedures in any country. Even leading industrial countries can be seriously weakened. What is taking place in large parts of Latin America shows what can happen, and for those who think that the Latin American experience lacks comparability, let me suggest here that a highly industrialized, democratic Germany under the Weimar Republic would not have gone to pieces so absolutely when confronted by Nazi subversion without the ghastly inflation of 1919-1923—an inflation that ate away the real core of people's faith that this society was standing on decent principles. The same process is now going on in a number of Latin American countries.

Part of the difficulty is, of course, that no country can control inflation by itself unless it wants to isolate itself. To cope with inflation requires the cooperation of the other countries.

Balance-of-payments difficulties are another partly related source of weakness. I believe the American dollar has been weakened. Everyone knows it has been hobbling for some time on crutches. Of course, the United States has had the cooperation and support of the leading NATO countries, but not without cost to our diplomatic stature. We have needed the help of the French, the British, and the German governments.

More recently, the disease of inflation has spread into Italy, France, and Germany, and it is still nibbling at United States resources, though at a much reduced rate. Compared with others, we may be better off, but inflation's threat to NATO cohesion continues to exist. Our relations with European countries could reach the point at which they were in 1932-1933. It is worth recalling that the World Economic Conference in London failed because the United States felt compelled to "go it alone" and devalue the dollar. From that moment, all countries "went it alone" and the disaster of World War II began.

Uri: There is one point on which I would agree with Mr. Brandt. It is clearly very useful to have a common purpose in this Atlantic world. But I am afraid it is just about the only point on which I would agree with him.

I am very much afraid that there is little chance of creating a community of purpose along the lines which he proposes. I do not think that there is very much to be gained for our world in denying some of the very real problems which have been posed at the United Nations conference in Geneva.

If we insist that the only philosophy on which we can create unity is complete reliance on free trade and the free enterprise system, I am sure we will not find much support in the rest of the world. I think we need to be much more concrete regarding ends which we seek, and much more flexible regarding the means we are prepared to employ.

That brings me back to the problem of success or failure in the Kennedy Round of trade negotiations. In my view, the major obstacle to success is our approach. If our countries were fully conscious of their real interests, as distinguished from the defense of certain particular or private interests, there should really be no conflict at all; we should be able to get agreement on tariff reductions which could have very dramatic consequences for the prosperity of our world.

Unfortunately, the countries negotiating in Geneva still think in the old terms of commercial advantage, which means gaining more in the way of export markets than they surrender in opening their own markets. This is readily apparent from the discussions that have gone on so far. If we really believed in reductions of trade obstacles as a very essential element in achieving greater effectiveness of our own economies, there would be much less haggling about whether tariffs should be reduced by this much or that much. Everyone would realize that it is advantageous to receive goods produced more cheaply elsewhere, provided, however, that some fundamental problems of policy are correctly solved.

A viable approach to the liberalization of trade requires common policies for expansion. It also requires a more reliable international monetary system so that transitory imbalances stemming from freer trade can be corrected before deflation spreads. What we really need is an over-all policy of world economic expansion. As regards the developing countries, that policy cannot be only one of aid; trade and commercial policy toward underdeveloped areas must be an integral element in such an over-all scheme.

In the GATT negotiations at Geneva, it may well turn out that industrial goods will not present insurmountable obstacles to the success of the Kennedy Round. Of course, the scope of what is possible here is limited due to the fact that Britain is not a member of the European Economic Community as anticipated when the U.S. Trade Expansion Act of 1962 was framed. As a result, the so-called "80 per cent clause," which allows tariff reductions without limitations where the Community and the United States, taken together, account for more than 80 per cent of total world exports, does not apply. With Britain outside of the Community, this clause is not applicable except in two or three cases. The situation that confronts the negotiators is therefore a rather rigid one, implying as it does that U.S. tariff reductions are limited to one-half of the initial tariff level. This is unfortunate because it prevents a linking of deeper reductions on some types of goods with lesser reduction on others. In view of the much discussed problem of disparity in the tariff rate structure as between the United States and European countries, this loss of freedom to maneuver is a distinct handicap.

Much more serious, however, are the difficulties in regard to agricultural products. The differences of approach in this area are fundamental. There are very good reasons why agricultural products should be included in the negotiations. They are a very important part of United States trade, and represent one of the fields in which the United States probably has great comparative advantages.

In short, agricultural commodities cannot be excluded from the negotiations. But, we have to see exactly on what basis those products should be included. Trade in agricultural products, at least in some of them, is unfortunately not the same thing as trade in manufactures. There are fundamental economic reasons for this difference. One market is dynamic and the other is much less dynamic. Moreover the fact of life is that all governments intervene in the field of agricultural production. There is a great difference between free trade according to costs, which is roughly speaking what trade in manufactures means, and competition between the different public treasuries, which is roughly what trade in agricultural products means. The price differentials from country to country of a great many agricultural commodities is proportionate to the amount of subsidies which the respective treasuries are able to serve up to the producers or exporters. If we want to succeed in the negotiations regarding these commodities, therefore, we have to realize that here the approach cannot be one of trying to sell a little more of this or that without regard to the adjustments required elsewhere. In agriculture there is a common problem of farm policy to be solved.

None of the countries on either side of the Atlantic can be too proud of its agricultural policy. Simply instituting free trade under existing conditions would result in their trying to sell to each other just what they should not produce as each one attempts to market surplus production stemming not from comparative advantage but from farm subsidies.

The problem of the farmer is much more than a problem of finding outlets for agricultural production. Initially, the countries involved should address themselves to the task of progressively reducing the proportion of the active population engaged in agriculture. This in itself would change the problem greatly. An effort should also be made to redirect our production—away from things which are in surplus, such as wheat, to things in comparatively short supply, such as meat, the demand for which is highly correlated with rising income.

Finally, there is the problem of using our over-all capacity to produce food, which contrasts so sharply with both the hunger in a large part of the world and with the inability of Communist countries to raise the level of their agricultural production even to cover the barest needs.

In a hungry world, there are better ways of using our own capacity to produce. This must be an important consideration in the effort to adjust agricultural production and to enlarge markets. Agricultural trade between countries should not only be increased, it should also be made more meaningful.

It is important to be clear about the concrete issues posed by the inclusion of agricultural commodities in the negotiations at Geneva. Unless we succeed here along the lines indicated, we might very well doom the Kennedy Round to failure. To see the danger, one merely has to look at the difficulties within the European Economic Community in this regard.

EEC has machinery to arrive at a common agricultural policy. Tariffs on agricultural imports are to be essentially a variable levy which would bring import prices in line with the level established for the Community. Obviously this levy remains indeterminate until EEC farm prices are agreed upon. Agreement is difficult to achieve because agricultural prices differ substantially as between EEC members. German prices, in particular, will have to be reduced in substantial measure, and this is a hazardous step for the German Government before the elections take place in 1965.

In the absence of an agreement within EEC on a common price policy, negotiations on agricultural import levies at Geneva will also be delayed. This could play into the hands of those who want to drag their feet by giving them the best reason for not really entering into the negotiations. The great danger is that procrastination will extend from agricultural goods to other areas of tariff negotiation.

These are presently the facts, and I think they amount to a dangerous situation. Let me emphasize again what we really want: not simply freer trade, but more meaningful trade. The transformations required for the latter are going to be achieved only if we address ourselves together to the problems of agricultural policy in a more reasonable way than we have been able to do up to now, acting separately.

Brandt: I do not believe that we can have in a few years anything like all-around free trade and free enterprise. Nevertheless, NATO countries should face up to the problem of choosing a basic approach to the economic issues confronting them. In which direction should these countries move? Should their lead be toward more state trading; toward more political decision-making by governmental agencies, for example, toward price-fixing under international commodity agreements? Or, should they move in the direction of reducing impediments to international trade? In my judgment, one of the greatest achievements since World War II is the far-reaching progress made in eliminating foreign exchange controls, hardening currencies to convertibility, and trade liberalization, i.e., abolition of import quotas. Success has not been easy, but the effort was worthwhile. World trade could not have expanded so immensely without it.

Now we are in a new phase of development in which the temptation to revert to the managed approach becomes stronger. For example, one speaks so emphatically of arranging for better trade of agricultural commodities. I agree with Mr. Uri that agricultural policies all around have had unfortunate results. But let us not forget that their aim was precisely to arrange better trading conditions for farmers. The wheat agreements, for example, were supposed to stabilize wheat trade by adjusting production to consumption. Actually quite the opposite has taken place. Large surpluses are being produced under this international cartel and some 30 per cent of all international transactions are "under the table" at concession prices that differ significantly from agreement price ranges. In addition, wheat is disposed of by outright gifts, or on the basis of ten-year credit agreements, or by practically any other device that can move wheat. I cannot agree that the right road to travel is one which leads to more and bigger international commodity cartels and similar institutions.

The question of what direction policy shall take is surely relevant if the countries in NATO have any economic aims in common. I do not believe that the pragmatic choice of the basic commodity approach with price fixing, though it may for the moment be an expedient solution of particular problems, is the right way to achieve more agreement regarding these aims.

Allais: There are in fact two different problems: the first is the problem of the deficit in the American balance of payments; the second is the problem of short-term liquidities.

These two problems are difficult to discuss in a few words. I intend to limit my remarks to particular aspects of what are very complicated questions.

As far as the persistent deficit in the American balance of payments is concerned, I would say that unfortunately this problem will probably be solved by inflation in Europe. If so, there will be no difficulty.

Of course, inflationary pressures in Europe may remain under sufficient control. In this case, there are only two solutions: the first is devaluation of the dollar vis-à-vis other countries' currencies; the second is increased imports on the part of Europe from the United States.

The first solution, in my opinion, is not so bad as some people believe. If the United States were to devalue the dollar, it would have a strong currency overnight. If this solution is not adopted, the only possibility is to increase U.S. exports to Europe. I would say, however, that strong policy action along this line would encounter a great deal of resistance.

I think that efforts to liberalize world trade without some common institutions will achieve very little. The Kennedy Round may achieve certain improvements in trade agreements, but I think that we cannot expect as much as many people seem to believe. The obstacles here are similar to those encountered by Great Britain in its bid to join the Common Market or by the British proposal to bring the European Free Trade Area into the Common Market.

I am convinced that without some common political framework it is impossible to stabilize international commodity trade to any considerable extent.

As far as the international liquidity situation is concerned, even if the United States balance-of-payments deficit is solved, the liquidity problem will continue to pose a threat. In my view, the only reasonable solution is to raise the price of gold by a factor of two or three. I do not see another solution.

Krause: International liquidity is a problem because balances of payments do not adjust themselves quickly in a world in which fixed exchange rates are an accepted arrangement. Leaving the issue of flexible exchange rates versus fixed exchange rates to one side, let me simply stress that when exchange rates are fixed, balance-of-payments adjustments are necessarily somewhat slow; and since they are slow, liquidity reserves are needed to carry on while imbalance is overcome.

All developed countries recognize this and everyone agrees that the international financial mechanism needs improvement. But the problem looks different to debtor countries than it does to creditor countries. Creditors always talk about discipline and debtors always talk about ease of borrowing. It would be helpful if creditor nations remembered what it was like when they were debtors.

The United States may be in the process of shifting out of its deficit position. Our balance of payments has improved, and although the strong showing made during the early months of this year may not continue through the remainder of 1964, there has been a change for the better. It is also encouraging that, for the first time, the United States has expressed concern about international liquidity and is willing to think about helping to improve liquidity arrangements.

Of course, we may forget this concern if we should move into a strong creditor position; but I submit that liquidity will remain a central problem in a world fully committed to fixed exchange rates.

Burgess: I disagree with the views just expressed by both previous speakers.

With respect to Mr. Allais' very interesting discussion, there are several items in the U.S. balance of payments that are subject to some degree of adjustment by direct policy action. In my judgment, the great problem here is not the commercial balance. Here we have done extremely well, with a plus balance of five billion dollars a year on trade.

If we keep that up in the face of increased competition, we shall be doing extremely well.

Our difficultities stem from some of the other items in the balance of payments and I think there is some flexibility here that may have been overlooked in the previous discussion. We have been so enthusiastic in our investments abroad that we have poured something like two to three billion dollars a year into long-term investments, borrowing short to finance the transfer of these funds. To that must be added our military and aid programs amounting to another three or four billion dollars a year. Taking all of these together, the United States is somewhat overcommitted.

I do not think, however, that the overcommitment is terribly serious for the long run because we still have very large resources. But I do think that adjustments can be made in the area of investments, loans, and grants and that we should certainly not change the value of the dollar. I couldn't disagree more on this point with Mr. Allais. The consequences of changing the gold value of the dollar would be extremely serious for the entire world. Such a move could produce reactions that would seriously dislocate world commerce.

As to Mr. Krause's views regarding the need for greatly expanded liquidity, we have done better in our international financial relations than in any other area. The International Monetary Fund,[13] for example, is almost a miracle in its operation. Here sovereignty has been surrendered with hardly a whimper. Virtually all Western nations are members of the Fund and its sister institution, the World Bank.[14] Nearly a hundred countries now have paid in their contribution, and these funds are voted out by a board of directors. I was recently told that negative votes never occur. The procedures are worked out so carefully that agreement is reached without difficulty. Yet no one shouts about this surrender of sovereignty.

I feel very strongly about the success of the International Monetary Fund because I was a member of His Majesty's Loyal Opposition in 1945 when the Fund was under discussion. Some of us feared then that the IMF might turn out to be more of a relief agency than a nine billion dollar financial institution. I am delighted that I was wrong. Not only has IMF worked as it should, but it has been tremendously enlarged, first by 50 per cent and more recently, through voluntary agreements, by the equivalent of another 50 per cent. In this way, the amount of international liquidity has been increased enormously. IMF provides a basis for credit the world around without fear of currency devaluations, and thus permits an appropriate credit expansion on the given gold base.

---

[13] The International Monetary Fund (IMF) has a membership of 102 countries.
[14] *I.e.*, the International Bank for Reconstruction and Development (IBRD), also with a membership of 102 countries.

I would suggest, therefore, that we first look at what has been done to increase international liquidity. I cannot agree with the statement that nobody is satisfied with the present situation.

Allais: I recognize that it is very unpopular to speak about the devaluation of the dollar. But the United States gold reserve amounts to less than $16 billion at the present time, and the over-all value of reserves held by other countries in dollars convertible into gold is about $25 billion. Thus, from one day to the next the United States could be placed in a very difficult position. Fundamentally the present situation is an unstable one. But if we could accept an increase in the value of gold in terms of the various currencies, the problem would be solved.

This is not a popular proposal. I recognize that. But, again, popularity is one thing and the truth is another.

Uri: Of course, there is risk in the present situation. The short-term dollar claims on the gold reserves of the United States are large—larger, in fact, than the gold reserves held by the U.S. Treasury, even if they could be used entirely. There is the risk that any one government may suddenly want to convert its claims into gold. But this does not mean that the only way out is to wipe out a large part of those liabilities by a decision making gold worth three times as much as it is now. The whole effort in international cooperation is to find procedures or rules or common institutions which are going to prevent that kind of individual move and the chain reactions to which it could give rise.

In other words, it is a question of finding informal or more formal ways of consolidating those claims without, at the same time, preventing them from being used as means of settlement.

Regarding the revaluation of gold as the only way of dealing with the liquidity problem, the redistributive effects of such an action are so undesirable that I would want to see it avoided if at all possible. If our respective countries are so rich that they would deprive themselves tomorrow for the same quantity of gold of three times the value in exports—which were produced with some toil—I submit that this generosity might be used in better ways than giving it to the Russians, the South Africans, and the Swiss.

If we are really able to spare those goods in exchange for what is after all just nominal value, the problem of aid to developing countries could easily be solved. Even apart from this, it is not clear why the price of gold needs to be changed because of the comparative size of foreign dollar holdings. After all, modern banking systems operate with scarcely ever a run on a bank even though it is normal for banks to work with cash on hand that amounts to only a fraction of their demand liabilities.

Rather than raise the price of gold, let us join our heads and develop more modern systems of international liquidity than one which involves, as Keynes put it, digging more gold out of holes just to be able to bury it again in other holes.

Allais: First of all, I agree, of course, that there are other solutions to the balance-of-payments and the liquidity problems than devaluating the U.S. dollar and raising the gold price. As far as the balance-of-payments deficit is concerned, I mentioned one alternative earlier. Let me point out, however, that the difficulties we have been discussing have been with us for some six years at least. No solution has been found in that time and I see no reason why next year's efforts will produce the answer.

My second point is in relation to Soviet Russia. It is true that raising the price of gold can help Soviet Russia. But, in the last months some countries have increased their trade with Soviet Russia and that helps the Soviets too. This policy is open to exactly the same criticism. I see no reason why a distinction should be made between trade and gold price appreciation.

Third, as matters now stand, the American economic situation is very much dependent on the actions of other nations. America's capability for leadership is thereby weakened. If the value of gold were increased, this dependence would disappear. I would agree, of course, that if very close agreement existed between NATO and a number of other countries on basic policy objectives, there would be no problem at all, but no such agreement exists at the present time.

A NATO Policy of Trade and Aid Toward the "Third World?"

Briefs: The major issues of economic policy so far considered are not primarily NATO problems. They nevertheless affect NATO profoundly in that they have far-reaching consequences for the character and development of international economic organization and for the effectiveness of initiatives taken in the West. Assistance to underdeveloped countries, however, could call for a coordinated NATO effort. At any rate, the question should be explored. The statements that follow call attention to several of the issues involved.

> Between 1950 and 1958, the rate of annual increase in the world population was 1.7 per cent. Today it is probably in the neighborhood of 2 per cent, and we fear that in the near future the figures will rise even higher. . . . No matter what the state of technological progress may be, the world is running blindly toward an untenable situation.

* * *

> The politicians who determine Western strategy continue to assert that in any reasonably dynamic economy, the rate of annual growth should average 5 per cent per year; and taking into account all their statements, the results seem to

> be that within a short period of time, if the West agrees to certain appropriate endeavors, the underdeveloped countries will reach a standard of living comparable to ours. . . .
> In promulgating such shining hopes which are carelessly reasoned out and, to say the least, foolish, we take upon ourselves obligations we are not prepared to meet and we run the risk of seeing ascribed to the very principles of Western civilization (based on the decentralization of decisions, a market economy, the price mechanism, and private property) the responsibility for a defeat, and thus the arousing of the resentment and hate of hundreds of millions of people.
>
> To be effective, this common policy [toward underdeveloped countries] must be based on *true* Western ideology. From this point of view, the essential articulation of the aid that the West must give to the Third World should rest on wide liberalization of exchange and on lowering of its tariff barriers. . . .
>
> The reciprocal liberalization of exchanges between the West and the Third World constitutes probably the only really effective way of development. It is, in addition, the only one which can lead to an effective redistribution of burdens.
>
> Maurice Allais

Uri: These are indeed challenging statements. Instead of a golden age ahead of us, population projections seem to promise a decline in the world standard of living, at least on the average. Fortunately, projections are only good for a certain term of time. If we always projected accurately, we should all be rich in a relatively short time. But by the same process, it would also be shown that the earth's surface would not suffice to house the world's population, cheek to jowl.

As regards population trends over the next three to four decades, the question that needs answering is: How far will the population explosion go before its driving force weakens? In the meantime, the only thing one can do is to go on trying to improve living standards, hoping that with improvement will come a reduction in the growth rate of the population.

Regarding the last of Mr. Allais' statements above, it is important to know what is meant by the role of freer trade, and the role of "true Western ideology."

If the point is that we must open our markets more widely to the goods of developing countries, I could not agree more. It would be a completely contradictory and ineffective policy to provide major assistance for the industrialization of developing countries and then to refuse them outlets for the resulting industrial production.

We all realize that opening our markets to these new industries will not be easy. The newly established industry will be disadvantaged by relatively high costs. But in other cases rapid progress is being made, and there is no reason why many of the industries in developing countries, in an environment of comparatively much lower wages, cannot be just as productive as ours. In fact, the lower wage levels may make them highly competitive.

In these circumstances I believe that the only course to follow is one leading to the all-around opening of our markets to developing countries. Only in this way can these imports be spread over an area large enough to dilute their impact. I also believe that we should implement this policy gradually. Given enough time, displaced resources can be re-employed in more productive uses without painful and costly transitional difficulties.

What troubles me in Mr. Allais' last statement above are the words "reciprocal liberalization." I thought there was rather general agreement that the "infant industry" argument is sound in the case of developing countries.

When industries are started in non-industrialized countries, they suffer from a lot of disadvantages. Something needs to be done to overcome those initial difficulties. Otherwise many of these efforts would be doomed to failure.

I would think, therefore, that at the start we should accept as reasonable a policy of *non-reciprocal* trade liberalization, i.e., without demanding reciprocity, at least for a certain period of time. Or better, let us agree that there should be some staggering of tariff reductions by the developing countries as their own level of production rises. Such an arrangement, after all, would be to the advantage of developing countries as they expand industrially within the growth pattern of the more advanced countries.

Allais: In reply to Mr. Uri's first point, the factual evidence available to us now leads, in my opinion, to a gloomy view of the future. Maybe we can have twenty or thirty more years of prosperity, but it is highly probable that by the end of the century serious difficulties will have developed. We must be able to face the problems of the end of the century, and that is why I think the nations of the West should unite in some way to prepare for a future which is less bright than some people think. Perhaps I am wrong on timing. Perhaps we can have a golden age for fifty years. But in the end there will be many difficulties, especially in what are now the underdeveloped areas of the world. Many of the problems that are bound to arise will be very difficult to solve.

As for Mr. Uri's second point, we must accept some trade liberalization vis-à-vis developing countries. But I do not agree at all that acquiescence in their protectionism is a good way to help them develop their economies. Many industries are viable in those countries without any protection, if we are ready to accept their exports. There are many examples of that. The crucial question is: Is the West ready to accept their exports? Here lies the real difficulty.

Brandt: When we talk about the rate of economic development in underdeveloped countries, we encounter one very serious difficulty. The measure one uses is the gross-national-product concept. GNP is defined as the total national output of goods and services valued at market prices. By and large, this limits the concept to items that make up the exchange economy of a country. In most underdeveloped countries, however, the proportion of goods and services "exchanged" is relatively small. By definition the majority of the goods and services produced are consumed without passing through a market, or at any rate through a market whose transactions are statistically discernible.

Because of these and other statistical impasses, the available measures of output—per capita income and capital formation—lead to crippling distortions in the view we have of economic developments in these areas, and of the potential development that could take place with the proper sort of aid.

This has disastrous consequences. With all the emphasis on measurable economic advance, the tendency is to stress almost exclusively efforts to expand the urban sectors of underdeveloped economies. In this process, agricultural and related sectors are deprived even of locally accumulated capital. The result is that the whole structure of these countries is undermined, i.e., the old socio-economic structures crumble and the new structures in and around population centers threaten to become unworkable both economically and politically.

Yet we support this type of development. For instance, we transfer capital, government to government, to India. We do this in order to support five-year plans that are specifically designed to socialize the Indian economy, with most of the investment going to urban centers. The result is that indigenous Indian capital also rushes into the cities where it helps to create the vast new slums around industrial centers and proletarianizes the population. Meanwhile the hundreds of millions who live in rural areas are deprived of the means of livelihood and of development. In my judgment this process can only lead to social ferment and worse conditions than would exist in the absence of five-year plans.

Brugmans: I agree that our development policy would be less than inspired if our help went to heavy industry only. Raising the standard of living in rural areas would be much more profitable to the well-being of the populations concerned. It is unfortunately true, however, that if this were our declared philosophy and policy, we would run into great difficulties with the governments of recipient countries. For the most part, they are not looking for unspectacular ways to improve the living standard of their rural population; they are much more interested in the political sex appeal of certain large-scale projects, such as constructing dams and building up heavy industry. This is true even though comparatively little manpower is required for the operation of such projects.

There is also another side to this problem. The aid-granting industrial countries of the West are unilaterally interested in selling their machinery in underdeveloped areas. This leads to a kind of unhealthy solidarity between some Western governments on the one hand and the governments of developing countries on the other as they want to have splendid photographs of their successes. The risk is that we may become both ineffective because we help to propagate too rapid industrialization and unpopular because our competition may prove that some of these ventures are destined to remain uneconomic.

If we wish to work out a wise philosophy and policy in regard to these problems, we can do it only if we reduce the involvement of our own political and military institutions in this matter to a minimum. I am not sure that NATO as such should be involved; for instance, any coordinated effort should by all means include the Swedes and Swiss. The Organization for Economic Cooperation and Development [15] might be a more appropriate framework, but unfortunately its machinery is not strong enough to be successful in an area as heavily political as this one.

Knorr: I do not want to say anything about economic development in the Atlantic world. With very few exceptions, development is proceeding satisfactorily. We hope it will continue to do so in the foreseeable future. This is an area in which, before long, we will have to do some new thinking.

Obviously, it would be very good if some of our European friends would do more in aiding the economically less advanced countries, although quite a few of the European countries are doing a great deal; some of them, relative to their national incomes, are doing even more than the United States is doing at the present time. In any case, Europe as a whole is doing more along this line than ever before.

What I would like to do is to make a slightly heretical remark about the policy NATO countries should pursue toward the Third World. This is an area in which we do not want to over-organize things. A great deal is to be said for an approach that would permit different points of initiative, so that different countries can bring to bear their own experience in various parts of the underdeveloped world. In short, I do not see any need here for highly organized, agreed-upon policies.

[15] The Organization for Economic Cooperation and Development (OECD) began its official existence in September 1961, with a membership of twenty European countries. Japan has since joined OECD.

Were we to try to get such agreement, I am sure we would achieve a great deal of delay and a great deal of compromise which, in the end, would preclude doing very much of anything in this area.

In this respect de Gaulle has a point. Although I do not agree with all the initiatives de Gaulle has taken, especially in the economic area, he is clearly right when he insists on many points of initiative as far as transactions of Western countries with the rest of the world are concerned.

Furthermore, if we want to organize anything, in economic matters let us please not do it within NATO. NATO seems to me altogether unsuited as a framework for coordinating economic development policies. There are problems enough within NATO, just straightening out issues of defense and strategy. I do not think it would help matters were we to complicate those negotiations by disagreements about how to coordinate efforts to assist in the development efforts of less developed areas.

If we must organize, there are after all other institutional structures available, including agencies of the United Nations and such institutions as IMF, the World Bank, and the like.

Holmes: All I want to say to Mr. Knorr is amen. I think his succinct statement deals very nicely with the Canadian endeavor to make something of the economic function of NATO, an effort known as the Canadian heresy. We are wise to repress the urge to implement Article 2 of the North Atlantic Treaty. I never really believed in the soundness of the Canadian proposal, though as a good civil servant I wrote memoranda in its favor.

Burgess: I also agree with Mr. Knorr's general approach to the problem of development assistance. I think the work being done in the Development Assistance Committee of OECD should be mentioned in this connection. One of its accomplishments has been to open up some of the European financial centers to underdeveloped countries. Another has been the organization of investment syndicates to undertake particular projects. I think these efforts illustrate the success of the principle Professor Knorr has emphasized, namely of letting individuals deal with their opposite numbers.

East-West Trade as NATO Problem

Briefs: In the context of this discussion, the issues that have arisen about East-West trade cluster about two interrelated questions.

First, how should one assess what appears to be a degree of disarray within the Soviet bloc? And, second, what can be done effectively in response to this situation in terms of trade and other relationships?

The following statement will serve to get the discussion under way.

First of all, the success of the European Economic Community and the manifold problems which beset the Soviet Union at home and abroad have significantly altered the general relationship between the two parts of Europe. The dynamism of the Common Market has taken the Soviet rulers aback. Nothing indeed in their ideological books or in their political and diplomatic expectations has prepared them to see a society "condemned by history" emerge as the most inventive region in the world.

* * *

On both the ideological and practical levels the Soviet theoreticians and practitioners of politics have been unable to cope coherently with [the dynamism of the Common Market] and to determine their course of conduct accordingly.

. . . Psychologically, the very success of the Common Market, i.e., its pragmatic and working economic integration, contrasts oddly with the Soviet bloc's admitted inability to progress along the same road, Khrushchev's insistence notwithstanding.

Milorad M. Drachkovitch

Our main problem is not how to get through to the East Europeans, but in which style to approach them. . . .

Traditional Western diplomacy is hardly prepared to carry out tasks—be it only in the cultural and economical spheres—which would be considered "interference in another state's internal affairs." Indeed, we do want to "interfere."

Hendrik Brugmans

What the West should try to accomplish . . . , taking into account variations in the individual situations of every country in East-Central Europe, would be to open the flow of human contacts, and to convince particularly the technical strata within the Communist regimes that it is in their interest to seek closer ties with the West.

While any incitement of captive nations to rebel against their masters must be radically rejected, the West should convey to them the sense of a common destiny and the promise of a common and free European future.

Milorad M. Drachkovitch

Drachkovitch: There is a tendency in the Western world to be rather gloomy about everything we do. Very often we do not realize that our problems, though they are very real, are actually the result of our successes.

I recall a discussion in 1951, when I was living in Belgium, with a former Belgian Prime Minister in which he predicted that the European Coal and Steel Commuınty would have catastrophic consequences for Belgium, leading to total economic chaos in a few years. This remark illustrates how truly remarkable the success story of Europe is.

One of the aspects of this story that deserves careful study is the way in which Soviet ideologists and Soviet diplomats have reacted to Europe's renaissance. At the beginning, the Soviets were convinced that the internal contradictions of Western society would make it impossible to develop in the direction of economic integration. They considered Western Europe as nothing more than an appendage of American imperialism. More recent statements on this subject, however, offer a remarkable contrast. During the last two or three years, comments about the Common Market that have appeared in the Soviet press point to a host of disquieting implications for the Soviet ideological vision of the world.

A second fact, which may be even more telling, is that the plan for economic integration that the Soviet leadership has been pursuing in Eastern Europe has undergone remarkable changes within the last two years. For example, beginning in 1962, one of its policy objectives was to push for rapid progress toward the supranational integration of the bloc area, i.e., toward the socialist division of labor according to one central planning scheme. It is truly remarkable that by 1963 Khrushchev had all but shelved this effort because Rumania, formerly one of the most subservient satellites, offered strong resistance.

Let me underscore, as dramatically as I can, still another dimension of Soviet Russia's problems. You have all seen the newspaper accounts recently, of 3,000 Czech students battling with the police. You may also have read that thirty-four of the most prominent Polish intellectuals are asking for a certain number of basic intellectual freedoms. Several thousand Bulgarians recently fought a pitched battle with the Communist police who wanted to prevent them from attending Easter midnight Mass. Something is on the move in the Eastern bloc.

These and other considerations suggest that our appraisal of conditions in the Soviet sphere in Europe should take account of cleavages within the bloc at three levels. First of all, there are the divergences within the Soviet Union, the head of the bloc. Secondly, there are telling disagreements between the Kremlin and the satellite governments, with the latter showing perhaps for the first time a certain degree of independence. I think it is extremely significant that a Communist regime in Eastern Europe, such as Albania, does not necessarily have to be pro-Soviet. Finally, and perhaps most important of all, we have the cleavage between the people of the satellite countries and their regimes. These people never stopped believing that they have every right to choose their own government. Perhaps they have also come to believe that they have a chance for bringing about some changes in their situation. In short, I believe a new situation of flux exists within the Soviet bloc, a situation which offers the West opportunities for new moves against the Communist threat in Europe.[16]

Brugmans: I know that The Center for Strategic Studies has devoted a considerable research effort to the problem of trade relations between East and West. At the College of Europe we just published a book on the Common Market and the Eastern bloc. But the main reason for my interest, of course, is that for Europeans this problem is emotionally crucial. Eastern Europe is part of what we still feel to be our common European cultural area.

If we want to define an acceptable and fruitful policy for the future, we should start by defining the limits within which a possible solution might lie.

On the one hand, it has sometimes been proposed that we build a wall around nasty countries and impose a maximum of trade restrictions on them. This has proved unworkable. The West tried this strategy during the first years of the Soviet regime, and tried it again after World War II against the Franco regime in Spain. In both instances it failed. The basic trend toward trade between countries, regardless of regime, is very powerful, too powerful to make trade quarantines workable. I remember a cartoon—I think it was in *Punch*—in which a British ship, loaded with buses for Cuba, passes another ship. The captain asks what the second ship might be, and the answer is: "It carries wheat from America, bound for the Soviet Union."

On the other hand, if trade embargo is no solution, one might think the opposite policy, namely "business as usual" with the bloc as with anyone else, is indicated. Such a policy might appeal to dogmatic advocates of free trade and free enterprise, but I do not think this approach workable either. Efforts to open the bloc area to such a policy are bound to be misunderstood by the governments in the East, who consider that *anything* is political, be it cultural exchange or exchange of goods; and I think in the present situation they are right. Everything is political as far as East-West relations are concerned, in any field.

So if these two extremes are excluded, there is only one approach left. This consists of promoting various "package deals" between bloc countries and ourselves, in which we would link our deliveries (excluding strategic goods, of course) to concessions in which we are interested.

---

[16] In response to a question, Mr. Drachkovitch warned against the delusion that the thrust behind Soviet imperialism would weaken more or less automatically. He argued that on the contrary, such developments as de-Stalinization and the conflict with China actually strengthen the Kremlin and the Communist parties in Western Europe because they help to overcome the latter's isolation by making possible popular front arrangements and similar devices that increase Communist effectiveness in the West.

For instance, why shouldn't we link a purely economic transaction with a student exchange program, our students going there and their students coming here? A few years ago, many Polish students came to the West under a Ford Foundation program. The consequences of their visit are still felt in Poland. To take another illustration, why shouldn't we suggest that in addition to trading in certain products, joint conferences concerning such trade be organized? The purpose would be to compare the methods, philosophies, and results obtained on both sides with COMECON [Council for Mutual Economic Assistance] on the one hand and the Common Market on the other. The objective should not be to take advantage of the impact that our success has had by trying to impose on those countries Western ways of economic organization. The conferences I have in mind are desirable in themselves; they should be a training in undogmatic thinking; and we should link them to specific trading arrangements that might be negotiated.

Who should make package deals of the kind described? It would be unwise to have each Western country negotiate on a bilateral basis with the other side. We should try to work out a general Western philosophy, and a technique on how to deal with the problems involved. In this way we may be able to do consciously and in a coordinated, orderly fashion what is going to happen anyway.

Would it be necessary to develop supranational institutions of some kind on the pattern of the Coal and Steel Community? That would certainly be preferable since an institution can, better than an "ad hoc" working party, learn from its own experiences. Let me add that close and permanent collaboration in a field as important as this could also be decisively important to stimulate Western cooperation. Mr. Schuman's declaration on May 9, 1950 is relevant here. He said at that time that the European Coal and Steel Community was a step closer to the integration of the Western European nations, and he emphasized the fact that the initiative was taken "in a limited but decisive field."

Drachkovitch: A policy of expanded East-West Trade and other contacts needs carefully considered guidelines. What should be avoided and what should we look for in pursuing such a policy? In one of his flourishing speeches, Nikita Khrushchev referred to West Berlin as a bone in his throat. I believe the entire satellite area is becoming a big bone for Soviet Russia's throat.

Let me emphasize, however, that no attempt at a solution should involve a call to rebel. The West does not have the moral right to ask for or to encourage revolt when it cannot help the insurgents militarily. We saw the results in 1953 and 1956. If not rebellion, then what? First, the Western countries should pursue a policy suggested by some leading American experts in the field of "peaceful engagement" in East-Central Europe. They should also remind the Soviet Union and the world that the great principle of self-determination is and should be valid not only for Asia and Africa, but for Eastern Europe as well. Western countries, and the United States in particular, should avoid the Soviet trap of a NATO-Warsaw Pact nonaggression treaty, for it would mean the freezing of the present abnormal situation of Europe, or what some people call, not without reason, a "second Yalta."

A second and coordinated move should follow the lines suggested by Mr. Brugmans. But here let us remember that man does not live by bread alone. A key feature of our approach to people from satellite countries should be to offer them the vision of a unified Europe. Nothing could have more appeal in East Central Europe than the idea of reunification with the rest of Europe. This may be a major consideration in de Gaulle's political strategy in Europe. As long as we have only the global confrontation of NATO and the Soviet bloc, it seems impossible to achieve any type of disengagement. But with the mounting internal difficulties encountered by the Soviet leaders, it may well be that they would not regard as unacceptable a unified Europe so long as it posed no military threat to Russia.

Possony: When we use the word "trade," we have to keep in mind that trade between the United States and Britain, say, is not the same thing as trade between a free country and the Soviet Union. The Soviet Union is operating through a trading monopoly. It does not engage in trade but implements its strategy through "trade"; it also has a trade strategy. That strategy, essentially, is to use the free world as a reserve into which the Soviet Union and other Communist countries can dip whenever they have a need to do so.

Now, the fact is that there is a basic disagreement among the allies in regard to trade with the East. Unfortunately, when we discuss these differences in terms of whether or not trade with the Soviet Union is less dangerous than trade with Hungary, for example, the question that should be discussed is often overlooked. The key question is: Can such trade be used to further our (i.e. NATO) strategic objectives vis-à-vis the Soviet Union? The advantage of considering trade as an arm of strategy is that it provides operational principles for deciding what the trade policy should be. On the negative side, for example, one would —or should—eliminate those types of exports which could be used by the Soviets to increase their war-making capacity.

But it is the positive side of this approach that needs to be stressed. The question is this: Does there exist a sort of trade which poses relatively low risks of contributing to Soviet war-making power? Are there low-risk exports that ever could help us in what we are trying to achieve, namely the gradual liquidation of the Communist dictatorship?

I think such types of trade exist. At the present moment the Soviets are trying to redefine priorities for investment because there just is not enough capital for the various purposes. We could aggravate their investment quandary if our trade with them took the form of consumers' durables, ice boxes, automobiles, and the like. To do so would be good business, provided they pay. But, more important, by stimulating consumer demand we would strengthen the power of the consumer in the Soviet Union.

The practicality of such an approach obviously is predicated on the existence of an enormous hunger in the Soviet Union for consumer goods of this sort. I think this hunger exists. It offers us an opening to use trade imaginatively. I fully realize that the definition of a consumer durable is difficult, as is the problem of guarding against our output being substituted for Russian output so as to free resources for strategic production. Wheat is used as food, but it can also be converted into alcohol for use as missile fuel. But I still find it a little difficult to see the same danger in the case of ice boxes and automobiles. In any case, I believe there are many classes of goods that are relatively impervious to substitution. In fact, there are important goods, such as pre-fabricated housing and automobiles, that might divert resources from armaments. Such diversion is our objective, and it may be reached through some types of trade.

Morgenthau: I would suggest a different approach to the problems of East-West trade. I think one has to start from the recognition that for the Soviet Union, as for all Communist nations, trade is something fundamentally different from what it is for us. Foreign trade for a Communist nation is first of all a political act; it is used as a political weapon. This explains why Mr. Khrushchev, in private communications and diplomatic dispatches, used to hammer upon the necessity or desirability of trade with the West, and why he berated Western governments continually for their refusal to trade freely with the Soviet Union.

Now, as regards the restrictions on East-West trade, I would not say that these have proved unworkable. It all depends on how you define the standard of evaluation. Certainly, those restrictions have constituted a very considerable handicap for Soviet economic development and frequently for military and political development as well. Let us not forget that the Soviet Union has chosen the economic field as the arena in which to gain a decisive victory over the West, and that the Soviet Union believes this strategy is workable.

Now, it is very easy to make general statements of the kind I have just made, and it is very difficult to translate them into a concrete trade policy. The fact is that there is absolutely no agreement among the members of the Atlantic alliance on trade with the Communist world. I think that this is itself an index of disarray in the alliance. If there were a rational policy, if there were a community of interests translatable into a common policy amongst the nations of the West, I would think that trade with the Communist bloc ought to be used as a political weapon. One could certainly hold out to Russia offers to make available certain items in exchange for what we want, or we could respond to a request on Russia's part with a proposal for a political *quid pro quo*. We might sell chemical plants, which they need, for military concessions. Pulling down the Berlin Wall comes to mind here. The Soviet Union would probably cry out that such a demand is typical of Wall Street war-mongers who only want to negotiate from strength. But it so happens that only fools refuse to negotiate from strength and attempt to negotiate from weakness.

I am unimpressed by such arguments on the part of the Soviet Union and I am dismayed by the echo they produce in the West. The indiscriminate rush into trade with Russia and with Communist China as well reminds me very much of the mindless trade we carried on in the thirties with Japan, exporting scrap iron with which American soldiers were killed when the war broke out.

If I may say a word about trading with China: It is by no means a foregone conclusion that China can transform herself into a modern industrial nation using her own resources only. The Soviet Union has given us an example in refusing to continue aid and trade with China. Russia does not want to build up a competitor in the form of an industrialized China. It would seem to me close to absurdity if the West now continued where the Soviet Union left off, helping to build for narrow reasons of financial gain the powerful economy which China may not be able to build up through her own efforts.

Knorr: It is true, of course, that trade conducted by the Soviet Union or other Communist countries is something quite different from trade as conducted by Western countries. At least this is potentially so, and has to be watched for this reason. As a factual matter, however, it appears that the trade carried on by the Soviet Union over the past ten years has been dictated almost entirely by economic rather than political considerations. But because Soviet trade policy can be a political and strategic weapon, a serious problem arises on our side if trade with the Soviet Union is increased. Mr. Brugmans has explained what kind of problem we face here. I would like to argue that our policy toward the Soviet Union should perhaps be less restrictive than it is at the present time. I confine my remarks to trade with the Soviet Union rather than Communist countries in general because different countries present us with different policy problems. For example, we have always understood that trade with Yugoslavia was a special case, and the same may be true for Rumania as a result of recent developments.

Now, if one thinks about restricting trade with the Soviet Union, one certainly wants to prohibit military goods. But as regards other goods, it is not entirely clear that the refusal to trade makes a great deal of sense.

If there were more trade between the Soviet Union on the one hand and the United States and West European countries on the other, this would have to be based on the mutual advantage. Trade always depends on mutual advantage. Now, what sort of advantage will the Soviet Union derive from us? Obviously, if the Soviet Union traded a great deal more with Western Europe and the United States than she does at the present, her own economic resources would become marginally more efficient than they are.

To my mind this is not a very good reason why we *should* increase our trade with them because I, for one, do not believe that this will make the Soviet Union richer quicker, or that a richer Soviet Union will be more peaceful. It is not quite that simple. On the other hand, I am impressed by the fact that what the Soviet Union would gain would indeed be only of marginal significance in the sense in which I have used that term.

Now what might we gain by lifting some of the restrictions that the United States at least favors at the present time? Obviously, we ourselves would realize a marginal gain for the same reason that the Soviet Union would gain. This may not be terribly important to us, but it cannot be said to be of no consequence whatever.

In addition, there are the possibilities Dr. Possony pointed out, namely, if we export more consumer goods to the Soviet Union this may serve to increase the pressure in the Soviet Union for increased Soviet output of such items. Here, of course, the question of substitution of resources becomes important. It is not necessarily true that expanded imports of consumer goods would mean that the total supply of consumer goods to Soviet citizens will be increased. Nevertheless, there are definite possibilities here.

Finally, I think we stand to gain enormously in such things as diplomacy. For example, the United States would have far less trouble with her allies who obviously are very reluctant to go along with American proposals for limitations on trade. The point I think Mr. Morgenthau made is very important here. If we were willing to expand trade with the Soviet Union we could bargain for political and other advantages to our side.

Brandt: May I add a few thoughts to this discussion. Even if one goes in the direction of exploring the possibilities for more trade with the Soviet Union, there are still some types of products which should be taboo. It would be highly desirable, therefore, to have continuing discussions among the allies about questions of this sort. I for one regret profoundly that the successor to OEEC [Organization for European Economic Cooperation], the OECD, was not transformed into an agency to study, develop, and coordinate an Atlantic trade strategy that makes sense and is effective.

Another issue NATO allies must face when it comes to trading with the Soviets is: Should credit be extended? How can we avoid situations in which the gains from trade are one-sided because loans are not repaid, as substantial former ones by the United States are simply dead claims? I believe joint action to guard against this risk is advisable in order not to march separately and be defeated jointly.

Another area in which coordination of economic relations among Western countries vis-à-vis the East is imperative is that of the supply of energy-bearing minerals, particularly oil and gas. It makes a difference whether a part of the supply of gas and oil in the pipelines on which the Western European energy system depends can be stopped at will by the Soviet Union. Short of that economic squeeze, the Soviets can engage in all sorts of power politics with various shadings of pressure to disunite Western Europe and the United States. In this and similar areas all NATO countries have a common stake which provides ample reason for closest mutual consultation on policy alternatives.

Mosely: Mr. Knorr has made a statement that I would like to reinforce, namely that the foreign trade of the Soviet Union is not a very large item in world trade. But since we cannot disregard the political and strategic factors involved, attention should be focused on the relative importance of these considerations.

I think that one of the assumptions commonly made about trade with totalitarian systems is that it will build their total war-making capacity in a way that is dangerous to us. This is something we should have considered more carefully prior to 1914 or 1939. In the present situation, however, if one of the dangers is nuclear war, we should remember that the first stage of such a war would destroy a tremendous amount of accumulated industrial and other capacity—as well as people—and that, therefore, the marginal gain or loss from engaging in trade or refusing to do so is a very much smaller factor than it would be in case of a protracted conventional war.

A second argument against easing trade restrictions is that any trade with the Soviet Union, to take the most important Communist country as an example, simply increases its ability to achieve its purposes. If Russia gets certain commodities, even refrigerators and vacuum cleaners, then resources can be diverted to other purposes such as space, defense, and aid to uncommitted countries. This is a risk we would have to take. Yet the size of this risk is really very small today. Apropos vacuum cleaners, let me add parenthetically that the Soviet Union has no incentive to meet her needs for consumer goods, and especially durable consumer goods, by importation. The Russians are producing substantial amounts in these fields and will gradually expand their production except perhaps in the field of automobiles. Soviet trade will be directed toward importing industrial producers' goods. That is where their real interests lie, except for emergency items such as wheat.

In view of these considerations, it seems to me we have to take into account other factors that may have a marginal value for us. For example, one marginal value which we would have lost had we refused to sell grain to the Soviet Union last year is the relatively favorable image which ordinary Soviet people have of America. Visitors to the Soviet Union are always struck by the very widespread trust and liking for Americans they find among people they meet. In fact, one of the main reasons for the incessant anti-American propaganda carried on by the Soviet party machine is the felt need to offset this underlying sympathy. If the Soviet leadership could have said to their own people: "Look, we need the food, we are willing to buy it for you, and the Americans have it to sell. But they are unwilling to sell it because they do not like you—they want you to suffer"—this would have offset several decades of very friendly and rather trustful feelings on the part of ordinary Russians. So when it comes to a particular item of this kind, we have to consider the costs of refusing to sell.

Furthermore, we always said that food is not a strategic item. I believe we are willing to sell it even to Cuba if the Cuban government will pay for it without recourse to barter.

To sum up, therefore, I believe that some increase in trade, watched over carefully from the point of view of denying strategic items, has a very modest and marginal value in promoting those currents in Soviet thinking that tend to postpone world revolution or attach less importance to it, and that tend to attach more importance to raising their own standard of living.

As regards the distribution of our trade: whatever the increase in trade with the Soviet Union, I think we should do more trading with the countries of East Central Europe, except East Germany.

In a situation of growing polycentrism within the Communist grouping—we cannot really say "bloc" anymore—each Communist regime will have to come to terms with its own people in one way or another. Of course, this may work in unfavorable as well as favorable directions. The growth of polycentrism may actually lead to a stiffening of Communist controls in some countries because of the deterioration it implies in the basic acceptance of Russia's right to rule. In Poland, for example, there has been a tightening up of party controls over intellectual activity, including an abortive attempt to limit intellectual exchange with the West. In short, polycentrism, instead of leading to greater freedom, can lead in some cases to a tightening of controls. This process can take different forms in different countries. We have to think about this when we consider policies to increase trade with satellite countries. Generally speaking, and except for East Germany, I would say that we should do a little more trading with the satellites than we do with the Soviet Union.

In my judgment the situation in East Germany will become unmanageable for the Soviet Union. East Germany is going to remain a source of danger, and a time may come when Russia will decide that the costs of trying to maintain that area as a satellite are too great. I favor exerting every kind of pressure against East Germany and the attempt to give it a legitimate status in international affairs or in the eyes of its own people.

Cuba, in my view, is a Western Hemisphere problem. Supporting Cuba costs the Soviet Union and East European countries a good deal in the way of resources, and for this reason as much pressure as possible should be brought to bear on Cuba even if our allies do not agree. We do not have to quarrel with them, but we should keep up the pressures because to that extent we may be deterring certain other arrangements that would make it easier for the Kremlin to manage its Western Hemisphere satellite.

In sum, I would suggest a differentiated approach in this matter of trade with Communist-sphere countries.

Knorr: Mr. Brandt raised the question of loans to the Soviet Union, and I agree with him that there is a great difference between straight trade agreements and Western trade financed by credits. If loans are involved, the Soviet Union, for example, does not put equivalent resources into the production of exports or of gold, at least not until repayment is made. In the meantime, therefore, the gain to Russia in terms of resources is equivalent to the loan; in fact, it is presumably greater because of the efficiency gain by the Soviet economy due to the imports. In a straightforward exchange situation, only the relatively small margin of net resources released through the gain in efficiency by the Soviet economy becomes freely disposable. The purposes to which the Soviet Government is likely to put this margin of gain depends obviously on the pressures experienced at any time. It could increase defense and space production. It might do something else.

Brugmans: I think we need a strategy that would get down to the grassroots of life in the countries behind the Curtain. Situations in those countries differ greatly. But I am sure that if such items as nylons, deep-freezers, transistors, and plastic household materials had been developed first in any of these countries, this would have been a source of immense propaganda for these Communist regimes. Now, if we were to sell limited quantities of such goods, the fact that these were imported from the West would certainly get around in public opinion. As a result, we could reap some of the same propaganda advantages; in fact, the scarcity of these items would increase this propaganda value. Moreover, since trade agreements along these lines may have to be negotiated between individual Western and Eastern countries—at least for the present—a basic operating procedure should be developed which should include spreading information about what is being done. It is a sign of laziness to conclude too easily that the countries behind the Curtain will not know what our policy is. We should systematically inform the largest possible number of people in those countries that we have insisted on selling to their governments the types of goods selected because we think not only in terms of our financial gain but also in terms of benefiting their personal lives.

Krause: I would like to argue that it is totally unrealistic to distinguish between the kinds of goods in which we should and should not trade. One cannot draw a distinction between consumers' and producers' goods, for example. The only distinction worth making is between those goods that save resources when they are traded and those that do not. If you are going to try to prevent the Soviet Union and her European associates from saving resources, nothing short of a total embargo will do, and it has been indicated how impossible this is, not to mention the gains we would forgo.

My second comment concerns the suggestion that we might link expansion of our trade with the satellite area to a program of student exchange. In effect, we would offer so much wheat and a few students thrown in, and if the other side refused to take the students, we would refuse to sell the wheat. But we would also have to prevent the Communist country in question from buying wheat elsewhere. This would require more than a consulting group on the Western side. We would need a trading organization that could prevent some countries from making a better offer—wheat without students, say. I am not sure what the outcome would be, but it certainly is not an easy matter to provide for the linking of trade expansion with the East and other activities designed to promote a less aggressive spirit in Communist countries.

Strausz-Hupé: We are talking about covering a well into which the cow has fallen for good. I do not think that any discussion of policies which the West ought to pursue about East-West trade will at this juncture be rewarded by fruitful results. Our Western allies are panting to do whatever trade they can do with the Soviet Union and her satellites. This is a condition and not a theory, and I do not think we can do anything about it. The floodgates have been opened and the trade is going to be done. I am sure that there are many principles by which we collectively should abide in order to be sure that our trade with the Communist bloc will be attended by the right kind of political and human results. But I am afraid these principles will not be observed.

I do not agree that the trade which the Soviet bloc or the Soviet Union engages in with the West is marginal. It is marginal, if you will, in purely statistical terms. But it is extremely important in strategic terms.

How are you going to evaluate thirty or forty British Rolls-Royce engines exported to the Soviet Union? That is a very small item relative to Soviet manufacturing output or any of the usual standards of comparison. Nevertheless, I am sure it was an exceedingly important strategic item for the Soviets. I could not agree more heartily with Mr. Morgenthau that this is a matter which goes to the very heart of Western cooperation.

Sir John Slessor, a few years ago, suggested in one of his writings that these matters are very much a concern of NATO. We have heard quite a lot of observations today that this and that economic matter should not be entrusted to NATO. We have OECD; we have the International Monetary Fund and similar institutions. These agencies perform very important functions. But they are no substitutes for a political-economic warfare general staff in NATO. Matters of trade with the Soviet Union which have been on the agenda for a good many years may well have been discussed in NATO with all the strategic implications of that trade in mind. But if so, these consultations have remained without effective results. The fact is, trading is going on, it will go on, and it will increase.

I believe we will have to get back to our primary base. We have to establish a new agreement on our joint political objectives as an alliance and then work our way back toward a trade policy vis-à-vis the Communist bloc. If we will not do that, then I am quite sure that all the political conditions which we individually would like to attach to the export of so many bushels of wheat, automobiles or refrigerators—these conditions will not be met by the Soviets and the other Communist states.

But let us not forget that the Soviet Union and even the satellite states are still in control of their respective propaganda machines. They can very readily present goods that are being imported from the West as being the results of clever moves executed by their respective governments. As a matter of fact, shortly after the wheat deal was concluded, the Soviet press dwelt at great length on the weaknesses of capitalism which make it necessary for America to sell wheat to the Soviet Union. The idea that the Soviet people would have been shocked if we had withheld the wheat because this would have meant indifference to their dietary plight cannot be substantiated from the reactions of both Mr. Khrushchev and the Soviet press in general. As a matter of fact,

Khrushchev said, "We have plenty of wheat; we really don't need American wheat. We really need it only as a kind of reserve, and those poor Americans have got to sell it anyway; as a matter of fact, it is we who are saving the American farmer from starvation." In short, I do not believe that our trade even under pressing circumstances will enhance our image in the Communist world, not even in satellite countries.

Holmes: I think we tend, now, to neglect some of the things which in fact NATO has achieved. It has been stated, for instance, that there is no coordination on trade policies with Communist countries. As a matter of fact, our policies on strategic items have been coordinated within NATO for a great many years. The list agreed to, for example, is even observed by members in trading with Cuba.

A good deal is to be said for coordinating our general trade policy in nonstrategic matters as well, and I think this has been the subject of very frequent discussions in NATO circles and in the NATO Council. I think it would be a good thing if we could do this effectively. Some of the advantages have been pointed out above.

If I may make another observation, it has been said that Soviet trade is always a political act. I entirely agree that in theory the Soviet leaders would like to have it that way. But I seriously doubt that their policy in the last few years has been a calculated political act. Is it, in fact, a calculated political act to scrounge all over the Western world trying to buy wheat? It is humiliating to have to do this. As far as the attitudes on our side are concerned, in Canada it would have been quite impossible to convince the population that wheat should not be sold to Russia. It was a good commercial deal, which does not mean that it was a narrow, selfish act neglecting higher interests. I am quite sure we would have forgone this sale, had we thought it would endanger the situation. The Canadian view represents merely a different calculation of the strategic importance of sales of this kind.

Let me add that I respect Mr. Strausz-Hupé's views on this subject. I understand a recent political joke in Moscow was to this effect: "Why is it that our Nikita Khrushchev is able to perform miracles?" The answer is: "Because he can sow wheat in Kazakstan and reap it in Saskatchewan."

Possony: I would like to associate myself with the view that NATO does need what you might call a board of economic warfare.

May I also say that so far foreign trade was perhaps not too important in the Soviet scheme. As the Soviet Union develops economically, however, foreign trade will become more and more significant and perhaps crucial—the evidence indicates this clearly. From the point of view of the problem under discussion, therefore, our trade with the Soviet Union is important. Our proposals and our ideas on this issue must be worked out in terms of ten, twenty years, or even longer periods of time.

Additional comments on two points may be indicated. First, with respect to the question of resource diversion, it has been said above that any time we sell something to the Soviets, they can divert production toward a military use. I do not think this is correct. For example, if we were to sell them a great many cars and prefabricated houses, the effect would be, I think, to introduce a new demand into the Soviet system, and resources may come to be diverted away from other uses, including perhaps, military production. After all, automobiles have to be serviced; the whole structure that goes with automobile transportation needs to be erected. In the case of prefabricated houses, the need for equipment of various types arises. I think the point is clear. If these commodities were bought in large quantity, there would be substantial diversion of resources away from armaments.

My second point is in the form of a proposal that relates to a comment made above by Mr. Mosely. As Mr. Mosely brought out, East Germany is definitely a deficit proposition for the Soviet Union. We know that every year, after a great deal of planning and an East German pilgrimage to Moscow, large under-the-table credits are extended by the Soviet Union. It seems East Germany is costing Soviet Russia upwards from one billion rubles a year. At some stage, conceivably, the Soviets might be willing to trade off this East Germany liability. This Communist experiment is not working too well. Now, it seems to me that if such thoughts—namely, a Soviet disinterest in East Germany—are being entertained, we should encourage them. I have submitted a proposal concerning this possibility, and I was told that Chancellor Erhard has been thinking in similar terms. My suggestion by way of an offer was $20 billion in the form of commercial credits made available over a period of time. Such an offer, if accepted, would represent an enormous influx of capital into the Soviet Union. The total strategic situation would be changed as a result of it. At the same time the liberation of East Germany is worth a big price. "Paris vaut bien une messe."

Let me add that I present this concept as the type of idea we should be thinking about. At the present moment we have an impasse in Europe. Sooner or later the question of reunification or of a changed status for East Germany will arise again. If at that moment we have a well thought out proposal, and if the Soviets feel sufficiently unhappy about the economic drain which they must be plugging, they may be willing to negotiate an agreement, provided it offers a reasonable *quid pro quo*.

Note, please, that the Austrian peace treaty was secured through a similar approach.

The Political Dimension

Cerny: To a very large extent, the previous discussion on The Nuclear Question and Economic Problems has unavoidably considered important political, as well as military and economic, aspects of the NATO alliance. In the present exchange of views we wish to concentrate on those political aspects that are treated in the essays included in this volume and that have thus far received insufficient attention in the dialogue. The following two-part outline serves as a framework for the discussion.

American Political Leadership
Consultation, Partnership, or Atlantic Federation

American Political Leadership

In our past discussions, the continuing role of the United States as leader of the NATO alliance has been emphasized despite fundamental changes that have taken place and possible reforms that might be undertaken. Moreover, when specific United States policies have been criticized, there has likewise been the frequent suggestion that the pursuit of such policies is incompatible with American leadership of the alliance. At this stage in our dialogue, it seems appropriate to focus more explicitly on this issue of American political leadership. More specifically: to what extent is the present disunity of the NATO alliance attributable to the inadequacies of American leadership? To launch the discussion we have selected some challenging statements from Mr. Strausz-Hupé and Mr. Kissinger that suggest a re-examination of American leadership is very much in order.

> Inevitably, America's dual role as the leading member of NATO and as the greatest independent world power is fraught with ambiguity. To play this role convincingly, more is needed than mere diplomatic virtuosity. . . . What, in the judgment of the United States, comes first: the making of the Atlantic Community, or the bouquets handed by the Afro-Asians to the United States whenever, in the name of anti-colonialism, it sides against a NATO member? . . . the increased military strength and closer political cohesiveness of NATO, or the United States' quest for a détente with the Soviet Union?
>
> Robert Strausz-Hupé

> Drastic changes in United States strategic doctrine or developments without adequate consultation—such as the removal of IRBM's from Italy and Turkey or the withdrawal of troops from Germany—create either a sense of impotence or pressures for more autonomy. Bilateral United States dealings with the Soviets from which our allies are excluded or about which they are informed only at the last moment are bound to magnify Third Force tendencies.
>
> Henry A. Kissinger

> General de Gaulle has been cast in the role of saboteur of the Atlantic alliance. Yet, NATO's dilemma is rooted in causes of much longer standing than de Gaulle's commitment to France's *Force de Dissuasion* and polemic against *les Anglo-Saxons*. . . . The United States has never pursued a NATO policy—if by such a term is meant the fostering of the growth and solidarity of the Western alliance.
>
> Robert Strausz-Hupé

Strausz-Hupé: No alliance is more cohesive than the leader of the alliance is purposeful. In his address to us, Secretary Ball cited a passage from Pericles, predicting the inevitability of decay of classical alliances such as the Delian League.[17] I think that there is something Pericles, a good politician, omitted to say; namely, that the principal guilt for the dissolution of the Delian League was the spectacular mismanagement by Athens of alliance policy.

In our day, the United States has failed to transform the NATO alliance into a vital union. And we failed to do so when the alliance was

---

[17] Secretary Ball continued: "Pericles's prediction . . . is not applicable to NATO, since NATO is not—or, at least, not merely—a classical alliance. We should never forget that it is something more—something quite different." See p. 11.

malleable. Ten years ago we could have transformed the Western alliance into our own image because we held preponderant power. If the European allies now behave as if the threat to the alliance has been greatly diminished and that thus the alliance no longer needs to command the sacrifices of its members which once seemed necessary, the responsibility for this state of affairs is traceable to some of the statements and hints emanating from what are called responsible quarters in our own country.

Certainly these statements have increased the impression of a dissolving alliance. For every myth dissipated, a new one has been conjured up. Yet not all of the ideas that we and our allies are now invited to disown may prove to have been myth. The principal enemy of the West is still communism. Some of the attempts now being made to dissociate Soviet communism from various other kinds of communism are downright ludicrous; polycentrism is much too complex a phenomenon to warrant hasty analysis. Moreover, loose talk on our side of the water is not conducive to strengthening the resolution of the allies. It is grist to the mill of all those in Europe who never liked NATO anyway and who do not like us.

If the United States, the strongest among the allies, falters, can we be surprised that our European allies falter in their allegiance to the idea of a united West? A very good example is the unfortunate preamble to the Test Ban Treaty which hints at the desirability of a nonaggression pact between the Atlantic alliance and the Warsaw Pact group.[18] The very fact that, in our official discussion and in reports from allegedly reliable quarters, NATO is equated with the Warsaw Pact expresses a judgment on the part of this country regarding the work of the alliance which most certainly does not redound to its credit in the eyes of our European allies.

The cure most certainly is not to pour the baby out with the bath water. We should not just simply wash our hands and retreat into a neo-isolationism dressed up as flexible, imaginative, *realpolitik.* We should rather clarify our priorities and stick to them. We should champion worthwhile reforms that increase the cohesion of the alliance. I have already suggested what we can do in the field of nuclear coordination and control. Let me give another example. Although I agree that organizational measures alone will not cure the ills of the alliance—and most certainly will not renew its spirit—there are certain organizational improvements which have been proposed for a long time and which should be applied now. The United States should put its weight behind

---

[18] Formed in 1955 under the title of Conference of European Powers for the Assurance of Peace and Security in Europe. Its original members were Albania, Bulgaria, Czechoslovakia, East Germany, Hungary, Poland, Rumania, and the USSR.

these improvements to show its good will and to show especially its concern with the evolution, the growth of NATO. Most certainly one of these improvements would be to strengthen the Secretariat General of NATO and to make it something akin to a cabinet with multinational ministries. Here is definitely something that could be done without too great difficulty and that would demonstrate the strength of purpose of American leadership.

Kissinger: As leaders of the alliance we have to keep in mind two separate problems: the soundness of our views and the steadiness of our judgments. To insure the cohesion of the alliance, I would think that the steadiness of our judgments may be much the more important problem. Regardless of their convictions, allied leaders are deeply concerned over the predictability and reliability of American policy. For example, in 1958 the United States advanced one strategic theory; three or four years later we advanced with equal fervor a radically or substantially different strategic theory. At the same time our intelligence estimates fluctuated from the superiority of 175 Soviet divisions to a Western conventional superiority on the Central European front. Rightly or wrongly, the question arises among our allies whether our intelligence estimates guide or follow our strategic policy. But the more damaging question—even among those who seem to agree with our latest view—is that if we can substantially change our position within three or four years on one issue, we are perfectly capable of changing our view again in three or four years on the same or other issues.

Every allied leader who agrees with an American policy not only agrees with the merits of our policy but he also stakes in part his domestic prestige on the fact of his agreement with the United States. When it becomes known that the United States is capable of changing major policies unilaterally and without adequate consultation, our allies —quite apart from their views on the correctness of our policies—have a vested interest to buy reinsurance so that their domestic position is protected.

The intellectual restlessness of some of our policymakers is therefore an inherent element of instability in NATO affairs regardless of whether I agree with the last view that they have advanced or with the next to the last view. I do not have to be in favor of liquid-fueled missiles in Italy to be concerned over a process by which missiles that were put into Italy under great opposition from the left-wing parties are pulled out with essentially the same arguments that were made by the left-wing opposition in the first place. I do not have to have any particular view about first or second strikes in order to worry about the wisdom of removing the Italian missiles two months after the conclusion of the Cuban missile crisis. In other words I should like to call attention to the fact that as leaders of the alliance we have an enormous requirement for steadiness and that there is a fundamental difference between leading an alliance and engaging in a permanent seminar about the latest fashionable strategic theories.

I also believe that we have established the wrong priorities. We have staked American prestige on creating a unitary strategic system which is designed to deprive our allies of the physical capability of autonomous action. But around the world, situations have developed in which we emphasize the political capability for bilateral action. I do not understand how we can at one and the same time urge the Germans to join the multilateral force and urge them to be flexible toward the Soviet Union. I do not see how we can at one and the same time speak for unity in the alliance and pretend that we negotiate separately with the Soviet Union, announcing the plutonium cutback, for example, with the comment that only the British were consulted on this issue. (Once again my criticism here is quite independent of what I think about the merits of the cutback of nuclear production.)

Our priorities should be reversed. Our top priority should be close political consultation and a much closer relationship in the political realm whereupon strategic issues would fall into proper place. But when from the Congo to Viet Nam to trade policy it is demonstrated that a unity of policy does not exist, when flexibility becomes identified in every country with the possibility of developing one's own approaches to the Soviet Union, it seems to me inconceivable that a unitary strategic system, if it could be achieved, would do anything else except enhance the sense of impotence of our allies.

In seeking a closer political relationship, moreover, we must avoid the kind of consultation in which our allies are asked to give their formal consent after we have accomplished a *fait accompli.* In such situations, our allies are confronted with a problem of either disagreeing with us publicly and thereby adding disunity to their already deep concern, or agreeing with us reluctantly. Consultation must come to mean that our allies have a real opportunity to express their views; it must become something else than elaborating a blueprint.

Knorr: In listening to the two preceding speakers, particularly in listening to Dr. Strausz-Hupé, I wonder whether they are not a bit too harsh in their criticism of American policy. For example, Dr. Strausz-Hupé started out by saying that "no alliance is more cohesive than the alliance leader is purposeful." This conception of leadership among free sovereign countries that have concluded a military alliance seems to me to be a highly unrealistic conception of what a leader can properly and possibly do in an alliance.

I think that we have to recognize the fact that the various members of this alliance, although they may hold some interests in common, do have different interests. Even to the extent that they face common problems, they may quite properly react in different ways. First of all, the way in which the common problem is perceived is necessarily a highly subjective matter. We know, for example, that not all allies in the NATO coalition view the Soviet threat in exactly the same way; in fact, there are considerable differences of opinion among the countries. And when it comes, secondly, to evaluating alternative courses of action that are open to the alliance, here again it is quite clear that the genuine and legitimate interests of these various countries may properly diverge.

Partly because of geographic location, partly because of other problems, they do not evaluate the available alternatives in the same way. Again, to give just one example that was mentioned in our discussion on The Nuclear Question, Europeans are chiefly interested in the deterrence of Soviet aggression; in the event that deterrence fails, they have very little interest in defense. On the other hand, the United States wishes other choices open to the alliance; it is interested in defense as well as deterrence, particularly defense in the case of local and relatively limited conflicts. European countries do not consider such conflicts to be very limited; they involve a degree of destruction that makes European countries react to this alternative in a quite different way from the United States or Canada.

It is hardly surprising therefore that on very many concrete issues our allies do not all try to push the United States in one particular direction. On the contrary, what is usually the case is that some allies try to pull us in one direction and other allies try to push us in another direction. Let me again give an example. In the matter of negotiating with the Soviet Union, we all know that the British and Canadians are very much in favor of the search for some sort of détente that in their view is in the interests of the United States and its allies. But we also know that if the United States gives way to their pressure, the Germans and the French will become extremely suspicious.

It is not my intention to get into the substantive merits of this issue; I wish merely to illustrate that things are not quite as simple as they have been suggested to be. The different allies do have different interests. They see even their common interests differently and therefore are in favor of different positions. This is a political fact of life which must be recognized and which makes the leadership of an alliance, if there can be such a thing, a far more complex and difficult thing than I think Dr. Strausz-Hupé has suggested.

Linebarger: [19] A great number of the preceding comments have been based on logic. Yet in my view, the presence of personality is an

[19] Paul Linebarger is Professor of Asiatic Politics at Johns Hopkins University. He is the author of *Psychological Warfare* (1948) and co-author of *Far Eastern Governments and Politics* (1954).

equally important factor in analyzing American leadership and the future of NATO.

I would like to suggest that men usually do—even if they are presidents or prime ministers—what they must do. They do things because of their emotional bias, and not because of logic or treaties. General Eisenhower, as a presidential candidate, said, "I will go to Korea." The function of presidential candidates in Korea—whether elected or not—still remains constitutionally undefined. But General Eisenhower won the election. In the Kennedy age of enthusiasm, we had a brilliant President with tremendous intellectual acumen and a zest for good talk. Yet President Kennedy utterly mismanaged our South American policy. Under Lyndon Johnson we have much less brilliant leadership but perhaps much wiser leadership. We have already solved a great part of the problem of Panama.

Who lives and who dies are emotional matters; they crystalize the feelings of large parts of the public. The death of Mao, the death of Salazar, the death even of Chiang Kai-shek, the death of General Franco, the death of General de Gaulle, the death of even another American President—these events cannot be ignored in considering the future of NATO. A different Johnson and a different Soviet leader might conclude an ideal treaty, a treaty which would be greeted with tears of joy in Moscow and Leningrad, New York and Washington. The treaty might be a simple agreement that in case of war the United States would not fire at the Soviet Union and the Russians would not fire at the continental forty-eight states. Instead they would fire at each other's allies. (The effect of such an agreement on Peking and Paris can well be imagined.) I do not trust any such proposal; I do not think anyone would trust it. But if somebody had an election to win in Washington, or a conspiracy to win for the succession in Moscow, then this kind of proposal may lie within the realm of possibility during the next half-dozen or dozen years.

I repeat therefore that people do things because of their emotional bias. I can predict fairly infallibly what Mr. Rusk will do next or what Mao Tse-tung will do next. I cannot predict what Lyndon Johnson will do next; it depends on how much the man exposes his cards. After the leaders have made the decision, then they call in the experts like us to tell them what they have decided on. And we figure it out and put it down in treaties and protocols. I find it significant that no one, least of all General Marshall, had the faintest idea what the Marshall Plan was to be when it started, and that no one has ever remembered what the first three points of Point IV were.

Consultation, Partnership, or Atlantic Federation

Cerny: In moving to the second topic of our outline we are chiefly interested in the question of how best to improve the institutional framework of the NATO alliance. To an extent, this question was already considered when we discussed the topic of nuclear coordination and control. Obviously, however, the question of institutional reorganization applies as well to economic and diplomatic policy fields. Indeed, in his statement of the U. S. attitude, Secretary Ball noted that apart from solving the problem of managing the nuclear deterrent power of the West, the second most important unfinished piece of business in the NATO alliance is to find ways of perfecting "NATO as an instrument by which the member nations can concert policies with respect to problems that arise not merely within the NATO area but elsewhere in the world." [20] With a view to considering the organizational improvement of NATO in this wider context, we have selected statements from Mr. Holmes, Mr. Allais, and Mr. Brugmans. Hopefully, these statements will spark a discussion of the relative merits of alternative institutional approaches.

> In the field of diplomacy, the interests of member nations are far more diversified, and a common foreign policy has proved impossible to achieve. It is persistently assumed, nevertheless, that it would be a good thing if we could achieve it. One cannot, of course, argue against perfection, and if we could all think in unison on Cyprus, chickens, or Mozambique, that would indeed be a heavenly situation. On earth we are not going to, however, and it is not just rationalization to argue that we are stronger as a team for our diversity.
>
> John W. Holmes

> On the political level, three basic measures could be envisaged: first of all, the creation of a NATO Council empowered, on questions of common interest, in specified fields, to make decisions by a qualified majority; second, the creation of a "Commission" suitably empowered to study common problems and make recommendations; third, the creation of an Atlantic Parliamentary Assembly whose role would be only advisory and whose members would be designated by the national parliaments.
>
> Maurice Allais

> Neither the United States nor any of the other allies could accept North Atlantic institutions in which decisions were made by simple majority or even a weighted majority because the United States, which has a near monopoly of the crucial weapons, could not permit a veto on its freedom of move-

---

[20] *Cf.*, p. 14.

> ment and the rest of us could not in such an unequal situation give up our right to dissent and contract out. . . . Are not we all . . . better off coping with the facts of [U.S.] priority which may be adjustable than with established definitions of what really goes on which would be offensive to admit?
>
> John W. Holmes

> Whereas America is a "nation" from coast to coast just as much as a "union," there is no European "nation" in the making, let alone an Atlantic one. If Western Europe is ever to federate, it will be through institutions extremely different from those of the American type. . . . On both shores of the ocean, statehood is of a different nature so that the building materials of an Atlantic union are not fifty-odd States on the one side, and six or sixteen on the other. The material has to be two-fold: Europe and America, boh of them "united." What, then, has to be done if disunity means ruin and Atlantic federation remains utopian? . . . The only long-range perspective seems to be a free world confederacy, based on regional, continental federations rather than on individual nation-states.
>
> Hendrik Brugmans

Holmes: In discussing the question of unity within NATO from the vantage point of a smaller country, I am not suggesting that we all happily go off on our own without any consultation at all. I assume that there will be more and more consultation. I also think that General Beaufre gave us a very good definition of the kind of consultation that is necessary: the need to try to work out policies together, to study them together. This has been very useful in NATO councils. And if I might perhaps add a note here, the fault with present-day consultation is not all on one side. The fault is sometimes on the side of the smaller countries that have not done their homework, or are not capable of doing as much homework. Sometimes the fault is on the side of the United States that confuses consultation with a briefing session. Thus we are confronted with a lecture, with the use of maps, and with colonels with illuminated pointers. All this is very interesting, but it is not consultation.

But assuming that we have more and proper consultation, the question still remains: how do we induce agreement? In my view, there is too much tendency to assume that if we cannot get agreement through consultation, we can get it by some kind of constitutional means. We always seem to run off in the direction of some kind of federalism. I think it is perhaps too often forgotten that in my country we have had a kind of pilot project for the last two hundred years in having two of the major peoples of Europe living together. I can assure you that federation does not induce agreement. We are finding this out very much at the present time.

In my essay I have suggested that it is not just a rationalization to say that there are advantages in diversity. Partly, of course, it is indeed a rationalization. If we could somehow or other have perfect agreement, if we could all agree on every matter of foreign policy, this would be splendid. And undoubtedly we should work toward such agreement. But I do think that if we cannot have it, we ought not to drive ourselves mad wanting and insisting on it, because there are advantages in diversity—even in a tightly-knit team.

More particularly, we have to look at the roles of the smaller powers, and even of the other major powers. For instance, we should look very carefully at General de Gaulle's effort and ask whether this is so contrary to the interest of NATO as has been assumed. The United States, it seems to me, does need help in Latin America. The relations between the United States and Latin America appear to some of us on the outside—I do not blame the United States for this situation—to have become extremely neurotic. It seems to me that the United States does need some kind of outside force and that it should be welcomed. General de Gaulle's influence on Latin American thinking is much more likely to make Mr. Castro unhappy than the United States. In the same way, we should appreciate the very special role that the British play in the world, the kind of influence which they have in Africa particularly at the present time.

I should also like to call attention to the special function of all the smaller powers in the NATO alliance. It is of course important that we be loyal members of NATO. Yet we also have particular peace-keeping functions which are becoming more and more important. It is essential for NATO that the Norwegians and the Danes and ourselves, for instance, be able to take part in these operations. I am not sure that there is anything that Canada has ever done to help NATO that has been more useful than having a thousand troops ready to go into Cyprus. If Canada is going to be accepted for this kind of role, she must have a certain independence of policy, a certain independence of position.

Obviously, there are limitations to this proposition. Certainly we cannot allow too much freedom on anything as essential as the position of West Berlin, because we must be very tightly united on a matter of that kind. But it does not necessarily follow that we have to follow a single policy on everything else. I might say that it is this worship of unity of policy as an end in itself, unity in the abstract, that bothers me—not that I am opposed to our trying to reach unity.

To deal with the diversity of interests and policies of the NATO allies clearly requires a great deal of tact and judgment on the part of everybody concerned. Unfortunately we all have our besetting sins. The besetting sin of the lesser powers may well be irresponsibility, a tendency to enjoy twisting the eagle's feathers, a delight in exercising our own independence. We should instead always consider the effect of any particular policy on United States policy because of the peculiarly decisive nature of United States responsibilities. Quite frequently such consideration may mean conforming with American policy even when we do not happen to agree with it. We must be prepared to do so—but by no means all the time.

On the other hand, I think a besetting sin of the United States, if I may speak bluntly about it, tends to be a certain moral arrogance, which I think was partially displayed in Secretary Ball's address to us.[21] I think it is essential for the United States to recognize that other countries are not merely acting in their own national interests. I do not know what on earth Canadian troops are doing in Cyprus, or why we have been in Indochina for ten years—unless it is perhaps assumed that we happen to be on the purer side of the Atlantic. Yet a man as great as General de Gaulle does not follow a policy solely out of the pursuit of narrow national interest, or just to make Americans unhappy. Perhaps he is truly concerned about Latin America; perhaps he is truly concerned about China. I do think it is important to recognize the function that has been played by the Commonwealth of Nations in trying to keep this world together; it has complemented the function of the United States.

I certainly would not want to suggest that United States policy in the world is merely in the national interest. But at the same time I don't see why it should be assumed that what Britain is doing in Malaysia is any more a matter of narrow national interest than what the United States is doing in Panama. If we would at least assume that the other side is acting honestly in its own interest, and not pursuing merely selfish national interests, we would be able to consult far more happily.

Allais: At least for the foreseeable future, the real struggle between East and West will probably be on the economic, social, and ideological planes. In my opinion, if the West is to wage this struggle successfully, two important and radical changes are necessary: first, a liberalization of trade throughout the Atlantic area; and second, some common political structure.

I do not share the widely held assumption that what is indispensable for the economic relations of continental European countries would be invalid for the economic relations of the Atlantic nations. On the contrary, an appropriate institutional framework would be *more necessary* on this broader level. In itself, the functional approach cannot constitute a valid solution. The functional approach can be effective *only* if associated with a vast *political* conception of unity, and

---

[21] See p. 18.

only if a certain degree of political integration is carried out at the same time.

Contrary to a widely held opinion, the realization of an Atlantic Common Market is a *feasible operation* and it would certainly be very advantageous for all its participants. But the implementation of Atlantic-wide trade liberalization would lead to profound transformations, and in fact it could be advantageous only if such transformations took place. This solution would be acceptable *only* if the participating countries were assured that these transformations were really permanent and could not be challenged overnight.

From this point of view, I must emphasize that any economy-wide liberalization is possible, can be advantageous, can be accepted, and can be maintained only if a certain degree of political integration is carried out at the same time. One should have no illusions about the possible success of the Kennedy Round in strengthening and extending the economic ties between Europe and the United States substantially and durably.

Any progress to be realized from an economic partnership that is not reinforced by a political partnership will of necessity be marginal.

These considerations bring me to Mr. Holmes' comments. I must confess that I have been impressed by his very interesting essay. It presents some very appealing arguments against an Atlantic federation to which it is very difficult not to subscribe.

Nevertheless, if I have understood his point of view correctly, he is in fact recommending some kind of status quo. In any case, he calls the federalist solution the federalist fallacy. I would ask two questions: Is it possible to say that the federalist solution has been a fallacy for the United States? Does he really think that the two World Wars would have been possible if there would have been some federation of the West in 1914 and 1939?

In these two cases should we not speak of the fallacy of the traditional policies?

Holmes: Although we must certainly learn lessons from history, one of the mistakes which we have made a great deal lately is to draw the wrong analogies. Of course I would not want to say that the federation did not work for the United States. But I think that we should also remind ourselves that within the American federation there was the most disastrous war of the Nineteenth Century over the question of sovereignty. Moreover, the North Atlantic organization is very different from the American colonies of the 1770's and 1780's. I just do not see the kind of cohesion, the kind of common approach, common understanding and common interest that would make a similar federation workable. Finally, is it really that self-evident which countries should become members of an Atlantic federation? I myself cannot see how Canada could be part of a federation with Turkey which did not include Australia. I do not see how the United States, with its interest in Latin America and other parts of the world, could be tied to a federation which included only a few countries on either side of the Atlantic.

Allais: Admittedly there are many drawbacks and obstacles to establishing very close cooperation between Europe and the United States. And I agree completely with the specific points that have been raised by Mr. Holmes. But we have to choose between different solutions, and the danger is that we might choose the worst. In politics, there are never completely good solutions; in fact, we must search for the least bad ones. In my view, despite the many obstacles to close cooperation between Europe and the United States, it is the goal of cooperation which we should choose and seek to achieve. Yet in listening to Mr. Holmes (and in reading his essay) I gained the distinct impression that in his view diversity among the allies is a good thing after all, and that there is nothing to be gained from closer cooperation. Such a conclusion cannot be taken very seriously in the light of today's realities. Even in the Eighteenth Century, there were many disagreements between the different American states; yet the Union proved to be most advantageous for the common interests of all the states.

Finally, with respect to Mr. Holmes' point that it is difficult to define the Atlantic Community in geographic terms, there is also the implied point that any effort at definition leaves the members of the Community open to the criticism of placing their particular interests above the interests of the entire world. In my opinion, however, we cannot tolerate disunity and anarchy among us just to please the rest of the world. As the Cuban example showed, decisive American leadership brought United States prestige to an all-time high. The people of this world respect strength and success, not weakness and disunity. Thus our first step should be to establish closer cooperation among the nations of the Atlantic Community.

Holmes: When we talk about federal institutions and the surrender of sovereignty to supranational institutions, I think we have to realize what we are in fact doing. We are extending American control and domination formally instead of informally within the alliance. In any federal organization, the United States decision is bound to be decisive, not because Americans want it this way but because it is a fact of life. What would have happened over Suez if we had had consultation in a federal-type system? Britain would have given way to the American point of view. (In this instance, I happen to think it would have been desirable.) Similarly, on all current issues, whether Vietnam or China, we would have to give way to the American point of view. Therefore when we surrender our sovereignty to a federal system, we are surrendering quite a bit. In practice, we of course do accept the fact that the United States is our champion. But I think it is better to accept this fact informally rather than formally.

Having criticized the federal solution, I don't mean to suggest that the alternative is to maintain the status quo. The status quo is not ideal—even if it is not quite as bad as it is sometimes made out to be. My own view is that we should seek to improve the status quo by proceeding according to the functionalist theory. NATO is essentially a military organization; decisions on whether and how to strengthen NATO should be based on the test whether the reforms will enable NATO to perform its major function better. On the other hand, if we wish to improve our economic coordination, then I would rather see the Organization for Economic Cooperation and Development strengthened. Moreover, one of the things which I like most about OECD is that it has included Japan, thereby suggesting that it is not a prisoner of the geographic conception of an Atlantic Community.

Uri: I doubt that any of us here disagrees with Mr. Allais' view that closer cooperation should be the goal of the Western alliance. I also think that we must all be very thankful to Mr. Holmes for pointing to the real difficulties in achieving closer cooperation, because there is absolutely no advantage in ignoring them. In political terms, therefore, the real problem before us is to find the means of discussing important issues in common without facing a situation in which suddenly one ally thinks that he has the right policy and the other allies are faced with a *fait accompli.* After all, the policy may not prove to be the best; yet once launched, it will prove difficult to change.

In seeking a practical solution to our problem, I wish to reinforce Mr. Holmes' warning that we should not be misled by false analogies. In the immediate postwar period, we Europeans often thought in terms of federation and of the example of the United States. We have discovered that fortunately we have invented something new. In an earlier comment, Mr. Brugmans coined the term "communitarian" to describe this new phenomenon. He was right in searching for a new word because we have not copied the American federal constitution. For example, we do not have a President and a bicameral Congress. Rather we developed a set of institutions in which there is a constant dialogue between one organ (i.e., the European Commission of the Common Market) which is in charge of the common interest, and another organ (i.e., the Council of Ministers) whose representatives are in charge of presenting the particular views and special problems of their respective governments.

This experience leads me to suggest that in approaching any problem—whether economic, financial, institutional, or political—the first question to ask ourselves is the extent to which our immediate problem differs from the one that we solved the last time. I would be frightened by the proposition that we should proceed on the Atlantic level in the same way that we have been proceeding on the European level.

Moreover, we should not try to hide behind rather vague solutions to our problem. We should only be satisfied that we have offered a solution when we have made it perfectly precise and operational. In the Common Market we have not only the general formula of a supranational body representing the common interest; we also have very precise rules defining the functions of the Commission and the voting procedure of the Council of Ministers. Unless we can point to specific institutions and precise procedures, we cannot say that we have any solution to problems such as a European nuclear force or a common policy on foreign affairs in any part of the world.

I am quite sure that the institutions and procedures to achieve closer cooperation between the United States and Europe are going to be different from those established in Europe. How can we really imagine that the United States will accept the possibility of being in a minority position? The United States represents half the population of the Atlantic world, more than half its production, and much more than half its defense expenditure. I don't know of any democratic rule that could persuade the United States under these conditions to accept a decision taken by others. It would not be rule of the majority but of the minority. Conversely, I do not believe that it is possible that one country and one country alone in an Atlantic organization could have a veto. Even if it could be justified, the political fact of life is that other countries, although granting the predominant power of the United States, will nevertheless insist that they cannot be treated on the same basis as tiny Luxemburg.

For these reasons, the organization of closer cooperation between the United States and Europe is bound to be different from the solution of the European Common Market. For the same reasons, I think that there is real value in the concept of partnership between the United States and Europe. Here is a special solution for what is a new and different problem. According to this concept, there are two groups that are roughly equal. Each group has to find its own way for making decisions and the final decision is an agreement between two partners. This concept is probably the only way out of our dilemma. If, on the other hand, we insist on trying to copy institutions that were intended to solve different problems, we are apt to be very badly mistaken.

THE HUNT LIBRARY
CARNEGIE INSTITUTE OF TECHNOLOGY

Allais: Mr. Uri's comments are not very convincing. We Europeans are perfectly aware that the problem of organizing the Atlantic Community is different from the problem of organizing Europe. Furthermore, Mr. Uri exaggerates the possible reluctance of the United States to joining an organization in which it might be in a minority position. As Mr. Holmes has made quite clear, a federal system could not prevent the United States from exercising a decisive voice. And as for the impact of a federal system on the various NATO countries, I should like to read the following sentences from my essay:

> Whatever the possible solution may be, there could be no question of any sudden change. It is a matter of advancing cautiously in a new direction. At the start, any delegation of rights would have to be limited and carefully hedged, as all international agreements are, by safeguarding clauses to preserve each nation from that which it could not accept.[22]

If we move cautiously therefore and make allowance for the possible adverse effect of federal decisions on the interests of individual countries, we should be able to soften considerably the full impact of the surrender of sovereignty.

Finally, what does Mr. Uri mean by "partnership"? It is not a federation; it is not a confederation. In fact, as far as I can see, it is at most an alliance. As such I don't see clearly what the difference is between this future "partnership" and the present situation.

Possony: I do not believe that the goal of a partnership between the United States and a united Europe will be achieved in our lifetime. Furthermore, I do not believe that it is necessarily advisable even for the future. We must distinguish between supranationality and supranational institutions. Today, the sociological and psychological reality of the Western world is the nation and the nation-state. Admittedly, the nation-state is in many ways out of date. National sovereignty—in the sense of a state being able to do whatever it wants—no longer exists. In any event, such sovereignty has been much curtailed. But the idea that the European nation-states are going to form one nation is utopian. These nation-states are historic entities; there is no reason why these nations should be merged and for all I know they will not be merged. And perhaps the merger is not culturally, institutionally, and linguistically feasible. Since there will be no such thing as a surrender of sovereignty, every member of the alliance will continue to have a *de facto* veto. The making of national decisions can indeed be temporarily transferred to another institution. However, the decisions of such an institution will not be carried out if they lack popular support in particular national entities.

---

[22] P. 374, below.

The building of supranational institutions is quite different from seeking to achieve the supranational idea of a united Europe. Supranational institutions presuppose acceptance of, or are compatible with, the sociological and psychological reality of the nation-state. Rather than presupposing that the nation-state can be dissolved, these institutions provide links between the various nations. In this way, nations can cooperate in achieving goals that are beyond the capacity of any one of them. In this way too, nations—or nationhood—can be strengthened rather than weakened.

Let us be clear therefore that our task is to build supranational institutions, not supranationality. And of course we are already building them. We are building them in NATO and in the OECD. Our task is really to build many more. Moreover, let me suggest that whether we can build such institutions depends on something more than convincing the executive officials of different countries. Our discussion is at times slightly reminiscent of eighteenth-century cabinet policy. We talk as though political reality is vested in the executive departments and we ignore the importance of national legislatures. Yet one of the reasons why such supranational institutions as we have—including supranational parliaments—do not function very well in terms of alliance requirements is that one parliament does not know what the other one is doing.

If we are agreed that we must start solving our problems in a gradual, evolutionary manner, then one of our first steps should be to start bringing our national parliaments together. After all, every advance in building supranational institutions will require national legislation in every participating nation. The coordination of parliamentary activities is as necessary as the coordination of executive activities. When one particular parliament is involved in deciding a given issue, it should know what other parliaments are doing or not doing with the problem. For example, in the United States Senate hearings on the Test Ban Treaty, it would have been useful for people from foreign nations to testify on how the treaty would affect their security. There are many other ways in which the parliaments of the free world can start cooperating. The important thing is that we place this item at the top of our agenda for reorganizing the relationships of the Western world.

Strausz-Hupé: In our earlier discussion on The Nuclear Question, Mr. Morgenthau called upon us to think creatively, to encourage creative statesmanship. I should like to take up Mr. Uri's challenge. Is the model of the European community really so unacceptable a solution for the problem of the Atlantic Community? Conceivably it might fit.

I do not wish to see my country in a minority in any kind of institution. However, I do not believe that in the nature of things the

United States conceivably could ever find itself in a minority within the structure of an Atlantic-wide community. To those who might argue that I am therefore merely reasserting the principle of American hegemony, I would answer that there is a great difference as to whether a country constitutes the majority within a community or imposes its will outside of a community. Even if this is only a psychological difference, it is still fundamentally important since it points to the prerequisite of successful consultation.

The fact is that the peoples of the Western alliance have thus far been incredibly lucky. During the past sixteen or seventeen years, the relationship of forces has been such that the alliance could afford some thumping errors, including Suez, the Congo, and now, Cyprus. Alliances do not go to war because of some technical deficiencies, because the right buttons are not being pressed, or even because there are no war plans. Alliances go to war because some well-identifiable, well-known international issues have been permitted to accumulate and to reach an intensity where there is no alternative to war. We of the West can no longer rely on past good fortune; we need the kind of consultation that will prevent explosive issues from accumulating.

Past experience would indicate that what we need is consultation in some improved institutional form. It is for this reason that I should like to align myself with Mr. Allais. To be sure, his solution may not be ideal. Yet there is no such thing as an ideal solution for the problem raised by national sovereignty on the one hand and the common interest of the Western people on the other. And I do believe that precisely because time is running out, because we are no longer in the "Golden Fifties," we have to opt for the goal of cooperation that Mr. Allais has outlined. Instead of maintaining the status quo, we have to think creatively, namely, how to institutionalize the consultative procedures of the Western alliance on at least a minimum rudimentary basis. Here is our core problem. In my opinion, the problem of the control of nuclear weapons or the control of nuclear strategy is of less significance than the problem of achieving agreement on how to conduct joint policies on such fundamental issues as East Germany, Eastern Europe, the Sino-Soviet bloc, and Southeast Asia. It is all very good to say that individual nations, by virtue of their own accumulated wisdom, can introduce valuable ideas into the councils of the allies. But let us not forget that such procedure is always a luxury and that we no longer have such luxury available to us.

Brugmans: I fully agree that we need some kind of institutional framework within the Atlantic Community to improve cooperation. To be sure, institutions cannot do everything. But they certainly can do a bit more than just reflect and embody the present state of forces active in the political field. They can also promote certain forces and restrain others. For example, if consultation takes place only occasionally, the process of building consensus can hardly develop. Moreover, if the institutional framework is such that an ally must defend his policies in the presence of his partners, not only today or tomorrow, but for an indefinite period, then the institutional framework facilitates the search for agreement. In this "communitarian" context, minorities are less likely to feel that they are unduly forced to accept majority agreement. A spirit of understanding and compromise develops.

At the outset I would not insist too much on rigid constitutional schemes with complicated voting procedures. The task of building a framework requires a more pragmatic and flexible approach. However, in advocating such an approach, I do not mean to imply that we should aim solely at achieving efficiency; we should likewise aim at securing democratic control. Although I am prepared to praise the provisional institutions of the European communities, I think it is essential that they be democratized. The real power in the European Economic Community is the Council of Ministers. But as an institution, it cannot be held responsible for its deeds or misdeeds. Its responsibility is hidden behind the smokescreen of national responsibilities which is no adequate substitute for supranational control by an independent supranational assembly. And I would urge that there is a similar need for democratic control in the case of NATO. It is a disturbing fact that while we oppose the Communist world under the banner of democracy, the processes of integration that are taking place in the West are failing to provide for adequate democratic control.

There is one other point that we should not lose sight of in attempting to establish an institutional framework within the Atlantic Community. We must recognize that the building of such a community will not be the end of our task. The whole world is moving toward a system of regional federations. Admittedly, the European communities are still only provisional; the Arab League has only approached the stage of the Council of Europe; the South American common market is very far from the stage that we have reached in Europe. Nevertheless, if we think in terms of decades and generations, the pattern of evolution is clearly toward the organization of continents and sub-continents as regional entities. As they form, we will face the task of finding ways and means to organize consultation between them, to come to mutual agreements and to coordinate activities.

Slessor: I think it is desirable to remind ourselves of a document called the Declaration of Paris. In January 1962, a number of us met in Paris as members of our national commissions to the Atlantic Convention of NATO nations. We were appointed by our governments and instructed to report to our governments. We came up with a unanimous recommendation to the effect that we should take immediate steps to create a true

Atlantic Community, with its own institutions and with the object of harmonizing policies in the political, economic, and military spheres affecting the community as a whole. We did not come up with recommendations for a federal system, or for decisions by majority vote, or anything else. We recognized that some of these community institutions would have to be developed, and we recognized that they could not be the same as those of existing organizations, either the Common Market or NATO or EDC.[23] Obviously, a hundred people meeting for a fortnight in Paris could not possibly work out a detailed blueprint for the kingdom of heaven tomorrow morning. What we recommended therefore was that our governments should set up a special intergovernmental commission which should get to work at once and within a two-year period produce a plan defining the nature of the Atlantic Community's institutions and the manner of their operation.

As far as my own government is concerned, the Prime Minister got up in the House of Lords and stated that the Declaration of Paris was a splendid document, and that the British Government could not be more completely in agreement with its recommendations. Yet absolutely nothing has been done from that date to this. Moreover, as far as I know, nothing has been done in any of the other countries who were represented at that Atlantic Convention. I know that the Atlantic Council of the United States and also the British Atlantic Committee in London have tried to put pressure on their governments to appoint the special governmental commission that was recommended by the Declaration of Paris. But again nothing has happened. My bet is that unless some very strong pressure is applied nothing will happen for another two and a half years.

Since it is highly unlikely that there will be an officially appointed governmental commission for a long time to come, I urge that something should be undertaken on the nonofficial level, perhaps in the Atlantic Institute, perhaps in the Atlantic Council of the United States, with some provision for allied representation. My suggestion is the establishment of a small group which would get down to some of the preliminary and rather unglamorous groundwork that would have to be done in any event by the special intergovernmental commission. To do any good, such an unofficial group would obviously require governmental blessing since it would have to have access to the State Department, Foreign Office, and so on. Governmental cooperation of this type, however, seems unlikely to be withheld and we will not have postponed indefinitely consideration of the structure of an Atlantic Community.

Brandt: To Sir John Slessor's admonition that we begin to think about the details of establishing the structure of an Atlantic Community, I

---

[23] European Defense Community.

should like to add the admonition that we begin to use the OECD for the purpose of planning joint solutions for serious economic problems that threaten the future of the alliance. Just as time has been wasted since 1962 in implementing the Atlantic Community Declaration of Paris of January 20 of that year, so too time has been wasted in coming to grips with economic problems that can presently be anticipated. In economics, to waste time may mean something more than delay; time may run out before we can prepare effective countermeasures.

Of the problems that can be anticipated, I would point, first of all, to the ever mounting competition for markets throughout the world. Since 1958, the United States has slowly come to recognize that the European nations are fully restored economically, that they are capable of competing effectively, and that some of our own industries have to begin making necessary adjustments to avoid serious economic decline. This growth of competition can be expected to increase as all the industrialized nations seek markets among themselves and in the underdeveloped countries. China, Soviet Russia, and the COMECON satellites cannot be ignored either; and we should once and for all dispel the myth that by opening the market of China every producer can sell all his producer goods and solve the problem of competition.

Still a second problem that can be anticipated is that capital funds are unlikely to continue being transferred to the underdeveloped countries on a government-to-government basis. If I am not mistaken, the American electorate will refuse to support such government aid indefinitely. We must start thinking about methods of facilitating the transfer of capital funds through the ordinary channels—through the banking institutions and private corporations of the different countries in the world. Political leaders in the underdeveloped countries may not as yet be aware of this impending development; they will however have to face the prospect of adjusting to hard necessity.

One other problem that deserves mention is the extent to which the American people have in a sudden sway begun to act on the assumption that inflation is built into our economy. Bonds have been exchanged against stocks. Due to limited supply, stock prices have been driven to the sky. Yet, as the first half of 1962 indicated, the whole edifice can crumble quickly and tens of millions of dollars can disappear overnight in a way that is generally assumed to be no longer possible after the experience of 1929. Fortunately we have pulled out of the crash of 1962 and we are probably going on for another year of a boom—or maybe two. We must deal, however, with the problem of built-in inflation; nor should we ignore its impact on the wider problem of our competitive position.

Unless the necessary intellectual work is done beforehand in the OECD, these economic problems to which I have referred may accumulate to the point of causing a serious recession. Indeed, the economy of the United States is of such enormous size that the beginning of a recession in this country may mean disaster for many other countries. Therefore we must plan now to cooperate with our allies in dealing with problems that we can anticipate. The alternative is a real diplomatic disintegration of the Atlantic Community as each country tries vainly to pursue protectionist policies in a situation where the capacity of the world market will be too small and the continuing social ferment will threaten political stability.

In my view, the greatest mistake of United States foreign policy has been that we have permitted cooperation within the OECD to be sidetracked. It is simply not enough that the OECD publish learned reports which are read and enjoyed by specialists. Through persevering consultation we must find areas of agreement on points of economic policy that deserve priority. It is equally important that we find the sensitive points where one nation must frankly warn the others in time not to interfere if the process of consultation is to continue. Such efforts require hard work and the use of precious time. The Treaty of Rome establishing the Europeon Economic Community was not established overnight. It required six months of patient advance preparation by specialists and statesmen at Messina. In the same way, if the OECD countries are to make effective use of the time that is still available, they must begin *now* to explore joint solutions to impending foreign economic problems.

Streit: [24] I should like to associate myself right at the outset with various points made during this discussion by Mr. Allais, Mr. Brandt, Mr. Strausz-Hupé, Sir John Slessor, and Mr. Brugmans. And I would like to comment a little more fully on some of the statements made by Mr. Holmes and Mr. Uri.

I was very much impressed by Mr. Uri's comments regarding recent European experience with establishing integrated communities. We are all very deeply indebted to the trail-blazing and the experimentation that the European communities have made. Yet, if we are going to base ourselves on the record of experience, then surely the federal system has a much better record. With all that we owe to the European communities, they have not yet stood the kind of test that the federal system has in the United States for 175 years and in Canada for well-nigh a hundred years.

In my view therefore the sensible thing is first to see what we can do to establish a federal system on an Atlantic scale. If we do not succeed, then we can proceed to develop new programs. When I speak of federalism, I do not mean that we should slavishly follow the

[24] Clarence Streit is President of Federal Union, Inc., editor of *Freedom and Union,* board member of the Atlantic Union Committee, and President of the International Movement for Atlantic Union.

example of the United States in the manner that was criticized by Mr. Uri. The Swiss federal union rests on a quite different basis. So too does the Canadian system which is adapted to the parliamentary system. Although Mr. Holmes seems to take a rather doubtful view of the possibility of federation around the Atlantic, there have been other Canadians, such as Patrick Nichols and Alistair Stewart, who have made eloquent pleas on behalf of Atlantic federation. They too made it clear that the Canadian and American examples should not be blindly followed. Of course, there are differences of opinion on these matters. But we cannot dismiss the possibility of Atlantic federation unless the effort has been made not only by Europeans but also by Canadians and Americans who have had actual experience with federalism and who are quite used to thinking in federal terms.

In criticizing the federal solution Mr. Uri spoke of the dilemma facing Americans who will not accept a minority position and Europeans who will not accept an American veto. If we are really thinking of a federal solution, however, Mr. Uri has posed a false dilemma. In a federal union there is a balance between the United States Senate and House of Representatives. The Senate is weighted on the side of the small states; the House, on the side of the more populous states. Yet neither chamber represents the governments of those states. Let us suppose, for example, that we had a House of Representatives for an Atlantic federal union and that the United States would be represented on the basis of one representative for every million inhabitants. The 190 American representatives would indeed not constitute a majority in the House. On the other hand they would not consider themselves as a distinct minority. They would be elected in 190 districts of this country; they would belong to different parties. Cutting across their common bond as American representatives would be ties of economic and party interest that would bind them to the representatives of other countries. Thus the problem of the United States occupying a minority position is far less of a problem in a federal system than in an alliance or partnership system.

On his part, Mr. Holmes, in questioning the feasibility of a federal system, called attention to the American Civil War. I could of course answer that practically all the great powers have had civil wars. The more important answer, however, is that the United States managed to effect a lasting peace. And one of the reasons that peace has lasted is that the North, although dominant and having won the war, chose after a brief experience with reconstruction not to impose its will in an immediate and total fashion. The American people learned something from that Civil War: to avoid dominating their fellow citizens, to handle problems pragmatically, and to play down the theoretical rights of majorities over minorities.

These considerations lead me to the point that was made by Mr. Strausz-Hupé. He dared to think the unthinkable. If I may change the phrasing, we had better cease to blink at the unblinkable. The unblinkable fact, as Mr. Strausz-Hupé has so rightly stated, is that we cannot count on having all the time in the world. Yet I submit that the basic assumption underlying present policy throughout the Atlantic Community is that we have time to proceed step by step through I do not know how many decades; at the end of the process we will still manage to avoid economic or military catastrophe. Surely, however, we should all remember that one of the characteristics of a democratic people is to do too little too late. We persistently face the grave danger of letting the golden years go by while we exercise our freedom of discussion but get to no action.

Let us then not be too confident that we have all the time in the world. By all means, let us do what we can step by step. But let us also realize that evolution some times moves at a swifter rate. In my judgment, it is not a very sound view to consider only the slow part of evolution and not the more rapid part which is called the revolution. The chick in an egg gently evolves from the yolk into a chick; but there is a time in coming out of the shell which is relatively rapid. In the same way, there is a distinction between slow progress in achieving better cooperation within the Atlantic Community and progress in opting for a federal solution.

How can we best achieve both the evolutionary and revolutionary solutions for the Atlantic Community? I would propose that we call a conference of all the NATO countries for the purpose of seeking agreement that a full federal union is the eventual goal of the Atlantic Community. Having secured that agreement we should then set up timetables for achieving the goal—for example, ten years to achieve a common currency, twenty years to achieve a common market. Here we can learn some lessons from the European communities which have not only set up timetables but have also established machinery for meeting them. If we have a goal, some tentative timetables and some machinery for meeting them, then we do not become paralyzed with problems of transition which we know will take time but which should not prevent us from starting in a realistic way.

On this 400th anniversary of Shakespeare, I should like to conclude with this passage: "There is a time in the affairs of men which taken at the flood leads to fortune. Omitted, all the voyage of their life is bound in shallows and in miseries. On such a full sea are we now afloat, and we must take the current when it serves or lose our ventures."

III

American and European Essays

The Crisis of the Alliance

—*HANS J. MORGENTHAU*

The Western alliance has ceased to be an instrument for policies to be pursued in common by its members. A *tour d'horizon* of the world scene presents a shocking picture of disintegration. There is not a single of the outstanding issues of world politics on which all members of the alliance see eye to eye. The United States stands alone in its policies vis-à-vis China, South Vietnam, and Cuba. The United States stands also alone in its policies concerning trade with the Communist nations. Great Britain, on the one hand, and West Germany and France, on the other, have taken contradictory positions with regard to Berlin. As concerns the German question as a whole and the over-all relations between the West and the Soviet Union, irreconcilable divergencies of interest and policies have made abstention from initiative and a passive commitment to the status quo the order of the day. Greece and Turkey have been on the brink of war over Cyprus. In Africa, the allies go their separate ways; Portugal, in particular, stands virtually alone. The policies of the United States and France toward the United Nations are diametrically opposed. A similar cleavage separates France from the United States and Great Britain in the field of disarmament. As concerns military strategy and the policies implementing it, the United States is at loggerheads with its major European allies on two basic questions: the role of conventional forces and the disposition of nuclear weapons.

The members of the Western alliance have only one obvious interest in common: protection from Communist aggression and subversion.

But such an interest is not a policy; it is an objective requiring common policies for its realization. It is both illuminating and disturbing to note that the allies come closest to pursuing common policies, of however dubious value in themselves, in the conventional military field which is least likely to require common action in the foreseeable future, and that it is almost completely lacking in common policies in the political and economic spheres, which the Soviet Union itself has declared to be the arena where the fate of the world will be decided.

The Problem of Risks

What accounts for this decline in the fortunes of an alliance which a decade ago still appeared as the indispensable foundation for the security of the West? The decisive factor in this decline has been the transformation of the American nuclear monopoly, one of the foundation stones of the Western alliance, into a bipolar nuclear threat. That new "balance of terror" has rendered the Western alliance, as presently constituted, obsolete.

In the pre-nuclear age, nations who had certain interests in common would try to defend and promote these interests by coordinating or pooling their diplomatic and military resources. Thus nation *A* would go to war on behalf of the interests of nation *B*, or vice versa, when it thought that the defense and promotion of the other nation's interests were in its own as well. By thus reasoning, a nation would take a double risk: it could be mistaken about the identity of the interests involved and be drawn into a war without its own interests being sufficiently engaged, or it could miscalculate the distribution of power on either side and allow itself to get involved in a war which it would lose. What a nation had to guard against in its relations with its allies was a diplomatic blunder or a military miscalculation. If it failed to do so, it would as a rule risk at worst defeat in war with the consequent loss of an army or of territory.

The availability of nuclear weapons has radically transformed these traditional relations among allies and the risks resulting from them. Nuclear nation *A* which enters into an alliance with nation *B*, nuclear or non-nuclear, runs a double risk different in kind from the risks a member of a traditional alliance must face. In honoring the alliance, it might have to fight a nuclear war against nuclear power *C*, thereby forfeiting its own existence. Or ally *B* may provoke a war with nuclear power *C* on behalf of interests other than those contemplated by the alliance and thereby force *A's* hand, involving it in a nuclear war on behalf of interests other than its own. That latter risk is magnified if *B* is also a nuclear power, of however small dimensions. If *B* were to threaten or attack *C* with nuclear weapons, *C* might, rightly or wrongly, consider *B's* military power as a mere extension of *A's* and anticipate and partly prevent the commitment of *A* through a first strike against

A. Or *A*, anticipating *C's* reaction against itself or seeking to save *B* through nuclear deterrence, may commit its own nuclear arsenal against *C*. In either case, *B*, however weak as a nuclear power, has the ability to act as a trigger for a general nuclear war.

B, on the other hand, too, faces a double risk. It may forfeit its existence in a nuclear war fought by *A* on behalf of its interests. Or it may find itself abandoned by *A*, should *A* refuse to run the risk of its own destruction on behalf of the interests of *B*.

It is this radical difference in the risks taken by allies in the pre-nuclear and nuclear age which has led to a radical difference in the reliability of alliances. In the pre-nuclear age, ally *A* could be expected with a very high degree of certainty to come to the aid of ally *B* at the risk of defeat in war. In the nuclear age, ally *A* cannot be expected with the same degree of certainty to come to the aid of ally *B* at the risk of its own destruction. Here we contemplate the reverse side of the mechanics of deterrence. The very same doubt that deters *C* disheartens *B*. *C* cannot be certain that *A* will not actually forfeit its existence by resorting to nuclear war and, hence, is deterred. *B*, on the other hand, cannot be certain that *A* is willing to forfeit its existence by resorting to nuclear war and, hence, is disaffected.

It is ironic that the event which foreshadowed the decline of the Western alliance virtually coincided with the establishment of that alliance: the first explosion of a nuclear device by the Soviet Union in September 1949. While the destructive effects this event was bound to have upon the Western alliance could be, and actually were, predicted, the policies of the Western allies for almost a decade took no account of these effects. Three new facts were required to open the eyes of Western statesmen to the ever more acute contrast between the official declarations of unity of purpose and the institutions intended to serve common military action, on the one hand, and the crumbling political and military foundations, on the other. These facts are the new foreign policy of the Soviet Union, the Suez Crisis of 1956, and de Gaulle's initiative of January 14, 1963.

Soviet Foreign Policy Since Stalin

The foreign policy of the Soviet Union has fundamentally changed since Stalin's death in 1953. The greatest asset upon which the foreign policies of the nations of Western Europe could bank was the foreign policy of Stalin. Whenever there was a slackening in the Western effort, whenever there appeared cracks in the fabric of the Western alliance, Stalin could be counted upon to make a drastic aggressive move demonstrating to the members of the Western alliance how necessary for their survival the alliance was.

Kremlin policy since Stalin is of a different nature. It is not, at least for the time being, a policy of direct military aggression or serious military threats. Soviet leadership has explicitly and emphatically ruled out nuclear war as an instrument of policy. Their policies are aimed not so much, as were Stalin's, at the conquest of territories contiguous to the Soviet empire by diplomatic pressure or military threats as at the subversion of the whole non-Communist world through the impact which Soviet power, derived primarily from its technological and economic accomplishments, makes upon that world.

That policy of "peaceful" or "competitive coexistence" has been widely misunderstood as indicating a radical change not only in the tactics but in the goals of Soviet foreign policy as well. We have tended to read into "coexistence" a measure of permanency, which, as Mr. Khrushchev reminded us emphatically many times, it cannot have in the philosophy of communism; it is intended to be an intermediate tactical stage in the inevitable decay of capitalism. Thus we took genuine "coexistence" to be an accomplished fact rather than a state of affairs to be striven for and to be achieved only if the West has become so strong that the Soviet Union has no choice but to "coexist" with it. In consequence of this misunderstanding, the association with the United States appears to some of our European allies less vital than it once was. Thus the absence of unmistakable pressure, primarily of a military nature, at the confines where the Western alliance and the Soviet empire meet, has contributed to loosening the ties of the Western alliance.

Suez and its Aftermath

The intervention of the United States, in conjunction with the Soviet Union, against Great Britain and France during the Suez Crisis of 1956 provided what might be called "the moment of truth" as concerns the political vitality of the Western alliance. It made empirically obvious what before could only be deduced from general principles—that the United States was not willing to risk its own existence on behalf of interests which were peculiar to its allies. The Western alliance proved to be much less comprehensive, cohesive, and reliable than official ideology and the array of common institutions had indicated.

From the state of affairs thus revealed, de Gaulle drew two alternative conclusions. The Western alliance, in order to regain its vitality, required a worldwide coordination of the policies of its major members, and to that end he proposed in 1958 a political triumvirate of the United States, France, and Great Britain. Since that proposal remained stillborn (the United States did not even dignify it with an answer) de Gaulle turned to the other alternative: the national nuclear deterrent. President de Gaulle, in his press conference of January 14, 1963 and subsequent statements, has declared traditional alliances for all practical purposes to be obsolete and has proposed to replace them with national nuclear deterrents. He proposes to assimilate nuclear weapons to conventional ones in that at least their deterrent function be controlled by national governments on behalf of traditional national interests. France would use its nuclear weapons, as it has used its army, navy, and air force in the past, for the purpose of exerting pressure upon a prospective enemy.

How has the United States reacted to this crisis of the Western alliance? As long as the crisis was not acute, the United States proceeded as though the foundations upon which the Western alliance had been erected in 1949 were a kind of immutable datum of nature and as though the factors which would make the crisis sooner or later inevitable did not exist. The extraordinary complacency and sterility which characterized the alliance policy of the United States in the 1950's not only precluded changes in policy taking into account the objective changes that had already occurred, and anticipating those which were sure to occur in the future, but also caused American power to be abused or not to be used at all for the purposes of the alliance.

Our intervention in the Suez crisis in 1956 is but the most spectacular and disastrous example of the capricious and devious disregard of the interests of our allies which marked that period of American foreign policy. Yet it is but the other side of the same medal of complacency and sterility that the United States during this period failed to exert within the alliance that positive political leadership which was its due by dint of its predominance and which its allies expected of it. Now that the leadership of the Western alliance has slipped from its hands, it is a cause for melancholy regret to remember how anxious our allies were then for American leadership to assert itself, and how often, during the crises of that period, publications such as the London *Economist* implored the United States to that effect—and did so in vain.

Some U.S. Policy Choices

Now that the crisis of the Western alliance has become acute, five possibilities offer themselves to American policy: restoration of the status quo, drift, isolation, "Atlantic Union," pragmatic cooperation with a united Europe. Of these possibilities, only the last two present feasible policies.

In order to do justice to these possibilities, it is necessary to remind oneself that the momentous event which has transformed the objective nature of international relations and undermined the foundations of the Western alliance is the availability of nuclear weapons to more than one nation. This transformation, while recognized in the abstract, has not been able to affect our traditional modes of thought and action. Hence the dilemma which the Western alliance faces. On the one hand, the unity of the West is as necessary in the face of Communist subversion as it was in the face of military threats, now temporarily shelved. On the other hand, for the reasons mentioned above, that unity of interest can no longer be translated into common policies through the instrumentality of a traditional alliance. Where, then, can a new foundation for Western unity be found?

The Proliferation of Nuclear Weapons

On rational grounds, there is much to be said in favor of a return to the *status quo ante* January 14, 1963, that is, nuclear bipolarity. The use of nuclear weapons as instruments of national policy by more than two nations greatly increases the risk of nuclear war, for erected into a general principle of statecraft to be followed by any number of nations, it would issue in the indiscriminate proliferation of nuclear weapons and thereby destroy the very mechanics of mutual deterrence. These mechanics repose upon the bipolarity of nuclear power. Detection systems, such as radar and sonar, are capable of identifying nuclear delivery systems in action, but they cannot identify their national identity, except in a limited way through the calculation of the projectory of land-based missiles. In consequence, retaliation requires that *a priori* determination of national identity, which bipolarity provides. Thus an anonymous explosion, caused by a seaborne delivery vehicle and destroying parts of the east coast of the United States, would automatically be attributed to the Soviet Union, calling forth nuclear retaliation. If a multiplicity of nations possessed such devices and the United States had tense relations with only two of them, such an anonymous explosion could with certainty be attributed to no one nation, however much suspicion might point to a particular one. And a new nuclear diplomacy would try its best to deflect suspicion and retaliation from the guilty to an innocent nation. In the face of such a contingency, a rational nuclear policy would become impossible.

Yet, however great the risks of nuclear proliferation are and however much nuclear bipolarity is to be preferred to nuclear proliferation, the latter could have been prevented only through nuclear disarmament or at least the enforceable prohibition of nuclear tests. In the absence of either, it is futile to oppose proliferation. What is necessary—and also difficult—is to create political conditions likely to minimize the risks of proliferation and in the end to deprive proliferation even within the Western alliance of its rational justification.

The Multilateral Force

Yet we have insisted upon trying to restore the status quo. As the instrument for that restoration, we have chosen the multilateral seaborne nuclear force (MLF), a fleet of surface vessels armed with nuclear missiles and manned by mixed crews recruited from different allied nations. This force is intended to serve three main purposes: the retention of the ultimate control over the use of nuclear weapons in American hands; the prevention of the proliferation of nuclear weapons by giving the allies a share in planning and operations; and the satisfaction of the alleged nuclear appetite of Germany without giving her actual control over nuclear weapons. This is not the place to enter into a discussion of the technical, military, and specific political shortcomings of this device and the improbability of its success. It is only necessary here to point to two of its qualities, which shed an illuminating light upon the deficiencies of our foreign policy: the commitment to a status quo which has been bypassed by history, and the attempt to meet a political problem with a military device.

It is easier, both intellectually and in the short run politically, not to face up to the impossibility of restoring the *status quo ante* January 14, 1963, to keep the legal facade of the Western alliance intact, and to leave the crucial problems unattended. This policy of drift into which a stymied policy of restoration is likely to degenerate is of all the possibilities before us the most dangerous, for it combines in an incompatible interconnection the legal commitments of a traditional alliance with nuclear proliferation. It gives those of our allies who possess nuclear weapons the power to reduce to a minimum our freedom of choice with regard to nuclear war. Both France and Great Britain see the main purpose of the national nuclear deterrent in their ability to use that deterrent as a trigger with which to activate the nuclear deterrent of the United States. As the British White Paper on defense put it on February 13, 1964: "If there were no power in Europe capable of inflicting unacceptable damage on a potential enemy," the enemy might be tempted "to attack in the mistaken belief that the United States would not act unless America herself were attacked." [1] Or as the London *Economist* said in commenting on this White Paper: "The bombers also give Britain the ability to involve the United States in a nuclear war for which the Americans have no stomach, the argument being that the Russians would be led to loose off an attack on the United States if any foreign nuclear bombs went off on their territory, since they would not have time to see the Union Jack painted on its warhead." [2] In other words, proliferation combined with traditional alliance commitments turns the obsolescence of the Western alliance, as presently constituted, against the survival of the United States. Allies of the United States armed with nuclear weapons could virtually decide whether the United States shall live or die.

Isolation or Atlantic Partnership

Faced with this unacceptable possibility, the United States has two alternative courses of action. It can try to escape the risks its present policies vis-à-vis Western Europe entail by severing the ties

---

[1] *The New York Times,* February 14, 1964, p. 1.

[2] *The Economist,* February 15, 1964, p. 587.

of the alliance and retreating into isolation. This alternative is likely to become more tempting as frustrations multiply and awareness of the risks sinks in. Intercontinental nuclear strategy, taken as the sole determinant, would indeed make this alternative feasible. The military security of the United States would not be appreciably affected by whatever course the nations of Western Europe, separated from the United States, would take.

Yet the worldwide conflict in which we are engaged is not primarily of a military nature. It concerns two different conceptions of man and society, and in that conflict the survival of our way of life is at stake. That way of life is an upshot of Western civilization, of which Western Europe is the fountainhead. It is an open question whether our civilization, still unsure of itself, could survive without being able to draw upon the example and the cultural resources of Western Europe. It is even more doubtful whether our civilization could survive in a world which, after the defection of Western Europe, would be either indifferent or hostile to it. It is for this ultimate reason that isolation, however tempting in the short run, is no longer an acceptable alternative for the United States.

The other alternative is presented by the grand design of Atlantic partnership which John F. Kennedy formulated on July 4, 1962 in his "Declaration of Interdependence." That design has remained in the realm of political rhetoric, but it contains a political concept which alone promises to combine Western unity with nuclear power. In order to understand its import, it is first necessary to remind ourselves again of the political character of the crisis of the Western alliance.

The Western alliance is in disarray not because the United States has monopolistic control over the nuclear deterrent, but because the members of the alliance pursue different and sometimes incompatible policies, on behalf of which they might want to use the nuclear deterrent. If the policies of the members of the alliance were in harmony, the issue of the locus of the nuclear decision would lose its present political sting and de Gaulle would have had no need to raise the issue of the national nuclear deterrent. For the nations of Western Europe, either severally or united, would then consider using nuclear weapons for the same purpose as the United States, and vice versa, and the issue of the locus of the decision would be of technical, but no longer of substantive importance. This is, then, the crucial question: how can the different policies of the members of the Western alliance be brought into harmony?

The Need for Statesmanship

Members of alliances have had to face this question since time immemorial, and insofar as they were successful, they have answered it by a supreme effort of statesmanship. For it is one of the great constructive tasks of the statesman to transform an inchoate and implicit community of interests into the actuality of operating policies. This is the task before us today. However, it must be doubted that we shall be able to perform it. Four facts support that doubt.

Statesmanship, that is, the ability to think and act in the specific terms appropriate to foreign policy, has been at all times and in all places an extremely rare commodity. For reasons which are imbedded in our historic experience and the political folklore stemming from it, it has always been in particularly short supply in Washington. It is unlikely, although it is not altogether impossible, that of the few among us who possess the intellectual qualities of statesmanship, one will rise to that eminence of political influence and power that would be necessary to equip the foreign policy of the United States for that creative task.

The chances for the achievement of that task are further diminished by the unprecedented complexity and diversity of the policies to be harmonized. This task cannot be achieved, as de Gaulle recognized in 1958, through the ordinary processes of diplomacy. It requires a virtual fusion of the foreign policies of the members of the Western alliance under centralized direction. In the heyday of NATO, we could at least hope for a political "Atlantic Union" to form a permanent political foundation for the military alliance. In the heyday of a revived nationalism, the leading members of the Western alliance, short of being faced with a direct military threat against them all, are not likely to bring forth simultaneously the political vision, determination, and skill necessary to achieve this rationally required goal.

Two further factors militate against this likelihood: the increase in the political and economic strength of the nations of Western Europe and the corresponding decline of that of the United States. The forging of a political "Atlantic Union" out of several independent political units requires, as de Gaulle has correctly seen, a paramount power which is willing and able to impose its will, if need be, upon a recalcitrant member. In other words, in such an "Atlantic Union" the United States would of necessity be predominant. Yet when in the 1950's the United States had the power, and when its allies urged it to play that predominant role, the United States did not have the will to do so. Now even if it had the will, it would not have the power to make its will prevail.

It is exactly because an "Atlantic Union" would be dominated by the United States that de Gaulle is opposed to it in no uncertain terms. The opposition of the other major European powers has remained implicit. But their desire for emancipation from the United States is obviously incompatible with the pursuit of a political "Atlantic Union."

Goals for the United States

The United States cannot afford to lose sight of political "Atlantic Union" as the ultimate goal; for nuclear proliferation, inevitable as it is likely to be, can be rendered tolerable only if its centrifugal and anarchic consequences are counterbalanced by the politically unified use of proliferated nuclear weapons. As long as political union is unobtainable and since traditional alliance commitments joined with nuclear prolification, as pointed out above, are intolerable, the United States must strive for three goals: to mitigate the consequences of proliferation by limiting the number of independent nuclear deterrents, to bring its alliance commitments for the time being into harmony with the interests it has actually or potentially in common with its allies, and in the end to render proliferation innocuous through united political control.

The first goal requires of the United States active support for the political unification of Europe. For since proliferation appears to be inevitable and political "Atlantic Union" unattainable, a European nuclear deterrent controlled by a European political authority is the best attainable alternative. Such support implies a radical change in our present policies which, by trying to isolate France, render the political unification of Europe impossible and seek in vain to restore the Atlantic alliance on foundations which no longer exist.

The second goal requires similarly a radical change from the dogmatic insistence upon the restoration of an unrestorable status quo to the pragmatic adaptation to circumstances which for the time being are not subject to our control. We must narrow the gap between our comprehensive legal commitments and the limited sphere within which our interests and policies still coincide with those of our allies. Otherwise we shall run the risk, to which improvident great powers have succumbed in the past, *vide* Germany in 1914, of getting involved in a war not of our making and on behalf of interests not our own.

Finally, we must look beyond these short-term adaptations to the ultimate goal not only of our alliance policy but of our over-all foreign policies as well: the minimization of the risk of nuclear war. The substitution of a European nuclear deterrent for a multiplicity of national ones is a step in this direction. Political "Atlantic Union" would be another step, impossible to achieve at present but to be sought for a not too distant future.

In the end, we must look for a settlement or at least decontamination of the great political issues which at present divide the world and conjure up the risk of nuclear war. We shall thus deprive the nuclear powers of the incentive to use nuclear weapons as instruments of their national policies. And we shall deal with the present crisis of the Western alliance, seeking first to take into account the new circumstances of the crisis and, then, to overcome the crisis itself not only as isolated moves aimed at short-term goals but also as steps toward the ultimate goal of banishing nuclear war itself.

The Crisis of Political Leadership

—*ROBERT STRAUSZ-HUPÉ*

Limiting Factors in Sovereignty

Except for birth and death, most everything in life is a matter of degree. There is always someone richer, handsomer, and cleverer than we; there is always someone less favored than we. This also holds for international life. In theory, the distinction between sovereign and subject, between a state's absolute right to do what it pleases and a people's submission to a writ which is not its own, is as sharp as a razor. All member states of the United Nations are sovereign. The United Nations Charter, although it assigns special privileges to a small elite in the Security Council, does not quibble on the one indispensable qualification for admission, namely the exercise of national sovereignty. Under the law of the United Nations, every member is every other member's peer. For national sovereignty, like Gertrude Stein's rose, is what it is. If it is not exactly what it is, then it is nothing.

One need only to step outside of the United Nations or, for that matter, into the lobbies and corridors bounding its tiered chambers to discover that some members behave as if they were more sovereign, and others as if they were less sovereign, than they are supposed to be inside. In theory, there is only one standard unit of measurement. In practice, there are about as many kinds of sovereignty as there are states.

Obviously, there exists among nations a great inequality in the exercise of sovereignty. Most every laborer in the diplomatic vineyard knows that nowadays the overwhelming majority of states are beholden for their sovereign status to the self-restraint of a few mighty ones among them—and hence to the prevailing balance of power. Some national sovereignties exist only by courtesy of the United Nations, the Ukraine and Byelorussia being the most flagrant though not the only examples. One need not be endowed with second sight to predict the fortunes of the 120-odd national sovereignties which now elbow one another upon the globe, if the present balance of world power were to be upset by some cataclysmic event. Let us assume that the United States had vanished from the international scene, would then any state care to contest the Soviet Union's interpretation of national sovereignty?

Even the most powerful states do not always enjoy the undiluted blessings of sovereignty. Perhaps the most familiar symbol of United States sovereignty is the dollar. Yet, countries far less powerful than the United States can, if they so choose, subvert U.S. sovereignty in fiscal and monetary matters. France, West Germany, and Japan, if they decided to withdraw their gold holdings from Fort Knox and liquidate their dollar credits, could abridge the most sovereign of all the sovereign rights of the United States, namely to manage its domestic finances: they could knock down the dollar and plunge the domestic economy of the United States into a severe financial crisis. Moreover, they could wreak such a disaster without contravening international law. Thus, the sovereignty of even so great a country as the United States is not as unlimited as, according to Webster's dictionary, it is supposed to be. The more closely we look at sovereignty, the more shadowy grow its features. Yet, we cannot do without it. Sovereignty is one of those indispensable concepts without which we can neither analyze nor operate the international system. All states, even the pseudo-states within the Communist bloc, act *as if* national sovereignty were the standard unit of international relations. De la Rochefoucauld said that hypocrisy is the compliment which vice pays to virtue. Even the most aggressive and savage states tend to respect, at least by the gestures of their formal diplomacy and by their demeanor in the open sessions of the United Nations, the national sovereignty of other states. Their hypocrisy pays homage to the ideal of international legality. Their pretense might be worth little; it is better than nothing.

Sovereignty, like the doctrine of free will, comes to life only within the context of limiting conditions. To be truly sovereign is to be able to do what one pleases. No prince has ever been able to do quite that; no sovereign people can do quite that now.

Effect of Alliances on Sovereignty

The most effective international organizations of our times are standing alliances endowed with permanent secretariats and other durable devices for deliberation and coordination. These coalitions—NATO, the Organization of American States, SEATO, the Warsaw Pact, and the Arab League—differ considerably from one another as regards their contractual arrangements for the military and political cooperation of their respective members. In each, the members have subordinated their national sovereignty to the collective purpose. True, this is a matter of degree, and the members, availing themselves of their sovereignty, can quit the alliance whenever they choose. But abrogating an alliance is always a troublesome business, especially for democratic countries. In the latter, the conclusion of an alliance is usually preceded by fulsome, official statements pointing out the benefits to be derived from teaming up with like-and-right-minded people. In the United States, for example, it is said that foreign treaties duly ratified and signed, become "the law of the land." Among foreign treaties, pacts of alliance are vested with special solemnity. Thus, a democratic government can disengage itself from an alliance, as long as the alliance partner has not grossly violated his pledge, at the risk only of injurious public criticism. For example, Daladier's desertion of Czechoslovakia shook the Third Republic to its foundations and engendered that moral disintegration which proved to be the Nazis' strongest ally in their conquest of France.

A country's trustworthiness as an ally is its most precious asset in foreign policy. In this century, Italy ratted twice on her alliance obligations. The low regard in which she is held to this day in interational politics, though well deserved, deeply rankles her people and underlies her national inferiority complex which, on various occasions, has diminished her status and influence in the council of nations. Thus, an alliance does mortgage national sovereignty. It is easier to contract in than to "contract out."

The Credit Side of NATO

No alliance of modern times represents as large an investment in political good will as does NATO. Never in peace time has as much collective and costly effort gone into the caring and feeding of an alliance. These facts as well as timeless historical experience weigh heavily upon proposals for strengthening or overhauling, not to speak of liquidating the Atlantic alliance. For better or worse, NATO represents the one and only concrete token of Western unity. The strains upon the alliance have been many. They have opened large cracks. The West's roof is leaking. And it is the only roof the West has got. So intense and, in certain quarters, so morbid has become the preoccupation with NATO's weaknesses and failures that Western publics now tend to give scant attention to NATO's shining achievements. NATO has been strong enough to persuade the Soviet Union not to test its weaknesses. Not so surprisingly, the Soviet Union has let it be known that it never intended to do so anyway. Be that as it may, the Communists, who elsewhere kept gaining ground, have not made any territorial advances in Europe and have confined their offensive against the European status quo to nonviolent strategems. Furthermore, the Soviets, contained in Europe, have not been able to compensate for the chronic malfunction of their domestic economy by valuable foreign conquests. Confined to Russia and Eastern Europe, the Soviets have been forced to live at home. And no worse fate can befall the Communists. Thus kept from capturing the great industrial establishments of Europe—especially Germany, which Lenin acclaimed as the greatest prize of world revolution—the Soviets had to yield to the Chinese a good deal of the initiative in revolutionary ventures. It is this circumstance more than any other which has aggravated the tensions within the Communist bloc. NATO can claim the lion's share in the causation of the Sino-Soviet split. Incidentally, it should be obvious that Western gains which might accrue from the fight within the World Communist Party, will be quickly dissipated if NATO, the true author of the Moscow-Peking controversy, were to fall apart.

Shortcomings in NATO

The Communists have been making hay only in those fields which are not specifically covered by the writ of NATO. Wherever the sovereign states of the West do not stand together, Communists have either gained ground or, at least, remained on the offensive. This simple fact has been illustrated so richly by global experience from 1949 to this day that one wonders at what precisely those who vow their devotion to the ideal of world order and propose for its realization all kinds of alternatives—except the preservation and strengthening of NATO—have been reading in the papers.

The present and growing confusion about the Atlantic alliance has been heightened by the West's signal failure in the field of public relations. Western promotional genius, which can sell virtually anybody on anything from brassieres to bulldozers to better mousetraps, has been remarkably awkward and listless in promoting the goodness of NATO. The reasons for this fiasco are many. Suffice that infatuation with global togetherness, paradoxically teamed with parochial nationalism, has reduced the powerful voices of Western publicity and information, when they speak of NATO at all, to an incoherent stutter.

It is generally agreed among experts on publicity that, given a chance, a good product sells itself. The only plausible explanation for

NATO's troubles in gaining public acceptance is that NATO, though good, is not good enough. Indeed, the image of NATO has been marred by several flaws which, with the passage of years, have become more noticeable and disconcerting.

NATO, born as a military alliance, has not been able to develop into a more highly differentiated organism—and this notwithstanding the fact that the Atlantic Pact envisaged the growing together of the organs performing the military function with those serving the political and economic purposes of the Atlantic Community. The military stigma has estranged from NATO those large sectors of Western public opinion who like to think of themselves as constructively progressive-minded. Diminishing public support now makes it all the more difficult for NATO to remedy the very imperfections which are responsible for its low popularity rating.

The most grievous imperfection of NATO is one which sooner or later pains every alliance: the national interests of the members differ from one another. In 1949, the alliance would not have been concluded, then and there, had these differing interests not been smothered by common overriding purpose. But, over time—and NATO is one of the longest lived alliances of modern history—differing national interests reassert themselves. So they must—if for no other reason but geography and history. It is difficult to translate Turkey's traditional hostility toward Russia into the code of Portuguese and Icelandic foreign policy. West Germany's economic stake in East Germany, not to speak of her people's emotional commitment to their enslaved fellow countrymen, cannot be equated with, let us say, Britain's irrepressible quest for foreign markets including any and all Communist ones. These geographical-historical disparities grow even sharper when traditional regional concerns of a member supersede his strategic commitments to NATO. French and British policy in the Suez crisis is a case in point. France fought her war in Algeria against the better judgment and without the support of her strongest NATO allies. In their predicament, the French derived little solace from, for example, the American interpretation of the Atlantic Pact's specific guarantee of the security of French Algeria, and the vocal advocacy by highly placed Americans of the rebel cause. Yet, France could point to unassailable evidence of foreign intervention, Tunisian, Moroccan and Egyptian, not to speak of massive arms shipments to the rebels from East European ports. France's allies chose to cleave to the letter rather than to the spirit of the alliance treaty. Although a good case can be made that Cuba is situated in NATO waters, the United States dealt unilaterally with the Soviet presence on that island, a presence which, incidentally, might have been spared the Cubans and us had the Atlantic Pact defined more specifically the breadth and width of the North Atlantic waters. Although all European NATO members professed themselves satisfied with the outcome of the missile crisis, not all were pleased with having been "informed" rather than "consulted."

The very fact that the members of an alliance are, by necessity, domiciled in various geographical localities, makes it unavoidable that they see issues confronting the alliance as a whole in differing perspectives. Far from abnormal, this is perfectly natural. Differences in geographical perspectives may divide the people of one and the same alliance member. Thus, for example, during World War II, the general public of the West Coast was far more concerned with fighting the war against Japan than with fighting the Germans. Thanks to strong leadership and a deeply rooted national consensus, these differences in geographical outlook were not allowed to hamper the American war effort and to weaken the coalition against Hitler. Thus, what might be called the locational strains on NATO are inherent in the vast geographical scope of the alliance. That these strains have not, thus far, damaged irreparably the alliance is largely due to the high value which, in their foreign policies, individual members have consistently assigned to their good standing in the alliance.

Unfortunately, the leader of the alliance, namely the United States, on many an occasion, has shown itself incapable of performing the simplest operation in international psychology, namely, imagining oneself in someone else's place.

Western Europe consists of several narrow, densely populated peninsulas, rooted in the Eurasian land mass. As seen from these promontories, the vast Soviet bloc appears in perspectives which differ markedly from those visible to American eyes. In part, at least, the American-European controversy over NATO strategy, and especially over the control and possession of nuclear weapons, has been exacerbated by the conspicuous lack of empathy for Europe's geographical consciousness reflected by American diplomacy. It is difficult for Europeans to conceive of nuclear weapons, even low yield and tactical ones, as other than area weapons. The neat hypotheses of controlled response to Soviet aggression, aesthetically satisfying as they might be to the sophisticates in the Pentagon, do not quite still the doubts of the Europeans, acutely and uncomfortably aware of their close exposure to Soviet might. Since a Soviet nuclear attack upon Western Europe could not help but be indiscriminate, European military thought has been drawn to the extreme ends of the strategic spectrum: the removal of all nuclear weapons from European soil, culminating in the neutralization of Europe, or the build-up of an indigenous nuclear force chiefly designed for wreaking punishment upon Soviet cities. Both of these conceptions may lack those finer shadings which grace American strategy, complexly poised between the concepts of counterforce and of finite deterrence. Yet, to the peoples crowded into peninsular Europe, they seem more convincing than do the more subtle arguments of the official spokesmen of America, a country far less densely settled and five times the size of Western Europe. This European feeling of being more exposed and more vulnerable to Soviet nuclear power, irrational as it might seem to American military logicians, explains a good deal, though not everything, about the "Ban the Bombers" in Britain on the one hand, and the popular appeal of de Gaulle's intransigence in the face of American homilies on the folly of nuclear proliferation.

Optimum Size of Alliances

Although no one has been able to define the optimum size of alliances—just as no one has been able to define the objective optimum conditions for marriage—it is obvious that NATO could function more efficiently if its membership were less numerous.

When NATO was formed, the size of its membership was determined by strategic and political considerations which then seemed perfectly valid. What mattered then was to obtain the largest possible area coverage from the Lincoln Sea to Cape St. Vincent and to Lake Van in Turkey and from there all the way north to the North Cape. In order to assemble this vast agglomerate of bases, staging areas, and forward positions, and to block all kinds of conceivable Soviet thrusts, the architect of the alliance, i.e., the United States, fitted the whole together from all kinds of building blocks which differed widely in size and quality. A fairly wide gap separates, for example, Norway, Iceland and Portugal on one hand, and Greece and Turkey on the other, as regards their strategic importance, contribution, and even psychological commitment to the alliance. This particular deficiency of NATO is generic, and, as long as the alliance remains politically as amorphous as it has been since its creation, incurable. It has greatly complicated the alliance diplomacy of the United States: to retain the cooperation, mostly passive, of the non-dues-paying members of NATO, the United States has incurred considerable financial expenses, unrequited by commensurate returns to the military strength of the alliance. Not the least unfortunate aspect of this problem has been its destabilizing effect upon the American diplomatic psyche: at times, the United States, harassed by the pusillanimity of its lesser allies, has hectored the NATO Council with the arbitrariness of an irritable schoolmaster. Thus, in turn, United States conduct has engendered psychological tensions which have contributed as much to the malaise of NATO as have the controversies over the proper place and the control of nuclear weapons in NATO strategy.

Views of General de Gaulle

President de Gaulle's proposal for a Tripartite Directorate in NATO, advanced shortly upon his accession to power in 1958, registered France's claim to a share in the leadership of the alliance. De Gaulle spoke of France. Yet, he also voiced publicly and vigorously what the other alliance members had felt for a long time but, cowed by the United States, had not dared to express unequivocally, namely, that the alliance consisted of several categories of members and the United States belonged to a category all its own. The short shrift given by the United States to President de Gaulle's proposal merely confirmed this impression.

Explicitly, the French President addressed his proposal for the informal reorganization of NATO to a long standing and increasingly more obvious shortcoming of NATO, namely the haphazard limitation of its geographical scope. For the United States, NATO signified—and signifies to this day—the defense of Europe against Soviet military aggression. Ever since NATO was established, some of the most serious threats to the national interests of certain members and to Western Europe as a whole have been posed not by Soviet military power deployed along the Iron Curtain but by developments in other parts of the world, notably South Asia and Africa, not specifically covered by the Atlantic Pact. Surely, the Mediterranean is as much a European as it is an African and an Asian Sea. Yet, NATO has ignored discreetly the goings-on in Algeria and Cyprus, not to speak of the rambunctious behavior at the West's expense of various Arab leaders. This has been true even though a good case can be made for the contention that the various North African and Middle Eastern crises were actually touched off by the Communists, or at least kept going by war materiel supplied by the Soviet bloc.

Long before de Gaulle appointed himself the spokesman of non-Anglo-Saxon Europe, other West European statesmen had argued that most anything of importance that happens in South and East Asia and in Africa concerns NATO Europe as much as it does NATO America. Over the years, NATO has developed all kinds of common positions on such matters as force goals and even so ticklish an issue as the defense of West Berlin. Yet, NATO has never agreed on the most rudimentary common approach to such problems as decolonization and the West's residual interests in Asia and Africa. Certainly, Holland, Belgium, and Portugal have not found membership in NATO a precious boon in their dealings with their colonial or ex-colonial wards. To the contrary, with pained surprise, they have watched their NATO ally, the United States, disassociate itself from what they deemed to be their legitimate interests. Nor were they consoled by the fact that the United

States, rather than backing them in their troubles overseas, referred them to the United Nations. Invariably, they met with an unsympathetic reception. Rejecting the charge of having ditched its unhappy NATO allies, the United States has pointed to its wider international commitments such as its undivided responsibilities in East Asia, its unique role as the wielder of the nuclear deterrent, and its *de facto* custodianship of the United Nations. Although there is a great deal of truth in the American apology for an independent course in extra-NATO matters, it is not all of the truth.

Inevitably, America's dual role as the leading member of NATO and as the greatest independent world power is fraught with ambiguity. To play this role convincingly, more is needed than mere diplomatic virtuosity, namely, a fine discrimination between those things that must come first and those that must come second. What, in the judgment of the United States, comes first: the making of the Atlantic Community, or the bouquets handed by the Afro-Asians to the United States whenever, in the name of anticolonialism, it sides against a NATO member? More specifically, what comes first: the increased military strength and closer political cohesiveness of NATO, or the United States' quest for a détente with the Soviet Union? Is it not these unanswered questions rather than the idiosyncrasies of individual statesmen which have given rise to the current and gravest crisis of NATO? If, since 1949, nothing had changed in the NATO circle and the world outside, these unanswered questions could be shoved back under the great diplomatic rug. Instead, they are now in a fair way of wrecking the great alliance.

Other Leadership Problems

Although U.S. diplomacy has been slow in taking cognizance of it, the world has changed and the United States has changed with it. The Europeans, a threadbare lot in 1949, have become richer; the dollar has become less influential in international economics; nuclear weapons have become not only more destructive but also more available; Soviet capabilities of annihilation have become more formidable; and, despite intra-bloc controversies, the presence of communism has become more ubiquitous than it has ever been. Not all of these developments may have been foreseeable; some of them were. To govern is to foresee. It *was* foreseeable that an alliance as hastily assembled and as oddly assorted as NATO depended upon the exercise of inspired leadership and organizational ingenuity for its survival. For a while, the stuff was malleable. Capable hands could have pressed it into an enduring mould. For a while—during the "Golden Fifties"—the United States could have shaped the Atlantic alliance into its own image, a "wider union." If this had been the American purpose, no one in

Europe could have gainsaid it. To be sure, such American purpose could have been accomplished only if the United States had cared to surrender certain of its sovereign rights in exchange for the place of first among equals in the Atlantic Community. Then, a gesture might have sufficed. In all essential matters, the vote cast by the United States would have decided the issue before the Community's Council. It can be argued that only the form but not the substance of NATO would have been changed. Under any and all then conceivable arrangements, the United States would still have retained the physical possession and, in the last resort, the political control of the nuclear deterrent. But, a people so well versed in the lore of public relations and attractive packaging as the Americans should be able to appreciate the importance of form in international relations.

No one has yet been able to explain satisfactorily how any cooperative undertaking can be made more effective and enduring without making more effective and enduring the authority which presides over it. In the process, the participants will have to yield to one another some of their rights to independent, noncooperative action. Hardly ever will they do so spontaneously.

Historically, durable associations of states have always been forged by a leading state. After World War II, the creation of the various European economic communities and the spectacular achievements of the European Common Market have given rise to a good many misapprehensions about international integration. Among these, the most erroneous is the idea that common tariff and trade policies—doing more and better business with one another—will lead, in the fullness of time and as a matter of course, to more intimate political association of states and, finally, to their political union. History does not teach this lesson. The German Zollverein, for example, was a political failure. Prussian political and military leadership forged the German Federation. It is, to say the least, an open question as to whether the European Common Market owes its existence to the force of economic logic or to the leadership of French and German statesmen inspired by the vision of European political union.

Sovereign states do not grow together into a federation by some self-generating process, but only by the exercise of political will. It is the leadership of one or a small minority—the strongest—among them which persuades the many to become one. No one should know this better than Americans who cherish the memory of the Founders. Could the United States, had it forthrightly espoused the role of federating power, have created that wider union of the Atlantic peoples which President Kennedy, in his celebrated speech of July 4, 1962, at Independence Hall, Philadelphia, acclaimed as the goal of American policy? This would be a pointless question had the United States tried and succeeded—or tried and failed. The fact is that the United States never did try. It has been argued that the American people, jealous of every particle of their national sovereignty, would not have supported so bold an initiative. Determined leadership persuaded them to embrace the United Nations, a radical departure from national precedent. Since the idea of Atlantic union never enjoyed such resolute and fervent sponsorship in high places, it is a moot question as to whether the American public would have opted for or against membership in Atlantic union. As it was, the American public was never asked. The European experience in the making of communities is instructive: a handful of men—the so-called Europeans, i.e., political leaders such as Robert Schuman, Konrad Adenauer, and Alcide de Gasperi, and technical experts such as Jean Monnet and his small elite of devoted aides—conceived the plan of attack, enlisted the support of influential interest groups, and *led* their peoples, who had as yet hardly overcome their mutual enmities, into mutual cooperation. It was their determination which evoked "European consciousness" stirring at the grass roots. They took their chance on the public mood. They went ahead. With each step forward, they won ever larger popular support.

In the United States, the Atlantic idea failed to fire political and intellectual leadership with that crusading zeal which enlivened the campaign for public approval of the United Nations Charter. In truth, despite the vague murmurings of those in high places on the beatitudes of closer Atlantic cooperation, the idea of Atlantic union never got off the ground. Presidents, Secretaries of State, and leaders of Congress agreed that it was a good idea. And this is about as far as they cared to go. Thus, the United States contented itself with nursing the NATO status quo.

The Multilateral Force

Paradoxically, it has been the deterioration of the Atlantic alliance which has spurred the makers of American foreign policy to seek political devices wherewith to shore it up. The U.S. proposal for a multilateral force (MLF) serves a political rather than a military purpose, namely, the satisfaction of European demands for a greater share in strategy decisions, especially a share in the decision to launch nuclear war. By offering its European allies a token membership in the nuclear club, the United States has sought to head off pressures for independent, national strategic forces—and thus to isolate de Gaulle. Skirting the delicate question of exactly where the sovereign writ of the United States—the right to pull or not to pull the trigger—ends and the collective writ begins, the American proponents of MLF have stressed the technical excellence of the hardware to be purchased at considerable cost by the Europeans. Thus, they invited technical criticism. The invitation was accepted. The American and European critics of the MLF, resting their case on technical grounds, proceeded to tear the proposal apart. Their task was eased by the flagrant inconsistency of the arguments advanced in favor of the proposal by the spokesmen of the United States Administration. What is sauce for the goose is sauce for the gander! If, in view of the vast nuclear capabilities of the United States, an independent European national or European collective deterrent is unnecessary, then the MLF, too, is a drug on the market. But it is not the technical shortcomings of the MLF proposal which defeat its avowed purpose, namely, to offer a basis for American-European cooperation in matters of highest common strategic concern. The proposal does not yield one iota of the United States' absolute control over the alliance's nuclear strategy. Far from advancing the search for a true, politically meaningful NATO deterrent, it blocks it.

Stubbornly, the proponents of the MLF clutch at the NATO status quo, the very status quo which is now breaking up under the eyes of the Western peoples and their enemies. Worse, the proposal now assigns to Germany a role which neither the founders of NATO, nor those very German leaders who gained their country's readmittance to civilized Western society, meant Germany to play. France is not interested in the MLF. The limitations of Britain's military budget, not to speak of the uncertainties of her domestic political future, preclude the allocation of significant British funds to the building of the MLF. Thus, nearly the entire European share of the costs to be incurred by the MLF will be borne by the *Bundesrepublik*. Perhaps, as some will have it, the West Germans are really so eager to "get their foot in the nuclear door," as to be willing to foot the bill for MLF to the tune of several hundreds of millions of dollars. Certainly, if they will do as they are told to do by the United States, they are justified in expecting—as a *quid pro quo* for their largesse—to emerge from this transaction as the United States' principal NATO ally. Hardly any more ingenious method could have been found for chilling the hearts of Germany's neighbors and blighting the residual hopes for preserving Western harmony, if not building a better Atlantic world.

It is not surprising that, in America, the growing crisis of NATO has set off the hunt for suitable foreign scapegoats. General de Gaulle has been cast in the role of saboteur of the Atlantic alliance. Yet, NATO's dilemma is rooted in causes of much longer standing than de Gaulle's commitment to France's *"Force de Dissuasion"* and polemic against *les Anglo-Saxons*. The worth of the MLF is not attested by the mere fact that de Gaulle opposes and ridicules it. The wisdom of United States adherence to the test ban treaty is not borne out by de Gaulle's refusal to sign it. America's NATO policy has not been sabotaged by the "narrow nationalism" of an obstreperous ally. In fact, the United States has never pursued a NATO policy—if by such a term is meant the fostering of the growth and solidarity of the Western alliance. If there is one true cause of the crisis of NATO—the crisis of the West—it is the failure of American political will and imagination. Why American political will and imagination succeeded so brilliantly in restoring the wealth of Europe and forging the greatest peacetime alliance of history only to stop short of the crowning achievement, namely the unification of the West—this question goes to the heart of democracy's most crucial problem: the role of leadership in a free society. But this is another matter.

Perspective on Nuclear Policy

—KLAUS KNORR

NATO after Fifteen Years

It is obvious that the Western Europe of the mid-1960's—rich and innovative, full of self-confidence and *élan*—is, in these vital respects, utterly different from the Western Europe of 1949 when NATO was founded. The Europe of 15 years ago was still suffering from many wounds inflicted during the war; it was impoverished, disillusioned, played out; it lacked nerve. What is not so obvious, especially to many people on this side of the Atlantic, is that the extraordinary change that has occurred in the state of Europe calls for a radical transformation of the NATO alliance, if indeed the alliance will continue for long to serve sufficiently common purposes. The evolution of NATO in the 1950's reflected realities that have undergone considerable change. At the present time, to be sure, the military recovery of Western Europe is lagging far behind its recovered and growing vitality in nonmilitary activities, and its security still seems to depend heavily on the military power of the United States. However, there have been appreciable changes, in recent years, in European conceptions of the European security problem and in the realities of which these conceptions take account.

On the one hand, there is an inclination, especially in Britain, France, and Italy, to discount the threat of deliberate Soviet aggression for either one of two reasons or for both. Some influential groups view Soviet Russia as a state having undergone profound internal changes since World War II, having become pragmatically preoccupied with problems internal to itself and to what used to be called the Sino-Soviet bloc, having lost much of its revolutionary zeal and, as Peking has noted disapprovingly, showing signs of turning bourgeois in its orientations. Others believe that Soviet leaders have realized the vulnerability of their society in a nuclear war, a war that could be precipitated by minor conflicts, and, not wishing to jeopardize their substantial achievements in modernizing their country, are deterred from risky courses of military action.

On the other hand, many Europeans have realized that, despite official U.S. assurances to the contrary, the U.S. "nuclear guarantee" of Europe is at least ambiguous, now that the United States also has become vulnerable in a large-scale nuclear war. This impression is reinforced by the recent U.S. insistence in NATO councils that the West requires other options than the threat of massive reprisal in the event of Soviet aggression in Europe. Europeans understand that, in order to cope with such contingencies, the United States might prefer to do so by means of a war limited to Europe and, if possible, waged with conventional arms whose employment may be less likely than tactical nuclear arms to induce escalation to strategic nuclear war. But it is hard for Europeans to share this preference. A limited war conducted in the heart of Europe would cause enormous local destruction. At the moment, at any rate, many knowledgeable Europeans are less interested than the United States in the *defense* of Western Europe. They prefer the unrestricted balance of terror—the threat of city destruction—to deter aggression altogether.

According to these changes, partly in military realities and partly in their subjective evaluation, both the threat to Western Europe's security and the value of U.S. protection seem to have declined. Under these circumstances, the costs to Europeans of military dependence on the United States are naturally registered more sharply than before. These costs, again subjective as well as objective, are far from negligible even though the United States has used its dominance, on the whole, with considerable circumspection, and even though the European allies opposed many similar proposals for improving the defenses of Western Europe either by outright rejection or, more frequently, by silent noncooperation. The facts are nevertheless that the military dominance of the United States has reduced its allies' freedom of action in foreign and military affairs, that American policy abroad frequently does not serve European interests or arouse European admiration, and that the role of military client was bound to frustrate the gathering sense of European pride, dignity, and self-assertion.

General de Gaulle's Position and European Self-Defense

European forces pressing toward a basic re-evaluation of relations with the United States are, of course, most manifest in the stand of General de Gaulle, who lets few opportunities pass without underscoring French independence from the United States. No other country in Western Europe is, at present, ready to follow the General's lead. In the Federal Republic and in most of the smaller countries, dependence on U.S. military protection is still keenly appreciated, while Britain, although both major parties feel an urgent need for redressing the balance of military decision-making in NATO, is not enamored of the Gaullist posture. Yet, unless the United States responds constructively to growing pressures, France might soon make converts. There is, after all, an influential French "party" in Germany which, though at present inferior to the American "party" in appeal and influence, might well grow at the expense of its rival.

In order to reach a realistic appraisal of the security problem faced by the United States and by the West European nations, we must recognize that it is possible for the Western European countries, within the next five or ten years, to provide for their military security without *formal* alignment with the United States and, at the same time, to gain a freedom of action uncurbed by such ties.

Continuing Dependence on the United States

Before explaining the reasons leading to this assumption, I must stress two important qualifications implied in my statement. First, even if NATO were abandoned or, though formally continued, became looser and less cohesive, Western Europe would not necessarily forfeit a degree of military protection by the United States. In both World War I and World War II, the United States came to the aid of Western European nations with which it was not formally allied. American intervention, to be sure, was hesitant and tardy in both instances. Yet the posture of the United States was then one of neutrality and its military preparedness at a minimum. Today, the United States sees its interest best promoted by involvement (in Europe at least) and it is highly armed for instant action. Even though the protection now afforded by the United States to its allies has become ambiguous in the sense that neither the Europeans nor the Kremlin can be sure that the United States will risk its own destruction in order to protect its allies under all circumstances, this ambiguous protection probably still commands a great deal of deterrent power. Moreover, even though this protection became less dependable, should the formal alliance lapse, it is, in view of strong American self-interests, unlikely to disappear. The very possibility of American intervention, however uncertain, might suffice to deter Soviet aggression under most, if not all, circumstances, and might, indeed, do so more effectively than any capabilities for retaliation and defense established by the Europeans. My second qualification is that although it is *possible* for our NATO allies in due time to provide for their military security without formal ties with the United States, it is not certain that they *can* and it is not certain that they *will,* even if they can.

French Role in a Militarily Independent Europe

What is the West European potential for a measure of military independence? Let us begin with the case of France. Some years ago, when France began its efforts toward nuclear independence, there were good reasons to doubt both the feasibility and the value of the goal. The enormous expenses incurred year after year by the United States and Russia, and the bitter experience of the British, suggested strong skepticism. Now, however, it is not at all clear that the French endeavor makes no sense, and the inclination to belittle this endeavor, frequently met with in Britain and the United States, may be governed more by wishfulness than by cold analysis. Uncertainty, to be sure, cuts both ways. It is impossible to demonstrate convincingly that the *force de frappe* is or is not economically feasible or that, if feasible, it will or will not have appreciable military utility.

In 1963, France's atomic arms program claimed about 15 per cent of her military budget, which, in turn, amounted to less than 7 per cent of her gross national product. Future costs are planned to rise steeply and to these must be added, of course, rising expenditures on delivery vehicles and infrastructure. It may turn out that required outlays will expand much more than the French now anticipate and that other and urgent claimants to the French national income will inhibit the allocation of much larger proportions to defense. It is possible, therefore, that the French program will be stretched out over time, retrenched in scale, and end up producing a capability of symbolic significance perhaps, but of very little military consequence. On the other hand, the French may be able to spend on the *force de frappe* a large share of a rapidly expanding income and, benefiting from a position of imitating rather than innovating arms technology, may succeed in keeping costs within tolerable limits. Equally controversial is the question of technological feasibility. Can the *force de frappe* achieve appreciable military value? At least as long as the delivery of French atomic bombs is limited to a force of Mirage IV's, critics point to the vulnerability of the French retaliatory capability to a disarming first strike and to the great difficulties that aircraft would encounter in penetrating Soviet air defense.

In view of short geographic distances and warning times, a French retaliatory force dependent on the Mirage bombers would no doubt be vulnerable. But, at a cost, vulnerability can be diminished by various measures and, for the period after the 1960's, the French hope to shift to missiles, probably mounted on submarines. Moreover, for the Soviet Union to initiate a disarming strike against France would constitute an extraordinarily aggressive and, in view of the U.S. posture, extremely risky action. Unless the USSR drastically changes its character as a militarily cautious power, it is hard to imagine circumstances desperate enough to make such an act more than an exceedingly remote contingency. Nor, except under unusual conditions, could the Soviet Union be sure of landing a good enough knockout blow. As for penetration, though the sum of expert opinion leans toward downgrading the future usefulness of manned aircraft compared with missiles, there seems to be no reliable defense against fast and low-flying bombers at the present time. On the basis of known technology, then, the French may be able to build a striking force good enough to give the Kremlin pause because it could not be certain of not losing a few large Soviet cities to French reprisal.

This qualified conclusion is, however, sensitive to further and radical advances in relevant arms technology. There is a widespread assumption that both the United States and Soviet Russia are at present on a plateau of arms technology, that further refinements of known weapons systems will be achieved, but that no major breakthroughs—such as an economical defense against low-flying aircraft and against rockets—are now probable. If this assumption turns out to be correct, the French are facing no prohibitive technological obstacles. If it is disproved by unforeseen events, France may find herself lagging seriously in technology and, despite vigorous effort, commanding no more than an obsolete or obsolescent force of little military worth.

The military value of the *force de frappe* is not, of course, only a matter of technological feasibility. It is also a question of what the force would be good for. As it is hard to conceive of situations in which a prudent Kremlin would decide to launch a disarming first strike against France, so it is difficult to imagine circumstances under which the French would find it rational to threaten a counter-city first strike in response to lesser forms of Soviet aggression in Europe or, indeed, in which their threat to retaliate with a counter-city attack against a Soviet counterforce strike would have strong credibility. In all probability, its credibility would be exceedingly low. Moreover, as observed in the foregoing, French security may continue to rest primarily on American protection, however ambiguous. The question may well be raised, therefore, of whether the French program makes sense, in terms of French interests, even if the building of the *force de frappe* does not run into insuperable obstacles on economic and technological grounds.

On this matter, again, uncertainties preclude safe prediction. But a French *force de frappe* possessed of a measure of survivability and penetration power surely would add to the Soviet Union's problem if it contemplated aggressive moves in Europe, although how much it could add would depend on various conditions—notably, the degree to which the Soviet Union was deterred by uncertainties about American countermoves. Likewise, France would surely feel less awed by Soviet attempts at nuclear blackmail or, for that matter, by any United States threats of withdrawing support from her; and whatever choices might be open to the United States in a crisis menacing Europe's integrity, France would be capable of some measures of independent initiative and response. However, the fat dividends from her investment in nuclear power would seem to accrue when no dangerous crisis prevails, and that means most of the time. These dividends would be political rather than military. Enjoying a greater degree of military independence, France would be freer to pursue national interests conflicting with American policy. She would fortify her position as a leading European power, command a stronger voice in international negotiations on disarmament, the organization of Central Europe, and many other matters important to her and, above all, as long as she craved such status, she would have the subjective satisfaction of knowing herself to be an independent nuclear power.

There are, of course, notable drawbacks to the French nuclear posture. Thus, France may have to neglect investment in education and other bases of strength. She may suddenly find herself disarmed by technological progress. She may give West Germany an emulative incentive. She may push the United States into a dangerously isolationist mood. She must bear the moral compunctions arising from the possession of nuclear weapons. She forgoes the advantage of being a nonnuclear country—the advantage, that is, of being spared nuclear devastation which may be worse than military defeat. Nevertheless, an independent nuclear posture may confer sizable net advantages. One would have to be French and clairvoyant to be sure, one way or the other.

The European Case for Nuclear Independence

If there is a plausible French case for a degree of nuclear independence, it does not, of course, follow automatically that there is an equally or more plausible European case for such a posture. Beyond doubt, what is—in terms of economic and technological constraints—feasible for France is, in these terms, feasible for Britain and, given time to catch up, for the Federal Republic, perhaps even for some other European countries. Again in these terms, any collaborative or collective European effort would improve feasibility if by "collaborative effort" we mean cooperation toward the production of separate national forces, and by "collective effort" an attempt to produce a joint nuclear force. It must be noted, however, that collaborative and collective programs are apt to involve delay.

What is doubtful is that several West European states, or Western Europe as a whole, would derive as much benefit as France from a measure of nuclear independence. This follows from the subjective values on the basis of which various benefits are necessarily measured. Not all Europeans hold the same preferences. Other countries may not derive as much enjoyment as France does from asserting their independence from the United States or from the status of being a nuclear power. They may agree with de Gaulle that the independent nation-state remains a strategic organization for social-striving but, unlike him, perceive great advantage in a high integration of national efforts. They may be more sensitive to any loss of United States protection that might result from the assumption of an independent, or at least quasi-independent, or pseudo-independent, military posture. Some nations may be more susceptible than France to the moral burden of participating in, and perhaps encouraging, a spreading nuclear arms race. Clearly, the utility to be drawn from an equivalent independent nuclear capability differs with the objective situations of various countries and, besides, is in large measure subjective. Therefore, what is good for the French is not necessarily good for the Germans or the Norwegians—as, indeed, the value of an independent nuclear force is assessed differently by different groups in the same country. For instance, neither the French socialists nor M. Monnet and his friends agree with the Gaullists on this matter, and the British Labor Party is at present hostile to British nuclear independence while the Tory leadership apparently is not.

Because of such differences in situation and preference, the West Europeans as a whole may not opt for the French model even though they are increasingly impatient with their status as military clients of the dominant United States. Some Europeans favor adjustments that would give Europe a greater share in the management of U.S. deterrent power. Others prefer a collective capability—whether a NATO or a European force—although the problem of making decisions on the employment of a collective capability may defy a solution that would not impede its employment and hence reduce the credibility of its use and its military utility. Still others are amenable to "neutralist" arguments.

Nobody can foresee now how our Western European allies will settle their military problem. Yet American behavior will certainly figure importantly among the determining factors. It should be noted that United States policy in and toward NATO will be only one element in what I have called American "behavior." The European public is highly attentive to a wide variety of United States moods and actions, such as, currently, our policy toward Cuba, Peking, and Panama, our record in Southeast Asia, our policy on foreign trade and disarmament, and even to such domestic matters as the Negro problem and the choice of President. Some actions clash directly with European interests while others affect the degree of respect we inspire in European publics.

Determinative as these matters are of the American ability to deal with European governments, this essay concentrates on United States policy in and toward NATO. Regarding this policy, what are the main American interests involved, and by which means are these interests best served?

U.S. Policy Considerations

In recent years, U.S. policy has been emphatically opposed to the establishment of further independent nuclear forces by our NATO allies and, in order to accommodate some contrary European interests and demands, the United States has pushed the plan for a multilateral nuclear force as a preferred alternative. Among the considerations that have led to this position, five seem to have been of great importance.

First, we are convinced that any proliferation of independent nuclear forces will increase the chance of nuclear war breaking out by accident or design, and hence will make this small planet a less safe place to live on. Second, to the extent that arms control and disarmament may offer opportunities for improving security, we have felt that the more independent nuclear powers there are, the harder it will be to negotiate and police such arrangements. Third, the increasing realization that cities anywhere, including our own, are virtually defenseless in general nuclear war has made us interested in the possibility of conducting such a war, should it break out, on the basis of a strategy favoring the destruction of military targets and the sparing of cities. Our European allies, however, are unable to afford strategic forces of a kind and size required by this strategy and, besides, regard the threat of retaliatory city destruction as most likely to deter aggression. Fourth, in order to avoid, as much as possible, situations in which the West would face a stark choice between accepting defeat or invoking the mutually destructive balance of terror, the United States has also advocated the expansion of limited-war forces and frowned on European interest in adding to strategic nuclear capabilities for fear that the large expense of doing so would preclude a substantial strengthening of the NATO shield. Finally, the United States has been apprehensive lest the establishment of independent nuclear capabilities in Western Europe would corrode cohesion in the alliance, particularly if such independent capabilities could not be denied to Germany, which, divided in two, cannot be expected to tolerate the present territorial status quo and might, sooner or later, adopt courses of action dangerous not only to herself but to the entire alliance.

Differing Interests

If these considerations chiefly govern U.S. interests in NATO, the first point to notice is that European interests do not necessarily coincide with ours and that NATO is bound to become moribund if we insist that, where interests diverge, NATO must primarily serve our own. Of course, we sometimes persuade ourselves that the true interests of our allies do coincide with ours—that we, in other words, know better what the true European interests are. This is a dangerous delusion. To be sure, we may know more than our allies about nuclear weapons and other relevant matters. But if we do, the sensible thing would be to communicate such knowledge to the proper authorities. After all, like everyone else, the Europeans must be expected to act upon their interests as they see them. One suspects, however, that differences of interest mostly reflect differences in situations, including geographic location, and differences in values that determine the utility of alternative courses of action. A limited conventional war in the heart of Europe is a different prospect to West Germany than to the United States. If the U.S. "nuclear guarantee" of Europe has become ambiguous, this is bound to be more worrisome to Europeans than to us. If dependence on U.S. nuclear power limits European freedom of action in foreign policy, this is easier for the United States to accept than for France or Britain.

The second point to notice is that the considerations governing our interests are not immutable and that they require, therefore, continuous review in the light of new circumstances. For instance, the conception of a spare-cities strategy did not emerge until after the Kennedy Administration took office and may lose appeal in the future if changes in the structure of opposing forces diminish its feasibility. Similarly, the recent U.S. preference for waging limited conflicts by means of conventional arms may be abandoned if both potential opponents and our allies refuse to take it seriously and to equip themselves for it.

The third point to consider is that we should not let our preoccupation with U.S. interests, formulated some time ago, shut our eyes to the advantages to the United States that may result from the contrary policies of its allies. Thus, provided a combination of economic and technological constraints does not condemn to failure the independent effort of countries of France's size, it should in some measure bolster the deterrent power of the West, especially since the U.S. "nuclear guarantee" of Europe has become ambiguous. With several governments capable of independent action on the nuclear level, the Soviet Union faces a more complicated and less predictable situation, and the United States may be relieved, in certain crises, from the necessity of making hasty decisions of formidable consequence. Moreover, if Europeans wish to discard their role of protegé and instead assume chief responsibility for their own military security—for which they do command the economic, scientific, and technological resources—they may come to require less American support and perhaps to agree to the repatriation of American divisions. Surely, such a development would not be altogether bad for the United States. Indeed, if such developments materialized over time, the very termination of the NATO alliance would not be without compensating gains. After all, the alliance limits the freedom of action not only of its European members but also of the United States, and it might constrain the United States more in the future than in the past as our position of domination diminishes. Finally, the entire world and the entire West, including the United States, might be better off if the European states, singly or jointly, enjoy the freedom and possess the military basis necessary to bring European imagination and resources to bear on the solution of a large variety of international problems. Close alignment may promote strength, though it does not do so necessarily, but it may also produce endless delays and uninspired compromises when it comes to meeting new external challenges. An effective pluralistic structure among the Western nations may well be as healthy and productive as it is within each national community.

These points are not made to prove that on balance recent United States policies in and toward NATO frustrate rather than further American interests. Many of the conditions just discussed refer only to possibilities, not to present-day realities. But, looking sufficiently far ahead, it is not so clear along which directions of policy the net advantages to the United States may lie; and, in any case, the differences in American benefits to be gained from several divergent lines of development may not be as great as is often assumed.

Nevertheless, how well European countries will perform in taking on a larger responsibility and burden for their own security remains uncertain, and the considerations that have impelled the United States to oppose a multiplicity of independent nuclear forces in Western Europe are, taken together, unquestionably weighty at the present time. Nor is there anything wrong about the United States' promoting its own interests even when they run counter to those of its European allies, just as there is nothing wrong about France or other European nations pressing their interests in opposition to the United States.

Alternatives for the United States

What has kept us from recognizing and acting upon these plain facts of international life has been, on the one hand, the remarkable degree of deference that European countries, at least until the renewed rise to power of General de Gaulle, have paid to United States leadership of the alliance. Accustomed to this deference, we may register its diminution with some pain. On the other hand, we have been handicapped by some subtle misconceptions about the nature of the alliance—misconceptions anchored in a great deal of loose talk and wishful thinking about the so-called "Atlantic Community." We are on reasonably safe ground if we mean by this term no more than that among many of the countries bordering on the North Atlantic there is an appreciable sharing of values originating in a more or less common heritage, a certain similarity of outlook derived from a high degree of scientific and industrial development, and some congruity of interest in confronting major problems arising outside the region or facing mankind as a whole. However, if by "community" we mean a structure in which an important category of decisions is subject to a supranational scheme, then an Atlantic Community does not exist even in a rudimentary form. The United States surely has never displayed much eagerness to participate in a community that abridges its national prerogatives, and the current trend in Europe is away from rather than toward such a development.

Within the alliance, the United States must obviously yield to European demands, present and future, for a greater role in safeguarding European security. If it does not, the United States nevertheless stands to lose its dominant position as the military director of the North Atlantic alliance and, besides, will find the pursuit of its own national interests grievously frustrated and its authority incessantly challenged. If, on the other hand, the United States is ready for imaginative adjustments, it will cede a degree of its previous dominance in return for constructive compromises between American and European interests. It can then hope to minimize the disadvantages, and maximize the advantages to itself, of Europe's self-assertion.

Whether in its present form the idea of the MLF represents a constructive compromise remains to be seen, and the matter is certainly open to question even though it expresses a genuine American move in the right direction. The crucial test is whether or not it will satisfy actual and potential European demands. Little would seem to be gained if some sort of MLF did come about with only partial and half-hearted European participation, and with the French and perhaps the British unwilling to forgo an independent nuclear role. On the other hand, if the MLF can be made more attractive, possibly by ridding it of a special U.S. veto over its employment, and if it received genuine backing from Germany, Britain, and Italy among the larger countries, the fact that France (and perhaps the United Kingdom) continued to maintain a small independent force might then turn out to be of little more than symbolic significance, and the incentive to nurture these separate forces might gradually diminish.

Conclusions

However, except for this illustration, I do not propose in this paper to examine specific policies and schemes. What I have been concerned with is setting out a basic perspective which, in my opinion, should guide the search for specific policies. My conclusions on perspective may be summarized as follows. The powerful influence over Europe held by the United States in the past rested in large part on anomalous and transient conditions. If the West is taken as a whole, the diminution of this influence is in all probability a sign of vitality. Instead of feeling frustrated and peeved at the passing of United States hegemony, we might derive some pride from it, for this country has contributed significantly to the recovery of Europe, including France, by giving generous economic aid at the critical time and by affording military protection which Europe was incapable of providing for itself. We should begin by acknowledging the basic change in the position of Europe, and we might then announce to our European friends that the United States is prepared to consider any European demands for reorganizing NATO, even for letting the alliance lapse if this is what most West European nations want; and that the United States is ready to conclude any military arrangements that are in keeping with its own interests as well as those of its allies. If the air were thus cleared, it is my guess that the United States would occupy a strong bargaining position.

The Military Effectiveness of NATO

—*JAMES E. MOORE*

Preface

NATO military policy must be considered in the context of an alliance made up of countries which, although they have subscribed to it military forces in order to provide for their collective defense, have not surrendered to NATO their national sovereignty. The NATO powers not only vary greatly, insofar as their individual military capabilities are concerned, but they also have many diverse national interests, responsibilities, and aspirations. It is difficult to believe that the member countries will, in the foreseeable future, take those steps which would be necessary to make NATO a supranational political entity. The fact that all the nations must continue to agree to any common course of action is thus a most important limitation to be considered in the planning and execution of allied defense measures. That they do agree in allied councils is an indication of the effectiveness of NATO.

NATO's problems are all complex and interrelated and there are many constraints placed on the allied planners who must take into account numerous factors in addition to the purely military. The determination of the threat, together with the forces and strategy necessary to cope with it, is, in itself, a task requiring considerable background. There also must be an appreciation of the political, economic, psychological, and other factors involved if the plans are to be realistic.

Since the expertise in these fields is ordinarily found in the civilian ranks, the civil-military relations in NATO and in the nations themselves become an important aspect of the alliance. While this fact is, in my view, generally appreciated by the military, the reverse is not always true. Too often we have proposed unilateral solutions to political and economic problems which have grave military implications for the alliance as a whole.

I propose to discuss several aspects of the current military questions facing NATO in its development of nuclear and conventional forces. In evaluating these problems, however, it is important that we first understand something about the machinery the alliance has developed to handle defense matters. It has been said that the most remarkable thing about the NATO military establishment is the fact that it works at all. But it does work and its effectiveness has increased through the years. *How* it works, however, is not too well understood by many.

The Military Structure

At the top of the military structure, reporting directly to the North Atlantic Council, is the Military Committee consisting of the Chiefs of Defense Staffs of the nations contributing forces to the alliance. It has as its executive agent the Standing Group, composed of senior officers from the United States, the United Kingdom, and France. The Standing Group is charged with responsibility for "the highest strategic guidance in areas where allied NATO forces operate." Since it is located in Washington it has a representative, assisted by an allied staff, stationed in Paris to maintain liaison with the Council in Permanent Session.

The three major NATO commanders, the Supreme Allied Commanders Europe and Atlantic, and the Commander-in-Chief Channel, who are charged with preparing and finalizing defense plans for their areas, determining force requirements, and deploying and exercising the forces under their command, report through the Standing Group. They do, however, have the right of direct access to the Chiefs of Defense Staff and Ministers of Defense and, in certain circumstances, to the heads of government of the NATO countries.

In both the Standing Group and the Military Committee there must be complete agreement before any NATO decision is made; but as in the Council itself, it requires only one "reservation" to prevent positive action. By the same token, once an allied position on NATO strategy or other matter has been established, it cannot be changed unless all concur. None of the representatives in these two bodies can make a military decision or, for that matter, a military judgment unless it is in accord with the views of his government. Nevertheless, while the consensus may represent the lowest common denominator of all national views, the machinery is there to develop an agreed NATO position.

If the Secretary General and the international NATO staff, or the members of the Council themselves, desire what has been referred to as "pure military advice," they can't get it at the Standing Group level or above. This isn't as disturbing, since they would probably go to SHAPE anyhow, as is the fact that all the requests and recommendations of the major allied commanders must be processed through the Standing Group, and the more important ones through the Military Committee, before they get to the Council. Since the individual members of these groups must go to their governments for instructions, this can take a very long time and, because of lack of agreement, it is even possible that no action at all will be taken by them.

The approval of force requirements for NATO is illustrative. The three major allied commanders, in close coordination with each other and the international staff, develop the over-all requirements and country programs for the provision of the forces necessary to meet the threat. However, neither of the two highest military bodies, because of their very nature, will approve or disapprove these requirements before sending them on to the Council and the nations.

Each member of the Standing Group and of the Military Committee might, as individuals, agree for planning purposes with the total military requirement and perhaps with that for every country except his own. If he indorsed the country force programs submitted, however, this might be interpreted to mean that his particular nation was making a firm commitment for the future. The members of the Council thus do not get the recommendations from the highest military echelons to which they are entitled and must necessarily look to the major allied commanders for advice on this subject.

If the Standing Group, and perhaps the Military Committee, would consider the commanders' over-all force requirements by regions, before the programming by individual countries was undertaken, they might be able to reach agreement in a reasonable length of time. The matter of adjusting the force requirements by nations could then be worked out by the major commands and the international staff. With an approved military determination of the minimum forces needed to meet the threat in each area, one source of dissension would be removed. The big question would still remain, however: what should each country provide?

Various suggestions for improvement of the top military organization have been advanced.

The appointment of a NATO Minister of Defense to solve the politico-military problems with which the alliance must contend is one of these. It is doubtful, however, that any nation would delegate to such an individual sufficient authority to make his appointment worthwhile. NATO is not a true political body so he could not, as the responsible member of "the government," control the size of the forces, the expenditure of funds, nor accept any risks which might be involved. These are responsibilities which the national Defense Ministers can not and should not relinquish.

The organization of a committee of the major NATO commanders to replace the Standing Group and the elimination of the Military Committee in Permanent Session, has also been put forward as a way to reduce bottlenecks and to furnish the Council with more objective allied advice. This has not been found acceptable, partly because of the nationalities of the individuals involved—there are two American commanders and one British but no French—and also the fact that the demands placed on the Chiefs of Defense Staffs themselves, in the reconciliation of national military views, would be too time consuming.

Increasing the size of the Standing Group to give representation to additional countries, although it might appear to have political merit, would probably only make matters worse. In this connection, it should be noted that the three Standing Group nations are the occupying powers in Berlin, potentially the most explosive area in NATO, and still have certain residual occupational responsibilities in the Federal Republic of Germany. There is the closest cooperation among the three nations in the exercise of these national responsibilities and, in times of real stress, they have always stood shoulder to shoulder agreeing promptly in just about every important decision.

It is at the level of the major allied command headquarters that we first find an organization which is subject to the authority of a single individual and which looks at its problems from a purely allied point of view. My comments are based on my experience in Allied Command Europe, but I know the other major commands function in much the same manner.

General Lyman L. Lemnitzer is presently the Supreme Allied Commander Europe (SACEUR). Because of U.S. national responsibilities with respect to atomic matters, Berlin and West Germany, and the fact that U.S. authorities should hold only one military man responsible in Europe, he also is the Commander-in-Chief of all United States forces in this theatre. The Europeans, however, look upon him primarily as SACEUR, the allied commander charged with the defense of the entire European area. The acceptance by them of an American commander as one who has the collective interest of the alliance uppermost in his mind is a tribute to the individuals who have occupied this position. As SACEUR, General Lemnitzer reports to and receives his instructions from the NATO authorities, *not* from the United States.

Unfortunately, there are some in Washington who do not appreciate this fact and, on occasion, put great strains on the alliance by failing to check first to see if proposed U.S. military directives to Europe are in accord with current allied policies.

The present representation of the different countries on the staff at SHAPE is determined by a carefully worked out formula which seeks to allot positions in accordance with national capabilities and contributions to the alliance. This is a complex problem with a great many variables, but it was developed by an allied staff, approved by an allied commander and is generally accepted by the nations as being realistic and fair. The staff is completely integrated, multilateral if you will, and is imbued with a sense of devotion to the alliance and loyalty to its commander which is truly amazing. It must be experienced to be believed.

Also located at SHAPE are the National Military Representatives of the nations having forces in Allied Command Europe. They are there to maintain liaison between SACEUR and their own Ministers of Defense but are not a part of the SHAPE staff. This arrangement makes it easier for the officers who are assigned to SHAPE to look at the allied problems objectively—they know their own country's interests are being handled by the National Military Representatives.

While the SHAPE staff itself is integrated, the company-sized troop contingents which support the headquarters are not. It is generally accepted that these men and women, living in barracks, who have different customs, speak different languages, eat different foods, drink different beverages, and receive different rates of pay, function better when they are organized into national units under an allied headquarters commandant. This is a point to be remembered when considering multilateral forces.

The chain of command from SHAPE down through the various allied headquarters is quite clear and operational procedures are well understood. The combat formations, ground, sea, and air, are of course all under their own national commanders. This is not only a matter of insuring that they have the greatest possible combat effectiveness, but matters of administration and logistics, which are national responsibilities, are also involved.

While there have been, and will continue to be, honest differences of opinion, the individual members of the NATO allied forces have, through the years, worked together extremely well. There have been times when there were rather severe divergencies between certain of the NATO powers, but this has had little effect on the nationals of those countries insofar as their work in the allied commands was concerned. They have kept their eyes on the Soviet threat and have cooperated wholeheartedly in developing and executing the plans of the NATO commanders to meet this threat.

Each year hundreds of military personnel "graduate" from the NATO commands and return to national assignments. They have been broadened in their outlook and imbued with the importance of the alliance to its members and to the free world. While recognizing its many limitations, they are for the most part convinced that, on the military side, it can and must be made to function effectively. The allied military organization is undoubtedly the most cohesive influence in NATO.

Some Nuclear Issues

The nuclear problems in NATO, both real and imaginary, are, of course, under continuing consideration by both the political and military authorities of the alliance. The IRBM's have been removed from England, Italy, and Turkey and, since the missile threat has not diminished but is increasing, must be replaced. Polaris submarines have come into the picture and the matter of European deterrents is under active discussion. It might be useful to take a very brief, pragmatic look at a few of these issues.

Independent nuclear deterrent may be a useful term politically to describe a national nuclear force but the reasoning behind the creation and maintenance of such a force should be kept in mind. Despite the many assurances given by the United States, there is concern on the part of certain Europeans that the American strategic forces might not be employed in the event of a nuclear attack on Western Europe. Or, to put it in terms more palatable for Americans, that the USSR might well have doubts that the United States, when considering the destruction which would surely be visited on North America, would honor its commitments to Europe. Both Great Britain and France, then, have felt that they must have "independent" strategic nuclear forces in order better to provide for their security and also to add weight to their views in the international arena. These forces, they state, will greatly enhance the deterrent to a Soviet attack on Europe.

There is only one nuclear deterrent force in the free world today which militarily can be considered "independent"—that of the United States. Knowing this, it does not seem possible that either the United Kingdom or France would use their strategic nuclear forces against the Soviet Union unless they were assured of U.S. support. To contemplate their employment independently elsewhere is difficult. At the same time, it is unrealistic to think that the United States would not consult with its allies before committing her own strategic forces.

I think it is generally agreed that, from a NATO viewpoint, the funds required for the development of the French *force de frappe* or the British Polaris submarines might better be expended on other defense projects. It does not appear, however, that any military arguments or any number of cost-effectiveness studies are going to deter the United Kingdom or France, at any rate, from going ahead with programs to provide their own "independent deterrents." It now seems to be primarily a matter of national prestige.

The United States takes a dim view of any further proliferation of nuclear weapons. It also feels that the centralized civilian control of all these weapons is most important. The picture of the American President and the Soviet Chairman making moves up—and hopefully down—the escalation ladder, as in a telegraphic chess match, becomes a bit cloudy if others also are to play a part. At the same time, the United States recognizes the legitimate wishes of the Europeans to participate more fully in nuclear planning; so certain steps were taken at the meeting of the Council in Ottawa in 1963 to accommodate these desires.

European participation in NATO nuclear matters has not been generally appreciated. For years the allied commanders of the various regions, together with the allied staff at SHAPE, had developed the nuclear strike program for Allied Command Europe. Throughout the command there were, according to General Lemnitzer, over 1,000 allied officers participating in nuclear planning and other nuclear activities. SACEUR has had his representatives at Omaha ever since this single U.S. operational headquarters was established and has *coordinated* his allied plans with those of the U.S. strategic forces. The Strategic Air Command has always had a liaison team in SHAPE. At Ottawa notice was taken of the fact that this was going on and United States approval was given to a previous SACEUR proposal that allied representatives at Omaha consist of officers of both United States and other nationalities

The appointment of a nuclear deputy to SACEUR may have had some political merit, in a vague sort of way, but it never made military sense. As a matter of fact, the SHAPE staff had just been reorganized to bring all planning and operations closer together and to readjust national representation. It also was hoped to get away from any idea of a U.S. monopoly of allied nuclear matters by giving even greater authority in this field to officers of other nations. SHAPE is not unaccustomed to handling superfluous deputies of one kind of another, however, so they should be able to adjust to this requirement without upsetting the functioning of the staff too much. Hopefully, this can be done without degrading the position of the senior German general at SHAPE, the Deputy Chief of Staff for Plans and Operations who was charged with the supervision of all planning, including nuclear planning. After all, one of the underlying reasons for the steps taken at Ottawa was the desire to satisfy what was expected to be future German nuclear aspirations without actually giving them the weapons.

The multilateral sea-borne force, which has been proposed, undoubtedly has considerable appeal to many who feel that it provides for greater European participation in strategic nuclear decisions. This increased participation is more apparent than real, however, as long as the United States retains the sole authority to direct the use of the nuclear weapons. There will be no real difference, as far as the political decision to fire is concerned, between these weapons and those with which a Dutch or a German nuclear strike squadron may be armed. The strikes all are targeted by the responsible allied commander and coordinated with those of external forces, but none of the U.S. owned weapons may be released by the American custodial units except by authority of the President of the United States. If a "corporation" consisting of the participants in the multilateral force were to be given the political authority over the weapons now held by the United States, we would have greater proliferation and the problem could become even more complicated for NATO as a whole.

While I am sure SACEUR will welcome the addition to his command of any force with two hundred missiles, militarily the idea of multilateral manning has many shortcomings. In all other types of forces we achieve the greatest effectiveness by organizing them in national units. If an arrangement like that used as an expedient by the U.S. Army in Korea is envisioned, that is, U.S. units with "fillers" of some other nationalities, the force will not only fail to achieve its political objectives but its very organization will be counter-productive. Should there be any idea that a single ship can be commanded by more than one captain, in other words that we can have multilateral control at this level, we will have what Professor Kissinger so appropriately calls "control through the threat of mutiny." Admiral Arleigh Burke, former U.S. Chief of Naval Operations, has stated:

> One cannot have a multiple manning or mixed manning of a submarine which will serve two purposes: first as an effective ship, and second to have national representatives on that ship control the situation, particularly in this kind of an organization. In this kind of organization the man who has the key, the captain, controls the situation, and everything depends entirely on what the captain wants to do. Either that ship is effective and obeys the orders of the captain or the ship is not effective and you can have multiple control. If there is going to be some way for a multinational force, it must be at a level which decides when to shoot and then the orders go out to all ships that now is the time to shoot.

The principal nuclear threat to Europe today is the hundreds of IRBM's, of various types and vintages, in the western USSR. These are point targets which should be engaged by weapons of great accuracy—the less accuracy, the more weapons or the greater the yields that must be used. Now that the Jupiters and Thors have been removed, the only missiles in Europe by which these IRBM's and other fixed targets in the USSR may be engaged are carried in Polaris submarines.

There should be a "mix" of both land- and sea-based mobile MRBM's, under SACEUR's command, to attack the targets which directly threaten Europe. Ideally these weapons should be deployed in considerable depth. The land-based missiles should be true counterforce weapons designed to fire with great precision from previously located points. They would be an evident deterrent force but, since they would move around, would be far less vulnerable than any airfield. They would, of course, have less survivability than a Polaris submarine. In comparing the vulnerability to detection of a land-based mobile MRBM and a surface missile ship, General Norstad suggested that essentially it is the difference between locating a needle in a hay stack and a needle on a billiard table.

From both a military and cost-effectiveness point of view, a mobile, land-based MRBM appears to be the best weapon system to take out the fixed enemy missile emplacements, airfields, and communication centers. It also could be used against certain enemy air defense installations and thereby enhance the effectiveness of the manned bomber forces.

The argument, admittedly oversimplified, for the sea-borne force with *no* land-based missiles, goes something like this: Stationary land-based missiles would draw hostile fire; so no country would want them on its soil. Mobile missiles, moving around on land, would have the problem of national boundaries to contend with, and without French participation could not be deployed in depth; therefore, send them all to sea. But a national ship at sea, like those belonging to the United States, could be sailed outside the control of the alliance and the captain might go off and start a nuclear war of his own, thus the ship must be multilaterally manned so the crew can prevent any such action.

SACEUR directly controls an allied nuclear force now and frequent exercises are held to make certain that it functions properly. He, as are his subordinate regional commanders, is served by a multilateral allied staff. With the forces which would be available to him in Allied Command Europe, he has the capability, in a matter of minutes, of initiating conventional war, the selective use of nuclear weapons, or all-out nuclear war. Frequent checks are made to insure that he at all times has positive control over the use of nuclear weapons of any type. All these procedures work now and are constantly being improved.

But before he can undertake any type of military action, SACEUR must be authorized to do so by the NATO political authorities. Before he, as the United States Commander-in-Chief of Europe, can direct the release of nuclear weapons to any allied commander, including United

States commanders, he must have a positive directive from the President of the United States.

The *military* part of the nuclear problem, i.e., the targeting, the organization of the forces, the procedures for committing them, etc., has been satisfactorily solved. Everyone knows exactly what to do when ordered. It is the *political* part of the problem which has not been solved, at least not to the satisfaction of some of the NATO nations.

The Secretary General, the Council and the international staff have long sought a realistic answer to this difficult question. Because it is recognized that with fifteen fingers on the trigger, or the safety catch, the NATO organization is too cumbersome to function effectively in an emergency, various ideas for streamlining procedures have been advanced. Weighted voting by the members of the Council, as a way to speed up the decision making process, appeals to some but not all. The development of NATO-agreed guidelines for an "executive agent," such as the President of the United States, is another solution which would, in effect, recognize the existing situation.

General Norstad, in an address to the Atlantic Council in January 1963, suggested that the authority over the nuclear capability which supports NATO defense plans should be vested in the alliance itself. To act for the Council in time of emergency he recommended an executive body which would be responsive to it, consisting of representatives of the nations contributing nuclear weapons. The Secretary General could preside over this group but not necessarily as a voting member. Variants of the plan would provide for German representation and perhaps that of one or two other countries elected on a rotating basis.

The threat list must be covered while this problem of NATO political control is being worked on, which will probably be for some time. If NATO-assigned forces, using for the most part American owned weapons, can't take care of the threat, the national forces of the United States must assume the responsibility. But the other two Standing Group nations either now have or will have a national nuclear capability. The British Bomber Command has been assigned to SACEUR, with a string attached so that it can still be called an "independent" national force, but it covers essentially the same targets as it did prior to such assignment. The five new British Polaris submarines are to be part of a national deterrent, but presumably their targeting also will be coordinated with those of other nuclear strike forces so that there are not duplications in one area at the expense of gaps in others.

What of the French? It appears that they are eventually going to have a national nuclear capability no matter what the cost may be. Is there any reason to feel that they would not want to coordinate their strike plans with those of the other free world forces? They do not wish to place their strategic nuclear forces under NATO command, as they have their tactical nuclear units which deliver U.S. weapons, but, if Cuba and Berlin are any criteria, they certainly appreciate the need for cooperation in any endeavor of a magnitude requiring the use of nuclear weapons.

Fifty Mirage bombers are not exactly what is required in Europe, however. Their airfields will be vulnerable to Soviet IRBM attack and their ability to penetrate to a defended target at any depth is questionable. Fifty—or preferably more—mobile MRBM's, on the other hand, would help fill a real military requirement and would complement the other national forces of the United States and the United Kingdom. But how do the French get the missiles, with the proper warheads, in time to be of any material help? About the only way seems to be to let them buy them, or the "know-how" of manufacture, from the United States, giving such assurances of cooperation in the planning and execution of strikes as may be expected from the British with their national forces.

This, of course, may sound like a reward for bad behavior to many U.S. and NATO authorities and perhaps is impracticable in the existing political climate. Americans, in particular, would balk at any such action if they had the feeling that in some way blackmail was involved. Logically, however, if the United States can justify the sale of wheat to the USSR because it is *not* of strategic importance, it would seem that it could justify the selling of missiles to an ally because they are. Legally, if it could be administratively determined under the terms of the Atomic Energy Act that the French have progressed to the extent that they are now qualified to receive nuclear assistance, it could benefit the United States in two ways. First, since the United States evidently has a capacity for the production of surplus fissionable material, the balance of payments would be helped if we were to exchange some of this surplus for French gold. Secondly, every target that was taken over by French missile forces would be just one less for the United States to cover at increased range and increased cost.

As a practical matter, there doesn't seem to be any doubt but that the United States, Great Britain, and France, would consult, at least with each other and with the Secretary General, before taking any decision to commit their nuclear forces. In the event of a "bolt from the blue," a massive nuclear attack, there should be no question but that we would immediately respond in kind. If our conventional forces were in danger of defeat, we should certainly use at least tactical nuclear weapons. In other cases there should be some time for consultation. Since the Council has and should continue to develop general guidelines for the employment of NATO military power, the decision making process perhaps is not as dark as some would paint it.

Germany is not in the same position treaty-wise as Britain or France. It has certain limitations placed on its armaments and is specifically prohibited from manufacturing nuclear weapons. It does have tactical nuclear delivery vehicles, some of rather considerable range, but the weapons themselves are in United States custody. While some, or all, of these tactical nuclear weapons might be released for use prior to the employment of the strategic nuclear forces, it is hard to picture them being withheld if the situation required the use of such forces. The German officers on the allied staffs at SHAPE and elsewhere have a very important voice in the military planning of nuclear strikes. Whether or not this will be sufficient to take care of future German aspirations, I do not know. So far, I have heard no expression of a desire by the Germans to have their own nuclear weapons.

Conventional Forces

There is a tendency to devote so much attention to the more intriguing nuclear issues that matters such as the provision of adequate conventional forces and logistics support, which in the long term are probably more important, have not been and are not being given sufficient consideration. If we seek to achieve political flexibility at the moment of truth, however, we must have the necessary military formations and supplies in being and in the proper locations. When tensions rise sufficiently, the task does not appear at all insurmountable; when they subside, there are a thousand reasons why the goals cannot be achieved. We've missed Soviet sabre rattling for some time now so the problem is not moving toward a solution as fast as it should.

Nations rationalize shortcomings in conventional forces very simply by going back to the "trip-wire" and "massive retaliation" concept, with one minor difference. Thus, "If any Soviet attack is launched it must, because of the great differences in the strength of the conventional forces, be met initially with at least tactical nuclear weapons. This means that immediately there is great danger of escalation to all-out thermonuclear war. The Soviets realize this and will not, therefore, risk even a limited conventional attack." The fact that since the creation of NATO there has been no Soviet attack of any kind is cited to support this argument.

The allied military authorities in Europe do not consider this reasoning to be valid, however. They feel that war could come as a result of a lesser undertaking; it might develop from an accidental clash of forces, or from a probing operation which, though intended to remain small, might get out of hand. It could happen as a result of an error of judgment or a miscalculation of NATO will and determination.

The so-called "shield forces" have always been a requirement to give flexibility to NATO response and provide credibility to the over-all nuclear deterrent. Without these forces, reaction to attack would be on an all or nothing basis and NATO would be faced with a choice of extreme alternatives: accepting defeat or initiating general war. The "pause" which shield forces would permit, however, has never been defined precisely in terms of time or space; it might last for a few hours or possibly a few days. It might even be obvious, because of the build-up of forces, that the period of contemplation of the awful consequences of his act had already passed before the enemy ever launched his attack. While the allies should employ only conventional forces if they are adequate to the situation, there should be no question but that nuclear weapons will be used if they are required to stop a hostile advance.

Commencing immediately west of the Iron Curtain are the population centers, the national resources, the great industrial complexes, and the ports of central Europe which, if lost to the Soviets, would be a tremendous blow to the whole of the Western world. SACEUR, who from the very beginning of NATO has been directed to defend as far forward as possible, has recently established stronger covering forces and has ordered that allied ground forces plan to conduct a mobile defense commencing just west of the Iron Curtain. This concept of a more forward defense, of course, calls for adequate forces properly deployed; some 30 M-Day divisions and comparable air forces.

To be most effective, the peacetime stations of the forces should be as close as possible to the areas in which they are expected to fight. However, the locations of most non-German troop units were originally determined by postwar occupation missions and early defense plans. Through the years considerable sums have been invested in their development so that changes or exchanges will not be an easy matter.

The logistics systems of the different countries, particularly that of the Federal Republic, must also be taken into consideration. The matter of wartime supply is difficult at best—in the Central Region it is particularly complicated. If the equipment in NATO were completely standardized, the problem would be considerably easier of solution. As it is, serious difficulties would be created in time of war if, in locating units, steps are not taken to insure that they can be readily supplied with the particular types of ammunition and equipment they require. Because of the costs involved, it will probably be many years before a completely satisfactory peacetime deployment is achieved. In the meantime, it is hoped that any conflict will be preceded by a period of tension sufficiently long to allow the movement of the forces from their current locations to the area they are to defend.

Unfortunately, many of the European nations are not now providing in the Central Region the forces which they can and should provide. There has been some modernization of the existing units and the United States has not only stockpiled the equipment for two additional divisions in Europe, but has also successfully conducted massive trans-Atlantic lifts to exercise the troops in the use of this equipment. The total available forces, however, still fall short of the established goals.

In the United States this fact exasperates those who feel that if the European countries will not accept what many Americans consider to be their fair share of the burden of defending the Central Region, there is no sense in the United States trying to do it for them. Some, including one former SACEUR, mindful of the gold-flow problem, believe that several U.S. divisions should be withdrawn from Europe now. Others seem to think that through the introduction of more realistic budgetary procedures, the lagging nations can be made to see their way clear to improving their defense posture.

The withdrawal from Europe of any significant numbers of U.S. forces could have disastrous effects on the alliance. This would probably be the one area where American leadership would be followed with alacrity by many of her allies. Rather than being spurred on to greater efforts in the face of a U.S. pull back, many of the Europeans would quickly justify further curtailments in their own forces. Those who have doubted that the United States would meet its NATO commitments for nuclear forces would be quick to say, "I told you so."

Reductions in the number of indigenous civilians employed by United States forces can have a more subtle but similar effect. Unless the activity in which they work is to be eliminated or curtailed, these civilians will have to be replaced by military personnel. There may be a possible saving of gold, but there is a certain concomitant loss in the combat effectiveness of the total force. This follows because it just happens to work out that for every civilian employee replaced by a soldier there is one less fighting man in the combat units. If a price tag could be put on combat effectiveness, this would be identified as a very expensive operation.

Various alternative suggestions have been made for the improvement of the defenses of Europe without increasing the strength of the regular forces. A "barrage" or barrier of atomic demolitions along a sizeable stretch of the front would permit the reduction of forces in that area and their use elsewhere. Its emplacement in time of peace, and perhaps in time of tension, is not feasible for political reasons. The establishment of a fortified zone along the entire Iron Curtain has also been advocated but there are both military and political objections to this.

Although the Germans have made great strides in the build-up of their active units, they continue to be limited by the shortage of trained officers and non-commissioned officers. The booming economy, with its demands for manpower, also makes it difficult for them to increase the size of the armed forces much above what it is right now. More combat and service support units are needed to achieve a balanced force, however; too much reliance is still being placed on the United States.

Steps are being taken to create reserve units, composed of men who have completed their active duty tours, to help fill this gap.

While SACEUR has directed that in case of ground attack a mobile defense be conducted, the cities of the Federal Republic are not going to move and no matter what is said they, and perhaps others, will have to be defended. There will be people living in the cities who could do much to provide for this defense in time of war—men who have served their tour in the active army and the first line reserve and who could be organized in militia units for this specific purpose. They could be composed of individuals who were not physically fit for full field duty, like the "stomach battalions" of World War II, but could give a good account of themselves in the defense of their own homes. With these organizations, the commanders of the active regular field forces would have much greater flexibility and could conduct a truly mobile defense in depth. Like the Swiss militia, such a self-defense force could contribute to the deterrent with a graduated response in periods of tension. It would certainly make evident the will of the people to resist. In time of peace, the labor force would not be affected.

There may be some, particularly in Europe, who will look askance at this build-up of German military strength. If this is a cause for concern, one way to counter it would be for the other European powers to increase the size of their own forces. The shortfalls in the Central Region could be overcome if the participating nations would make the necessary effort. France alone, if she would match but half the German contribution to NATO, could balance the books.

Summary

1. NATO has developed as an important and effective organization which does surprisingly well from a military viewpoint in developing workable plans and policies to meet the common threat. There is a constant exchange going on between the political and military sides of the NATO house during which the many practical aspects of attaining a viable defense posture are examined. As a result, a mutual understanding, at least of what is involved, has developed. This understanding has proved much more important in times of crisis than any set of specific directives which might have been drawn up.

Although the alliance machinery may at times turn slowly and creak rather loudly, if it were consistently used by all the nations in keeping with the spirit of the treaty, it could be made to operate more effectively. Many of our problems are created because the NATO machinery is disregarded or is not used properly by one or more of the allies.

2. The nuclear issues are primarily political, not military, and, to quote an old Army saying, "the buck is never passed down." Mili-

tary measures proposed as answers to political problems should be examined critically to determine their impact on the combat effectiveness of the forces and to ascertain whether they do, indeed, solve anything politically.

There is a requirement for a credible nuclear deterrent in Europe. This should consist of a combination of both land- and sea-based MRBM's to meet the Soviet threat effectively and at the lowest cost.

3. European conventional forces should be built up and modernized, particularly in the Central Region. In addition to regular formations, reserve forces also should be organized.

Rather than encouraging the Europeans to assume a greater share of the NATO defense burden, the withdrawal from Europe of any substantial number of U.S. troops would have the opposite effect.

Practical Considerations about Cooperation

—*W. RANDOLPH BURGESS*

In this memorandum I propose to discuss the following: NATO as a mechanism for insuring cohesion of free Western nations; NATO as an agency for coordinating and safeguarding the use of nuclear weapons; NATO as an organ for the harmonization of political policies.

NATO as a Mechanism for Insuring Cohesion of Free Western Nations

In all the discussions of the cold war, or in fact of other phases of international political and economic relationships, one conclusion is universal. It is that the countries of the free Western world must find the means of working closely together. "United we stand, divided we fall." The policy of the Soviet has time after time showed itself to be "divide and conquer."

At the present time the critical nature of this basic need for common understanding and action is particularly evident. For Western unity is threatened. It is threatened by a détente, a feeling that the danger of aggressive action by the Soviet is greatly lessened. The conclusion of the treaty for the limitation of nuclear testing has led to the hope that the world may be moving in the direction of less tension and genuine peaceful coexistence. The coming of great prosperity to Europe has lightened economic pressures for cooperative action. The two adjectives *fat* and *lazy* go naturally together.

Another divisive factor has been the difficulty of a number of the problems the West is now encountering as it attempts to take the next steps toward united action. For example, the Common Market is only now beginning to apply its rules to the storm-tossed area of agriculture, where politics has triumphed over economics in almost every country in the world. The Common Market is also moving further into the zone where more and more decisions become subject to majority vote, and national sovereignty has to yield ground. It is face to face with the nationalistic ideas of General de Gaulle.

These are some of the reasons why the Western alliance appears now to have lost some of that great impetus which carried it so magnificently out of the postwar disorganization and depression, that surge of activity and unity with which it countered and overcame the Soviet threat to Greece, to Scandinavia, to Berlin, and to the whole West.

So the first order of business of the NATO nations today is a reexamination of the available methods for preserving and stimulating anew their power for joint action and forward progress as an alliance.

About the United Nations

Before considering other agencies, a word should perhaps be said about the United Nations. For just after the war it was widely believed that that agency was the one which might bring all nations together in the cause of peace. The United Nations has played a most useful role as a sounding board for opinion, and as a mechanism for certain types of cooperation, as in Korea, Suez, and the Congo. But years of experience have shown its limitations. More than 100 vetoes by the Soviet Union in the Security Council have made it impossible for the United Nations to take positive positions in many situations. Moreover, the huge and increasing membership of inexperienced nations sets a limit on the kinds of action which the organization can take.

The inescapable conclusion has been that for effective unity of action on important questions related to the basic issues of today, it is necessary to look to some smaller regional grouping of nations, with the cohesion that arises from a common background of culture, ideals, and objectives. In effect, this has meant turning to the Atlantic Community with its background of understanding and responsibility rooted in the Judæo-Christian religions. It is this group of nations which in practice has found it possible to agree on most objectives and on a great deal of common action—military, economic, and cultural.

Even within this group the road to unity has been a narrow and tortuous one, and, as indicated above, there is now a loss of forward impetus that threatens a breakdown of the machinery of coordination. So we need to review this machinery to see how it can best be restimulated. It is a very complicated setup, consisting of a whole series of organizations of varied kinds. We need to determine which of these organizations offer most promise for continued and effective action.

The Federal or Functional Approach?

Among the organizations which have grown up since the war, one can distinguish two different approaches to a solution of the problem. These two approaches date back fifteen years to the time when the Council of Europe was debating the form of future European organization. The Council was split down the middle between those who favored what was called "federalism" and those who preferred a form of organization known as "functionalism."

The idea of "federalism" was the application to Europe of the American political idea of the relationship between the states and a central government, as embodied in the Constitution. The application of this idea to world organization was advocated years ago by the New England historian John Fiske, and many times since then by many people.

As early as March 1943 Winston Churchill proposed a Council of Europe as follows:

> A really effective league, with all the strongest forces concerned woven into its texture, with a High Court to adjust disputes, and with armed forces, national or international, or both, held ready to impose their decisions and prevent armed aggression and the preparation of future wars.

Churchill continued to press this idea, calling it in 1945 a "United States of Europe." This general idea was supported abroad by a group of organizations such as the United Europe Movement, the European Union of Federalists, etc. A similar approach was taken in the United States by the movement for "Union Now"—except that this latter organization thought in terms of the whole *Atlantic* Community, rather than Europe alone.

The philosophy behind these movements was the recognition that the West, in order to achieve the strength necessary to maintain its freedom from domination by any international threat, had to find a way to subordinate national sovereignty to some form of over-all "federal" organization.

This was the background for a spirited debate in the newly created Council of Europe in 1949 and 1950. In this debate representatives of France, Italy, and the Benelux countries espoused the idea of a federal organization with centralized power, i.e., supranationality. On the other side in the debate were the British and Scandinavian spokesmen, who favored cooperative organization for specific tasks, but without surrender of sovereignty by the participating nations. They called this type of organization "functional."

Those countries favoring the federal idea went on from this point to organize the European "communities," starting with the Coal and Steel Community and moving on to Euratom and the Treaty of Rome.

Over the past fourteen years they have moved far and brilliantly in this direction. Other European countries joined with Britain in EFTA (European Free Trade Association) for the specific function of reducing tariffs, but with less convincing results than those achieved by the Common Market.

In fact, the achievements of the European communities were so great as to capture the imagination of people all over the world. Little "common markets" sprang up in other places. It seemed to many that here was a pattern that might be susceptible of expansion to larger areas, perhaps even to the Atlantic Community as a whole, starting with the inclusion of the United Kingdom in the Common Market. The imagination of the people of the United States was stirred to a point where the Trade Bill of 1962 was passed, conferring unprecedented powers on the President to negotiate reductions in trade barriers. The Common Market was to be the core of a United Europe, with which the United States might deal as an equal "partner."

Then in January 1963 General de Gaulle blocked British entry as a member of the Common Market, and in addition made it clear that while favoring some closer political cooperation, he was out of sympathy with the supranational character of the organization. His conception of a Europe of sovereign countries is far afield from the spirit of the Treaty of Rome.

But General de Gaulle's action was not the only disturbing sign. The Common Market has also run into serious problems in attempting to carry through on schedule the standardization of tariffs and the harmonization of national policies on agricultural products.

So, the Common Market has, at least for a time, lost its halo. Two searching questions about it are being raised. The first is whether in fact the member countries are prepared to carry out the rigorous terms of the Treaty of Rome when it impinges seriously on their national interests. Is the called-for supranationality really practical and attainable?

The second question is whether the plan is sufficiently outward looking. Is it of a character that can expand to include a number of other countries, and furnish the kind of pattern necessary for the full establishment of an Atlantic Community? Or does the Common Market owe its success in large measure to the benefits which its members derive from lower tariff barriers among themselves, while they enjoy protection from the goods from other countries? To what extent is it acting as a self-serving customs union? Does its success rest on the specific *functions* it performs more than on its political *federalism?*

It is still too early to know the answers to these questions. Certainly many of the leaders of the Common Market are thinking in broad international terms, and General de Gaulle appears to be largely isolated in his position. However, we need to keep our minds open, and to use whatever influence the United States may have to encourage the development of the European communities in the direction where so much hope has seemed to lie.

But recent developments suggest the wisdom of not betting all our money on this particular horse. They indicate that we might well take a good hard look at that other school of thought for Atlantic cooperation, i.e., the functional one.

As we examine these two approaches toward international objectives, we need to consider their applicability not to Europe alone, but to the United States as well. Which of them represents the most suitable vehicle for United States participation? For it should be noted that while this country has changed tremendously in its international outlook, it is still reluctant to surrender any national sovereignty. This is illustrated by the refusal of Congress to agree to commit the country to abide by all the decisions of the World Court at The Hague.

Interesting evidence is also contained in a public opinion poll conducted by Elmo Roper for the Atlantic Council of the United States in the autumn of 1963. This poll showed that the United States, neither as a whole, nor in any geographic area, can any longer be considered isolationist. The American people are thoroughly sold on the United Nations, NATO, and other agencies for international cooperation. There was 79 per cent concurrence in the following statement:

> We are more certain to remain a strong and democratic country if we continue our alliances with other countries.

On the other hand, the response was quite different to the following question:

> Do you feel that the world situation is going to make it necessary to give up some of our national sovereignty, or do you feel that we should hold on to our national sovereignty at all costs?

Only 12 per cent replied that it was necessary to give up some of our sovereignty; 67 per cent answered that we should hold on to it at all costs.

The findings of this poll are amply supported by opinions revealed in Congressional discussions. In the hearings during the Spring of 1961 on the bill confirming U.S. membership in the new OECD, the sections of the charter relating to *decisions* were scrutinized with minute care to make sure they involved no surrender of *sovereignty*.

It would clearly require a very substantial change in American public opinion before this country would be willing to become a member of the Common Market under the terms of the Treaty of Rome, which involve certain specific surrender of sovereignty to the central organization. Thus when we consider the possible use of the Common Market as a unifying force, it is not realistic under present conditions to think of it as expanding to include the whole of the Atlantic Community. It is more realistic to think of the Common Market as—in time—unifying Western Europe. The United States could then deal with the Common Market as an "equal partner," as was suggested in a number of statements by President Kennedy and members of his Administration.

This concept, however, involves some serious difficulties. It will be a long time before the Common Market could possibly constitute the whole of Western Europe. Furthermore, an Atlantic Community consisting of organized groups of countries bargaining with each other, is remote from the concept of true community, which implies harmony and unity of action.

The Functional Approach

Now for an equally searching scrutiny of the functional approach to international cooperation. As the name implies, this approach is in terms of organization for the accomplishment of certain specific purposes: defense, trade, economic cooperation, etc.

A vigorous presentation of this point of view was made by Senator William Fulbright in an article in *Foreign Affairs,* for October 1961, entitled, "For a Concert of Free Nations." Senator Fulbright reviews the failure of the United Nations to accomplish the high purposes set for it.

He then develops the concept of organization by *function,* citing as evidence the organization of the Allies and Associated Powers in the two world wars:

> The experience of the joint war effort points to the efficacy of a functional approach towards the building of an international community. Common efforts to deal with specific concrete problems are likely to be more productive in the long run than comprehensive and spectacular attempts at world constitution making.

Further on he applies this reasoning to the organization of the Atlantic Community:

> The North Atlantic Nations represent an almost existing community, and because they do, they can press forward in the development of supranational institutions. Because their community is fragile, these institutions for the time being should be functional rather than federal, piecemeal and pragmatic rather than general.

A similar principle was voiced recently by a European statesman when he said, "The Atlantic Community, if it succeeds, will grow out of what we actually do."

With this background, Senator Fulbright comes to the logical conclusion that the necessary machinery for an Atlantic Community is already available in NATO, the OECD, and existing organs of the European communities. There may be added also a number of the agencies with wider membership, such as the IMF, the IBRD, and GATT, the core of which consists of the Atlantic countries.

It is my belief that the Fulbright conclusion is correct, and amply supported by experience, particularly in the case of NATO. The alliance of necessity conducts most of its business in closed session without publicity. As a consequence there is a general failure on the part of the world outside to appreciate the scope and the depth of its activities, and its enormous value as an instrument for Atlantic cooperation. Therefore, I propose to describe a few of the attributes of NATO, as revealed in the fifteen years of its life since it was established in 1949. This will not be a comprehensive review of NATO, but rather a survey of some of the most vital features.

The Basic Motivation of NATO

It seems almost unnecessary to remind people that NATO has been, and still is, the bulwark of the free world against Soviet aggression. It is this basic fact which gives it fundamental strength, vitality, and cohesion beyond that of any other international organization. NATO is essential to the self-preservation of the Atlantic Community.

NATO legally has no supranational powers—and its Treaty requires no surrender of sovereignty by its members. And yet the pledge in Article 5 of the Treaty that an armed attack against any one or more of the members "shall be considered an attack against them all," and the agreement of each one to take "such action as it deems necessary, including the use of armed force, to restore and maintain the security of the North Atlantic area," is a strong commitment, prescribing action under specified circumstances, and thus in fact limiting the freedom of action of each member of the alliance.

The basic cohesion of the members is indicated by the fact that, in spite of serious differences of opinion from time to time, the alliance has held firmly together for the fifteen years since its inauguration in 1949. The Treaty provides that after ten years any member country may make proposals for amendments. Although this date line was passed nearly five years ago, no country has yet formally proposed any amendments. The Treaty also provides that after twenty years—in 1969—any country can withdraw on a year's notice, and there is some expectation that General de Gaulle may make major proposals in anticipation of that time. Thus far, he has asserted the need for changes, but has not made his proposals specific.

Some commentators have mistakenly stated that the Treaty terminates at the end of twenty years and will require renewal. This is not so, and the provisions the Treaty contains are similar to those in many other treaties, providing for the possibility of orderly changes. Unless positive moves are made for changes, the Treaty continues indefinitely in its present form. The very fact that no one has taken advantage of the opportunity to offer amendments is persuasive testimony that its basic structure is sound, and is so regarded by the member countries.

I propose to review certain of the more convincing aspects of the alliance as an instrument of Western cohesion, some of them controversial, some of them taken for granted, or often overlooked.

The Practice of Cohesion

The strength of the alliance has been built up out of a strange mixture of accumulated, inconspicuous hard work, and intensive effort to meet a series of crises.

One of the earliest of the great forward steps was the admission of West Germany as a member, and this accomplishment grew out of a crisis. The circumstances were as follows. As soon as joint command was established for the NATO forces under General Eisenhower in 1951, and a realistic appraisal was made of the military forces required by the alliance to carry out its mission, it became convincingly clear that German forces were needed. But this was not easy to bring about, because there was natural, widespread, and very strong resistance to the rebuilding of a German national army. Furthermore, in West Germany itself, which had suffered military domination, there was reluctance.

An ingenious method for overcoming this difficulty had its origin in France. The proposal took the form of a European Defense Community (EDC) in which the various national military forces of Western Europe were to be integrated, and Germany would participate in small units. Thus no national German army would be organized. The organization would follow the "community" pattern, with certain subordination of national sovereignty. This plan seemed to accomplish the essential purpose so well that it won endorsement on all sides. The United States backed it heavily. Then in 1954 the French Assembly voted against it. In passing, it may be noted that General de Gaulle was not blamed for this action, even though it was consistent with his later position. He was at that time in retirement in his country home.

The rejection of the EDC seemed to be a serious blow to the strength of the West, for it appeared to shut off the much needed German strength. Secretary Dulles suggested that the unreadiness of the European countries to go ahead with this plan might call for an "agonizing reappraisal" of American policies.

But the crisis was finally met, in a different way. There were weeks of conferences of statesmen, with Anthony Eden playing an important role. Through the machinery of the Western European Union treaty, limitations were laid down as to the character of the German rearmament. Thus, after weeks of discussion, the way was opened so that NATO members were finally convinced of the wisdom of making Germany a full member of NATO. This was agreed upon late in 1954, and put into effect in early 1955. So, in order to strengthen the whole organization, conditions were set whereby it became possible to admit a former foe into NATO as a participant, bearing its full share of the load and the responsibility. This, I believe, will prove in the long run a better solution of the problem than the EDC. It avoided the separation of different blocs of NATO members, European and American and Canadian, which would have been involved in the EDC. It provided for Germany a more self-respecting position. And above all it signified a healing of the wounds of war, and nurtured the spirit of Western unity, essential to meet the pressures from the East. Thus NATO became in truth a cornerstone of Western security.

A quite different type of successful achievement on the part of NATO is to be seen in the day-to-day steady building of cohesion. One of the first such steps was the assembling of a military command staff at SHAPE. This group of high officers of all the NATO nationalities, who have learned to work together day by day and month by month, with rotation from national high commands, has built an invaluable *esprit de corps.* Added to them are the more than 1,000 graduates from the six months courses of the NATO Defense College, who constitute in all the member countries an elite group of understanding and enthusiastic supporters of NATO and Atlantic cooperation.

A somewhat similar growth of the habit of cooperation is embodied in the development of what is termed the "infrastructure" of the alliance. When NATO first assumed the responsibility for the defense of the NATO area there were glaring deficiencies in airfields, pipelines for aviation and other fuel, communication facilities, and other logistic requirements for any substantial armed forces. There was promptly undertaken a common program, jointly financed, to supply some of this operating machinery needed by all. Year by year this program has moved gradually forward in spite of many arguments every inch of the way about costs, and about the nature of the facilities. There has been no supranational means by which any single country could be ordered to supply the money or the technicians or the terrain needed for the job. But by persuasion and discussion and moral pressure, the work has been done. The latest step has been the approval by the NATO Council (reluctantly of course) of NADGE (NATO Air Defense Ground Environment) at a cost of about $300,000,000. This will supply needed equipment, radar, electronic, etc., for air defense. All told, the infrastructure of NATO is physically extremely impressive, but perhaps even more so is the habit of cooperation which has been developed with it. It is notable that over the years the proportion of the costs borne by the European countries has been increased, and the U.S. share reduced from 43.7 to 30.9 per cent.

NATO as an Agency for Coordinating and Safeguarding the Use of Nuclear Weapons

With these preliminaries we may well plunge into the hottest subject of discussion, that of atomic weapons. In the public eye, this is the making or breaking of the future of NATO, of its power to weld together the Atlantic Community.

On this topic it is most desirable to set the record straight. Throughout current discussion one finds the statement that the United States has reserved for itself a monopoly of nuclear weapons. This is a dangerous half truth.

The facts are that from the early days of NATO the United States has had a realization of the critical importance of nuclear arms for NATO. Of necessity the first policy had to be one of massive retaliation—a clear cut assurance that aggression on the part of the Soviet could be met by nuclear retaliation. That was the only feasible policy at that time, for the alliance did not then possess the means of a graduated response. The military doctrine at that time was that there could be no such thing as a "limited war" on the Central European front. To meet this requirement, the only substantial nuclear power was American, though British bombers became a useful supplement.

But the United States and the other allies were aware that as NATO international forces developed, nuclear arms would have their crucial place through those forces.

Plans for arming NATO with nuclear weapons began to take shape as early as 1954 and 1955, when it was decided by the NATO Council that NATO must be equipped with the most modern weapons. Accordingly, nuclear arms were woven into the plans drawn up for NATO forces by the international military staffs and commanders. These were approved by the Military Committee (composed of the chiefs of staff of all countries), and recommended by them to the NATO Council, which adopted them. Thus the allocation and strategy of these weapons became, after full consultation, a part of the established program.

The next important step was in December 1957, right after Sputnik, when the heads of government of the NATO countries, including President Eisenhower, Chancellor Adenauer, Prime Ministers Macmillan and Gaillard, took the unusual action of meeting in Paris with their Foreign Ministers, Defense Ministers, and Finance Ministers. One of their resolutions accepted a proposal by which the United States would make available in Europe stockpiles of nuclear warheads needed for the weapons systems owned by certain of our allies.

The 1957 resolution, after citing the Soviets' announced intention of arming their forces with the most modern and destructive weapons, continued as follows:

> As long as the Soviet Union persists in this attitude, we have no alternative but to remain vigilant and to look at our defenses. We are therefore resolved to achieve the most effective pattern of NATO military defensive strength, taking into account the most recent developments in weapons and techniques.
>
> To this end, NATO has decided to establish stocks of nuclear warheads, which will be readily available for the defense of the alliance in case of need.
>
> In view of the present Soviet policies in the field of new weapons, the Council has also decided that intermediate range ballistic missiles will have to be put at the disposal of the Supreme Allied Commander in Europe.
>
> The deployment of these stocks and missiles and arrangements for their use will accordingly be decided in conformity with NATO defense plans and in agreement with the states directly concerned.

The programs for both delivery systems and warheads have moved forward on schedule, and in accordance with signed agreements between the United States and the other NATO countries. These agreements have all been submitted to the U.S. Congress and became effective only after sixty days had been allowed for Congressional consideration.

The planes and missiles with nuclear capability in the hands of the allied forces were at first for the most part donated or sold to them by the United States. The U.S. stockpiles of warheads have become available, at our expense and under our control, as fast as were the vehicles for their delivery in time of war. All the allies are kept informed of the status of nuclear armament, first by reports on progress in the general plan, and second through the more detailed military reviews of each country's efforts.

As a result of this plan substantial and increasing amounts of planes and missiles with nuclear capability, largely tactical missiles, are now in the hands of the forces of nine NATO countries, including the United States and Canada. The warheads are accessible, and the forces are trained in the operations necessary to put them to use should the need arise. This formula is applicable to French forces stationed in Germany, though it has not been accepted by the French for their other forces. Its further extension to French territory would make nuclear power widely available to French forces, and other NATO forces on French territory, and so strengthen the alliance.

This formula also provides for placing nuclear-capable weapons in the hands of German forces on the same basis as those of other NATO partners, always with the safeguard that the warheads are under U.S. custody.

So, with respect to the missiles and planes of our allies which are served by U.S. stockpiles, the decision for use *is shared.* The use of nuclear power requires the joint action of the commander of the national forces having the missiles or planes, and the U.S. commander in charge of the stockpile of nuclear warheads. Each of them would be subject to his own civil authority (in our case, the President).

But sharing nuclear decisions has gone beyond that. In the case of those weapons held for use by U.S. forces, we have made agreements with certain countries to launch such weapons from their soil only *with their consent.* To clear up frequent misunderstandings, it should be said that the proposal to base nuclear weapons on French soil has always contained that stipulation.

Lest this degree of sharing should seem to run the risk of veto of use, let me point out that the amount of our own nuclear power *not* subject to this reservation is sufficient to assure a massive response when necessary, even without the use of weapons subject to these consents. But the essential point here is that each NATO country already has the opportunity to become a direct partner with the United States in nuclear armaments, and that such participation involves sharing in the development of strategic concepts and plans.

The whole NATO military operation in Europe is under the Supreme Allied Commander (SACEUR), who works with an international staff in the planning and execution of plans. For example, the selection of targets for nuclear weapons in Europe, a highly secret undertaking, is a concern of the international military staff.

Thus, in all these arrangements, there has developed more sharing than is usually recognized, while at the same time the interests of the United States are fully protected.

The foregoing arrangements, which have been worked out by the NATO Council and the military commanders over the years, have been, I believe, acceptable to most of our allies. Admittedly these procedures do leave to the President of the United States final decision as to a preponderant part of nuclear power, because the great weight of such power is in the hands of the United States.

In addition to this plan for nuclear stockpiles, a number of other steps have been taken in the direction of nuclear sharing, as follows.

The United States, by arrangement through the NATO Council and bilaterally, stationed a number of squadrons of Jupiter and Thor intermediate range missiles in the United Kingdom, Italy, and Turkey, under the joint control of the United States and the allies concerned, and with crews partly American and partly of these other nationalities. These weapons were maintained in service until 1963 when they were retired simultaneously with the stationing of Polaris submarines in these areas, with a more than equal firepower and much greater invulnerability.

Also, following the December 1957 meeting, a sustained effort was made to agree upon the joint production of IRBM's in Europe. The United States offered its cooperation, but the plan encountered insuperable difficulties, first because of rapid changes in technology which made it hard to decide which weapons to produce; second, difficulties in setting up European capacity to produce such complicated weapons, and third, disagreement as to whether all of such production should be for NATO requirements.

Meanwhile a number of other joint allied production efforts were successful, including that for the Hawk and Sidewinder missiles. It was finally decided to turn the European effort to the production of the F104G fighter bomber plane, capable of carrying atomic weapons. The production has been by a syndicate in which Belgium, Germany, Italy, and the Netherlands have been participants, with technical assistance from the United States. This is a NATO program.

Squadrons now in service equipped with these planes have available, if required, the nuclear warheads in nearby NATO stockpiles—under U.S. control. In this case, as with the tactical weapons and IRBM's, use of nuclear power would require the decision of the country concerned as well as the United States. These squadrons are a part of NATO forces under command of SACEUR for training and in time of war.

The Multilateral Force (MLF)

During this period there was increased discussion in NATO, in governments, and by the public, of the whole problem of the nuclear armament of NATO and the control of such arms. This was partly in response to the announced determination of General de Gaulle to go ahead with the development of an independent nuclear capacity for France, which ran counter to the widely expressed hope that the proliferation of nuclear arms could be limited. Much of the discussion also arose out of the growing strength and feeling of self-reliance of the European NATO countries. With that has come a desire to have a larger share in decisions of such overwhelming significance as the use of nuclear weapons. It became difficult to escape the natural human reaction that the control of nuclear power carried great national prestige.

Recognizing the political importance of this discussion and underlying sentiment, the United States agencies concerned have examined this whole question with great care. The State Department and Defense Department staffs have given it high priority. My own office in Paris and that of SACEUR reviewed it thoroughly. It was vigorously discussed by the NATO Council, privately and in meetings of the Council.

The end result of these efforts was the gradual development of a proposal later called the Multilateral Force (MLF). This had a first objective of providing for the NATO European Command, Medium Range Ballistic Missiles (MRBM) to replace the liquid fuel IRBM's as they were phased out by obsolescence, and to offset the large force of such missiles held by the Soviet Union. A second objective was the more political aim of carrying one step further the joint development of nuclear strategy among the allied countries.

The first offer of this plan was made to NATO by the United States at the Ministers Meeting in December 1960. The proposal was made by Secretary Herter and Secretary Gates in rather general terms in order not to tie the hands of the new U.S. Administration which was coming into power in January. The proposal was, in brief, that the United States was prepared to assign five Polaris submarines to the NATO command and was also prepared to work with other members of the alliance in building up a multilateral seaborne force of medium-range ballistic missiles jointly owned and operated by the allies and under NATO command.

Upon assuming office, the Kennedy Administration appointed a committee chaired by former Secretary of State Dean Acheson to review the United States' policy with respect to NATO. Certain conclusions of that study appear in an address that the President made in Ottawa on May 17, 1961. On this subject he said;

> We must make certain that nuclear weapons will continue to be available for the defense of the entire Treaty area, and that these weapons are at all times under close and flexible political control that meets the needs of all NATO countries. We are prepared to join our allies in working out suitable arrangements for this purpose.
>
> To make clear our own intentions and commitments, the United States will commit to the NATO command area five—and subsequently still more—Polaris atomic-missile submarines, subject to any agreed NATO guidelines on their control and use, and responsive to the needs of all members but still credible in an emergency.
>
> Beyond this, we look to the possibility of eventually establishing a NATO sea-borne missile force, which would be truly multilateral in ownership and control, if this should be desired and found feasible by our allies once NATO's non-nuclear goals have been achieved.

This statement by President Kennedy was most welcome to those of us who had been coping with these problems during the Eisenhower Administration. For this statement by President Kennedy followed, as indicated above, a searching review by the new Administration. Happily they came out in substantial agreement with the policies which had been wrought out over preceding years. They specifically confirmed the proposals as to Polaris submarines, and a potential multilateral force which had been laid before the NATO Ministers Meeting the preceding December by Secretaries Herter and Gates. United States policy on these important questions has had the virtue of consistency and continuity.

The policy announced at Ottawa by President Kennedy has been followed up by statements to the NATO Council and by public announcements. There has been no prompt nor general acceptance of the proposals by member countries, though several, especially Germany, have approved in principle, and there have been extended informal exchanges of views. Our Administration has not yet pressed for decisions, recognizing the technical, military, political, and financial implications for each country. It is clear that the plan, if carried out, would require an increase in military budgets of participating countries, though not by huge amounts. An estimate is that three billion dollars would be called for in the first eight years to put into operation and maintain a fleet of surface vessels carrying 200 missiles. Finding these additional funds poses a political problem for the European countries.

It is not proposed here to examine in detail the whole MLF proposal. That would require a separate presentation. We are only interested here in the question of how this fits into the broad program for the sharing of nuclear capacity in the alliance. As to the details of the plan, suffice it to say that it stands up well under the analysis it has been given. These vessels would supply a significant part of the strategic firepower called for by alliance military plans, though it can be argued that they are not essential from a military point of view, as an equal power could be provided by additional U.S. long-range missiles, at U.S. expense. The most important advantage is political. This program would tie into the alliance, subject to joint control, a force that could not be withdrawn by unilateral action. It also would involve many members of NATO in the understanding of these weapons, and the strategy of their operation.

The installation of the MLF weapons would constitute a next logical step to those which have already been taken in the sharing of nuclear capacity as described above. It is not very far between the plan for the provision of tactical weapons, in the hands of member countries, with U.S. stockpiles of warheads nearby, to a somewhat similar plan on a ship, where there might be three or more nationalities involved instead of two. While the NATO command of this small fleet would involve what might be called a NATO Navy Department, there is already in existence in SHAPE, as mentioned above, a joint staff for the planning of operations of nuclear weapons.

The Ultimate Control

While the MLF proposal has gone a long step further in the sharing of nuclear strategy, it has not satisfied all the critics. Certainly it has not dissuaded General de Gaulle from his determination to have independent French weapons. So the debate continues on whether there may be found some method of giving to European members of NATO the power of decision not subject to U.S. veto.

In the quotation above from President Kennedy's speech at Ottawa in May 1961, it may be noted that he did not spell out the precise mechanism involved in joint control of the weapons he discusses. This presumably came under the phrase, "We are prepared to join our allies in working out suitable arrangements for this purpose." There has been no deviation from this position, though Secretary McNamara at the meeting of the NATO Ministers in May 1962, and a few weeks later, in a speech at Ann Arbor, clearly indicated firm U.S. opposition to any steps leading to the proliferation of the control of nuclear weapons.

Statements by some other government officials have left this point a little fuzzy, suggesting that future experience in cooperation may lead to a wider sharing of controls. But the implication up to this point is that, in any present plan, the United States would retain a veto in the final decision as to use, which indeed other participants would have also. Certainly there is no indication that the U.S. Congress is prepared to hand over to any other country the terrifying means of acting independently of the United States in the discharge of such weapons—a matter of life or death for many millions. The Atomic Energy Act recognized the United Kingdom as a special case, because they had already developed nuclear power.

Many hours have been spent in the NATO Council and the military commands, in governments, and in academic circles seeking formulae which might apportion final responsibility for use of nuclear weapons more generally in the alliance. Thus far it is fair to say this search has not yielded results convincing to either the United States or its NATO partners that went beyond the arrangements of dual or multiple control, which have been described here.

Everybody agrees that there may be cases which afford time for discussion in the NATO Council, but no government has proposed decision of such a critical issue by majority vote. The idea of leaving such a decision to a select committee is not acceptable to other members of NATO (not on the committee), whether by majority vote or not.

Another suggestion that the power to decide on use of these weapons be given to the Supreme Allied Commander for Europe (SACEUR) under certain defined conditions, has been countered, in the Congress of NATO Parliamentarians, by the answer that this decision must remain in the hands of the political authorities. President Kennedy, in his statement quoted above, also made this point clear.

Does all of this mean that nothing more can be done in this broad area to assure the mutual understanding and cohesion of the NATO allies? My own belief is that much more progress can be made; but that the most promising field is not so much in the formulae and mechanisms relating to the final act of pulling the trigger of nuclear weapons, but in perfecting and broadening political and strategic consultation in NATO. This is now the key factor in the unity of the alliance. It is here that our partners are least happy about the working of NATO.

It is necessary to be realistic. If, and when, the moment for the trigger to be pulled should actually arrive, it would usually be too late for effective consultation; matters would have gone too far by then and would dictate a practically automatic response. The time for consultation is in the prior weeks and months and years when policies are being formed. That is when consultation can effect results, without the risk of holding up, and thereby jeopardizing action. If this consultation leads to strategic consensus, the *deterrent* will be more effective and the moment of *use* need never come.

NATO as an Organ for the Harmonization of Strategic and Political Policies

Consultation in NATO has a long history—and a checkered one. The principles are clear and agreed to by all. They have been restated at almost every meeting of the NATO Council at ministerial level or higher. They have been reviewed by two committees of "Wise Men," whose findings have been unanimously approved. The basic idea is that NATO partners should consult together about their mutual problems before—and not after—the event.

The communique issued after the Heads of Government meeting in December 1957 included the following paragraphs:

> Although progress has been made, further improvement is needed in our political consultation. We are resolved to bring this about. Our Permanent Representatives will be kept fully informed of all government policies which materially affect the Alliance and its members. In this way, we shall be able to draw fully on each other's political experience and to ensure a broad coordination of our policies in the interest, not only of the Alliance, but of the free world as a whole.
>
> In addition, to strengthen the cohesion of the Alliance, the permanent Council and the Secretary General should ensure effective consultation, including, where necessary, procedures of conciliation at an early stage.

These same principles have been restated over and over again. The present U.S. Administration has made clear to the NATO Council its agreement with them. Indeed, as this is being written, the United States is in the midst of consultations with its NATO partners on the MLF and many current problems.

Consultation sounds easy in theory, but in practice is sometimes far from it, as all U.S. representatives to NATO or to other international organizations can testify. For one thing, governments move too slowly and news agencies move too fast. While our President is still consulting his Cabinet and selected members of the Congress on any policy, the newspapers are already out with positive statements of what the United States is going to do. This being so, how can we give our partners in NATO the feeling that they are being consulted: furthermore, if we wait until a firm U.S. position has been decided upon, what is the value of consultation with our partners? It is necessary to distinguish between *informing* them and *consulting* them.

These are the circumstances under which every NATO Ambassador and the responsible officials in Washington have struggled to consult with our partners in time, so that their reaction can be considered and their views taken into account before the U.S. decision is finally made. The U.S. representative in NATO has had to tear State Department officials from their beds at 3 A.M., Washington time, to get authority for statements to the NATO Council that very morning on U.S. news dispatches which had already appeared in the Paris papers five to six hours ahead of Washington. The role played by this time differential is an important fact—sometime for, sometime against—effective international operation.

So, consultation in NATO has had its ups and downs. The case of Lebanon and Jordan was one of the successes. Three weeks before the United States and the United Kingdom moved in there, the British and the U.S. Ambassadors had exposed the whole situation to the NATO Council. They did it again two weeks before, and again one week before, as well as on the day of action. In that way, there was understanding—and no recriminations. While this was not the type of case in which we could reasonably have asked for NATO approval, the understanding of our NATO allies was essential, and it was most useful to give them a chance to express their views.

The United States also consulted satisfactorily with our NATO partners in the case of Quemoy and Matsu. It was a more difficult case, but we told the whole story promptly, and won a great deal of sympathy. Consequently, there was no break in the NATO ranks on that very serious issue.

Another case, which did not so immediately involve the United States, was one of the most difficult political problems ever thrown on the NATO Council table. It was the long drawn out three-way dispute over Cyprus, in which three NATO member countries were immediately and seriously concerned, with the Soviet waiting in the wings to see whether it could pick up a cue for entrance. After months of effort, the patient discussion in the Council and in smaller groups finally yielded results, largely due to the statesmanship of the President of the Council, Mr. Spaak, and to the Permanent Representatives of the United Kingdom, Greece, and Turkey, who were ready to take some personal risks to press their own governments for a settlement. Thus, NATO consultation was effective, and a highly explosive situation was solved, though recent evidence shows that such problems do not always stay solved.

Over the years, probably the most satisfactory and useful political consultations have concerned the various phases of the relations with the Soviets. The many exchanges of notes between Mr. Khrushchev and the allied countries have been discussed in the NATO Council. Drafts of the replies which different member countries were proposing to send have been submitted to the NATO Council for suggestions, and have been brought into harmony as the result of NATO discussion. In this way, the allies have been able to present a united front.

Similarly, as to negotiations with Russia on disarmament, nuclear testing, surprise attack, and Berlin, the members countries participating in the negotiations have kept the NATO Permanent Council informed, have sought its advice, and have profited by it. Consultation has included military plans for contingencies.

One important finding from these experiences is that the NATO Council can be trusted with these top secret problems. The record shows a minimum of leaks of information, either directly from the Council, or through the fifteen national capitals, which are fully informed of Council discussions.

But consultation has had its failures. Let me quote as witness a man of well informed and objective mind, who served for years as Secretary General of the Atlantic Treaty Association, Mr. John Eppstein. His annual report for 1960 was very frank. He said:

> I am sure that the members of our Association as a whole sympathize with Monsieur Paul Henri Spaak in the disappointment which he experienced in his endeavours to maintain real and effective political consultation within the North Atlantic Council leading to a coordination of policies between the Member Governments . . . .
>
> Before the Belgian Government took its grave decision to grant independence to the Congo on the 30th June, 1960—with results which have greatly embittered the international situation—was any serious attempt made to secure cohesion between the Western Powers regarding preparation for this step, the timing of it and its political consequences? Did the United States, Britain and France offer their cooperation to the Belgians in effecting the

dangerous political transition? When chaos ensued and the battle of propaganda moved to the United Nations, did the United States and Britain show any sympathy or solidarity with their ally?

On the contrary, each Western government in dealing with Africa appears to go to extreme pains to avoid even the appearance of having any common understanding with its partners.

Disregarding details, about which there may be differences of opinion, we must admit that the Congo did great damage to NATO's sense of cohesion. It would have done even more damage if members of the Council, working with Mr. Spaak, had not done their utmost to bring about better understanding and a gradual modification of public positions.

This was typical of the greatest failures in NATO consultation. They have often occurred when the symbol of colonialism reared its head. The most serious misunderstandings in which the United States was involved in recent years have been with France on Algeria, with the Netherlands on Indonesia and West New Guinea, with Belgium on the Congo, and recently with Portugal on Angola. In each case our NATO ally has felt with some justice, that he has not been treated as a partner by this country.

In each of these cases, the United States' obligation to our established NATO partners for sympathetic understanding has clashed with our other policy directed toward winning and maintaining the friendship of Asian and African countries, which are making a religion of breaking away from colonialism. There is no easy way of sidestepping this fundamental dilemma, especially when it appears to call for sudden action in the United Nations.

With the worldwide obligations of the United States, and our earnest efforts to further national aspirations and counter the challenge of communism in the less developed countries, there are bound to be at times conflicts of interests with some of our NATO partners.

But, in furthering the long-term health and effectiveness of the alliance, the least that can be expected in the relation between partners is that they should avoid like the plague altercations with each other. That sort of behavior not only weakens the cohesion of the alliance, but encourages the Communists in their belief that they can win by splitting the West.

The solemn commitments which have been made by all the NATO partners clearly bind them to use the machinery of consultation, both in the NATO Council and privately, to seek solutions of differences earnestly and persistently. Experience has proved that when this has been done, even rather belatedly as in the case of Belgium and the Congo, agreements have often been reached and tensions reduced. I suggest that such experiences may also show that sympathetic treatment of one NATO ally by another has not really damaged the relationships of our countries with African and Asian countries, but that, on the contrary, we get further when we work together.

The Cuban case proved to be one where the national interests were in a sense reversed. It was one in which the United States found herself in need of the sympathetic understanding by her allies in dealing with a recalcitrant neighbor. The case involved an area outside the Atlantic Treaty area, and included economic as well as political and military problems. The allied countries responded with considerable reluctance when the question of economic sanctions was raised. But when a critical emergency arose with the planting of Soviet missiles in Cuba, all the countries of the alliance were prompt and unanimous in their support of the U.S. position.

The foregoing experience with NATO consultation has been traced in some detail here because it seems to me to contain elements of enormous importance in the development of the Atlantic Community. A good beginning has been made in the establishment of habits of mutual consultation and cooperation. Each crisis that has been met has helped to create precedents to guide future decisions, just as the British Constitution is created by the accumulation of laws and legal decisions.

The Need for a Common Nuclear Strategy

—*FRIEDRICH RUGE*

What is Nuclear Policy?

Nuclear policy is part of a country's national policy; its task is to help secure the national objectives. When a country is a member of an alliance, its national policy should accord with the general objectives of the alliance insofar as possible. This presupposes a clear-cut common policy (grand strategy), or at least a generally recognized scale of political priorities. The more partners there are the more difficult it will be to reach a common policy and to fix priorities. In a coordinated alliance of equal partners, such as NATO, a consensus is especially difficult of achievement. The decisions of the NATO Council can be made by unanimous vote only, and its members are subject to the directives of their own governments. On a somewhat lower level the same applies to the NATO Military Council. In contrast, the Warsaw Pact is a subordinated alliance, a hegemony; its "council" has an advisory capacity only, and there is a single supreme commander who is always a Russian marshal and gets his orders from the Kremlin without any discussion by the council.

This disparity makes it all the more necessary for NATO to develop a common grand strategy, and for its members to adapt the national policies to the broad objectives of this strategy.

U.S. Nuclear Policy

When NATO was founded the United States Government had already committed itself to a distinct nuclear policy in accordance with its over-all policy of trying to establish world peace and promote social progress, better living standards, and greater freedom by means of the United Nations. Under the impression of the frightful havoc atomic bombs had wrought on Japanese cities, President Truman endeavored to bring atomic energy under international control and effective supervision. In this way, he hoped its use for destructive purposes could be prevented. He felt that he could not make this effort and at the same time continue full exchange of nuclear knowledge with the British as during the war, for they planned to produce fissionable material for military as well as for peaceful purposes. In the fall of 1945, therefore, the U.S. Government terminated this cooperation in spite of previous agreements.

The McMahon Bill "for the control and development of atomic energy" introduced in the Senate on December 20, 1945 left some latitude by stipulating that a Board of Atomic Information should "provide for the dissemination of related technical information with the utmost liberality as freely as may be consistent with the foreign and domestic policies as established by the President." In the Atomic Energy Act, however, passed on August 1, 1946, the section title "Dissemination of Information" had not only been altered to "Control of Information" but its contents had also been greatly changed to prevent atomic knowledge from getting into the wrong heads. Distribution of fissionable materials to any foreign government, the British included, was strictly prohibited.

There were two reasons for this reversal of policy. One was that attempts to control atomic energy by international agreement and supervision continued under the Baruch Plan. The other was that many Senators considered interchange of atomic knowledge a threat to security. This was vividly demonstrated by the fact that Alan Nunn May, a British physicist working on nuclear problems in Canada, had been discovered giving information on nuclear matters to the Soviets.

As early as November 1945, Molotov had announced that the Soviet Union would soon have atomic energy. This declaration in conjunction with Nunn's treason gave the first warning of future developments deeply affecting nuclear policy, although at the same time the Soviet Government showed itself willing to cooperate on the problem of a commission on atomic energy.

The United States had embarked on an idealistic attempt to harness nuclear energy for peaceful purposes and the welfare of humanity. To achieve this goal, it had put up with the bad feelings of its British allies, but had neither prevented the British from pursuing their plans nor the Soviets from gaining access to nuclear secrets. Moreover, even then it could be expected that other nations would before long have nuclear weapons.

Other Major U.S. Postwar Policies

In the same period immediately after the war, the Soviet Union ruthlessly seized as much territory as possible. The United States Government, finally aroused by the Soviet Union's wholesale annexation and subjugation of East European nations and by its attempts to gain a foothold in Turkey, Iran, and Greece, carried out two decisive operations as part of a far-sighted grand strategy: the implementation of the Marshall Plan and the creation of NATO. The objectives of the Marshall Plan were to effect European recovery, and, in the long run, to establish and maintain closer economic and political cooperation in Europe. The objectives of the Atlantic alliance were (and still are): furthering stability and well-being, strengthening the free institutions, preserving the peace and security, and maintaining the collective defense of the North Atlantic area.

In view of persistent Communist aggression NATO had been preoccupied with defense problems, although ultimately other objectives should prevail. As a result nuclear policy has been considered part of military strategy only, whereas it is actually part of the grand strategy of the alliance.

In the first years of NATO's existence this caused hardly any difficulties. The British had reconciled themselves to the fact that their own progress in nuclear matters was slowed down and that costs were much higher than with American assistance. Their first bomb was detonated in 1952. The other European allies, still suffering greatly from the ravages and aftereffects of World War II, were only too glad to rely on American leadership and protection. In fact, they put more trust in the concept of "massive nuclear deterrence" than the situation warranted, and took their time about rearming themselves. However, the detonation of the first Soviet nuclear bomb in the fall of 1949 ended American monopoly much earlier than had been expected. The Communist attack on South Korea in 1950 indicated what might happen to ill-prepared nations. The war in Korea also showed that the atomic bomb was not a panacea for every difficult situation, and that massive retaliation might be a policy of doubtful value. The doubts increased when the Soviets followed with a hydrogen bomb early in 1953, only a few months after the Americans. This had been made possible because several scientists in addition to Alan Nunn May betrayed nuclear secrets to the Russians. How much classified material was stolen by Soviet agents will probably never be known.

The United States intensified its efforts and has kept the lead in the nuclear race by a wide margin. For a long time, however, it did not change in the least its nuclear policy laid down by the McMahon Act, although the situation had varied fundamentally, from the political as well as from the military viewpoint.

Effects of U.S. Policy

The aims of the inspired national policy that created the Marshall Plan and NATO had been to give Europe strength and unity. The aims of the nuclear policy expressed by the Baruch Plan and the Atomic Energy Act had been to give the world controlled atomic energy for peaceful purposes, and to prevent its use for military weapons and its abuse for power politics. Whereas NATO and especially the Marshall Plan had succeeded beyond expectation, the Soviet Union had put an end to the Baruch Plan, and the Atomic Energy Act had proved a failure. It had not stopped developments in the Communist bloc where Soviet Russia evidently was in possession of most nuclear secrets and a growing number of weapons. Red China received Soviet assistance for building up its own nuclear potential. No neutral country could be prevented from going in for nuclear research which might result in the construction of weapons. Technical progress was bound to continue.

Within NATO, on the other hand, United States nuclear policy annoyed important allies, to the detriment of good relations in the alliance. It did not end nuclear research and development in Great Britain and France, but it caused duplication and triplication of this most expensive kind of work, and thus set back conventional armaments to a high degree.

Nuclear Weapons in NATO

As NATO is not a hegemony like the Warsaw Pact, mutual trust and confidence play an important part in keeping alive the spirit of the alliance. It is not surprising that the McMahon Act did nothing to promote such mutual trust, for it was conceived as part of the national policy of a single country prior to the formation of the NATO alliance. It proved unfortunate, however, that it was not revised after the United States had changed its national policy fundamentally. This decisive step had been made possible by Resolution 239 introduced by Senator Vandenberg and adopted on June 11, 1948, by an overwhelming majority in the United States Senate. Contrary to the old policy of "non-entanglement" going back to Washington's testament and to the Monroe Doctrine, Resolution 239 authorized the President to join alliances in the interests of national security and within the Charter of the United Nations.

No corresponding measure was taken with respect to nuclear policy, although this might have been the time to reconsider the whole problem in its political effects. A way could have been found to permit those allies who occupied themselves with nuclear development to share some U.S. knowledge, and thus bind them together more closely in the interests of the alliance—at the same time stipulating that they spend more money on conventional armament. No such step was taken, and Great Britain and France went their separate ways in nuclear matters.

Thus it came about that not only the least satisfactory of the possible roads was taken but also the changeover to either a NATO nuclear force or a double nuclear force consisting of a United States and a European component was rendered difficult. There has never been any doubt that NATO needs strong nuclear forces as the sword of retaliation, supplemented by effective conventional forces as the shield in a military strategy which is essentially defensive. At first the conventional land forces were far too weak but United States nuclear superiority was so overwhelming that the European allies felt secure under this protection. With the increase of Soviet nuclear and missile power, the United States itself was threatened and its nuclear strength lost much of its practical value as Europe was more and more exposed to Soviet medium- and short-range missiles. At the end of 1955, the NATO Council decided to equip the Atlantic forces with atomic weapons, and two years later it decided to establish stocks of atomic warheads readily available for the defense of the alliance in case of need. Medium range ballistic missiles were put at the disposal of the Supreme Allied Commander in Europe (SACEUR), but the weapons remained in U.S. hands and under U.S. control. Only the President could give orders to launch them.

In the meantime, a number of countries had shown interest in creating their own facilities for developing nuclear power. Outside the NATO area, Red China was resolved to use it for military purposes. Within NATO, France followed Great Britain and began to form her own *force de frappe*. This was a most expensive undertaking because attempts to bring about Franco-British collaboration were not crowned with success.

Again, the weakest part of NATO suffered most. The conventional land forces in Central Europe have not yet reached the strength called for by the NATO Council in 1952. As a consequence of their nuclear policy, the British have never been able to bring their Army on the Rhine up to full strength. They have 180 V-bombers equipped with nuclear weapons, and they have started on a program of four submarines with twelve Polaris missiles each. The French are giving their armed forces a completely new look. They have cut down the number of their active divisions to six—very mobile, highly mechanized, and equipped with atomic weapons of their own. In addition, there will be fifty-four nuclear bombers of the Mirage type, and three submarines, each with sixteen missiles similar to Polaris. The cost of this nuclear force will rise from 13 per cent of the defense budget in 1963 to 25 per cent in 1970.

When finished and ready, each of these two forces will represent only a tiny fraction of the American nuclear potential. On the other hand, taken together, they will probably come up to 10 to 15 per cent of Soviet nuclear strength. To some extent, these figures are an explanation of the contrasting views on the value of the West European nuclear forces.

The American opinion is that the United States possesses such strong and variegated nuclear armaments that there is no need for national nuclear forces in Europe. At best, these are too small to be effective; at worst, they are dangerous for our own side because they might invite the Soviet Union to take pre-emptive action, and thus precipitate rather than prevent an all-out war. In any case, they are very expensive and uneconomical. Moreover, countries developing an independent nuclear force have been unable to contribute their full share to conventional defense in Western Europe.

On the whole, the nuclear efforts of Great Britain and France have been considered superfluous from an economic and military viewpoint and from the standpoint of attempting to gain undue influence on United States political decisions. Even at a high level, it has been said that they are "inimical to NATO."

British Views on Nuclear Strategy

That is one side of the coin. The other looks somewhat different. As far back as 1955, Churchill expressed the British idea that since behind the Iron Curtain there are large administrative and industrial targets, an effective policy of deterrence must include the capability of paralyzing them at the outset of a conflict, or very shortly thereafter. Churchill expressed the belief that unless the British furnished their own contribution, they could not be certain that in an emergency the weapons of other nations would be used in complete accord with British wishes—or that the targets most threatening to Britain would be attacked first.

And the British *Statement on Defense, 1964,* presented to Parliament by command of Her Majesty, February 1964, states:

> The keystone of this policy is the prevention of war. If we and our allies fail to prevent major war, none of the other objectives can be attained. Nuclear weapons are so devastating that, unless we prevent them from being used, we shall not be able to secure the homeland or carry out our obligations to those who rely on us. Yet, until true disarmament becomes a reality, it is the overwhelming power of these very weapons and the determination of the nations not to provoke their own destruction that keep the peace . . . and in the present state of the world no other realistic policy is apparent. Early and provident fear, as Burke said, is the mother of safety.
>
> It is the Government's policy not only to contribute forces to the main strategic deterrent, but to maintain an independent British deterrent. . . .

. . . To suggest that the independent deterrent might be abandoned in the interests of non-dissemination overlooks the fact that if there were no power in Europe capable of inflicting unacceptable damage on a potential enemy he might be tempted—if not now then perhaps at some time in the future—to attack in the mistaken belief that the United States would not act unless America herself were attacked. The V-bombers by themselves are, and the Polaris submarines will be, capable of inflicting greater damage than any potential aggressor would consider acceptable. For this reason the British nuclear forces make a unique contribution to the main deterrent.

French Views on Nuclear Strategy

The French views are rather similar. They see the European nuclear forces as a European security problem, not at all directed against United States policy, but necessary to give the Soviet leaders something to think about. An efficient force deployed in Europe and not subject to an American veto would serve as a warning. Whatever ideas the Soviet Union might have about the United States, there would be another nuclear force ready to strike back at once.

The French acknowledge that U.S. deterrence will cover at least 90 per cent of the European security risks. It is the task of the national nuclear forces to give a somewhat greater percentage of security. To wipe out European national nuclear forces without incurring unacceptable damage, the Soviet Union would be compelled to use such a large part of its own forces as to be decidedly weakened against the United States. Thus the national nuclear forces would constitute an additional risk to the Soviet Union and add perceptibly to the deterrent. It goes without saying that such forces must be really efficient and capable of causing enough damage to handicap Soviet action. Sufficiently strong national nuclear forces would help to allay the widespread European doubts whether the United States would use nuclear weapons unless America were immediately threatened.

In this context it may be mentioned that, in the Federal Republic of Germany, President Kennedy's declaration in Frankfurt and Berlin in the summer of 1963 did much to disperse similar doubts. Besides, a sober evaluation of the situation is bound to show that the United States simply cannot afford a Soviet advance into NATO Europe which would give the Communists an advantage in position and an increase in power that would imperil the American continent.

German Views on Nuclear Strategy

The position of the Federal Republic of Germany is different from that of Great Britain and France. In the Paris Treaty of 1955, by which Germany joined the Western European Union prior to NATO, it undertook not to produce any atomic, biological, and chemical

(ABC) weapons. The German attitude has not changed, and in view of the delicacy of the nuclear problem for Germany, is not likely to change. There is no foundation whatever for the allegations sometimes heard in allied countries that the Federal Republic is striving hard for the possession of nuclear weapons (which, incidentally, is not forbidden under existing treaties). Such allegations help the Communists in their barrage of unfounded assertions of West German "militarism" and "revanchism." What actually has happened is that the Federal Government and especially the Minister of Defense repeatedly have stressed the importance of tactical nuclear weapons in the shield forces. Their reason is that certain knowledge that there were no tactical nuclear weapons in the three German Army Corps sectors would give the Soviet Union an undeserved and dangerous advantage, which would enable them to concentrate their forces for a breakthrough far more easily than if opposed by tactical nuclear weapons.

The Soviet Union is known to possess such weapons. Therefore, the defense must be widely dispersed. Denying tactical nuclear weapons to the German sectors would be a grave disadvantage to the whole of the Central European front.

It should be made quite clear that the Government of the Federal Republic has never asked for the control or possession of these weapons, believing that they should remain in American hands, although control might be delegated to SACEUR under certain circumstances. Mutual trust and confidence within the alliance are considered far more valuable to the Federal Republic than the possession of a few atom bombs.

In this context it may be mentioned that it would be appreciated (and worthwhile politically) if our allies took a more determined stand against the endlessly repeated and never substantiated attacks against the "militarists and revanchists in the Federal Republic"; e.g., in the United Nations and at Geneva where the Federal Republic is not represented. This is part of the Communist anti-NATO and anti-nuclear campaign (i.e., as long as these weapons are not in their own hands). It can be expected at every conference, and it is not enough simply to wave it aside. A much better answer would be that it was Khrushchev himself who in 1959 said that he could incinerate the whole of the Federal Republic with eight hydrogen bombs.

Far too often these Soviet allegations are repeated without discrimination. Politicians and journalists acknowledge that so far the Federal Republic has kept its word but darkly hint at an "appetite for nuclear weapons that will grow." There are enough safeguards against any tendencies of that kind in the Western European Union (WEU) and NATO treaties. Any changes in this sector of nuclear policy have to be discussed in the Councils, and reouire a two-thirds majority in WEU and a unanimous vote in the NATO Council.

What Is the Soviet Nuclear Strategy?

It would seem more valuable—but nobody appears to take much interest in it—to get an answer to several questions on Soviet nuclear policy: how is control of nuclear weapons regulated behind the Iron Curtain; how many fingers are on the trigger over there; how far can a dictator afford to delegate this kind of power? Will the next dictator feel himself bound by the signature of his predecessor and what might be the consequences of a not-impossible de-Khrushchevization? Together with the fact that Marxist-Leninists consider coexistence another form of class war with no holds barred (except all-out war) this tends to show that as long as the tension between East and West is not really eased all attempts at pulling the nuclear teeth of deterrence by creating nuclear-free zones are to be viewed with the greatest distrust, for they can be supervised with far less reliability than a nuclear test ban.

All this has a direct influence on nuclear policy as part of NATO policy. It is always in the mind of the statesmen in the government of the Federal Republic which, after all, is not more than a narrow strip of territory, densely populated, directly in the path of a Soviet main thrust in a possible war, and always in the path of the Communist main thrust in the actual cold war. Therefore, West Germany is far more interested in successful deterrence than in powerful retaliation. Nuclear weapons are indispensable, but they are only part of the deterrence. To be successful it must be implemented by impressive conventional forces (and by an adequate civil defense). In addition, political strength is imperative, expressed by a homogeneous grand strategy (including a nuclear policy), a firm attitude of government and citizens, and flexibility in political action in the widest sense.

NATO Goals

Apprehension has resulted from a blurring of the goals of the alliance in recent years, from a decrease rather than an increase in the stability sought in the treaty, and from the failure of nuclear policy to take into account the problem of a stronger and more self-confident Europe. Nuclear policy has, in fact, exerted a somewhat disruptive influence, more in the political than in the military field.

In the *Revue de Défence Nationale* of February 1962, Général André Beaufre, formerly Deputy Chief of Staff at SHAPE and later French member of the Standing Group, wrote:

> The decision to use atomic arms has too many political consequences to be automatically delegated to one of the allies, even if this one possesses almost all the atomic resources. . . .
>
> The atomic autonomy of the U.S.A. involves as a corollary the autonomy of its partners: the limited nature of the alliance means leaving outside it one of the most important military factors.

And one of the most important political factors, it may be added.

It does not seem quite logical that the Americans do everything for a full economic partnership—that in the military field they integrate their conventional forces and put a considerable part under NATO command—and at the same time keep their nuclear forces entirely under national command.

Certainly, nuclear weapons do not fit into the old concepts because of their enormous military effects and political consequences. However, we have to find ways and means to manage these problems, for technical progress will go on. Even the Swiss are of the opinion that today every army must possess nuclear weapons because only in this way can a country show its resolution to defend its liberty under any circumstances. In 1963 they disclosed that from raw materials to scientists they have all the prerequisites to manufacture small atom bombs and shells. In a plebiscite, the majority of the people voted against prohibiting atomic weapons.

In NATO, the United States has gained its short-term goal of preventing an all-out war, but more by its technical and military superiority than by superior policy and exploitation of the ever-changing situation. However, it has paid rather a high price, for by its nuclear policy it has contributed to some disjunction within the alliance. This is not so severe that it could not be remedied, and it is easier to judge after the event than in the middle of a development. By laying too much emphasis on massive nuclear reaction, the United States has realized rather late that it has contributed to driving underground the war which the Communists wage on the rest of the world. The results have been reverses in Southeast Asia, where nuclear arms cannot influence the situation, and in Cuba where they could do so only when the Soviet Union tried to install its own nuclear arms on the island.

National Goals within NATO

Two of the most important NATO allies went their own nuclear way, the British with less commotion than the French. There were several reasons for their actions. Nuclear armaments seem to be considered the ticket of admission to the status of a great power, or an indispensable sign of national sovereignty, regardless of the fact that nowadays not even the two super-powers command the degree of independence formerly enjoyed by all members of the "Concert of Great Powers." However, the most important reason is lack of confidence in the United States. Some of the European members of NATO have grave doubts whether the Americans would actually commit everything they have in the case of a Soviet attack on Europe alone. This distrust has been augmented by lack of knowledge concerning U.S. nuclear means and plans. The comparative lack of public discussion of strategic questions in European countries may have contributed to this deficiency. In the Federal Republic, for example, strategic studies are not emphasized by research groups or universities. As a consequence, problems of technical and military strategy are generally judged more from sentiment than from reason.

By setting up their own nuclear forces, Great Britain and especially France have reintroduced nationalistic tendencies which seemed passé in the Europe of the Schuman Plan, the Common Market, and the Western European Union, thus slowing down the process of European unification—a long-range target of U.S. grand strategy. It is most important to overcome these setbacks and to improve the cohesion of the alliance. Only a strong unbroken front with a pronounced resolution to act in case of need will impress the Communists, for they are over-sensitive to power.

It is to be regretted that General de Gaulle's 1958 suggestion that Atlantic unity be consolidated through the creation of a political directorate composed of France, Great Britain, and the United States "never received even the courtesy of an acknowledgement" [W. W. Rostow]. For a considerable time, the consequences of United States nuclear policy were not foreseen. Not until 1960 were the first steps taken to remedy the situation. After that, a number of measures followed which lead in the right direction although they do not yet constitute a full solution of these knotty problems.

Dawn of a New Nuclear Policy

The first was an agreement with Great Britain to make Polaris missiles available on a continuing basis, which was a distinct move away from the McMahon Act. That it was a deliberate beginning of a new policy is shown by the stipulation to develop new and closer arrangements for the organization and control of strategic Western defense. It was explicitly stated that such arrangements could in turn make a major contribution to political cohesion among the nations of the alliance. As a first measure, the 180 British V-bombers (with British nuclear weapons) were assigned to NATO.

The British Government reserved the right to use this force "at discretion" if supreme national interests were at stake. Unfortunately, this reservation was noticed mainly in the other European countries, as was the simultaneous scratching of the Skybolt project. From a military and economic viewpoint this was probably right, but it was published by the European press in a rather unpropitious form.

The allocation of the British V-bombers and five U.S. Polaris submarines to NATO was the beginning of a multinational force which in the course of time might develop into a genuine NATO nuclear force. In the eyes of the other countries its main disadvantage is that the nuclear weapons of these forces remain under the control of their own governments and can be withdrawn at any time.

MLF

As an alternative, the United States suggested a multilateral force (MLF) in the form of submarines or surface vessels with Polaris missiles. The crews were to be composed of men of the countries sharing the costs, and the nuclear weapons were to be furnished by the United States and to remain under United States control. This plan was probably sprung too suddenly on the world and at first met with considerable criticism in the countries that were meant to participate. Subsequently criticism gave way to a more sober evaluation of MLF possibilities.

The submarine project was soon dropped as too expensive and too difficult in the training of the crews. The surface ships are much easier to handle and cheaper to build and run. Their military value is lower than that of the submarines (at least as long as anti-submarine warfare does not make considerable progress). With Polaris III they have a range from the waters west of the Iberian peninsula to Central Russia. This gives them a wide area of ocean to hide in. To shadow them constantly would mean an enormous Soviet expenditure. Tactically, they serve not as a substitute for Polaris submarines but as a valuable supplement. In the light of the experience of German sailors in several allied navies in the last years, very few human difficulties are to be expected, and none that cannot be solved by a careful selection of the men.

The main drawback of the MLF project would seem to be that it does not provide a satisfactory solution for the recurrent problem of creating a NATO authority entitled to order the use of nuclear weapons.

Opinion of the MLF varies. A British publication, *The Navy,* has described it as "politically undesirable and militarily indefensible." Several governments have given MLF a somewhat guarded acceptance. Mr. von Hassel, the German Minister of Defense, says that it is not the task of MLF to solve all the problems of cohesion and defense. Yet it would help to give an answer to the Soviet MRBM's which threaten Central Europe in increasing numbers, and it would represent a strong military potential in any case. Jean Monnet, the President of the Executive Committee of a United Europe, says that the differences in the question of nuclear armaments concern our existence, our safety, and our liberty because they prevent the unification of Europe and moreover the political and military association of our two continents. Europe must participate in and contribute to nuclear armament. A common action of the West is indispensable. In the present difficult situation the proposed MLF can, in his opinion, perhaps constitute a temporary solution and fill a dangerous gap.

The British Government intends to participate in the experiment of training a mixed crew in a United States destroyer to gain some firsthand knowledge of how it works, and experience for the actual MLF. Objections from various sides (e.g., Mr. Nelson Rockefeller) that with the MLF there would be too many different nuclear forces in NATO are not quite valid in the light of the experience with the far more variegated "crazy-quilt" of conventional forces in NATO. Given clear directives, the military in the integrated staffs will take this problem in their stride. Their cooperation is more advanced and running more smoothly than many people realize. In this respect, there is true progress in NATO.

The vociferous objections of the Soviet Union to the MLF can be taken as a sign that it is not quite so inadequate as sometimes considered in the West. It should be emphasized that it is not an unlawful road for the Germans to gain admission to the atom club. The German line is neither to press for the MLF nor to turn it down, but to cooperate within the frame of the obligations accepted by the Federal Republic. There is one point, however, which has hardly been mentioned. Forward defense and the situation in Central Europe make it imperative to have strong conventional forces all along the Iron Curtain. To increase the number of active divisions to more than thirty would be very expensive, and there is hardly room enough for them. The best solution would be an efficient territorial defense, somewhat like in Switzerland or in the Scandinavian countries. This would not be cheap, either, if these men are to be well-armed and ready for action within a few hours in an emergency. It should be carefully examined, therefore, how much German money is to go into this kind of defense, and how much into the MLF. This problem of finding an optimum can be solved only with political cooperation on the basis of mutual confidence.

From the political point of view, the MLF gains importance in combination with two other measures made possible by the change in U.S. nuclear policy. They are the appointment of allied officers to the Joint Strategic Targeting and Planning Section at the Headquarters of Strategic Air Command at Omaha, Nebraska, and the institution of a Nuclear Deputy to Supreme Allied Commander Europe at SHAPE near Paris. So far, not enough attention has been given to these improvements by the European public. They are most important, however, for from now on, Europeans will participate far more in forming nuclear strategy. It may be mentioned that cooperation in target planning has not been neglected in the past. In this respect, too, the military have gone about their duties in a matter of fact way; they have acted and reacted flexibly.

In the ups and downs of nuclear policy the removal of the old-fashioned liquid-fuel missiles from Turkey and Italy after the Cuba affair and the lack of visible consultation at the test ban negotiations influenced European opinion negatively. The declarations of Secretary of Defense McNamara on the immense nuclear strength of the United States and on the increase of the nuclear potential in Western Europe have greatly contributed to clearing the atmosphere again. Taken together, all these details show how many-sided nuclear policy has to be, how many seeming trivia have to be watched. It might be noted that Americans because of their shorter and simpler history are inclined to be more optimistic in foreign politics than Europeans with over 2,000 years of sad experience behind them.

Conclusions

All the measures mentioned above are tactical moves showing a change in the direction of nuclear strategy, which however has not yet been formulated. Nor has the grand strategy of the alliance been formulated; rather, it has been obscured. Stability, freedom, and common defense are still the goals, but they cannot be reached without cohesion and cooperation. There is general agreement that over-all policy should strive at avoiding the use of nuclear weapons as long as possible, and that there should be a nuclear strategy permitting a flexible reaction in case of nuclear attack from the other side—although there is slight hope to keep nuclear war limited once it has begun.

As evidenced by Marshal Sokolovsky's book *Military Strategy* (1962), the Soviet military leaders are prepared almost exclusively for an all-out atomic war without any restrictions. They are evidently adherents of a counter-city strategy. It appears, however, that Khrushchev himself has a clearer picture of the situation, quite apart from the fact that as a rule the Soviet leaders do not like to take great risks.

True, they were overconfident in Korea and in Cuba. It is all the more important to show them a firm determination to prevent more misunderstandings of that kind. A main prerequisite would be to tell them unequivocally whose finger is on which nuclear trigger, and that the owner or owners are resolved to act at a certain fixed point according to the situation. "There must not be the slightest doubt in the minds of the Communist leaders that our system of collective security is efficient" [Minister von Hassel].

In theory, the ideal solution would be a political integration of the Atlantic nations. This is a distant aim, hardly feasible in the near future. A closer integration of Western Europe seems more practicable. It had already started on various roads and made good progress until it got stuck for various reasons, among them American nuclear isolationism. At the moment, strengthening the position of the NATO Council does not seem very hopeful, but it should be kept in view. In the political field, improved consultation will have to follow nuclear strategic coordination. There are also possibilities in the NATO Committee of Political Advisers.

In December 1963, for the control of nuclear armament, General Norstad suggested a solution somewhere between a single national authority acting for the alliance, and common and equal responsibility of the fifteen members. He sees it in a small, responsible group composed of one representative each from the United States, France, and Great Britain, with the Secretary General of NATO as coordinator.

The WEU assembly in Paris early in December 1963 considered NATO strategy and nuclear forces and recommended:

> that NATO defense planning . . . provide the political authority with the widest possible choice of action;
>
> that there be developed within NATO a unified strategic planning system aimed at the development of a common strategy;
>
> that to this end NATO governments undertake consultations toward the elevation of the NATO Council into a high-level allied forum for unified strategic planning with appropriate military advisory staff, the membership of such a revised NATO Council to be drawn from the highest levels of government;
>
> that such a revised NATO Council should engage in strategic planning in the broadest sense: political as well as military planning on questions affecting war and peace.

These objectives can be reached only with cooperation, coordination, and cohesion which in NATO are not yet sufficiently strong. They are good in the military sphere, probably because military defense has been much in the foreground. That holds for nuclear armament, too, which has been considered mainly a military means of combat. But that is not enough. Evidently, we are in a new phase of political relations between the nations. As Secretary of Defense McNamara said:

> There is no true historical parallel to the drive of Soviet Communist imperialism to colonize the world. This is not the first time that ambitious dictators have sought to dominate the globe. But none has ever been so well organized; possessed so many instruments of destruction; or been so adept at disguising ignoble motives and objectives with noble words and phrases.

The Soviet Union has never been reticent in using force where it will pay. However, technical progress has created weapons which are practically useless for war because they will leave broken and vanquished peoples, if any life at all. Therefore, all-out war is improbable, and yet, as an act of desperation or misjudgment, not impossible. We can be sure that the Soviet drive will continue as a different type of war, with ideological, subversive, and economic means, and with hot war used as a threat.

The free world is confronted with the danger of being annihilated physically by a nuclear holocaust or being destroyed spiritually by the methods of the cold war. Therefore, it must employ a strategy which deters military aggression effectively, and which resists and overcomes all forms of ideological and subversive war. This will be a long process, and we have before us a kind of limited war in which—as it did 200 years ago—clever maneuvering will play a role at least as important as military weapons. In these operations the nuclear threat is an important tactical maneuver.

This new situation is bound to influence all deliberations and decisions on the sharing of nuclear control within the alliance. It is often said that first a United Europe should be created, with a supranational government endowed with authority to receive nuclear knowledge and weapons. As the Communist menace is shaping, this might take too much time and be too late. Of course, European unification is to be promoted in all possible ways, and NATO integration not neglected. But simultaneously, ways should be explored to let the allies participate in nuclear responsibility, and to handle nuclear policy not only as a military, but also as a political and psychological instrument.

Nuclear Deterrence and World Strategy

—*ANDRÉ BEAUFRE*

The General Framework

Up to the present, NATO has been an organization of limited responsibility. It is defensive in nature, restricted to a given geographic area, and does not establish the means that each nation will employ for the defense of all concerned. However, this definition has proven to be too narrow in scope to meet with present day problems. Hence any serious study on the subject of NATO must first be considered in its true framework of world strategy.

The Principal Factors

Since 1945, world strategy has been dominated by two opposing forces, namely the United States and Russia. But this notion constitutes a simplification further and further removed from reality.

Actually, the present situation is characterized by the simultaneous emergence of several important factors.

The fall of Europe after two world wars resulted in a vacuum in Central Europe into which the Soviet Union rushed, and in the collapse of Europe's world empire. Western Europe, while recovered economically and politically, remains weak from the military point of view.

The emergence of the United States and Russia as superpowers. Their mutual opposition has led them to take reciprocal security measures in Europe and in Asia. But the inherent nature of the problems of nuclear warfare is leading them to establish among themselves a new kind of relationship.

The awakening of the Third World, instigated by its contact with European civilization, rendered possible by Europe's downfall and the mutual neutralization of the nuclear balance, and provoked by the old restraints of colonialism. The Third World is striving simultaneously for Europeanization and for a rediscovery of its old traditions. The Europeanization of the Third World nations wavers between the Western and the Soviet models. In the Third World, several giants of the future are slowly emerging, although they are still more or less in their infancy: China, India, and the Arab World. But elsewhere, the general perspective is one of chaos, offering numerous opportunities to the indirect strategies of the two principal political camps.

The development of economics of plenty, thanks to modern technology. This development, which has engendered American prosperity, Soviet power, and the rapid recovery of Europe, is ill suited to the conditions of the Third World, which lacks technicians, capital, and adequate resources, while their rapidly expanding populations, resulting from modern health improvements, present virtually insoluble problems. Hence we have a dangerous disparity between economies of abundance and the economies of the underdeveloped nations. Then again, the Third World nations waver between American techniques of production and those of Soviet socialism more or less adapted by the Chinese.

The development of the Marxist ideology, a materialist interpretation, and secularization of Christian ideals leading to a messianism of historical evolution through the complete overthrow of old values: property, profit, etc. This ideology seems to be becoming the credo of the proletarian peoples.

The advent of nuclear weapons (and more generally the development of scientific resources serving military technology) leading to the creation of means of destruction which are disproportionate to the political objectives of war. This has resulted in a still incompletely realized new balance with specific problems of considerable importance.

These six principal factors combine to give the world its present character: on the one hand, a basic instability due to political and economic factors; on the other hand, an almost total stabilization due to nuclear weapons, where there is the knowledge of how to use their power.

This situation leads to a world strategy which brings to view two complementary and interdependent aspects: on the one hand, a direct strategy of deterrence, essentially nuclear, aiming at a military balance among the great economic and political potentials by means of an arms race which constitutes an increasingly heavy burden on the most advanced countries; on the other hand, an indirect strategy, essentially political and economic, possibly violent, whose intensity depends on the degree of neutralization established by the military balance—a strategy that utilizes to the maximum the factors of instability, especially in the Third World.

In this perspective, world strategy depends upon (or should depend upon) two principal factors: the long-term political objective, and the internal laws governing contemporary strategy, particularly nuclear and indirect strategy.

The Long-Range Political Objective

The determination of this objective is purely political, not strategic, in nature. Hence it is not pertinent to the framework of this study. From the strategic point of view, one can merely state that it is unfortunate that such an objective has been defined only in uncertain and often contradictory terms. The reasons for this are obvious: the divergence of views among the United States and the former colonial powers; propaganda disputes; and illusions as to the possibilities of resolving simultaneously all existing problems, especially those of the Third World.

It is evident that the big problem will be to determine what, in the years ahead, is to be the nature of the civilization of the third millennium which is developing under the mark of productivity and technology in a shrinking and overpopulated world, and to determine whether our Græco-Roman and Christian heritage will endure.

From this point of view, the unity and the prosperity of Europe and the Atlantic Community seem to be essential, as does the stemming of poverty in the Third World.

This implies long-range options and it is only in the light of such political options that we can define a strategy.

The New Strategic Laws

We have already noted in passing the fundamental duality of current strategy.

The Nuclear Problem

Regarding the nuclear question, we are often led into error by the vestiges of our former (and now obsolete) ideas on war.

Modern means of destruction are much too powerful to be used. Furthermore, technological advance has introduced a completely new concept of enormous and inevitable reciprocal risks, which obviates the old notion of the victor and the vanquished. A war of this nature has become unthinkable, so unthinkable that we risk losing the stabilizing advantages of the nuclear deterrent, thus introducing once again the possibility of violent non-nuclear conflict.

Our interest, then, is centered on two conclusions which are, unfortunately, contradictory.

1. The use of nuclear weapons is unthinkable.

2. The threat of the use of nuclear weapons is indispensable.

Hence it is necessary to sustain the credibility of a first strike without actually bringing the threat to fruition.

There exist but three ways to resolve this contradiction:

1. To render rational the possibility of a first strike by possession of a counterforce capability sufficient to diminish significantly the effect of retaliatory measures. This solution is very difficult to achieve and is limited to the major nuclear powers.

2. To make others believe in the possibility of an irrational decision to launch the first strike. This is the only possible choice for the smaller powers.

3. By humanizing or mollifying the first strike, to make it not unthinkable, declaring in advance its limited design in order not to incite massive retaliation. Such a solution (of a limited first strike) renounces the possibility of achieving absolute deterrence.

Each of these three possible solutions has advantages and disadvantages. The error generally made has been to present one of these possibilities as the only worthy solution. Actually, an effective deterrent must embrace all three. From this point of view, the tactical nuclear weapon is absolutely indispensable if conventional forces are to enjoy the stability which only the fear of nuclear risk can bestow during a period of nuclear balance.

By contrast, if we were forced to resort to nuclear weapons, it would be essential to play a humanitarian and compromising role in order to stop the conflict at the lowest possible level.

This consideration naturally applies to the use of tactical nuclear weapons which, in any case, should be extremely limited.

Conventional Forces Problem

Conventional forces are essential to the achievement of nuclear deterrence. But the difficulty is to foresee the importance of this necessary complement.

As long as the policy of nuclear deterrence is sufficient to influence the conventional level, the use of conventional forces by the enemy is almost inconceivable.

But the nuclear balance could be such that the use of nuclear weapons might appear impossible, at least for small stakes. In this case, the strength of conventional forces, reinforced if necessary by tactical nuclear weapons, should be sufficient to discourage minor aggression not covered by the policy of nuclear deterrence.

If the nuclear stalemate should become total or almost total, the threatened use of conventional force could rise considerably, leading to the possibility of substantial conventional warfare. At any rate, the existence of strategic nuclear forces would nevertheless create a danger such that these conflicts would be stopped short and would be limited in their political objectives. Hence, we would not revert to the condition which prevailed during the two world wars, but to the need for a greater conventional force level.

Finally, in the areas where nuclear deterrence does not apply (for want of know-how) conventional forces must be capable of operating alone. The possession of highly mobile conventional strategic reserves is essential to the operation of indirect strategy. In certain instances, these forces must be able to be reinforced by substantial effective forces.

Since it is impossible to choose from among these alternatives in advance, it is easy to see the need for having available a minimum level of conventional forces which can be augmented as required by developments in the nuclear balance of power.

The Cold War Problem

The cold war persists under changing aspects and intensity. This is to be expected in the age of nuclear deterrence. Political, economic, diplomatic, and military factors are brought into play—but the military means play only an auxiliary role. Foremost is the political-psychological factor—that is, the adopted political strategy.

Strategically, freedom of action depends above all on the scheme followed on the world chessboard, outside the disputed area. There, where the defense is difficult and the balance precarious, it is especially necessary to have the initiative.

Problems of NATO

In spite of its diverse limitations NATO can be understood and organized only within the general framework described above.

Since 1950, in fact if not in theory, NATO has been an organization directed exclusively by the United States, whose force has been and still is preponderant. The United States has strictly reserved nuclear strategy for itself and has carried out its world strategy with complete independence, generally without consulting with its allies, and sometimes even in direct conflict with some of them. The economic and political recovery of Europe—thanks, to some extent, to the Marshall Plan—has made it impossible to continue this way. NATO must find a formula for achieving a new balance in its policy and strategy. This is what General de Gaulle proposed in his November 1958 statement, which has never been effectively answered. The two issues he raised deal with the direction of world strategy and nuclear strategy—solutions for which still must be found.

World Strategy

World strategy is essentially that indirect strategy which, within the context of the cold war, seeks to promote a new balance of power required by world change. It is in this area of "indirect strategy" that we must re-establish a profitable Western initiative. If we acknowledge that national independence must be safeguarded, three solutions are possible: widespread unilateral action; consultation within the NATO framework; formation of a joint strategic policy wherever possible.

Because of failure to adopt a joint strategic policy (as had been suggested by General de Gaulle), an attempt has been made at a system of consultation within the framework of NATO which has not really worked, and which, moreover, could hardly have practical results since within NATO interest in extra-European questions is constantly changing. Thus, we have returned to a policy of disunity, the shortcomings of which are obvious.

The only logical solution (although admittedly difficult to achieve) is a return to consultation on common strategy among nations having worldwide interests, subsequently restating that strategy to apply regionally for other nations with allied interests—all of which presupposes appropriate vehicles for carrying out such a solution. (The remarkable task accomplished in regard to the Berlin issue constitutes an interesting precedent and shows how a practical solution could be found.)

Nuclear Strategy

The issue of nuclear strategy presents the same difficulty. In this area, NATO suffers because up to now the Americans have considered nuclear strategy to be strictly national, although it constitutes the basis of NATO joint strategy. It is no longer possible to restrict NATO's sphere of influence to the question of the tactical defense of Europe when NATO's strategic framework is much more extensive. The problem arises now in the atomic sphere because of the French independent nuclear force, but it is in fact a problem for the whole alliance to the extent of a developing strategic awareness within the various European nations.

Since 1960 the development of American thought in this area has served to complicate rather than to resolve the problem. Of prime concern are two essential considerations: the fear of nuclear proliferation and the necessity for a completely centralized nuclear control. These preoccupations are partly unfounded, and there exist other considerations which are at least as important.

The fundamental error has been to think that: politically it would be possible to maintain indefinitely the complete authority that the United States has exerted in the nuclear sphere; materially it would be possible to prevent France from carrying out its nuclear program. This error has precluded consideration of alternative solutions which will be necessary sooner or later.

On the other hand, the fact that the allies of the United States (except perhaps Great Britain) had not closely followed the development of American ideas with regard to nuclear force has produced a dangerous intellectual gap which is manifested by the divergence of opinion which in many cases could have been avoided by a joint study of these problems years before.

The formation of alliance nuclear strategy raises two problems: the theoretical one, the role of allied and independent nuclear forces; and the practical one, the possibilities of coordination of allied nuclear strategies.

The Role of Allied and Independent Nuclear Forces

Theoretical studies made by the French Institute of Strategic Studies regarding nuclear deterrence have brought to light certain laws concerning multilateral deterrence.

When two principal and opposing nuclear forces are in a counterbalancing deterrent position, the existence of a third nuclear influence allied to one of the two forces, although remaining independent as far as decisions are concerned, presents to the deterrence problem some very important modifications which are not proportionate to the destructive capacity of the third force. In effect, the resulting phenomena can be compared to the influence of a catalytic agent in chemistry.

To a *potential aggressor,* desiring to avoid an all-out nuclear war, the existence of several focal points of independent decision complicates the deterrence problem to the point of preventing even plausible predictions. This uncertainty is for all intents and purposes a deterrent and stabilizing force.

In bringing to light the potential risks of attacking the vital interests of this third partner, the independent nuclear capability prevents an error of judgment, which would endanger these interests even if they appeared secondary for its principal opponent.

In creating an element of uncertainty, small as it may be, with regard to the possible reactions of the third partner, the existence of a focal point of independent decisions serves to confer upon the principal ally's nuclear forces (more or less neutralized by the existing balance), a more extensive deterrent power. In fact, the existence of a third partner considerably augments the opponent's belief in the possibility of a first strike.

This combination of possible consequences serves to fortify deterrence considerably.

As far as the *principal ally* is concerned, the existence in his camp of a focal point of independent nuclear decisions creates the need for effective coordination between the deterrent strategies of the two allies in order to prevent the adversary's uncertainty from spreading into the allied camp. This necessary coordination tightens the bond between the two allies, resulting in a powerful, organic solidarity. In the event of serious tension, the existence of two or more centers of decision allows for graduated pressure, leaving the enemy in doubt about the degree of coordination, and makes it possible (if it is deemed useful) for the principal ally to refrain from or delay participation.

This combination of possible consequences serves to make allied deterrent measures both more flexible and more efficient, while, at the same time reinforcing alliance cohesion.

The Problem of Coordination of Deterrent Strategies

Up to the present, this problem has been approached by the United States only to the extent of their trying to avoid it by complete integration of allied nuclear forces. The main reason behind this unifying tendency has been the fear of seeing the subtle and terribly dangerous game of deterrence confused and compromised by dangerous initiatives of one or more allied nations acting independently.

Hence we have cast doubt upon the maturity and judgment of the nuclear allies, although there are many compelling reasons for their fear that they would be the hardest-hit victims in the event of a nuclear conflict. Furthermore, it should be noted that the American reaction of distrust of their European allies is very similar to the attitude which existed in several of the European countries with regard to the United States when the theory of massive retaliation held sway. To a great extent it had been caused by threatening statements of deterrent intentions, as well as the undeniably privileged position which the United States enjoyed. But above all, the present error is a result of ignoring or forgetting the real nature of nuclear weapons, whose role is not to wage a war which would be unthinkable, but to prevent war through a policy of deterrence. It is in this context of deterrence that the coordination of strategies, resting in several decision centers, must be viewed.

In order that the allies might maneuver in confidence and freely converge their efforts for the prospect of maximum deterrence, it is necessary first of all that they have a full understanding of the phenomenon which they seek to direct. This presupposes thorough joint study and frank discussion aimed at deriving understanding of the true collective interests of the alliance in the nuclear realm. This stage of reciprocal education is indispensable and should not be short-lived, for nuclear truths demand a long incubation period. Let us say that up to now the surface has hardly been scratched.

Thanks to this preparation—the duration of which is no longer that of material accomplishments—the nuclear allies could form a team ready to win together the game of deterring the enemy—like a real football team, and not like a bunch of robots under the remote control of a single will.

Naturally, appropriate vehicles would be necessary; on the one hand for the *study and preparation phase* (similar, probably, to the quadripartite group in Berlin), and on the other hand for the *coordination of the operation* of deterrence, thanks to various communications systems which make possible instantaneous communication between the various government heads and their chain of command. It would not be a question of impairing the freedom of the various participants and even less of allowing an arbitrary veto right, but rather of allowing concerted or planned decisions.

Hence it follows that the coordinated *use* of forces would be planned for the improbable eventuality that nuclear deterrence would fail; but, as we have mentioned above, it is from the viewpoint of *deterrence* and not of *use* that the whole system must be conceived.

Conclusion

This brief study, intentionally limited to the plan of basic principles, has attempted to emphasize the principal gaps in the alliance and to seek over-all solutions which would fill these gaps within the scope of world strategy and of nuclear deterrence.

In fact, it is the problem of establishing a formula for a truly collective control or coordination within each of these spheres, rather than limiting interallied action to operational problems of local defense in the European theater. The fact that nuclear strategy has evolved from defense to deterrence makes this adjustment absolutely necessary, while the creation of independent nuclear forces compels the establishment of a system of coordination.

In spite of the prejudices which persist in this area, it is self-evident that a multipolar nuclear system, harmonizing the initiative of the allies, thanks to a common concept, could achieve a deterrent more complete and more stable than a strictly bipolar system. Some organizational schemes seem to be achievable. Besides, a more intensive analysis would show that there exists only a difference of degree, but not of kind, between the coordination which prevailed on the conventional level (with regard to Berlin, for example) and that which it would be necessary to achieve on the nuclear level.

If these needs, as well as the very real advantages which could be gained from them, were recognized, the obstacles which are currently presented to technical osmosis between allies would be lifted, and the entire alliance could benefit greatly from the large sums spent on armaments.

But it is probable that the road leading in this direction is still quite long, since some minds are not yet ready for such solutions. However, one needs to realize that it is only in this direction that NATO will be able to bring to fruition a more cohesive organization. If this road is not taken, nuclear and world initiatives run the risk of becoming more and more uncoordinated, and therefore dangerously divergent.

The Problem of the Nuclear Trigger

—*STEFAN T. POSSONY*

The plans we are making today will be executed at a time when the current crop of statesmen no longer will be in action. Hence it is not particularly useful to discuss strategic planning in terms of personalities and evanescent political situations. Geography and technology are more durable foundations of long-range strategic planning.

Proximity to the Communist threat is the salient geographic feature of continental NATO. The geometric configuration of the continental NATO countries which spells an initial inability to concentrate the full force in the main theater is a second salient feature. For example, the ground forces of Germany and France would not be immediately additive to stop a sudden attack. Disregarding the French units in Germany, the full weight of the Soviet attack would fall first on the German forces and subsequently on the French, Belgian, and Dutch forces. "Forward deployments" may mitigate this danger; they cannot, even if they were to last, fully overcome it. Thus, piecemeal destruction of one army after the other is a hazard that is inscribed on the map of Europe.

Similar considerations apply to the air battle, though in this case echeloning in depth would provide some significant advantages.

The difficulties of this geographic situation are compounded by the destructiveness of nuclear weapons and the technology of fast air delivery and rapid ground advance.

If the German front were to hold, all NATO forces could be used simultaneously *in the end*. But this would require that Germany's twelve divisions (together with U.S. and other forward contingents) must be able to withstand a Soviet assault launched by a force two or three times stronger.

A Soviet attack would be designed to be extremely fast-moving and devastating. It would be launched to achieve surprise which means that the NATO forces may be attacked when they are in a less-than-optimal posture.

Red forces equipped with nuclear weapons could defeat stronger NATO forces to whom nuclear weapons are denied. Even denial during "only" the initial two hours could mean decisive victory for the aggressor. In fact, during the critical few minutes when the warheads of 700-odd Soviet MRBM's are re-entering the atmosphere, denial could be fatal.

It is not unrealistic to assume that there will be some warning about an impending Soviet attack, but it is hazardous to assume that there *must* be warning and that such warning will be *adequate* and *unambiguous*. There is no need to plan exclusively against the most unmanageable threats and assume that there can be only "zero warning," but it would be unrealistic to expect that unambiguous warning would allow us more than a few minutes to ready the parry. It would be entirely impractical to plan on anything but instantaneous defense "response."

In order of magnitude figures, the United States would obtain tactical warning of about fifteen minutes at worst and about twenty minutes at best. If the United States were struck first, European warning times *could* be somewhat longer. But this is unlikely because Soviet strategy probably will be aiming at simultaneity of European and American warning. If so, European warning times would be on the order of five minutes or one-third of American warning times.

If there were a NATO space warning system, European warning time could be increased to approximately eight minutes; U.S. warning times would still be about three times longer.

Precise warning times are, of course, variables depending upon locations of bases, targets, and radars, as well as delivery systems. In Europe the warning times of Turkey, Greece, Norway, Denmark, and Germany are, almost inevitably, far shorter than those of Spain and Portugal, while in the United States the warning time of Seattle would be dependent on whether the city were attacked from the Chukhotsk area or from, say, south of the Urals. The United States benefits from its ability to put warning systems forward into unpopulated and ocean areas. European warning is derived from systems that must be deployed along the iron curtain, and is particularly unsatisfactory against low level air attack, a type of threat which, for reasons of range, is far more difficult to mount against the United States than against Europe. On the other hand, a submarine attack on the United States might nullify our tactical warning advantages, but if the mass sortie of hostile submarines were observed near their base of departure, a very comfortable strategic warning could be obtained.

But there is a tactical *first* warning which, if everything is well organized, alerts the whole system; and this first warning is almost unmanageably short for Europe.

Add to this hazard the impact of population density on European security. Add lack of space which hinders deployment and maneuver, and precludes dispersal. Add further the importance of areas that are situated close to the hostile borders.

I doubt that the United States has a real awareness of the European defense problem. I even doubt that the United States is fully aware of the defense problem that exists for the U.S. forces in Europe. The public discourses on balances of power (or terror) which conveniently neglect to mention the Soviet MRBM threat, indicate considerable lack of comprehension. And is it not certain that prior to attack this MRBM threat would grow?

It used to be asserted that the U.S. deterrent was not "credible" because the USSR could effectively attack North America. I submit that the present disintegration of NATO is attributable, at least in part, to the fact that the Soviet threat against America is less imminent than against Europe—if the estimates are correct. Perhaps the riddle of why the Soviets have not yet built a larger ICBM force, may be explained by strictly political strategy: the present Soviet posture effectively intimidates Europe and invites a U.S. policy of accommodation. Even if the Soviet Union should run out of war potential, the political effect of the imbalance in Soviet capabilities has already been to unbalance NATO.

How can the alliance be defended *in toto* if at the moment of truth, national strategies of *sauve qui peut* might enhance the chances of survival or, at least, the hopes for survival?

For Europe to hold and survive, there must be a capability in Europe to ward off missile attack instantly, effectively oppose airborne attack within one or two hours, intercept air attack within minutes and up to two or three hours, and stop ground attack within a few short hours. The times for defense against submarine-launched missiles may vary from a few seconds to hours and days.

The implication is that present arrangements, according to which nuclear weapons are to be released from Washington, can be practical only for *some* types of defense. Unfortunately, the *most important* types of defense, notably missile defense, cannot work without automatic and immediate nuclear response. Except in case of a delay in the Soviet attack on Europe, no immediate and effective counteraction is possible if authorization for weapon use must be requested from Washington.

Present trigger arrangements cannot be expected to work even if tactical warning operates at perfection. They might work if there were strategic warning, and if the authorization were given ahead of time. They must fail if in case of tactical warning only the President is delayed and if the enemy succeeds in interfering with communications.

An unexpected and disturbing implication has been brought out by recent unhappy events. A large-scale attack may be preceded by, or be predicated on, the assassination or, for that matter, the medical incapacitation of the President of the United States. It is conceivable that the President may not have the physical capability of issuing the requisite orders without delay; for example, he may be under an anesthetic. Yet legally no one may act on his behalf. It would seem that we are asking a great deal of our allies by insisting that they accept our good faith on complete trust, when at the same time we are neglecting to institute those constitutional and legal changes that are necessary to insure fulfillment of our commitments.

The question is whether there may be solutions through which, while the United States retains control over its nuclear weapons, the Europeans may be acquiring that degree of security to which they are entitled.

Before proceeding, I would like to state that opposition to the "proliferation" of nuclear weapons reminds me of Don Quixote's fight with the windmills. The whole point of Cervantes' story was that Don Quixote was unable to halt technological change.

Since technology always spreads sooner or later, military forces, to be effective, will have to include nuclear weapons ultimately and must be prepared to fight nuclear engagements. Forces without modern arms will be little more than police establishments. There may be reason for delaying this process in a period of reasonably assured peace, but it makes little sense to withhold arms from peaceful people who need them for defense and deterrence.

On the other hand, this danger of proliferation is in part chimerical because many of the nations which have the scientists to construct nuclear weapons, lack the necessary funds, while many of those who have the funds, lack the industrial capacity to produce modern delivery systems. And quite a few nations lack the will to obtain modern arms.

Thus, additional nations will have nuclear weapons but there will not be a "prolific" spread of nuclear capabilities. There will be less of a "proliferation" than occurred with aircraft, heavy artillery, and modern naval weapons, e.g., carriers and submarines. All in all, "proliferation" may be a matter of two dozen nations and probably far less.

Presently less then ten nations are able to produce effective modern weapons. Not more than five can build the *whole* set of weapons systems required for all-out conflict.

There is, obviously, no need for the United States to distribute nuclear weapons like so much foreign aid. Nor is it to be overlooked that most of our allies remain woefully uninformed about the strategic, tactical, and organizational correlates of nuclear weaponry—a situation which has allowed the United States to stick far too long to impractical policies but which does not now require undue haste in correction.

Finally, I see no pressing reason for transfer of ownership of U.S. produced equipment. The Europeans need nuclear weapons, but, with a few exceptions, they are not ready to pay for them. The Europeans have yet to take adequate steps to pool their resources, and some members of NATO do not devote much attention to the exigencies of modern war.

But I do see a very strong requirement to (1) keep the alliance going by allowing to each member his legitimate share of security; (2) help the allies set up requisite R & D and production facilities or, if it be advisable to keep certain types of facilities within the Western Hemisphere, to sell them, at cost price, the weapons they do need for their defense; (3) abstain from interfering with, and blocking allied efforts in modern weaponry; and (4) forgo the making of unilateral decisions in key defense problems.

There is not too much disagreement that the nuclear problem is the root cause of the various factors causing the gradual disintegration of NATO. This does not mean that each European army now wants or needs nuclear weapons of its own. But forces that are not properly armed cannot defend themselves; moreover, a disarmed Europe does not add to U.S. strength. Since an alliance is supposed to strengthen *all* partners, NATO is becoming increasingly useless.

It is quite true that the national interest of the United States demands the protection of Europe from Communist conquest. Under present arrangements we have to perform this job virtually unaided, granted that the overseas bases are a prerequisite for doing the job at all, and granted, too, that we just might be able to arm our allies in time. But we remain, within NATO, the monopolist of power. Given a monopoly of power, it creates only trouble and paralysis if the monopolist "concerts" or "coordinates" his policies with those he is protecting or, in fact, commanding; and so long as he remains the monopolist, he carries all the significant expenses—though by no means all the risks.

The policy of nuclear "monopoly" (within the free world) can be but a transitional policy; or else we shall help world peace better by dissolving NATO and inviting the Europeans to provide for their own defense.

The proper solution, of course, is to keep and revitalize NATO. President Kennedy, who was anything but friendly toward modern arms, stated on May 17, 1961, that we "must make certain . . . nuclear weapons will continue to be available for the defense of the entire treaty area"; control of these weapons must be such that "the needs of all NATO countries" will be met. This is the correct approach.

The nuclear problem has numerous ramifications. I suggest, however, that the so-called "trigger" problem is the central issue within the nuclear complex. Once the trigger problem has been disposed of satisfactorily, other solutions will come more easily. Therefore, I want to devote the rest of this essay to the "trigger."

The Trigger Problem

If NATO were to embark on offensive war, there would be ample time to make that decision jointly. The same is true if a single NATO member were deciding to resort to war: that government would have time enough to make its decision and transmit the orders, and it also would have the opportunity to consult its allies. In fact, no NATO member would embark on war without previous consultation, and hardly any NATO partner would take the risk of plunging into conflict without being assured of allied support. Therefore, *the so-called "trigger" problem arises only within the framework of a defensive or a "second strike" strategy against sudden and rapid aggression.* In this case, the task is to take immediate counteractions through which the sequence of the enemy offensive can be disturbed and friendly forces, blood, and treasure protected.

This requires that enemy missiles and aircraft be shot down as soon as they penetrate into friendly space, and notably that nuclear attacks against storage sites, troop concentrations, and ships be neutralized.

The second requirement is that as soon as the warning whistle sounds, weapons-equipped aircraft take off. A little reflection shows that even if the weapons were already loaded, many aircraft would lack the time to get off the ground before the runways were under attack. Naturally, those aircraft which are kept on airborne alert and which, by definition, would be sent aloft prior to explicit warning, must carry the nuclear weapons on board. The situation is the same for ships that leave port *in extremis* or are at sea.

Upon warning—and this is the third requirement—ground forces would deploy to battle positions. Thus, they too must be furnished immediately with the nuclear components of their combat weapons.

All this is commonplace. For example, the whole agitation about such questions as "fail-safe" arose precisely because U.S. alert bombers carry the bomb on *ante-bellum* flights. Instant readiness, therefore, is a clear-cut defense requirement not only for American forces in America, but also for Europe. The requirement applies to NATO as a whole. Indeed, unless this requirement is satisfied, NATO would probably fall apart under the first blows.

I propose that a solution be sought along the following lines:

As a fundamental step forward, NATO builds up a joint warning system, including space capabilities, a NATO-wide data-handling system, and a net of intelligence situation rooms that are attached to each major decision-maker and are interconnected in such a way that each change will be automatically registered in each room. Given adequate warning times, the allies consult through a NATO-wide net of Presidential hot lines and make joint decisions, including those designed to persuade the aggressor to desist.

In the absence of early warning and in the face of an unfolding "bolt from the blue" attack, smooth and dependable cooperation is brought about in the following manner:

1. The principle is accepted that upon invasion of friendly airspace and territory, all invading weapons and forces will automatically be opposed with suitable counter-weapons, the explosions to occur on *our* side of the border. This principle applies to anti-missile and anti-aircraft weapons, ground mines, and short-range tactical weapons, as well as to their nuclear components.
2. The immediate response weapons are of such yields that they would be unsatisfactory for attack on enemy ground targets across the border. They should be clean. Whenever possible, delivery means positioned in the border zone should be of such ranges and should incorporate such other control features, that offensive utilization would not be feasible. (This type of arrangement could be incorporated into an "arms control" agreement, or a *modus vivendi,* with the Warsaw Pact countries.)
3. These weapons should be constantly guarded and in some key locations operated by American troops. There should be daily or, if the situation demands, hourly checks on whether the nuclear components remain in place. The system could be similar to that used by night watchmen recording their rounds. The warheads themselves could be tied to an electronic system that would report whenever the components are being handled.
4. To guard the weapon designs whenever this is required, the nuclear components should be handled by U.S. personnel only.
5. On multiple-seat aircraft, the weapon should be under the control of an American officer. Single-seat loaded aircraft would be flown by Americans.

6. A serious difficulty would arise with respect to long-range missiles. It is to be presumed that NATO missile sites would be among the primary targets of sudden aggression. Hence, unless the friendly missiles were launched immediately, the sites would be hit and a portion of the NATO missile force would be destroyed before it could be used. On the other hand, if the missile force were committed automatically, the ability to control the response would be lost. This difficulty may be reduced through mobility, i.e., Europe-based missiles should not be in fixed sites but should be airborne and shipborne, and perhaps, truck or railroad-borne. This does not exclude fixed sites in all those locations where the launchers actually can be hardened economically to withstand the impact caused by a given combination of yield and accuracy. (In other words: future sites must be hardened far beyond present standards. Furthermore, there is an urgent need for long-endurance aircraft with highly accurate air-to-ground missiles.)
7. It is agreed that a limited number of suspect radar tracks and other indicators of attack, or limited border violations, need not lead to automatic response, on the grounds that there may be an inadvertent mistake or a false signal. However, if there are agreed-upon indicators of serious attack, and these indicators reach a certain quantitative level, the defense will be ordered into action immediately. Let me repeat: hostile targets initially would be destroyed only within friendly space.
8. Given evidence of an all-out attack—that is, the number of incoming weapons exceeds a certain limit—the retaliatory force is ordered into action, notably the long-range missiles that are in fixed installations. (Obviously, many of the long-range missile sites should be to the rear to allow maximum time for decision-making and launch. A few should be forward to draw fire and render the "warning" unequivocal.)
9. To insure timely and comprehensive response, radar signals, impact and damage reports, and other indicators should be piped into an electronic command-control-communications (CCC) system, fed into computers, and tallied against previously made response decisions that were programmed into the computers at an earlier time. *The computers would determine the nature of the attack and, according to NATO-wide agreements made beforehand, issue specific response "go" signals into the command channels; simultaneously, the pertinent nuclear weapons would be "unlocked" for mounting, deployment, and detonation.*
10. Response decisions could be graduated according to the weight of attack, as well as according to other criteria.
11. Arrangements should exist to allow the President to "override" pre-programmed decisions.
12. Arrangements might be made to prevent the computers from

issuing response "go" decisions in all those cases where recorded events depart markedly from anticipated situations.

13. After the pre-programmed response decisions have gone into effect, "live decisions" could be made with respect to retaliatory and counter-offensive operations.
14. Pre-programmed decisions could be made in case the President of the United States is unable to issue his orders or communicate his "live" decisions. In the absence of the principal decision-maker in Washington, as well as in other NATO capitals, deputies must be readily available to the CCC system, preferably at secret command posts that are relatively safe from attack. (This sort of continuous manning is routine in the Fire Department but remains to be organized at the summits of strategic leadership.)
15. The computers and related CCC systems must be highly secure and "invulnerable," and should be several times duplicative.
16. Each computer must be so programmed that in case of attack upon the computer installation, or any tampering with the machine, the particular computer turns itself off. Simultaneously a warning would be flashed to the other computer installations.

Is this gadgetry to solve a political problem? To fend off a combined missile-air-ground attack with any degree of success, the defender requires an elaborate system consisting of radars and other sensors, CCC, data handling, and computers. Given the facts of modern technology, such a system is mandatory. Indeed, systems of this type are being built or are in existence. Hence, the "gadgetry" is, or will become, part of national and international life.

The change that is proposed here is not that certain decisions be pre-programmed; pre-programming is by no means a novelty, on the contrary, it is becoming part of human existence.

Nor is it, concept-wise, a real novelty to pre-program Presidential decisions. It stands to reason that the particulars of foreseeable response decisions must be thought out and programmed beforehand: this is the nature of a war plan. Improvisation is *not* a war plan and usually is not even feasible; if attempted, it often leads to disaster. Hence, in an emergency not much can be done to change existing plans, except to hold up execution of the war plan or make a fast choice between alternate "pre-programmed" plans. *The novelty, therefore, is only that the "go" signal and the choice of plan are pre-programmed; and furthermore, that a system of this sort can be used to achieve allied unity with respect to the major threat and to facilitate, accelerate and render more meaningful, allied consultations with respect to any and all threats.*

Pre-programming of responses can be accomplished with considerable effectiveness. Actually, the computers have a greater capability than human brains of handling a mass of confusing data rapidly. Therefore, they are better able to decide than the President, the Secretary of Defense, and the Joint Chiefs, which war plan fits the best; and it is clear that in a threat situation which is developing with supersonic speed, no one can invent a new war plan. Even if the intuition were to occur with the speed of light, the implementation of a new concept or a single major change requires months: "Order—counter-order—disorder," Napoleon used to say. The formula is still correct, and we had better keep it in mind. Pre-programming offers the best insurance we can devise against over- and under-reactions or false reactions to concrete military challenges.

It must be stressed that this concept of pre-programming does *not* presuppose predictability of future situations which, indeed, cannot be foreseen. The proposal envisages that pre-programming be done on a continuous basis; ideally, therefore, the decisions develop with the situation. It is also envisaged that in case the type of developing threat was unpredicted—in spite of systematic attempts to identify a maximum number of typical attack situations—the programmed decisions can be suspended; the computers would order "no-go," i.e., only precautionary actions would be put into effect.

Furthermore, the computers would perform only in those instances where deliberate command decisions *are not feasible.* They would be used by decision-makers whenever those decision-makers are able to act, but they would *not* substitute for them. Finally, pre-programming would *not* extend beyond the initial encounters.

Hence the computers, as usual, do *not* replace man, but rather support him. In this particular case, the computers would operate as substitutes *if,* and *to the extent* that, the President were unable to act. This does not mean, of course, that human substitutes for the President should not also be used. But the assignment of the most vital Presidential action to another person, be it only on a contingency basis, would raise more or less insoluble questions. *Pre-programmed decision making is entirely within the prerogative of the President.*

Perhaps the predictability problem can be clarified in still another way. Far from being tied to prophecy, the computers would react to a set of hypotheses: "if—then." The NATO members would agree, for example, that x missile tracks moving within y seconds from Soviet bases to targets in Europe and North America, call for immediate alert; that $2x$ tracks within $2y$ seconds call for interception; and that $3x$ tracks within $3y$ seconds call for a full "go" signal. This is a simplified model, of course, but it still describes the essence of the challenge.

Responses could also be planned against single tracks directed at such targets as Washington, London, Paris, and Bonn. However, these types of "minimum situations" are less important than responses that are pre-programmed against large numbers of tracks.

The point, be it repeated, is that pre-programmed decisions would be made *only* with respect to those threats that allow no time for any other type of decision making. By and large, the solution applies only to the threat of massive air-missile attack. All threats that move slowly enough to allow deliberation would be answered in the customary manner. Moreover, the pre-programmed decision would be invoked only if the threat exceeds a certain quantitative level.

Under this scheme, then, it is not necessary to predict "situations." It is merely necessary to agree that a certain number of incoming missiles (and bombers and spacecraft) calls for certain counter-actions.

In its essence, this scheme is not different from the type of instruction that for centuries has been given to frontier guards.

Such pre-programming (with the possibility of override) is entirely in our own U.S. survival interest. This nation cannot afford that the President, for whatever reason, may be delayed in making a decision whose precise timing could make all the difference in the world. Nor can we afford for our forces in Europe to be destroyed because we denied to them the authority to attempt an optimal defense.

In view of the enormous strain under which a President would labor in a "clear warning" situation, and the probability that he himself would be a target for physical or psychological attack, and in view of the possibility that an attack might occur when the President is, for example, in surgery or under the influence of anesthesia, it would be preferable to make the vital or fatal response decision under conditions that allow rational deliberation.

A pre-programmed decision would be a far better decision than one made in panic—especially if the panic were to grip the decision-makers of all major NATO countries simultaneously.

Knowledge on the part of the enemy that response decisions have been pre-programmed would strengthen deterrence of aggression, render less attractive a possible recourse to assassination or psychological pressure on the President of the United States, and preclude a number of conceivable radical methods of attack. Thus, the United States, in its own self-interest, needs the pre-programming of military response decisions.

In turn, the pre-programming of defensive responses would allow the solidification of the NATO alliance. The main powers could, at leisure, debate the precise circumstances under which automatic nuclear defense would or would not be resorted to. The United States would be able to determine with precision what sort of enemy attack our allies want to have repelled, and with what means. Mutual agreements could then be hammered out, even to a point where *different* responses are pre-programmed with different nations.

Under this procedure, all participants would assume mutual obligations, and pre-programmed arrangements would be considered binding on all governments that did agree. It is NATO policy even now that agreed-upon decisions can be changed only through the concurrence of all, just as it is NATO policy to have the Council develop "guidelines" for the employment of military power. Why should there be objection to putting such "guidelines" on computers in the CCC system?

There could be different types of commitments, some of them binding until formally renegotiated, others subject to limited modifications during an emergency. There could be mechanisms to allow final consultation between the main capitals, and special buttons to record confirmation or cancellation. The methodology and the decisions must be refined constantly by re-evaluating enemy attack strategies and friendly defensive measures and by changing pre-programmed decisions as new technologies and situations arise.

It could be provided that the arrangement be reviewed after each major change of government.

Another refinement would be to have the President confirm specifically—and electronically—his pre-programmed decisions daily after the regular intelligence briefing; to put a "button" at his disposal whenever during the day a development induces him to suspend any pre-programmed decision; and to have such hold action communicated instantly to the leading allies. (Such immediate and automatic communication denotes what is, or *should* be, meant by the word "consultation" within the NATO alliance.)

Once instant death is precluded through immediate response arrangements, subsequent decisions can be made more leisurely and also more safely, including last minute attempts to stop the war that seems to have begun. Even the "pause" can be rendered more effective if the enemy knows that pre-programming reduces the prospects of a successful, sudden mass attack.

Political agreement (practically everybody stresses this) is the key to an effective NATO strategy. But it seems to be rather difficult to obtain such agreement. Apparently, the methodology of seeking consensus remains that of traditional diplomacy, with a few "standing groups" thrown in. I presume that, as a technique, diplomacy is adequate—and indispensable—to achieve agreement about trade policies and about such military matters as a decision to defend a certain piece of real estate. I am reasonably certain, however, that bureaucratic diplomacy, even if it were practiced by soldiers and not by military amateurs, is not suited for the planning of effective response actions against air-missile-space attack.

A great deal of strategic disagreement is derived from the fact that the various nations operate on only partially convergent intelligence data and often on highly divergent intelligence estimates. The primary decision-makers usually are not aware of the nature and causes of these intelligence differences and do not properly understand the methodology of modern intelligence. For that matter, only a few of them devote much time to this whole complex of questions, or even realize the crucial importance of intelligence (in lieu of snap judgments). I suggest that intelligence divergence is among the main causes of our strategic troubles. With present arrangements, ineffectiveness of the alliance is almost inevitable.

It is all too easy to reject a plea for a novel approach as "utopianism." I consider it eminently practical to establish compatible situation rooms in the White House and Elysées of the main allies. I believe that once a month, or once a week, on closed TV circuits, the principal decision-makers, supported by the art of simultaneous translation, are capable of participating in systematic intelligence discussions. I think it is feasible to rotate among the main members of the alliance intelligence briefings presented to the NATO heads. I am convinced that it would be useful to identify divergence in the interpretations. The nature of the threat, in most of its aspects, is subject to objective determination. I would presume that these intelligence sessions could be used, for example, through presentation of simulated war games, to evaluate the nature and effectiveness of agreed-upon responses.

These debates would be informal sessions and there would be no decisions unless a formal procedure were invoked. The principal decision-makers would discuss their variances and they might exchange ideas. They could educate each other in their respective strategic problems. *They would be communicating on the most important problems facing our nations.* In this age of communication, leaders of state still remain isolated from one another.

I do not know whether this sort of methodology would culminate in a meeting of the minds. Since one and the same set of facts may lend itself to different courses of action, divergence may—and perhaps should—continue. But if NATO is ever to arrive at effective response actions and if there is to be mutual confidence, some such system is necessary. Once there is a common "data base" and mutual comprehension, there exists a better chance of agreement on the essential points and of preserving confidence in the face of disagreement on minor points.

It is attractive to think that electronics could partially replace bureaucratic "channels" and "layers" and involve the heads of state in the realistic and concrete aspects of the problems about which, all too often, they are given but hazy information. Perhaps the method might be applicable to areas other than strategy. Has it not yet dawned on us that a yearly or biannual face-to-face meeting with a crowded agenda is *not* an adequate method of communication and is not likely to result in "rapport"?

This is not the place to argue with those who would contend that such a joint intelligence and warning effort at the NATO summit would not be feasible for assorted reasons of security. I do not deny that serious security problems are involved, but I believe that those would be soluble. It is more difficult to get the heads of state to agree on a standardized procedure, or even to indulge in frequent bilateral or multilateral telephone conversations.

An equally important point is that the findings of intelligence, including estimates about the severity and timing of the threat, are not matters that, in democracies, should be kept classified. For NATO to work effectively, popular consensus is needed—and many voters in all the member countries do not even know NATO exists, let alone what it is good for. To achieve this consensus, the best information must be made available, just as it is now recognized that for virtually all civilian activities statistical information is indispensable. (Stalin used to classify census data; sometimes we are almost as silly.) The fact is that the United States does release some basic estimates through Department of Defense testimony before Congress, usually at the beginning of each year. So why not do a really good job and persuade our allies that the principles of the open society also apply to our common tasks in security? Let us keep the *real* secrets classified, but let us eliminate those bureaucratic practices of unnecessary pseudo-security, which in addition to offering opportunities to defeatist propaganda, preclude strategic unity within the alliance and deny popular support to NATO's most important security decisions. We cannot preserve an open society when the most vital type of information is needlessly kept secret.

We do live in an age of political and strategic interdependence; but if this interdependence is to become a reality that transcends hidebound traditions, sonorous phrases, and inspired speeches, we must use new techniques and technologies, and must apply those when there still is time. More than ever, war must be won (or better still, averted) by the decisions that are made in peace.

We must look forward to threats and techniques. But we must also look backward to the best tradition of the Western world—a tradition, alas, that we have nearly forgotten, and that was persuasively expressed by Lord Chesterfield: "Never put off till tomorrow what you can do today."

The Case for a Multinational Nuclear Strike Force

—*SIR JOHN SLESSOR*

Clausewitz showed convincingly and logically that political superiority, acquired through a country's foreign policy, is an essential element of war. . . . Today a great power's foreign policy can only be a policy of coalition, and this involves accepting certain limitations of national sovereignty, a fact of which the German leaders in both world wars were still completely unaware.

General F. Von Senger und Etterlin,
Neither Fear nor Hope.

The Relevance of History

In this nuclear age, most of the history of past wars is wholly irrelevant to the future. But we can still learn something from it in one critically important field—that of political reactions and human behavior under the stress of war or the threat of imminent war. World War II was the first great war of which it was clear in advance that death and destruction would not be confined to the military forces in the field, but would have a direct and immediate impact on the civilian populations at home; so the history of what actually happened in that context before and after its outbreak in September 1939 is, to my mind, an indispensable background to any realistic examination of strategic policy in an age when the vital need is the prevention of war—which, unhappily, still involves the capacity to fight it effectively if it is forced upon us.

The tendency of history to repeat itself is a reason to welcome one of the decisions agreed at Nassau in December 1962, namely, the agreement to assign Bomber Command of the RAF to NATO.

Crisis in 1939-40

In 1939 I was Director of Plans on the Air Staff in London. As such I was appointed the Air Force member of the British team in the shockingly belated Anglo-French Staff Conversations in the spring of that year. Looking back on it today it seems almost incredible that up to that time, six months before the outbreak of war, there had been virtually no contacts between the British and French Staffs, except some tentative administrative arrangements—expressly without commitment—in connection with a possible dispatch to France of two divisions and the twenty light-bomber squadrons of the Advanced Air Striking Force (AASF) of Bomber Command in the event of war. That bore no relation to any common policy. There was no formal alliance, no commitment on our part to send an Army Expeditionary Force and Air Contingent to France, and, in short, no combined strategic planning to meet German aggression against either France or Britain.

The British Air Staff had, of course, for several years been planning for the employment of Bomber Command in the event of war. And our conception of its role—perhaps naturally in view of the lack of any combined policy or planning with the French—had been one of direct attack on Germany, or more accurately counterattack, because of the widespread apprehension in Britain about the possibility of what was called a "knockout blow" by the German Air Force against our Island. Today, in the light of experience of air warfare that we then lacked, we may smile at those fears; it might, however, be salutary to look back and remember them before we in Britain or France talk too lightheartedly about independent nuclear deterrents.

But the point here is this: We know that we were in no position to fight Nazi Germany except in combination with France, and we made the reasonable assumption that we should be able to count on the use of French airfields in war—in fact, as I have said, we had actually held some discussions about the matter with the French Staff on the administrative level. But what we wanted those airfields for, in the absence of any combined plan, was to base our short-range light bombers nearer to their German targets than they could be in our own country, to play their part in our plans for counterattack against the German air force, war industry, oil resources, and so forth.

When, at last, pressure by our Chiefs of Staff, supported by Mr. Eden as Foreign Secretary, resulted in agreement to undertake combined strategic planning (and our first meeting was not till March 29, 1939), it was perhaps natural that we British officers should lay more stress on the possibility of a knockout blow against England, and that our French colleagues should emphasize more strongly the dangers of an invasion of France—and they, of course, as it turned out, were right.

But we were agreed on the possibility of an enemy offensive through Belgium and Holland into France; and the French were quite naturally and rightly obsessed with the need to halt that invasion. And that led them—again I think perhaps naturally—to entertain some suspicions of our intentions for the use of Bomber Command. We had previously been at pains to make clear to them that the object of sending the AASF to France was to bomb Germany, not to support the French Army, which we thought was the job of the French Air Force. But I hope my French friends will forgive me for saying that the Armée de l'Air was not very strong in 1939—which was more the fault of the politicians than of General Vuillemin and the French Air Staff. And our colleagues in the Staff Conversations clearly saw visions of our carrying on from some of their airfields a sort of private war—a *guerre de course*—against Germany, leaving their very inadequate Air Force to support their *Couverture* divisions in resisting the invasion.

I had some difficulty in persuading them that as members of an alliance we should certainly not do any such thing, and finally handed them a memorandum containing a formal undertaking of which I need quote only the last paragraph: "A German attack by land and air in great force directed against France . . . would constitute a decisive situation and, in these circumstances, collaboration with the French Army and Air Force in stemming the invasion would become the primary commitment of the British Bomber Command."

Eleven years later, as Chief of the Air Staff, I attended one of the early conferences of NATO General Officers, at the RAF School of Land-Air Warfare. I found there a hint of the same sort of suspicions on the part of our European allies about our intentions for the use of Bomber Command, this time in relation to the threat of a Russian invasion of Germany. And I found it necessary to repeat in almost identical words the formal assurance that I had given to the French eleven years earlier.

Now, in order to point more clearly the moral I want to draw from this, I must go back to what actually did happen when the German invasion put an end to the *drole de guerre* in May 1940.

The light-bomber squadrons based in France with obsolete Fairey

Battles were immediately thrown into the battle in direct support of the armies, and were virtually wiped out in the process; we need not here concern ourselves further with them, except to note that their crews died because we had failed to provide them with a more modern type in time. The problem of the employment of the remainder of Bomber Command from bases in England was less straightforward; and it was the subject of protracted discussions with General Gamelin and the French Government during the opening months of the war, in fact almost up to the time when it was clear that the battle of France was over. By that time the RAF had lost in only about four weeks of fighting nearly 1,000 aircraft, about 400 of which were of Bomber Command, whose total first line strength was then only about 500—most of the balance being fighters which we desperately needed for the defense of Britain in the battle we knew must follow.

During and subsequent to the Anglo-French Conversations we in the Air Staff had come to the conclusion that the best way of delaying the advance of the German armies into the Low Countries, which all agreed would be the *Schwerpunkt* of the invasion (and we knew we could do no more than delay it), would be to attack the Ruhr with its network of rail and road communications. Let me emphasize here that the accusation sometimes leveled against us, that we indulged a passion for "strategic" bombing at the expense of our ability to stem the invasion, is wholly unjustified. Our appreciation of the situation led us honestly to believe—and there is still no evidence that we were wrong—that we could do more to dislocate and delay the communications serving the enemy's advance through Belgium and Holland (what we should now call interdiction) in this area than in any other; and in this belief we had the powerful support of no less a person than the CIGS, General Ironside—right up to the very last moment when he suddenly and unaccountably changed his mind.

This policy was approved in October 1939 by a committee of the British War Cabinet, and in the subsequent months was repeatedly pressed upon the French authorities. For six months they strongly resisted it on the grounds that the inevitable retaliation by the enemy would, to begin with, endanger the deployment of the French Army, and then lay open their cities to a scale of attack against which they were in no position to defend themselves. It was not until April 23—less than three weeks before the invasion started—that the Allied Supreme War Council approved a somewhat watered-down version of the plan for attack on the Ruhr communications.

Even when the invasion began on May 10, the British War Cabinet (including, be it noted, Mr. Churchill who could hardly be accused of lacking offensive spirit) still withheld authority to put this plan into effect; and it was not until after the German bombing of Rotterdam four days later that the first attacks on the Ruhr were made—a delay which might have proved disastrous had there in fact been any chance of any plan being really effective in the circumstances of that time, which of course we now know there was not.

Even so we were not allowed to continue for more than two nights in the face of the desperate—and humanly understandable—pressure from the French for closer support in the immediate battle zone. From then on the main effort of Bomber Command was directed to trying vainly to make what were known as *coupures* on roads, railways, bridges, etc., close behind the battlefield—a task for which the primitive aircraft of the day were quite unfitted, which had been the reason for our resistance to this course of action in the earlier discussions with the French.

Another fact about the campaign of 1940 which, I am afraid, has not yet impressed itself sufficiently strongly on some of our governments, is that the German armies of that day whose government had appreciated the realities of what was then modern war went, like a hot knife through butter, through the armies of Britain and France, whose governments had refused to face up to the costs involved. It is difficult now to believe that we British, who invented the tank in 1916 (as we pioneered the technique of air support of armies in the desert a quarter of a century later), went to war in 1939 without a single armored division.

There is one bit of history of this grim time to which I must refer, because I think it also contains a lesson which is too often forgotten in present-day discussions about the use of "independent" national deterrents. That is the story of the operation with the unromantic code-name of "Haddock."

By the end of May 1940 it was pretty clear that Mussolini was going to intervene against us. On May 31 the Allied Supreme War Council agreed that in that event the RAF should immediately bomb the industrial cities of Northern Italy. The shorter range Wellington squadrons were to operate from an advanced refueling base in the Marseilles area, and on June 3 a Wing Headquarters and servicing echelon was dispatched to Salon. Italy declared war on June 10. And immediately the plan for the Haddock operation met with violent opposition from the French authorities, from the government, from General Vuillemin's headquarters, and from the local French Bomber Group Commander, on the grounds that Italian retaliation would fall on Marseilles, Lyons, and Paris. Mr. Churchill insisted that the operations should proceed in view of the agreement in the Supreme War Council; but on the night of June 11 when the first Wellingtons taxied into position, the French drove trucks onto the runways so that they could not take off.

I am not blaming the French for this, nor claiming that the British action was right; as a matter of fact I am sure, looking back on it, that we were wrong to press on with the operation with the totally inadequate resources available—indeed the few raids that did go to Milan and Turin before operations were suspended on the opening of negotiations for an armistice are rightly described in the British Official History as "singularly unprofitable." I tell the story merely to point a moral that we should never overlook when we are tempted to talk lightly about attacking independently an enormously more powerful enemy, whose retaliation today would be unthinkably more catastrophic than anything could have been in June 1940.

Cuba

Before going on to suggest some of the lessons we should learn from the experience of 1939-40, I must jump forward twenty-two years into the megaton age and recall one other bit of much more recent history, which I think holds out one of the most important lessons of all. I mean the Cuba episode. I hope none of us Europeans were foolish enough to believe that Cuba to Europe is what poor Mr. Chamberlain thought Czechoslovakia was to Britain in 1938—a faraway country of which we know nothing and which is not really of any direct concern to us. The Cuba issue was literally vital to each one of us; suffice it to ask what would have become of our confidence in America's ability to fulfill her obligations in the defense of Europe, had she been unable to face the implications of confronting such a direct and brazen threat to her own local security.

Very few people know what was in the famous unpublished letter from Khrushchev to Mr. Kennedy. But there is not the least doubt that in that awful week he looked over the brink at the genuine possibility of nuclear war, and was absolutely appalled at what he saw. It was a first and classic example of a nuclear deterrent in operation. That is the first point to remember.

The second is that there is neither evidence in history nor reason in common sense for a belief that the possibility of the British Bomber Command joining the U.S. Strategic Air Command in a nuclear war arising out of Cuba ever entered into Khrushchev's calculations. I have no doubt we would have done so, and in fact the Command was brought quietly but promptly to a high state of readiness. But I don't believe it ever occurred to Khrushchev, faced as he was with the colossal strength of American nuclear power.

A third point is that Khrushchev was, nevertheless, surely far too intelligent and shrewd an operator to have failed to draw the right conclusions from the fact that Mr. Kennedy received the solid and astonishingly prompt support of his allies in NATO and the Organization of American States.

A fourth is that the Cuba episode eliminated, or at least enormously reduced, the chances of war arising from miscalculation. Perhaps the most dangerous possibility of miscalculation used to lie in the idea that the United States was a "paper tiger"—that the Americans were soft and would not face the risk of nuclear war if or when the time ever came. Khrushchev at any rate clearly no longer cherished any illusions about that.

Now let me suggest some lessons which I think we should have learned—but am afraid some of us have not learned—from all this.

Counterattack on Heartland

The first and most obvious lesson for the future from Cuba is that the West must retain for as long as may be necessary (which means until comprehensive multilateral disarmament is a reality) the capacity to inflict nuclear catastrophe on the heartland of Russia in the event of a Russian attempt to inflict any sort of catastrophe on us. This is what is commonly but misleadingly described as *the* deterrent; it is an essential element in the deterrent, but not the only one. I do not propose to argue the need for it, because that is accepted by all but an insignificant minority.

On the other hand, it is time-honored principle that the force required to do any military job must clearly be enough to serve the purpose, but should be no more. "Enough," as Eisenhower once said, "is plenty." It is certainly unwise to have more than plenty in one element of military power at the expense of failure to have enough in another. No weight of heavy artillery in an army is any good if the infantry is hopelessly inadequate. Moreover, military thinkers from Sun Tzu in 400 B.C. to Vannevar Bush in 1950 A.D. have warned us against the self-defeating implications of overinsurance in armaments. In considering the problem of the strength necessary for this element of the deterrent, we are bound to take into account the fact that the issues at stake are so appalling compared to anything in history that it would be criminal folly to take any chances; we must allow a most generous margin for misjudgment in a situation which has no precedents to guide us. But margin piled upon margins can add up to political, economic, and military lunacy. In this element of the deterrent the United States now has, and still more when the Minutemen and Polaris programs are completed will have, more than enough—an enormous overkill potential, including second strike capacity.

We should never forget in this connection that a primary aim of Western policy is to work toward general comprehensive disarmament, which alone can give the world real security in the long term. That should mean that any military program, and particularly any increase over existing programs, should be subjected to the test of two questions:

First, is it absolutely indispensable to our security within the period before any really substantial measure of disarmament is conceivable? And secondly, is it likely to improve the chances of achieving general disarmament, or the reverse? There will always be a nice balance between the two; like most things in life this is not a straightforward matter of either—or. But I cannot avoid the impression that the second question seldom receives the consideration it deserves.

The moral is surely that anything more than American nuclear capacity, for the purpose of inflicting catastrophic punishment on Russia, is wholly unnecessary. And this applies more particularly to additions to allied strength which are solely for this purpose, or anyway can be useful for nothing else—into which category obviously fall the multilateral force (MLF) and the British Polaris submarine program. For the first, even its most ardent advocates hardly claim any military value; it is designed as a diplomatic or political measure—surely the most expensive and in my view the least necessary ever devised—and as such I shall touch on it later in this essay. The second raises the thorny problem of "independent national nuclear deterrents" to which I must now turn.

"Independent" National Deterrence

This seems to me to be the subject of more muddled thinking than any military problem in my experience. So much so that it seems necessary to emphasize the truism that an independent deterrent, to mean anything, must have two qualities: It must be really independent, and it must be a credible deterrent—something that really is able to deter.

Let us look first at the question of *independence*. That, if it means anything, must mean that the nation owning the nuclear force concerned must be politically and militarily capable in the last resort of *using* it independently, singlehandedly and, if necessary, against the wishes of its allies, to carry nuclear devastation into the heart of an enemy country—which, for all practical purposes as far as we are now concerned, we can take to be Russia (I am assuming for the purpose of this essay that China will not be a first-rate nuclear power within the next twenty years).

It could, I suppose, be argued that one of the nuclear powers might wish to use it, or the threat of it, against some nation other than Russia; against Egypt, for instance, to deter an attack on Israel, or China in a crisis over Formosa or Hong Kong, or Indonesia to curb Sukarno's ambitions to extend his lebensraum to the Philippines and the Thai border. I do not deny that a strictly limited use of some lower yield nuclear weapons is conceivable in certain circumstances in any of those areas. But I find it very difficult (to say the least) to visualize nuclear deterrence in the generally accepted sense of the term being employed in such circumstances. And my personal memories of the occasion in which I was involved many years ago, before Russia had an effective nuclear capacity, when some people in the United States wished to use atomic bombs against the Chinese at a critical stage of the Korean war, makes me tolerably certain that nuclear weapons would not in fact be used anywhere by any one nuclear power against the wishes of the others.

Now what do we mean by "deterrence"? General de Gaulle has defined it well. France, he has said, is a country "that could be destroyed at any moment unless the aggressor were turned from the attack by the certainty that he also would suffer destruction," and he added that the certainty must exist "that a riposte of the same kind and the same degree would be immediately released." Exactly! It would be impossible to define nuclear deterrence more clearly or correctly. The certainty must exist that a counterattack would in fact be launched that would bring equivalent destruction on Russia—or, at the very least, a high degree of uncertainty must exist that it would not be. It is no good basing a policy on a threat which you hope you will never have to implement—taking refuge in catch phrases about ability to inflict "unacceptable" damage on Russia. Who is going to decide, if the awful moment ever comes, what the Kremlin would regard as "unacceptable"? It is wholly unwise to ignore the possibility that the deterrent *might* fail to deter, and then the government of the country claiming nuclear independence would have to make the appalling decision to launch its nuclear strike force in a bilateral exchange with Russia, accepting (in the case of any ally but America) the certainty of virtually complete elimination. For the United States and Russia, with their vast strength and huge areas, the prospect would be a degree less gloomy; for Britain and France, the only advantage of a small missile-submarine force seems to me to be that it would afford us the doubtful consolation of a posthumous revenge—devastating no doubt but not lethal—after our countries and the bulk of our population had been obliterated.

I believe the whole military power of the Western alliance can be an effective deterrent because of the knowledge that, if it failed to deter, it could inflict far more total destruction upon Russia than she could impose upon the alliance as a whole. But frankly I do not believe that there is such a thing as independent nuclear deterrence, even for the United States. This may seem a contradiction of what I have just said about the Cuban affair. But I think that episode was *sui generis,* and do not believe the Kremlin will ever again be so stupid as to offer a challenge in an area where they are at such a hopeless disadvantage as they were in the Caribbean.

Anyway, suppose things had not turned out as they did in October 1962. Suppose there had been a Chamberlain in Britain and a Daladier in France and someone less tough than old Adenauer in Bonn, and those three allies had taken the line that Cuba was no business of theirs —would Mr. Kennedy have been able to sustain his courageous resolution to the point of nuclear war? Suppose there had been a Stalin instead of Khrushchev in Moscow, and his reaction to the American threat of blockade had been to seal the Berlin autobahn and move thirty or forty armored and motorized divisions up to the partition line —what then? Surely at least there must be serious doubt about the answer, and there should be no room for serious doubt in this equation. To me, the only thing about which there is no doubt is that in facing up to the threat of nuclear war we must do so, not individually, but as an alliance—*bras dessus bras dessous* as old Foch used to say.

If that is accepted—and I cannot see how it can be denied—it has a direct bearing on the problem of control of nuclear strategy, which I shall discuss later in this essay.

The French attitude to nuclear independence has, to me, an air of almost total unreality, and I doubt whether more than a very few people outside the Elysée really believe in it. I wonder whether the truth is not that General de Gaulle does not believe in the possibility of war as long as the United States retains her nuclear capacity, but that he regards his theoretical independence as a political symbol of the greatness of France and of her influence in world affairs. Looking back on Operation Haddock and the arguments about the Ruhr plan in 1940, does anyone really believe that even that indomitable man could actually launch his *force de frappe* in a singlehanded forlorn hope against the nuclear might of Russia?

As for the British position, it must, I think, be very difficult for foreigners to understand—it is difficult enough for many Englishmen, including myself; to me, and to many others who think like me, it seems (to put it mildly) to be equivocal.

There is one point on which I am in complete agreement with the British Government,* namely, their claim that our nuclear status and record gives us a special position of influence in the world, particularly in relation to negotiations about disarmament, the test ban, and so on. I have never suggested—and would never agree—that we British should throw away our nuclear capacity, short of effective general disarmament; goodness knows we are not now contributing such an effective share of the military burdens of the alliance as to entitle us to do that. But what gives us added influence in these world affairs is the fact that we are a formidable and very experienced nuclear power—not our pretensions to an independence that in point of fact we can never possess. And that in due course will also be true of France, when the *force de frappe* is a reality.

But apart from that, I confess I simply do not understand the

* The final version of this essay was completed in the late summer of 1964.

British Government's attitude. It was on their sensible if belated suggestion at Nassau that Bomber Command, elements of the U.S. Strategic Air Command and of Tactical Air Forces based in Europe were assigned as "part of a NATO nuclear force"—what in the jargon of today would be called a multinational force. But at Nassau also the multilateral force and the British Polaris submarine project first saw the light of day. The latter was to be part of the former, but in paragraph 9 of the Bahamas Statement: "The Prime Minister made it clear" (not, be it noted, "The President and the Prime Minister agreed" as in earlier paragraphs) that it could be withdrawn from "international defense of the Western Alliance" if the British Government decided at any time that "supreme national interests are at stake." Apparently the idea behind this extraordinary paragraph is that, despite the cancellation of Skybolt, the British Government retains an "Independent Nuclear Deterrent" of its own—or will when the Polaris submarines are built and the V-bombers can no longer penetrate Russian defenses without prohibitive loss. What else paragraph 9 means I do not pretend to understand. In any case, I should have thought there is only one "supreme national interest" and that is national survival, which can only be secured within the context of the Atlantic alliance. But apparently the theory is that some day in some part of the world (and some politicians have even mentioned Kuwait in this connection) a situation might arise in which the United States would say it is no concern of theirs, but we should regard the issue as being so nearly supreme a national interest that we should go it alone with Polaris submarines in the Persian Gulf or India Ocean or Far Eastern waters.

I have said enough earlier in this essay and elsewhere to make it clear that I simply cannot take this seriously. Perhaps the assumption is that we could indulge in a little private nuclear war with Sukarno, for instance, without any risk of Russian intervention against us. But is this a safe assumption? It may be. But is it a risk that any British Government would really take? If they miscalculated—what then? In coming to a decision to accept any risk of all-out nuclear war, it is literally vital to hold the strongest possible cards and for the stake to be no less than a matter of life or death. Cuba showed that as part of an alliance we would face the risk; independently, I do not for a moment believe we should.

If there is any risk of Russian intervention against us, we British and French can only face it as part of the alliance. Whether or not you are sure (as I am) that the Americans would not default on their obligations to NATO, whatever you may feel about the need to depend on the American alliance, we should be practical and mature enough to recognize that we can't do without it. Sir Alec Douglas-Home, when he was Foreign Secretary, said in a speech in Ottawa in May 1963 that a Russian missile threat against Britain would be so colossal that it would be deterred only by the combination of United States and British nuclear power. And in October he said in another speech that "without the closest alliance between the U.S. and Britain there is no balance of power and therefore no security. There is no substitute for NATO. Nothing less than an Atlantic alliance will do. That is vital to the security of our island." That is obviously true, and it is the more curious that he should still subscribe to paragraph 9 of the Nassau agreement, still insist on the need for Britain to have an "independent deterrent." So wise a statesman can hardly believe that as part of an allied deterrent four British Polaris submarines could possibly tip the scale either way. And as for *using* them independently against Russia, does anyone really believe we should do so—remembering that a man like Churchill and his colleagues in the British Cabinet, at a time when the threat we faced amounted to a few thousand tons of primitive conventional bombs, hesitated for five days to authorize bombing of Germany, though we were already at war and facing a brutal invasion of Europe?

I may be asked why, if we are so unlikely to act independently, need anyone worry about the British and French claim to nuclear independence? The answer is simple. As recent events have proved, this claim bedevils the unity of the alliance; tends to result in similar claims by other people and leads to proliferation of nuclear weapons; gives rise to absurdities like the MLF and the British Polaris submarine which, as sure as tomorrow's dawn, can only be at the expense of other really important contributions which we Europeans should be making to the common defense; and gravely prejudices our chances of making genuine progress toward comprehensive disarmament.

Direct Defense of Europe

Let me now turn to the other, and in my view equally important element of the deterrent—namely, our ability to present a really formidable direct defense against any attempt at invasion of Western Europe. I hope I have made it clear that I am not for a moment suggesting anything so silly as that we British should discard our very efficient nuclear strike force, or that the French should cancel theirs before they have it. On the contrary, I think they both have a critically important part to play in this other element of the deterrent.

I have already suggested in connection with Cuba that the first element could be incredible and ineffective unless the second is credible and effective. The plain fact is that, while we are talking of spending huge sums on Polaris surface ships and submarines, the second element of the deterrent is still neither credible nor effective. The presence of six excellent American divisions should not blind us to the probability that, at present, the rest of what we used to call the Shield would not be much more effective in stemming a Russian invasion tomorrow than the French and British armies were in stemming a German invasion twenty-four years ago. And let us not think solely in terms of divisions; we should know from bitter experience in World War II that divisions are cold meat without adequate air support.

I gave the assurance to which I have referred earlier in this essay —to the French twenty-five years ago and to the NATO Generals fourteen years ago—because I was (and remain) absolutely certain that, whatever might be the theoretically ideal employment of Bomber Command, in actual fact when the time came and the alliance was in danger from massive invasion of Europe, it would be politically impossible to use it for any other purpose than for stemming that invasion. May 1940 proved me right—so much so that we were forced by political pressure when the time came to use our bombers in a way that we knew was technically and tactically hopeless. But what we were trying to do with Bomber Command before we were diverted to the *coupure* policy might very well have been effective then if our aircraft had been of present day types, and would certainly be an essential requirement tomorrow—namely interdiction.

The allied armies today, even at their present strength, could be made capable of putting up an infinitely more formidable defense on the battlefield than they were able to in 1940, if they were properly deployed and endowed with good cross-country mobility and modern armor. The British battle forces, especially, could be made enormously more effective on the battlefield, with little if any increase in manpower, if we spent our money on adequate numbers of the really important things—V/STOL close-support aircraft, tactical missiles like Blue Water and antitank weapons like Swingfire—instead of squandering it on grossly expensive white elephants like Polaris submarines which, for us British, have absolutely no military justification whatsoever. But the forces under SHAPE exist to fight a battle if need be, and no battle plan is credible that does not provide for interdiction behind the battlefield, for stemming the forward flow of enemy reinforcements and supply, and paralyzing his movement of reserves.

I confess I am not clear—and doubt whether anybody is—about what this multilateral force, including the British submarines, is supposed to be going to do in war. I do not intend to argue whether or not mixed-manning is feasible, or whether all these Polaris vessels will be quickly sunk or not—all that sort of thing seems to me largely irrelevant. What I am clear about is that the last thing anyone who knows anything about air support of land operations would demand today for the purpose of tactical interdiction is a megaton missile floating about in or under the Atlantic or North Sea. On the other hand, for some years to come the V-bombers will remain well fitted for the interdiction role for which, owing to the shorter penetration involved,

Skybolt is not essential. And the Mirage IV's of the *force de frappe* will be even more suitable for that role.

A Realistic Plan for NATO

So that is what we should do. Forget these fancy gimmicks like mixed-manned ships and the British Polaris "deterrent," and instead use our resources for bringing our existing forces up to a condition in which they are fit to fight any future war in Europe, and to fulfill their essential obligations east of Suez. We should use what we have now, or are bound to require in any event to replace it, and make the multinational force a reality. I think we British are largely to blame for the pressure in favor of the MLF by our failure to put forward any alternative that would serve the political purpose without being a military monstrosity.

Here then is such an alternative.

We should leave the first element of the deterrent—the counterblow against the heartland of Russia—to the United States, accepting the reality that they would not use it if their allies were opposed to its use, and that we British and French could not use our nuclear weapons for that purpose except in combination with the United States. To those who object that a future President in Washington might be so unwise or so weak as to launch it against our express opposition or refuse to use it when he should, I would say that would be just too bad, but there is nothing we Europeans could do about it—having our own fractional "deterrents" would certainly not prevent that; what we should really need in the first case would be the ability to defend ourselves against the invasion which might well be the Russian riposte to an American threat. I need elaborate no further my utter disbelief that we should ever attack Russia independently of the United States.

We British and French should assign our Bomber Commands *unreservedly* to NATO, to form the hard core of an allied nuclear strike force under the command of SACEUR, with the primary role of defense against invasion. That force should also include all tactical air and missile forces of all the allies—other than the short-range "battlefield" weapons like Sergeant and Davy Crockett. It must include an American element; it must be a NATO force, not just a European one. The various national contingents should be grouped under a unified high command, subordinate to SACEUR, with a headquarters as fully international as SHAPE now is; and the commander should be a European officer, selected from among the principal European powers contributing forces to the command—who, of course, would include the Germans.

I do not speak parochially as an airman. I think it will be many years before the manned aircraft fades out for this sort of job, if it ever does; I look forward to seeing the allied interdiction force include the British TSR2 and the production version of the American TFX, and perhaps modern light bombers like the Buccaneer II. But it must also include the longer range tactical missiles like Pershing and Mace; and if or when technological advance leads us to the conclusion that tactical missiles can be effective from floating platforms, whether surface or submerged (and there would be obvious advantages in that), then they too should be included in this SHAPE force.

Our experience in 1940 underlines the obvious need for a firm, well-planned program of interdiction. But, like any well-conducted force, this command must also have alternative plans to meet varying contingencies, for which the necessary training must be carried out in peacetime. I do not mean only within the NATO area itself, to support the defense of the flanks in Turkey or Norway, for instance—that goes without saying. There must also be agreed arrangements whereby in certain circumstances some units—by no means necessarily only British—could be temporarily withdrawn to support Western obligations outside Europe, in the SEATO or CENTO area, for instance, or even to serve the interests of the free world elsewhere, as in the event of an attack by Indonesia on the Philippines or Malaysia, or a renewed attack by China against India.

The Problem of Control

Finally, I must refer to the key problem of the control of nuclear strategy. The thing that really bedevils this whole subject and is causing serious dissensions within the alliance is American insistence that the ultimate control in this quite vital matter must remain in American hands and American hands alone—the implication being (let us be frank) that their allies, except perhaps the British, cannot be trusted to handle these terrible toys. A distinguished American officer (General Ira Eaker) has recently described this attitude as being like a father saying to a retarded child, "you can only have an air gun; if I give you a .22 rifle, you might get into trouble." The United States really must come off this high horse—must accept the truth of what that great French architect of Atlantic unity, Jean Monnet, recently said. "You in the United States," he said in New York in January 1963, "must realize that the claims of Europe to share common responsibility and authority for decisions on defense, including the nuclear weapons, is natural, since any decision involves the very existence of the European peoples." With respect, it is no answer to say that the Congress will not have it. The alliance is as essential to American security as that of anyone else; and if Congressmen persist in an attitude that makes no sense, they cannot blame others for adopting attitudes that make no sense—and that may well end in the break-up of the alliance, as de Gaulle's reactions should have warned us.

Against the background of what I have said about our actually total interdependence in this business of nuclear strategy, I ask you to consider certain broad principles which I think I have learned from participation, at a pretty high level, in the working of a great alliance in war.

I submit that we only create unnecessary difficulties for ourselves when we insist on drawing blueprints in advance of exactly how decisions will be made in hypothetical circumstances, which are almost sure to be quite different if or when the time ever comes—circumstances, anyway, which will never arise if the alliance remains solid and strong. The supremely important condition is the unity and willing cohesion of the alliance—without willing cooperation an alliance simply does not work. To take a stand on rigid national positions, to insist in advance on inflexible systems of command organization, only inhibits cooperation. If we are really allies, pulling together as a team, almost any system of control will work—however untidy it may look in a diagram; if we are not, then no system will work, however theoretically perfect it may appear on paper. And we only handicap ourselves unnecessarily and weaken the alliance by indulging in unreasonable fears about what might or might not happen if some one ally at the last moment were to go crazy enough to want either to go it alone or stand out alone. Written agreements, when the chips are down under the stress of war or the threat of war, have an unhappy habit of meaning very little—another lesson from June 1940.

Now, the MLF project is designed to give the European allies, and apparently the Germans in particular, a share in that responsibility to which Jean Monnet referred. I believe it would do no such thing. I personally know of no evidence that responsible Germans are desperately concerned about having personal control of nuclear weapons of their own; but if they become so, they will surely not long be satisfied with a small but expensive share in the manning and command of an insignificantly small and militarily useless fraction of allied nuclear power, of which the ultimate control still rests in American hands. I submit that the alternative I have proposed will give them and all the European allies a more real "share of common responsibility and authority for decision on defense, including the nuclear weapons" at far less cost than this expensive contrivance would ever give them.

To serve this end—though not for that reason alone—certain quite drastic modifications are necessary in the system of direction and control in NATO. The first, which is anyway long overdue, is a remolding of the system at the top. The NATO Council must become a fully fledged Supreme War Council, strengthened on the civilian side for the proper exercise of political and economic control, and on the military side by reconstituting the Standing Group—transferred to Europe—as the highest echelon of an executive military staff working under the political direction of the Council.

If or when it ever comes to the real rub—to the point of the supreme crisis with which NATO exists to deal—there will, I believe, be more time for consultation than is commonly supposed. But it would be unrealistic to pretend that the final irrevocable decision to go to war could be made by a unanimous decision of the whole Council. That, by the way, is the real crux of the matter: *the decision to break off negotiations and accept the inevitability of war.* The consequential decision on the first use of nuclear weapons, which of course must rest with the highest political authority, would depend on the course of events in the opening stages of hostilities—like the decision to initiate bombing of Germany in 1940. That dreadful decision must in the last resort be delegated by the Council to a small cell representing the major partners and, whether we like it or not, it makes no sense to deny that the primary agent in that decision can only be the President of the United States, as incomparably the strongest partner. But the man or the few men who have the appalling responsibility of decision to pull the nuclear trigger or snap on the safety catch, must be able to do so on a clear basis of agreed policy.

This is the essential point—that all the allies whose lives depend on the decision of those few men must have a common knowledge of all the factors that should determine that decision if the need ever arises; they must all have a share in the formulation of the strategic policy to govern that decision, and in the broad planning of the action to give effect to it, including the action of SAC which should become a NATO force like everyone else. We made some limited steps in that direction in Athens and Ottawa; we must now carry them much further. Nobody pretends that will be easy, but it can be and has got to be done.

Lastly, there is one other major modification in the organization of the alliance which I believe to be of great psychological importance. It is obviously indispensable that we should retain the most rigorous system of control at all levels to safeguard against unauthorized firing of any nuclear weapon. But the allies of the United States will never be satisfied that they have a real share in the responsibility and authority for the use of nuclear weapons, as long as the control of the two-key system and the permissive electronic link rests solely in American hands. That control should be transferred to a specially recruited corps of international control officers under a NATO control agency answerable to the NATO Council. Ideally that system should be extended to

U.S. air and missile forces based in North America but that may be asking too much of the Congress, at least initially. It should certainly apply to all nuclear weapons based this side of the Atlantic, and I should like to see Britain give a lead by offering to place her nuclear weapons under the control of such a commission as soon as it could be formed.

This, I submit, is the way to satisfy all the allies that they have a real share in the responsibility and authority for nuclear strategy. It would be far more effective and economical, and could be brought to fruition much more quickly, than any newfangled multilateral force.

Requirements for a European Deterrent in the 1970's

—PHILIP E. MOSELY

At some time between 1970 and 1975, if Western Europe chooses to do so, and if the United States decides to help in this, it will, I believe, be possible for an integrated Western Europe to possess its own strategic deterrent. Whether this development is necessary is a separate question. Whether it is desirable is a third question. Whether it will turn out to be politically feasible is still a fourth question. What I propose to discuss here is a logically antecedent question: What would be the requirements for the creation of a West European nuclear deterrent by the 1970's?

Most discussions about an independent strategic deterrent for Europe start from the current situation. They deal primarily with the fact of the American near monopoly, within the Western alliance system, of the power and responsibility for nuclear deterrence. They often discuss various ways in which the power of decision about the possible use of the deterrent can be shared, or appear to be shared, by the United States with the major European members of NATO. Or else they consider the impact of present or potential national nuclear deterrents on the durability and operation of the alliance.

Looking Ahead

Many of the arguments for and against the creation of a seaborne multilateral nuclear force are centered on the first steps, rather than on its ultimate structure or its eventual impact on the balance of political influence within the Western alliance. What I propose to do here, instead, is to put the cart before the horse and to try to picture a West European deterrent which could be created between 1970 and 1975, and then to trace backward to the present some of the technological and political requirements that would have to be met.

This procedure, which is intellectually justifiable, is also logical in terms of political thinking. If Western Europe is to possess an independent strategic deterrent by 1975, it will have to set about procuring the equipment and training its integrated manpower by 1970. In order to begin these programs by 1970, both it and the United States will have to adopt a wide range of political and budgetary decisions between now and 1970. Finally, if representative democracies, with their gradual methods of achieving consensus, are to arrive at a whole series of unprecedented solutions to novel and complex problems of political and strategic power, they will have to discuss and debate them at length. Hence, it seems logical, if we arbitrarily choose the year 1975 for the establishment of an important new component of power, to begin discussing both its strategic modalities and its political implications without delay.

Western Europe even now has some of the elements required for creating and operating its own strategic deterrent. Its economic growth is proceeding at a steady pace, and it should be able by 1970 to bear the burden of providing for a separate nuclear deterrent. In addition, the establishment of a second Western deterrent should be much less costly than was the creation of the first deterrent force, that of the United States. The question of cost will be strongly influenced in turn by an American decision to cooperate or not to cooperate in this. The sharing by the United States of its accumulated scientific and technological knowledge and its strategic experience would greatly simplify and accelerate a similar European development, as well as make it far less costly. American trial-and-error experience with problems of command and control can also be transferred at a great saving of cost. Europe has the necessary skilled manpower, accustomed to military service, provided it wishes to use a part of that resource for this purpose. The main obstacles, then, are political, on both the European and the American side.

European Dependence and Western Strategy

That we are discussing a European deterrent at all is due to a major change in the strategic balance. For Europe, political dependence on the U.S. deterrent was a comfortable posture between 1945 and the late 1950's. It placed almost the entire burden of the strategic deterrent on the United States and left Europe free to concentrate on its economic and political recovery. The saving on the cost of strategic defense, together with Marshall Plan aid and Europe's own enlightened efforts to re-create "Europe" within its curtailed boundaries, allowed America's European allies to launch their part of the world into an economic revolution that has provided a most successful and dramatic refutation of Marxist predictions of disaster and of Communist hopes for expansion and eventual hegemony.

Since 1957 this posture of dependence has become an increasingly uncomfortable one. The emergence of an impressive Soviet nuclear-missile force made it clear that deterrence would henceforth be no longer a one-way street. This new factor raised the question whether America would stand willing in perpetuity to sacrifice its own cities and people for any issue short of its own survival. Put in a different way, the question was asked: What issues and interests would or would not constitute the *casus foederis* in a two-way nuclear war? Attempts, even minor ones, to bring about greater stability of antagonistic relations and even a partial relaxation of tensions between Moscow and Washington have also brought with them European suspicions and even accusations that the United States might be preparing to make a "deal" with Russia at the expense of Europe's interests, or at least over Europe's head. General de Gaulle and a good many other European spokesmen have asserted that the only way to assure respect for Europe's interests on the part of both the United States and the Soviet Union is for Europe to have its own nuclear deterrent, either national or regional in character.

This distrust seems to me unjust, unjustified, and dangerous. It is unjust because the United States has done and is doing far more than Europe to safeguard Europe's survival; it is not only providing the deterrent for the common defense of America and Europe but is also making a powerful and costly contribution to the defense of Europe on Europe's own soil. The distrust is unjustified because the lines between Western and Soviet power are so tightly drawn across Europe today that no substantial military move on either side can fail to be interpreted as an attempt to overturn the existing precarious balance.

This attitude of carping suspicion is dangerous because its constant repetition may some day persuade a Soviet political leader that certain partial encroachments on Western Europe would be tolerated by the United States and would lead to the panicky disintegration of the defenses of Western Europe. Be that as it may, a basic argument for establishing a West European deterrent would be to restore to an integrated Europe confidence in its ability to define its own spectrum of vital interests and to decide whether to defend those interests, with or without American participation. If Europe wishes to be independent of the American deterrent and to make its own basic decisions, it must possess a deterrent of its own.

Concern for European Interests

A second motive, the converse to the first, is the fear, not that the United States will refuse to use its strategic deterrent, but that it will actually use it and use it in places and for purposes that have little or nothing to do with Europe's own vital interests. The firm but restrained U.S. posture in the Cuban missile crisis of October 1962 swept away, at least for the time being, European fears that the U.S. deterrent was perhaps no longer adequate or that perhaps America was incapable politically of presenting an effective nuclear threat and making it stick.

In Europe the immediate reaction to the crisis was one of pride and relief at American power and at the skill and strength of will shown by the Kennedy Administration. Yet the backwash, especially among some influential groups, had some less favorable side-effects. Again the United States' action, however sound in purpose and execution, had demonstrated that the decision on war or peace rested solely in the hands of the American President, without any effective influence being exerted even by his most trusted allies. Europe's strategic weakness had again been made all too clear.

Paradoxically, the clarity and firmness of American decisiveness in the Cuban missile crisis heightened the feelings of dependence and impotence among many European policymakers and stressed to them the crucial difference between having and not having nuclear power in their own hands. Could American leadership and American opinion always be relied upon to act or react so effectively and yet so cautiously as it had in October 1962? Other crises might arise elsewhere in the world, in which the United States would feel impelled to bring to bear nuclear threats or even nuclear force. Would Europe again be exposed, in such circumstances, to the threat or reality of nuclear devastation, again without having a voice in deciding its own fate? Thoughtful Europeans and Americans are constantly aware that the relative abundance of Soviet intermediate-range missiles targeted on Western Europe makes free Europe, as Khrushchev has boasted, a hostage of American policy despite an American margin of superiority in intercontinental missiles.

The surest way to destroy NATO and thus to isolate North America politically from Western Europe would be to confront the two halves of the alliance with a prolonged and potentially nuclear crisis somewhere outside the North Atlantic area. In other words, if the United States felt obliged to use nuclear threats in order to protect a vital interest of the West in Asia, Africa, or the Middle East, its West European allies would feel even more strongly obliged to impose restraints on that policy and to make unmistakably clear to their own people and to Moscow that they were indeed successful in imposing those restraints on U.S. choices of action.

The result would be any or all of the following: the panicky adoption of a neutralist posture by Western Europe; the sacrifice of vital interests of the United States outside Europe; the loss of mutual faith between America and Europe; the breakdown of the Atlantic alliance; the adoption of a "go-it-alone" policy by the United States. If Communist aggressiveness and European fears in combination were to drive the United States into a "Fortress America" psychology, this major shift would bring closer the risks of nuclear war. In discussing this possibility we must note in passing that there is no indication that the Soviet leadership has given up its determination to disrupt the Atlantic alliance, or that Western Europe is willing to assume any nuclear risks either to defend its remaining interests outside Europe or to help the United States defend them. Western Europe has abandoned its claims to world power, and yet it is not reconciled to the status of "Little Europe."

The Chinese Capability

Factors operating outside European or American control may raise to a high pitch the danger of nuclear war in non-Atlantic areas. The achievement by Communist China of nuclear capability, for example, doubtless heightens the risk of a nuclear war in Asia. Although the Soviet leaders had their own national and ideological reasons for first promising, in 1957, to help China acquire a nuclear force and then, in 1959, for withdrawing from that commitment, the Kremlin had also become aware by 1959, as the United States had by 1951, that a "capability" is not a "deterrent." The Soviet leaders had concluded that a small Chinese deterrent, far from being an asset for Communist expansion, might merely serve to trigger off a far bigger war—one that would devastate the Soviet Union as well as the United States.

In the presence of new crises in Asia, the Soviet leaders now seem deeply concerned to limit the scope of such conflicts, or at least to hold them below the threshold of nuclear war. In pursuing this policy, the Kremlin is helping Communist China, whether Mao Tse-tung appreciates it or not, for by itself mainland China is in no position to withstand a nuclear attack. At the same time the Kremlin is thereby, for good reasons of its own, endeavoring to deprive American policy of any political opportunity to threaten the use of its most powerful and mobile instrument of force. Western Europe, basically, shares the Soviet purpose of holding any conflicts in Asia to a non-nuclear level.

The creation of an independent or even a semidetached European deterrent would do much to release U.S. policy from this predicament. An integrated Western Europe, armed with a credible deterrent, would cease to be a hostage to Soviet threats and a dependent of the U.S.

retaliatory force. In turn, American policy in Asia would no longer be a hostage to Soviet blackmail against Western Europe and to European fears. If Europe could provide for the deterrence of Soviet nuclear threats against itself, American policy could be exerted much more powerfully in other regions of the world. Europe would be able to give up its real or assumed veto on the exercise of American power outside Europe.

European Responsibility

At present European feelings are dangerously detached from accepting any real responsibility for what happens in the rest of the world. Indeed, Europeans are increasingly indifferent even to contributing adequately to the defense of their own continent. The longer Europe feels helplessly dependent on the American deterrent, the more it may be inclined to drift into an attitude of passivity and even neutralism, punctuated by sharp spasms of fear and resentment over American efforts to apply its strategic power politically to preventing the expansion of Soviet or Chinese Communist control to new areas.

If an integrated Western Europe must eventually have its own nuclear deterrent in order to take responsibility for its own survival, this is an uncomfortable price for American policy to pay. But it may turn out to be a reasonable price. On the other hand, if the United States prefers, at all political costs, to retain in its own hands a near monopoly of free-world deterrence, it will have to reconcile itself to the discomforts of Europe's distrust, its increasing detachment from American policies, and its possible acceptance of a relatively powerless and increasingly neutralist role in the world.

Integration a Prerequisite for European Deterrent

I must emphasize the word "integrated" in trying to define the potential importance of a nuclear deterrent for an integrated Western Europe. National deterrents, to be effective, require larger territories and greater resources than even the strongest countries of Western Europe can provide. This consideration is reinforced by the prospect that over the next decade a deterrent system, as distinct from the possession of some bombs or missiles, will become steadily more costly, burdensome and risky to create and operate. An integrated Western Europe can provide the resources needed to establish its nuclear independence; individual European countries cannot. There is, of course, an enormous gap between the present separate sovereignties of Western Europe and a future integrated grouping equipped politically to manage nuclear-missile power jointly. Nevertheless, if Europeans are as worried about preserving their sovereignty in a nuclear age as they are about losing that sovereignty permanently to either the United States or the Soviet Union, they will perhaps find in this worry a sufficiently strong reason for deciding to establish both an integrated European deterrent and an integrated political community capable of managing that deterrent.

Nature of European Deterrent

Although in a brief treatment it is difficult to go into detail about the technological characteristics of a European deterrent, or the steps through which it might be established, a number of possibilities come to mind. One of these is to "Europeanize" the proposed seaborne multilateral force. Indeed, spokesmen of the Administration in Washington have stated repeatedly that the seaborne multilateral force may be turned over some day to European control within NATO, provided the European partners to NATO decide how they would combine to exercise command-and-control. A big step beyond that would be to transform NATO itself into a primarily European alliance, with its own nuclear forces under its joint command, while maintaining close ties with the United States and Canada.

There is much room for uncertainty about the long-range viability of a seaborne missile force. However, it will probably provide a positive factor of strength for ten to fifteen years. In the meantime the range of the Polaris missile and the power of the warheads it can carry are being increased to make the force a substantial factor of power. Over the next decade other systems, underwater and airborne, may be adapted to back up and eventually to supplement a European seaborne force. The latter was itself substituted, after the Nassau Conference of December 1962, for an initial proposal to establish a jointly manned fleet of Polaris submarines. In any case, a mobile submarine system is within the range of early possibilities, provided the many political and technological problems can be solved. Other underwater launching systems have also been studied; one or more of them may prove effective by the 1970's in providing a second-strike deterrent to Soviet attack or Soviet nuclear threats against Europe. Finally, airborne systems may become important in the 1970's. All these systems have the advantage of locating the second-strike force outside Europe's own territory; they would not, of course, remove the Soviet threat to hold the people of Western Europe as hostages to mass annihilation.

Nor is it impossible that Western Europe could be equipped at some stage with a land-based deterrent, centered on later generations of Minuteman missiles, with increased hardening and elaborate systems of communication and control. There are many sparsely populated areas in Europe: The Massif Central, parts of the Alps, the Vosges, and the Pyrenees; parts of Wales and Northern Scotland. Large areas of Spain, provided a post-Franco regime were found eligible to join a Europeanized NATO, might be suitable for housing a second-strike force.

Cost Problem

Although I do not minimize the problems of joint training and manning, or joint doctrine and control, in this brief treatment I should like to make just a few comments on the general problem of cost. When analysts speak of the very great expense of establishing and maintaining a deterrent system, they are referring in part to the enormous and unpredictable costs that go into research and development. On the other hand, a large part of these original costs would be avoided by adapting an already proven system to create a second deterrent.

True, the cost of providing advanced systems of hardening, command and communications, and detection will probably be greater than the original cost of manufacturing the military hardware that goes into the new system. Nevertheless, the actual cost of a deterrent force to the European alliance would be greatly influenced by an American decision either to share U.S. knowledge and experience or to force Europe to "re-invent" each bit of equipment and to gain operating experience on its own. In any case, the cost projection of such a system should be carried out in a realistic way to provide political leaders in Western Europe and America with a feasibility study. It will then be up to the political leaders in Western Europe to decide in full knowledge whether nuclear independence is worth the price or not. It is not convincing simply to cite astronomical figures on the cost of creating a U.S. deterrent when, actually, a large proportion of these costs would not have to be duplicated in creating a European deterrent with U.S. cooperation.

On the other hand, some projected trends in strategic technology are going to make it more difficult and costly, rather than less so, to establish and operate a European deterrent by the 1970's. One of these factors is the growing cost of research and development. Missiles and warheads may not change decisively over the next decade or so; yet additional gains in their effectiveness will undoubtedly be achieved through intensive research, though at increasing cost. The weapons and vehicles are, however, only a part of any system of deterrence, and, as noted above, they may prove to be a relatively small part of the total systems cost. Research and development are not standing still, and they are also becoming more costly all the time. The question will therefore remain: Will America continue to bear this very large burden alone, and will it be willing to give Western Europe a "free ride" in the field of research and development? It will probably be unwilling to do so, and therefore an integrated Western Europe would have to share future research and development costs in some to-be-agreed pattern.

Detection

A second major factor relates to systems of warning and detection, which must be increasingly worldwide if they are to be effective. In this crucial field it would hardly be feasible for Western Europe to develop a self-contained system. Yet without such a system, or without access to the American system, it would be operating "blind." In any period of tension that might lead to nuclear threats or nuclear war, the question of adequate detection is just as vital as the ability to respond by a second strike. The question whether Western Europe can share in the American-operated warning system and still retain its nuclear independence is a very complex one and would require special study.

Antimissile Systems

A third factor militating against Europe's achieving full nuclear independence is the current and prospective development of antimissile systems. Whatever their other characteristics, it seems clear that these systems will have to be practically worldwide in scope in order to be effective at all. Geography alone makes it extremely unlikely that Western Europe can have an effective antimissile system, even if that should become possible in some undefined degree for North America and the Soviet Union. If Western Europe is to have its own nuclear-missile deterrent, it will at some stage also need to have an antimissile system or to share in a U.S. system. The two capabilities—missile and antimissile—cannot be considered in isolation one from the other if we are talking about an effective deterrent for the 1970's.

European Unity

Assuming for the moment that all these questions of technology and systems can eventually be resolved, one major nexus of questions remains: Is it politically feasible for Western Europe to possess and control an independent nuclear deterrent? Is Europe sufficiently aware of a common danger and a common destiny to want to make the great changes that would be needed? The United States wants, its spokesmen say, to talk with "Europe" about its future defense when there is a Europe to talk with as an equal partner. Will it be or become one?

The path that a major part of Western Europe has been following so far in its search for a higher degree of unity has been that of economic integration. Yet the process of "creating Europe" has yet to reach the stage of creating a collective sovereignty, and it has so far left out several countries whose membership will be indispensable to a community of strategic self-defense.

One assumption underlying the remarkable emergence of a new and stronger Europe has been that economic integration will mean, in addition to the basic advantages of a much larger market and a more effective use of resources, that one day Europe or most of it will suddenly wake up to discover that it has become irreversibly a single unit. From that, it has been assumed, there would then flow imperative and new consequences in the fields of political and strategic unity. The question remains unanswered, however, whether nations like those of Europe, with their deep traditions of independence and diversity, can be led through these partial steps to merge their political sovereignties in a wider unity. Perhaps the challenge to Western Europe to take up the burden of its own strategic defense will have to be injected into the process of integration in its midcourse, rather than waiting for the completion of its economic integration. Perhaps the urge that many Europeans are beginning to feel, an urge to take Europe's strategic sovereignty into its collective hands, may provide the incentive to decide that a revived and strengthened Europe can and must assure the strategic underpinning of its own political will.

Political and Strategic Considerations

If, in addition to the gradual development of a community of economic, social, and cultural life, Europe is to regain its strategic independence, it should take a closer look at the problem of how it intends to establish political control over a joint strategic force. If the will is present, the methods may not be as complicated as they now appear. If the European deterrent is to be a second-strike retaliatory force, it can, like the U.S. deterrent of today, be used primarily to face down Soviet nuclear threats, or, in an extremity in which that retaliatory threat failed to deter Soviet aggression, to inflict equivalent destruction on the Soviet Union.

Under this assumption it should not be beyond the wit of statesmen to agree on a pre-programming of the role of the European retaliatory force. A direct Soviet attack on Western Europe as a whole, or even on neutrals such as Sweden or Austria, would be a signal that, discarding all past evidences of caution, the Soviet leadership had decided to risk both European and American retaliation in order to expand its control by military means. In that single and least likely case, there could be only one response, by both European and U.S. deterrents, and the decision-making process would be a correspondingly simple one, whether pre-programmed or not.

In this extreme contingency the European nuclear commander would have his instructions, but he would also have a few minutes in which to consult the heads of several major governments by a "hot line" network of his own. The pre-programming of the response would, of course, be quite well known to the Soviet political and strategic leaders, and we can assume that they would also have no doubt about a coordinated and simultaneous American response. To that extent, independent U.S. and European deterrents would exercise deterrence in much the same way as the U.S. deterrent exercises it today, but with a redoubled certainty of retaliatory damage to the Soviet Union.

Other and more likely contingencies would be less clear-cut.

Would the European community feel any urgency to join the U.S. deterrent force in responding to a Soviet attack defined in advance as leaving Europe untouched? Presumably U.S. strategic planning would not count on receiving a European backing equivalent to that it would give Western Europe. On the other hand, Soviet strategic planning could not leave the European deterrent out of account. It would have to reckon with the possibility of a decisive intervention by the West European deterrent after the Soviet Union had expended most of its missiles and had suffered widespread destruction from the American second-strike response. In that sense a reliable European deterrent even if smaller than the Soviet or American one, would weigh in the balance of Soviet calculations as an additional factor on the side of restraint or caution.

A third set of contingencies is even more difficult to define. They include, however, the real possibility that, having established its nuclear self-reliance, Western Europe might wish to use its new might elsewhere in the world, in the Middle East, for example, or Africa. Indeed, one of the emotions that has made many Europeans yearn for nuclear independence has been their resentment of the U.S. veto against the French-British-Israeli action at Suez.

If Europe—or France and Britain—had had their own nuclear power, they could have persisted, so this line of reasoning goes, a few days or a few weeks longer, long enough to achieve some of their goals at Suez. Actually, this seems to me a misreading, though a widespread and influential one, of what really happened. The British government of that day had expected and had discounted both the U.S. and the Soviet reactions. It was thrown off stride much more by the strong opposition of members of the Commonwealth and by the vehement criticism at home and in the United Nations. Be that as it may, the resentment engendered by the Suez crisis has fed the demands for nuclear independence. A similar emotion might influence its use after it had secured that independence.

A nuclear-armed Europe may well want to exercise a political influence derived from that nuclear power and to exercise it in ways that will be highly disagreeable to American opinion. That is a risk that will have to be taken if the larger decision is to be made. Three factors will, however, serve to moderate the extent of that risk. One is that the nations of Western Europe have abandoned or compromised most of the non-European interests for which they might have been willing, even in 1956, to risk war. A second is that it would be very difficult to persuade a group of European powers to accept the risks of using nuclear weapons for any purpose except to safeguard Western Europe against being overrun by Soviet power. That is one reason why de Gaulle insists on a national rather than a regional deterrent.

A third factor to keep in mind is that the possession of nuclear power has operated so far, in the instances of the United States and the Soviet Union, to promote a growing sense of vulnerability, caution, and responsibility. There is no reason to suppose that this factor will work any differently in the thinking of West Europeans, once the awesome duty of decision is placed in their hands.

Many political changes would have to take place within Western Europe before it could erect the political framework necessary for exercising a collective strategic sovereignty. In France a post de Gaulle leadership would have to make several basic and difficult decisions. It would have to conclude, assuming that de Gaulle might be correct in asserting that an American deterrent would not be available forever to defend Europe, that it would be better to rely on a regional and jointly controlled force in which France would certainly have an important but not exclusive place of leadership, than on a small national one. De Gaulle's successors would have to be convinced by the reasoning of scientific prediction and strategic thinking that a national deterrent would be too weak, too unreliable, too costly, and too soon obsolete to take on the sole responsibility of substituting for the American deterrent in the defense of Europe. These changes in French thinking would be painful for many, but possible.

Leading people in Great Britain would also have to rethink many current assumptions. They would have to consider whether Britain can have greater influence in the world through possessing a small national deterrent, which in turn depends on American technological assistance; whether this nation would be stronger as an experienced leader within an integrated European community. They would have to consider whether they really need a separate, modest and not very independent deterrent merely in order to trigger a U.S. retaliation against a Soviet attack on Western Europe. In reviewing Britain's still very important positions in the non-European world they would have to decide whether nuclear power is henceforth going to be very useful in preserving its influence and interests.

For the German Federal Republic and Italy the basic question will be whether their security can be enhanced by full membership in a European strategic community, or whether their security needs are best met as at present, by a unilateral American guarantee. For the smaller tries a fair share of influence in the decisions that might lead up to the ultimate one of whether or not to stand fast against nuclear threats to European members of NATO the problem will be to assure their coun- the security of Western Europe.

The idea of a more or less completely independent or coordinate European deterrent has been very unwelcome to American opinion and policy. With all its recurrent risks of destruction, the two-power possession of major nuclear-missile forces has by now become a customary situation. Nevertheless, the two-power division of nuclear might may not remain as stable as it now seems. Some analysts foresee a substantial proliferation of nuclear weapons by the 1970's. If their predictions are sound, it would be the better part of wisdom for the United States to work for a cautious and limited proliferation—for example, by assisting Western Europe into a position of nuclear independence—rather than wage a rearguard action against any and all proliferation. That is especially true if a delaying action seems likely to lead to its own defeat in the end.

By assisting Western Europe to supplement its growing economic vigor with strategic and therefore political independence from direct American tutelage, the United States may hope to avoid a heritage of bitterness that Europeans would feel if they had to struggle long and hard to achieve that independence against American-imposed obstacles. Because of the close cultural, economic and political links, because of shared values and dangers, North America and Western Europe, even if they should become wholly or partially independent in the strategic sense, are certain to understand each other quickly and to find ways to work together in cooperation. The United States has repeatedly affirmed its desire to act in close partnership with an "equal" Europe, but it has not defined "equality" in any clear terms.

In putting forward these thoughts for discussion, I have many doubts and uncertainties. I have also made many assumptions, technological, budgetary and political, that need to be examined much more closely and critically than I have time to do here. On the other hand, for Americans and Europeans to consider together, in realistic detail, what it would mean concretely for Europe to acquire nuclear independence, and what that would cost in terms of strategic risks, political transformations, and economic burdens, can help restore an effective dialogue on these matters between the great nations that border the North Atlantic. Without a dialogue of this kind our European friends will continue to believe that America is fully satisfied to have their nations as its strategic clients, and they will exercise the privilege of the protected to criticize their protector in all ways fair and unfair. Once both sides of the Atlantic are engaged in a frank examination of new possibilities for the 1970's, they will both be challenged to make their full contributions to the defense of freedom in the decades ahead.

European Integration and Atlantic Partnership

—*KURT BIRRENBACH*

The political sovereignty of the member states of NATO and the leadership of the alliance by the United States of America on the basis of her superior political, economic, and military power were unequivocally the foundation of the Atlantic alliance at the beginning of the 1950's. The synthesis of these factors made possible the collaboration of the member states which has become the functional principle of the alliance. For the sake of clarity, these terms require a somewhat more detailed interpretation.

Sovereignty

The concept of sovereignty is complex and controversial. Its substance can be interpreted in a positive or negative sense—in the negative as freedom from outward compulsion, in the positive as the very essence of national power. Sovereignty is both a political and a legal concept, and can be taken as absolute or relative.[1] In this context, it is the negative content and the political aspect which arouses our interest rather than the legal aspect. Since we are concerned with states in the West, states which have subordinated their legal order to international law, the term sovereignty must be taken as relative, not absolute.

[1] George Schwarzenberger, *The Forms of Sovereignty in Current Legal Problems,* X (1957), p. 246ff.

> Sovereignty in the sense of international law can mean, as far as limited by international law, not an absolute, but only a relative supreme authority. Supreme means in this context insofar as it is not subjected to the legal authority of any other states; and the state is then sovereign when it is subjected to international law, not to the national law of any other state.[2]

In the narrow sense of the word, political sovereignty presupposes that a state can freely and independently shape its external relations with other states. But can states, in particular medium-sized and small states, which no longer possess power in the real sense of the word or even the power to decide whether to go to war or remain at peace, still be termed sovereign? This degree of independence has never in the past been so problematical as it is today in view of the might of continental powers, the development of military techniques in a nuclear age, and the ideological conflict between East and West. As recently as the last century even a small state could evade the pressure of another state or groups of states by choosing neutral status or by changing its alliance commitments.[3] It is by no means axiomatic nowadays that a state can extricate itself from a web of political entanglement by choosing neutrality. Transition in a neuralgic zone of world politics from one ideological bloc to another can be a step toward the end of liberty.

Thus, not only the small states, but also the larger ones, are bereft of this way of escape, so that political sovereignty in the sense of genuine independence from external influence is extremely problematic. In this context, in the world today, when the association of groups of states is the rule and not the exception, another restriction on political sovereignty is possible. Can one speak of politically sovereign states when such states relinquish their sovereignty by participating in long-term treaties or by sharing it with others? Modern constitutional theory admits the possibility of political sovereignty in both cases. On this basis, neither the restriction on the actual external freedom of action of a state nor a temporary contractual restriction on its exercise of sovereign rights deprives it of its sovereignty, as long as the state in question is not subjected to the national law of any other state.

> For despite a massive pressure which is today exerted in so many forms on the smaller and middle-sized states, these states still retain the possibility of replying to such pressure with their political "no," regardless of the consequences which may possibly arise for them from the adoption of such an

[2] Hans Kelsen, "The Principle of Sovereign Equality of States as a Basis for International Organization," *Yale Law Review,* LIII (1944), p. 207ff.

[3] Georg Erler, "Staatssouveränität und internationale Wirtschaftsverflechtung," *Berichte der deutschen Gesellschaft fur Völkerrecht,* Heft 1 (Karlsruhe, 1957), p. 39ff.

attitude. As long as a state still retains in the political-existential sphere the possibility of issuing such a refusal, it can still justifiably lay claim to being considered a sovereign state.

The fact that judicial obligations exist between and within states is not sufficient to call into question the essentials of sovereignty, for so long as a state retains the capacity to have the final word on the political plane, that state remains sovereign.[4]

Cooperation and Integration

"Cooperation," the result of the interplay between political sovereignty of the member nations and the leadership exercised by the United States, means, for our purposes, the working together of politically independent states, in principle on the basis of unanimity. I say in principle because none of the smaller member states has thus far in practice used its veto to delay or obstruct a majority decision in the alliance. Any negative decision on the part of one of the smaller states would merely enable the state in question to withdraw from the implementation of a decision taken by the alliance as a whole. That a veto by one of the larger states such as Britain or France would, in view of the unanimity principle laid down in the treaty, make a resolution impossible, has been clearly demonstrated by the experience of recent years.[5]

The counter notion to *cooperation* is *integration*. In a narrower sense, this term means, in the realm of international law, the transfer of sovereign rights and functions from the competence of a single partner state to common organs of a community or association of several states. In part of NATO, especially in the field of military command structure, integration was first achieved after the resolutions of the 1952 NATO conference. Here integration would mean the beginning of institutionalized decision making with obligatory consequences for all members. Thus one must ascertain in this context whether the principle of collaboration will and can remain the functioning principle of NATO during the 1960's, especially after 1969, or to what extent as a whole or in partial areas of NATO activity the application of the integration principle is expedient and desirable, regardless of whether its application is acclaimed by all the members of the alliance.

---

[4] Gerhard Liebholz, "Sovereignty and European Integration," *Sciences Humaines et Integration Européenne* (Leyden, 1960).

[5] The adoption of the principle of Article 6.2 of the OECD Treaty to NATO, proposed recently by Secretary General Stikker, would improve substantially the functioning of the alliance.

Leadership

The very real American superiority founded on the United States monopoly in nuclear weapons, which was actually overwhelming during the first decade of the alliance, compensated for all practical purposes any divergence in the specific interests of the smaller member states until the end of the 1950's. The ultimate result was that American superiority made possible a more or less uniform will within the alliance which gave the United States the right to assume the role of leader of the Western alliance against the Soviet-led Eastern alliance.

The uncontested American leadership of the alliance can be divided into two distinct periods: the period dating from the foundation of the alliance until the Korean war, and the period dating from the Korean war until 1958. During the first period, the NATO alliance was for all practical purposes purely a guarantee pact; i.e., the legal form in which the United States of America clothed her military obligations in Europe, while the other member states contributed but little to the military effort of the alliance. During this period, America's nuclear potential was both the shield and the sword of the alliance. Thus it was correct at the time to describe NATO in its essentials as

> the traditional guarantee pact committing its members, particularly the United States, to come to each one's assistance on the basis of the minimal peacetime collaboration. The commitment of the United States was the essential feature of the defense system.[6]

As noted above, this situation changed after the outbreak of hostilities in Korea when, due to the establishment of a central headquarters (SHAPE) in 1951, and other supreme commands (SACLANT and Chan-Command) in 1952, NATO assumed the attributes of a semi-integrated military organization. The requirement of an integrated defense of the North Atlantic area gave impetus to the establishment, in September 1949, of an elaborate structure of civilian and military committees and planning groups. After the creation of a permanent civilian body (the council deputies for the daily coordination of the work of the subsidiary bodies of the alliance) the North Atlantic Council was made, at the Lisbon Conference, a permanent body with permanent representatives and a secretary general.[7]

However, it must not be overlooked that even the partial application of the principle of integration within the scope of the alliance did not result in any fundamental change in the features just described. "The impact of supreme power and leadership, exercised by the United States, remained the basis of coherence of the alliance essentially as the

---

[6] Robert Endicott Osgood, *NATO—The Entangling Alliance,* p. 21ff .
[7] *Ibid.*

multilateral framework for reinforcing America's guarantee to involve herself in the defense of Europe."[8] By no means the least of the pillars upholding the credibility of American obligations in Europe is the formal tie entered into by the United States within the system of mutual obligations in conjunction with more than fourteen countries.

With few exceptions, at no time during the 1950's did the European NATO countries contribute to the general armament effort by as much as they might have done. Rather, they concentrated their energy on the economic reconstruction of Europe. The rearmament of the European nations served first and foremost to reduce Europe's vulnerability to subversion, indirect attack, and very limited direct attack.

The confidence of the European allies in the alliance, and especially in the leadership of the United States, was essentially weakened by two events of historical importance. The first was the emergence of the Soviet Union as a nuclear power, and, to an even greater degree, the success of the Soviet Union in building up delivery systems for nuclear weapons; the second was the economic and political consolidation of Western Europe.

The implication of this evolution was not immediately understood. It was only when the Kennedy Administration promulgated the McNamara doctrine, which displaced the strategy of massive retaliation as formulated under John Foster Dulles and Admiral Radford, that the European nations were aware of their new strategic situation.

This weakened the decisive component within the alliance system, the fact of United States leadership, while, on the other hand, the claims of a number of the member states to sovereignty were more strongly emphasized. This is a development which would be even more evident if there were European development toward political unity. NATO was therefore subjected to a dangerous and simultaneous weakening from two sides. The crisis in NATO arose essentially over two questions. One was the disunity of the NATO partners regarding the substance of military strategy, the other the question of the control of nuclear weapons. Even if it were possible to bring about agreement among the member states of NATO regarding military strategy—and this is not only a purely organizational problem—there would still be the question of the control of nuclear weapons, which, although primarily a political and military problem, also has important organizational ramifications. The difficulties of solving these problems are enhanced by the fact that the NATO member states do not agree on the extent of the threat posed by the Soviet bloc. The less seriously that threat is taken the greater will be the reluctance within the alliance to enter into any far-reaching obligations.

---

[8] *Ibid.*

The Question of Organization

Quite apart from problems of a purely military nature, the malaise within NATO has a specific political ground: some of the NATO member states feel that they are not sufficiently consulted on vital matters of foreign policy. If one asks whether technical collaboration is the ideal form of organization for NATO (and that is the implicit theme of this essay), one should determine, before dealing with material problems, whether an organizational reform of NATO has become necessary, and whether and to what extent such a reform could solve NATO's problems. Political and organizational matters are closely interwoven within the complex of NATO problems.

If one were to compose an inventory of the present situation in NATO, bearing in mind the question of whether we want collaboration or integration, one would arrive at this conclusion. Within NATO itself, three forms of organization have evolved: collaboration, integration, and the purely national sphere of influence.[9] If we proceed from the loosest to the most highly developed form of organization in the light of the alliance goals, we find that there are areas completely removed from the process of internationalization and reserved for purely national control: the build-up and training of the armed forces, the type and duration of military service, the payment of the troops, the form of the high command and its relationship to civilian authority, and finally the disposition of the armed forces under the condition that their deployment requires the consent of the NATO command. In addition, there are the further military considerations of the national infrastructure organization, logistics, and the production of armaments.

The system of international collaboration on the basis of unanimity had its place in alliances of bygone days. Lack of cohesion in this organizational form is reduced by coordination of the alliance as a whole by the Secretary General. Added to this, we have funding on the basis of an annual review and mutual assistance where this is a part of NATO agreements; logistical supply and production in limited form in specific areas, with collaboration being implemented less in the overall framework of NATO than within the more limited framework of specific groups of countries; a limited degree of standardization of certain military equipment; and loose collaboration in the fields of technical research and development, armaments production, the coordination of air traffic within the European NATO area, civilian emergency planning, and—the most important element—political planning and consultation among all the allies.

What about the third stage—integration? Even in peacetime there are integrated staffs for units above the division level. These integrated

[9] Eberhard Menzel, "Nationale und internationale Strukturformen der NATO," *Europa Archiv* (August 25, 1963).

staffs have no command control of their own in peacetime, but general staff planning for all nations is carried out around them, and the practicability of this arrangement is tested in joint exercises. Although the degree of integration of command structure in peacetime cannot be compared with that of previous alliances, it is relatively small (particularly in peacetime) when compared with the complete fusion of national prerogatives. There is a high degree of integration, however, in the so-called common infrastructures, which are commonly funded and administered by the alliance organizations (airfields, telecommunications facilities, pipelines and fuel dumps, naval facilities, radar warning facilities, air defense ground installations, special ammunition dumps, rocket, launchers, etc.). Military planning may also be regarded as integrated to a certain degree, since it is the basis for joint operations by the alliance as a whole in the event of war.

The entire strategic deterrent of the United States—with the exception of the British V-bomber force—is outside the competence of the alliance, as is the developing French atomic strike force. Since NATO's conventional forces as such are below the level which formerly was regarded as indispensable to the shield function of the alliance, a decisive weapon is removed from the realm of both alliance cooperation and alliance integration.

Since the ultimate decision to use tactical atomic weapons also lies with the President of the United States, NATO's scope of effect must be regarded as limited. It is hardly surprising that this is one of the reasons for the uneasiness—justified or unjustified—of the parties to the alliance. An attempt at a solution for this problem will be discussed below.

All previous efforts to achieve genuine integration within the alliance in peacetime, especially in the fields of logistics, production, equipment, and command structure, have proved fruitless. The division between national and international decision-making powers on the question of war and peace remains unclear and will continue to remain unclear. Every NATO country reserves the right in her constitution—whether written or unwritten—to make the ultimate decision whether to remain at peace or to go to war.

Article 5 of the North Atlantic Treaty contains no automatic obligation to have recourse to arms. Unlike Article 4 of the Brussels Treaty, the North Atlantic Treaty contains a series of conditions which do not constitute a complete military assistance obligation. It is agreed that an armed attack on any one or more of the partners constitutes an attack against all.

The absence of appropriate provisions is partly compensated by the regulations governing the immediate preparation of the alliance for an imminent outbreak of hostilities. Depending upon the degree of urgency involved, an imminent outbreak of hostilities will lead to a formal alarm resolution in the NATO Council or to a state of military alert which SACEUR can declare in its sphere of command while simultaneously informing the ministers of defense of the countries concerned. Any alert resolution places the NATO alliance, or part of it, in a state of alert, and automatically entails—depending upon the degree of alert—the subordination of the command structure to SACEUR. In these fields, the standardizing power of the factual plays a more important part than the integrating factor of the NATO alliance. But it cannot be denied that even here NATO lacks, for very understandable reasons, an absolutely clear delineation of areas of responsibility. At any rate, this points to the tremendous importance of the presence of United States forces in Europe.

Equitable Burden Distribution

Where in NATO is the transfer of functions from one area of responsibility to another most important? The retention of certain national responsibilities has slowly but surely developed to the point of threatening the cohesion of the alliance as such. The order of competence reflects the priority of the interests of the specific countries. The NATO countries have joined together in the cause of common defense. If the NATO partners have united for the purpose of common defense, then the alliance can operate harmoniously only when duties as well as rights have been distributed equitably. The problem of equality is certainly not purely quantitative today. The only reasonable way of appraising all the factors (which are complicated to an even greater degree by the balance of payments problems) is to distribute the burdens according to highly differentiated criteria. But it is even more important to insure that such distribution is carried out not on the basis of bilateral negotiations, but exclusively by multilateral consultation.

There are two ways of transferring functions hitherto performed by individual countries to the level of collaboration or integration. The first is to lay down the type and extent of the financial effort to be made in the field of armaments, and the second is to determine the form and duration of armed service. The one-sided efforts of the United States to secure a more equitable distribution have so far failed to achieve any signal success. That is why all the parties to NATO will have to come to grips with this vital question and get down to the establishment of a fundamentally new system of distributing the alliance burden.

Financial requirements could be considerably reduced if the degree of weapons and equipment standardization were to be increased. The present chaos in specifications, even in the light of understandable national interests, is inexcusable in view of the possible consequences in the event of war. That applies in particular to ammunition, small arms, machine guns, and vehicles.

The process of internationalizing research and development in the field of weapons and equipment must be rapidly accelerated, even if the framework of NATO should prove to be too large for this task, in view of the differences in military requirements. The need for the concentration of research and development on a regional basis or for specific projects is becoming increasingly urgent, particularly in view of the constant increase in the cost of modern weapons.

In the future NATO should refrain from authorizing any further weapons development unless such development—and here I exclude the United States—is accepted on the basis of joint production for a major region and is jointly financed. This is a unique opportunity for international coordination of all new developments. Joint development and research projects automatically lead to coordinated or even common forms of production. We have had proof of the feasibility of such joint action not only in the development of the F104G, but also in the design and construction of the Hawk, the European Sidewinder, and the Fiat G-91 fighter. This development could be accomplished either through the manufacture of American weapons under license, or on the basis of original European developments. With all due recognition of the necessity for relieving some of the strain on the American balance of payments position by purchasing weapons, one must ask whether it might not be a good idea, and even in the interests of the United States, to have European industry develop and produce weapons to a greater extent. The best way of arriving at a constructive solution in this matter would appear to be the division of the tasks involved. Effective progress may be expected more quickly in the field of armaments production as well if it is placed on a regional (European) basis.

A serious weakness in NATO's organization lies in the fact that logistics is primarily the responsibility of the individual nations. Operational command and logistics are two inseparable factors in modern warfare. The NATO commanders have no immediate control over supplies, stocks, and facilities, during peacetime; and, in time of war, their control is confined to supplies in the combat zone.[10]

Lines of supply are under national control, as is transportation. To be sure, in recent years, a certain amount of progress has been made in these fields: the development of a common infrastructure, as well as a common network of pipelines for fuel supply, and the establishment of a common telecommunications system in the European command area. But this is not enough. It is simply incomprehensible that the command of the forces should be entrusted to integrated staffs while the materiel needed by the troops remains unintegrated. The integration of logistics would of necessity entail a higher degree of standardization of weapons and equipment. It was in this spirit that the Western

[10] Frederick W. Mulley, *The Politics of Western Defense* (London, 1962).

European Union (WEU) Assembly passed Recommendation No. 56 on December 1, 1960, recommending to the NATO Council that

> allied commanders be given adequate control in peace and full control in war over all logistics resources earmarked for forces assigned to their command, and that the logistics system in the allied forces be integrated.

The formation of the logistics centers within the SACEUR area of command, coupled with the creation of a European transportation division under a European head vested with adequate powers, would constitute a purposeful initial step toward such a new development. That a development of this kind would call for a fundamental change in NATO practice is axiomatic. Special attention would have to be devoted to the question of insuring a common and adequate stockpile of, and service maintenance for, advanced weapons under the control of SHAPE. Beyond the framework of Europe, it would be advisable to have a long-term NATO plan for all logistical requirements and a system for requisitioning and reporting would be especially advisable, to mention just the most important measures that could be taken. If a European collective defense authority were set up on the basis of the ideas generated by the Institute for Strategic Studies in London,[11] it could, without in any way jeopardizing the cohesion of NATO, assume important tasks in the field of planning and developing European armaments production and in the standardizing of modern weapons systems. Thus, an important initial step toward adapting the NATO structure to the structure of Europe (which has changed since the NATO treaty was signed)—a step which would be in the direction of realizing a European-American partnership—could be taken. Europe's importance as a whole would be enhanced and the European nations would be accorded a higher degree of responsibility which might provide a greater degree of self-assurance.

Additional Reforms

Other NATO reforms are necessary in addition to these changes. The most urgent is the strengthening of NATO's administrative machinery. This could be brought about by strengthening the status of the NATO Council and the position of the Secretary General; by modifying the command structure; by changing the functions of SACEUR; and by eliminating the Standing Group in Washington, replacing it by fully integrated chiefs of staff responsible to the civilian authorities of NATO. The proposals put forward by Alastair Buchan would seem to merit serious consideration.[12]

---

[11] Alastair Buchan, "Partners and Allies," *Foreign Affairs* (July 1963).
[12] Alastair Buchan, "Reform of NATO," *Foreign Affairs* (January 1962).

There is no doubt that changing competences and the implementation of the ideas sketched above would constitute an important step toward the internal consolidation of the alliance. Nevertheless, the decisive reasons underlying present malaise would persist. One such reason is the absence of a universally acknowledged military strategy for the NATO *European* area; another lies in the fact that nuclear weapons-the deciding factor in any war today—are not, with the exception of the British V-bombers, under NATO command; and still another lies in the lack of adequate consultation and coordination in the foreign policies of the member states. If we do not succeed in the course of the coming years in arriving at unanimous, satisfactory solutions to these problems, the present trend of internal loosening will continue in NATO. The Western world simply cannot afford to risk the political and military consequences of such a development.

Consequences of the New Nuclear Strategy

Only in recent years has the relinquishing of the strategy of massive retaliation—a logical consequence of the military and technological developments which since 1957 have made the United States of America, for the first time in her history, immediately vulnerable—become clear, in all its implications, to the European nations. It was the development of a comprehensive nuclear strategy under the Kennedy Administration which brought about this realization. The strategy of graduated deterrence or controlled nuclear response brings to light the possibility of conflicts of interest between Europe—especially the continental European states—and the United States of America. It shows that the United States and Europe are no longer in the same boat, as they once seemed to be. Although the concepts of a threshold and a pause and the idea of waiving a first-strike strategy appear reasonable and understandable in Europe when considered in the abstract, they are somewhat doubtful in several respects when viewed concretely in the perspective of European interests. The decisive questions for any European appraisal of the merits of this strategy are: Where exactly is the atomic threshold within the framework of American strategy, and how is the "pause" calculated for the use of atomic weapons?

> The concept of counterforce strategy is well fitted to the deterrence of attack on the United States itself and it can be soundly based on the assumption of an American second strike. But it is more dubious as a protective strategy for Europe unless the United States is prepared to strike first when large-scale hostilities break out.[13]

---

[13] Alastair Buchan and Philip Windsor, *Arms and Stability in Europe* (London, 1963), p. 73.

Furthermore, with regard to the European countries, one is confronted with the question of what would become of the counterforce strategy should the Soviet Union succeed in rendering its own retaliatory forces invulnerable. The prospects of more or less conventional major military operations in Europe, beyond defending a probing action or some other kind of limited operation, have called forth considerable concern in Europe, a concern which has gradually been realized by the people themselves. Added to this is a rationally unjustifiable but nonetheless latent distrust of the political dialogue (which is actually regarded as reasonable) between the two atomic superpowers on a large number of questions affecting the fate of Europe. This last point is an extremely complicated phenomenon deriving from a multiplicity of psychological factors which, given their explosive nature, could in the long run jeopardize the atmosphere of trust and confidence on which the alliance is based. The most important reason for the NATO crisis is, after all, a lack of consensus concerning military strategy and all its political implications. Writing in *Foreign Affairs* in July 1963, Buchan says:

> There is little difficulty in tracing this uneasiness to its original source: On the European side, it springs from the sense of irritation, impotence, and even despair, which the individual allied countries feel in doing business with a nation which has many times their own strength and resources, a nation which is self-sufficient to an extent they can no longer hope to be, and whose policy, once painfully evolved by a cumbrous process of internal debate, is extremely hard to alter.

The military authorities of NATO have worked out a plan which would have reduced the differences in NATO strategy for the central area of Europe to reasonable proportions. Unfortunately, this plan has been vetoed by one NATO power. This, for the reasons explained before, is deeply to be regretted because otherwise one of the most important causes for the crisis in NATO would have been eliminated.

This brings up the problem of the integration of nuclear weapons in NATO, and especially the problem of their control. The United States should try to understand the fact (regardless of whether it is still an unalterable fact) that the European nations, situated as they are on the front line, find it difficult to accept the fact that the ultimate decision on the effective defense of their territory should lie with a political authority separated from their coasts by a vast ocean. It is a fact which is more easily accepted by a country such as the Federal Republic of Germany—which is in greater jeopardy than all the other European countries, and whose national tradition has been broken by a deep hiatus caused by the disaster of national socialism and the last World War—and even more readily accepted by the smaller European countries than by countries such as Britain and France. All the same, it cannot be denied that this fact constitutes for every country a problem which is primarily divorced from the question of trust in American leadership. That is why large sections of Europe had pinned such great hopes on the grand design of President Kennedy, who would ultimately have extended the partnership to the military field so that, in the long run, it would have been impossible to exclude nuclear weapons. The crisis of the Western unity movement since the breakdown of the Brussels negotiations in January 1963 is therefore much more serious than is generally supposed.

The MLF and National Deterrents

In the Federal Republic of Germany it is not thought that the differences between American strategy and a legitimate European need for security are so great that they cannot be reduced to a tolerable minimum given good will on both sides. However, it has become so very urgent to try to clear up this difference in strategy that any lengthy delay would be bound to entail serious consequences. The United States proposal to form a multilateral atomic striking force, and the resolutions passed at the Athens and Ottawa NATO conferences to bring the non-nuclear powers into the central planning and control of American atomic strategy, have the full approval of the Federal German Republic, the Parliament, and, in the main, public opinion.

Both United States proposals imply the possibility of taking into consideration not only European national interests but also supranational interests within the scope of the decision-making process if there is to be a true and comprehensive unification of Europe. Jean Monnet, the President of the Committee for the United States of Europe, to which prominent political leaders from every party and from the free trade unions of Common Market Europe belong, proposed in his speech in Bonn on February 25, 1964 that a specific clause on Europe be included in any future agreement on the formation of an MLF.

In this context, it was naturally understood in Europe that the offer of the American government on July 4, 1962 of partnership between the United States of America and Europe presupposed that Europe would be able to speak "with one voice."

This in turn presupposes the inclusion of Great Britain and the other European states which have stated their willingness to join the European Common Market in any future European political union, and it also presupposes their organization on the basis of true political integration. In this way the road to a solution to the nuclear problem in NATO would be opened—a road which was hinted at in the speech made by the American Vice President in Brussels on November 8, 1963, as well as in the speeches made by McGeorge Bundy in Copenhagen on September 27, 1962; George W. Ball in Bonn on April 2, 1962; Robert

Schaetzel in Enstone and Berlin in August 1963, and in the works of Robert Bowie [14] and Henry Kissinger.[15]

For the time being, the only constructive solution to the problem of nuclear weapons in Europe is the American idea of an MLF. In a final phase, many years from now, if a genuinely politically united Europe should come into being, the MLF would then rest on two pillars—a European and an American one—because a united Europe would replace the individual European nations who originally participated in this venture. A collective European atomic defense community would then be the partner of American nuclear forces assigned to NATO, with both closely integrated into the Western alliance under a centralized command. The ultimate decision on the use of nuclear weapons within the framework of NATO would then rest with the President of the United States on the one hand, and with the competent organ of the European political union in the form of a collective defense community on the other. Such a system of decision making would correspond to the practice adopted during the last war, whereby the President of the United States and the British Prime Minister were responsible for reaching decisions on the most important military questions. Since the order to employ nuclear weapons can in its ultimate form come from only one person, it should be left to the decision of the American President, who would thus be regarded as the executive organ of an American-European partnership.

The alternative—national deterrent powers in Europe (even if they were combined)—is not, in the long run, desirable. It seems to me dubious whether this course of action would offer a transitional solution to the problem, as suggested by Henry Kissinger. This applies particularly if one looks at the matter from the European perspective. One cannot separate the development within NATO from the evolution of a united Europe. National deterrents in Europe constitute an element of disintegration within Europe. This applies to France as well as to Great Britain. If there are European powers with a special status which qualitatively distinguishes them in a fundamental way from the other member states, the basic idea of a community within Europe will be endangered. Apart from differences of political, military, and economic strength, there cannot be two different classes of powers within Europe. A political Europe of tomorrow will be either a cooperative structure or it will not survive. That is also the main argument against the idea of a tripartite directorate inside or outside NATO. Bearing in mind the Athens and Ottawa resolutions, and the chance of a col-

[14] Robert R. Bowie, "Tensions within the Alliance," *Foreign Affairs* (October 1963), p. 49.

[15] Henry A. Kissinger, "NATO's Nuclear Dilemma," *National Security: Political, Military, and Economic Strategies in the Decade Ahead,* ed. David M. Abshire and Richard V. Allen (New York: Praeger, 1963), p. 293ff.

lective development such as that of an MLF, most of the European states, possibly even Britain and France, would sooner or later be prepared to accept the preponderance of the United States until final European political integration could be accomplished. A clearly worded American offer taking into consideration the situation set forth here would certainly facilitate such a development. However, let it be repeated that any dissolution or loosening of European-American ties in the defense of Europe would, from the European point of view, entail dangerous consequences. That is why any such development should be accompanied by a strengthening of Atlantic ties. This point of view is not accorded sufficient appreciation in certain places in Europe.

One point, however, must be clear: Important though the problem of strategy may be, it must in the final analysis be a reflex of the common policy of the NATO states. Military strategy is not an isolated or alienable function of alliances or their members; it is the integrating component of the over-all policy of allied partner states. After all, politics and military strategy are ultimately inseparable.

In the past, alliances were entered into for a given purpose valid only for a given period of time, with political goals and the coordination of military means in accord.

Today the conflict between East and West, which gave birth to NATO, has a global and all-embracing nature. It is not confined to countries, but is between two civilizations. It affects not only states, but whole continents. It is therefore not a matter for armies, but for entire peoples.

When we talk about the risk of victory or defeat, we are not concerned with the fate of armies, but—for the first time in history—with the destruction of the substance of entire nations. No alliance as comprehensive as this can in the long run continue to exist unless one succeeds in coordinating to a high degree, or even integrating, those member states' policies which are of significance to the alliance as a whole. The greater the differences in the interests of the individual partners, the more difficult the way to a common policy.

That it is difficult to coordinate the interests of a world power of continental dimensions such as the United States with those of the smaller European countries is obvious. That is why the unification of Europe in integrated form is of such fundamental importance to the ultimate consolidation of the NATO alliance itself.

Need for Consultation

In view of the waves of tension and relaxation of the conflict between East and West, such consolidation is made all the more important if it is a justifiable assumption that this total conflict with the Eastern bloc is a challenge which will last for at least a whole generation.

It is only the enormity of the risk and the danger that threatens all which facilitate cooperation among different nations. However, even these elementary facts are not sufficient alone to insure that collaboration.

The meaning of insufficient consultation for the coherence of the alliance has seldom been made clearer than in the course of the last years.

The Suez Crisis, the Nassau Agreement and its repercussions on France, the French veto in Brussels, the recognition of Peking by France, the course taken by the operations in the Congo, and the question of trade with Cuba, to cite a few examples, illustrate the fateful effects on the alliance of lack of consultation and coordination in Western policy. It is not that the importance of this question has not been recognized. In fact, the contrary is true. The results of investigations by the Committee of Three on Non-military Cooperation within the framework of NATO, accepted by the North Atlantic Council at a meeting held on August 13, 1956, constitute a classical text on the subject.

If one disregards contingency planning for Berlin, an agreed procedure on the policy to be adopted by the NATO countries in questions of disarmament, and the modest beginning of an attempt to settle issues and differences of opinion amicably between NATO member states, those recommendations are meaningless. The "Committee of Three Wise Men" came to the conclusion that

> greater unity can only develop by working constantly to achieve common policies through full and timely consultation on issues of common concern. Unless this is done, the very framework of cooperation in NATO, which has contributed so greatly to the cause of freedom, and which is so vital to its advancement in the future, will be endangered.
>
> Any changes in national strategy or policy which affect the coalition are made only after collective consideration.
>
> An alliance in which the members ignore each other's interests or engage in political or economic conflicts, or harbor suspicions of each other, cannot be effective either for deterrence or defense. Recent experience makes this clearer than ever before.
>
> From the very beginning of NATO, then, it was recognized that while defense cooperation was the first and most urgent requirement, this was not enough.[16]

The report boils down to the conclusion that the fate of NATO will ultimately depend upon whether we succeed in developing the

[16] *NATO—Facts about the North Atlantic Treaty Organization* (Paris: NATO Information Service, January 1962), p. 260.

alliance, in pursuance of the goals set forth in the North Atlantic Treaty, into an Atlantic community. Sometimes, say the authors of this report, it appears that the great lesson taught to the European states by two World Wars—that the age of national states, at least in Europe, is, in this age of nuclear science, gone forever—has fallen into oblivion.

In the opinion of the authors of the report, close Atlantic ties would by no means exclude regional ties within Europe: "The moves toward Atlantic cooperation and European unity should be parallel and complementary, not competitive or conflicting." This anticipates the idea of a partnership between Europe and the United States.

All these ideas were collated in the grand design of the late American President to form an over-all concept for the alliance. The failure of this idea for the time being is therefore of decisive importance to the cohesion of NATO.

If, then, in view of the present impossibility of finding a comprehensive solution to the problem, the importance attached to the principle of consultation is enhanced, one must clearly understand that consultation means more than an exchange of information, more than apprising the NATO Council of national decisions which have already been taken, and even more than an attempt to gain support for such decisions. According to paragraph 42 of the above mentioned report, it means "the collective discussion of problems in the early stages of policy formation, and before national positions become fixed."

In favorable cases, the recommendation in the conclusion stresses, such discussion will lead to collective decisions on matters of common interest to all the allies. "In favorable cases, it will insure that no member undertakes anything without previous knowledge of the views of the other members." These words demonstrate how far we still are from implementing the recommendations accepted by the NATO Council in 1956.

It is obvious that consultation has practical limits, since, for the time being and in the absence of more comprehensive solutions to the problem, ultimate decisions still rest with national governments. Since, however, most international political decisions affecting the immediate interests of the coalition are incapable of solution at the national level, the necessity for common decisions is all the more obvious. In other words, a system of collaboration on the basis of unrestricted sovereignty and the preponderance in power of the United States is no longer conducive to solving the problems of the alliance.

Economic Aspects

Finally, a word about the importance of the economic aspects of the alliance.

It is self-evident that politico-military collaboration cannot exist where there is economic friction. Not only in the military and political fields, but also in the field of economics, the recommendations contained in the report compiled by the Committee of Three (especially paragraph 61) are an anticipation of the conversion of OEEC into OECD, the goals of the Trade Expansion Act, and, if other chapters of the same report are taken into consideration, the foundation of an Atlantic community. We should also keep in mind that the fundamental importance of the speech made by the American President in Philadelphia on July 4, 1962 lies on the one hand in the fact that the creation of a future partnership between Europe and America has become an official American policy, and on the other in the fact that the proposal of a partnership of equals offers the functional principle on which such a community is to be based. The birth of a partnership of this kind would necessarily alter the entire structure of NATO, as noted in the previous discussion of the nuclear question.

The most important matter in connection with this fact is that the prerequisite to a partnership in the field of economics already exists. The European Economic Community alone, even without Britain, is the first trade power on earth. If the Brussels negotiations had not broken down in January 1963, the negotiations of the Kennedy Round would already bear the insignia of a trade partnership, which was the object of the Trade Expansion Act.

As long as Europe fails to fulfill the prerequisites on the basis of which the President of the United States offered a partnership among equals in his speeches in Philadelphia and Frankfurt, no trade partnership can be founded except in a still very inadequate form. The new constellation in the field of commerce and economics, however, makes possible an approach to the procedure of a partnership, at least in certain important sectors. The Kennedy Round will be the first test of the feasibility of setting up partnership relations between the two continents.

If one considers that economic collaboration embraces such important policy fields as currency, trade, agriculture, development, and economics in general, one sees clearly the measure in which the trend from all sides leads toward the development of ever closer links between Europe and the United States.

It is only when this development toward partnership has made further progress that the conflicts of interests which today seem insuperable will automatically die down or be completely extinguished. The complete maintenance of sovereignty and the priority of national interests in their entirety over regional group interests makes any permanent or ultimate solution to the problem impossible.

The answer, then, to the threat posed by the conflict between East and West, despite the polycentric development within the Communist bloc, can only be complete unity within the Atlantic world.

The Advantages of Diversity in NATO

—*JOHN W. HOLMES*

The Case for Heresy

One of the functions of a lesser ally is to be irresponsible in a thoroughly responsible way. It should be emboldened rather than cowed by the fact that its position is rarely decisive—provided, of course, that this freedom of speech and action is restrained by due deference to the obligations of those who carry the burden of power. A great power, the United States in particular, because it must sustain the framework of security, is, of necessity, more cautious and conservative than auxiliary powers in adopting strategic and diplomatic ideas which threaten the status quo with imponderable elements. This is not to say that Americans have in fact lacked boldness in exploring fresh concepts; recognition of the unique power of their own government to determine the nature of East-West relations has inspired Americans to a good deal more imaginative thinking than can be found elsewhere in fields such as arms control. Yet the United States Government must, by reason of its decisive responsibility, be canny about moving from tried to untried positions, more so than countries whose heresies cannot do mortal damage to the alliance if proved wrong. This special need to be conservative is something which allies must respect more patiently. They must recognize also that, because they are dependent on United States strength, they must not commit themselves to heresies without being confident that their commitment will not seriously embarrass their champion. They cannot, of course, leave to the United States Government the decision whether their actions will be embarrassing, because the latter would naturally disapprove of any policy it didn't happen at that moment to be supporting.

There is a nice balance of judgment and discretion involved in being a good ally, an obligation which a country ought not to abdicate by becoming a satellite. It has a duty in the common interest to explore independently the possibilities in fields where the United States must move with greater care. Needless to say, an important consideration in its calculation is whether its espousal of a position, or even its open interest in a position different from that of the United States or other major allies, would encourage antagonists of the alliance to boldness or blackmail to enable them to succeed in malevolent policies which would otherwise fail. This, however, should be regarded as an important but not necessarily absolute consideration. At any rate it should be a consideration based on the facts of the specific situation—whether it be disengagement in Europe, neutralization in Southeast Asia, or relations with China or Cuba—rather than on the blanket theory that it is *ipso facto* bad for members of an alliance at any time to pursue variant policies. It is not primarily a question, of course, of espousing positions contrary to the known views of the United States. What is much more important is that the lesser allies show enough imagination to produce for consideration or show an interest in proposals which the United States ought not to support until the consequences have been thoroughly examined. The lesser power can help also by introducing into international debate views held by minorities in the United States—a particularly valuable function if it is true, as Senator Fulbright has said, that the United States has been "narrowing the permissible bounds of public discussion, by relegating an increasing number of ideas and viewpoints to a growing category of unthinkable thoughts." That fresh ideas from lesser voices are not necessarily reckless may be illustrated by a reminder that the idea of the North Atlantic Treaty itself was first floated in public speeches by a Canadian prime minister before it was a subject ready for negotiation.

This argument for heresy from lesser voices is intended partly as justification in advance for some unorthodoxy in this paper. Governments and alliances are inevitably cliché-ridden. They must indeed be cautious about moving away from the established clichés about unity and purity—although they should also beware of creating by their rhetoric a hot-house atmosphere which smothers the critical faculty. My quarrel is not with NATO practice, but with NATO preaching. My purpose is to raise questions about fashionable assumptions of our alliance and point out what seem to me confusions in the canons, or at least the rhetoric, of contemporary Atlanticism. It is *a* Canadian perspective but certainly not *the* Canadian perspective; the public statements of Canadians are as rich as any in banalities about the North Atlantic world, although our policies are fortunately more pragmatic than our utterances. Nothing in this essay is intended to question the continuing and basic importance of the military alliance of the North Atlantic countries. At the moment, however, undiscriminating pleas for NATO unity are creating confusion and dismay because they conflict, and are bound to conflict, with the realities of members' policies in the North Atlantic and in the world at large.

The Variant Requirements of Defense and Diplomacy

There are in NATO contradictions between military and diplomatic requirements.

Unity of command and coordination all down the line obviously promote an effective fighting posture. The task of coordination would be simpler if NATO forces were responsible to a single federal government to which they were all subject—provided, of course, anything so unwieldly as a NATO government could have an effective and forthright policy. Most member governments recognize the necessity of surrendering more control over military matters than over political or economic policy. The genuine federal solution being out of the question, however, most are sensible enough to steer clear of a spurious federal solution, the worst of all methods for maintaining an alliance. While insisting on as much interallied coordination and consultation as possible, they shy away from the paralysis inherent in proposals for placing all hands on the trigger. Knowing that ultimately it is the strength and determination of the country that controls the crucial power rather than the unity of the alliance which acts as a deterrent, they accept, tacitly for the most part, the decisive role of the United States. Dissenters develop their "independent" nuclear power rather than hold out for multiple control. Whether or not these "independent" deterrents are wise or effective, it is better that dissent take this form than lead us too far into schemes for multipartite direction of policy which would break down in a crisis. Nevertheless, in the military field, the argument for as much centralized control as possible is strong.

In the field of diplomacy, the interests of member nations are far more diversified. A common foreign policy has proved impossible to achieve, but it is persistently assumed that it would be a good thing if we could achieve it. One cannot, of course, argue against perfection, and if we could all think in unison on Cyprus, chickens, or Mozambique, that would indeed be a heavenly situation. On earth we are not going to, however, and it is not entirely a process of rationalization to argue that we are stronger as a team for our diversity.

The Argument Against Uniformity

While there are, and always will be, real problems troubling NATO, some of them seem to be psychiatric. We are driven mad by abstractions—searching for symmetry and unity, making ends out of means, ignoring the virtue of untidiness in an untidy world, seeking to define the undefinable, and evoking a mood of despair about the fortunes of the Atlantic world when we might better feel the reasonable confidence justified by things as they have worked out in practice. This is not to say that the differences which threaten the alliance, and specifically the differences between France and the United States, should be ignored. It is healthier, however, to look at the practical results of this difference rather than judge it in the hysterical belief that every difference among the allies is fatal for us and an enormous boon to our antagonists. It is certainly better for the allies to agree than to disagree if they can, provided, of course, that the policy they agree on is a good one. It was better for them to be divided over Suez, the Congo, or the Bay of Pigs than, in accordance with an abstract belief in unity, present a common front in support of the unwise policies of one or more of their members. The apostles of unity tend to assume against all evidence that "unity" means we shall all be united behind policies which are eminently wise. There are times, however, when members should remain disengaged in order to do what they can to bail out their foolish partners and incidentally avoid the opprobrium which the latter have brought upon "the West."

On certain issues of crucial military importance such as the protection of Berlin or, even outside the NATO area, the confrontation over missiles in Cuba, it is highly desirable if not essential that the allies maintain a united front. The importance of unity in any given situation depends, however, on where strength lies. In the case of Berlin it would seem essential that at least the United States and Germany stand together, and highly desirable that the whole alliance be in agreement. In the case of Cuba the solidarity of the allies assisted the United States in its brinkmanship, but it is by no means certain that it was the major factor in the Soviet decision to back down. Khrushchev displayed a shrewd recognition that it is the strength of the United States rather than the fact of the alliance which is the decisive deterrent. It is true, of course, that the morale of the alliance will be sapped by persistent differences over major issues, but damage can also be done to the spirit of fraternity by the resentment of members against the compulsion to alignment against their own judgment. Permanent damage would be done if panicky demands for solidarity led members into the fallacy of believing that by setting up compulsive institutions they could induce uniformity in so inchoate a collection as the members of NATO or, more widely interpreted, the Atlantic Community.

It is by no means proved that General de Gaulle's differences with the United States over European affairs and his intervention in Latin America bring cheer to the Kremlin. As a third power in the fetid atmosphere of Pan America, Gaullism, if it has anything behind it, could be more of a threat to Castroism than to the United States. As for his attitude toward China, there is reason to conclude that it has been a good rather than a bad thing that Britain and other NATO allies have had relations of some kind with Peking when the United States had not: for instance, the imminent conquest of all Indo-China by the Communists in 1954 was probably forestalled by the Geneva truces because Sir Anthony Eden was able to talk to Chou En-lai while the Chinese were being frightened by U.S. threats of retaliation. Variations in the China policies of Britain, France, and the United States were tactically useful in persuading the Communists to a truce. On the other hand the withdrawal of the United States from a united front at the signature stage seriously prejudiced whatever chances there were of stabilizing the area on the basis of the truce. There is a good deal to be said at present for contact between a major Western leader and the outlaws in Peking, although this advantage must be weighed against the effect French deviation could have on the prospects for success of the uncompromising policy which the United States, in its own wisdom, has decided to pursue in Vietnam. The argument is not that diversity and disunity are advisable; it is that they are not always as bad as they are proclaimed to be in principle, and sometimes diversity strengthens the diplomatic arm of the West.

Some allowance should perhaps be made here for the fact that lesser powers in NATO have long been suspicious of cries for "NATO unity." To us this has been the siren call to support whatever our larger brothers wanted to do on their own. When the French used to expect us in the name of NATO to support them over Algeria, for instance, they never suggested that there should be any sharing of decisions on policy in Algeria. They could certainly not be blamed for failing to take Canada or Norway into their counsels on so delicate a matter as Algeria. It is necessary, however, to accept the consequences of the fact that where there is and can be no unity in policymaking, undeviating support can hardly be expected.

If what is wanted is a united Atlantic foreign policy, we cannot get around this fundamental dilemma with rhetoric about common purposes. Nor can we get around it by fondly believing that we can go much further than at present to achieve unity in policymaking. Even in a limited European political union it is doubtful if the product would be one strong nation with a single powerful policy toward the rest of the world acting as a beneficent "third force," as claimed by many Europeanists. It might very well turn out to be an association pledged to unity and therefore obliged to settle for something half way between Oslo and Lisbon—a policy based on the lowest common denominator, a collective voice weaker than that of the historic nations of Europe. In a century, or even a generation, Europeans might feel like a nation, but they cannot neglect the need to be strong in the crucial meantime.

We went through this issue of a common foreign policy in the Commonwealth and learned a good deal. During the last war and shortly after there were voices raised in Britain and Australia for a Commonwealth with a single foreign policy. The Australians thought this would give them some control over British policy, and the British advocates fondly thought of an empire in which the real decisions would be taken in London and supported in world councils by six or more votes instead of one—an ingenuous assumption one suspects is at the bottom of proposals from the greater powers now for a common NATO policy toward the world. The vision was dissipated in London when it became clear that British intentions under such an arrangement were subject to veto from distant and presumably irresponsible capitals. If in the Commonwealth we had prescribed unanimity, we would have prescribed a rigidity bound to crack at the first major test. When the goal is the achievement not of alignment but of a maximum amount of mutual understanding, then countries can remain in the association even after they have differed on an issue. It is true, of course, that the amount of common purpose achieved in the Commonwealth under this loose system has been well below maximum, but it does not follow that the results would have been better if we had been confined in a framework so tight that resignation was the only alternative to assert in an intolerable position—and Britain could have been the first member to resign. No analogy is exact, of course; NATO has a task that requires more cohesion than the Commonwealth, but it has to cope with political attitudes and interests hardly less diverse.

The Function of Lesser Powers

In the Atlantic Community we have great powers, middle powers, and small powers, each with its own historical and geographical associations, and I cannot think that the prospects of world peace would be improved if they were all welded into one mass—even a federalized mass. Great powers usually lack comprehension of the role of middle powers, while middle powers have a tendency to exaggerate their importance in the scheme of things. The role of a middle power may be more pacific, but it is no more virtuous than that of the large ally; it is not even possible without the great powers holding the ring. Nevertheless, the secondary role of the middle power in international diplomacy is worth preserving.

Would we be stronger today if the Scandinavian countries had been so tightly bound to a united Europe or Atlantica that the Swedes, Norwegians, Danes, and Finns would not have been acceptable in international truce forces or as mediators? What would the United Nations have achieved without Scandinavian secretaries general? Consider the remarkable contribution that Ireland has made not only in supplying forces for the Congo and Cyprus but in the emollient diplomacy of the

United Nations. It could not have done so if it had been bound to a united European or Atlantic foreign policy. Each country is unique, and there are unique ways in which it can serve the cause of peace. It is difficult to think of any country so useful in the world as Switzerland, and yet there are those with such an unreasoning prejudice against neutrality that they would penalize Switzerland within Europe for its services. We may yet have wars like Korea in which the Swiss can play their indispensable part, and we are certain to have need of them to act as they have for the French and British in Cairo and the Americans in Havana, or between French and Algerians. What would we do without Geneva—or Vienna—for diplomatic encounters impossible elsewhere? There is no need for any other country to follow the Swiss model, but let us not in our passion for unity and uniformity destroy what is unique and valuable. Some countries, such as Sweden, are more useful neutral than armed at our side. Even within NATO there is room for diversity short of neutrality. Norwegians, Danes, and Canadians have been able to participate effectively in various mediatory exercises while still contributing to NATO and remaining aligned on basic NATO issues. It is in our power to achieve more for the common good if we resist a policy of automatic alignment. It is not suggested that United Nations or other international truce or mediatory forces are a substitute for NATO force under present circumstances, but they play an indispensable and complementary part in the continuing struggle with anarchy in the world, and it is in NATO's interest that some states be in a position to furnish them with forces.

The Federalist Fallacy

The passion for uniformity is usually expressed in a credulous predilection for federalistic institutions, associated no doubt with the widespread assumption that progress in the international community must inevitably proceed through regional agglomerations to the monstrous leviathan of world federation. It may be that the world will eventually find salvation in federation, but to assume that this is inevitable is to close our minds to more imaginative and more functional means of making progress from our present difficulties. Trouble comes when the enthusiasts assume that the unity they devoutly wish for and which is essential if federation is to work does in fact exist. If there were even as much consensus from Sicily to Scotland as there exists from Florida to Oregon, the argument for a common Western European foreign policy would be strong. If Western Europe, however, has not revealed a consensus adequate to permit even the EEC members to submit to common decisions on foreign policy, how much more unreal would it be to act on the assumption that there is a consensus from Alaska to Turkey? To assume that it exists because it ought to exist or that a Council of Ministers could compel it to exist, and to establish institutions under the spell of that illusion, is to court disaster. Ancient nations and new nations alike need room to breathe. Agreement is induced more readily when they are tied together loosely than too tightly. In Canada after two centuries of a pilot project in European union involving two of the great peoples of that continent living within a single political framework, we are realizing that the corset must be adjusted for a two-way stretch.

The search for agreement is not helped by pious denunciations of sovereignty in the abstract. Exorcising national sovereignty is not going to remove the problems of jurisdiction or conflict of interests endemic in a world disorderly by nature. The bloodiest war of the nineteenth century was caused not by the assertion of national sovereignty but by the problem of jurisdiction within the sovereign state. Nor is the cause aided by unctuous pleas to rise above petty nationalism coming from large states which have cultivated more intense national feeling and more jealous regard for their sovereignty than their docile partners. The largest powers, furthermore, far from submerging their identity in a broader political organism, could confidently expect to dominate it politically and culturally. It would be grossly unfair to accuse the United States of calculating aggrandizement or even of hypocrisy when Americans call upon allies to surrender their sovereignty to common institutions, and yet lesser countries cannot fail to foresee that such institutions would in practice lead to no real diminution of American sovereignty but rather to an extension of the area in which the American writ would in fact run. No fair-minded person should argue that the United States in advocating a multilateral nuclear force is seeking to add to the forces under its control a polyglot fleet of mercenaries, but this seems what it would amount to. The incompatibility stems not from American arrogance but from American power. Congress is generous and internationalist, prepared to offer American aid and American protection but in no way to surrender its right to decide American foreign policy, because its worldwide interests are such that it dare not.

Neither the United States nor any other ally could accept North Atlantic institutions in which decisions were made by simple majority or even a weighted majority because the United States, which has a near monopoly of the crucial weapons, could not permit a veto on its freedom of movement and the rest of us could not in such an unequal situation give up our right to dissent and contract out. In practice, of course, and that is what matters, the United States is unlikely to act in ruthless disregard of the views of its allies; and the latter are unlikely to be reckless enough to put themselves beyond the bounds of the alliance. To acknowledge formally the priority of the United States among the allies would rouse even more trouble than the French proposal for accepting a tripartite leadership. Nevertheless, members of the alliance understand even when they do not admit the United States role. So why not leave well enough alone? Leaving well enough alone allows, furthermore, for the unostentatious adjustments which may be required to accord with shifts of power and policy within the alliance. It is doubtless easier for a Canadian, haunted by less history than a European and safer under the umbrella, to accept the American priority in Atlantic diplomacy and strategy. Are not we all, however, better off coping with the fact of that priority, which being unspecified may be adjustable, than formally acknowledging a relationship of inequality or proclaiming principles no one is likely to respect?

It must be recognized, of course, that failure to create decision-making bodies leaves the great powers free to make unilateral decisions. They are going to do so anyway, and it is better not to complicate crises with the bitterness of broken promises. Britain and France did not consult their allies from whom they wanted support over Suez, and the United States did not consult its allies over its reaction to Cuban missiles. In neither case was it simply because they didn't want to; it was because they couldn't. In operations of this kind governments don't even risk telling their own senior officials; how could they tell foreigners? This is a fact of life about the great decisions which we have to live with, but it doesn't follow that we cannot and should not consult about those continuing policies which shape the world and determine whether crises will erupt.

These facts of life are not altered by exaggerating the unity or danger of the Communist bloc as an argument for drastic measures on our part. There is a *non sequitur* in the apocalyptic argument that the threat is so great it must be met with federation. If desperate measures are needed, why try something least likely to succeed? It might better be argued that the threat is so great we should all, according to the Soviet model, become satellites of our all-powerful leader, the United States. That is neither an ideal nor a lasting formula, but if the worst came to the worst, I would have more confidence in it than in the paralysis of power resulting from an Atlantic federation.

When Is an Alliance Not an Alliance?

There are reasons for dropping the word "alliance" altogether in dealing with the NATO community because the concept of it as an alliance in the classical sense is misleading. It might be better to use—or at least to think in—Max Lerner's term "power cluster." One cannot, however, rally devotion to a "North Atlantic Power Cluster," and loyalty inspired by appeals to a supranational cause will be required from members so long as NATO serves an essential security function. We should not be so bemused, however, as to fail to see the reality beneath the rhetoric. NATO is not in any literal sense an association of "free and equal partners." It is a "power cluster" with the United States, in

Lerner's phrase, its "epicentre." We should not forget either, as Atlantic isolationists are inclined, that the "power cluster" of which the United States is "epicentre" includes countries in the Pacific, South Atlantic, and other regions as important in the American scheme of things as members of NATO. "The United States," according to William Lee Miller, "is technically one ally in a set of alliances, but actually a superpower with many lesser affiliated powers. She has in fact a large impact on her associates, but she is debarred by her own tradition and the nature of the association from the more blatant impositions of her will."[1]

The United States is not so much our ally as our "champion," as defined by the Oxford English Dictionary thus: "Person who fights, argues, etc., for another or for a cause." The resources of the United States and its allies are so disproportionate that the military contribution of most of the latter is marginal, justifiable more for political than military reasons. The contemporary role of the United States is threefold. It is able and disposed, although not necessarily committed, to defend its allies from attack and the threat of attack, out of concern for their welfare and for its own paramount interest in discouraging aggression anywhere. Secondly, it maintains its end of the duel of deterrence. A third function is to carry on the dialogue with the Soviet Union through which we might all hope to move on toward a more stable balance of forces. The United States role as "champion" is appropriate to a transitional stage out of which it is the common aim to break into a more stable world order wherein right and justice are less directly associated with pressure and compromise. In the meantime, nevertheless, the allies of the United States must bear in mind constantly the significance of American strength for whatever stability they have in the world.

The phraseology of alliance implies more of a community effort in the raising of levies and the determination of policy than is obtainable or even desirable. NATO military and strategic policies may be the product of combined decisions in theory, but these decisions are largely dictated by the national policies of those who control not only the decisive forces but also the rhythm of technological development. One reason for obscurity is the reluctance of the United States, for sound diplomatic reasons and out of a disinclination to assume the global burden, to define candidly its position in the "alliance." By its actions it makes clear its view of the relationship, as for instance in its unhesitating adherence to its own policy in the Cuban crisis or its determination to pursue limited talks with the Russians in spite of the reservations of Paris and Bonn. The United States would prefer to act in

---

[1] *Alliance Policy in the Cold War, ed.* Arnold Wolfers (Baltimore, 1959), p. 33.

concert with its allies, but if it can't it may be expected to act anyway. The allies are valuable to the United States even if the alliance is something of a mirage. The United States Administration is strengthened in dealing with Congress and in appealing to world opinion by appearing as one member of a strong association. And whatever the military realities, "the West" is politically stronger if it can appear as a mutual-benefit association. Herein lies an inescapable paradox.

Alignment or Nonalignment

In the enormous dialogue into which the world may be moving, one voice may be better than several both for strategy and negotiation. The illusion that there can be a clear, firm voice emanating from the collectivity of NATO dies hard. In present circumstances the United States has the responsibility almost alone to match actions and words, calculate threats and promises. It has the specialized information and expertise against which allies find difficulty even in maintaining an argument. The logic for the allies to remain docile is clear but quite unacceptable. Nations persist and cannot be wished away. Their pride and sense of responsibility are as much a force for good in the world as for ill.

Sensible allies will, however, recognize limits to their freedom of action, and herein lies the significance of the Cuban crisis of October 1962. From the beginning of the Castro regime there had been tactical differences between policies of the United States and those of the NATO allies toward Cuba. Although Castro is regarded with apprehension, a majority of Western Europeans and Canadians have doubted the wisdom of United States policy toward the troublesome island. Consultation—or rather explanation—is continuous among the allies on dangerous situations, but the allies were never seriously engaged in the formulation of American policy or tactics toward Cuba. The matter was treated as one of the OAS rather than NATO, a course justified by the rules both of OAS and NATO but of dubious strategic validity nevertheless. However, when the crisis came in 1962 and the gauntlet was thrown, the allies recognized that the ranks had to be closed. The NATO nations knew they had to take cover with their champion right or wrong. Deductions from this experience, however, should be discriminating. To assume that since in the "crunch" allies may be expected to stand with the United States they have no room for maneuver between crises is to ignore the facts of their behavior. Few of them, even after the crisis, have aligned their tactics toward Cuba with those of Washington. The Cuban crisis did not prove that the allies would or should seek agreement and act in concert in a moment of crisis. It proved simply that if the United States challenged a Communist opponent the allies would be likely to recognize a fundamental interest in supporting their champion right or wrong.

The argument for undeviating alignment within the alliance rests too often on an oversimplified view of the forces loose in the world. It assumes that the world is divided into two camps and that nothing else matters except the struggle for dominance between them. The need to maintain Western strength against the Communist threat may often be the determining factor, but to assume that any single frame of reference could guide all the decisions of a modern country in foreign policy is too much like Marxism for free people. The upheaval involved in the transition from an imperial world to a world of universal self-government makes the factors much more complex. Nor can one dissociate from political diplomacy the struggle for trade which divides the nations on non-cold-war lines. The bipolarization of the world is a dangerous and undesirable state of affairs which we should seek to avoid. The cracking of the monolithic structure of the Communist realm presents us with opportunities. The French assertion of independence may be looked upon as a dangerous disruption of unity or as an effort to break through the framework in which we have been congealed for too many years, to loosen international society, and, by permitting freedom of national expression, to reduce the danger of catastrophe. Close alignment, the unity of the West, cannot be lightly abandoned as principles, but the world will be better off when we can abandon them—when nations can join together for specific purposes and then realign themselves with other nations if different interests are involved, when the pragmatists triumph over the absolutists.

What Is the Atlantic Community?

The whole concept of an Atlantic Community requires respectful but skeptical examination. What we should seek to achieve by the idea of the Atlantic Community goes deeper than the concoction of a new political entity of any kind. It is the preservation and toughening of a civilization which, although it has its roots in the Mediterranean-North Atlantic area, is universally pervasive. Because that civilization is threatened by the military power of a bloc which only partially shares its tenets and by the danger of anarchy in the world at large, and because the vast preponderance of military power outside the Communist bloc is to be found in this area, countries of the North Atlantic must collaborate closely in military affairs. This is the persisting reason for NATO, and NATO is on the whole a satisfactory functional agency to achieve this purpose. Because it is also essential to maintain understanding and a sense of common purpose among the principal custodians of that civilization, we also need agencies like the NATO Council in which to discuss our policies together. We need bodies like the NATO Parliamentarians' Conference through which understanding can broaden into wider circles. Then there is the Organization for Economic Cooperation and Development (OECD), a body devoted to stimulating the wealth of Europe and America for the benefit of itself and the world at large. What is significant and encouraging, however, is that the OECD, originally a European and then a North Atlantic association, has recognized by inviting Japan to membership that its function cannot be geographically circumscribed. These functional bodies are, I suggest, all we need for our essential purposes—except for the will to understand, without which no conciliar bodies are of any use at all. The will to understand, however, requires study and unceasing exertion; too many people, therefore, concentrate not on the substance of unity but on the erection of shadowy constitutions which, they fondly assume, will circumvent disagreement by imposing unity.

The trouble with defining the Atlantic Community is that it has no bounds. Its political and cultural ideas are more deeply rooted in Delhi or Dakar than in some regions washed by the sacred waters of the North Atlantic. The concocters of North Atlantic unions usually pay lip service to this fact by adding, as a postscript, that other countries may graciously be permitted to come in later. What other countries? Is it imagined that states like Australia, Japan, Jamaica, or Uruguay will be flattered by honorary Atlantic status? When one tries to draw up a membership list, one realizes the futility of seeing this institution in geographical or in constitutional terms. How could we draw a frontier round the Atlantic spirit without destroying it? How could the United States, Britain, France, or even Canada tie itself to an entity which would limit its scope to find common cause with countries in the four corners of the earth? The act of definition would be essentially a separation of sheep from goats, but the creation of unity on a selective basis inevitably stimulates disunity on a broader basis. The tightening of the alliance of countries of West European origin can make more difficult conciliation and reconciliation with the other races; and this latter is the major problem of our time. It is often argued that the North Atlantic races must form their own bloc to defend themselves against blocs being formed in Africa, Asia, in Latin America, and by the combination of all of them in the United States. But how can one seriously compare the laudable but tentative endeavor of the weak and divided peoples of Africa, for instance, groping toward mutual understanding and collaboration among themselves, with the creation of a close federation of power and wealth in the North Atlantic? As for the so-called "Afro-Asian bloc" in the United Nations, there are real problems presented by the occasional united front of non-Europeans in what look to us like dubious causes, but too often this "bloc" is a myth and a bogey kept alive by those who want to shake free from a universal international organization and create a pure white substitute in the guise of a North Atlantic Community. This motive, justified only by panic, is an abdication of the mission of the North Atlantic peoples.

The Atlantic Community is a spiritual idea and it has a function. That function is to use the enormous wealth and power and skill of the area to stimulate prosperity for this and other areas and to protect the weak. Its function is initiative—to save the world, not itself alone. It can be the core of a new internationalism, or it can be the instrument of racial isolationism. Our function is to promote our mission rather than our unity. Our defense arrangements and our instruments of consultation are not perfect, and we may find better mechanisms; but the test of these mechanisms is whether they enable us better to play our part in the world rather than shut us off from it.

Economic Problems of the Alliance

—*LAWRENCE B. KRAUSE*

Introduction

The need for collective defense that gave rise to NATO in order to face the threat of Soviet expansionism in Europe has implications beyond the domain of military policy. A unified military posture demands coordinated diplomatic and economic positions on matters not military in the narrow sense. It is thus from derived importance that international economic problems have a bearing on NATO.

It is worthwhile noting that intimacy of economic relations among the NATO countries is not a goal in itself. The *economic* gains from harmonious economic relations among the NATO partners are no different from those that can be obtained from similar relations with Japan, Australia, Sweden, Switzerland, or indeed South Africa, the Soviet Union, Communist China, or Cuba. The fact that we draw diplomatic and military distinctions between NATO and other countries that carry over into economic policy should not hide the realization that no purely *economic* end is being served by these distinctions. When economic disputes occur among NATO countries, no special importance should be attached to them unless they have diplomatic or military implications.

The desire to keep economic relations distinct from diplomatic and military ties of the NATO countries has been recognized in the past. Not only is there no great advantage in combining economic functions within NATO—there would be an economic and political loss in discriminating against all non-NATO countries, many of whom are close friends of the alliance. But we must return to the reality that economic relations do have a bearing on our military position and cannot be excluded in an examination of NATO unity.

Changes in the Western Alliance

One need not be very observant of world affairs to recognize that the Western alliance has changed and is in the process of changing further. In military matters, diversity has replaced what once appeared to be a monolithic structure. Serious questions have been raised by the French as to the effectiveness of collective defense for the security of individual countries.[1] Indeed the Cyprus issue has made two NATO countries wonder whether the most immediate military threat to them is to be found outside or inside the alliance. Diplomatic changes have also been very marked. Recently, France has extended recognition to the Communist Government of China and thereby withdrawn recognition of Nationalist China without prior consultation in NATO.[2] While diversity on diplomatic questions has always been greater than on military issues within NATO, open differences on crucial East-West questions have been avoided in the past. The changes on the economic front have been just as great, although they do not appear as spectacular because they evolved more slowly over time. These changes have many implications for the unity of the alliance. Change by itself is neither good nor bad, but must be evaluated as to consequences. In economic matters as well as military and diplomatic ones, the changes have some elements that can be generally welcomed and others that seem less desirable.

The changes that have occurred can be traced to two sets of forces, one external and one internal. The Western alliance, particularly in its military and diplomatic aspects, is primarily a defensive alliance that owes its existence to the threat of Communist—mainly Soviet—power. The fact that this external threat is or appears to be less severe today than it was in years past has reduced the need for the alliance and, as a result, the individual members feel they can indulge themselves in the luxury of diversity. Another source of change has been the marked revision in the relative economic strengths of the member countries of the alliance. Europe has experiencd what is probably the most remarkable period of sustained economic growth in the history of mature capitalist countries. The standard of living within this

[1] Pierre M. Gallois, "The Raison d'Être of French Defense Policy," *International Affairs* (October 1963) and General Paul Stehlin, "The Evolution of Western Defense," *Foreign Affairs* (October 1963), pp. 70-83.

[2] Apparently there was also no consultation between Paris and Bonn on this issue. This makes one wonder what the meaning of the 1963 Franco-German Treaty may be when an issue of such great importance to both governments was not included within it.

area has increased to the point where the Europeans can carry a much larger share of the economic burdens of the alliance and rightly insist on a greater role in leading it. This change is not due to the fact that the United States has stagnated while Europe has advanced. To the contrary, the United States since the war has achieved better than average growth by its own historical standard. The difference has been solely the result of the exceptional economic dynamism in Europe which has enabled it to narrow the gap with the United States.

The evaluation of the military and diplomatic, as well as the economic changes requires detailed study and this has not been attempted. The first impression that one gets from viewing the military situation is that it is hard to recognize any advantages in diversity, but easy to see potential dangers from the weakening of NATO unity. A careful and critical re-examination of strategic planning is desirable, if it leads to beneficial changes; and to the degree that this would not have occurred otherwise, the crisis within NATO has improved our defense. However, the weakening of NATO may have seriously undermined our military posture if it has made us appear less resolute in the face of Communist pressure or if it has increased the chances of nuclear accidents.

The possible advantages of diversity of diplomatic positions among the members of the alliance are easier to contemplate. It is frequently difficult for a single country to amend a diplomatic position once taken, and this may be particularly true for the United States. But diplomatic positions should be changed if the conditions upon which they were predicated no longer exist. When the path to an improved position is embarked upon by a friendly country, other countries can follow without appearing to retreat in the face of hostile pressure. This allows the alliance to be flexible without being irresolute. There are real dangers to diversity, however. When an important member of the alliance takes a new diplomatic step, it will necessarily weaken the old position adopted by the alliance. If a great deal of power is required to hold the new position and the member making the diplomatic overture does not possess this power, then the alliance position may be weakened without a realistic alternative being presented in its place.

In contrast to military and diplomatic changes, the new economic situation appears to have only desirable consequences. When one country advances economically, all countries usually gain. Indeed, the economic advancement of Europe is an important goal of U.S. policy and has been due in some measure to Marshall Plan aid extended by the United States. The most important single outcome of the economic resurgence of Europe has been the creation of the European Economic Community (or Common Market) which until recently had the strong support of Washington. Nevertheless, our applause must be tempered with some caution for even a desirable change can frequently be improved upon and there are many features of the European Common Market that are less than optimal.

European Economic Community and the Unity of the West

The approval of the Treaty of Rome by the parliaments of West Germany, the Netherlands, Belgium, Italy, Luxembourg, and France can properly be regarded as a major victory for a group of European statesmen who were not only visionary thinkers but also practical politicians. This major step toward turning the idea of European unity into reality reflected past successes, such as the European Coal and Steel Community, and also past defeats ,such as the still-born European Defense Community. Yet the form of the EEC as specified in the Rome Treaty was not considered to be an ideal, but merely a beginning toward economic and political integration of all of Western Europe. Clearly, this larger purpose was the basis for U.S. support.[3]

The motivations that can be identified as being of some importance in the creation of the Common Market are in the main compatible with, and in part identical to, the goals of NATO. Of primary importance was the desire to prevent a recurrence of conflicts in Continental Europe. By immersing West Germany and her neighbors in an all-embracing institutional structure, it was hoped that independent aggressive action by a single country would no longer be possible. Certainly the cold war gave a sense of urgency to this desire since it became clear that West Germany would not only have to be rearmed, but would soon have the strongest conventional forces in Western Europe. Furthermore, it was hoped that the Common Market could help alleviate some of the problems caused by the East-West division of Germany. While the major goal of reunification could not be served—and might even be hindered—by the formation of the EEC, the Common Market could ease some of the frustration of division by giving the Germans an achievable goal in the form of a more unified Europe. This would provide an outlet for German nationalism without exacerbating the cold war. Economic motives also played a part in kindling enthusiasm for the Common Market. It was thought that by combining the separate markets of the member countries into one gigantic market, substantial economic benefits could be obtained. All of these motives were in keeping with United States interests and with the U.S. view of an integrated Europe.

A further motive involved in the formation of the EEC was the desire for independence and self-respect. It was all too apparent that only two countries survived the second World War as real powers—the United States and the USSR. In the face of their strength, the individual European countries could make little impact on the world

[3] Max Beloff, *The United States and the Unity of Europe* (Washington: The Brookings Institution, 1963).

scene. The reduced diplomatic role of Europe was graphically illustrated during the Suez Crisis when the United States refused to support the steps taken by France and Great Britain. The role of follower is never very satisfying, and countries previously at the center of world affairs may think it intolerable. While no single European country had hope of reaching superpower status, enough economic recovery and advancement had occurred in Europe by the mid-1950's to indicate that an amalgam of European nations would achieve this position if it could develop true political unity. The independent or third force idea has subsequently been most closely associated with President de Gaulle, but he is not the only Frenchman who feels this way, nor is France the only country in Europe where nationalism survives.[4] Jean Monnet avers that unity in Europe will not develop into a nineteenth-century type superstate and that the Common Market was developed in order to avoid nationalism.[5] But political unity in Europe will create power and how that power is used will depend on the desires of those political leaders able to direct it. President de Gaulle sees a unified Europe as a power base for spreading European —mainly French—influence throughout the world.

From the point of view of the United States, European independence has two faces. On the one hand, independence means that Europe will shoulder a much larger share of the costs of defense, will provide greater resources for the "have-not" nations, and will in general take on more of the responsibilities of the free world. On the other hand, independence also means a rejection of U.S. leadership and all that this implies.

The EEC and the Cleavage of Europe

The conflict of interest between the EEC and the United States stemming from the creation of the Common Market was overshadowed in the first instance by the cleavage within Europe itself among member and nonmember countries. The EEC included only six European countries, not because the members wanted to keep the club exclusive, but because the other European nations did not wish to join. Great Britain showed indifference to the customs union idea and great hostility to institutional arrangements which impinged upon its national sovereignty. The decision by Britain to stay out precluded Norway and Denmark from seriously considering joining. The European neutrals — Sweden, Switzerland, and Austria — felt that their mili-

---

[4] In a speech before the National Press Club, March 23, 1964, Gaston Defferre, the Socialist candidate for President of France, criticized President de Gaulle for the way that he attempts to assert French independence but not for the substance of his moves.

[5] Jean Monnet, "A Ferment of Change," *Journal of Common Market Studies*, Vol. 1, No. 3, pp. 203-11. Reprinted in *The Common Market: Progress and Controversy*, edited by Lawrence Krause.

tary status prevented them from participation. For the other European countries, either the weaknesses of their economies or their peculiar political position (or both) inhibited them from seeking membership. However, the Six recognized that the nonmember countries of Europe might someday change their minds and they included a provision in the Treaty of Rome for accepting new members.

When it became obvious that the EEC was going to become a reality, the implications of its existence for intra-European trade began to attract attention within the OEEC. In February 1957, the British Government unfolded a plan to prevent the trade split within Europe through the creation of a free trade area in which the EEC would be one member. The proposal accommodated all of Britain's needs by closing the trading breach without sacrificing Commonwealth preferences or the British agricultural system, and without the sacrifice of national sovereignty to a supernational organization. In this form, the proposal did not generate much support, either within the EEC or from the United States. The United States saw the free trade area as a means of spreading discrimination against U.S. exports and also as a means of weakening the movement toward political unity in Europe, both of which it opposed.

The EFTA Solution

Even though the free trade area proposal was modified during the negotiations to overcome some of its weaknesses, the basic objections of the EEC remained and the negotiations failed. The failure, unlike subsequent ones, was not marked with great bitterness. The nonmember countries which are most dependent on the EEC, Austria and Switzerland, accepted the failure almost with indifference. Nevertheless, a conference was called at Stockholm and eventually a rival trade organization was born, the European Free Trade Association. The purposes of EFTA were threefold: to provide an economic offset to the member countries for the loss that they might suffer from not being a member of the Common Market, to demonstrate the technical feasibility of the free trade area technique, and to provide a bargaining counterweight to the EEC. Actually, the bargaining power provided by EFTA is usable only in multilateral trade negotiations or in negotiating a wider free trade area, but not in negotiating for membership in the EEC as Britain found out subsequently.

Both the EEC and EFTA have proven to be successful and, on some grounds, more successful than could have been expected. For the Common Market, economic gains have been outstanding. Intracommunity trade has expanded at a remarkable rate which has contributed to and resulted from the rapid pace of economic growth of the member countries. This has made possible the accelerated removal of the barriers to intracommunity trade and the beginnings of a common agricultural policy. The EFTA has also made substantial progress in reducing trade barriers and increasing trade among its members, but, of course, has not resulted in the complete reorientation of the trade of those member countries dependent on the EEC. In addition, EFTA has scored an important diplomatic victory by negotiating the association of Finland to its group and thereby re-establishing the economic unity of Scandinavia, while at the same time staying clear of cold war problems.

The success of the two groups, however, made the economic cleavage of Europe more ominous. The more they succeeded in directing the trade of member countries toward other member countries, the greater became the welfare loss of trade diversion. Furthermore, the possibility of an aggressive trade war within Europe that might accompany a cessation of economic expansion was enhanced. Since NATO countries are found in both groups, the military and diplomatic consequences of overt economic hostility had to be recognized. Finding a bridge between the Six and the Seven became an important goal.

British Membership in the EEC

At this point Great Britain once again took the initiative. Having faced up to the fact that only a major proposal could succeed, Britain took a bold step and applied for membership in the EEC. This move was quickly followed by applications for membership or association from all the EFTA countries (except Portugal and Finland) and from other European countries then affiliated with neither group. It was clear from the start that the negotiations would be very difficult. Britain had trade commitments to the other EFTA countries and to the Commonwealth, which would be undermined by membership in the EEC unless special provision was made for them. Furthermore, Britain enjoyed a special relationship with the United States, particularly with respect to the sharing of nuclear secrets. If the political side of the Common Market was to have meaning, then this special relationship could not remain unaltered. The negotiations became protracted, with both sides bargaining very vigorously. Tentative settlements were reached on a number of technical points, usually following a British concession, but many difficult problems remained to be decided when the negotiations were abruptly halted in January 1963 by the unilateral action of President de Gaulle.

The De Gaulle Veto of Britain

It is difficult to know all the factors that went into de Gaulle's decision, but certainly the issue of nuclear armaments played a part. When the United States cancelled the Skybolt missile project, a crisis developed for British strategic planning since they were counting upon this missile as part of their nuclear weapons delivery system. The choice made by Prime Minister Macmillan at Nassau was to accept continued dependence upon the United States by agreeing to rely on Polaris-type missiles. President de Gaulle interpreted this move as a choice by Britain for collaboration with the United States at the expense of Europe and was reported to be personally angered because he thought Macmillan had agreed to consider a "détente nucléaire" with France.[6]

The ending of the Brussels negotiations led to a great deal of bitterness among the participants and most of it was directed against France. Many observers in Britain felt that the talks were on the road to success if not on its verge. They interpreted the de Gaulle veto to mean that France simply did not want Britain in the EEC and had been bargaining in bad faith. Certainly the Conservatives lost the election issue on which they hoped to be retained in office. Within the EEC, anger against France was directed especially toward the method by which the talks were ended. Unilateral action—particularly a pronouncement in such a form as a press conference—struck at the very heart of the Community spirit and therefore robbed the Common Market of the necessity for agreement. Without the "will to agree," all the basic weaknesses of the institutional procedures whereby decisions are made in the EEC came to the fore. A crisis of confidence resulted and is still having some effect on the operations of the Community.

The breakdown of the Brussels talks can be evaluated in terms of its possible consequences on economic policy of the European countries and its effect on relations among the Atlantic countries and the free world in general. On the surface, calm has returned to the diplomatic scene. The British economy survived the shock and expanded at a rapid pace during 1963 without excessive pressures from the balance of payments. While discussion of joining the EEC has ended in Britain, the public reaction to the failure was not so great as to prevent a subsequent attempt at entry after a reasonable lapse. Official British statements have indicated that they have not turned their back on European unity. Periodic discussions between the EEC and Britain have continued under the aegis of the Western European Union (WEU), which has kept a channel of communications open, though nothing of substance has resulted as yet. Even in Brussels a sense of normalcy reigns, but there certainly has not been a return to the *status quo ante.* Progress has been made on some of the problems facing the Community by working out carefully balanced programs to meet some of the needs of all of the countries. The "synchronization" approach, however, is slow and cumbersome and many important issues have yet to be dealt with. For the United States, the rejection of Britain by the

[6] Hal S. Nieburg, "Nuclear Exclusion and the Common Market," *Midwest Journal of Political Science,* VIII (February 1964), pp. 55-74.

EEC was a real disappointment; however, no obvious shifts in U.S. policy resulted from it.

Insight as to the importance of these recent developments can be gained by examining the major issues of economic policy individually and relating them to the general problem of the unity of the West. Five areas of economic policy are important:

1) trade in industrial products,
2) trade in temperate agricultural products,
3) international monetary mechanism,
4) international transmission of inflation and recessions, and
5) the relations of developed countries to less developed countries.

Trade in Industrial Products

Much progress has been made since the war in liberalizing restrictions on the flow of industrial products among the developed countries of the West. Quotas and dollar discriminations that were so much a part of the early postwar scene have all but disappeared. Tariffs have been reduced substantially through tariff bargaining in GATT. However, in a competitive world even moderate tariffs can be quite protective. The creation of the EEC and EFTA also raised the importance of the tariff barrier to trade since the tariffs of these trading groups are levied only against nonmembers, while trade among the members themselves is (or will be) free of restraints. Despite the need for further tariff reductions, the traditional mechanism for bringing this about, item-by-item bargaining, had reached the limit of its usefulness. The United States was particularly constrained in its ability to carry on fruitful tariff negotiations because of the limitations imposed on it by the Trade Agreements legislation under which it operated and especially by the "no injury" philosophy that it contained.

Recognizing the situation, President Kennedy proposed and the U.S. Congress accepted a new approach to tariff bargaining contained in the Trade Expansion Act of 1962. Under the new act, the United States can bargain for large tariff reductions on whole groups of products (the linear method), and the only item negotiations needed would be over those products whose tariffs were not to be reduced. This legislation was passed primarily as a tool for negotiating with the Common Market, since at the time of its enactment it was generally believed in the United States that the EFTA countries would in the main be absorbed within the EEC. However, the most-favored-nation principle was to be maintained, so all GATT countries would benefit from any tariff reductions negotiated and therefore would be urged to take part in the negotiations themselves as in the past. Even the method of tariff bargaining was patterned after that followed so successfully by the EEC in pursuing internal tariff reductions.

When de Gaulle vetoed British entry into the EEC, the Trade Expansion Act became much more important despite the fact that part of it was made inoperative. While it could not be used to heal the breach between the Six and the Seven, it could lead to substantial lowering of tariffs all around which would ease much of the pain of the separation. It also gave the EEC an opportunity to prove what it had long proclaimed, namely that it was liberal-minded with respect to trade with nonmembers. Being the largest trading bloc in the world —greater even than the United States—the importance of the commercial policy of the EEC for the prosperity of all countries is second to none.

The need for a new round of tariff negotiations was recognized by all of the GATT countries and in May 1963, a resolution was adopted at the GATT Ministerial Meeting calling for preparations to be started for such a negotiation, named the Kennedy Round, to be held the following year (1964). Since that time, very little has been accomplished by way of agreeing to rules which would ensure the success of the Kennedy Round. A major controversy has involved the rules to be used for cutting industrial tariffs. While the Common Market had found the linear method suitable for cutting internal tariffs to zero, it had reservations concerning the fairness of the method for use externally when a reduction to zero was not contemplated. The U.S. tariff is highly differentiated with many high and many low rates, and a 50 per cent cut of all rates would leave some tariffs quite high. The EEC external tariff, in contrast, has little dispersion and a 50 per cent cut would bring almost all of its rates to a moderate level which it feared would not be protective enough to induce further rounds of tariff negotiations. Thus, even though the average tariff levels of the United States and the EEC are identical, an equal cut was feared by the EEC because some U.S. tariffs would remain high and it would have no bargaining power to get them reduced.

Attempts to find a solution to the disparity problem have been complicated because a number of technical details are involved and because of the internal politics of the EEC itself. The characteristics of a good solution would be one that all parties felt was equitable, that did not unduly reduce the over-all level of the tariff reduction, that did not so complicate the negotiating procedure as to be unworkable, and that did not work a hardship on innocent third countries. Such a formula is conceivable. All that remains is the agreement to accept it. Solving the disparity problem will not insure the success of the Kennedy Round, but failure to reach an agreement on this problem will certainly cause a failure of the total negotiations.

If the negotiations are scuttled on this or some other technical issue, it will only be because there is no will for success. It is not clear that all countries do want the Kennedy Round to succeed. One gets the view that France is very reluctant and will agree only if forced by her Common Market partners. If this is true, then one must contemplate what failure might mean. The fragmentation of the West into trading blocs would take on added meaning in the event of a failure of the Kennedy Round. It would sharpen the split, partly because of the disappointment of expectations and partly because of the drift toward protectionism that might well occur in the absence of a major step in the other direction. The drift toward protectionism between rounds of tariff reductions has appeared in the past and is going on at present.[7] It is almost certain that the disappointment would sour members.

The form in which the bitterness might be expressed could be an attempt to isolate the country or countries whose policies caused the failure. If the country were France, then she might react by becoming more obstructionist and less committed to NATO. Alternatively it could force the United States to reconsider its policy of nondiscrimination in international trade and lead to the return to the conditional form of the most-favored-nations principle. The hint of such a suggestion was contained in a report by the Joint Economic Committee of Congress.[8] In any event, a failure of the Kennedy Round would shake the NATO alliance just when it might need strengthening.

Trade in Temperate Agricultural Products

International trade in temperate agricultural products has not benefited from the liberalization measures taken since the war. Codes of conduct long since deemed inappropriate for industrial products are still permitted in agriculture. Many agricultural products are still state traded (even in free enterprise economies), they are subject to import licensing and quotas, they are besieged by discriminatory health and mixing regulations, and their export is often subsidized. Nevertheless, the volume of agricultural products entering international trade has increased.

The trading situation merely reflects the position of the agricultural sector in the domestic economies of the Western countries. Methods of agricultural production have been improved to the point where an output revolution has occurred. These increases in output have been achieved with a labor supply that has been constantly shrinking. Despite these trends, economic rewards to agricultural pursuits in general have not kept pace with those in nonagricultural work. Under these circumstances practically all governments have policies to supplement farm income. These policies have led to a great deal of

[7] Since the Dillon Round of negotiations we have seen the carpet and glass controversy, the chicken war, the movement toward agricultural protectionism in Great Britain as well as the EEC, and the raising of steel tariffs by the ECSC.

diplomatic relations and possibly military relations among the NATO

[8] U.S. Congress, Joint Economic Committee, *The United States Balance of Payments*, 88th Congress, 2d Session, 1964.

governmental involvement in the business of agriculture and the interference in international trade is just another manifestation of this trend.

Before the advent of the EEC, agricultural protectionism in Europe was kept within reasonable limits. While few countries showed much restraint in stimulating increases in output of particular crops up to the point of self-sufficiency, most countries refused to continue artificial stimulants beyond this point. Further output could be disposed of only in foreign markets with export subsidies which would cause a substantial drain on their treasuries. While these policies closed many markets to the efficient world exporters, many other traditional markets remained open to them and they grew in size. The adoption of the Common Agricultural Policy by the EEC, however, threatened the markets of two of the most important of the traditional importers, the Netherlands and West Germany. What was needed for an enlightened policy was an agricultural program for the group that was *more* responsible than any of the countries had followed individually (except the Netherlands) because the power of the EEC to create mischief in world agricultural markets was greater than the sum of the powers of the countries separately. Instead the EEC adopted a policy of complete agricultural protectionism that in theory and possibly in practice can isolate the EEC markets entirely from international competitive forces.[9]

The first major clash over the new EEC policies occurred in 1963 in the now famous "chicken war." The United States during the preceding five years had developed a lucrative and expanding export trade in frozen poultry to West Germany. The Common Agricultural Policy, when applied to poultry, tripled the tariff on American chickens entering Germany and proved to be an insuperable barrier. The United States felt that the increase in tariff was unjustified, particularly in view of an explicit agreement to the contrary. The United States protested in vain and finally took steps within GATT to seek redress, which was finally obtained. The controversy raised tempers beyond what the importance of the product would justify because it was over an issue of principle and because of what the EEC action portended for other agricultural products.

The United States and other agricultural exporting countries came to the belief that agriculture could no longer take a back seat in international negotiations. The interests of agricultural producers are being threatened, and they are insisting that agriculture be treated on the same basis as industrial products in the Kennedy Round.

Agricultural trade is important to all the Western countries (despite the fact that many of them are highly industrialized with small farm

[9] Lawrence B. Krause, "The European Economic Community and American Agriculture," *Factors Affecting the United States Balance of Payments,* U.S. Congress, Joint Economic Committee, 87th Congress, 2d Session.

populations, in percentage terms) because of the magnified political importance of this group. Even the figure of President de Gaulle is not enough to calm the French peasants when they are angry over economic issues. This makes international negotiating very difficult because domestic political considerations limit the area of maneuver for all participants. Yet as difficult as the negotiations may be, the problem must be faced because there is probably no other economic issue that could poison the diplomatic relations of the Western countries more quickly than a wrangle over agriculture.

International Monetary Mechanism

The experience of currency markets in the 1930's was not a happy one; values were very unstable due to private speculative capital movements and attempts by governments to alleviate domestic unemployment through competitive depreciations. Recognizing that chaos in currency markets inhibits international trade and investment, the postwar monetary mechanism was designed to maintain fixed exchange rates to the greatest degree possible. The present system, the gold exchange standard, was patterned after the gold standard of the late 1920's and early 1930's but with the addition of the International Monetary Fund to aid in adjustment problems and, as it developed, with a greater role for key currencies, primarily the U.S. dollar.

It was hoped that the system would combine the advantages of the stability of the gold standard while avoiding its disadvantages. Domestic money supplies were not to be tied to gold and occasional changes in currency values were to be allowed to correct fundamental disequilibria in the balance of payments. The system seemed to work quite adequately in the early postwar years as alterations in the exchange rates of developed countries were infrequent and the U.S. dollar was able to supplement the small increases in new gold for official reserve purposes. Before 1958, the U.S. dollar was really the only international currency since all others were technically inconvertible and the dollar was as fully acceptable or was considered preferable to gold.[10] After the major European currencies were returned to convertibility, however, the situation changed. Not only did European currencies become more desirable, the U.S. dollar became less so because of the very large balance-of-payments deficit that the United States developed beginning in 1958.

With the changing status of the dollar, questions began to be raised as to the efficacy of the gold exchange standard itself.[11] It was recalled that an essentially similar system collapsed in 1933 and our

---

[10] The British pound and the Swiss franc also played an international role but much reduced from that of the dollar.

[11] Robert Triffin, *Gold and the Dollar Crisis* (New Haven: Yale University Press, 1960).

current system is not free of defects. Critics of the gold exchange standard claim that it combines the worst features of a gold and non-gold standard. It does not contain a quick-acting adjustment mechanism, does not provide enough liquidity to allow slow adjustments, and permits exchange rate changes only as an act of desperation leading to harmful speculative capital movements.

As the continued U.S. balance-of-payments deficit exposed the weaknesses of the system, attempts were made to strengthen it by improving the liquidity-creating mechanism. The resources of the International Monetary Fund were increased and special standby borrowing rights were created for it. A number of bilateral agreements were made between the United States and other developed countries to shore up the key currency status of the dollar. New borrowing instruments were created to enable the United States to limit its short term liabilities without a loss of gold. All of these measures, however, are of the nature of a rescue operation and have not added much basic strength to the system itself.

There is probably no other economic issue on which the basic interests of the Western countries correspond so closely as with the desire to improve the international monetary mechanism. The International Monetary Fund is studying methods to improve the system as is the Group of Ten.[12] The interests of the countries while close are not identical. If agreement cannot be reached on this issue, then it is a very bad omen for the unity of the West. On the other hand, the spirit of cooperation that could be kindled from a successful attack on this problem could carry over into other areas.

The International Transmission of Business Fluctuations

During the Great Depression, all countries learned the meaning of common destiny as economic distress was spread from one country to the next through the network of international trade and capital movements. After the war, most governments became committed to preventing large-scale unemployment. Newly investigated aggregate economic policies to influence the level of over-all economic activity offered them the instruments to bring this about. However, Keynesian economics does not provide a means of insulating domestic economies from changes in foreign business conditions. In the postwar period, inflations rather than depressions have been the major worry. If a rapid inflation begins in one country, it can quickly spread to other countries. To resist the inflation requires a country to allow its resources to be shifted abroad through involuntary foreign investments which it may be unwilling to do. Thus, the problem is still worthy of consideration.

[12] The United States, Canada, Belgium, the Netherlands, West Germany, France, Italy, the United Kingdom, Sweden, and Japan, with the cooperation of Switzerland.

It is certain that the science of economics will not develop in the near future to the point where economic growth can always be prevented from leading to inflation or economic constraint from bringing unwanted unemployment. Moreover, even if economics did always give the right answer, it is uncertain that the political will to take unpopular policies will be present. It is therefore of international concern that some countries will be experiencing domestic excesses in one direction or another. This concern can be harnessed for positive good if it can lead to better economic analysis and if it could bolster the will of governments to take proper actions. Some steps have been taken in this direction. In the framework of the OEEC and its successor, the OECD, the economic situations of the member countries are examined and governmental policies reviewed. This confrontation procedure imposes no obligations on countries deemed to be following improper policies, but the confrontation itself may nevertheless facilitate beneficial modifications.

This problem does not present a critical issue for the West since countries can continue to adjust to the excesses of other countries as they have in the past. It is an area, however, where great benefits could be obtained if international cooperation ever developed to the point of allowing meaningful consultations. This is a field of preventive medicine which promises reductions in balance-of-payments worries and help in achieving sustained economic growth if perfected.

Relations of Developed to the Less Developed Countries

The NATO alliance is directed at the East-West controversy, but another area of difficulty may have equally upsetting implications for the political stability of the world, the so-called North-South controversy. Within recent years the less developed countries have found that a slow attack on poverty is today not politically acceptable at home and therefore they are impatient to take rapid steps up the economic ladder. This they recognize cannot be done without foreign help. From the point of view of the "have-not" nations, the United States looks much like the Soviet Union, and West Germany like East Germany; they are all rich countries not doing much for the poor ones. Discontent in these countries can lead to internal revolutions or aggressive external actions. These conflagrations cannot be easily contained and quickly take on cold war characteristics as witnessed in the Congo, Cuba, Lebanon, and elsewhere. Issues involving the LDC's have also frequently led to squabbles among the advanced Western countries themselves.

Primarily what is involved is the desire by LDC's for better conditions for their trade of goods and services, greater and more liberal grants of aid and loans, and some LDC's desire larger receipts of foreign investments and technical aid. The United Nations Conference on Trade and Aid convened in March 1964 for the purpose of giving the LDC's a forum for expressing their desires in the hope that joint expression would bring concessions from the richer countries. It is apparent that there is a difference of view among the Western advanced countries on how help should be extended to the LDC's. On the one hand there is the method typified by the association of certain African countries to the EEC. Through this agreement grants and loans are extended and preferential treatment is given to the products of the associated LDC's when entering the Common Market. In contrast is the method of extending general aid without trying to tie the recipient country to any special arrangement to the donor country. This latter approach is preferred by the United States, balance of payments permitting. These different approaches have their counterpart in suggestions made at the U.N. Conference: one plan would extend preferential trading opportunities in advanced countries to the LDC's and they would be differentiated by degree of poverty; and the other plan would call for the general reduction of tariffs by the advanced countries on products of importance to LDC's without seeking compensation from the LDC's.

There is no need to coordinate Western policy to the point where only identical terms for export markets or loan conditions are being offered the LDC's. In fact, a substantial loss might be involved in doing this. It is the diversity of the West combined with competition for the markets of the LDC's that makes the West a much better commercial area for the LDC's than is the Communist bloc. Competition insures that the LDC's will get the most for their resources today and in the future. Yet there would be benefit from agreeing on a code of behavior that would discourage certain practices that could be quite detrimental to the Western alliance. Policies that further the economic development of one poor area at the expense of another poor area cause political animosity in the area being discriminated against. They may also bring resentment in the favored area if the arrangement yields commercial benefits to the advanced countries. Preferential trading arrangements are of this type and should be discouraged. Furthermore, any arrangement that ties an LDC in a special way to an advanced country, particularly if it mirrors a former colonial tie, may someday be the target of nationalist extremists in the LDC's as being a form of neo-imperialism. This may be an issue over which moderate leaders in the LDC's could be defeated to the detriment of the stability of the world. It would be naive to suggest that each developed country treat all underdeveloped countries equally, especially when traditional patterns have been established by reason of a common culture and the dictates of geography. However, it is only when traditional ties are not institutionalized in restrictive agreements that they can appear natural and desirable in the long run to the less developed countries.

Conclusion

Walter Hallstein has characterized NATO as an alliance that has demanded the highest degree of responsibility from one member and from the others the highest degree of trust.[13] In order to convert this nonsustainable position into one of lasting benefit, methods must be found of sharing responsibility and spreading mutual trust. It is clearly in the area of military policy and particularly with respect to nuclear weapons that the best opportunity exists for doing this. However, the NATO countries have economic and nonmilitary diplomatic relations which also can play a role in the transformation. Many economic problems have been discussed where differences, if compromised, could aid in the process. If in contrast the economic problems create lasting differences, NATO, although unlikely to be undermined, certainly will be hurt.

The NATO alliance has lasted for fifteen years, which is long as military alliances go, but is still too short to have stood the test of time. The NATO alliance could end and if its raison d'être were to cease, the demise would be the object of boundless happiness. However, NATO could end as an effective alliance without a diminution of the Soviet threat. Under these circumstances any joy that was expressed in the West would be short-lived. The seeds of NATO's destruction have already been sown. Mistrust and resentment are powerful poisons. Change must come and should be aided wherever possible.

[13] Walter Hallstein, "NATO and the European Economic Community," *Orbis,* VI (January 1963), reprinted in *The Common Market: Progress and Controversy,* edited by Lawrence Krause.

The Trend Toward Economic Cooperation

—*STANISLAW WASOWSKI*

At the time of this writing, the future of the Kennedy Round is uncertain. Students of international affairs generally wish it success and hope that the conclusion of the Kennedy Round will be followed by further steps to liberalize trade, to cooperate closely in monetary matters, and to determine a common policy on aid to the less-developed countries. Many believe that closer political links between the two shores of the northern Atlantic would follow directly, or be implied in such an economic rapprochement.

One cannot be satisfied with looking at this alternative alone. What is likely to happen if the process of building the intergovernmental links across the Atlantic proves to be a failure? Most people are silent about this unpleasant alternative. A few occasionally throw a furtive glance at the chasm. In his essay, Dr. Krause, for instance, foresees strong negative attitudes based on disappointment, the revival of protectionism, and a gloomy prospect of a return to the conditional form of the most-favored-nation clause. The prospect of fear and disappointment, if nothing else, should lead us to investigate the second alternative. Moreover, an economist always likes to consider alternatives if only to see how much one gains by not accepting them. Finally, it is not inappropriate in a volume devoted to strategic problems to mention a simple tactical one: at the negotiating table, having alternative strategies strengthens one's hand.

What follows is an attempt to scan the horizon and to point out some developments which are likely to occur, should there be failure in the negotiations aiming at some form of wider intergovernmental agreement about the economic aspect of the Atlantic union or community.

World Market for Manufactured Goods

Sophisticated manufactured goods today have two characteristics: they require large expenditure on research and development, and the economies of scale fully appear only when markets are very large. Advanced technology is often so expensive that there is no point to repeat the performance of others. At a time when the French have asserted their independence of the United States, the Mirage planes which are about to become a part of the independent French deterrent will be using American engines as well as American tanker-planes. Recently, an important French electronics firm, Machines Bull, which is heavily involved in the French defense effort, became closely linked with General Electric, an American firm.

The need for sizable markets is illustrated by the case of passenger jets. According to informed estimates, the annual demand for small jets is probably not higher than 100, and for big jets probably around forty. Therefore one wonders how many big jet producers can be profitably accommodated in the free world. This explains, perhaps, why the year 1963 saw not only the famous press conference of the French President, but also the decision to produce, together with Great Britain, a supersonic plane with the ominous name "Concord." Since, doubts have developed whether there is enough room both for the Concord and the American supersonic plane, now on drawing boards.

The market demand for some modern products is small in comparison to the most efficient scale of production. Sophisticated and capital-intensive goods might find the tariff walls relatively easy to scramble over. As Pierre Uri observed, due to a high degree of specialization, trade between industrialized countries is marked not by competition of industries, but by competition within industries.

While tariff barriers are getting increasingly inefficient when applied to capital-intensive products, labor-intensive manufactures at the other end of the spectrum might well become tariff-free. As the United Nations Conference on Trade and Development in Geneva has indicated all too clearly, the hope for the less-developed South depends to a large extent on their ability to export labor-intensive manufactures. Pressure for the eventual scrapping of all barriers for such products is strong, and has not been rejected in principle by the industrial North.

There are additional reasons for doubting the efficiency of the tariff barriers for many manufactured goods; they stem from considerations on the demand side of the international and national markets. With growing opulence on both sides of the Atlantic, the consumer finds that after he has taken care of the essentials, a substantial part of his purchasing power remains to satisfy less pressing needs. His spending on luxuries is not very price-margin conscious. If it is at all, it may be in the "wrong" direction: beverages, cameras, original furniture, good perfumes, woolens, and, on a less magnificant scale, razor blades, will be scaling tariff walls more nimbly than ever before.

As manufactured products become increasingly more complicated (high precision, electronics, etc.), good service more often turns out to be more important than lower price of the product. Organizations with excellent service departments have comparatively little reason to fear tariff walls. After all, the wild success of the Volkswagen "beetle" is due not so much to its enchanting beauty, nor even solely to its price (which in the United States is competitive with that of other small European cars), but to a large extent to its excellent service organization.

Closer Contacts Between Countries

Growing affluence means more spending on luxuries, including tourism, which leads not only to an increase in foreign exchange earnings but also to an interest in foreign ways of life and in goods produced in other countries. Tourism tends to lead to an increase in trade and, in democratic countries, would be one of the forces out of sympathy with higher tariffs. Increasing contacts between peoples and firms may lead to the realization that a good way to earn profits is not only by imitating somebody else's product and subsequently claiming protection, but also by differentiating products and by inducing interest in one's own brand beyond the political frontiers of one's own country.

International contacts are growing closer; this cannot be denied. It is significant that the first anniversary of the press conference which denied Great Britain entry to the Common Market was celebrated, a few days late, by the announcement that Great Britain and France had agreed to build a tunnel under the Channel.

Agricultural Products

The rejection of a North Atlantic understanding on agricultural trade barriers will leave the professional economists muttering unhappily about the misallocation of resources. Large groups of farmers and their political representatives will be rather disgruntled that the principle of protection working for their interest at home is mischieviously applied against them by foreigners. In the short run, and probably in the medium run, protectionism would celebrate a success.

Not so in the very long run, however. There are sound reasons for suggesting that protectionism in agriculture will not survive very long, at least in the form that allows high-cost production to be reflected in a high level of costs and prices. To put it briefly, the European Economic Community will one day pass its Corn Laws. The alternative would be to suffer an uncomfortable increase in costs resulting from high food prices, on top of the increase caused by a relatively slower growth of labor input in the EEC than in the United States.[1]

For the agricultural problem, European Corn Laws are not the only solution compatible with a decline of protectionism. European agriculture might become so competitive as not to require a high protective wall any longer. This could be achieved by modernizing agriculture and strengthening the present trend for the labor force to leave the soil. After all, Belgium has only about 11 per cent of its labor force on the farm, which is nearer to the proportion prevailing in the United States than to that in West Germany, France, or Italy. When the agriculture of the Six reaches a high level of efficiency, owing both to better methods of production and to an outflow of the labor force to the towns, the justification for the protection of the "infant agriculture" would disappear. The end of its privileged status would be more feasible, since a decrease in the percentage of the labor force employed in agriculture also means a decline in the political power of rural electoral districts. Thus in the long run the Community seems to face either the Corn Laws or a removal of some no longer necessary protection.

While the United States and other net food producers wait for these slow processes to evolve, the dearth of agricultural production in the world can be advantageously used to diminish the accumulation of surpluses and to introduce some free-market logic to our agriculture, for we are not without motes in our own eyes. A plan along lines proposed by Pierre Uri in his *Partnership for Progress* could be introduced on a voluntary basis by the surplus producers. Vouchers for food would be distributed as a part of aid; they could be used by recipients who, in their choice of the type of the product and its source, would take into consideration their needs and the prices of food. Such a plan would not need to wait for unanimous agreement. Any country or group of countries could start it.

Governmental Policies

Even if intergovernmental agreements concerning trade should not be accepted, areas of international cooperation exist and must continue to exist. With the worldwide spread of currency convertibility, dangers of hot-money movements, or of accumulation of unduly large reserves by some countries, would cause the governments of the industrialized North to continue to enlarge their cooperation in this field. It seems probable that some help to overcome short-term difficulties caused by interrupted growth as well as by sudden outflow of international reserves would be granted on a more or less regular *ad hoc* basis, even if the overconfident would shy away from a thorough extension of the International Monetary Fund.

---

[1] See J. Frederic Dewhurst, John O. Coppock, P. Lamartine Yates, *Europe's Needs and Resources* (New York: Twentieth Century Fund, 1961), Chapter 3.

One cannot disregard the present trend toward more awareness of consumer interests. Public reaction to magazines such as *Consumer Report, Which?,* or DM, as well as the interest shown by governments in the important and politically promising issue of consumer protection, indicate that the influence of the consumer on economic policy can only grow. In the long run, this should be a force working for a lowering of tariffs, or at least for maintaining the present level of tariffs.

Lastly, there is the unmentionable "conditional most-favored-nation clause." It is only fair to remind oneself of the proposal on this matter made by *The Economist* in the fall of 1963. Some countries (e.g., the United States, Canada, Great Britain, and the EFTA nations) could extend mutual linear tariff cuts, and make them available to other countries ready to reciprocate with equal cuts. Only a few exemptions in really touchy cases would be granted. The open, unrestricted, but conditional clause could win many friends for the free-trade solution. It would permit a lowering of production cost in the member countries and thus the level of their export prices. As the EEC countries are the largest trading group in the world, it would be a very telling argument for less protection on their part.

Hope in Lieu of Conclusion

Although the issues raised here require a thorough study, this brief review of the alternatives, should the Kennedy Round fail, permits a tentative conclusion. Gloom and despondency, evoked by a mere thought of the failure to bring about closer trade links within the Atlantic Community, might be justified only by our own attitudes and behavior. The facts about production, demand, changes in wealth, and habits seem to create a sufficient basis for even a unilateral pursuit of the non-protectionist solution. But these facts are not sufficient in themselves. They are merely the necessary condition. In the absence of an over-all intergovernmental agreement, a policy for the North Atlantic region could be hammered out to stave off protectionism as well as the fear of protectionism. The existence of such a policy could be a useful prop in trade negotiations.

An Economic Strategy for NATO

—*KARL BRANDT*

The preamble of the North Atlantic Treaty of 1949 appropriately and succinctly defined the ends to which this alliance and the twelve original signatories were dedicated.[1] It emphasized the determination of the signatory states to "safeguard the freedom, common heritage, and civilization of their peoples, founded on principles of democracy, individual liberty and the rule of law." The parties to the treaty also affirmed that they sought to promote "stability and well-being in the North Atlantic area," and that they were resolved to unite their efforts for collective defense and for the preservation of peace and security. Three days before its conclusion, the treaty prompted the Soviet Union to a formal protest declaring: "This treaty is directed against the Soviet Union."

While the irrevocable 25-year commitment of the parties gives the treaty at this time nine more years of validity until the first date for the opportunity of renunciation, it has been open to consultation and review for several years. Thorough consultation and candid review seem most urgently needed vis-à-vis the extraordinary changes in the international political panorama, the changed aspects of other alliances, and changes in the relations among the NATO allies themselves. What lawyers call the *clausula rebus sic stantibus*—the clause for invalidation of any contract due to circumstances, unforeseeable at the time of

[1] U.S., Congress, Senate, Committee on Foreign Relations, *North Atlantic Treaty: Documents relating to the North Atlantic Treaty,* Senate Document 48, 81st Cong., 1st Sess., 1949, p. 1.

its conclusion, which make fulfillment an unintended or unreasonable imposition—provides possibilities for revision at any time.

It may be taken for granted that insofar as the collective defense purpose is concerned, the ICBM superiority of the United States and the likelihood of tremendous destruction in the event of a Soviet or American decision to use nuclear weapons amounts to a *de facto* stalemate. This also implies the resulting prospect of multitudes of local or regional military conflicts conducted with conventional or entirely new weapons (with or without nuclear warheads) and short or medium range missiles which could be used by guerrilla forces. Indeed the rapidly emerging pattern of bleeding and exhausting the United States and the NATO defense capacity by pinning it down in as many guerrilla wars as possible in most distant spots of the globe and stifling requirements of supply lines and communications has all the earmarks of traditional Communist tactics.

The restoration of Western Europe's industrial and military strength and the new dynamic expansion of its capacity to produce and to export have given the leading European allies of the United States and Canada much greater stature and self-confidence. This fact combined with their additional military and economic strength resulting from the disengagement of several of them from most, if not all, of their colonial obligations, has inevitably diminished the prestige and the originally self-evident value of NATO among the allies. If this trend is not to lead within a short time to a serious weakening and obsolescence of the alliance for the defense of Western Europe against a Soviet attack on the one hand, and to grave jeopardy of the security of the United States on the other, it is high time to diagnose the existing afflictions and their causes and to take remedial action now. This applies particularly to the complex and numerous vexing problems and issues of economic policy.

Communist Strategy

However, in discussing economic affairs of the alliance and its members, it must be realized how profoundly they are rooted in ideas which motivate the gigantic worldwide power contest between the Communist system of government by coercion and the free world's defense of freedom and limited government under law. One hundred years after the formation of the First Socialist International, the emphasis on the means of world conquest has changed, but the ideological core of this revolution and its goal have not.

In the bewildering and confusing circumstances of an asserted change of climate in the cold war, meaningful discussion of issues of economic strategy requires the demarcation of clear assumptions concerning the contingencies of forms of conflict in the challenge of Western civilization. What, for example, is the present state of the global contest between the Communist powers and the NATO alliance? Have the Communist powers really abandoned the cold war? If so, for how long and for what reasons? The seductive diplomatic moves accompanying the crucial interval of a presidential election year in the world's leading industrial country with the greatest economic and military power create a convenient tranquilizing illusion. It is insinuated that the militant Communist movement, characterized by a determination to conquer and remake the world in the Marx-Lenin-Stalin-Khrushchev-Mao image is now in the process of shifting toward a realistic acceptance of "peaceful coexistence." Moreover, the chiefs of the two Communist empires confess as audibly as possible before the ears of the whole non-Communist world that each of them has economic difficulties at home and political trouble with its brother despotism. This amazing metamorphosis is alleged to lead to an era of lessening tensions, demilitarization, progressive opening of the iron and bamboo curtains, and maximum growth of economic and cultural intercourse among all countries.

Even if there were the barest minimum of tangible evidence for such total reversal, it would not entirely change the frame of reference for the following discussion of questions of economic strategy. Preparing national and mutual security requires prudence in weighing all potential dangers to the nation's existence, and strictly forbids toying with optimistic assumptions.

Therefore, not as the verdict of proven fact, but as a working hypothesis, I assume that the much-publicized symbolic symptoms of the "great thaw" are not deeds but astute and well-timed tactical maneuvers of the chiefs of the Soviet and Chinese states and their satellites. These diplomatic moves are true to their philosophy and to Lenin's strategic doctrine of long-term psychological warfare. Temporary compromises and even years of driving in reverse gear—as in the interim years of Lenin's New Economic Policy (NEP)—have always been included in the Soviet strategy of psychological warfare designed to throw the enemy off balance. Aside from such moves—synchronized with the changing situation in the several U.S. alliances in different areas—there are no indications of any weakening, reformation, or abandonment of the dogma of the inevitable ultimate victory of the dictatorship of the proletariat over the assertedly decaying democracies with their private capitalism and imperialism. The frustrating toil of United States diplomats for nuclear disarmament is hopelessly deadlocked by Soviet intransigence. Unmitigated in its stark reality, the concrete and barbed wire wall of shame stands in Berlin, erected as the twentieth-century symbol of inhumane tyranny, and as a deliberate insult to the United States and NATO as well as to the United Nations.

Even if there were reliable symptoms of evolutionary change toward more pacific goals inside the Communist realm of coercive state capitalism, the natural sense of mortal danger and the basic duty of Western statecraft would nevertheless require utmost vigilance and precautionary action to strengthen the collective security against the threat of reversion to a new phase—Communist militancy and aggression. This holds particularly since working out rational procedures for cooperation is a time-consuming process, while totalitarian surprises typically occur instantaneously.

As the solidarity of the leading NATO countries begins to relapse into separate nationalist and independently sovereign courses of policy, and as the Communist bloc powers take full advantage of this leeway for maneuver, it must be the paramount duty of self-preservation of the United States and the West European nations to restore and maintain NATO to full functional integrity. Its only purpose and exclusive justification for existence is today what it was originally in 1949: "to safeguard the freedom, common heritage, and civilization of their [the signatory governments'] peoples." These governments not only were founded on, but owe their proud and unequalled social and economic achievements more than ever to, respect for human dignity, protection of individual liberty, the institution of private property and means of production, limitations of the power of the state by the essential tenets of natural law, and the functioning of representative government by law.

Economic Policies

It is a widely accepted but totally erroneous assumption that economic policies and the conduct of economic affairs in the life of a society are a dimension of government which is more or less independent of the content of the Bill of Rights and have little if anything at all to do with the severity of law enforcement and the penal code. It is therefore also widely taken for granted by many that in the dimension of economic policies their governments are free to choose at will and with impunity any available methods, procedures, arrangements, and corrective actions which promise success—irrespective of the form of government, the principles on which it stands, or the accepted social credo. Sadly enough, this sort of pragmatic treatment of symptoms of social or economic maladjustments by *ad hoc* measures is equivalent to structural alterations in a well-designed building made by workmen without any knowledge of, or respect for, the architectural design or the safety margin of the static balance. The result is in both cases the emergence of a malfunctioning jerry-built construction.

But the interrelation of economic policies and the law of the land has another little known cause and effect circuit: the adoption of certain economic institutional arrangements—such as the partial abolition of private property, competition, or flexible market prices—in democracies leads very quickly to the necessity for brutal methods of law enforcement which ultimately abolish the integrity of life and liberty. This has been proven by past transitions from representative government to various forms of monolithic systems, irrespective whether fascist, socialist, or communist. These economic policies ignore basic traits of human nature, and hence lead inescapably to the need for subduing by force and punishment the natural inclination of "economical man" to utilize his private initiative opportunities for personal gain. This nexus means simply that economic measures which abolish the essence of private initiative, free enterprise, and a competitive market economy, and which banish decentralized decision making and consumer oriented resource allocation lead to the police state and political tyranny via the backdoor of economic decisions. It is one of the hard historical facts of life that freedom, which the NATO alliance is designed to safeguard, is inseparable from an economic system that relies basically on a system of order in which the free market offers incentives for private initiative and competitive free enterprise under the restraints and regulations of social responsibility.

Yet, while the NATO alliance is of vital importance for the security of the North Atlantic family of nations and thereby for the security of the free world, realistic appraisal also requires recognition of the fact that, in spite of its importance, this alliance inevitably has to confine itself to the wise orientation and coordination of vital policies, and that it cannot be a cure-all device for solving every member's specific needs. The United States as well as all its European allies have a multitude of other treaty relations with other states. The pattern of specific interests of individual states is complex and overlapping, or is sharply competitive. However, the intelligently interpreted self-interest of the allies, as well as a well defined broad basic and over-all economic orientation, ought to give the North Atlantic pact top priority rank among all treaties and other agreements in the foreign relations of the member states, as well as induce their governments to render such loyal service to its common cause that the Communist regimes have to respect its powers of unity and cohesion.

The Economics of Military Defense

In view of the extraordinary fluidity of the scientific and technical frontier in the search for effective defenses against new and even more powerful offensive weapons, utmost vigilance and suspicion must be combined with the allocation of a substantial proportion of scarce resources for military defense-oriented research and for even more costly development and production of reliable weapons in quantity. Tying up scarce resources for military tasks deprives the civilian economy of the benefits of their use. This major burden is at present carried by the industrially advanced countries of the West, primarily by the

United States. It lies in the interest of solidarity, with all allies as beneficiaries, that continual adjustments be made in sharing the costs as fairly and equitably as is politically feasible. This sharing ought to apply to the burden in terms of manpower, physical installations, functional performance, and materials. Procedures to arrive at agreement on gradually more fair and equitable distribution of shares in the burden call for continual consultation with candor, conference without fear of disunity, and constructive imagination.

But even more necessary is a balance between boldness in pursuing supremacy in deterrent power, irrespective of primarily economic considerations on one side and the inevitable thrift and avoidance of extravagance in shaping the aggregate defense budget of the alliance, on the other. The latter need demands that, in order to maintain an optimum deterrent and the ability to win if attacked, the individual member states abstain from the pursuit of narrow national ambitions designed to enhance their prestige.

It would not be necessary, certainly, to unify allied efforts in the field of weapons research and development in order to insure against the emergence of Communist weapons superiority; rather, active competition should be encouraged in this field, with a subsequent pooling and collective implementation of the results thus obtained. Thus, ruinous skyrocketing of armament expenditures can be avoided without a sacrifice in security.

Economics of Partnership

Beyond allocation of sufficient resources to armament development and upkeep of military strength and services of supply, the key problems of allied economic strategy involve preventing of separatism and the disintegration of solidarity by the establishment of contractual intra-alliance relations which would gradually approach a genuine partnership. To talk merely in euphonious terms of the "Atlantic Community" is little more than to project beautiful colors of a rainbow of pious hopes against the thunderhead clouds of a coming storm. While sounding programmatic, the Atlantic Community label is but a vague generality and a visionary abstraction, as was the ill-fated concept of "One World."

If the members of the alliance, including the United States, want to fortify themselves against the powerful temptation to pursue every day's hard necessities by independent bilateral transactions with Communist countries, thus impairing solidarity, two types of action are mandatory. The first is to put with bitter frankness before all signatories the adverse consequences of contemplated opportunistic deals of one individual ally for the others and the aggregate evil effects on the cause of the alliance itself. The second type of action consists in working out and agreeing on detailed principles and procedures on specific issues of economic policy among partners, and searching for compensatory action for sacrifices incurred. Such partnership procedures would amount to changes and adjustments in the pattern of existing practices, which, in order to be practical, would have to yield a substantial and tangible net gain for all partners, and which therefore could be expected to be politically approved by the majority of the people even in those countries which gain least.

To explore, shape, and adopt such procedures one needs representative agencies with the delegates of all allies. The first among such agencies is the Organization for Economic Cooperation and Development (OECD) in Paris, successor to the most successful Organization for European Economic Cooperation (OEEC).

What makes the effort to close ranks and to restore true working relationships within NATO particularly difficult for the United States is the existence of a sort of quadripartite regional subdivision of the 15 members. While militarily closely aligned and economically interdependent, the United States and Canada are far from close economic cooperation. Each faces independently and separately the European Economic Community of the six leading continental European signatory states of the Treaty of Rome (France, Germany, Italy, Benelux), with a considerable number of associated member states in Africa and the seven nations associated in the European Free Trade Association (the Scandinavian countries, Austria, Switzerland, Portugal, and the United Kingdom), composed of four NATO and three non-NATO members (Sweden, Austria, and Switzerland). The fourth group consists of three NATO member states (Iceland, Greece, and Turkey) which are not otherwise aligned, although Greece has applied for associate membership status in the EEC.

The attempt to arrive at meaningful and workable partnership arrangements under the mutual defense roof of NATO would have as its first task agreement on guideposts for major problems that call for adoption of a common policy. Among the multitudes of such problems, a few belong within the range of over-all strategy.

Currency Integrity and Containment of Inflation [2]

In the conduct of all economic affairs within NATO countries, a basic requirement is the morale and faith of the people in the justice and fairness of the rules and regulations of the market economy, as is the proper functioning and the healthy growth of each nation's economy so that the yardstick for the value of goods, services, and productive assets remains reasonably stable. This axiom amounts to the mainte-

[2] *Cf.* U.S., Department of Commerce, *Survey of Current Business,* "The Balance of Payments" (January 1964), pp. 3-4.

nance of the integrity of the currency as the measure of exchange value and as the actual medium of exchange of and substitute for goods, services, and capital in the domestic and foreign markets. Inflation, meaning the rise of the level of consumer prices or the decline of the purchasing power of the currency, irrespective of whether it proceeds rapidly for a shorter span of time or continually at a slower pace for longer periods, and irrespective of the particular causes, has a most corrosive impact on the coherence and *esprit de corps* of any society. This is true in spite of the tendency toward increasing employment and rising nominal wages. During the inflationary boom real wages decline. The seeming prosperity stimulated by inflation is a mirage which costs in reality a shrinkage in national wealth. Simultaneously inflation acts as a powerful force that distorts the formation as well as the movement, the allocation, and the necessary depreciation of capital. It vitiates and undermines long-term contractual obligations, lets creditors lose, debtors gain, and thereby upsets and disorganizes in varying degrees the orderly economic process in the afflicted country and in its foreign relations.

While inflation automatically depreciates long-term obligations—such as mortgage debts and bonds—it enhances the value of physical assets and shares, and causes, inadvertently and unpredictably, revolutionary changes in the distribution of wealth and income. These shifts introduce an element of fraud into contracting debts as well as the purchase of durable goods or, particularly, producer goods. The shifts also engender a feeling of instability and tendencies to social revolt and political turmoil, which even in lesser degrees impede economic growth and stability. But inflation leads further to a flight of the people from monetary assets to physical assets such as inventories of goods or real estate. It discourages thrift and the formation of capital, and it puts a premium on hand-to-mouth living. By corrosion of confidence in contracts and the stability of value of money, it destroys or disorganizes the proper functioning of capital markets, one of the vital necessities of any economic development in a non-coercive open society. This disorganization is worst in countries which have undergone one or several phases of rampant inflation, such as Germany and France, where capital markets are still thin and brittle, or in Latin American countries where capital markets hardly exist. But even in the United States, with a loss of purchasing power of the dollar of an order of magnitude of, say, 2.5 per cent per annum in twenty years, and with a very large and well-functioning capital market and the majority of all people participating in it, the memory of the calamitous devaluation of the dollar in 1933 caused fear of acceleration of inflation and perhaps another devaluation of the dollar. This massive shift from bonds to shares caused prices of common stock to skyrocket early in 1962 and to collapse in the spring and summer of the same year. Worse than this, inflation drives existing indigenous capital into foreign shelters which offer more security, but it will also scare and induce some capital into domestic investment, but not to the spots where it would contribute most to growth. Security of the principal even in the absence of any interest is more appealing than opportunity for earning even high interest rates.

Inflation tends also to deteriorate a country's balance of payments. If the shrinkage of the gold and foreign exchange reserves of the currency goes far enough in corroding the residual confidence in its stability, it leads to a crisis in which the fixed relationship between gold and the currency unit and the convertibility of banknotes into gold is at stake. Unless the crisis is solved by the surgery of changing the relation of the currency unit to gold, it is usually countered by a variety of measures which control the foreign exchange of goods, services, and money by quantitative import restrictions on top of flexible tariffs and supplementary measures in lieu of tariffs. While all these measures inevitably throttle foreign trade, the worst one is the rationing of foreign exchange by licenses. They all amount to abolition of the free convertibility of a currency.

This sorry sequence of events led in the past, in the period from 1928 to 1933 and following years, to the progressive deterioration of cooperation among the former Allies of World War I, with disastrous results for foreign trade, entrenchment in depression, and default in joint efforts to prevent World War II. Nothing is going to prevent a repetition of the sequence of concentration on domestic political affairs, economic nationalism, and the resulting deterioration of diplomatic relations among mutual security partners—nothing but the clairvoyant determination of the heads of state and the leaders in the parliaments to prevent such a disastrous course in the coming years.

The containment of inflation poses in all political democracies today one of the most complex problems of national self-discipline involving the self-restraint of the government at all levels—federal, state, and local—in its fiscal and monetary policy, of the large corporations and employer associations, of national and local labor unions, and of organizations of farmers. The attainment of full employment increases the propensity to set in motion the cost-push and demand-pull inflationary spiral of wages and prices. Compulsory arbitration, government seizure of factories, and enforcement of wage-price guidelines are all government interventions which tend to fetter the free labor market as well as the commodity markets. Since industrial countries are competing with each other, inflationary processes in one country very quickly affect conditions in neighboring and competing countries. While it is the responsibility of the national governments and their note-issuing banks to use the reins of fiscal and credit policy to keep inflation in check—even at the price of some unemployment, it is also a fact that coordinated policies of several governments promise to avoid extreme severities in case of independent national policies.

The same applies to the equally desirable avoidance of falling prices, i.e., rising purchasing power of the currency—or deflation. This process increases real wages for all those employed, but it also distorts all long-term obligations, causes illiquidity and bankruptcy of debtors and thus creates unemployment and recession.

The maintenance of conditions in which the national economies can grow with reasonable stability and the defense of the full and free convertibility of the national currencies of all member states is a common concern of all NATO countries.

Mutual Balance of Payments Assistance

The enormous efforts and financial aid from the United States have contributed a major share to the successful reconstruction and fabulous growth of the European economy, the convertibility of the leading European currencies, and the growth of currency reserves of the six EEC and the seven EFTA countries from $12.3 billion in 1954 to $27.5 billion in 1963. But in pouring out aid to European countries to overcome their postwar difficulty to earn enough dollars and closing the so-called "dollar gap," the United States has incurred a deficit in its balance of international payments every year since 1950, with 1957 a minor exception. From 1950 to 1963 the accrued deficit amounted to $26 billion. As one major result the gold and foreign exchange reserves of the U.S. currency have shrunk from $25 billion in 1949 to $15.5 billion in 1963, while in the same period the short-term liabilities to foreigners have increased from $7.5 billion to $25 billion.[3]

The delicate position of the currency of the leading power of the West is first of all a problem to be handled by the American government by its own fiscal and monetary policy, and secondly by its 8.5 million private business enterprises in agriculture, industry, commerce, and banking.

However, due to the unique proportions of the American economy, its performance inevitably has a powerful impact on the economic affairs of other industrial countries far beyond. This accounts for the high priority which the United States is attributing to a program for restoring equilibrium in its balance of payments and particularly for the fact that the corrective measures chosen inevitably become a matter of keenest interest to all European countries. It is obvious that the more the correction has to rely on measures confined to unilateral

---

[3] *Cf.* David L. Grove, An Address before Town Hall, Biltmore Hotel, Los Angeles (San Francisco: mimeographed, Federal Reserve Bank of S.F., September 24, 1963).

action of the United States, the more severe will be the impact on the economy of other NATO countries and on their foreign sphere of economic interest. By the same logic it follows that carefully coordinated multilateral action of NATO governments aimed at restoration of equilibrium in the balance of payments could succeed with a far smaller aggregate of costs.

Both sound economic growth and the posture of the United States as the leading power in the free world demand strengthening of the world's confidence in the existing gold parity of the U.S. dollar. To restore this precious confidence at home and abroad our government must begin by discarding any ideas of devaluation, of adoption of floating exchange rates, or of creating new international credit institutions. Since such sound monetary policy comprises the essential elements of the economic, military, and political strength of the free world, the NATO member nations should rededicate themselves to it and implement it. Again, the way to such solidarity in shaping and executing policies is paved by the working party of the OECD devoted to balance of payments and financial problems.[4] Continuous intensive exchange of information and critical analysis of economic developments and current policies by an alert team of experts are the prerequisites to mutual agreement and specific action.

Such general staff work on monetary affairs is particularly needed in view of the negotiations on trade and tariffs under GATT with EEC in the summer of 1964. The agenda of the preceding conference on trade and development to be held under the auspices of the United Nations in Geneva—led by enthusiasts for international dirigism—makes such OECD staff work even more necessary. There the economic strategists of the Soviet Union and the underdeveloped countries will try to set up institutions and lay down policies which will give the raw material exporters maximum bargaining leverage vis-à-vis the leading industrial countries of the NATO alliance.

The more NATO partners arrive at mutual agreement on monetary and balance of payments policies, the stronger their position will be on the board of the International Monetary Fund in efforts aimed at fortifying the defenses of the major currencies.

Coordination of Development Aid Policies

The necessary corrective actions on the U.S. balance of payments and the general question of international liquidity are hinged to the transfer of capital aid to developing countries. Here again the chief need from the standpoint of NATO strategy concerns over-all orientation rather than coordination of specific measures.

[4] *Cf.* Robert V. Roosa, Under Secretary of the U.S. Treasury for Monetary Affairs, "Assuring the Free World's Liquidity," *Business Review Supplement* (Philadelphia: Federal Reserve Bank of Phila., September 1962) p. 10 ff.

In spite of the fear of the "population explosion" predicted by long-range projections and in spite of the "explosion of expectations" in the newly independent states, it is an immutable axiom that the leading industrial countries of the free world have a vital interest in the improvement of the living conditions and well-being of the greatest number of individual human beings in those countries. This very interest militates against the endorsement or support by omission or commission of the economic policies of socialism, meaning the abolition of private property in the means of production and in resources, in favor of government owned and operated enterprises, and the resultant curtailment of freedom.

Western industrial countries have a natural selfish interest in an optimum of economic and social development in the underdeveloped primary producing countries and in the optimum exchange of goods and services with them. The former are making capital as well as technical assistance available to these countries. But their common interest requires that those scarce resources be used effectively and that they are neither wasted nor used to assist in tilting the scales in favor of communism. Here again adoption of some major guideposts of policy would avoid a course of marching separately and in the end being defeated jointly. Such guidelines could envisage the following kinds of action:

1. Shift capital aid as far as possible from government-to-government grants or loans to private investment or loans by individual enterprises or consortia of business enterprises.
2. Give additional incentive to private investment and loans. Allied insurance groups could underwrite a part of the political risk of losses. They should agree mutually on excluding any countries which expropriate foreign investors or lenders without paying prompt, adequate, and acceptable compensation.
3. Refuse to accede to demands for investing in industrial plants which are desired as prestige symbols only and which are bound to become white elephants which will exert a net drain on national income.
4. Make thorough investigations of the feasibility of profitable operation of new enterprises and secure managerial piloting until indigenous operation is firmly in the saddle.
5. Provide opportunity for acquisition of shares in foreign financed enterprises by nationals of the host country.
6. Support truly cooperative associations as a capitalistic form of enterprise, but discourage financial and technical support of collective state-controlled enterprises in agriculture as well as industry.
7. Strengthen the functioning of exchanges in primary commodities and particularly the trading in contracts for future de-

livery in such products as mining and agriculture as the best means to mitigate extreme fluctuations of prices.

8. Diminish all barriers to freer international trade, particularly non-tariff barriers, and liberalize trade in agricultural products.
9. Establish among private and public creditors in industrial nations in their financing activities of projects in developing countries effective cooperation by which they protect themselves against the risk of nationalization or other confiscation without prompt, adequate, and acceptable indemnification. This would amount to the adoption of the equivalent of the Hickenlooper Amendment of the Foreign Assistance Act.
10. Cooperate with those constructive and socially responsible leaders in business in the developing countries who are already well on their way to laying the foundations for healthy economic growth and stability.

Preference of private transfer of capital and of technical assistance is a wise orientation among NATO partners for two reasons. Waste, failure, and mismanagement, if not outright fraud and corruption, are almost inevitable corollaries in government-to-government aid. Neither in the industrial countries nor in the recipient developing countries does the government have available the very scarce managerial and technical skills that are essential to the decision-making process on investment in new enterprises. Such talent is also not in ample supply or at all available in the tight international market. The other reason lies in the strategic necessity to avoid the repetition of the disastrous errors of all Communist regimes in overdeveloping a few capital goods industries at the expense of bleeding agriculture of capital and retarding the right-of-way of land transport as well as all consumer goods industries.

Joint Defense of Open World Commodity Markets

Although they are each other's best customers, the industrially advanced countries of the free world have a vital interest in the steady and healthy expansion of foreign trade that demands far more than exclusive exchange among themselves. It calls for exchange of their manufactured and particularly investment or producer goods for primary materials and light industrial goods from the mining and agricultural economies. The disturbing feature since the Korean War is the great disparity between the rise in economic prosperity in the advanced countries and the very uneven and lagging economic progress in the majority of industrially retarded countries. Economists have searched for simplified models or blueprints that could explain the dominant causes of unsatisfactory growth of the economy in the underdeveloped countries. Yet, the historical record of development until this day has far more exceptions to the rules of even the most sophisticated models than examples that support these rules.

Among the criteria for qualifying as an industrially underdeveloped country is a high share of primary products in the value of exports and hence in the ability to earn foreign exchange to pay for industrial imports. One of the most visible and most accurately measurable indices of the changing fortunes of these countries is the fluctuation of the prices of their export commodities in the world market and resulting changes in their national income. The instability of prices of primary commodities is one of the earliest and best explored problems of international economics and foreign trade. It was closely related to certain hypotheses in the theory of the business cycle, particularly in the analysis of the origin of the Great Depression of the late nineteen twenties. Overexpansion of agricultural production capacity combined with the impact of weather cycles for export commodities was considered a major contributing cause.

In 1943 the International Labor Office published a book on Intergovernmental Commodity Control Agreements. At the end of World War II, in November 1946, the draft constitution for an International Trade Organization prepared in a conference at London devoted its longest chapter to International Commodity Agreements.[5] In 1947 the Economic and Social Council of the United Nations held a conference in Geneva with the aim of setting up the ITO. The illustrious Advisory Committee on Economics to the Committee on International Economic Policy jointly with the Carnegie Endowment for International Peace issued a new classic study by the eminent economist, Director of the Food Research Institute and later presidential adviser, Joseph S. Davis, entitled "International Commodity Agreements: Hope, Illusion or Menace?" After exhaustive analysis of the bewilderingly complex problems involved in the proposed international administrative intervention in world and national markets, after strong cautionary advice to adhere to the principles underlying a dynamic consumer oriented economy of freest competitive exchange, and after reference to Great Britain's resistance to some undesirable types of price-raising ICA's in bilateral import agreements, the study ended in the following uncannily prophetic statement:

> American agricultural policy presents serious obstacles to rational ICA's in most farm products that are produced here. This policy has been one of persistently promoting advances in prices of these products, and guaranteeing supports in case of pressure upon prices, at levels defined in terms of uneconomic parity formulas. An artificial price structure, largely unrelated to prices abroad, has thus been built up. American commercial exports of these products are well-nigh impossible except under subsidy or special arrangements. In the past, the threat of sub-

[5] *Cf.* Joseph S. Davis, *International Commodity Agreements: Hope, Illusion, or Menace?*, A Brochure by the Committee on International Economic Policy (New York: January 1, 1947).

sidized exports has been used, though seldom effectively, to induce other countries to agree to an ICA and to secure American export quotas under it, based on historical experience. Department of Agriculture officials have tended to advocate ICA's that would buttress and extend American agricultural controls, despite the fact that these have not worked well and have now created a dangerous situation. Time will be required to work out of this situation, and there is small prospect that ICA's can be adopted which will facilitate the needed readjustments. In general, ICA's are likely to be better if the Departments of State and Commerce strongly outweigh the Department of Agriculture in influence on their terms.

Today, seventeen years later, little has changed with reference to the issue, except that most other industrial countries have—insofar as they had not done so on their own initiative earlier—adopted protectionist and subsidizing agricultural policies similar to those of the United States and Great Britain. The net effect is the violation of principles of foreign trade by all parties concerned due to political compromises with vested interest groups, which shortsightedly buy subsidies at the cost of freedom of enterprise. To support the farmers' income, prices of farm commodities are fixed above equilibrium level, leading to excess output. Acreage controls are ineffective as brakes on output, as are marketing quotas. The excess supply is bought by the government, stored at exorbitant cost, and in the end dumped at additional expense in foreign markets either as gifts or by concessional deals. The United States will export in the fiscal year 1964 close to $6 billion worth of farm products, of which one-third are concessional exports including gifts, arranged largely by bilateral agreements.[6]

The EEC and the EFTA countries, as well as Canada, Australia, and New Zealand, all have similar policies with similar effects, though in different degrees. And there are two common markets in the making in Latin America and one in Malaysia.

From March 23 to June 15, 1964 in Geneva the 122 members of the United Nations are holding a Conference on Trade and Development, which, seventeen years after the one previously cited, will again try to establish an International Trade Organization. One of the major themes concerns the use of new trade policies for aid to development in developing countries. Pervading the preparations for the conference are theses advanced by its Secretary General, Dr. Raul Prebisch, which deny and reject the continued relevance of the principles of comparative advantage and freest multilateral trade, and militate toward industrial

[6] *Cf.* Karl Brandt, "The American Economy: Problems of Growth, Change, and Stability," An address presented at Stanford Research Institute Industrial conferences in Stockholm, Düsseldorf, Brussels, London, and Milan, May 1963 (Düsseldorf: Bundesverband der Deutschen Industrie e.V., 1963; Menlo Park; multilithed, Stanford Research Institute, 1963).

protectionism for underdeveloped countries, preferably organized in common markets. Simultaneously, support for ideas of correcting the adverse terms of trade for primary commodity exporting countries by international commodity agreements comes from the U.S. Department of State, from leading personalities in some EEC countries, and from underdeveloped countries. Limitation of space, the complexity of the issue, and the diversity of the situation for specific oil or food or fiber exporting countries forbid analyzing the multitude of reasons why international price lifting of raw materials would fail disastrously in boosting foreign exchange income of developing countries. However, it may be stated summarily that from the standpoint of the NATO countries nothing could be a greater disservice to their common cause of strengthening free governments and open societies than to submit to collective pressure of underdeveloped countries for international cartelization and price fixing for commodities. Such price fixing for a few individual commodities and commodity groups abolishes the equilibrating functions of the market and the price and disorganizes the relationships between fixed commodity prices and all other prices.[7] Without effective power of universal enforcement of production or trade restrictions, and with the strong incentive of exorbitant profits by their violation, smuggling and corrupt trading will discriminate against obedient producers, traders, and countries. Opportunities for economic development of agriculture and mining in efficient low cost producer countries will be frustrated by quota allocations in international cartel offices—unless regulation remains merely a decorative sham transaction.

The deadly weakness of all centrally controlled economic systems and commodity price fixing machinery lies in vastly underestimating the dynamic versatility of competition and the penetrating power of private initiative. For nearly all agricultural products, fixing prices leads to substitution of others, or worse, to substitution of synthetic products. Hence price supports actually subsidize the manufacture of substitutes. Competition among minerals does the same. Price fixing also leads inevitably to the accidental subsidization of shifts in location of production of the regulated commodity between countries and even continents—to the detriment of those meant to be the beneficiaries of the price pegging cartel.

If the NATO partners do not want to yield unwittingly to a gigantic squeeze play by a multitude of the peripheral underdeveloped countries, they must individually and jointly do everything they can to keep markets open and functioning with maximum freedom for private non-subsidized trade and private investment. They must recognize

[7] *Cf.* Karl Brandt, "The Instability of Primary Commodity Prices and the Enigma of Remedial Policies," An address before the Académie d'Agriculture at its session in Paris, May 27, 1964 (To be published in *Comptes Rendus Hebdomadaires des Séances de L'Académie d'Agriculture de France*, 1964).

the incompatibility of such sane and sound goals with international cartelization of commodity markets. They must retreat from this slippery road to socialism which reduces the living standards and stymies economic progress nowhere more than in underdeveloped countries.

What is needed is the removal of obstacles to a maximum flow of trade, not strictures or organizational innovations with more political machines to curtail freedom of economic action. Insofar as government support of income to any group of producers is concerned, any other method is preferable to the jamming of the price mechanism and the fettering of the competitive market function. The same applies to efforts at improving the balance of payments of raw material exporting countries. Here compensatory financing is one of the positive measures that leaves the market alone.

Joint Strategy toward Freer Trade and Foreign Investment

In the enigmatic period of a potential détente, the real strategic need of the industrial countries is basic agreement on the principles for expansion of foreign trade, not formation of more international agencies. The machinery of GATT should be adequate to arrive at such agreements as well as to negotiate some multilateral lowering of barriers by the initiative of the leading NATO powers. In view of the strict bilateralism of the Soviet Union and Communist China and the fact that among the seventy-three nations associated with GATT in some form are Czechoslovakia, Poland, and Yugoslavia, it will be essential, however, to amend the charter's unsatisfactory reference to transactions with state trading monopolies. It is high time to spell out the common interest in development in underdeveloped countries by opening the markets of the industrial countries to freer entry of agricultural and mineral products via private trade channels.

For NATO powers on both sides of the Atlantic the greatest temptation to yield to *Realpolitik* or practical expediency and *ad hoc* opportunism lies in the atmospheric pressure of the international political scene. This emotional fervor leads to assertions that no time is left to develop sound and reliable policies, and that only quick forceful action can satisfy the explosion of expectations and pacify the tumultuous political turbulence. It might be well to look at an example of unique success in withstanding such clamor for nearly two decades: the International Bank for Reconstruction and Development. It did not yield to pressure for wild expansion of operations. It is today one of the solid bastions of international finance and is expanding gradually and uncompromisingly in line with principles of prudent investment.

The members of the NATO alliance are at the crossroads of foreign economic policies at which they may separate without even recognizing it because they are in too great haste and do not even make the effort to see where the path ends. There is no question that energetic action is needed in foreign trade and foreign investment. But in the choice among many alternatives, decision must rest on a sound moral basis and be consistent with the principles or values to which the nations adhere. If the choice is between removing high consumption taxes on tropical products in an industrial capital exporting country and supporting a price-raising international commodity cartel, the decision should be derived from weighing its impact on freedom and human dignity at home and abroad. Moreover, the strategy for dealing with international problems should begin with honest analysis of the specific social, economic, and political facts in the case of each country, not with uncritical acceptance of generalizations, worldwide statistical averages, trends, models or projections. Many of the most serious problems defy accurate quantification, yet they demand action.

Decisions must be based on common sense and prudent judgment anchored in a few basic values.

Economic Dimensions of Atlantic Partnership

—*PIERRE URI*

The North Atlantic Treaty provides in Article 2 a very broad framework for political and economic cooperation, with a view to promoting conditions of stability and well-being and to eliminating conflict in international economic policies. However, very little has been done in this respect. The report of the "Three Wise Men" of 1956 broadly describes the aims which such actions should pursue: more freedom in trade and capital movements; better coordination and more effectiveness in aid to developing countries. The last objective named is of a broader character—that of building a good base for the working of free institutions. It recognizes that duplication with other institutions has to be avoided, particularly with the functions of what was then the Organization for European Economic Cooperation (OEEC), and which has developed into the Organization for Economic Cooperation and Development (OECD) through full American and Canadian membership.

In NATO itself, one may assume in all fairness that the main economic question which is directly dealt with is the capability of each member country to assume its share of defense and armaments expenditure. This is an exercise which was started on the eve of the Lisbon conference of 1952.

The Problem of Interdependence

The striking feature of the NATO alliance is the enormous disproportion between the power of the United States and that of any other member taken in isolation. Even after the great progress made in Europe, the relations between the United States and any one of the largest NATO powers is that of eight to one. Britain, France, and Germany are roughly equal, whereas Italy, with about the same population, and despite its economic progress by leaps and bounds, is still lagging behind. The difference is all the more striking if one considers Canada, which of course has a very high production per capita, but a reduced population, and even more the smaller countries, whether fully industrialized or still in the process of development. In general terms, the United States by itself represents about one half the population of the Atlantic world and much more than one half its total production.

In matters of defense, nothing has as yet emerged to bridge this gap, unless one subscribes to the theory of the equalizing effect of nuclear force, however limited the European proportion in this respect. In economic matters, the imbalance begins to be redressed by the progressive establishment of a large European unit. The Community of the Six, despite more rapid progress since 1955 than has been achieved in the United States, still represents about one half the total American production, with a hardly smaller population. British entry into the Common Market would have further closed the gap. This would have given full significance to the concept of Atlantic partnership. Of course, partnership may describe any kind of association between members, large or small. The more imaginative policy is that of partnership between equals, which in the Atlantic world could only mean a relationship between two large units on both sides of the Atlantic.

Whatever the way this notion originated, it gained historic significance when proposed by President Kennedy in his Philadelphia speech on the 1962 anniversary of the Declaration of Independence. Of course it extended far beyond the field of economic matters to include defense and policies toward the rest of the world. Thus, beyond a recognition of a move toward economic unity in Europe, it was an appeal to political unity as well. In this respect, progress is very slow, if not completely halted. In the economic field, the grand design included support for the entry of the United Kingdom into the European Community, the possible adverse effect on American exports being, however, limited by all-round reductions in tariffs. This hope too has been disappointed.

In political terms, the importance of President Kennedy's offer was to recognize the difficulties which arise from the very disproportion between allies, the reciprocal resentment which this may lead to on the part of those who feel too dependent, as well as those who feel too much depended upon. It was also a wise recognition that great decisions and far-reaching policies should be discussed to avoid the risk which Keynes described in the preface to his general theory—how incredible it is what foolish things one may think when he thinks too long alone.

From an over-all point of view, this is not so much a concept opposed to that of an Atlantic Community grouping together a large number of nations as such, as a practical way of organizing it, and an answer to a dilemma. There is no lack of international statements suggesting that the Atlantic Community could be run by some kind of high council where a majority rule could at some point be introduced. It is not quite clear whether the implications have been fully thought out. Looking at the share of the United States in total population, production, contribution to defense, etc., no democratic rule could force it to accept minority status. Now it is also a political fact that it would be inconceivable to give only one country a veto, while other nations which consider themselves great powers could be overruled. It is this very nature of things which commends the creation of a large European bloc, and the organization of the Atlantic Community as a continuing process of closer relationships and joint action. In this respect, there is no other procedure than agreement between two parties. The rise of the European Community begins to give significance in the economic field to a notion of partnership which would serve two purposes: avoiding conflict and furthering common interests.

Too much has been made of the blow dealt to this grand design by President de Gaulle's refusal in January 1963 of the British bid to join the Common Market. The one immediate implementation of the partnership concept was the proposal to negotiate tariff reductions under the authority granted to the President by the new American legislation. Under no circumstances could it have remained a purely bilateral affair between an enlarged Common Market and the Americans. In substance, the task remains the same.

It could even be argued that a British membership in the Common Market raised, or at least manifested, some fundamental issues which could not have been resolved even in such a powerful group as an enlarged community. Thus the path to Atlantic negotiations through British membership in Europe could as well be reversed, and an approach made to these large-scale issues in the broader framework of Atlantic cooperation.

Agricultural, Aid, and Monetary Considerations

The first case is that of agriculture. The negotiations between Great Britain and the Common Market revealed two aspects of it. On the one hand, there is support given to the income of the agricultural producers on both sides of the Channel, however much it may differ in form. Continental Europe raises income by raising the price through old and new ways of protection. Britain brings down the domestic price to the level of imported goods by deficiency payments which make up for the difference between this and the guaranteed receipt to the home producer. But even more important, there was a kind of scramble for the British Market which revealed the acute limitation of solvent outlets for agricultural production in the world at large. Home producers wanted to keep it, the Common Market farmers were eager to gain new access to it, the Commonwealth continued to look at it as their privilege, and the United States began to wonder why it should be discriminated against in favor of the Commonwealth. Clearly, new and expanding markets must be found if freer trade is ever to be established in agricultural products.

The second glaring case is the problem of money. It may appear astonishing that it was not officially raised in the negotiations. The Community of Six has had no real monetary problems. None of those countries possesses a reserve currency, and all of them since the franc devaluation at the end of 1958 have enjoyed a surplus which precluded any difficulties in their balance of payments, although now this situation appears to be deteriorating rather fast. The British case is just the reverse. The pound sterling is a world currency, used as a reserve by the members of a large trading area. Britain's dependence on foreign trade makes it very vulnerable to balance of payments difficulties as soon as its economy grows faster or its competitiveness weakens. There is no doubt that the British entry into the Common Market should have hastened the plans for some monetary arrangements between the members of the Community, perhaps some kind of a common reserve fund.

Still more broadly the ties and commitments which Britain has in all parts of the world would have added a new dimension to the outlook of the Community. The territories associated with the Common Market comprise less than sixty million inhabitants. Some former British African territories might have finally decided to accept an association which at first they had turned down. The links to the White Commonwealth and to such large countries as India and Pakistan would have come to the fore. It can be argued that a substantial part of day-to-day foreign policy has been transferred to the Community by the member countries, inasmuch as they have pledged themselves to develop a common commercial policy before the end of the transitional period. They would have been bound to take a broader view of world problems.

Agriculture, aid, and money are some of the fields in which neither Europe, nor the United States, nor Britain plus the Commonwealth, can solve the problems in isolation. There will not be any common action unless we go through the narrow gate of tariff negotiations based on the Trade Expansion Act. One will soon discover that tariff reductions are not enough, or even that they cannot be implemented, unless some understanding is reached which concerns agricultural policies, over-all policies (aid and otherwise) toward developing countries, and finally a reinforcement of the money and payments system.

The U.S. Trade Expansion Act of 1962

Whatever developments it may imply or necessitate in the field of common policies, there is no doubt that the Trade Expansion Act up to now is the one concrete step toward an Atlantic partnership. There is no doubt either that it was conceived against the background of British entry into the Common Market. Roughly speaking, it contained two main provisions: a general authorization given to the Administration to negotiate a reduction across the board of tariffs up to 50 per cent of their initial level; and the possibility of a further reduction, even down to zero, on products for which United States and Economic Community exports (as of the date when the reduction would apply) accounted for more than 80 per cent of total world exports, excluding intra-Community trade and exports of Communist countries. The 50 per cent limit is discarded for tariffs below 5 per cent or on agricultural or tropical products on which obviously the effective limit will be the degree of agreement which can be reached on parallel or reciprocal policies by all parties concerned.

The 80 per cent clause was so calculated that it was practically void unless the British joined the Common Market. Incidentally, Canada had been forgotten as one of the possible partners in computing the Atlantic share of world exports. In the present evolution of negotiations, the practical exclusion of this clause has very serious consequences.

Not only is there an absolute limit to the reductions which can be negotiated by the United States, item by item, but within the broad authority to negotiate reductions, without limit on products whose suppliers outside the Atlantic area proper were not important or actual competitors, a whole array of flexible formulae could have been devised to try and match the reciprocal concessions or accommodate the difficulties of the other side. A rigid limit leads to a great rigidity in the solutions which can be applied.

There is certainly great misunderstanding in Europe over the American insistence on applying a linear method of reduction. The fact that the American tariff is much more differentiated than the European one is easily concealed by averaging broad or even smaller categories of products. If, however, more appropriate statistical methods are applied, there are a lot of peaks in the American tariff, and in the British and Japanese ones as well. The common external tariff being roughly the arithmetic average of the four principal existing tariffs, it appears by virtue of its origin much flatter. It is often thought on the European side that the reduction of all duties by the same percentage would practically eliminate the protective nature of the European tariff by leaving a great many positions very effectively defended on the side of the other main negotiating parties. This interpretation should be dispelled.

The three major motives behind the American proposal appear to be as follows. On the one hand there seems to be a somewhat misleading analogy with a method which has proved successful in the establishment of the European Common Market. A certain flexibility had been provided for in the elimination of tariffs with a combination of a minimum percentage on each duty at every stage of reduction, and a minimum weighted average; in fact, the linear method has been consistently applied. But it should be remembered that there is no stop before the complete reduction to zero, so that the path followed is of merely secondary or passing interest. When, however, one is bound to stop half way, the method will determine the final position, i.e., the resulting comparative structure of tariffs.

But much more important to understand is the wish of the U.S. Administration to avoid, by means of a simple and rigid rule, the pressure of private interests and organized lobbies. This genuine concern for a far-reaching solution may not be fully appreciated in Europe.

There is finally an all-decisive factor. Once the 80 per cent clause was in fact discarded by the exclusion of Great Britain from the Common Market, any solution, other than linear cuts, is bound to limit even more the reductions achieved and leave one even further away from a 50 per cent target.

Tariffs and Trade

To clear up some of the misunderstandings, it may be useful to distinguish two purposes in the lowering of barriers to trade. The traditional one is to obtain as much increased access to other people's markets as can be skillfully bargained. With this approach, reciprocity is roughly measured by the amount of increased exports which each party may be given. Weighting the tariff rates by the volume of trade is not meaningless. The great unknown is how much water there is in some of the rates; if they do much more than compensate for differences in cost, their reduction is purely nominal; conversely, the reduction of even very high tariffs may be a very substantial concession, in cases where costs are extravagantly high.

The other line of reasoning is to accept the liberalization of trade for the sake of rationalization and for the sake of the shift to more productive or competitive activities which it entails. From that angle, increased imports have a real advantage, and it is not unreasonable to accept a much more than proportional reduction on the highest tariffs, whether they conceal a large safety margin or cover up highly uneconomic production.

This second line of approach would give more Atlantic significance to the exercise and justify a certain degree of harmonization of tariffs. Additional arguments stem from three other considerations. It is a fact that between industrialized countries there is a two-way trade in all fields; in other words, specialization applies within each industry, rather than between industries as a whole. It is a reasonable claim on the part of the industries concerned, if the market is to be opened up to their competitors, that their competitors' markets should be opened up to them on more or less similar terms. There is also the important case where the most formidable competitor may be a third country, particularly a developing one which in some sectors enjoys very low costs of production: a harmonization of tariffs between industrialized countries would spread more evenly between them the impact of cheap imports in such a case. Finally, whatever the way in which it may be precisely defined, there is always the fear of dumping—the main defense against it being the possibility of retaliation. If, however, one industry operates behind very high tariff walls, it gives the impression of an army in a fortress which may with impunity launch an attack on its neighbors!

In fact no clear choice is made between the two concepts. The consequence is that some compromise might be struck which will have at least the political appeal of apparent reciprocity. Even if it could be argued that the less differentiated a tariff is, the less protective it is, and the less it should be reduced, this is hard to sell to public opinion. Thus the hallmark of reciprocity would mainly be, between the main partners, the same over-all percentage of cuts on the existing tariffs. However, the difference in structure between the less differentiated and the more differentiated ones will be taken care of in a rather clumsy way on a basis of product-by-product disparities. The logic of harmonization would call for a deeper reduction of a higher tariff when on any particular product there is a large difference from the lower tariff. But because of the absolute limit of reductions authorized by the Trade Expansion Act, it will be the other way around: the lower tariff will be less reduced. Economically this leads to a rather queer consequence. Protection is less reduced by one partner, not because his competitive partner requires a high tariff, but because the other partner requires one. And, when the main supplier is a third party who has to overcome a high tariff in country *A*, he will again be penalized by having to overcome a less reduced tariff in country *B*. In fact this works only in principle and there will be more flexibility in the actual implementation. But as a final solution, it would make sense only if this exercise were considered a first step, and some more flexible legislation could be later adopted, or if the European Community could be enlarged in time so as to make up for the fact that the 80 per cent has practically no application. It remains to be seen also how far the parameter chosen to define the so-called disparities will take care of most of the cases which otherwise would have been produced as exceptions.

The difference between the Common Market and the scope of the Kennedy Round is clear.

On the one hand, there is complete elimination of all barriers to trade, which means a reduction to zero on the entire array of products. On the other hand, there is only a partial reduction of tariffs, with possible exceptions or limited rates of reduction. In the Common Market, complete final reciprocity is assured by the fact that all tariffs are eliminated in intra-Community trade, whereas there is for all member countries the same difference between the zero tariff and the common external tariff applying to goods imported from third countries. Whether in a transitional period equal rates of reduction, which on initially different tariffs result in unequal absolute reductions, lead to reciprocity or not, can be safely ignored. In the present negotiations, however, a problem arises as soon as the process stops half-way without any certainty as to the range of goods on which the maximum reduction applies. The old bargaining is revived by the fears of the kind of tariff structure one will be left with at the end of the negotiation. What complicates the problem further is that there is not even a clear answer to the question of the average level of protection provided by each tariff. If it is weighted by effective imports, this gives a very distorted picture. The real weight of high tariffs is not the imports they allow but the imports they prevent. This method gives undue weight to the lower rates under which the bulk of imports come in. Should one then resort to a simple arithmetical average? This approach too is distorted since it will in fact be weighted by the number of tariff lines devoted to the different categories of products. The correct assessment should be based on a difference between the imports which would take place if tariffs were zero and the actual imports realized under existing tariffs. This would unfortunately involve impossible calculations about the market and its elasticities. The spread between high and low tariffs can be assessed more accurately, but again there is an impossible problem of weighting.

An overriding question, however, is posed by the report of the Brookings Institution. This report recognizes that the common tariff was not deliberately set high, and that the arithmetic average could be a rather objective rule and has in fact been corrected downward by additional provisions. However, the report maintains that due to the very fact of a Common Market the external tariff affords a higher protection than did the four separate tariffs previously. The relevant factor is, which of the four groups had in any particular sector the most competitive industry? The others will have to adjust to its cost level if they are to stand its competition. If the common tariff is higher than was the tariff of the country in which the most competitive industry was located, then the ensuing protection is higher than it was before.

What this really amounts to is that the more productive and competitive an industry is, the higher its protection even if the apparent rate of the tariff is maintained or lowered. If this is just another way of saying that the increased competitiveness of European industry due to the operation of the Common Market is going to make the exports of other countries more difficult, it is a fair point. If however it is construed as an accusation of protectionism, then there is a hidden fallacy. If we take it to its logical conclusion, we could accuse of protectionism even a country which would have a zero tariff if its industries enjoyed low costs of production. Much more relevant would be to point out that tariffs should not be considered in isolation, but in conjunction with the rate of exchange and also in conjunction with relative prices. An undervalued currency is equivalent to a substratum of fixed customs duty, on the basis of which the different duties are established; it also affords a flat subsidy to exports. The same point detracts from some of the value of the arguments put forward by the European Community against the accusation of protectionism. It does not deny that intra-Community trade has increased much more than the trade with third countries. It points out however that trade with third countries has increased very rapidly, particularly on the import side. In fact, imports have grown even more than total internal production. The difference between the rates of growth of intra-Community trade and trade with third countries is obviously the effect of the Common Market. This does not necessarily mean that there is any diversion of trade at the expense of third countries. Increase in trade may be at the expense of the corresponding internal production in each of the member countries. But the accelerated increase in imports from third countries during the last year is not proof of the liberal intentions or policies of the community; it may be simply related to an increase in prices which has outrun the corresponding increase in other industrial countries of the world, particularly in the United States. But inflation is the last thing a country or group of countries could boast about.

Agricultural Tariffs

Agriculture has always been expected to present the most difficult problem. Even if both the United States and the Common Market claim to be fairly liberal in their tariff and import policy, this is a field where neither can disclaim guilt. There is no denying that the difficulties have their political side. It will be fascinating to see whether the redistribution of constituencies according to the ruling of the Supreme Court will make any difference! But the genuine problems cannot be ignored. The demand for most agricultural products is less elastic in relation to the increase in income than for manufactures or services. In other words, markets are limited. At the same time, technical progress has proceeded very fast. The theoretical solution is to reduce the number of people employed on the land, so as to raise their productivity and their income. But for human and social reasons this displacement cannot exceed a certain yearly rate. At that rate, productivity increases fast, so that total production is not decreased but stepped up. Hence all the devices to maintain the farmers' income. Unfortunately, they almost inevitably distort the pattern of production and lead to the accumulation of surpluses, at the same time as some products, the market for which expands much faster, like meat, remain in comparatively short supply.

There is some justification in the approach offered by the European Community, i.e., to look into the amount of support which each product enjoys in different countries. Free trade only leads to a better allocation of resources when it is based on costs of production, not on competition between public treasuries. The support can take the form either of outright external protection, as in the Common Market, or of subsidies in proportion to production, as in Britain, or acreage limitations accompanied by payments to those who refrain from producing, as in the United States. However, the Community's proposal is only to freeze the amounts of support, not to reduce them.

It is abundantly clear that, unless some new policies are devised in common, agriculture will be a stumbling block. The Common Market maintains at the same time that its own agricultural policy must be determined before negotiations get really started and that the problem can only be solved in a worldwide framework. As of now, there is only a verbal reconciliation between these two tenets, through an appeal to international agreements concerning prices, production, and outlets. It remains to be seen what the content of such agreements will be. This is clearly a case where joint action shall not mean a compromise between the behaviors of various governments, but an attempt to devise some better ways to open new markets, adjust production to demand and maintain the income of the farmers.

Unless we act together, the West could miss an historical opportunity and fail just where it could best demonstrate its capacity to face the needs of our world. There is in this world a tragic contrast between our countries burdened with surplus production and the hungry masses of so many continents. There is also a contrast between our capacity to overproduce and the inability of the Communist countries to step up their agricultural production. To be sure, a part of the surplus is already distributed in kind to some other developing countries. However, price policies and not demand determine the output, and this form of distribution maintains the rigidities of production. It is high time for all of our countries acting together to discover some more flexible way of helping the hungry, so that they get what they need and we produce what is wanted, instead of letting them get what is not wanted.

NATO Economic Policies: Impact on the Rest of the World

Thus, an important fact emerges. What begins as a settlement of reciprocal relations between Europe and the United States is bound to develop into a policy in regard to the rest of the world. This is clear in the case of agriculture. It is equally clear with industrial tariffs, which by virtue of the most-favored-nation clause, would be applicable to third parties as well. How far, acting together, we are prepared to accept gradually more of the goods which developing countries should be able to produce, will be the yardstick of our capacity for consistent action. It would be inconsistent to give aid for purposes of industrialization and then to close the markets to the resulting industrial production. The developed countries must follow this course jointly, so as to spread the impact of what in some cases may be formidable competition. But provided the process is gradual enough, and full employment is maintained in our own economies, it is a gain, not a loss, to redeploy our own resources toward more productive use and more sophisticated lines of production.

Freer trade, a formulated agricultural policy, a more consistent and effective over-all policy toward developing countries—all these require a high degree of employment and economic growth. This in turn requires a reasonable degree of price stability, in the absence of which expansion has periodically to be curbed, so as to avoid inflationary developments or disequilibrium in the balance of payments.

If freer trade is going to be established and maintained, then the autonomy of financial policies is going to be reduced, and more coordination will be necessary. In fact, the freedom which has to be abandoned is the freedom of making nonsense! Accelerated growth by concerted policies would make freer competition more readily acceptable. The larger swings in trade, as well as the unequal development of imports under the influence of changes in prices and of the rates of internal expansion, will call for greater and better administered credit facilities.

There is no lack of recognition of the various problems which this analysis has revealed step by step. What is lacking is the will to tackle them in their interrelationships instead of dealing with each of them in a dispersed and haphazard way. It is mostly from that point of view that the rejection of British entry into the Common Market must be deplored. We missed the opportunity to set up effective instruments of coordination in the trade and economic policies on the two sides of the Atlantic in the form of original institutions which would have embodied the concept of partnership between equals.

This should not deter us from thinking further about what we can do for our own people. There is still a great deal that we can learn about each other and, even more, from each other. There are still many misconceptions everywhere, even in Europe, about the workings of the American economy, though it has by and large probably achieved a greater degree of equality than most other countries. It should even be stressed that the United States tax system accomplishes a greater redistribution of income than is the case in some of the countries where socialists have influence or have on many occasions run the government. Take only one example: capital gains are in most cases tax free in the hands of individuals in Europe, whereas they have been taxed for a very long time in the United States.

On the other hand, there are a great many misconceptions on the American side of the Atlantic about the development of social services in Europe and elsewhere, and about the role of planning. The fear that development of social security would reduce the competitive thrust in the economy and retard economic expansion has been disproved by the experience of many countries as different as Japan, Italy, Germany, and France. State or mixed enterprises, totally or partly owned by the government, may be run effectively or in some sectors may even offer a capacity for rational decisions that surpasses the record of public utilities when privately operated. Finally, the insistence on the economic advantages of the free enterprise system may be somewhat overdone. There is no denying that it ensures the quality, the diversification, and the inventiveness of both goods and services, as well as an effective allocation of resources. But such considerations are static in character. It is demand (including investment) rather than the allocation of resources which really determines growth and a rapid rate of expansion. Some flexible forms of planning may bring about a convergent effort toward higher production targets by all interested parties than would have been possible for each of them in isolation.

The Challenge for the Future

We are all slow in recognizing that in the last twenty years we have developed a completely new economic system which has as yet no name in history. The first discovery was that our own markets can be indefinitely increased, so that any form of imperialism should be abandoned not only on moral and political, but on economic grounds. Full employment eliminates exploitation by raising the remuneration of labor. During the 1930's, it might well have been doubted whether the West could be capable of such a rate of growth as was evidenced by Soviet communism. Now, with some setbacks, we have entered a phase of rapid expansion and practically mastered the recessions which were considered the almost inevitable plague of a free economy.

But all this is not enough. Freedom itself is not enough. It will not be maintained unless we are able to hold the promise which for almost two centuries has been considered just as much of an essential element of democracy: this is the search for equality. Equality has to be more precisely defined, and reconciled with the requirements of increased production and the necessary incentives to effort and to risk-taking. Its meaning is twofold. First, a minimum coverage of the essential needs, not only for those at work, but also for those in old age and illness. This cannot be achieved by proclamations, but only by a formidable effort to increase over-all production. Now we have become rich enough to conquer poverty. The other meaning is very adequately covered by the concept of equality of opportunity. There was a time when the spreading of education could appear to run counter to the structure of the economy, where the predominance of manual jobs limited the outlet for skill and knowledge. Now the time has come when the progress in production depends on the progress of skills, which in turn can only be developed on the basis of general education. The requirements of economic efficiency thus coincide with the requirements of social justice.

We have to recognize that none of our countries lives up to this obligation. None of our systems of education, as different as they may be, as yet realizes completely the principle of equal access, on the basis of ability, nor reconciles the spread of education with the maintenance of its cultural level. On all this we unjustifiably lag behind some of the Communist countries. It is a matter not only of devoting more resources to this task, but also of inventing new structures and new techniques which alone can reconcile the quality of culture and its wider distribution. Our future lies not in the diversity of the gadgets which we put on the market, but in our continued ability to apply in our policies, and to implement in our organization, the principles which in the past have too often been belied by our actions.

Toward an Integrated Atlantic Community

—*MAURICE ALLAIS*

The purpose of this essay is to try to place the current problems of the Atlantic Community in long-range perspective; to show that it would be to the mutual interest of the Atlantic nations to tighten the political, economic, cultural, and military bonds which unite them, however loose these bonds may appear at present; and to specify what such an orientation implies.

The writer has no illusions about the actual possibilities, at least in the immediate future, of establishing such a policy. But he is convinced that without a clear picture of the common interests of the various nations of the Atlantic Community, present-day problems cannot be resolved satisfactorily.

If the writer appears skeptical of the real possibility of establishing among the North Atlantic nations a true Atlantic Community in the near future, he is still more skeptical of the possibility for these countries to solve the problems which will confront them if they do not succeed in establishing in some way such a community.

While this paper is oriented toward an essentially economic point of view, it takes into consideration the fact that the economic problems cannot be separated from the general political, sociological, and cultural framework. Special attention is given to a study of cooperation in relation to the principle of national sovereignty.[1]

[1] This essay takes up many arguments the author has presented elsewhere, in particular at the Atlantic Convention of NATO countries held in Paris, January 8-20, 1962.

The events of the last fifty years have clearly demonstrated that most basic problems of the respective Western countries are really Atlantic problems. This fact has become increasingly obvious and has led to a growing awareness of the strong interdependence among the interests of these nations.

For a half century these nations have continually been confronted, and are confronted still, by certain basic questions: Would it be to their advantage to tighten their bonds, and if so, what course of action should they take? What are the obstacles, and are they surmountable? The following basic points bearing on these questions will be discussed in this essay: the essentials of the current state of affairs, the traditional point of view, solving the problem of an Atlantic Community, the doctrine of national sovereignty, and finally, the present possibilities.

The Current State of Affairs

First of all, what is at issue? The issue is our Western civilization, our Atlantic civilization.

This civilization is based on one fundamental principle: respect for the human person. This principle has two corollaries. The first is the concern and respect for diversity, which is an essential factor explaining the extraordinary developments of the Atlantic civilization. The second corollary is the belief in the necessity and the possibility of peaceful resolution of conflicts between men and between societies within a framework of appropriate political and judicial machinery according to pre-established laws and procedures.

The Atlantic civilization is threatened today. To the future historian the Twentieth Century will appear to be characterized by a staggering decline in the political influence of the West.

What are the causes of the West's decline? We can distinguish three main reasons. The first two, for the most part, are external to the Western world. They are Communist totalitarianism and, in the decades to come, the growth of hunger and misery throughout the world; of these two, the latter is far more terrifying than even the present threat of communism. The third cause is internal in nature. It is our own demoralization, the basic mistrust which separates us from one another, our disunity, our refusal to sacrifice the trivial for the essential, our refusal to be loyal to the ideals of our own civilization.

The Communist Threat

The Communist threat manifests itself in very different forms, depending on whether it comes from the Soviet or Chinese sphere.

In the Soviet sphere the doctrine of Communist totalitarianism has already passed its zenith. Since the death of Stalin in 1953, a profound evolution has taken place in Russia, and a great liberal revolution has begun, the true nature of which has not yet been fully understood.

The historian of the future, however, will see this continuing and persisting evolution as the birth of a new era. Stalinist factions, however, are still powerful and oppose this liberal trend. Our dissensions could serve only to reinforce them. In fact, Western disunity could lead them to underestimate our real solidarity and thus contribute to some act of aggression on their part which might entail a disastrous conflict.

China's totalitarian communism appears far more dangerous. It is now at the same hard stage as was Soviet communism in the 1930's, but in the light of the current world situation and the possibility that China may become a nuclear power, the danger from this source is potentially much greater. This makes it all the more imperative that the West try to speed up the liberal evolution in Soviet Russia and in the satellite countries and to dismantle the Communist ideology *before* China achieves the rank of a full-fledged nuclear power.

The Growth of Poverty and Hunger

The second threat which will surely confront the Atlantic nations sooner or later is the spread of poverty and hunger in much of the world. This peril is even more ominous than the Communist threat because it results not from an ideology which we can combat but rather from developments that seem beyond our power to arrest.

The inequality of incomes today is far greater between countries than it is within the various countries. Approximately four-fifths of the world population has an income which amounts to less than one-fourth of the income of the average American; half of the population has an income which is less than one-twentieth the average American income; and perhaps one-fourth of the world's population has an income of less than one-fiftieth of the American income. At a time when the Western nations enjoy unprecedented prosperity, hundreds of millions of people live under the most miserable conditions.[2] To those of us who are aware of the importance of even a one to two ratio of inequality between average income in Europe and the United States, the above mentioned inequality seems to be considerable.

South America, Africa, and Asia, representing two-thirds of the world's population, are largely undernourished. Half of the world's population has a 20 per cent food deficit. Even more striking are comparisons in terms of industrial consumption between underdeveloped and developed countries. The average ratio is 1 to 20 for textiles, 1 to 16 for coal, 1 to 37 for steel, 1 to 332 for telephones, 1 to 150 for radios, and 1 to 230 for automobiles. In thinking about these statistics, one must keep in mind that the average difference in real income is only 1 to 20.

---

[2] All these figures and those which follow are taken from Maurice Allais, "Le tiers-Monde au Carrefour," *Cahiers Africains* (1962).

Comparative statistics on illiteracy, doctors per capita, and life expectancy are equally significant. While the illiteracy rate in the developed nations is approximately 3 per cent, the rate is nearly 80 per cent in the underdeveloped countries. The ratio of doctors per 1,000 persons is 1 to 7, and the life expectancy ratio is 1 to 2. In India, for example, life expectancy in the period 1941-1950 was 32 years, compared with 67 years in the United States.

Viewed in this perspective, the term "proletarian nations" seems to be far more appropriate than "proletarian masses." Fortunately the different peoples of the world live in different regions. Otherwise such great inequality would long since have provoked revolution of worldwide proportions. However, class war may yet come to be transferred to an international setting. "It is, above all, the awareness of economic inequalities," writes Mr. Mamadou Dia, one of the most qualified of African leaders, "that gives rise to a growing feeling of national proletarianism which will turn the nations of Africa and Asia—both faced with the same struggle—against the West. With the awareness of the problems of underdevelopment appears a new element, that of the proletarian nations grouped on 'the lifeline of imperialism,' in contrast to the prosperous nations and having a geographic location which widens the economic gap. We obviously find here the most original element of the revolution of the Twentieth Century. It is here that we become aware of the extreme gravity of the situation. It is here that we become aware of what is at stake: namely, world peace." [3]

Against this background, let us examine the pattern of population growth. The average annual growth rates of the world's population for the six 50-year periods between 1650 and 1950 are 2.66, 3.10, 4.40, 5.16, 6.32, and 7.98 per thousand. These six points are closely aligned on a logarithmic scale, which means that over the 300-year period both the population and the 50-year growth rates grew exponentially. If this trend continues, world population will have grown to roughly 4 and 7 billion by the years 2000 and 2050, respectively. This would mean more than a doubling of the world population one century from now.

World population recently seems to have been increasing at an even greater rate (17.0 per thousand from 1950 to 1960 as against only 8.0 per thousand between 1900 and 1950). If this rate were to persist, the population in the years 2000 and 2050 would be approximately 6 billion and 14 billion, respectively, or a fivefold increase within one century.

Let us assume, however, that population will reach only 4 billion by the year 2000. In that case, the food deficit will probably rise to 20 or 25 per thousand. The comparable figures were 1 per thousand in 1913, 11 per thousand in 1939, and 14 per thousand in 1955. It follows

---

[3] *Nations africaines et Solidarité mondiale,* p. 13.

that underfeeding throughout the world, already serious, is likely to increase to a very dangerous extent.[4]

The case of China deserves special attention. In 1954, the population of continental China was 583 million and is said to have reached 700 million by January 1960. The annual increase, which was about 12 million in 1954, is today at least 15 million, and probably will soon reach 20 million. Such a demographic explosion can only lead to growing economic difficulties. To an extent, these problems were already felt in 1960 and 1961, when China was forced to establish a rationing program. However, these are only the first warning signals.

The future is dark: it is dark for China and also for China's neighbors. Nobody can foresee today what one billion starving Chinese, convinced by agitators that the foreigner is responsible for their misfortunes, might do in the next few years.

We can only wish, zealously, for economic progress in underdeveloped nations. But significant progress would itself be a source of difficulties. To take only one example, on the basis of the 1960 world population, and assuming that living standards the world over could reach the 1960 United States average, the world's lead reserves would be exhausted within three years.

This aspect of the development of underdeveloped nations, until now, seems to have escaped the attention of the experts! It is easy enough to plan development programs, but nobody seems to be concerned with adding up the resource requirements. Under present day technological conditions and with today's population, it seems to be *physically impossible* that the entire world population could reach today's average American living standard.

That brings us to the question of technological advance, and here the point to be made is that the present rate of productivity gain cannot be maintained indefinitely. The average annual gain for the United States of 2.55 per cent (1913 to 1957) may not seem to be very striking, but for the long run it is bound to prove exceptionally large. The practical absurdity of basing extrapolations upon such a rate become immediately clear when one reflects on the fact that a gold sou, the weight of several postage stamps, invested in 4000 B.C. at the compound interest rate of 2.55 per cent per annum, would by 1961 yield a mass of gold equivalent to as many constellations (each composed of thousand billions of golden suns) as there have been billionths of seconds in the same period.

Taken together, all of these calculations regarding population, resource requirements, and technological progress show that ours must be an absolutely *exceptional* historical period which cannot last very

[4] Many people believe that overpopulation manifests itself only in countries such as India and China. It also exists in Western Europe, Russia, and the United States, particularly in the towns and cities, though on a much smaller scale, of course.

long. If population growth continues, and everything suggests that it will at least for the next few years, it is absolutely futile to hope for improved standards of living in large parts of the world. The only development we may anticipate is one of dreadful poverty. To say the least, it is completely illusory to believe that the problem of hunger in the world would be resolved without a halt to the population rise.

Yet, responsible Western politicians continue to assert that in any reasonably dynamic economy, the rate of annual growth should average 5 per cent per year. From all their statements it seems to follow that within a short period of time, if the West agrees to appropriate efforts, the underdeveloped countries will reach a standard of living comparable to ours, and that the problem of hunger, at least, could be resolved in one way or another.

To suggest that the world has become rich enough to eliminate widespread poverty is sheer demagoguery. By thus raising false hopes, we take upon ourselves obligations which we cannot possibly fulfill, and we run the risk of seeing ascribed to the very principles of Western civilization (based on decentralized decision making, a market economy, the price mechanism, and private property) the responsibility for failure. This could only bring upon us the resentment and hate of hundreds of millions of people.

As for the West's own outlook, whatever the speed of technological progress, population growth in the West is also rapid, and if the current trend continues, will bring about a very serious drop in real wages in the most developed present-day economies.[5] One or two centuries, perhaps only several decades, would be sufficient to bring about such a change. As in the past, the liberal system of the West is likely to be made responsible for the fall in living standards, regardless of the true facts.

But this internal danger is nothing compared with the external threat to Atlantic civilization posed by the demographic tidal wave which is sweeping over the rest of the world. I agree with Bertrand Russell that world population expansion represents a potential danger that is perhaps even greater than the danger posed by the atomic bomb.

The Demoralization of the West

The third danger stems from our own demoralization, our loss of confidence in the principles of our civilization, our mutual distrust, our general policies of protection against each other, and the failure to respect our own principles. It is a fact that a large segment of public opinion in Western Europe, and even in the United States, no longer adheres as strongly to the principles which have given force to Western

[5] A reader of the original version of this essay supported the opposite point of view. *Cf.* David Sarnoff, "By the End of the Twentieth Century." *Fortune* (May 1964).

civilization and which explain its extraordinary development during the last century.

For one thing, the Western nations seem troubled and demoralized by some of the successes of collectivist economies. The fact is, however, that, contrary to a widely held belief, the Soviet economy has not developed more rapidly than the U.S. economy, if one compares the two economies at comparable stages of development. Even if the same period in history (1913-1955) is considered, the most recent figures of the National Bureau of Economic Research show that the gain in production per worker has averaged only 1.7 per cent per annum in the Soviet Union, as against 2.8 per cent for the United States. If we consider output per manhour, these figures become 1.3 per cent for the Soviet Union as against 1.9 per cent for the United States.

To take another example, an economic system based on free markets and private property has permitted France to quintuple its real hourly wages between 1850 and 1957, to reduce its workday by nearly one-half in the course of one century, to reduce its percentage of illiteracy from 53 per cent in 1832 to less than 3 per cent at present, and to extend the life expectancy of the population as a whole from less than 23 years in 1835 to 68 years today. Similar advances were made in other Western countries. Meanwhile the population in Western Europe has doubled, and the population in North America has sextupled.

All of these figures, together with observations I developed elsewhere,[6] show that there is nothing whatever to indicate any superiority of the Soviet system over that of the West. In fact, quite the contrary appears to be true.

Not only has the efficiency of the Soviet system continued to be less than that of the Western economies, but its cost in human suffering from 1929 to 1953 has proved to be extremely heavy. Real wages in Soviet Russia have increased relatively slowly, and this slight progress is even less impressive in the light of the methods of coercion, based on mass deportations, forced labor camps, and mass executions, to which Soviet Russia has resorted.[7] These methods have been a permanent

[6] See in particular Maurice Allais, *L'Europe Unie, Route de la Prospérité* (Paris: *Calmann-Lévy,* 1960), Chap. 13; and Allais, "Le Tiers-Monde au Carrefour," *Cahiers Africains,* Annexe VII (1962).

[7] Thus, if the result of collectivization in the USSR between 1929 and 1940 was to reduce the percentage of the economically active population employed in agriculture from 80 per cent to 55 per cent, the counterpart of the elimination of the kulaks was famines, deportations, and mass executions. The corresponding loss of human life can be estimated at five million on the basis of the published figure for the Russian population in 1938. *Cf.* Lorimer, *The Population of the Soviet Union, History and Prospects* (United Nations, 1964). But the revision of the population figure for 1956 from 220 to 200 million raises the possibility that the 1938 figure was overestimated by several millions. If this is so, the estimate of the number of deaths would be far in excess of five million.

challenge to the principles of a civilization which has slowly emerged through the centuries.[8]

As far as we are able to judge today on the basis of the information at our disposal, the human toll in Communist China has not been less heavy.

Nevertheless, the West, paradoxically, appears to lack faith in its values and confidence in its system. It has taken them for granted for so long that their advantages have ceased to be assessed at their true value, and there is room for doubt whether, if the necessity arose, the sacrifices required to defend them would be forthcoming.

As for the factor of mutual distrust, it is clear that the actions of Western nations constantly have been crippled by a lack of trust. To take only one example, the Suez affair was carefully prepared by the British and French governments without the American government being informed. The date was chosen to coincide with the approaching elections in the United States with the expectation that the American government would be paralyzed. As it turned out, France and Great Britain succeeded in laying a smoke screen for Soviet intervention in Hungary and thereby helped to rescue Soviet communism from a heavy defeat.

What more could we say about the Congo, Algeria, Cuba, Cyprus, and Vietnam! Everywhere the Western nations have been, and continue to be, in more or less cunning opposition; and in defending their supposed interests, they achieve, over-all, the curtailment of the West's influence throughout the world.

The Western nations are defensive about many things. They protect themselves against each other economically, culturally, and politically.

At the economic level, the Europeans are afraid of being overwhelmed by American competition; they reject real freedom of trade with North America because they believe it will lead inevitably to the domination of the European economy by the American. Americans, on their part, are no less fearful of being submerged by a flood of goods from European countries. The fact that wages in Europe are relatively much lower gives rise to their concern.

These mutual fears are well founded only if immediate freedom of trade were contemplated. They have no foundation if this freedom is achieved gradually over a period of twenty or thirty years.

Many Americans are afraid of being impoverished if their economic ties with Europe become closer. The present differences in standards of living in Europe and the United States is about 1:2, but this ratio is constantly diminishing, owing to the vitality of the present day

[8] Maurice Allais, "Productivités, Niveaux de Vie et Rythmes de Croissance comparés en Russie soviétique, aux Etats-Unis et en France," *Travaux de l'Académie des Sciences Morales et Politiques,* 4th Series. (1956), pp. 137-163.

European economy. It is worth nothing that the differences between average incomes in various parts of the United States are even larger.[9]

Cultural protection, though not so easily recognized, is certainly greater than economic protection. Everywhere, in all Western countries, the education given to the young is for the most part on a narrowly nationalist basis. And on the political level, our protectionism is shown by the enclosing and isolation of our political systems and by the lack of common institutions.[10]

On all these levels we retire within ourselves. We are afraid to face outside competition and, wrapped up in our own particularism, we reject the free confrontation of our differences, and so deny a basic principle of our civilization and a prerequisite of any real progress.

No account of the West's demoralization can neglect the fact that we regularly proclaim our adherence to the fundamental principles of our civilization, and just as regularly violate them.

To mention only recent examples, at the end of World War II, a tribunal was instituted at Nuremberg to judge war crimes. The judges composing this tribunal included representatives of a country whose government had been responsible for innumerable crimes and millions of deaths in its own country.[11] This tribunal rendered judgments in an unprecedented way, in that it allowed citizens of vanquished countries no possibility to introduce any consideration whatsoever based on the very ethic to which this tribunal was appealing.

In another instance, Western radio stations for many years had broadcast propaganda in an attempt to incite the Hungarian people to revolt. But in 1956 the West closed its ears to the pathetic appeals of a people, many of whom died for liberty believing that they had been the subject of a shameful and cowardly betrayal.[12]

At exactly the same moment, the amazing Franco-British invasion of Suez violated both the letter and spirit of the United Nations Charter, not to mention Article I of the NATO treaty.

Again, however justifiable and necessary American action may have been in the Cuban affair, there is a question, at least, whether the form it took was consistent with the fundamental principles of the UN Charter. Certainly it was no less a breach of the NATO treaty than the earlier Franco-British Suez intervention had been.[13]

---

[9] In 1962, average per-capita income in the United States was $2,366, but in Mississippi it was only $1,285 and in Arkansas it was $1,504. The comparable figures for California, Connecticut, and Delaware were $2,898, $3,089, and $3,102 respectively. *The Economic Almanac* (1964), p. 140.

[10] This applies at the political and not at the economic, cultural, and military levels.

[11] See Note 7, above.

[12] See Maurice Allais, "Le Bilan d'une Politique et les Conditions de Survie du Monde libre," *Monde Nouveau,* No. 206 (December 1956), pp. 55-98.

[13] Maurice Allais, *Les Leçons de l'Affaire cubaine et la Politique de l'Occident.*

France's role in Algeria will perhaps serve as a final illustration. For many years, France acted both as plaintiff and judge in that country. Throughout that period, the legitimate demands of those among the Algerians seeking independence were refused, although at the time they could have been satisfied by the institution of a federal system, or even by some kind of partition. In the end, this policy led to an inhuman war which lasted for seven years, and whose settlement treaty was no more than a scrap of paper. Within a few days, 800,000 persons fled the country of their birth, in shocking conditions, while several hundred thousand Moslems were abandoned and left to face the most brutal reprisals. No segment of Western opinion which could be considered representative was heard to protest against an agreement which in effect delivered one minority group, tied, bound, and without any real safeguards, into the hands of a majority, and, to all intents and purposes, decreed the deportation of a hundred thousand persons.[14] From the point of view of the ethics of Western civilization, the settlement of the Algerian question was a setback. This failure takes on added significance at a time when the same problem, just as deep-rooted, has to be resolved in South Africa, in Cyprus, and elsewhere.

In all these cases, as in so many others, the West betrayed its own principles. There are grounds for at least some skepticism as to whether Western policies, invariably oriented to short-term advantages and too narrowly nationalistic in outlook, have really served the basic long-term interest of Western countries *considered as a whole*.

Regardless of how one ranks the danger due to the Communist threat, the growth of hunger and misery, or the demoralization of the West, the future is undoubtedly much more disquieting than we might want to believe. Faced with such perspectives, what can we do? First of all, we must be able to distinguish clearly between the possible courses of action and be aware of what they actually imply. Two main courses of action are open to us: the traditional path, or the realization of an effective Atlantic Community.

The Traditional View

The first course of action open to us is to take the traditional path followed up to the present, that of agreements and treaties between sovereign states.

This approach is at first glance the more enticing, for it has the advantage of flexibility. It offers to each nation the possibility of adapting itself to local conditions and to new situations. Another advantage is that it respects national differences, an important consideration for all nations that adhere to the principles of a free society. In short, this course of action appears to be the simplest since it does not entail any radical modification of national policy.

---

[14] Maurice Allais, *L'Algérie d'Evian* (Paris: Editions de l'Esprit Nouveau, 1962).

However, various factors combine to cast doubt upon the long-range effectiveness of this approach, particularly in view of the new technological state of the modern world.

Two world wars have unfortunately demonstrated that it is fruitless to expect from simple treaties and alliances an effective guarantee of peace. These two wars, which in effect were civil wars for Europe, have shown that the true interest of the European nations is to be found in areas other than the belief in absolute national sovereignty.

Nevertheless, and notwithstanding the fact that the state of affairs in 1964 is potentially more dangerous than ever before, the solutions which are being proposed continue to be inspired by a narrow nationalism.

During the past twenty years, the Western nations have anxiously tried to preserve the autonomy of their national policies. But if we judge these policies not on the basis of motives (which have been and are now highly respectable) but on the basis of results, we may justifiably doubt their effectiveness, precisely from the point of view of the nationalistic interests they intended to preserve.

At the heart of the Atlantic alliance, the United States wants to maintain ultimate authority with regard to the utilization of atomic arms, and we must recognize that, *in view of the present state of affairs,* it might be an error for the United States to relinquish this authority. Nevertheless, such a situation inevitably creates feelings of uneasiness; it creates irresistible centrifugal forces which tend dangerously to divide the West. The author of this essay has no particular sympathy for the foreign policy of General de Gaulle, but some of de Gaulle's basic contentions are far from groundless. If it is validly unacceptable for an American to run the risk of having basic U.S. interests jeopardized by too close a union with America's European allies, it is completely unacceptable for a European that the decision to resort ultimately to nuclear weapons in defense of Europe's major interests should be left almost solely to American authority.[15]

Can the West Europeans be absolutely certain that the Americans would back them with as much determination as Americans evidenced during the Cuban crisis? Who could say beyond any doubt that the United States would risk having its territory partially destroyed in a nuclear war for the defense of Europe? For want of an assurance which should be tantamount to certainty—a simple promise can never be equivalent to certainty—one can be sure that the forces of disintegration already active within NATO will continue to develop.

---

[15] It is often suggested, rightly, that national deterrents in Europe constitute an element of disintegration within Europe, and that a genuine European Community is inconceivable if certain powers such as Great Britain and France are granted a special nuclear status. This proposition is true *a fortiori* for the Atlantic Community and the United States.

If the fundamental problem of nuclear control today lacks a solution that is unanimously accepted, is not the basic reason a fundamental misconception of what the nature and the direction of the relationships among the Western countries should be? The fact of the matter is that a common military organization is inconceivable in the absence of common policies; and common policies imply a certain degree of political integration.

The most basic question facing us is that of the proliferation of atomic weapons in the world. But in the absence of fully accepted agreements, which would not merely be verbal statements or commitments to a temporary state of affairs, who can validly refuse France, for example, the right to have her own atomic weapons? Should not what was valid yesterday for the United States and Great Britain be valid today for France, and tomorrow for Germany, Italy, and the other countries? Besides, who can be certain that tomorrow a new and revolutionary method will not be devised which will make the atomic bomb available to every country?

The progressive accession of every nation to atomic weapons, together with the unlimited application of the prevailing principle of national sovereignty, can only lead, in the end, to a third world war, an atomic war. This forecast appears much too probable, unless an essential change takes place in the policies of the various nations.

It is a commonplace to point to the growth of communication between all parts of the world. But if this fact is to become significant, its essential role must be accepted. The past political concepts of national self-sufficiency are no longer adaptable to new conditions. The possibilities of contact and consequently of differences among political groups have been multiplied and call for an institutional framework in which disputes can be peacefully settled according to predetermined procedures.

The writer is not inclined to side with various forms of centralized organization which stifle individual action and suppress the legitimate aspirations of minorities. On the contrary, his entire philosophy is opposed to the Jacobin conception of a centralized state, and he is convinced that the organization of any community should be as decentralized as possible. But he cannot help asking himself whether, in the world today, the best means of preserving these inestimable advantages—the respect for individuality and a wide decentralization of decisions—could be furnished through the unrestricted application of the principles of national sovereignty. Yet, this is the principle which seems to guide the basic policies of the United States, no less than those of General de Gaulle. One may doubt, to say the least, whether solutions to the problems facing the Atlantic world can be found by continuing along the traditional paths.

The Solution of an Atlantic Community

The other alternative before the North Atlantic nations is an Atlantic Community. At the present time, and in view of the state of public opinion, this alternative appears difficult to realize. Still, it is valid to ask ourselves whether an Atlantic Community will not constitute, at least in the long run, a viable solution which must be examined and discussed. In particular, we can ask whether the question of national sovereignty is well defined when presented to the public as a choice between all or nothing.

First of all, if our security today can be based only upon our determination to oppose force with force, an all-out war (barring the unexpected) hardly seems likely, at least for the next decade; for the havoc of such a war would leave the conqueror of tomorrow in a worse situation than the vanquished of yesterday.

In the foreseeable future at least, the real struggle between the democratic West and the totalitarian East will probably be fought on the economic, social, and ideological planes. The Western system can win out if, while satisfying the imperative demands of its own security, it shows decisive superiority on the economic, social, and human levels —in scientific progress and efficiency, in raising standards of living, and in effectively liberating man from the material or political constraints which enslave or threaten him.

If the West wants to survive, therefore, it must strive to maintain, strengthen, and extend the system of a free society, based on the decentralization of decisions and the maximum utilization of human initiative and individual effort, a system which has permitted unprecedented growth in standards of living and cultural possibilities.

The maintenance, strengthening, and extension of this type of social framework imply, on the international level, the disappearance of all obstacles to the most efficient utilization of material resources and the most complete development of individuality. Modern societies have been able to reach their degree of developmnt only by abolishing all the trade obstacles among the various regions within each nation. The same stage must be reached today in trade between states.

In the fight for democratic ideals, the military factor, important as it may be, is not sufficient. As necessary as it actually is, it is in itself only a negative factor. The decisive factor is, and can only be, the psychological strength and the effective functioning of the ideals in question.

If a true Atlantic Community were to be established economically, culturally, and politically, it would make our Atlantic world a powerful pole of attraction, capable—through its very existence and taking into account the enormous prosperity which it would possess—of breaking up little by little the totalitarian world of the East. The means for destroying the totalitarian ideology in peaceful ways are probably within reach, and they do not require spending hundreds of millions of francs, marks, pounds, and dollars.

Furthermore, an effective Atlantic Community could compensate for its growing numerical inferiority which may become even more of a handicap politically as industrial development in the other continents enable those areas to enlarge their military potential.

Also, the realization of an effective Atlantic Community would bring unprecedented prosperity, permitting a very rapid rise in the standard of living in both Europe and North America. Whatever the prospects may be for the utilization of inexpensive atomic energy—these prospects are nothing when compared to the possibilities offered by a careful and gradual removal of the barriers to trade between Western Europe and North America.

Only the prosperity brought about by such a development would enable the North Atlantic nations to face simultaneously the three conditions necessary for preserving social and international peace: improving national living standards, substantial assistance to under-developed countries, and armaments which the lesson of past years unfortunately thrusts upon the free world.

Such an Atlantic Community would represent a new stage in the progress of Western civilization, progress which in the past has consisted of gradually settling differences among men within the framework of a political and judicial structure. The refusal to establish a true Atlantic Community would amount to a refusal to apply the very principles of our own civilization. It should be established even if the horizon before us were not laden with so many ominous storm clouds. Atlantic civilization cannot survive if it seeks to attain only negative objectives, such as the containment of communism, or the minimization of the risk of nuclear war. The goals must be positive ones; they must be sufficiently attractive in and of themselves.

To summarize, a true Atlantic Community appears to be extremely desirable for at least three reasons:

(1) Through its very presence, through the force of attraction it would have, through the very power of its example, it would strongly contribute to the breaking up of the totalitarian ideology which is already in serious difficulties.

(2) Through the strength of its numbers, it would compensate, at least in part, for the disequilibrium of forces resulting from the stronger population expansion in the rest of the world.

(3) It would constitute progress in itself and be a source of many kinds of progress—social, economic, and cultural; it would represent a new stage in Western civilization, leading to a fuller realization of its possibilities; and it would serve the entire world as an example to follow in order to assure progress and peace.

The Implications of a True Atlantic Community

Obviously there will be disagreement as to what the institutional machinery of a true Atlantic Community ought to be. But whatever the institutions, and allowing a necessary period of transition, a real Atlantic Community would have to be based on: (1) an Atlantic common market, and (2) a basic minimum of common political institutions.

As suggested above, an actual Atlantic Community would imply, on the economic level, a situation in which all artificial obstacles to international movements of goods and factors of production are effectively eliminated. Contrary to an opinion too widely held, the realization of an Atlantic common market is *feasible* and, as far as can be judged, would be *very advantageous* for all its participants. Setting up such a market will inevitably create very serious problems; a complete and immediate opening of frontiers is therefore out of the question. But the problems involved are not beyond mastery. The same problems result from the suppression of trade barriers, tariffs, and quotas in Europe. In the case of an Atlantic market, of course, they would occur on a much larger scale; the advantages for all the participants, however, whatever their level of development, are probably also much greater.

The extensive studies pursued for the past twenty years on achieving a European Common Market show that such problems are technically soluble and that they would be even easier to resolve within the larger framework of an Atlantic Community. Understandably, these studies stress the necessity of a stage-by-stage approach. In this connection, the greater the progress achieved in the first stage of Europe's economic integration—an essential preliminary stage in the total process—the easier will be the implementation of a common Atlantic market.

On the political level, the existence of an effective Atlantic Community would imply extending to the management of all common interests the principles of democratic policy adhered to in each country. In such an Atlantic Community, the participating nations should accept the arrangements made in their common interest and settle differences on the basis of mutually accepted laws and procedures. Such a solution would imply that decisions affecting the common interest would be reached by a weighted, qualified majority among the participating countries.

All of this, obviously, requires the creation of a certain minimum of common political institutions. The discussion of these institutions is outside the scope of the present paper. Suffice it to say that their establishment could only be gradual.

The important point here is that the establishment of a political community, however limited its conception, would mean the transfer of some sovereign rights to a common political authority having *limited but real* powers.

Any confusion that might arise concerning this point should be cleared up at once. In speaking of the transfer of certain sovereign rights belonging to the respective states, it must be understood that this transfer is limited to the *minimum* of rights implied by the effective joint pursuit of the common objectives which have been defined. It must also be understood that *the larger the geographic zone we are considering, the more this transfer can and must be reduced.*

Thus there can be no question of contemplating the transfer to an Atlantic political authority of a body of rights equivalent to the one presently assumed by the American Federal Government,[16] nor even the one which a majority in the "European Six" seem prepared to transfer to the European community. Such a transfer is neither necessary nor desirable. *It is simply a matter of delegating a minimum of rights which, taking into account the experience already acquired, can be considered indispensable for the effective attainment of common objectives.*

Whatever the possible solution may be, there could be no question of any sudden change. It is a matter of advancing cautiously in a new direction. At the outset, any delegation of rights would have to be limited and carefully hedged, as all international agreements are, by safeguarding clauses to preserve each nation from that which it could not accept.

It is also clear that the United Nations cannot provide the West with the institutional framework required to further its common interests. The institutions needed must be specifically geared to the Atlantic Community.

Political Priority

The creation of an Atlantic common market, or even of Atlantic-wide trade liberalization, could lead to profound transformations and could in fact be advantageous only if such transformations took place. *Consequently, it would be acceptable only if the participating countries were assured that these transformations were to be, in effect, permanent, that they could not be challenged overnight.*

Economic ties in themselves are fragile. A true common market, or even extensive trade liberalization, are really acceptable only if they are reasonably stable. It follows that economic integration can be accepted and maintained as advantageous only if a certain degree of political integration is carried out at the same time.

Whatever progress has already been made by the European Common Market, *a complete economic integration of Western Europe is conceivable only within the framework of a certain degree of political*

[16] Many Americans hold, correctly so the author believes, that for the size of the country the concentration of power in the hands of the Federal government is tending to become excessive.

integration. Even if all the objectives of the Common Market Treaty were attained, one would still be quite far from a true common market. For example, while customs duties are eventually to be abolished, permanent fiscal compensation will still have to be accorded various commodities under certain conditions when the common market is achieved. The December 1963 negotiations of the "Six" on agriculture, and Chancellor Erhard's statements of March 19, 1964 about the impossibility of Germany's accepting a reduction of some of its agricultural prices for 1964 and 1965, are other examples. Even in the European Community of Coal and Steel, after eight years of existence, one is still very far from a true common market.

It is not sufficiently realized that progress toward a European Common Market has benefited from a very favorable circumstance, namely, the almost continuous economic expansion that has taken place. A depression could break the established ties very rapidly. Under such conditions there is great danger that the egotistical forces of nationalism would prevail over any regard for European cohesion. The bitter experience since World War I should serve as a lesson for the future. We must carefully analyze the reasons why our past efforts to eliminate the obstacles to free movement of the means of production have failed and glean the lessons pertinent to our course of action. We must remember that it is vain to hope for efficiency and stability when agreements may be broken at any time.

Furthermore, it is doubtful whether one can efficiently prepare a certain degree of political integration by starting in the economic sphere. On the contrary, economic integration reinforces the awareness of the various different national self-interests and, consequently, jeopardizes the development of a real community. In my opinion, *the establishment of at least a minimum of common political institutions must precede, or at least accompany, economic union*. This is an essential condition. The widely held opinion to the contrary is a dangerous illusion.[17]

Seen in this light, one should have no illusion about the possible success of the Kennedy Round in strengthening and extending in a substantial and durable manner the economic ties between Europe and North America. The progress that can be derived from an economic partnership not reinforced by a political partnership will necessarily remain marginal.

I cannot agree with those who maintain that the institutional prerequisite of closer economic interrelations among European countries would not be required in the case of similar relations across the Atlantic. Quite the contrary. In the event of even a relatively moderate policy of trade liberalization, the risks encountered on both sides of the Atlantic would be greater and some of the institutional guarantees which

---

[17] *Cf.* Maurice Allais, *L'Europe Unie, Route de la Prospérité, op. cit.*

have been considered necessary by the "Six" would be even more indispensable on this broader level.

For the past twenty years the writer of this paper has constantly defended the principle of free trade on national and international levels, advocating a policy of expanding trade on the Atlantic scale. But he would consider as absolutely unrealistic any serious attempts to broaden trade without previously setting up appropriate common economic and political institutions.

The same stricture applies to those who suggest that the functional approach is a valid solution. *The functional approach can be effective only if associated with a vast political conception of unity.* In and by itself, it can achieve only very limited results. It is unstable and completely unadaptable to the real needs of the peoples of the North Atlantic.

This view does not imply that the general and political approach is easy, or even that it is immediately workable. It simply means that at present the chances of maintaining and strengthening the cohesiveness of the Atlantic alliance are not good, and that it would be very dangerous to think that—for lack of a general and political approach, said to be impossible—traditional policies can provide a valid solution. Who would maintain that without the general approach of the Treaty of Rome the few strides taken thus far toward a Common Market could have been taken?

Steps to an Atlantic Community

If we agree that an effective Atlantic Community would bring positive advantages to the participating nations, it is essential that we see very clearly what its preliminary stages are.

The first necessary step is the transformation, as soon as possible, of the economic Europe of the Six into a political Europe.[18] Without this transformation, one may well doubt whether a true economic Europe is possible, and, *a fortiori,* whether trade liberalization on an Atlantic scale can be accomplished.

The second step is to open the "European Six" to any European nation (particularly to Great Britain) which would accept its fundamental economic and political principles. Only a solidly structured Europe could constitute a desirable and acceptable partner for the United States, and only such a solidly structured Europe could discard

[18] A necessary condition for such a political Europe is the establishment of a bicameral European parliament, with one house composed of representatives of member countries, the other elected by direct universal suffrage. This is the truly decisive step which the European Congress at The Hague, after heated discussion, refused to take in 1948. Fortunately, this mode of election is explicitly provided for in the Treaty of Rome signed nine years later. It is to be regretted that this provision has not yet been activated, for there is no doubt that it governs the effective formation of a true European Community.

the fear of losing its own personality in a closer association with the United States.

The next step would be a substantial effort on the informational and cultural levels. A closer association of Europe and North America would imply a considerable change in the various public opinions.

To state these conditions is to underscore the difficulties. But no human enterprise can succeed without delays, or materialize without some preparation of mind and of the facts. Unless the North Atlantic nations now make the effort to prepare their future with clarity of vision, it is all too probable that they will find themselves disunited and weak at crucial moments. An Atlantic common market and a real Atlantic Community are possible, but not without an effective and permanent political willingness to achieve them by all the participants.

The Dogma of Absolute and Unlimited National Sovereignty

The establishment of a real Atlantic Community and the transfer of certain of the states' sovereign rights to a supranational authority, even on a limited basis, naturally raise numerous objections on which I would like to comment briefly.

An effective Atlantic Community would imply the renunciation of the principle of unlimited national autonomy. But the actual significance of this renunciation is much smaller than appears at first sight.

First of all, the various nations of the West have already renounced a certain part of their national sovereignty. Clearly, Belgium in the Congo, France in Algeria, Germany in Berlin, the United States in Cuba, have all accepted limitations in their choice of policy. All must take into account the position of their partners in the Atlantic alliance. But this renunciation, however real it may be, is worthless if it is carried on in confusion, disorder, and mutual distrust. Not being related to any real joint action, it is purely negative and serves little purpose. Each of the Western nations suffers the disadvantages of surrendering the principle of unlimited national sovereignty without thereby securing the many advantages which they might reap within an appropriate common political institution.

Secondly, at issue is not so much a surrender of national sovereignty as the delegation by the citizens themselves of a part of their inalienable rights to a superior political authority. In reality, it is simply a transfer, not a surrender. The real objective is not to limit national sovereignty in itself; it is to promote material prosperity and to safeguard fundamental political liberties, peace, and finally, as stressed in the American Constitution, the happiness of the people. The objective is that system of political institutions which is most appropriate to these ends. And if it appears that an Atlantic political community of a certain type might better succeed than our own national institutions, would it not be in the interest of all citizens of the nations involved to support its creation?

In any case, and even within the framework of traditional policies, any treaty, any international obligation is a real limitation of sovereignty the moment one has the positive intention to respect it. Public opinion seems to exaggerate completely the difference between the partial renunciation of national sovereignty implied by respect for treaties and the functioning of an Atlantic Community. Given appropriate safeguards, one wonders if, in all these discussions about a limited renunciation of national sovereignty, we do not attribute more weight to appearances than to realities.

Also, in setting up mutual political arrangements of the type implied by an Atlantic Community, the actual constraints on real independence are far less important than the letter of the agreement might suggest. As the operation of the European Coal and Steel Community has shown, when the fundamental interests of a participating country were in question, the other countries have always renounced the literal application of the Treaty. Each country knows that if today it fails to take account of its neighbor's difficulties, it may itself be treated similarly in the future. Whatever the situation, the possibility of withdrawal in the course of time is always sufficient to prevent the unreasonable application of the letter of such treaties.

Finally, one of the essential principles of our common civilization is the peaceful settlement of differences on the basis of established rules and procedures. In this frame of reference, the delegation of certain limited but real powers to a common political authority would appear to be a *necessary* consequence of the very principle of our civilization.

America's Real Interest

In viewing this question strictly in American terms, two points need emphasis.

First, there is a real danger that Europe might turn toward nationalism and a self-sufficiency which may be anti-American. Europeans are strongly tempted to shut themselves up in their own community, perhaps even to establish a Third Force as many in Europe have been suggesting. It might be easy, and in the short run at least it may appear politically advantageous, for someone or for one or another group or nation to advocate a policy of independence toward the two blocs and to attempt some vast association with the Third World. Clearly, a drift in this direction could prove very disadvantageous to the United States. A split of the West into two separate and opposing groups would leave the United States dangerously isolated. The basic question facing the United States is unmistakable. Can the United States follow a policy designed to retain absolute independence of action and at the same time maintain and develop friendly ties with her allies?

Secondly, who can say what the American people would answer if asked to choose between the traditional policy based on the dogma of unlimited national sovereignty and an important breakthrough toward an Atlantic Community? Between the burden of increased military spending and the possibility of a rapid dismantling of the Communist ideology? Between the evident dangers of a divided West and the formal renunciation of a limited part of national sovereignty which in fact has already been renounced?

It is true that according to a recent sampling of public opinion, only about one-ninth of the American people seemed to feel that the world situation will make it necessary to give up some of the nation's sovereignty, while two-thirds believed that the U.S. should hold on to her sovereignty at all costs. At the same time, however, almost four-fifths considered it highly desirable to maintain U.S. alliances. One wonders what these four-fifths would do if retaining national sovereignty "at all costs" were in the end to lead to the liquidation of America's principal alliance.

In any case, public opinion sampling must be interpreted in the light of the information available at the time of the survey. It cannot be dissociated from this information. After two "suicidal" wars, Europeans have begun to understand that there was something erroneous and dangerous in the myth of unlimited national sovereignty. Perhaps this difficult lesson can be of value to the United States.

Europe's Real Interest

Europe's apprehensions regarding an eventual Atlantic Community are no less great than those of the United States; *they are probably even greater.*[19]

Paralyzed by a kind of inferiority complex and subjected, throughout Europe, to skillful and tenacious anti-American propaganda which is by no means the work of the Communists alone, Europeans are anxious not to be dominated by the United States.

Viewed realistically on the political as well as on the economic level, these apprehensions about United States domination of an Atlantic Community appear to be unjustified. In terms of population, material resources, and culture, as well as technical know-how, the United States could certainly not dominate the countries associated in such a Community. Actually, the result would be a mutual balancing of the various Atlantic Community members, which would prevent the predominance of any one nation or the formation of any totalitarian governments.

These fears, on both sides of the Atlantic, are really trivial when compared to the importance of what is at stake. If, at the beginning

---

[19] One could even say that the U.S. today is probably more favorable to Atlantic cooperation than ever before, whereas in Europe, each dawn sees the further growth of dangerously nationalistic forces.

of this century, the Atlantic nations had united themselves in a common political organization based on the principles of their civilization, the two world wars could have been avoided. Must we wait for the colossal destruction of a third world war with the virtual annihilation of all mankind in order to understand how trifling our hesitations really are?

Objections of the Third World

The decision to form a true Atlantic Community, were it taken, would surely be greeted with the accusation that it is motivated by selfish interests. However true this may be, the danger implicit in such a charge is actually far smaller than might appear.

First of all, if by this decision the threat of a third world war were removed for at least two or three decades, the value of such a Community for all mankind should be clear.

Furthermore, the aid which the West would be able to provide to the third world will be sufficient to meet their real needs only if the economies of the Atlantic nations are made as effective as possible; and this efficiency can be accomplished only within the framework of a true Community. Also, we should not forget that the influence of the Atlantic World on the Third World is a function of its own efficiency and prosperity. Disunited, the Western nations would descredit themselves in the eyes of the rest of the world. The world really respects only power and success.

Finally, the Community which is to be formed must remain *open*. When fully established, it must be able to include, by means of appropriate processes, the other countries holding the same values and dedicated to the same democratic principles. For the moment, however, we must be realistic and begin where it is actually possible to begin.

Safeguarding National Diversities in an Atlantic Community

If we accept the proposition that an Atlantic Community is possible, the only essential problem is the safeguarding of our national diversities.

We all passionately love our own soil, our own language and customs, our own diversities, fully convinced that the maintenance of these diversities is essential. Western civilization is based on respect for diversities. They have enabled our civilization to become what it is and to attain unprecedented levels of progress. These diversities themselves result from the fundamental principle of respect for human individuality which is at the very base of our civilization.

Unfortunately, confronted by a simplistic ideology and by an environment whose organization is based on totalitarian principles—the very negation of diversity—a government which is too decentralized and too diversified represents a serious handicap in the implacable war to which we are exposed.

The challenge, therefore, is this: *Is it possible to define institutional ties which effectively preserve national diversities, at least those which are essential, while assuring the effectiveness of united action in defense of common interests?* Can a political agreement be worked out which would allay the fears of smaller nations that they may be dominated by the larger ones, and of larger nations that they may be stifled by the smaller ones?

The appropriate reply to this question would seem to be in the affirmative. The United States and Switzerland have demonstrated that it is possible to organize a true community on the basis of the general principles of a free society, and that such communities can be highly effective.[20]

History demonstrates, furthermore, that only such a political organization could offer the people guarantees to preserve their true freedom, their particular way of life, and their own civilization. Moreover, if the organization is democratic, the more extensive the community, the more effective will be its opposition to totalitarian tendencies. The concept of the separation and balance of powers, one of the main principles of democracy, is of special importance here, for without it the democratic organization of free people is inconceivable.

What the Western Nations Can Do in the Meantime

The establishment of a true Atlantic Community undoubtedly would enable us to meet the challenge we face. Public opinion, however, is not ready for such a solution—either in Europe or in the United States. We may well deplore it, but we must look at facts as they are. For the time being, therefore, we must unfortunately be satisfied with measures which, though certainly less ambitious, can at least lead us in the right direction. The delay involved might prove disastrous, but all we can do is to realize that it is inevitable and to strive for our common salvation with all our strength and will.

In the author's opinion, immediate action could and should be taken on three different levels: the economic, the political, and the cultural.

On the economic level, there are these major areas of desirable cooperation: an enlarged Atlantic mutual aid program; the maximum possible degree of association between North America and the Common Market even though this might amount to very little; and finally, a common policy for the development of the Third World.

---

[20] The example of Canada and Cyprus are no less instructive by highlighting the problems to be resolved where ethnic or linguistic minorities are present if a federal type of organization is to be viable. From this point of view, it is quite likely that any Atlantic Community which included both the U.S. and U.K. would only be acceptable to the continental Europeans if it also included some European countries over and above the "Europe of the Six."

Regarding the first of these, whether common institutions are set up or not, the Atlantic nations must furnish each other with mutual assistance of the widest variety in order that they may better face their problems.

This was the objective of the generous aid an enlightened America provided under the Marshall Plan. The same objective should be pursued today by the European nations by effectively aiding the United States to solve its balance-of-payments problems and by cooperating to provide greater international liquidity as required by the functioning of the gold exchange standard in a world of fixed exchange rates.

Regarding the former, and neglecting such undesirable alternatives as inflation in Europe relative to the United States, there exist only two means for remedying the deficit in the American balance of payments: a devaluation of the dollar in relation to the other currencies which would permit increased United States exports, and a lowering of the tariff barriers by countries friendly to the United States.[21]

The countries friendly to the United States are in a position to help her substantially. Besides, for Europe it is only a question of discharging a debt of gratitude. Certainly, lowering European tariffs so as to benefit American exports would meet with strong opposition, at least by a part of European public opinion.[22] But this opposition could be surmounted if the agreement to be reached could be put *on a reciprocal basis,* i.e., if it were understood that in case of a reversal of the balance-of-payments situation, the United States would lower its protective tariffs to help Europe in return.

The problem posed by the large volume of short-term claims in dollars held abroad is even more difficult. Under the "gold exchange standard" the United States must honor widespread requests for turning these claims into gold and this could bring about an embargo on U.S. gold exports.[23] As matters stand, we face a *dangerous and unstable*

---

[21] The author believes that devaluation of the U.S. dollar would not have the disastrous effects usually suggested, whether it was done by a move to a new fixed exchange rate or by letting the dollar find its level in a free market. The only effect would be to turn the dollar overnight into the strongest currency in the world, and at the same time to free the United States policy of military and economic foreign aid from balance-of-payments restraints; such a move would also strengthen its policy of internal expansion.

This is not an isolated opinion; it is shared by a growing number of American economists. See in particular the statement of Professor Milton Friedman on November 14, 1963, before the Joint Economic Committee, the 88th Congress, on the occasion of its Hearings on Balance of Payments.

[22] The effort which would have to be made is likely to be smaller than one might think. In 1963 the U.S. balance-of-payments deficit, some $3 billion, was only about 5 per cent of the total imports of the EEC and EFTA.

[23] In December 1964, the over-all reserves in dollars convertible into gold held by other countries were almost $29 billion, whereas the U.S. gold reserves amounted only to $15.4 billion. Of this amount $15.1 billion would have been earmarked under U.S. law to cover internal money supply. However, recent legislation reduced gold cover requirements to about $9 billion.

situation, the more so since the balance-of-payments deficit and the probem just indicated aggravate each other.[24]

Europe can give very effective aid to the American economy by measures to alleviate both of these difficulties. We should be aware, however, that the support presently given by Europe rests only on unwritten rules of good neighborliness. In an economic crisis this aid may dwindle overnight. The situation would be quite different in the case of a real Atlantic Community.[25]

In regard to the second line of action mentioned above—developing the association between North America and the Common Market—it appears that under present conditions a very extensive reduction of trade barriers covering the Atlantic area would be difficult if not impossible. Such a step would amount to superimposing on a European Common Market still in process of economic and political formation a much more inclusive free-trade zone without benefit of common political institutions.

The difficulties involved are exactly similar to those that became apparent when Great Britain's entry into the Common Market was being negotiated.[26] The economic Europe of the Common Market ought to be transformed without delay into as inclusive a political Europe as possible. From this point of view, any economic or political agreement between nations that could compromise the development of a political Europe ought to be avoided. This was, and still is in the eyes of many on the Continent, the obstacle in the way of Great Britain's full participation in the Common Market. Adherence to the Treaty of Rome cannot be reduced simply to an economic formula. *Above all* there must be adherence to the political spirit of the Treaty which in turn constitutes only one step toward a politically integrated Europe.

Analogous objections apply to very sweeping reductions of trade barriers on an Atlantic area-wide basis. The Common Market finds it difficult enough, in spite of the existence of common institutions, to ad-

---

[24] It seems to the author that, other than a de facto renunciation of international convertibility into gold of major currencies, the only reasonable remedy for the present situation *for Western countries as a whole,* is a 2- to 3-fold revaluation of gold in terms of the various currencies. The arguments which have been put forward against such a measure—the windfall gains to be realized by South Africa and the Soviet Union—are of no significance compared with the dangers inherent in the present situation. A 3 to 1 revaluation would settle liquidity problems for many years to come for both the United States and Europe. Only the existence of taboos can account for our failure to accept so reasonable a solution.

[25] See Clarence Streit's remarkable article "The Danger to the Dollar and How to End it," *Freedom and Union* (November 1963).

[26] For essentially the same reasons, much of the difficulty presently experienced at Geneva in reducing trade barriers results from the dogma of the most-favored-nation clause, whose systematic application has the effect of rendering impossible any real trade liberalization. Any large-scale liberalization can only be regional, not worldwide, at least for a long time to come. Here as elsewhere, as the French proverb has it, "the best is the good's worst enemy."

vance its own development without the additional problems such reductions would imply.

The idea of partnership between North America and Europe, though in itself very seductive, has never been clearly defined. In its present formulation it is no more than a myth, possibly of some use politically but otherwise devoid of meaning. One must not conceal the fact that without common institutions, and in the absence of an over-all political design, the concrete possibilities for this idea are very limited.

In sum, there are serious reasons to believe that in the second area of action, looking toward an Atlantic Community, we must be satisfied with marginal advances. If things go well in Geneva, for example, a useful but limited trade agreement between the United States and the Common Market countries may prove possible.

In the third area, that of assisting underdeveloped countries, it seems essential that the North Atlantic nations define and implement a common policy. To be effective, such common policy must be based on true Western ideology: that is, the basic articulation of Western aid to the Third World should be in terms of a wide liberalization of trade with regard to the products that the Third World can advantageously export—mainly raw materials and especially tropical products, products of skilled crafts, and labor intensive manufactures.

The effort required by the West obviously poses difficult problems. However, reciprocal trade liberalization between the West and the Third World probably constitutes the only really effective approach to development in the countries of the Third World as well as in Western countries. In addition, it is the only way which can lead to an effective and acceptable redistribution of the burdens involved.

On the political level, three basic measures could be envisaged: First, the creation of a council in NATO, empowered, on questions of common interest and in specific fields, to make decisions by a qualified majority; second, the creation of a "Commission" suitably empowered to study common problems and make recommendations; and third, the creation of an Atlantic Parliamentary Assembly with advisory functions whose members would be designated by the respective national parliaments. The details here matter little at this point. What is needed is a beginning from which we can progress. Very useful proposals, not only along this line but also in regard to economic and cultural matters, are contained in the Declaration of the Atlantic Convention held in January, 1962.[27]

The most effective steps on the cultural level would be to increase cultural exchanges on a vast scale. The costs of these programs are nothing compared with the decisive gains to be made. A real Community could not possibly be negotiated at the top and brought into

---

[27] *Cf.* the Declaration of the Atlantic Convention of the One Hundred Citizens of NATO (Paris: January 20, 1962), presided over by Mr. Herter.

being by law. It is through learning to know each other better that people in various countries can erase the misunderstandings which separate them, and become accustomed to appreciating and liking each other. Cultural cooperation can take many and diverse forms. For example, it would be desirable to have the Atlantic nations agree that henceforward no advanced academic degree may be conferred without at least one year's study in another Atlantic country. A minimum representation of professors from other Atlantic universities might also be required, with some of them teaching in their own language. In addition, substantial numbers of workers and executives should undergo a period of training in a neighboring country. Every citizen of an Atlantic nation might be taught to speak a second language. A final example would be to provide for the translation of all writings of value into another Atlantic language.

Summary and Conclusions

The view here presented of the dangers and issues which the Atlantic nations face leads to a number of simple and basic conclusions.

First, the political leaders of the West should not lose themselves in technical details, nor should they content themselves merely to identify certain new arrangements that might improve the present situation. Their true task is to deal effectively with the basic questions of our times, those which involve our liberties and our very lives.

Second, we should all learn from history that the root source of our difficulties has been our unfaithfulness to our own principles. Marxist communism had its origin in, and drew its strength from, the inhuman organization of our societies at the beginning of the industrial era. Our inability to adjust our differences peaceably has led to two world wars —totalitarian communism was born of the first war and emerged stronger than ever from the second. Today it is our differences and our disunity which constitute the essential strength of the ideology of totalitarian communism. If the West is to be faithful to the principles of its own civilization, it must be capable of passing through a further stage of historical development: that of the unity of the Atlantic World.

Third, our future depends on us. It depends neither upon the Communist world, nor upon the Third World. The broad outlines of the solution to our basic problems are evident. The Atlantic World must realize that disunited it heads inevitably towards disaster, that the international policies of the great democratic nations can be effective only if pursued in concert. To do so requires that the West reinforce its political, economic, and military cohesion. We must surmount all the inherited feelings of false nationalism and head resolutely toward an Atlantic Community. If such a solution were chosen, a new worldwide conflict could be avoided. The peoples of the North Atlantic could then come to know, at least in the next decades, a "golden age" without precedent in the history of mankind. The question is: Can we grasp that it depends upon us alone whether the apogee of Western civilization is yet to arrive or has already passed?

Fourth, nothing could be more dangerous for the West today than to limit its action to half measures under cover of a false realism, and to postpone decisions which alone can decisively change the course of events. Such an easygoing policy would only divert public opinion from real problems and genuine solutions. Meanwhile, half measures run everywhere into roadblocks. The problems we face remain unsolved, and the basic reason is that so long as we adhere to the doctrine of absolute national sovereignty, any really effective solution is blocked.

Fifth, to conclude that a true Atlantic Community is impossible in the future because of its present impossibility is to beg the question. Yesterday the Common Market was only a chimera. Today it has begun to be a reality. An Atlantic Community, as I have defined it, is certainly possible a few years from now. But there must be sufficient vision to begin preparing for it now; there must be the political will to make progress toward the realization of that vision. A radical and immediate change of public opinion in the United States and in Europe is probably unthinkable, but education to bring about this change is possible.

Finally, the sacrifices which must be made in order to build an Atlantic Community are slight compared with our freedom and our lives. Let us not, for the sake of appearances more than realities, persist in outdated solutions which in the end will solve nothing and will involve the risk of catastrophe. We must sacrifice the trivial in order to safeguard the essential. The question is, will we be lucid enough to see the problem for what it is, clairvoyant enough to perceive the solution, and courageous enough to defend this solution in the face of public opinion? Or shall we be like the Byzantine monks who gathered to discuss the sex of angels while the Turks were besieging Constantinople?

Toward Constructive World Leadership

—*HENDRIK BRUGMANS*

The Present Situation

Certain problems of the modern world—such as widespread hunger and underdevelopment—are perhaps theoretically more important than the East-West conflict, and surely more of an inspiration to young Westerners who are anxious to contribute their share to a better standard of living and greater liberty for mankind. Moreover, in the struggle against communism we face a deadlock. Actions against economic and social backwardness require immediate measures in several fields: more investments, better vocational training, stabilization of prices of tropical products and raw materials, etc. On the one hand, there seems to exist a guardian duty to be patiently performed. On the other, there appears a multiplicity of concrete tasks to be fulfilled.

The rivalry between the two systems has global repercussions, disrupting every normal human intercourse between nations, races, and continents, and influencing (or rather politicizing) any initiative made to improve living conditions of the underprivileged. On our side of the Iron and Bamboo Curtains, "the front is everywhere."

The ubiquitous rivalry between the two systems of values has a very particular character which can hardly be compared with any other conflict in world history. Although the ironic mind may resent its harshness, this rivalry will continue to divide humanity as long as Peking and Moscow aim at world revolution; i.e., for a period which may last indefinitely. Moreover, we are not facing here a "problem" to be "solved" by means of intellectual ingenuity. (In that sense, it obscures the terminology to speak about a Berlin or a Formosa "question." [*Cf.* Bertrand de Jouvenel, "The Myth of the Solution," *The Pure Theory of Politics.*]) We face a power, political, and ideological conflict. Ideas and the force behind them will shape the fate of mankind, at the very moment when we enter "the era of global history." [Hans Kohn]

What Stalin used to call "peaceful competition" does not differ basically from what the Kremlin today terms "thaw," "peaceful coexistence," or "détente." Time and again, the present Soviet leadership has clearly stated the view that there could be no end to "ideological class struggle" before the final defeat of capitalism. This, they said, was true both in the field of intellectual and artistic life inside the USSR ("fight against the remnants of bourgeois ideology") as well as international relations. We would be naive to hope for greater, lasting toleration, or even for a lasting division of the world into "spheres of influence." In fact, any "de-tension" or "détente" at all results exclusively from a weakening of Communist dictatorship, as Khrushchev did not wield as much power as his predecessor used to enjoy. Stalinism without Stalin, as he would like to have it, is utopian. Similarly, East European countries could not be kept down after the events of 1956—at least not as before. We would be equally as foolish to believe in a change of heart of the Communist leaders, as to act as if their regime would be monolithic and not subject to the historical laws of change and evolution.

The only chance we have to decrease tensions lies in a change of the balance of powers to the detriment of the Communists; i.e., in a further weakening of the Communist bloc or in a strengthening of our side or both—making our opponents realize that the times of victorious advance are over and that, consequently, a more "flexible" attitude is desirable. In other words, "liberalization" of a dictatorship (and a totalitarian, ideologically obsessed dictatorship at that) can never be obtained other than by its internal disintegration or by a series of external defeats.

Finally, the conflict between Moscow and Peking, far from making the former more Western minded, may well force the Soviet leaders to insist on their implacable loyalty to the principles and doctrines of Marxism-Leninism. Any ideological weakness on their part will immediately be interpreted as fresh evidence of their "revisionism" and their having become unworthy of bearing the banner of world revolution in the "Third World." Such a humiliation would mean a major catastrophe for the Kremlin, since being considered "heretical" would mean to forsake the spoils of the capitalist world.

"The Communist system is therefore already on what is practically a war footing." This statement, made by a Chatham House study group in 1950, when Stalinism was at its zenith, appears to be valid still, even if the wording of Khrushchev and his successors may sometimes be less aggressive than Stalin's, since they have greater difficulties to face with less absolute power. It might even be advocated that these circumstances will not always diminish but rather might increase Communist aggressiveness toward the outside world. In a comparable way, the French Revolution entered its most aggressive phase after Thermidor, when the crusading spirit of Jacobinism was on the wane and the Paris Government wavering.

Communist pressure will normally make itself felt in any area where a power, political, or ideological vacuum appears, since our opponent is likely to attack our weakest spots. Analyzing the world situation, we therefore have to ask ourselves where such weak spots appear.

Their Strength and Our Weaknesses

Some time ago a Dutch cartoonist portrayed Mr. Khrushchev, sitting at a control board wondering which button to push—Berlin, Vietnam, Cuba, etc. Today, the artist might have presented the same control board—adding perhaps a few new buttons (Zanzibar for instance and Kasai)—but showing two quarreling technicians behind it, as Mao has now come into the competition for world conquest. In any case, whatever the number of buttons and button-pushers, they do have the means to open or close an incident in numerous parts of the world, as they dispose of local "agents" who freely and even enthusiastically accept leadership of "the people" on the spot, organize mass movements, and follow instructions, even while using their own initiative. In other words, the "buttons" are made of human convictions, organizational skill, and energetic devotion, at least as much as of bribery and intimidation.

Outside our own realm, we in the West can at best count on governments, sometime though not always corrupt, sometimes though not always successful, but hardly ever on spontaneous popular movements. This is only too understandable. The underdeveloped regions, where de-colonization more often than not has left anti-imperialism, chaos, and incompetence—and consequently a power-political vacuum—are ruled by men who desperately look out for a "regime" to establish and to believe in. In their view, mature representative democracy hardly offers any solution. For that conviction they have at least two main arguments. (1) Western Democracy is represented either by ex-colonial countries or by the United States, which is too powerful not to be interested in economic expansion and to covet new overseas markets. In any case, the West is suspect and does not arouse the enthusiasm which is indispensable in an emotion laden world. ((2) These freshly emerged countries cannot afford the luxury of opposition groups out of office, as all available political and technically skilled forces must be permanently mobilized for the common goal. Pluriformity and open criticism against the Government—values which we cherish as essential prerequisites for freedom—in their view amount to disloyalty and disruption. Consequently our main argument against communism (or against fascism for that matter), that it does not provide room for free public debate, falls flat when the state is recent and the income per capita low. By contrast, communism appears to offer the passionately desired short-cut toward political and administrative order, industrialization, and prosperity. True, Asians and Africans begin dimly to realize that communism does not shrink from using the violent methods we have learned to discard. But in the new countries, violence and coercion are considered inevitable in any case. With an "ideology" in mind, it seems to become easier to run a country and whip up national energy.

When we review the situation, it may therefore seem that communism, whether Russian or Chinese, has too formidable trump cards not to win. In fact, it sometimes seems that it is progressively winning over the "non-committed" peoples. This, however, is not necessarily our conclusion. Especially in Africa, experience with Communist "help" has aroused doubts, to say the least, as to whether these "allies in the struggle against neo-colonialism" are as disinterested, as competent, and as humane as was thought from a distance. Nonetheless, we would be unwise and intellectually lazy should we reassure ourselves too easily, relying on the blunders which our opponents doubtlessly make and will repeat. What then are the conditions for an inspiring, imaginative, and constructive world policy from our side?

Before considering what a Western program for the world should positively contain, we must first indicate the obstacles that stand in our way and hamper our progress. In other words, what are the weak spots at home which enable Communist propaganda to recover rapidly from tactical defeat? This implies that there is a close relation between our inner strength and the success of our statecraft abroad. In fact, we contend that the present world political situation forces us to consider anew our traditional concepts of "foreign" as opposed to "home" policy. We live in a glass house and should know that anything is likely to be used against us, so that the realm of "internal" affairs has been narrowed down more drastically than the average citizen in the West suspects.

This is particularly, though by no means exclusively, the case as far as interracial intercourse is concerned. A clash between Jamaicans and English rowdies in Manchester is no longer a local police affair; it is world news. "Little Rock" is worth several rockets for the Communist cause, and Governor Barnett is better known in Africa than President Johnson.

By contrast, General de Gaulle enjoys an enormous prestige in the "Third World." This is partly due to his purposeful energy (the Third World does respect authority if it is strongly affirmed), but also (perhaps above all) to the fact that without any color consciousness he presided over the Brazzaville conference in 1942, and in 1962 granted independence to Algeria, helping this country afterwards in spite of its socialist regime. Consequently the West should realize that any strike, any social conflict, any setback in economic expansion, means a world political defeat for the forces of freedom we have to lead, whereas any success on the home front is a battle won in the struggle for the world. Of course this does not imply that we should transform our press into a propaganda machine or establish an authoritarian regime of any kind. We cannot expel the Devil with Beelzebub, nor communism with fascism. It does mean, however, that generosity always pays, whereas prejudice and discrimination never do.

For What Is the West Ready to "Fight"?

These problems however, important though they are, are perhaps not part of the essential structures of Western society. In a way they are only incidental *Schönheitsfehler,* and one might imagine a moment to come when they would have been eliminated. Another phenomenon is far more fundamental, namely the fact that so many Westerners—especially Europeans—have lost their self-confidence, their certitude to stand for a good cause, their faith in the future and the values of their civilization. Here lie the roots of a widespread defeatism which sometimes materializes in pacifist illusions, sometimes in moral skepticism. In any case, a great many young Europeans perform their military duties without the slightest conviction and with the feeling of losing time. Both the "how" and "why" of our military system have become problematic.

This psychological situation greatly differs from the one which prevailed in the thirties, when violent anti-fascist feelings flourished. True, even such emotion was not always powerful enough to prevent the sometimes shameful collapse of the Allied armies on the Continent in 1940. But there at least existed a source of inspiration for future resistance. Today only few desire the triumph of communism, but many regard it with a certain sympathy and consider it an historical necessity.

These feelings are reflected in the purely defensive attitude of the West. One might say that today the American deterrent plays the role which the Maginot Line performed in French public opinion thirty years ago. It looks as if the West was unable to produce a strategy, other than the classical answer of defense against aggression—trying to protect its territories, its spheres of influence, its vital interests, against enemy infiltration. Consciously or unconsciously, we have stuck to the old methods of *cordon sanitaire,* the best we could hope for being to achieve a military insurance for political *status quo.* [*Cf.* André Kostolany, *La Paix du Dollar.*] True, when this *status quo* had been challenged by our less scrupulous and more dynamic opponents—in Berlin, Indochina, Korea, Cuba, or the Indrapura Valley—we suddenly awoke and sometimes even scored a defensive victory. But each time, immediately after the shock, everything returned to normalcy again. We consequently make the impression of relying exclusively and placidly on material defense and weapons of mass destruction, leaving the political initiative to communism.

Communism, by contrast, looks more idealistic and less militaristic, since it has imagination and conquering faith. Facing it, we seem to hide behind the nuclear wall and to have retired inside a "fortress West," trying to hold our own and continue our *dolce vita* as long as possible. Consequently, in a world conflict which is rightly felt to be first and foremost a political and spiritual struggle, Western reliance on nuclear defense appears as a form of moral escapism and lazy materialism.

Nothing could be more disastrous. Outside our boundaries every child knows that the challenge is a spiritual one. Infinitely more drastically than Nazism ever did, communism puts before us the basic problem of the defensibility of our civilization. Nazism and fascism never presented a universal message, and when they were militarily defeated, few of their former enthusiasts stuck to their guns [*Cf.* Ernst Nolte, *Der Faschismus in seiner Epoche*], whereas communism has its impact all over the world, "promising" while the West can only "give" [Raymond Aron]. If European morale is low, its defeatism is exactly proportional to the prestige of the ideological enemy. Europe, in fact, though not a spiritual vacuum, is badly in need of a banner around which to rally. Nationalism, although still strong enough to prevent rapid progress toward supranational integration, no longer provides a source of popular inspiration. European patriotism is slow to crystallize. Consequently, the question whether the West is ready to "fight" coincides with another one: "What does the West oppose to communism? What are its peace aims?"

As an answer to this question, it is sometimes said that we would be better off if we had a uniform ideology. The other side has one, so why not we? The author was even invited, some time ago, to join a panel of "experts" in order to elaborate one! Nothing could be more sterile. As political freedom is the basis of our society, and freedom implies pluriformity, there can never be a uniform Western creed. Moreover, the main wickedness of totalitarian movements lies in their ambition to offer a pseudo-religion, with its "orthodoxy" and its "heresies." Such an ersatz, whatever its precise contents, would be totally unacceptable to Christians who would denounce its "idolatrous" character, as well as to non-Christian humanists, who would probably reject it for other reasons.

Although it is true that politics—even the noblest kind of politics—should never be inflated to a *Weltanschauung,* this does not imply that we should be content with occasional, improvised hand-to-mouth solutions, half-hearted compromises, reluctant retreats, moral sermons and incidental, defensive local successes. "Decline begins when people no longer ask 'What shall we do?' but 'What is going to happen?' " [Denis de Rougemont].

Why did President Kennedy so rapidly become popular and why did his death come as such a shock to all of us? He embodied the hope for a Western renovation, based upon two complementary requirements: a moral revival and a practical, long-run program of action. He too suffered occasional defeats such as the Cuba landing, but he seemed to have put an end to the disheartened feeling of our being constantly outwitted and taken by surprise by an opponent who seems to play a cat-and-mouse game with us. He too, of course, gave considerable attention to the problems of material defense, as do the Russians—but he realized that no increase of divisions or missiles, no modernization of equipment could enable us to win the war of ideas. Military over-equipment might even be a political disadvantage.

This leads us to a closer examination of the *duo necessaria* mentioned above.

Moral Revival and a Long-Range Program

Civilizations are built on ethical values [*Cf.* Ernest Bieri, Hendrik Brugmans, Milorad Drachkovitch, Hans Kohn, Leo Moulin, *Basic Values of the Atlantic Community*] and ethics in turn have their roots in religion. Therefore it is hardly possible that the moral revival of the West should not coincide with religious rebirth. Societies live as long as they take their own inspiration seriously, and there are no cultures based on skepticism. Of course, individual ethical consciousness is not necessarily linked to revealed religion, but ethical systems as a social phenomenon have never maintained themselves outside religion or *Weltanschauung.*

True, such *Weltanschauungen* are by definition universal and not "Western" or "European": this is even specifically the case with present-day Christendom, as it is freeing itself from its historic—Mediterranean, Atlantic, and white man's—past. Nonetheless, moral inspiration, in our part of the world, has always been linked with the preaching of the Gospel rather than with the Koran or the Upanishad, and it is difficult to imagine an ethical and religious renaissance in our countries that would not bear the mark of Jerusalem. In fact, such a renaissance is clearly underway, both in the Jewish, the Protestant and the Roman Catholic communities. However this problem is outside our range here.

As to the practical program: in order to be effective, it has to be both political (as opposed to inspired by economic interest) and international (as opposed to inspired by national interest).

We must learn to put the political interests of the free world before anything else. We must learn to become "disinterested" as far as immediate business profits are concerned. Of course, it can be said with a large amount of good sense that the Communists are very far from being disinterested in their world policy; they pursue their own national aims too, so that their supporters become those "nationalists of a foreign power" whom Léon Blum denounced. But the fact remains that these supporters have freely allowed themselves to be persuaded that the Communist empires are not empires but ideologically progressive communities. By contrast, wherever the United States, Britain, or France operate, they will regularly be accused of serving the cause of well defined "capitalist" groups, such as United Fruit Company, Shell, Michelin, Firestone, or Unilever. What is worse, such criticism may well be justified up to a certain degree. Consequently, it is only fair to say that our unpopularity results partly from the confusion which appears between our foreign policy and the requirements of our "profit-making, worker-exploiting" regime.

First things first. If we believe that the most important item on the list of our priorities consists of promoting prosperity everywhere, developing civil liberties, increasing social responsibility, and thereby repelling the Communist onslaught, we must draw the consequences therefrom. Although the interests of our great firms do not necessarily conflict with the political aims we pursue, neither do they necessarily coincide. In cases of conflict between the two, the priority must lie with our political aspirations—which means that private business has to be subjected to political supervision as soon as it operates in particularly "hot" spots where competition with communism is fiercest.

Neither should we forget that the conflict is not between communism and one particular country in the West, not between America and Russia, but between the West in general and communism as a whole. It therefore is a dangerous illusion to be disillusioned by one's allies and consequently decide to "go it alone." This holds true for the smaller countries of the alliance, such as France—and also for its leader, the United States. Understandably enough, each nation has its own geographical position, its historic background, and therefore its special sensitiveness. Nonetheless, the fact that President Kennedy, in his Cuba broadcast, constantly referred to "this hemisphere" and to the direct threat which Castro's Russian missiles meant to "this nation" rather than to the free world at large, suggested to many European listeners that, after all, they were not directly involved in this quarrel. And this conclusion did much to clear the ground for Gaullist "separatism" within the West.

In this context three remarks are in order.

First, a plan for deliberate internationalism in Western policy is by no means incompatible with the acceptance of nationalism as a positive force elsewhere. It is both honest and effective to strengthen movements for national independence outside the free world, even while making interdependence the keynote of our own efforts. In fact, the word "nationalism" is ambiguous, and in mature nations connotes insularism and reaction. In newly emancipated territories, however, it will represent progress and human dignity.

"Algeria for the Algerians," for example, is a potentially anti-Communist slogan, as it may inspire a refusal of Chinese or Russian interference. "Britain for the British" has an entirely different meaning if it has any at all. In other words, nationalism, however naive, is an indispensable force of state building in regions where that process has still to be started, whereas it constitutes only a factor of disintegration and disruption in well established political communities.

Second, however, even in countries where a minimum of (national) order has to be built and where national idealism is a source of strength and self-confidence, nationalism is not enough, and movements like Pan-Africanism should be supported. For example, priority aid has to be given to those development plans in which more than one state participates.

Third, the principle of Western cooperation should include a fair amount of division of labor among different countries. We are in the same boat, but we are not identical in our possibilities. Curiously enough, the former colonial powers do enjoy a growing prestige in their former possessions, and the economic ties between them and the former motherlands are far from negligible.

It was therefore natural that Britain should intervene in East Africa and that French-speaking nations of West Africa should continue to have their eyes fixed on Paris. Even the Dutch seem to recapture a certain privileged position in Indonesia, after the transfer of West Irian. No doubt these favorable positions should be used to the utmost, in the general framework of a coherent common Western policy.

Forms of Western Cooperation and Confederation

It might be asked whether any attempt to strengthen the West through closer cooperation and unity would not be looked upon with suspicion in the "Third World." In fact, regional concentrations such as the European Community and Atlantic partnership, whatever their precise institutional forms, obviously represent power political blocs. This will initially frighten newcomers in historic life, as they want to dream—and want us to dream—in terms of "idealistic" weakness. Let us, however, not allow ourselves to be too much disturbed by such reactions. In practice, respect for power belongs to the fundamentals of public action, and—although power may corrupt the sinful human soul—it is not evil in itself. On the contrary, it is the indispensable instrument of any policy, either good or bad. [*Cf.* Bertrand de Jouvenel, *On Power*.]

Recent events confirm this observation. The United States was never more respected than in October 1962 when it brought the world, rightly, to the verge of war. China's operation against India brought discredit rather than pity to Nehru, whose moralistic pacifism then appeared as what it was: the "ideological superstructure" of military unpreparedness and political inadequacy. Consequently, as together we are powerful—and therefore suspected anyway—we should use our power in a convincing manner, rather than try to hide it. Guilt complexes in that respect only make us less efficient, certainly not more popular.

Therefore, the only real problem remaining is how to use our power, which in itself will never be too strong. The answer to this question is that we should use our strength by producing and trying to enforce a scheme of institutional world order.

Does this necessarily mean World Government? By no means. True, some basic issues in the modern world—such as the struggle against hunger, illiteracy, and underdevelopment—can be dealt with only on a global scale, and this is the case even more for the threat of nuclear warfare. But the Communist states do not dream of sharing any part of their sovereignty with their capitalist opponents. We cannot blame them for that: supranationality is only possible—and even then far from easy—among nations who have at least some basic values in common and therefore share a degree of mutual confidence. We have to limit our cooperation with the Communist bloc to technical and politically neutral matters, and to fields where both accept the practicing of "peaceful competition." (On this last point, the West can afford to be very liberal, even culturally aggressive, as its methods will prove to be more efficient than those of the totalitarians—at least in the long run.)

But even around the Atlantic Ocean, free-world government would be difficult to establish, as it is unlikely that the medium states in Europe are prepared to enter a federation where one already "united" power—America—is predominant. Naturally enough, they consider such an enterprise an attempt to institutionalize American hegemony, whereas the United States would not unnaturally argue that no effective administration can work without an executive who is able to decide and carry out its decisions.

What then? Unite the European countries, one by one, with the fifty-odd "states" of the American federation? Let not the word "federalism" deceive us. Whereas America is a "nation" from coast to coast just as much as a "union," there is no European "nation" in the making, let alone an Atlantic one. If Western Europe is ever to federate, it will be through institutions extremely different from those of the American type. The European and Atlantic institutions, in fact, should not only provide a high amount of inner, administrative decentralization—a more or less technical device after all—they should, on our side of the ocean, also assure the continuity of ancient fatherlands, each of them with its own secular history, its cultural personality, its language of languages. It would therefore be wholly unrealistic to put the European "states" on the same footing as those that formed their "more perfect union" in North America around 1780, or to merge both types into one federation, "The United 'States' of the Atlantic." The French would call such an operation "the marriage between carp and rabbit." In fact, the building materials of an Atlantic union are not fifty-odd states on the one side, and six or sixteen on the other. The material has to be two-fold: Europe and America, both of them "united."

What, then, has to be done if disunity means ruin and Atlantic federation remains utopian? Let us clearly specify our answer: the only long-range perspective seems to be a free world confederacy, based on regional, continental (European, Latin American, and North American) federations rather than on individual nation-states. This requires an undogmatic analysis of how different functions could best be performed and by whom—"undogmatic" in the sense that there should be no global doctrine as to who does what: no nationalism but no systematic "Europeanism" either, as well as no uncompromising "Atlanticism." The only principle to be respected is "subsidiarity": when in doubt, choose the smaller community, which is likely to be closer to people's hearts and more easily equipped for democratic control. For the rest, efficiency is the supreme rule.

Let us take, for instance, the military problem.

It might be considered useful to lay the responsibility for the protection of Western Europe in the hands of a renewed European Defense Community, having at its disposal plurinational supplies and standardized armaments, including tactical nuclear weapons. There also would exist an "integrated" European command. However, the Community should immediately conclude an agreement with the United States, in view of a renewed, better balanced NATO. At the same time, as it seems undesirable that nuclear deterrents should remain in the hands of any individual state—be it America, France, or Britain, control of strategic nuclear weapons should be handed over to an Atlantic authority "with limited function but real power," as the classical phrase runs. In this field, technical cooperation between the allies should be total, and the elaboration of a common world policy for the maintenance of peace based on Atlantic partnership and dialogue.

Such plans, like the ones rejected above, may be said to be utopian. And indeed, in the present state of affairs we seem to be far away from their practical application. However, the aim of this essay, as the writer understood it, was not to provide possible compromises for diplomatic intercourse here and now, but rather to outline a long-range program which would be audacious enough to be inspiring, and at the same time sufficiently close to the lasting realities of the Western world. Whatever the concrete political situation after General de Gaulle's latest press conference, or after the forthcoming elections in Britain, or after the possible success or collapse of the Italian *apertura a sinistra,* the author thinks that his basic arguments will remain valid. One coherent although diversified Western policy, even if it is open to criticism, is preferable to continuing the present cacophonia—the multiplicity of conflicting methods, doctrines, and approaches in world affairs, the chaos through which no policy can really develop its full potentialities. (The recent Anglo-American dispute on Cuba is an example.)

Action Behind the Curtains

Whatever forms the West may finally adopt for its consultation, cooperation, and integration, the body responsible for Western political strategy will find one problem on its table: the attitude to adopt toward the countries behind the Iron and Bamboo Curtains. Let us suppose, for argument's sake, that the institutional problems are settled and that it has become impossible for members of the democratic community to deal with Communist countries in competition with other Atlantic nations. Whatever our policy, it would have become a common one. All of us, or none of us, would have recognized Continental China. All of us, or none of us, would have the possibility of exporting pipelines to Russia. A considerable step forward would have been made. But the main job would remain to be done—namely, to define the contents of such a common policy. It seems useful to devote some thought to this problem. As the writer does not feel competent to discuss China, he will concentrate on Eastern and Central Europe.

This policy should be free of the "Maginot mentality" we mentioned earlier. It should be politically "aggressive." This is elementary strategic common sense: in a life-or-death battle, victory can be won only by those who are able to grasp the offensive. If, therefore, the West should consider the Communist countries as definitely "lost," whereas the Communists from their part consider any country a potential field of propaganda, a territory to be "freed" later or earlier—the final result cannot be doubtful. Moreover, such a purely defensive attitude on our side would neglect the fact that the inner stability of the Communist regimes is far from assured. Especially in the so-called satellite countries, mental resistance to communism is widespread, although it cannot take the active forms which organized resistance took during the war, when the masses in the Nazi-occupied countries waited for military liberation. In this case, military liberation is, of course, ruled out, and the peoples knew it, at least since October 1956. Nonetheless, they have lost their illusions about a system of government and production which, in Asia, Africa, and Latin America, is often considered the most "progressive" in the world. The population in Eastern and Central Europe—located "behind the enemy lines," to speak in military terms—amounts to 120 million men and women. It is of supreme importance for its own sake. It also influences deeply the policy of the USSR.

Bringing "our secret allies" into the picture does not imply that we should recruit "agents" among them, either for national spy nets or for an "integrated" intelligence service. This would be morally wrong and politically short-sighted. The peoples behind the Curtain have become extremely sensitive to being "used" by anybody. They know that the USSR, far from having "liberated" them from "the bondage of capitalism," far from having in mind their happiness and well-being, simply and cynically makes them a piece on their chessboard, a trump in their game, a unit in their campaigning forces. But Communist propaganda has probably been successful in so far as the "capitalist" West is no longer thought to be altruistic. Consequently, any attempt to win over individual citizens to our side and make them "work" for us remains far below the standards which we claim to be ours.

Moreover, in our dealing with the peoples under Communist domination, we should make it clear that we do not think an economic and social restoration either possible or desirable. Those who reject the totalitarian forms of socialism—no doubt the majority, at least among the thinking élite, including those in the working class—remain convinced that private ownership of the means of production and an economy for individual profit constitute a wicked regime. They may consider that private capitalism is probably less harsh than the state capitalism they live under—nonetheless, they do not dream of replacing one sort of capitalism by another. The Hungarian Revolution has taught us a significant lesson in that respect: whereas disgust of the Rakosi regime was unanimous, there was hardly any "looking backward" among those who fought the Russian tanks. Consequently, our action in East and Central Europe should aim at providing the peoples concerned with the real freedom to choose the production system they prefer.

It is sometimes thought that the Communist dictatorships have successfully locked the frontiers of their empire, so as to prevent any news from the West from penetrating. This may have been their intention and sometimes even the result of their action, but today this is less true than before. Touristic intercourse is increasing in both directions, and "reading between lines" in the state-controlled press supplies useful knowledge. Even if Western broadcasts are jammed, this is not always done drastically enough to prevent a good many comments from oozing through. For example, the success of the European Common Market is much more widely known than pessimists might have foreseen. Consequently, our main problem is not how to get through to the East Europeans, but in which style to approach them. It is this writer's opinion that the problem of communication can be dealt with successfully only by men and women who know and love the peoples behind the Iron Curtain, and who, above all, display the mental attitude we would describe as post-Communistic. They should not consider communism an intermezzo, but an essential phase in history, one day to be integrated in Europe's living past.

Traditional Western diplomacy is hardly prepared to carry out tasks—be it only in the cultural and economic spheres—which would be considered "interference in another state's internal affairs." Indeed, we do want to "interfere." From their point of view the Communist regimes rightly consider the success of a well-presented piece of American technology, a French *chansonnier,* an Austrian opera, an exhibition of Dutch abstract paintings, or a German lecturer, as political setbacks. But that is no reason not to pursue a policy of cultural exchange: just the opposite. In any case, our national possibilities and methods should carefully be compared, adapted to the circumstances, and "integrated," again leaving room for well-planned inter-Western division of labor. In any case, we may be assured that the population behind the Curtain looks to the West as a whole for the modest amount of fresh air it longs for.

The same is true for commercial relations [*Cf.* John P. de Gara, *Trade Relations Between the Common Market and the Eastern Bloc*] where we should try to escape the thoughtless and sterile alternatives of either economic boycott, or "business as usual." Here again, political motives should prevail on the immediate interests of one firm or one nation. The days of uncontrolled trade, when Lenin was justified in saying that "capitalists would even sell the rope with which they are hanged," should rapidly be brought to a close, whatever policy one might wish to pursue. [*Cf. U.S. News and World Report,* December 30, 1963: "British bankers and industrialists are straining at the leash to go to Khrushchev's aid."]

Our commercial behavior toward the bloc should be part of our world strategy. There, it is an illusion to think that "ideas follow the goods" and that there would exist an automatic relation between material and spiritual intercourse. On the other hand, the tighter the frontiers, the less chance we have to reach our friends in the East. Since the rulers there are desperately in need of Western aid and trade, we should make this a means to re-establish the contact with those Europeans who are separated from us, politically, for the time being, but should realize that they are still considered part of our cultural community.

Let us repeat our main point. Western defeatism is the main cause of our weakness. Whereas public opinion in the bloc countries, after many years of uninterrupted propaganda and pressure, remains able to distinguish between official facts and the real ones, the West seems to consider them "lost." Whereas Mr. Khrushchev went on repeating that he was going to bury us, we have hardly ever shown that our conviction is the opposite. A combative self-confident spirit has to inspire our attitude in this field. Not impressed by ideological intimidation, we should constantly show the serene certitude that "we'll bury them." The considerable prestige of General de Gaulle east of the Curtain is due to his strongly affirmed belief in France's future, his total "un-impressedness" in the face of Communist boasting.

In Conclusion

The fundamental problem of the West in the struggle for the world is the following: it has to transform its inner diversities from a disadvantage into an asset.

In military as well as in political warfare, democratic communities are bad starters, as they have considerable difficulty in imposing discipline on their diverging components. Freedom as to each individual's, each group's, each nation's "pursuit of happiness" means that nobody wants initially to give up his prejudices, his special interests, and his way of life. Instinctively we incline toward an attitude of "live and let live." Some of our European states are tempted by isolationism, now that colonialism is over. Some of the smaller ones feel happy to look at the world from their balcony and enjoy their prosperity. The United States itself feels hurt, as it is accused of being so immensely powerful and therefore constantly forced to interfere with other people's business.

Unfortunately—or rather fortunately—we belong to a world which, for the first time in history, has a common destiny. Wars have become world wars, economic depressions are world depressions, revolutions world revolutions. Consequently, nationalism has become parochial and even continental integration may develop into a new form of provincialism. Meanwhile, in this uniting world, freedom is constantly in retreat.

On the other hand, it might well be that the Communist bloc has entered a period of inner disintegration, whereas ours painfully and reluctantly chooses the road of integration. The rift between Belgrade, Moscow, and Peking not only weakens Communist power politically, but is in complete contradiction with the very principle of "proletarian internationalism." It also defeats their fundamental contention that conflicts between states, inseparable from capitalist anarchy, would automatically disappear after the rise to power of the working class. Consequently, Marxism-Leninism will more and more lose the prestige of its self-awarded infallibility, as it is losing control over the evolution it has provoked. So much the more reason for us not to be too impressed by the trumpeting of Khrushchev and his successors. On the other hand, the internal difficulties in the Communist bloc only give us time to act, and if we do not act wisely and energetically, our opponents may recover. In that case, it would be small consolation to think that, after our defeat, the victorious Communist powers might quarrel over our spoils.

Our trump cards are diversity and adaptability, but our weakness is disorganization. National pride and state sovereignty, the illusion that we can at the same time be faithful allies and unrestricted competitors, and mental laziness and lack of imagination, are the main obstacles which prevent us from having in the world the authority we deserve and need.

The first step toward the necessary concentration of Western strength is a pooling of our intellectual resources. A recent example: the Atlantic Institute in Paris undertook a large study on educational aid to developing countries. It is simply scandalous that up till now billions of dollars have been spent in ignorance upon an essential item like this. We therefore should start with a systematic stock-taking of our problems so as to examine them, one by one, in working parties where different national, confessional, political, and intellectual tendencies would be confronted. Our own meeting gives the model of such a procedure, but this method should be applied on a larger scale.

The second step is to provide adequate organizational machinery for action in the sphere of government. In this field, the highest degree of pragmatism is recommended, as every pre-established dogma (be it of national sovereignty *per se,* or European federalism *a priori*) has to stand the test of its applicability *ad hoc*. This machinery has to meet two requirements. On the one hand it should give room for adequate consultation among all members of the Western group: nothing would be more fatal than the institutionalization of a hegemonist-satellites position between the United States and her allies. Not being consulted or being consulted only *pro forma* creates feelings of frustration which disrupt the alliance. On the other hand, an efficient executive body should be set up, speaking for the West as a whole, in any field where neither America nor Europe would be able to take full responsibility alone. However, the prerequiste of such a worldwide "integration" is a United Europe, speaking with one voice and handling her own affairs. Organized Atlantic partnership, which becomes possible once the Europeans will have recovered strength and established unity, constitutes the strongest concentration of know-how, natural resources, and maybe even political wisdom, in the world. It would be unbeatable.

Finally, we have to educate public opinion in view of these perspectives. It would be senseless to unite the West under the banner of democracy, while allowing democratic control to be undermined, as is the case now. Free-world government, based on intercontinental partnership, has to deal with a limited number of problems—indeed, world problems—but it cannot stand for freedom if it does not allow public opinion to criticize it and, possibly, force it to modify its political line. True the problems of emerging international parliamentarianism have hardly been approached so far [*Cf.* Kenneth Lindsay, *European Parliamentarianism,* and Murray Forsyth, *The Parliament of the European Communities*] but they are not much more disturbing than were those of America when the frontier was reached and conditions of transport were still primitive. In Europe, an experiment of this nature is being carried out and, although the difficulties remain numerous, evidence exists now that a supranational assembly can function where the dividing lines between the competing parties do not always coincide with the ones traditionally valid in the member states. There is no doubt that the average American or European has not yet been brought to think in those new terms. More often than not, their interest still goes to the familiar debates within the familiar community. Nonetheless, uneasiness about national parliamentarianism is already widespread, as it is instinctively realized that our assemblies are no longer "sovereign" on the most essential issues. The decline of our national democracies even leads to skepticism toward the democratic ideal as such. Consequently, the growth of European and Atlantic democracy—both in institutions to be set up, and in public opinion to be informed—constitutes perhaps the greatest contribution we could make to the rebirth of the liberal West.

NATO and East-Central Europe

—*MILORAD DRACHKOVITCH*

There are two kinds of realists: those who manipulate facts and those who create them. The West requires nothing so much as men able to create their own reality.

Henry A. Kissinger

An event in East-Central Europe—the *coup de Prague* of February 1948—was the decisive political fact which prompted the Western European and North American nations to begin urgent and formal negotiations which ended a year later with the establishment of the defensive Atlantic alliance. During the ensuing fifteen years, the Western and Soviet blocs faced each other in the middle of Europe, and although the dividing line on the river Elbe remained stable, both blocs experienced momentous changes in their internal structures and relations.

This essay will explore three important facets of these changes: (1) the emerging dispute between NATO's Anglo-American and Franco-German members concerning the policies to be adopted toward the Soviet or Communist-dominated East-Central Europe; (2) internal developments in the Soviet bloc itself; (3) the relevance of Western disputes and intra-Soviet bloc problems for the future of both the Atlantic alliance and Western and Eastern Europe.

The aim of the essay is thus to show why the events and prospects of East-Central Europe should attract attention of Western policymakers no less today than a decade and a half ago.

Disagreements Within Atlantic Alliance About East-Central Europe

Since the establishment of NATO, its very defensive character has fitted perfectly well with the United States' "containment" policy toward the Soviet Union. Nobody among the U.S. partners in the alliance has challenged that policy; and even when for a while, in 1952 and after, it was rebaptized as "liberation" its basically static character did not change. The rebellions of Soviet satellites in 1953 and 1956, and the repressions by the Red Army, were followed by dismay or anger in the West, but no Western government nurtured any intention to interfere in what was tacitly acknowledged as Soviet imperial domain. Toward divided Germany, Berlin, and the "people's democracies" the Western attitude was twofold: morally, the West could not approve the postwar changes in Eastern Europe, because they were obviously imposed on the population by force, and because the Soviet Union had patently violated its international obligations by creating the satellite realm; politically, the West was resigned to accept the *status quo* under the condition of not recognizing it formally. The right of self-determination which the U.S. government advocated so strongly in Asia and Africa, often even against the governmental policies of its NATO partners, was never considered as anything but a rhetorical exercise when dealing with the Soviet Union. The Western European nations were too weak, and thus unwilling, to ask on their own account the Soviet Union to "de-Stalinize" its foreign policy. On their part, the Soviet rulers, particularly after the experiences of 1956, pressed for international agreements which would officially consecrate the *status quo* in East-Central Europe and thus dispose of the problem of the legitimacy of their satellites.

During the last several years prominent public figures in the Western world have suggested more or less elaborate plans of "disengagement" in Central Europe.[1] These plans have been designed to eliminate the direct confrontation of the antagonistic nuclear powers in the heart of Europe, and to contribute in this way to lessening of international tensions and increasing the chances for serious negotiations about disarmament and genuine peaceful solution of problems. Although the plans have remained essentially as material for academic discussions, the United States Government under the Kennedy Administration, in agreement with the British and even if *a posteriori,* with some of the Western European governments, has shown an inclination to explore in direct talks with the Soviets the possibility of some new arrangements, particularly concerning the problems of Berlin and Germany in gen-

[1] For a useful survey of various "disengagement" proposals, see Eugene Hinterhoff, *Disengagement* (London: Stevens and Sons, Ltd., 1959). — An excellent article on the same issue is James E. Dougherty, "Zonal Arms Limitations in Europe," *Orbis,* Fall 1963.

eral, which should achieve some of the results that the individual proponents of "disengagement" advocated. In 1962 and 1963, however, the plans favored by the United States were opposed, once obliquely, the second time openly and vigorously, by Western Germany and, especially, France. Open opposition of two leading Western European powers to the ideas of American diplomacy was indeed something new in the post-war history of the Atlantic alliance. It merits careful scrutiny.

The first instance of Western European suspicions concerning American direct talks with the Soviets over Berlin occurred in April 1962, when the Germans leaked to the press the original U.S. scheme for an International Access Authority to Berlin as a means of torpedoing it.[2] The plan provided for the establishment of an authority in which East Germany would enjoy the same status as the Federal Republic, the creation of several East-West German commissions to deal with German problems, a nonaggression treaty between NATO and the Warsaw Pact countries, and an agreement to prevent the spread of nuclear weapons to other countries.

The suspicion of the French and German governments that bilateral U.S.-Soviet negotiations could lead to an accommodation at their expense led the French government to take a series of strong attitudes during the first half of 1963. In the first place, General de Gaulle, in the famous press conference of January 14, 1963, in which he turned down as premature the British application for membership in the European Economic Community, also criticized sternly any idea of a "colossal Atlantic Community under American dependence and leadership which would soon completely swallow up the European Community." He emphasized at the same time that what France wanted and was working for was "a strictly European construction" and denounced the idea of a NATO multilateral atomic force.[3] Only a few days later, on January 22, a treaty between the French Republic and the Federal Republic of Germany was signed, with three fields of application: foreign policy, defense, and education and youth. Commenting on the treaty before the French National Assembly on June 12, Maurice Couve de Murville, French Minister of Foreign Affairs, made some precise statements about the deeper meaning of the treaty:

> Europe—that signifies two things: the union of the free Europe first, then a stable European settlement, when the Soviets will have changed sufficiently, that is to say, the establishment of a relative balance between the Russian Empire to the East and the united free Europe to the West. In order for the European union

[2] *Cf.* Henry A. Kissinger, "The Essentials of Solidarity in the Western Alliance," *The Conservative Papers* (Garden City, New York: Doubleday and Company, Inc., 1964), pp. 20-22.

[3] See the entire text of the press conference in *Speeches and Press Conferences*, No. 185, published by the Service of Press and Information, French Embassy, New York.

> to be constituted, in order for the balance to be established, Germany must necessarily be on our side, that is to say, linked to France. If Germany should turn toward the East, the Western fringe which we represent will be submerged sooner or later. If Germany does not make a choice, the threat will be permanent, and we also know how we will end. . . .
>
> If French-German cooperation succeeds as we intend, that is, evolves toward a real political union of Western Europe, far-reaching transformations will take place, for the good of all, firstly in the relations of the participating European countries themselves, then between them and their allies—and first of all the United States. The final result of this would be *the alliance of Europe and America in every domain on an equal footing.*[4]

The same set of ideas, but with a still greater precision, was affirmed by General de Gaulle during his next press conference, held on July 29, 1963. After taxing the Yalta conference as "deplorable," and stating that the Atlantic alliance was at the same time "an elemental necessity" and in need of "important modifications," he spoke of "great changes which modify the character of hegemonic solidarity which, since the last World War, has marked the United States relations with France." Before discussing the agreement banning nuclear tests which was just about to be signed between the United States, the Soviet Union, and Great Britain and explaining the reasons why France would not join the treaty and would continue to equip itself with nuclear weapons, General de Gaulle made the following statement, which touches upon a vital part of the problems with which this essay deals:

> The United States which, since Yalta and Potsdam, has nothing, after all, to ask from the Soviets, the United States sees tempting prospects opening up before it. Hence, for instance, all the separate negotiations between the Anglo-Saxons and the Soviets, which, starting with the limited agreement on nuclear testing, seem likely to be extended to other questions, notably European ones, until now in the absence of the Europeans, which clearly goes against the views of France.
>
> France, in effect, has for a long time believed that the day might come when a real détente, and even a sincere entente, will enable the relations between East and West in Europe to be completely changed and it intends, if this day comes, . . . to make constructive proposals with regard to the peace balance, and destiny of Europe. But, for the time being, *France will not subscribe to any arrangement that would be made above its head and which would concern Europe and particularly Germany.* As

[4] *French Affairs,* No. 158, published by the same French Press Service in New York, pp.2-3 and 5. Italics added.

> for a draft nonaggression pact—which we are told was discussed in Moscow—between the States belonging to NATO and the leaders of the countries subjected to the Kremlin's yoke, I must say right away that France does not appreciate this assimilation between the Atlantic Alliance and Communist servitude.[5]

These sentences of the French President—which are so typical of his statecraft: precise statements of present policy coupled with vague hints about future diplomatic initiatives—acquire even greater interest in relation to an article written by an ardent French *gaullist* (of Polish origin) and published in the distinguished French review *Politique Etrangère*.[6] Under the significant title "For an Independent and Reunified Europe" the author, Alexander Kawalkowski, tried to present in unequivocal terms what he believed were the deeper thoughts and strategic and tactical intentions of the French President. According to Mr. Kawalkowski, any agreement between Washington and Moscow, with British participation, tending to freeze the Elbe line as a definitive boundary between the Atlantic and Soviet blocs would represent a "new Yalta" and would be detrimental and unacceptable to Europe:

> The present iron curtain, strengthened by an eventual new political agreement, would serve as a boundary between the United States and the Soviet Union. Today's Europe, cut in two pieces, but without abandoning hope for reunification, would be definitely replaced by two Europes: the American and the Soviet.

The policy which the author ascribes to General de Gaulle is to "open an alternative with regard to the deadlock of the American-Soviet system, the deadlock which worsens in proportion with the consolidation of the system." Mentioning the famous speech made by General de Gaulle on March 25, 1959, in which he terms German reunification a "normal destiny of the German people" under the condition that the reunified Germany "does not open the question of its present frontiers;" i.e., recognize the Oder-Neisse frontier between Poland and Germany—Kawalkowski offers then a vision which, whether he ascribes it to de Gaulle or offers it as a suggestion to him, is certainly worth quoting here:

> A Europe, inspired by the idea of its independence would have the means to pay the price of its complete liberation. Once in possession of its own means of defense, classical and nuclear (the latter thanks to France), but not before, Europe will realize that the Atlantic Alliance is no longer an indispensable condition for its security. From this moment on, Europe will be in a position to propose to the Soviet Union a new solution which would rep-

[5] *Speeches and Press Conferences,* No. 192, p. 8.
[6] *Politique Etrangère*, Paris, No. 3, 1963, pp. 195-220.

> resent an alternative to the system USA—USSR. The principal points of these projects would be the following: the Russian troops would evacuate Eastern Germany and all the European satellite countries, primarily those adjoining the European Economic Community . . . These countries would recover the free exercise of their national sovereignty and would be free to associate themselves with Europe economically and even politically. The Atlantic Pact as well as that of Warsaw would be dissolved. The American troops would be evacuated. Europe, enlarged by the admission of former Soviet satellites would bring to Russia massive economic aid.

The author forsees that the Soviet rulers could reject the entire idea, but asserts that in that case the perspective of European reunification would "revive not only the hopes but also a genuine fermentation capable of generating the powerful internal pressures behind the iron curtain." These pressures could convince the Soviet Union that it was in its own interest to accept the scheme of European unity.

Kawalkowski's article merits extended attention, because it puts the finger on some sore points within the Atlantic alliance (the European suspicions about a "new Yalta" which the American diplomacy is allegedly tempted to conclude), indicates the new vitality of Europe as a genuine partner of the United States and potential negotiator with the Soviet Union on equal footing, and hints that the Soviet Union has lost the ideological and economic game in East-Central Europe. This certainly optimistic conclusion serves as a good introduction to a dispassionate analysis of Soviet policies toward the satellites under Stalin and Khrushchev.

The Shifting Scene of East-Central Europe

"The most outstanding single fact about East-Central Europe in the last fifteen years has been that despite the total foreign and domestic Communist domination and Western inability to influence directly its destiny, the region and its peoples have witnessed an amazing degree of active and passive resistance to ideological indoctrination and absorption in the Soviet bloc."[7] To justify this assertion and to emphasize its multiple meaning we will review briefly the most important aspects of the satellites' existence under Stalin and after.

Stalinism

The first couple of postwar years in East-Central Europe saw a transition from genuine coalition regimes to monolithic Communist rule (with the exception of Yugoslavia and Albania where the Communists were in the saddle from the beginning). These years have been followed, with seemingly increasing efficiency between 1947-48 and

[7] Milorad M. Drachkovitch, "Soviet Satellites: Challenge to U.S. Policy," *The Conservative Papers*, p. 39.

the death of Stalin, by a distinctive process of political subjugation of East-Central European states to the Soviet empire. To what extent the imposed pattern of uniformity corresponded to Stalin's growing distrustfulness may be seen from his angry indictment of a Communist Balkan Federation discussed rather vaguely by Tito and Dimitrov at the end of 1947 and beginning of 1948. This absolute unwillingness to allow any independent move, even if inspired by the greatest zeal to serve the Communist cause, led in June 1948 to the spectacular excommunication of the most militant Communist regime, Tito's in Yugoslavia, from the Cominform. Thereafter, the screws were progressively tightened on all the satellites, and the closest bilateral relations between Moscow and every East-Central European country were established. In January 1949 the Council of Mutual Economic Aid (COMECON) was founded as a counterpoise to the OEEC and West European economic consolidation under the Marshall Plan; but, contrary to the functioning of new mechanisms in Western Europe, COMECON remained for several years chiefly a sponsor of bilateral trade agreements concluded between its Eastern European members.

One of the most important characteristics of this period of Stalinist domination was the multiplication of similar economic structures in East-Central Europe, each country having to become a sort of "miniature reproduction" of the USSR. "The unprecedented and unlimited power over all means of production in this very large part of the world has not been used to integrate internationally the economies of the several countries contained within it."[8] The underpinning of economic collectivization was political terror, applied against all real or potential political enemies and including more or less violent purges of the Communist parties themselves. As the counterweight to terror—or, if one prefers, terrorism in its more subtle aspect—systematic efforts were made to inculcate in the young generations of East-Central Europeans a primary loyalty to the Soviet Union.

At the same time, overt or camouflaged exploitation of individual countries by the USSR was a current practice and had several aspects: the imposed shift in the trading directions of the region; the overpricing of Soviet goods and underpricing of products coming from East-Central Europe; the functioning of joint companies in Hungary, Rumania, and Bulgaria; the maintenance of Soviet troops and technical advisers, etc. Such an over-all economic relationship permitted the Soviet Union to gain during the 1945-1956 period a total of $20-25 billion through the exploitation of the satellites.[9] To realize the full scope of this gain, one should notice that the volume of Soviet aid to the bloc between 1946 and 1955 amounted to about $2 billion, or about $200 million

[8] Gunnar Myrdal, *An International Economy* (New York: Harper & Brothers, 1956), p. 147.

[9] Jan Wszelaki, *Communist Economic Strategy: the Role of East-Central Europe* (Washington, D.C.: National Planning Association, 1959), p. 71 ff.

a year.[10] This is, among other things, what Tito had in mind when at the Sixth Congress of the Communist Party of Yugoslavia, in November 1952, he declared:

> In reality, this enslavement of little peoples, as was shown by the enslavement of Poland, Rumania, Hungary, Bulgaria, Czechoslovakia, and so on, has only one aim, which certainly is not world revolution, but world hegemony and mastership by the Soviet Union, as an imperialist power, over other peoples.[11]

Domestic autarky worked out under total subservience to the Soviet Union had brought some results similar to those in the Soviet Union under its early Plans: significant increases in industrial production—especially in heavy industry and engineering; rapid growth of the industrial working class; rapid urbanization; uneven but significant progress toward land collectivization; etc. Moreover, through the sociopolitical changes accomplished during a brief period of time, the image of revolutionary history in the making served both the cause of the Soviet empire and gladdened the hearts of Communist parties around the world, unswervingly following Stalin's leadership. On the other hand, the list of shortcomings or overt failures has been no less impressive: the low level of agricultural output; the general neglect of consumers' goods production; currency "reform"; elaborate, expensive, and unfulfilled schemes such as the Danube-Black Sea canal project in Rumania; extraordinary inefficiency and waste; the production of goods of poor quality; forced labor—particularly in Bulgaria, Rumania, and Czechoslovakia, etc.[12] In consequence, along with the average decline in the standard of living went a growing feeling of apathy or bitter dissatisfaction, the cynical realization of the gap between professed goals—still boasted of by the official propaganda—and the reality of everyday life. The rulers in Moscow must have realized even before Stalin's death that unless prompt and effective measures were taken to bring about a change, the entire "people's democratic" system was verging on catastrophe, or, as Nikita Khrushchev expressed in his usual colorful way: "We should have been booted out summarily."[13] Stalin's death, in March 1953, came at the right moment to speed up the salvage operation.

The "New Course" and the Gathering and Subsiding of the Storm

Very soon, indeed, after Stalin's exit from the stage, his successors inaugurated both internally in Russia and in the satellite realm the

---

[10] Joseph S. Berliner, *Soviet Economic Aid* (New York: Praeger, 1958), p. 51.
[11] Sixth Congress of the Yugoslav Communist Party, November 2-7, 1962. Stenographic notes (in Serbo-Croatian), Belgrade, 1952, p. 38.
[12] *Cf.* Robert F. Byrnes, "The Climax of Stalinism, 1950-1953," *The Annals of the American Academy of Political and Social Science,* May 1958, pp. 9-10.
[13] As quoted in Imre Nagy, *On Communism: In Defense of the New Course* (New York: Praeger, 1957), p. 66.

so-called "new course," which has had uneven applications and results in East-Central Europe. In 1953 the workers' riots in the Czechoslovak cities Pilsen and Ostrava in May and June, the uprisings throughout East Germany on and around June 17, the most unusual speech which the new Hungarian Premier Imre Nagy delivered before the National Assembly on July 4, criticizing some basic tenets of Stalinist practice—all this indicated that the days of Stalinist calm and uniformity were over. Still, the "new course" was far from meaning something identical for all the countries. In Czechslovakia, Rumania, and Bulgaria the reforms were limited to technical improvements within the established Stalinist framework; in Poland and Hungary the "new course" went deeper and in reality attacked some of the basic Stalinist evils. Whether "technical" or "substantial" in form, the "new course" meant concessions to agriculture and peasantry, an increase in consumer goods production, a rise in living standards, and a new respect for the "forms of Socialist legality."[14] Timidly at first, but with growing intensity, a nonconformist movement among intellectuals began together with these official measures. The deep-rooted awareness of suppressed national feelings and the irresistible yearnings for freedom, which both seemed to be withering away as long as Stalin lived, pushed their way forward everywhere. The Stalinist seed resulted in "bitter harvest."[15]

The "new course" was, however, neither coherent nor efficient. With Khrushchev's replacement of Malenkov in February 1955, it appeared that the clock would be turned back to Stalinism, especially because emphasis was again put on the priority of heavy industry. This seemingly backward turn was certainly most spectacular in Hungary, with the comeback of Rakosi in April 1955 and Nagy's indictment for "rightist, opportunist policies" and exclusion from the Party. It was impossible, however, to revert to Stalinism without Stalin. Very soon, Nikita Khrushchev himself, with his remarkable intuition of threatening political realities, inaugurated his own "new course," going beyond Malenkov in opening safety valves through the dangerous game of de-Stalinization. His spectacular reconciliation with Tito in May 1955 and his denunciation of Stalin's "cult of personality" in his historic secret speech at the Twentieth Congress of the CPSU were the two most daring elements of his new political line. It seemed, indeed, during the first nine months of 1956, that Khrushchev's policies, and particularly his endorsement of the Titoist concept of "different roads" toward

[14] *Cf.* Edmund O. Stillman, "The Beginning of the 'Thaw,' 1953-1955." *The Annals of the American Academy of Political and Social Science,* May 1958, p. 13.

[15] *Cf.* Edmund Stillman *(ed.) Bitter Harvest: The Intellectual Revolt Behind the Iron Curtain* (New York: Praeger, 1959). This volume is a real anthology of essays, poems, and short stories written by "angry" intellectuals in Communist countries throughout the world.

Socialism, were to lead to the dismantling of Stalin's empire. And while for him, as for Tito, the new approach had as its purpose the reformation of the satellites in order to make the Communist regimes more acceptable and more efficient, the Hungarian revolution went a qualitative step further and, beyond "national communism," seemed to represent, in Milovan Djilas's words, "the beginning of the end of Communism."[16]

These cataclysmic events, particularly in Hungary and Poland, had another fundamental aspect of which nobody in the West was aware at the time, but which was revealed seven years later, during one of the bitter attacks of Chinese Communist leadership against the Soviet. In September 1963, the Chinese leaders accused the Russians of committing "grave errors" in the fall of 1956. The propensity of the Soviets to use their troops in Poland was termed the "error of great power chauvinism," an error which was avoided owing to Chinese influence and the support they gave to Wladislaw Gomulka. In Hungary, to the contrary, according to the Chinese, the Soviet leaders "intended to adopt a policy of capitulation and abandon Socialist Hungary to counter-revolution," while it was Peking that "insisted on taking all necessary measures to smash the counter-revolutionary rebellion," implying that the Chinese forced the Soviet intervention of November 4, 1956 which crushed the Hungarian Revolution.[17]

Three conclusions with enduring and again actual consequences may be drawn from these history-making events: the vacillating Soviet leaders were on the verge of blundering in both the Polish and Hungarian cases; the West has been totally inactive at the moment when a bold and imaginative policy could have been fruitful; the Chinese had begun, even if unconsciously at the time, their second "long march" on the road to leadership of the Communist world movement.

Khrushchev's "Grand Design"

As an indirect proof of Soviet embarrassments, the Hungarian revolt, despite the brutal suppression of it, did not lead to the reimposition of Stalinist terror. To the contrary, it convinced the Soviet leaders, Khruschhev in particular, of the absolute necessity to reform Soviet-satellite relations in at least two respects: to give to

[16] "The Storm in Eastern Europe," *New Leader*, November 19, 1956.

[17] The Chinese attack was published simultaneously in Peking's *People's Daily* and *Red Flag*, on September 6, 1963, in an article entitled "The Origin and Development of the Differences Between the Leadership of the CPSU and Ourselves." See also Harry Schwartz, *Tsars, Mandarins, and Commissars*. A History of Chinese-Russian Relations. (Philadelphia and New York: J. B. Lippincott Company, 1964), p. 159. — David Floyd, *Mao Against Khrushchev*. A Short History of the Sino-Soviet Conflict (New York: Praeger, 1963), p. 40 — Donald Zagoria, *The Sino-Soviet Conflict, 1956-1961* (Princeton University Press, 1962), p. 338.

individual Communist leaders greater freedom in shaping domestic affairs, under the condition that they remain faithful to the essentials of solidarity within the Soviet bloc; and to de-Stalinize the pattern of economic relations between the USSR and the smaller states of the bloc. What Khrushchev must have had in mind was not simply to employ the classic "carrot and stick" policy,[18] but to go beyond and to devise subtler and more efficient ways to foster imperial cohesiveness for which some techniques of Western European economic integration offered an example worth emulating.

Already in 1955 Khrushchev had discovered that the dormant COMECON (there was only one plenary session of the Council of the COMECON between August 1949 and March 1954) might be resuscitated as a convenient means of coordinating the economic activities of the various bloc countries. The ferment of the year 1956 and the October thunderbolt finally convinced him that COMECON was potentially an ideal—and strangely forgotten—method of binding the Communist states together. After several conferences at various levels during 1957, the real beginning of the new phase of COMECON activities came in May 1958 during a conference in Moscow on economic cooperation attended by First Party Secretaries and Premiers of COMECON countries and by high-level observers from Communist China, Mongolia, North Korea, and North Vietnam. The basic principle which emerged from that meeting was a "bloc-wide economic integration through extra-long-term supranational planning."[19] The target to be attained was the elimination of differences in the level of development of individual countries, and the means was the concept of the "socialist division of labor," i.e., increased specialization in various fields of production among the COMECON members. This specialization should be the combined result of both short-term and broad "perspective" planning for the entire huge territory of the USSR and East-Central Europe.

It is beyond the scope of this essay to try to outline how the practical work of the COMECON unfolded. Suffice it to say that the bursting activities of the organization's multiple permanent and specialized commissions and subcommissions, covering practically all the fields of economic life, were matched only by the secrecy in which they con-

[18] The changed Soviet attitude toward the most restive satellites, even before the 1956 events, took various forms: exemption from the domestic contribution to the maintenance of Soviet occupation troops (East Germany), emergency loans (Hungary), postponement of payments of past debts (Poland). This has led a Western expert to call these three countries a new "net liability region" to USSR, while the more docile Czechoslovakia, Rumania, and Bulgaria continued to be "net asset regions" from the point of view of Soviet domestic economic interest. Victor Winston, "The Soviet Satellites—Economic Liability?" *Problems of Communism,* No. 1 (January-February 1958), pp. 14-20.

[19] *Cf.* Alfred Zauberman, "Economic Integration: Problems and Prospects," *Problems of Communism,* VIII, No. 4 (July-August 1959), p. 23.

ducted their difficult work of economic coordination. Perhaps a supreme initial difficulty was that COMECON was built on the principle of national sovereignty and that its decisions were conditioned by the unanimity rule, so that the absence of a central authority with decision-making powers was paralyzing any progress toward genuine supranationalism in the economic realm. More than anybody else, Nikita Khrushchev was aware of the shortcomings of such a state of affairs. To remedy it a summit meeting of the First Party Secretaries of the COMECON countries was convened in Moscow in June 1962. The most significant decision of the meeting was the creation of an Executive Committee as a superior authority of the organization. The obvious aim which Khrushchev pursued by pushing toward centralization and decision-making powers for the COMECON was clearly outlined in his famous article published in the September 1962 issue of the *World Marxist Review* under the title "Vital Questions of the Development of the Socialist World System." The central theme of the article, which may be legitimately considered as the most authentic formulation of his "grand design" for the future of the Soviet bloc, was outlined in the following two paragraphs:

> The socialist countries are now at a stage when the conditions have ripened for raising their economic and political co-operation to a new and higher level. At this level a special significance is acquired by co-ordinated national-economic plans, socialist international division of labor, and by co-ordination and specialization of production which will guarantee successful organic development of the socialist countries.
>
> The socialist world system is now at a stage when it is no longer possible correctly to chart its development by merely adding up the national economies. The task now is to do everything to consolidate the national economy of each, broaden its relations and gradually advance towards that single world-wide organism embracing the system as a whole which Lenin's genius foresaw.

It seems, however, that the aforementioned Moscow "summit meeting" of June 1962 fell short of Khrushchev's expectations. Speaking before the Plenary Session of the Central Committee of the CPSU on November 19, 1962, he urged the necessity of new COMECON meetings at the highest level for taking other steps forward along the path of developing economic cooperation. And again he insisted: "We must move more boldly toward establishing a single planning agency for all the countries in common."[20] There were indeed many reasons for risking "bolder moves," for his ingenious plan was encountering mounting problems and opposition.

[20] *The Current Digest of the Soviet Press*, XIV, No. 48 (December 26, 1962), p. 11.

The Difficulties of East-European Integration

To assess the scope and depth of difficulties the Soviet Union is facing in the attempt to integrate its economy with the economies of the satellites involves a great number of problems, both economic and political. Some of them existed from the beginning, others are piling up; some were created by local conditions, and still others are the result of international circumstances. Since it is impossible within the scope of this essay to analyze this maze of problems, we will merely enumerate them, and this quantitative enumeration will demonstrate their qualitative importance.

To begin with, the countries of East-Central Europe are unequal in size. The distribution of their national resources is uneven, and there are considerable differences in the level of their industrialization. (Taking Eastern Germany's industrial production per capita as 100, the percentages of other countries were in 1960: Czechoslovakia 110, Poland 60, Hungary 55, Rumania 36, Bulgaria 33.) Moreover, their economic life has unfolded according to strictly national, autarkic plans, and the planning techniques employed differ. The question of prices and profits, now in the foreground of economic discussion in the Soviet Union,[21] poses grave problems in the smaller countries of the bloc as well.[22] It is obvious that the economic basis of self-sufficiency in every single country offers insuperable obstacles to an integrated, centrally-planned socialist economy of the Soviet bloc as a whole. There are many problems which cannot be solved in a non-market economy, unless a central supranational body has the authority to impose the solutions. And even in that case the magnitude of problems is certainly enormous: how to determine in which country investment in a given branch of productive activity will be most fruitful; how, in view of the fact that prices in the Soviet bloc are divorced from the outside world, to determine and compare production costs; how to achieve greater mobility of capital, labor, and managerial, and technical skills, when the USSR is already a "capital-hungry state"; how to achieve the goal of more rapid growth of less developed bloc countries while adhering to the principle of specialization. Other no less difficult questions arise: how much industrialization, how much decentralization, how much increase in wages, how much consumer goods? With increased intra- and extra-bloc ambitions will it be possible to solve all these problems without again overburdening the industrial

[21] *Cf.* Marshall I. Goldman, "Economic Controversy in the Soviet Union," *Foreign Affairs,* April 1963.
[22] *Cf.* Wolfgang Berger, "Socialist Economy and International Cooperation," *World Marxist Review* (February 1964). This article is an unusually frank discussion of difficult and unresolved problems existing both in East Germany and in the Soviet bloc at large.

workers and frustrating growing consumer demands?[23] Difficult under any circumstances, these problems are unsolvable as long as the principle of national sovereignty in economic affairs is observed. Here lies indeed a basic paradox: Stalin, who had totally disregarded the national sovereignty of his satellites, did not think it necessary to impose upon them a genuine supranational economic integration, although he had at his disposal all the political means to implement such an economic end. Khrushchev has a clear vision in this respect, but he could not use the political pre-eminence of his country in the same way Stalin did. Today's Soviet representatives in the COMECON must argue, try to convince, be ready to make concessions and be satisfied with the compromises—and not simply give orders. Even the supreme argument of force fades in the light of the successful Albanian defiance and the increasing challenge of Chinese Communists. The emergence of a competitor to the Soviet Union within the Communist world offers the satellites an opportunity to maneuver which they would not have had without the Sino-Soviet rift. And the specter of a dynamic Western Europe certainly does not alleviate the Kremlin's problems.

The preceding considerations are clearly reflected in the case of Rumania's successful opposition to Khrushchev's "grand design." This opposition stems from the unwillingness of the Rumanian rulers to accept the basic premise of the "socialist division of labor" which would mean that instead of their ambitious program of industrial expansion, Rumania should concentrate on the production of oil, petrochemicals, light industry, and foodstuffs. But to assess the peculiar nature of that opposition one must take into account that the Rumanian Communist regime is one which has been most reluctant in recent years to implement the policy of de-Stalinization, and, contrary to other satellite countries, the victims of Stalinist purges have not been rehabilitated in Rumania. One can say therefore that the Rumanian regime, headed by Gheorghe Gheorghiu-Dej (who as an uninterrupted leader of the Party organization since 1945 has shown supreme ability to remain at the top and to survive in the deadly game of Communist politics), continues to pursue the old Stalinist concept of economic autarky with the emphasis on heavy industry producing capital goods. In this sense the Rumanian six-year plan, covering the period 1960 through 1965, anticipates in particular an increase in the volume of electrical power and iron ore production, while the main target was

[23] The following articles offer rich documentation about COMECON's problems: Alfred Zauberman, "The Soviet Bloc and the Common Market," *The World Today* (London, January 1963); A. Alexeyev, "The Council of Mutual Economic Assistance: Tasks and Prospects," *International Affairs,* September 1963; Stefan C. Stolte, "Liberman and Comecon," *Bulletin* (Institute for the Study of the USSR, Munich), November 1963; Robert S. Jaster, "The Defeat of Khrushchev's Plan to Integrate Eastern Europe," *The World Today,* December 1963; S. C. Stolte, "Economic Cooperation in the Communist World," *Bulletin,* February 1964; Michael Gamarnikow, "Comecon Today," *East Europe,* March 1964.

and remains the construction of the huge Galati Steel Works in the eastern part of Rumania. Machinery and equipment in considerable quantity were to be supplied for the Galati project, according to an agreement, by Soviet Russia. But, if recent information is correct, the original agreement failed to materialize, and Western firms and experts are replacing the Soviets.[24]

The self-appointed role of the Rumanian Communists in the spring of 1964 to be the "honest brokers" between Moscow and Peking, as well as a series of internal measures in Rumania tending to limit the Soviet Russian cultural and political influence while stressing the theme of Rumanian nationalism, are other indications that the relations between the Soviet Union and one of its reputedly most subservient satellites have entered a new phase which could be termed neither integration nor rebellion.[25]

The Rumanian attitude which epitomizes the viewpoint of industrially less developed countries of the Soviet bloc, as opposed to the regimes of highly industrialized states which are much more favorably inclined to the scheme of economic "specialization," has convinced the Soviet Union that for the time being it would be best not to impose supranational integration. Thus, an official communiqué issued after a meeting of First Party Secretaries which took place in July 1963, stated that "the best possible basis for multilateral coordination of plans is provided by bilateral consultations between member nations."[26] This decision has been followed by a series of bilateral agreements and the creation of intergovernmental commissions for economic and scientific-technical cooperation between the Soviet government and the individual satellite states (Czechoslovakia, Hungary, Bulgaria). At the moment when these lines are written, the old approach of bilateralism has taken precedence, at least for the time being, over the new scheme of integration.

It would be erroneous however, to conclude that Khrushchev's retreat from 1962 plans represents their abandonment or that the pivotal role and the interests of the Soviet Union in East-Central Europe are seriously jeopardized because of satellite reluctance to obey unconditionally. In fact, the USSR continues to enjoy a distinctly privileged position within the bloc. Although the Western experts disagree about the causes and scope of the continuous Soviet economic discrimination vis-à-vis the satellites, it is incontrovertible that the Soviet Union reaps

[24]*Cf.* "Rumänien und die COMECON—Integration," *Wissenschaftliche Dienst Südosteuropa,* April 1963; "Rumänien und die COMECON—Planung," *Ibid.,* July-August 1963; J. F. Brown, "Rumania Steps Out of Line," *Survey,* October 1963; Louis Ramerie, "Tensions an sein du Comecon: Le Cas Roumain," *Politique Etrangère,* No. 3 (1963).

[25]*Cf.* Valentin Toma, "Rumänien zwischen Rebellion and Integration," *Europa Archiv,* November 10, 1963.

[26]*Pravda,* July 28, 1963.

commercial advantages at the expense of other bloc states, or prevents their trade benefits by channeling their exports to a large extent toward the USSR.[27] Likewise, "the rate of growth for the USSR [in 1962] was the highest or one of the highest, although in view of the trend toward equalization of the economies of the countries concerned the reverse should theoretically be the case."[28] Finally, despite the setback in full-fledged integration, the economic coordination within the bloc and satellite dependence upon the USSR have advanced. The establishment of the International Bank of Economic Cooperation in Moscow, which began functioning on January 1, 1964, should facilitate multilateral trade settlements (based on the Soviet ruble), although here again the initially planned credit-dispensing function of the bank has not been accepted. Second, the recently completed "Friendship Pipeline" linking the USSR with Poland, Czechoslovakia, East Germany, and Hungary, i.e., bringing Soviet crude oil to East-Central Europe, will not only represent a technical improvement in transportation methods, but will increase the economic dependence of these countries on the Soviet Union. The completion of the intra-bloc electric power grid, and considerable improvement achieved in the field of various modes of traffic and transportation,[29] will have the same effect. The feverish activity of COMECON organs (over 170 meetings held during 1963) was certainly not devoted only to overcoming disagreements, and the project (to be completed in 1965) to build in Moscow a 25-story, 350-foot high palace for COMECON, is another proof that Soviet leaders have postponed but not abandoned the hope to succeed where Stalin had failed.

Alternative Policies Toward East-Central Europe

In one of his famous 1957 Reith BBC lectures, George F. Kennan has discussed the "dangerous and unsatisfactory situation from everyone's standpoint" in East-Central Europe. His rather gloomy prediction

[27] According to Dr. H. Mendershausen's calculations ("The Germs of Soviet-Satellite Trade: A Broadened Analysis," *The Review of Economic Statistics* (Cambridge, Mass., May 1960), the satellite countries paid between 7 and 16 per cent more during the period 1955-58 for their imports from the USSR than the countries of Western Europe. Aleksander Kutt used similar methods in his analysis of Soviet foreign trade statistics. His conclusion was that "the East European countries lost in the six-year period 1955-60, a total of more than five billion dollars in their trade with the USSR." ("Exploitation in Soviet-Bloc Trade," *East Europe,* May 1962). Professor Franklyn D. Holzman has disputed these findings, but has concluded on his own that the bloc countries must be losers in foreign trade because of the "Soviet-imposed policy of forcing the members of the bloc to conduct the bulk of their trade within the bloc. This is where blame on the Soviets should be focused." (From his letter to the editor of *East Europe,* June 1962.) See on the same subject the already quoted article of Stefan C. Stolte, "Liberman and Comecon."

[28] Stefan C. Stolte, "Economic Cooperation in the Communist World," p. 21.

[29] *Cf.* Werner Gumpel, "Das Verkehrswesen im Integrationsprozess der Comecon-Staaten," *Osteuropa Wirtschaft,* June 1963, pp. 81-101.

at that time was that the state of the satellites could not remain unchanged for a long period of time and that "there must either be further violent efforts by people in that area to take things into their own hands and to achieve independence by their own means, or there must be the beginning of some process of real adjustment to the fact of Soviet domination."[30] Both prospects seemed "appalling" to Mr. Kenan, for in the case of the former the West would again be unable to render effectual aid to the insurgents, while the latter alternative seemed to him morally intolerable. Seven years after this pessimistic judgment, changes in both Western and Eastern Europe suggest the possibility of an emerging third alternative. Let us examine some of the aspects of such an alternative.

First of all, the success of the European Economic Community and the manifold problems which beset the Soviet Union at home and abroad have significantly altered the general relationship between the two parts of Europe. The dynamism of the Common Market has taken the Soviet rules aback. Nothing indeed in their ideological books or in their political and diplomatic expectations has prepared them to see a society "condemned by history" emerge as the most inventive region in the world. Western Europe's capability to surmount its seemingly insuperable fratricidal tendencies, its ingeniousness to devise pragmatically the most stimulating forms of economic and social progress, even its present propensity to question the "hegemonic leadership" of the United States without whose help it would have been unable to gallop along the road of history—all this has been a continuous repudiation of the favorite theme of the decaying bourgeois society of the West. On both the ideological and practical levels the Soviet theoreticians and practitioners of politics have been unable to cope coherently with that phenomenon and to determine their course of conduct accordingly.[31]

What was initially considered a simple extension of American imperialism in Europe and an unworkable capitalistic patchwork, was suddenly transformed into a workable concern—workable to such an extent as to present a threat to the Soviet Union. On the political level, the Franco-German alliance has adopted a much tougher line in dealing with Soviet diplomacy than the more distant "Anglo-Saxon" powers. Economically, the mechanism of the Common Market and particularly its moving toward unified prices and rising trade barriers, is weakening the over-all trade positions of the Soviet bloc vis-à-vis

[30] George F. Kennan, *Russia, the Atom and the West* (New York: Harper & Brothers, 1957), pp. 34-35.

[31] The following two articles analyze thoroughly the discrepant approaches employed by Soviet official sources in recent years in discussing the process of integration in Western Europe: Marshall D. Shulman, "The Communist States and Western Integration," *International Organization,* III, (1963); Zbigniew Brzezinski, "Russia and Europe," *Foreign Affairs,* April 1964.

Western Europe. "The basic fact [is] that while East-West trade constitutes about one-fifth of the total trade of the Soviet bloc, it is only a marginal fraction—about one twenty-fifth of the total—of Western European trade. Furthermore, the commodity pattern being what it is, the bloc suffers from the long-range trend in the world market which works distinctly against the seller of primary produce."[32] Psychologically, the very success of the Common Market, i.e., its pragmatic and working economic integration, contrasts oddly with the Soviet bloc's admitted inability to progress along the same road, the Kremlin's insistence notwithstanding.

The challenge of Western Europe should be compounded with a series of other problems which confront the Soviet Union domestically and internationally: the slowdown in the rate of Soviet economic growth and the obvious failure of agriculture; the foreign aid commitments to Afro-Asian states and Cuba, which are not all paying the expected political dividends while representing an obvious burden to the Soviet treasury; heavy allocations of the productive capacity to military purposes which handicap the prospects of "peaceful economic competition" with capitalism; the already analyzed setbacks in the scheme of integration with the satellites; and last but not least, the ugly quarrel with China.

All this certainly does not mean that the resourceful and imaginative Soviet leaders are left holding only worthless and unusuable cards. There are too many places in the world where the disputes among the Atlantic partners or loss of American influence and prestige compensate for their own troubles with their obstreperous Chinese rival. Curiously enough, the same conflict with China, which in the world at large threatens Soviet pre-eminence in the international Communist movement, helps the Soviet leaders in some of their political and diplomatic initiatives in Europe. The result they have achieved thus far should by no means be underestimated. If they have failed to subvert the regime of Enver Hoxha in Albania (which Khrushchev certainly tried to do in 1960),[33] they have succeeded in neutralizing the impact of Tito's heresy, and aligning Yugoslavia's foreign policy on the Soviet in all essential issues. As for Western Europe, Khrushchev's de-Stalinization has considerably facilitated the work of local Communist parties, especially in Italy and France. Thus the concept of the "popular front," which seemed a few years ago to have been totally buried, should not be discarded under the present circumstances. It might emerge indeed as a major political if not governmental force in these two countries. The "soft" line of that old Comintern professional Palmiro Togliatti,

[32] Alfred Zauberman, "The Soviet Bloc and the Common Market," p. 35.

[33] *Cf.* William E. Griffith, *Albania and the Sino-Soviet Rift* (Cambridge, Mass.: MIT Press, 1963), p. 47.

and the present trend toward a new "popular front" in France[34] could, if successful, create confusion in Western Europe and paralyze the progress of the Common Market. Likewise, the Rapacki plan, whose essential target was always to detach the Federal Republic of Germany from the Atlantic alliance,[35] was revived in March of this year with some very encouraging effects, from the Soviet viewpoint, in the Western world.

Most important, however, has been Khrushchev's attempt "to maneuver the United States into a position of joint sponsorship of the division of Europe, in the hope of stabilizing the present partition and, perhaps, eventually creating new political opportunities for Soviet diplomacy."[36]

This brings us back to our initial examination of French and German suspicions that the United States might indeed be ready to cooperate with the Soviets in freezing the European *status quo*. The situation is rendered even more intricate and tense because the Franco-German partnership and General de Gaulle's views in particular are assailed in other quarters of the Common Market, the most vigorous attacks coming from the Belgian Minister of Foreign Affairs, Paul-Henri Spaak, former Secretary General of NATO, and reputedly a man highly regarded by Washington. What makes things truly paradoxical and puts the American leadership and NATO's cohesion under particular stress, are some specific aspects of de Gaulle's and Spaak's behavior.

De Gaulle, who is systematically accused both in Europe and the United States of undermining Western solidarity and consequently helping the Soviets in their pursuit of one of their perennial diplomatic aims, represents at the present moment a particular hindrance to the Soviet Union because of their opposition to new "Yalta" solutions and because of their policy of closest alliance with Western Germany. On the other hand, Mr. Spaak, for years the incarnation of Atlantic solidarity and opposition to Soviet plans, today endorses some of the basic tenets of Soviet policies in Europe. He has recently accused General de Gaulle in one of the most influential American magazines, of being the chief cause of the "most serious crisis that the Atlantic alliance and the European community have so far experienced."[37] And not satisfied with this indictment, in an interview given on May 15, 1963 to a correspondent of *Izvestia,* he found it advisable to qualify the Franco-German January 1963 treaty as a "bad thing." He went on also endorsing the principle of peaceful coexistence in the form suggested by

[34] Edmond Taylor has demonstrated a peculiar political acumen in describing this phenomenon in two of his articles in *The Reporter* Magazine: "A New Popular Front?" June 20, 1963, and "Rumblings on the Left," January 2, 1964.
[35] See in this sense Adam Rapacki's article, "The Polish Plan for a Nuclear-Free Zone Today," *International Affairs,* January 1963.
[36] Zbigniew Brzezinski, "Russia and Europe," p. 442.
[37] Paul-Henri Spaak, "Hold Fast," *Foreign Affairs,* July 1963, p. 619.

his interviewer, supporting "without hesitation" the Soviet proposal for a non-aggression pact between NATO and the Warsaw bloc, and calling "useful" the Rapacki plan for a denuclearized zone in Central Europe, which as Secretary General of NATO he had denounced as a Soviet device to undermine the Atlantic alliance.

It would be absurd, of course, to accuse Mr. Spaak of pro-Communism (just as it would have been absurd to accuse Neville Chamberlain and Edouard Daladier in 1938 of pro-Nazism). What the versatile Belgian statesman probably had in mind was that Nikita Khrushchev was the best partner the West could possibly have in the Kremlin; that he was a man genuinely dedicated to peace; that a non-aggression pact between the two blocs would be desirable because it would contribute to the lessening of international tensions and the further mellowing of the Soviet bloc; and that the Common Market should foster direct contacts with COMECON, while the individual Western European countries should establish commercial relations of "perfect normality" with the individual COMECON members, as the Belgian Minister of Foreign Trade declared recently in Warsaw on the occasion of signing a new three-year trade pact between Benelux and Poland.[38] Mr. Spaak's ideas are certainly not isolated; they represent a sort of consensus of many official and public opinions on both sides of the Atlantic (the brilliant *Reporter* European correspondent, Edmund Taylor, informs his American readers that the Belgian minister is sometimes called "Polaris" Spaak among the European diplomats because of his championing of the Kennedy Administration's defense policies, and also that "Spaak can be looked upon as a kind of outrider for the British Foreign Office").

The conflict between the views of the visionary de Gaulle and pedestrian Spaak is presently irreconcilable (not merely for reasons already discussed), although it is not easy to pinpoint de Gaulle's real plans and it is even more difficult to foresee his moves so often made abruptly and to everybody's astonishment. The closest, perhaps, we can come in penetrating de Gaulle's perspective of the future is to quote from his 1964 New Year's message:

> Without yielding to delusions indulged in by the weaklings, but also without losing the hope that human freedom and dignity will finally triumph everywhere, we should envision the day when, perhaps, in Warsaw, Prague, Pankow, Budapest, Bucharest, Sofia, Belgrade, Tirana, Moscow, the Communist totalitarian regime which still constrains the captive peoples, will bit by bit evolve in a sense compatible with our own transformation. Then will be opened to the entire Europe the perspectives compatible with its resources and its abilities.[39]

[38] *Cf.* "Monsieur Spaak goes to Warsaw," *East Europe,* January 1964, p. 21.
[39] *Le Monde,* January 2, 1964.

A few weeks later, Maurice Couve de Murville, rejected in most categorical terms any idea of neutralization of Central Europe, meaning above all Germany:

> For us, Central Europe is vital because it is a question of life or death. It is a question of our survival. We think that neutrality means a vacuum, and it would be a vacuum between the immense mass of Soviet military might and what would be left of Western Europe, that is, France, the Benelux countries, and Italy.[40]

With these remarks in mind, the difference of approach to the problems of the Soviet bloc between the French President and the former NATO Secretary General, becomes even sharper, particularly on one specific point. For General de Gaulle, who is certainly not opposed to contacts of various kinds with the Communist states, these contacts are subordinate to waging bigger historical battles. Whatever might be his intimate and narrower purposes, and whatever one may think about the disproportion between his aims and the means at his disposal, he challenges the Kremlin on the scale of a continent. De Gaulle refuses to facilitate the USSR's plans in Europe, and when he opposes any settlement of European problems without the participation of Europeans themselves, he opens the only historical perspective which in the final analysis may pull down the Iron Curtain. In this sense—a supplementary paradox—he, the French "chauvinist," emerges as a much more genuine European that the champion of Western European integration, Paul-Henri Spaak. When de Gaulle denounces Yalta (old or new), the *people* in East-Central Europe understand the language of freedom it implies; Spaak to the contrary seems satisfied to deal with *governments,* and his European message to captive nations fails to reach or move anyone.

This distinction between the Communist regimes and their motives, and the peoples in East-Central Europe and their aspirations, is, in the opinion of this writer, of crucial importance for a successful Western policy. Here also the scene is shifting and new situations are arising. This is what a competent and on-the-spot observer has recently expressed in the following way:

---

[40] From an interview given to the magazine *U. S. News and World Report,* March 16, 1964, pp. 71-72.—In his March 25, 1959 press conference, General de Gaulle has unequivocally expressed his hostility to "recognize this [Pankow] regime as a sovereign and independent state because it could not have been born and could not exist except by virtue of the Soviet occupation and because of an implacable dictatorship." He added then his sentence, already mentioned, that the "reunification of the two parts into a single Germany which would be entirely free seems to us the normal destiny of the German people, provided they do not reopen the question of their present frontiers to the west, the east, the north, and the south, and that they move toward integrating themselves one day in a contractual organization of all Europe for cooperation, liberty, and peace," *Speeches and Press Conferences,* No. 128, p. 3.

> Despite these emerging differences among them, the Communist nations remain Communist. In each, the writ of the party central committee is law, leadership is self-perpetuating, the courts and press are politically controlled, the secret police is ubiquitous if no longer omnipotent. Voluntary association is sharply curbed, and travel remains a privilege rather than a right. In the domain of political freedom, the atmosphere at its best approaches that of Franco Spain. . . .
>
> Has Eastern Europe's increasing variety made the Kremlin stronger or weaker? In the short run, the answer seems clear. The situation today is considerably less explosive than it was at Stalin's death. . . .
>
> However, the Soviet leader has purchased this relative security at the price of ideological disunity, the rise of nationalism and an unmistakable decline in Russian authority.[41]

These diagnostics convey two different aspects of political reality not to be overlooked. One is that *all* Communist regimes are determined to maintain their monopoly of political power, and their curbing of conspicuous Soviet influence is essentially the "removal of unnecessary irritants without any tangible loss for the regime or for the Kremlin."[42] The emphasis on "nationalism" is therefore used as a safe device to subdue or frustrate the authentic popular patriotic feelings. The fact, however, that some of the Communist regimes are adopting measures which flatter national (without quotation marks) consciousness and thus defy Soviet plans is no less significant. Even if these measures are taken with a view to winning people's allegiance and enlarging the Communist power-base, they also mean that the regimes are aware of a "far more popular ferment than is visible on the surface. A sense of injured national pride, disgust with the incompetence of the bureaucrats who rule economic life, revulsion against past and present injustices, and the desire for the rights of free men, all play a role in this ferment."[43] The recent challenge of thirty-four outstanding Polish intellectuals to Gomulka to recognize "the existence of public opinion, the right of free discussion and honest information"; the clash between thousands of Czech students and police in Prague on May 1; the rioting of hundreds of Bulgarians when armed policemen prevented them from attending a midnight mass in the cathedral of Sofia in observance of the Orthodox Easter; the strikes of workers in Yugoslavia—all this indicates the radicalization of popular mood in East-Central Europe, with all the problems it creates for the Communist regimes.

---

[41] Anatole Shub, "Moscow's Satellites—In and Out of Orbit," *New York Times Magazine,* March 15, 1964.

[42] "1963 in East-Central Europe," Assembly of Captive European Nations *News,* New York, Nos. 105-107, January-March 1964, p. 12.

[43] "Evolution in Eastern Europe," *New York Times* editorial, March 27, 1964.

Moreover, the cracking monolithism of the Communist world movement is necessarily accompanied by the decreasing cohesion within every single Communist party. If Imre Nagy reposes with a Soviet bullet in his head, and Milovan Djilas rests in jail, it does not mean that their heretical ideas are not present in the minds of many Communists in East-Central Europe, even among those who are the official guardians of Party orthodoxy. The myth of the "class solidarity" of the bourgeoisie has today its counterpart: the exploding myth of Communist "class solidarity." Is it not, then, obvious that the Soviet leadership needs to achieve these political (the conclusion of a non-aggression pact) and economic (Western economic help in various forms, from the already concluded wheat deal to the still only rumored multibillion dollar loan) agreements with the West in order to gain time, acquire supplementary means, and secure free hands to right things at home and tighten control over East-Central Europe. If history teaches us anything, it would be so easy to demonstrate that the Soviet leaders behave today as their Bolshevik predecessors did many times before when they needed, and obtained, capitalist help to overcome Communist shortcomings.

The picture of disarray in both Soviet and Western blocs, outlined briefly on the preceding pages, shows how vulnerable both sides are, and how in the months and years ahead the present flux in inter- and intra-bloc relations could decidedly tip the scale in favor of either side. The decisive question will indeed be which side will better succeed in putting its own house in order while profiting from the obvious contradictions within the enemy camp. The fluidity of the relations observable today within the Soviet bloc, and to a varied degree within every Communist party of the bloc, poses the crucial question of the most appropriate Western attitude toward the bloc and its individual parts. The problem is of course extremely delicate and complex, and the absence of a real consensus within the Atlantic alliance on how to tackle it makes things even worse. There are three approaches to that question, and they should be briefly expounded as a sort of conclusion to this essay.

There are first of all those who, although from totally opposite motives, advocate a simple wait-and-see attitude on the part of the West. Because they are indifferent to the fate of East-Central Europe, or because their emotional reaction to communism is such that they refuse every contact with it, their attitude may be characterized as total "immobilism," whose final result could only be the fulfillment of either of two alternatives suggested by George Kennan.

The second approach corresponds roughly to Mr. Spaak's ideas. Its essential shortcomings, in the writer's opinion, are threefold. First, it makes a vital political and psychological concession to Soviet policies by formally recognizing the division of Europe. Second, it is based on wishful thinking that appeasement of communism will make it necessarily more acceptable and will push the Communist regimes toward genuine democratization. Third, it implies that doing business with the Communists on the usual and strictly apolitical basis, or even that extending to them aid and other economic privileges will make them friendlier to the West. Such a policy seems to us self-defeating; it facilitates rather than complicates the tasks of Soviet diplomacy and helps the Communist regimes, particularly their most conservative elements, to consolidate their presently uneasy situations. Everyone in the Communist bloc—the Kremlin, its faithful or wavering followers in the bloc, dissident Communists—and the overwhelming majority of people, non-Communists as well as anti-Communists, could have only contempt for such a timorous attitude. To grant the Soviet Union and the Communist bloc leaders, politically and morally, the right to perpetuate their domination within the bloc, while the Western European Communist parties continue and increase their undermining work, would reveal Western Europe's lack of wisdom and courage. And this in the final analysis could not but have catastrophic consequences. In this case, also, Mr. Kennan's two alternatives remain the only choice.

The third approach (which does not necessarily coincide with General de Gaulle's ideas) would require the use of diplomatic and political means in the service of the great cause of European unity. The United States would have to play a crucial role here. Its first task would be to refuse to accept the present Soviet proposals and to refuse to cooperate with the Kremlin in denying to East-Central Europe the right of self-determination. Zbigniew Brzezinski has with his usual keen insight described the possible consequences of such an American policy: "By striving for a Soviet-American rapprochement, based on an acceptance by Washington of the division of Europe, the Franco-German challenge might be converted into a destructive feud inside the Western alliance and possibly might even lead ultimately to a new Rapallo."[44] In fact the Atlantic alliance should strive to achieve a broad consensus on a coherent common policy toward the Soviet bloc, functioning on three levels: negotiating with the Soviet government which holds the key of East-Central European destiny; entering into multiple relations with the satellite governments because of their political power at home; speaking to the captive nations above the heads of their rulers whom they have never freely chosen.

Negotiations with the Soviet Union have usually been an exercise in futility, for the essential Soviet attitude has been contained in the simple Leninist principle which Nikita Khrushchev made the cornerstone of his foreign policy: "What is mine is mine, and what is yours is negotiable." The diplomatic contacts we advocate here pre-

[44] Zbigniew Brzezinski, "Russia and Europe," p. 442.

suppose a patient but firm effort to arrive at a settlement which would mean neither a NATO nor a Warsaw Pact victory over its rival but their "disengagement" through the establishment of a unified Europe, whose both parts could then cease to be members of military alliances which, by the same token, would have lost their initial purposes. The Soviet rulers would certainly reject any thought of such an accommodation as long as they think they could obtain Western assent to absorb the satellites definitively. If to the contrary, the West refuses to acquiesce in Soviet imperialist desires, and if the conflict with China worsens, and if some other Communist party within the bloc shows anti-Soviet inclinations, such a multiplicity of pressures might convince the Soviet leaders that a genuine agreement with the West and a writing-off of satellites who have become an economic burden and political liability, could be an acceptable policy. On the Western side, "the dissolution of NATO would not be a disaster if the alliance no longer faced a threat and hence had outlived its *raison d'être*."[45]

On the second level, contacts with satellite governments would again presuppose Western initiatives designed to facilitate the goal of European unification. What the West should try to accomplish here, taking into account variations in the individual situations of every country in East-Central Europe, would be to open the flow of human contacts, and to convince particularly the technical strata within the Communist regimes that it is in their interest to seek closer ties with the West.

Finally, while any incitement of captive nations to rebel against their masters must be radically rejected, the West should convey to them the sense of a common destiny and the promise of a common and free European future. The longshoreman from San Francisco, Eric Hoffer, has expressed it in a superb fashion:

> It seems to me that the ideal object of identification for the people in the satellite countries is the vision of United Europe: a closely federated sub-continent, beautiful and powerful, possessed of more talent, skill, and learning than any other part of the world, and with a history unequal in brilliance and achievement. A Europe, moreover, in which people can work, study, teach, build, trade, travel, and play wherever they please, and feel at home everywhere.[46]

Such a vision, as Hoffer himself states, does not rise of itself. It must be projected and diffused by a vigorous movement in the non-Communist part of Europe, and must have the full support of the United States. For the latter country, a genuine and integral unification of Europe would mean the accomplishment of the entire American task,

---

[45] S. F. Giffin, "Untangling an Alliance," *Orbis*, Fall 1963, pp. 473-474.
[46] Eric Hoffer, *The Ordeal of Change* (New York: Harper & Brothers, 1963), p. 88.

its first half being brilliantly achieved by the success of the Marshall Plan. For peoples of East-Central Europe such a vision already has and could acquire even greater attraction. In the final analysis, even the people of Russia, looking to the clouds of the Far East, might realize that the "westernizing" trend, which has always existed as one of the components of Russian history, represents the real guarantee of a better and freer future. Furthermore, the Soviet leaders themselves, if Western firmness and self-confidence thwart their expanding ambitions, may realize that in the age of nuclear weapons, Chinese peril, and technical progress, a genuine understanding with the West, bringing peace and prosperity to all, is more important than the worn-out ideological slogans.

All this seems remote from reality in the light of the present state of affairs in the West. Still, the West has at its disposal all the ingredients to pursue successfully a global policy which would lead to the results depicted above. The tools are in Western hands. Western courage and wisdom, or lack of them, will determine the shape of the future.

Background for Atlantic Partnership

—*ROBERT KLEIMAN*

Few diplomatic bombshells since the war have produced as much surprise, shock, dismay, and universal puzzlement—or have caused as much havoc—as the January 1963 press conference at which President de Gaulle vetoed Britain's entry into the Common Market and rejected the Nassau offer of Polaris missiles. For months afterward —and to this day—observers near and far have asked, "What happened? What went wrong with the Kennedy 'Grand Design'?". There is not space here for the detailed narrative and analysis needed to unravel this mystery—the multiple errors of the British, the ambitions of de Gaulle, the Kennedy-de Gaulle conflict, the defection of Adenauer, the Nassau Conference.* What follows is an attempt simply to identify some of the American misconceptions that, in my view, contributed to the disaster and still shackle American policy in this field.

The origin of the phrase "Kennedy's Grand Design" has been lost to man. It was a misnomer when it entered common use. Some in Europe, including General de Gaulle, read into it objectives that were foreign to its aims. Others, at times, wondered whether there was any grand design at all.

Dean Acheson was asked about it in May 1962 and, according to *The Times* of London, he replied: It "comes from the Press Club bar. Walt Rostow [State Department director of policy planning] has inherited a project of trying to write down everything that has gone on

---

* See Robert Kleiman, *Atlantic Crisis: American Diplomacy Confronts a Resurgent Europe* (New York: Norton, 1964).

and trying to tie it together. I believe the psychiatrists call this rationalization."

Acheson's quip contained some truth. The core of the "Grand Design" was the idea of an Atlantic partnership. It began to come into focus for some Administration officials in the fall of 1961. But it was many months later before President Kennedy embraced the concept. And, until January 1963, the Grand Design remained a direction rather than a policy, a perspective toward the future rather than a concrete program to be implemented. The setback it suffered, in this writer's view, stemmed as much from this flaw as from the machinations of Charles de Gaulle.

The Grand Design grew out of Britain's decision in the summer of 1961, to seek entry into the Common Market. This decision dramatized for Washington the beginnings of a united Europe, which promised to place a new giant on the world stage.

Within the Common Market, the European nations were eliminating tariffs among themselves. To reduce discrimination against American goods, they offered to negotiate substantial across-the-board tariff cuts with the United States. The President had inadequate authority to take up this offer under the expiring Reciprocal Trade Agreements Act. A radical new bill was drafted, with authority to reduce most tariffs up to 50 per cent and some to zero. And the Trade Expansion Act was made the centerpiece of the Kennedy legislative program for 1962.

To some of the President's advisers, the prospect of an unprecedented trade deal between the United States and a united Europe opened vistas of a far broader nature. America's commitments abroad had led to a chronic payments imbalance and a dangerous outflow of gold and dollars. The dollar outflow hampered efforts to stimulate the lagging growth rate of the American economy. It was becoming evident that the United States could not indefinitely carry worldwide defense and aid burdens alone. But little additional help was to be expected from the European allies individually. Britain's entry into a united Europe, it was thought, would bring into being a partner capable of sharing the load.

President Kennedy gave public support to the idea in his July 4, 1962 speech in Philadelphia:

> Acting on our own, by ourselves, we cannot establish justice throughout the world; we cannot ensure its domestic tranquility, or provide for its common defense, or promote its general welfare, or secure the blessings of liberty to ourselves and our posterity. But joined with other free men, we can do all this and more. We can assist the developing nations to throw off the yoke of poverty. We can balance our world-

> wide trade and payments at the highest possible level of growth. We can mount a deterrent powerful enough to deter any aggression. . . .
>
> I will say here and now, on this day of Independence, that the United States will be ready for a declaration of interdependence, that we will be prepared to discuss with a united Europe the ways and means of forming a concrete Atlantic partnership.

What has thwarted this concept of the Atlantic future so far has been, in large part, a conflict between Gaullist France on the one hand and the United States and Britain on the other. In this conflict—which originated in de Gaulle's 1958 proposals for a tripartite U.S.-British-French directorate for the West—the personality and nationalist ambitions of the French President have played a corrosive role. But there is also an underlying ideological dispute that must be grasped if the United States is to come to terms with the rest of Common Market Europe, dissuade the continent as a whole from taking a Gaullist direction and, most important, lay the basis for the Atlantic partnership that, in my view, should continue to be the central focus of American policy in the world.

De Gaulle

Charles de Gaulle has been described as "a man of the day-before-yesterday and of the day-after-tomorrow." He lives in the past and in the future. Much has been said, with justice, of his nineteenth-century views, of his archaic nationalism. But it is important to understand something of his "futurism," as well.

Again and again in de Gaulle's eloquent speeches and memoirs, he talks of "the current of history" which must guide nations and leaders in their great decisions. De Gaulle's genius has been his ability at crucial moments to sense and ride with history's tide. In 1933 he foresaw the role of mechanized armor in World War II. Before most of his compatriots, he sensed the coming doom of the Hitler era in 1940 and the collapse of the colonial era in the years preceding his return to power in 1958. He was the first statesman of note to predict the current Sino-Soviet conflict. "De Gaulle's decisions are often wrong," one of his Cabinet Ministers said recently, "his predictions—never."

The historic tide that de Gaulle senses now is a shift in the balance of power within the Western world. The American dominance that marked the 'forties and 'fifties is challenged in the 'sixties. A new power is foreshadowed in the West, a strong, united Europe, increasingly independent of the United States financially, economically, and, perhaps ultimately, in other fields.

The "little" Common Market, as now constituted, is not as small as it often seems with Britain subtracted from it. Its population is 170,-

000,000. Its economy is about as powerful as Russia's, its living standards much higher. Its growth rate over the past decade has been twice that of the United States. Its gold and foreign currency reserves have soared to a level significantly higher than those of the United States; in 1952, even after the Marshall Plan, they were less than one-sixth as large.

The backing of Europe's central banks and treasuries today stiffens the dollar and the British pound somewhat as U.S. aid supported Europe's currencies during the Marshall Plan years. There has been a dramatic reversal of roles. During the 1961-63 period, the United States had to ask continental Europe first for a $3 billion line of credit and then for another $1.9 billion in treasury bond purchases and swap arrangements. It was the Continent that put up almost $2 billion of the $3 billion needed to save Britain's pound from a dangerous devaluation in November 1964.

In the financial and economic fields, therefore, the balance of power within the West already has shifted significantly. Another decade of growth combined with real progress toward political unity could make the six-nation Common Market, without Britain, an entity more nearly approaching the dimensions of the United States and the Soviet Union, whether or not it matches them in all fields.

Roughly equal status with the U.S. and Russia in world affairs has long been de Gaulle's chief ambition for the European power he sees ahead. He seeks to advance French "grandeur" by uniting Europe. Although he talks of "independence," he realizes that a nation of forty-seven million with a national income one-ninth that of the United States can only be a second-class power if it stands alone. But, unwilling to merge the French identity in the kind of federal union most non-Gaullist Continentals want, he has proposed a loose "Union of States" leading toward confederation. He was prepared for a time to accept British participation and he knows that ultimately it may be unavoidable both for defense purposes and to counterbalance a Germany more powerful than France. But he prefers the present six-nation configuration because he believes it is, as has been said, "small enough for France to lead and big enough to lead Europe."

De Gaulle's bid for leadership so far has been rejected by Europe because of his efforts at dominance, his exclusion of Britain, and, most of all, his opposition to the federal principle. De Gaulle's tactics have been deplored; his methods have been attacked as ruthless, Machiavellian, and destructive of the community spirit on which, alone, unity can thrive. But it must be recognized that the objective the French President seeks—equal status for Europe in a world of continental giants—evokes a powerful response both in the Common Market and Britain. De Gaulle was by no means the first to see this even if, when he did, he moved purposefully to encourage and exploit Europe's desires. This deep European desire for equality with America is a major reason why Harold Macmillan wanted to be inside Europe, rather than outside looking in. De Gaulle's effort to hasten the unification of Europe, under French leadership, helped provoke Britain's Common Market bid. Macmillan stated his own thesis, so similar to de Gaulle's, this way: "Are we now to isolate ourselves from Europe, at a time when our own strength is no longer self-sufficient and when the leading European countries are joining together? . . . There remain only two national units which can claim to be world powers in their own right, namely the United States and Soviet Russia. . . . A divided Europe would stand no chance of competing with these great concentrations of power. But in this new European Community . . . a new organization is rapidly developing with the ability to stand on an equal footing with the great power groupings of the world."

Equal status is the aim that has led many Europeans, including the "father" of the new Europe, Jean Monnet, to favor integrated European nuclear deterrent as one possible solution for the Atlantic nuclear problem. They see it as a way to escape the proliferation of national forces—small, inefficient, expensive, and dangerous—without remaining forever dependent on the United States for their entire nuclear defense.

"A [U.S.-European] relationship of two separate but equally powerful entities." This is not a phrase used by de Gaulle to advocate a "separatist" Europe. It is the concept of his chief organized opposition in the six nations of the Common Market. It is the phrase used by Monnet's Action Committee for a United States of Europe to describe its ultimate objective, an Atlantic "partnership," a word de Gaulle never employs.

The United States, under the Eisenhower Administration and initially under Kennedy, tended to respond to this challenge, if at all, in "Atlantic Community" terms, as did many Britons. What this signified to de Gaulle and a steadily increasing number of Europeans can be seen in the fifteen-nation NATO Council, where all nations theoretically are equal, but one, the United States, is more equal than the others. This structure has meant American leadership or none.

It has meant an alliance where, as de Gaulle sees it, "everything is commanded by the Americans and where the Americans control the use of the principal weapons, that is, atomic arms."

Nuclear Weapons and Strategy

De Gaulle was the first European leader to make this a public issue. But it would be a profound error to believe that he is alone in this view or that this genie can be put back into the bottle.

Nor can de Gaulle's argument be destroyed by accusations that he is seeking to create a "Third Force." De Gaulle's opposition to communism is as strong as was Kennedy's. If he were one day to engage independent negotiations with Moscow, it would be for reasons parallel to those used by Kennedy to justify his unilateral talks with the Soviets. As one of de Gaulle's cabinet ministers put it:

"De Gaulle is not trying to build a Third Force. He is trying to build a Second Force in the West."

Dr. Walter Hallstein, President of the Common Market Commission and hardly a Gaullist, has asked: "Given a fully united Europe . . . should it be integrated—some would say 'dissolved'—into a so-called 'Atlantic Community' . . . a system which harnesses one giant with a number of comparative dwarfs?" His answer was to propose "a new system" which "joins in partnership . . . twin units which today are already comparable and which one day will be equal," namely the United States and the new Europe.

After eighteen months in office, President Kennedy seemed to accept this concept. At Philadelphia, on July 4, 1962, he spoke of "interdependence" and a "partnership" of "full equality" with Europe. But he was speaking of a distant "goal" to be sought after British entry and a further tightening of Europe's bonds. His speech was filled with such words as "premature" and "some day" and "not built overnight." At no point prior to de Gaulle's January 1963 veto was there a dynamic, imaginative effort to accord progressively equal status immediately to a Europe whose strength and unity, in the White House view, were thought to lie in the somewhat distant future. Yet that is precisely what a majority of Europeans—not de Gaulle alone—wished to see.

The fact is that Washington, as London, simply failed to react in time to the trend. Not until Britain applied to join the Common Market did the United States see itself seriously affected by the new Europe. Even then, the assumption was that there need be no hurry in adjusting the U.S.-European power relationship.

Yet, with or without de Gaulle, the likelihood has always existed that a revived and united Europe, increasingly independent of the United States, one day might go its own way. It was inevitable that the growth of a second Atlantic giant would crack the mold in which a dominant America had shaped the unity of the West in the postwar period. Before this happened, it was vital for the United States and its friends in Europe to find a new structure for unity. It was essential to devise and forge new links of interdependence across the Atlantic more appropriate to the new day.

Foresighted Americans and Europeans such as General Lauris Norstad and Jean Monnet recognized this in the late 'fifties and drew pertinent conclusions. There were voices in Washington and elsewhere which supported their views. But public policy lagged behind.

As early as 1957-58 and again in 1959-60, General Norstad made formal proposals to give the European allies a real voice in the nuclear weapons field. The Eisenhower Administration in its last weeks in office and the Kennedy Administration in 1961 paid lip service to one aspect of this idea: a NATO multilateral nuclear force. But both Administrations were divided on the issue, and little was done to bring such a force into being. It is ironic now, but as late as December 1962, a few days before Nassau, Secretary of Defense McNamara tried to discourage the project. He told the NATO Ministerial Council that there was no military requirement for a NATO nuclear force.

In this same discourse, McNamara turned inside-out the 1956-57 NATO strategic concept of a "shield" of conventional and tactical nuclear forces, designed to hold briefly, and a strategic nuclear "sword" to defeat the aggressor. He spoke of a nuclear shield, to deter Soviet use of atomic weapons, and a conventional sword to fight the war. He indicated elsewhere that an all-out Soviet conventional attack could be held for three to six months, and even defeated, by stepped-up NATO conventional forces. And he urged the Europeans to satisfy themselves with a conventional role in Atlantic defense. Whether this was good or bad strategic doctrine may be arguable. But it clearly was poor alliance politics for it weakened confidence in American willingness to use nuclear weapons—and risk American cities—to defend Europe.

When McNamara took office he found the U.S. Army preparing to fight a two-year war, while the U.S. Air Force was prepared for a war of a few weeks. A new, unified strategic doctrine for the U.S. Armed Forces undoubtedly was necessary. But the day had long since passed when a strategy made in Washington without consulting the allies could be imposed on Europe.

Some elements of the Administration sought a different approach. In March 1961, Dean Acheson spoke to General de Gaulle of his plan for a NATO nuclear force controlled by a five-nation "war cabinet." He gave de Gaulle the impression that there would be no single-nation veto, for he indicated that the European elements would be able to commit the U.S. Strategic Air Command by striking alone, if necessary. But despite other, similar hints, the issue of the veto was never clarified. Later, de Gaulle was accused of building a small independent deterrent to "trigger" American nuclear strength.

In September 1962, White House Security Advisor McGeorge Bundy went so far as to suggest that the United States, under certain conditions, would accept, within NATO, a European nuclear force in which the U.S. neither would participate nor possess a veto. But the central thrust of U.S. policy before January 1963 remained the opposite of sharing nuclear responsibility with Europe. It was a policy of maintaining the American nuclear monopoly—with a British appendage that, it was hoped, would ultimately disappear.

American reluctance to share control of nuclear weapons was paralleled by a reluctance to share sovereignty in the economic field, even though the stakes were much smaller and did not involve the country's physical survival.

The Road to Economic Unity

In the economic field, Jean Monnet launched the concept of "partnership" with the United States as early as 1957 and, more precisely, in June 1959, shortly after the Common Market began to function—and long before Britain applied for membership. The West European nations, he said then, "no longer dependents . . . are ready for the full responsibilities of partnership." For this "new era" he urged a "new Atlantic initiative" to face "new problems common both to Europe and America."

"The creation of the Common Market," Monnet said, "has already had substantial repercussions in nonmember countries. These repercussions are likely to increase rather than diminish." The Common Market Six, he pointed out, "are on the way to establishing new political arrangements under which policies as well as resources will be merged."

"A new institutional approach is necessary," Monnet said, to "concert policies" among "the *major* Western industrial powers on both sides of the Atlantic" in a limited number of critical fields: monetary stability, economic growth, aid to underdeveloped areas, and world commodity stabilization—as well as tariff arrangements. "What is at stake," said the Action Committee for a United States of Europe, "is no longer simply the question of how trade problems should be settled . . . but rather how to solve the economic problems facing all the countries of the West, including the United States."

Monnet's chief objective was one which the Common Market Commission endorsed in its First Memorandum in February 1959. It was, as the Commission put it, nothing less than to bring together for "joint action" the "three great units" which are "the motive force of the economy of the free world: the United States, the United Kingdom and the [European] Community." This objective, which preceded Britain's application to join the Common Market, has increased pertinence now, after the failure of Britain's Brussels bid and the election of a Labor Government which has no desire to enter the new Europe.

Monnet's proposal was taken up by Douglas Dillon, then the U.S. Undersecretary of State. It led in 1960 to the reorganization of the eighteen-nation OEEC as the twenty-nation Organization for Economic Cooperation and Development (OECD), with the United States and Canada joining the Europeans as full members. But the OECD, despite some useful work, has failed to perform the essential tasks for which it was conceived. The reasons for failure include a weak secretariat, a too-numerous membership and a loose charter. Two key elements suggested by Monnet were missing: the Six refused to sit as a Community, acting as one; and a small policy council to bring the United States, Britain, and the Common Market together for joint decisions was never set up. But, above all, what the OECD has lacked has been a mandate for action. The weak OEEC charter, which permitted binding decisions only by unanimity, was watered down further to satisfy the United States: the OECD was not authorized to make binding decisions at all; it can only consult and recommend.

The chief American negotiator in creating OECD, Ambassador John Tuthill, made this public comment in the spring of 1963 about OECD consultation: "The United States Government, in my view, was slow in concluding that this type of consultation was needed. Even (in 1960) in the negotiation for the establishment of the OECD, there remained skeptics in certain parts of our government who questioned whether we should consult in this intimate fashion on such highly sensitive issues as policies in agriculture, finance, economic growth, etc."

Tuthill went on to say that the Kennedy Administration, unlike the Eisenhower Administration, had no hesitancy about consultation. And this was true. The New Frontier sought to use the OECD machinery to influence European monetary, economic, and foreign-aid policy. It even sought European recommendations to influence the U.S. Congress. It was willing to talk about international programs for stabilization of agricultural and other commodities, something that was anathema to the Eisenhower cabinet. But talk can only be a first step. Except in one important instance, the Kennedy Administration prior to January 1963 held back from real partnership, the kind that involves action and a sharing both of responsibility and the power of decision. This single instance occurred in the monetary field.

In January 1961, Jean Monnet saw in the continuing U.S. dollar crisis a mounting threat to the West and an opportunity to advance Atlantic unity. A spectacular run from the dollar in the fall of 1960 had lifted U.S. gold losses to an annual rate of $6 billion. In an interview with this writer in *U.S. News & World Report*, Monnet urged "a joint approach by the Governments of Europe, including Britain, in partnership with the United States" to strengthen confidence in the dollar and to "stabilize the currencies of the West."

What should be done—many national and international techniques had been advanced in the preceding year or two by monetary experts—seemed less important to Monnet than *who* could do it effectively. He added:

> While we must examine solutions involving the International Monetary Fund, we should as a first step think of what we can do quickly to the same ends by reinforcing the partnership of Europe and America. . . .

> The principal actors in the monetary dramas of recent years have been the U.S., Britain, the Common Market countries, Switzerland and Canada. While gold reserves have shifted back and forth among these countries, they always have had almost nine-tenths of the gold of the non-Communist world. By acting together, these countries have the power to put the free world's monetary system on a sound and stable basis. . . .
>
> During and after the war, gold flowed from Europe to the U.S. We had the famous 'dollar gap' that was closed by the Marshall Plan. Now the flow is in the other direction. One day, it could easily be reversed again.
>
> It should be possible to solve these problems without periodically endangering the whole economic structure of the West. We need permanent machinery that will enable the U.S. and Europe to cooperate in this field on a continuous, rather than a crisis, basis.

The Kennedy Administration discussed this problem with its Atlantic allies in the then nine-nation OECD monetary committee. But it sought action in another forum—the sixty-seven-nation International Monetary Fund, which was dominated by the United States and Britain. The United States proposed that the continental European countries make some $3 billion of their currencies available to the IMF in the form of stand-by credits. It amounted to a doubling of the European currency in the Fund upon which the United States could draw, if necessary. The United States, Britain, and Canada were also to pledge about $3 billion in their own currencies for reverse circumstances. But it was not expected that these funds would be used in any immediate future.

The key issue, argued out during the IMF conference in Vienna in September 1961, was whether the IMF or the lending countries would decide on use of the new reserves. The United States and Britain, as the chief prospective borrowers, wanted something close to automatic drawing rights under normal IMF procedures. Most of the Common Market countries—with little voting strength in the IMF—insisted on a wide range of safeguards, including consultation before their currencies were drawn out. French Finance Minister Wilfrid Baumgartner—a longtime Governor of the Bank of France and no Gaullist; he left the French Government a few months later—demanded a veto. He insisted that "each country should remain judge . . . of the use of its own currency."

The compromise agreement that was reached took the route Monnet had proposed eight months earlier. It provided for IMF machinery to handle the mechanics. But the decision on each drawing of funds was made the multilateral responsibility of the ten nations contributing to the new reserves. France yielded on the veto. The United States and Britain yielded on automaticity. It was agreed that decisions by the new ten-nation "Paris Club" could be made by qualified majority votes—the votes of seven countries which had contributed sixty per cent of the new reserves. In effect, the agreement was a step toward a limited kind of Atlantic reserve fund. And the same countries, meeting in the OECD monetary committee, thus acquired an added incentive for the day-to-day cooperation by Finance Ministries and central banks that subsequently gave OECD its only significant continuing success.

Most important, an *ad hoc* Atlantic institution had been created with decision-making machinery that, for the first time, reflected the new balance of financial power in the West. Sovereignty had been pooled in a way new to the Atlantic area.

This beginning in true Atlantic partnership could have set a precedent for action on other critical economic problems as well as more permanent monetary reform. Further steps toward an Atlantic reserve fund, for example, could have strengthened the dollar and pound, forced the pace toward joint business-cycle policy and stimulated common policies for balanced economic growth on both sides of the Atlantic. But the precedent of the "Paris Club" was not followed up in any field, not even in the field of stopgap monetary measures. In building further defenses for the dollar, U.S. Undersecretary of the Treasury Robert Roosa sought increases in IMF quotas and bilateral deals with European countries individually through swap arrangements and sales of U.S. Treasury obligations. He opposed new Atlantic machinery to deal on a permanent basis either with Atlantic monetary problems or the world's long-term "liquidity" problem.

U. S. Trade Expansion Act

The main thrust of U.S. policy in the Atlantic economic field turned in October 1961 toward the Trade Expansion Act—a measure that skirted the central issue posed by Europe's union and aroused some suspicion of America's aims.

The Trade Expansion Act repeated, five years later, one of the errors Britain had made in its initial reaction to the Common Market. To many Europeans, Washington's plan looked like London's Free Trade Area scheme in another and even broader form.

There was an important difference, which America's friends recognized but Gaullists and some others ignored. The British in 1956-58 sought to dissolve the Common Market in a wider commercial grouping, a move that would have destroyed the burgeoning economic and political union of the Six. Washington from the start had favored Europe's union and had encouraged Britain to join; the Trade Expansion Act was an attempt initially to limit the trade damages to the United States and, later, to achieve increased exchanges. Freer trade, it was hoped, would open the way toward cooperation in other fields. But the timing of the measure was bad. And one provision—authorizing zero tariffs—cast a shadow over a project that, otherwise, might have been well received.

Under Secretary of State George Ball evidently suspected it was a mistake to rush trade legislation on the heels of Britain's Common Market bid. A well-informed observer, writing early in 1962, reported that "The Ball Group . . . was concerned lest precipitate American action in 1962 complicate the entry of Britain into the Common Market. To gain time, it favored letting the 1958 Trade Act expire, and then writing a new bill for submission to a new Congress in 1963."

But when President Kennedy ruled otherwise, even Ball was surprised at the nature of Europe's reaction. The Europeans welcomed plans to negotiate toward a fifty per cent reciprocal tariff cut. They were pleased at the turn away from escape clauses and peril points. They found, in the plans for adjustment assistance, an Administration intention to reduce tariffs even when it hurt. But all this got less attention than the provisions permitting zero tariffs on products in which the United States and the Common Market conducted eighty per cent of world trade. That provision—if Britain had entered the Common Market—would have covered a large part of U.S.-European trade in manufactured goods.

To Europeans this seemed like an attempt to create an Atlantic Free Trade Area, wiping out much of the Common Market's external tariff. The external tariff was considered one of the vital elements in unifying the economies of the member countries over the next decade.

Ball hastened to Europe to reassure Common Market leaders. He said that the Administration had merely sought the widest possible bargaining authority. He argued that most-favored-nation treatment would extend the tariff cuts to the whole world, proving that there was no thought of an Atlantic free-trade area.

But with zero tariffs projected for products traded most heavily in the Atlantic area, many Europeans were not convinced. Some suspected a fine British hand had been involved in shaping that part of the Trade Act; French diplomats in Washington reported that the initial draft had been "written in the British Embassy." There was fear that West Germany and Holland would be tempted by Atlantic zero tariffs as they had been by the European zero tariffs in Britain's free-trade-area scheme.

Oddly enough, Europe's opposition to the zero-tariff clause was little grasped in the United States. So well-informed a Congressman as Representative Henry Reuss of Wisconsin remained convinced, even after de Gaulle's veto, that the zero tariff provision was an incentive to the Common Market to admit Britain.

A fundamental error in comprehension in the United States was reflected in the Trade Expansion Act, which absorbed the Administration's energies for a year. Many in Washington evidently were bemused by the words "common market" and overlooked the true meaning and real title of the European Economic Community. The six nations of the new Europe were reducing their tariffs for each other not primarily as a means of increasing trade but as a step toward "a more perfect union."

"We're not in business; we're in politics." This widely quoted remark by Dr. Walter Hallstein should have pointed to the overriding objective of the new Europe. That objective was never simply a customs union, but a political union, first in the economic field. The contribution of Jean Monnet to the second half of the twentieth century was not a new trade scheme but a method of uniting nations. The Europeans recognized the legitimate American interest in reciprocal tariff reductions and were willing to go along—up to a point. But their real interest in relations with the United States lay elsewhere.

The essential political nature of Europe's union required a political response from the United States. That response had to face up to the new power balance developing in the West. It had to envisage a transformation of outmoded Atlantic patterns. It had to recognize the inevitable evolution toward a new relationship—"a relationship of two separate but equally powerful entities." Whatever the nostalgia for a bygone day, the United States had to realize that there was no future in "Atlantic Community" proposals which would disguise but maintain American rather than joint U.S.-European leadership.

Nothing has been more misleading since January 1963 than the general belief in the United States and Britain that the Common Market, under the French influence, is seeking an "inward-looking" Europe. Vested interests may lead France to resist too-rapid tariff cuts on some industrial products; German farmers may cling to high prices and protection. But the essential orientation of the Six is "outward-looking" in the sense that continental Europe is determined to play a more imporant role in the world. And this is at least as true of Gaullist France as it is of any of the other countries.

In his early months in office, President Kennedy admitted that "no one nation has the power or the wisdom to solve all the problems of the world or manage all its revolutionary tides." He later said repeatedly that the United States no longer could carry worldwide defense and aid burdens alone. Nor has the United States alone been able to solve the West's increasingly dangerous problems of monetary instability, farm surpluses, lagging growth rates, booms and slumps and declines in world commodity prices. Such declines in recent years—the result of a too-free market—have seen the industrial countries mulct the underdeveloped exporting nations of far more than they have given back in the form of grants-in-aid.

If the United States wanted Europe's help in such fields, it should have begun by proposing *ad hoc* institutions for these purposes in which Europe could have had an equal voice on the board.

A real burden-sharing partnership is impossible between one great power and numerous smaller nations, as in NATO, or on a bilateral basis. In such a relationship, the giant necessarily calls the tune—or fails to lead—and no one else can take its place. The others inevitably become submissive or resentful and, in any case, cannot assume responsibility. Whatever effort a small nation may make, its added contribution is bound to be so limited compared to the total that there is little incentive to sacrifice. This can be changed only by the uniting of Europe. As the new Europe senses its ability to influence events on the American scale, it will want to do so. That already is beginning to happen. But it cannot take the form of a European contribution to projects shaped in Washington. Either the strategy of the West will be shaped jointly by the United States and Europe in the political, economic, and military fields, or Europe ultimately will shape its own.

On December 6, 1961, in announcing his coming foreign trade program, President Kennedy said: "This is not speculation about some grand design for the future." And, in the mind of the President, it seems clear, there was no Grand Design at that time, whatever thoughts others below him may have had.

In the spring of 1962, a visitor told one of the President's closest advisers of Europe's skepticism about the Trade Act. Many Europeans, he said, felt the United States was interested in protecting American trade, but not in sharing power with Europe.

"They may be right," smiled the White House adviser.

But on July 4, 1962, President Kennedy said: "We believe that a united Europe will be capable of playing a greater role in the common defense, of responding more generously to the needs of poorer nations, of joining with the United States and others in lowering trade barriers, resolving problems of commerce and commodities and currency, and developing coordinated policies in all economic, political and diplomatic areas. We see in such a Europe a partner with whom we can deal on a basis of full equality in all the great and burdensome tasks of building and defending a community of free nations."

This was a Grand Design.

Yet, prior to January 1963, the United States still failed to face up to the implications of the united Europe—of the Six—that already was taking shape. President Kennedy had begun by seeking to restore American leadership at a time, in 1961, when a clear need already had arisen for common action and joint leadership with Europe. When this need finally was seen, its urgency was overlooked; action was delayed pending Britain's entry into the Common Market, mortgaging U.S. policy to London's dilatory methods. And, all this time, the Atlantic solidarity upon which partnership had to be based repeatedly was strained by the pursuit of other, conflicting objectives—felt to be of overriding importance—such as maintenance of the U.S. nuclear monopoly in the West and unilateral negotiations with Russia.

A Policy for the Future

It is too late to repair the errors of the past. But it is not too soon to shape a policy for the future. And, in this, the past can be a guide. While there have been important developments since January 1963—none more important than the tragic assassination of John F. Kennedy and his replacement by Lyndon B. Johnson, who now has been elected to a four-year term in his own right—most of the underlying factors remain the same:

(1) The Common Market of the Six is still a going concern. It is the only united Europe that exists or will exist for some time. There has been less Community spirit since de Gaulle's veto of Britain and more emphasis on reciprocity in national concessions. But forward movement has gone on and is likely to continue, despite predictable difficulties for 1965 over agriculture and tariff negotiations with the United States. A great thrust ahead—made as 1963 ended—was confirmed by detailed agreements in August 1964. Through a Franco-German compromise, the mainly industrial European Economic Community was extended to most of agriculture—averting a serious crisis over de Gaulle's July 1963 warning that otherwise the Common Market might "disappear." Agreement on a single grain price for the future, necessary to make the common market in agriculture operative, averted a new crisis in December 1964. And although a number of lesser farm issues remained, it then appeared clear that Europe's economic union—to use Jean Monnet's expression—had become "irreversible." All plans for the West must start from these facts of life.

(2) Political union of the Six is still on the agenda, even if progress is likely to be difficult and slow. As 1964 opened, President de Gaulle listed as his major objective abroad "the union of Europe . . . in the domains of politics, defense and culture as . . . in that of economics." But negotiations continued to be blocked, as they had been since 1962, by Dutch and Belgian insistence on a federal structure or British participation. The October 1964 victory of the British Labor Party, which had opposed entry into the Common Market, promised to reduce this impediment. Chancellor Erhard of Germany and Foreign Minister Spaak of Belgium in the fall of 1964 submitted fresh proposals for political union that called for action by the Six—without insisting on either British participation or a Federal union at the start. A new obstacle arose when the French in November 1964, as part of a campaign against the projected eight-nation multilateral force (MLF) of Polaris-armed surface ships, declared that West Germany's inclusion in an Atlantic nuclear force—whether the MLF or that proposed by Britain—would make a continental political-military union of the Six meaningless. But the French, on the other hand, showed an increasing willingness in 1964 to meet the desires of their Common Market part-

ners for a political structure that could evolve in a federal direction, as long as it began with something similar to the loose "Union of States" proposed by the Fouchet Plan of 1961-62. Pressure for a federal union is such, from the Five and within France, that de Gaulle's Prime Minister and his Foreign Minister now have been forced to pay lip service to "federation" rather than "confederation" as the ultimate goal. In the economic sphere, the fusion of the executive commissions of the three existing European Communities—to which France has agreed in principle—will consolidate and thus enhance the powers of the most vigorous federal institutions of the new Europe.

(3) British entry into the Common Market is off the agenda, probably for several years. The Conservative Party, which sought entry, has always been divided on the issue and has adopted an ambiguous position since de Gaulle's January 1963 veto. The Labor Party, now in power, remains opposed and is unlikely to change its position very soon, although it ultimately may do so. French terms for British entry have been raised since January 1963. A defense deal in the nuclear missile field is now the central condition and is likely to remain so as long as de Gaulle is in power. It can be undercut, if at all, only by a British proposal to participate in an integrated European deterrent—a proposal Jean Monnet unsuccessfully urged London to make after the January 1963 crisis. Despite some high level backing, both the Conservatives and the Laborites still oppose that now.

(4) U.S. negotiations with Russia face less opposition from Germany with Adenauer's departure from the Chancellorship. Though substantial elements of the Christian Democratic party remain hostile to East-West talks, there is a majority in all three German parties now for careful contact with Moscow—if there is advance agreement on objectives. Fear of a U.S.-Soviet deal at Germany's expense continues, as was demonstrated by the West German reaction to the nuclear test ban treaty in the summer of 1963. But the Bonn Government under Chancellor Erhard and Foreign Minister Schroeder is advancing its own views, becoming a subject as well as an object in international relations. And the United States now seems prepared to accept this. Since the spring of 1963, Washington has made a point of informing and consulting the Germans continuously. It has become clear—even to the Russians, as shown by Khrushchev's bid before his fall for a meeting with Erhard—that there can be no Berlin, German, or European settlement without West German acquiescence.

(5) Relations between the United States and France, after several ups and down, returned toward the end of 1964 to a crisis state almost as tense as that in January 1963—and then eased slightly. Although much had changed in the two interim years, the fundamental issues between Paris and Washington remained the same.

De Gaulle Between East and West

During the first half of 1963, as the first shock of de Gaulle's veto faded, President Kennedy decided to make a new effort to open a dialogue with the French leader and he sought to arrange a meeting with the General. Then, after the test ban agreement in July 1963, Kennedy for the first time recognized France as a nuclear power under the Atomic Energy Act. That meant new legislation no longer would be needed to grant France nuclear assistance similar to that given Britain. In a July 25 letter to de Gaulle and in his August 1 press conference, the President mentioned three conditions for U.S. aid. He wanted France to sign the test ban treaty and to halt atmospheric testing; to come to agreement on "the organization of the defense of the West"; and to join in "a cooperative effort" to satisfy the desires of West Germany and other non-nuclear NATO countries for participation in the West's nuclear deterrent. He also pointed out that Britain, in return for Polaris, had agreed at Nassau to place its V-bombers and its future Polaris force "under NATO." De Gaulle replied on August 2 that he intended to continue testing, presumably until the French H-bomb is developed in 1966-67. He said he would make no arrangements that would deprive the French deterrent of its independence. But he did not close the door on the offer. While neither side was prepared to move further immediately, it became clear to both that for the first time the way was open for a serious Franco-American discussion on defense. And, during the last months of the Kennedy Administration, events were moving toward the revival of a Franco-American dialogue for the first time since 1961. This trend was interrupted by the assassination. But the underlying circumstances are unlikely to change, and they deserve examination.

During 1963 and 1964, in the wake of the French veto, circumstances evolved unfavorably for Gaullist policy. Although the French President had his defenders in Europe, he was generally blamed for the way Britain was excluded, for the continued strain in French relations with the United States and NATO, and for the slowdown in progress toward European union. French ties with Bonn failed to develop as effectively as the General had hoped when he signed the Franco-German Treaty with Adenauer; even before Erhard became Chancellor, the West Germans increasingly showed a mind of their own. Closer relations between Bonn and Washington, actively sought by Kennedy and Johnson, led de Gaulle's cabinet ministers to talk with concern about the danger of Franco-American "competition" for German loyalty. Instead of achieving the leadership of Europe, aided by German backing, the General found himself threatened with isolation within Europe and within the Atlantic world.

At the same time, the French President became concerned lest the improvement in Anglo-American relations with Russia, stemming from the test ban treaty, lead to a deal over Germany in his absence—"another Yalta," his aides called it. With the West Germans participating in Western planning for talks with Moscow, de Gaulle began to feel that the French policy of total "nonparticipation" had outworn its usefulness. All these factors placed the General under pressure to re-enter the Anglo-American dialogue with Russia and to seek discussion of differences with the United States—steps that Bonn, particularly, urged upon him, as did many of his own officials.

One de Gaulle dilemma was that he remained as opposed as ever to negotiations with Russia on Berlin and Germany. The status quo—the *de facto* division of Germany—suited him very well; he saw no advantage for France in moves either toward legalizing the division or ending it. Moves toward reunification would present France with the prospect of a nation of eighty million Germans on its eastern frontier. Moves toward legal acceptance by the West of Germany's division increased the danger that Germans ultimately would look toward Moscow to reunite their country. One day, de Gaulle predicted, a Russia in trouble might become willing to make major concessions to a united West Europe. Until that distant day, the status quo would remain, for France, the best of all possible worlds.

De Gaulle saw his task, therefore, as one of re-entering the Western dialogue with Russia, if he could steer it away from the German problem. He moved to repair Franco-Soviet contacts through a trade agreement, finally concluded in the fall of 1964. And he made an attempt, starting in July 1963, to bring about a disarmament conference of the four (later five) "nuclear powers" in Paris. But this proposal received an unfavorable response and de Gaulle, a few months later, was forced to shelve it temporarily—until Peking's October 1964 proposal for a worldwide summit, following Communist China's first atomic explosion, gave him an opportunity to dust it off again briefly.

Meanwhile, the French President in mid-1963 began to yield to the necessity of renewed contact with the United States. He had rejected Kennedy's proposal of a meeting in Paris during the President's European tour in June 1963—a tour designed, de Gaulle felt, to organize Europe against him. But Kennedy's continued efforts to arrange a meeting intensified the French and European pressure on de Gaulle to re-open discussions with Washington. De Gaulle responded initially by sending his Foreign Minister to see Kennedy in May and October 1963. And during the latter meeting, Couve de Murville let it be known that the General would cross the Atlantic for a "working visit" with Kennedy early in 1964.

On November 20, only two days before his death, Kennedy discussed the projected visit with French Ambassador Hervé Alphand. De Gaulle was prepared to spend a working weekend at Hyannisport in March, a time when he expected the first Mirage IV unit of his *force de frappe* to become operational. The only remaining detail to be settled was whether or not de Gaulle would rescind his refusal to spend an additional day in Washington, as Kennedy urged. Kennedy told Alphand he wanted to stage a parade "to prove to the General that he is the most popular and respected foreign dignitary in the United States."

It is impossible to predict now what would have happened if this meeting—the first between the two Presidents in almost three years—could have taken place. Kennedy certainly had no illusions that one meeting could resolve the fundamental French conflicts with the United States, Europe, or NATO. He suspected that de Gaulle preferred for his own reasons to maintain tension between Washington and Paris. And he felt sure, as he told visitors, that the General did not want "an intimate relationship" with the United States. But here was an obvious need, after such a long lapse, to resume personal contact. And a beginning might have been made toward restoring a working arrangement between the two countries.

In one area of disagreement, the swift pace of technology had created a political opportunity that Kennedy was preparing to exploit. The Atomic Energy Commission in 1963 had achieved a breakthrough in underground nuclear testing, the only kind still permitted by the treaty with Russia banning tests in the atmosphere, under water, and in outer space. The AEC earlier had been convinced that nothing substantially larger than the 20-kiloton Hiroshima bomb could be exploded subterraneously. But prodding from the White House led AEC technicians to drill and emplace their test bombs ever deeper into the earth. By the fall of 1963, it had become clear that thermonuclear blasts of about a megaton could be contained without surface eruption. By extrapoltation, the data could even serve to replace tests of H-bombs many times larger.

Kennedy planned, when he met de Gaulle, to offer this know-how to the General in return for French signature of the test ban treaty. Hints of this, meanwhile, were given to French officials. Such aid, it was evident, would save France the great expense and opprobrium involved in atmospheric testing of H-bombs in the Pacific. And it promised to eliminate a major source of contention not only between Paris and Washington, but between Paris and Moscow as well.

The assassination of President Kennedy interrupted this evolution in Franco-American relations. The French President came to Washington for the Kennedy funeral and a few hours later had his first brief meeting—and first misunderstanding—with President Johnson. The 22-minute talk gave Johnson the impression, which he then announced publicly to some thirty American Governors, that de Gaulle had reconfirmed his agreement to visit the United States early in 1964. Within forty-eight hours, de Gaulle let it be known officially that he too felt a "thorough examination" of Franco-American differences was essential in 1964. But he wanted Johnson to come to Paris for their first substantive talk—as had Presidents Eisenhower and Kennedy and all of Europe's important leaders, except Chancellor Adenauer. Adenauer's reluctance in 1958 led to a meeting half-way between Bonn and Paris, but still on French soil, at de Gaulle's country home.

Early in December 1963, Johnson sent de Gaulle a note thanking him for coming to the Kennedy funeral, and he added: "I look for more thorough conversations with you next year." But, at the same time, he indicated at a news conference that he could not leave the country before the 1964 elections. He made the same response in January 1964 when the French Ambassador, on instructions, suggested a compromise —a meeting "half-way," on the French Caribbean island of Martinique during de Gaulle's projected trip to Mexico in March.

As the 1964 election approached, Johnson planned a November or December trip to Paris and Europe, then delayed it to permit more careful preparations. Simultaneously, de Gaulle prepared for the confrontation by launching a two-front war-of-nerves against Bonn and Washington on agriculture and the multilateral nuclear force. He implied that the future of the Common Market, the Kennedy Round, the Franco-German Treaty, European political union, and French cooperation with NATO all depended on satisfactory settlement of these issues—thus broadening the impending negotiation with the United States and West Germany to the widest possible basis. Then, in December 1964, after Bonn yielded on a common European grain price, and Washington postponed its early deadlines for creation of an Atlantic nuclear force, Paris proposed scheduling talks for late 1965 on target coordination between its projected *force de frappe* and the U.S. Strategic Air Command.

When the U.S. and French Presidents finally do confer, it will be vital to avoid one pitfall—the illusion, widely held, that significant French cooperation can be obtained in exchange for U.S. nuclear assistance. Nuclear aid is something de Gaulle personally never has asked, although he has permitted his Ministers and General to do so. De Gaulle has hinted privately that he prefers France to build its own deterrent. He has assumed a "don't-tempt-me" posture by saying that if he were the American President, he would not offer nuclear aid to a French national force. The truth is that de Gaulle fears he might compromise his freedom in an American nuclear embrace. As a result, he is not prepared to concede much for U.S. aid, although he is under considerable pressure from his cabinet and the French military to seek it. That being so, it would hardly be wise for the United States to trade away this valuable American asset for a few meaningless gestures. A much broader negotiation is indicated. Far more, for example, might be achieved one day by authorizing British nuclear cooperation with France—something de Gaulle has sought and wants—under conditions that would protect the general Western interest. One such condition could be a requirement that any Anglo-French nuclear cooperation take the form of an integrated force—European or Atlantic—open to the non-nuclear NATO nations on a basis of equality and closely linked with American nuclear forces. Important French and British Conservative cabinet ministers discussed related ideas of Franco-British nuclear cooperation in 1962-63. The advantage of this approach is that it could both open the door for British entry into the Common Market and accelerate the political union of Europe. A lesser result would scarcely warrant rewarding de Gaulle with nuclear aid. But nuclear aid alone, in this writer's opinion, will not be enough to extract significant cooperation from the General.

In relations with the United States, de Gaulle's primary objective has always been, and remains, not nuclear assistance, but policy coordination that enhances French and European influence in the world. This was the condition for French cooperation with NATO laid down by de Gaulle in his September 1958 memorandum to Eisenhower and Macmillan; when his proposal for a tripartite U.S.-British-French directorate was evaded, he withdrew his Mediterranean Fleet from NATO and refused to permit nuclear stockpiles for U.S. fighter-bombers and missiles on French soil. Global policy coordination remains, in a somewhat different form, de Gaulle's objective today. The General retains his old idea of a tripartite U.S.-British-French "directorate" to undertake global decision-making for the Atlantic alliance, as his Foreign Minister twice confirmed publicly in 1964. But since 1962 he has felt that it could be brought about only by making the Europe of the Six under French leadership into a world power with which the United States would feel compelled to consult, if only to discourage independent policies running at cross-purposes to its own.

De Gaulle's recognition of Communist China, his proposals for a Vietnamese settlement, and many of his other "independent" moves in recent years originated, this writer believes, in a desire to show Washington that a France (and, later, a Europe) denied an equal voice in joint policymaking for the West could conduct a policy of its own—a policy that might make as unpalatable reading in Washington at times as U.S. policies often had made in Paris.

The General's immediate aim, as a result, is to "complete" the economic union of Europe—by extending it fully to agriculture—and to resume his efforts for a political-military "Union of States." As for the United States, his proposal is to "concert" policy and to "coordinate" nuclear strategy. It is not clear whether he still is determined to exclude Bonn from the "directorate" or whether he still insists, as in 1959-60, on a veto over U.S. use of nuclear weapons anywhere in the world. Only a prolonged negotiation of a kind that has yet to occur could discover his "fall-back" positions on these issues.

As 1964 opened the French President restated his chief objectives as follows:

> France, because she can do so, because she is France, should conduct amidst the world a world policy. . . . We must assist our Western Europe, from the time that it is united, in practicing with America a truly concerted political, economic, and strategic entente.

What Is To Be Done?

In a word, if the United States wants de Gaulle's cooperation, it will have to cater to the prestige of France—directly and through the person of its President. Some cooperation could be obtained cheaply that way. Prestige is important to the General. He considers it "the mainspring" of leadership; and leadership of Europe is one of his central aims. French leadership in Europe is something the United States could support again, as it did a decade ago, if it is a leadership of the first among equals, not a cover for domination, and if there is a clear understanding in advance as to where Europe will be led. Under these conditions, the West Germans would be prepared to go along. The new German leaders want friendship with France, their channel to unity with West Europe, as well as a close alliance with the United States, their military protector. They do not want to choose between Paris and Washington. On the contrary, it is in their interest to bring the United States and France together, and they would be prepared to do a great deal toward this end.

None of this means that Washington must surrender to Gaullist ambitions that run counter to the interests of the West as a whole. While Briain must come to terms with France before it can come to terms with Europe, the United States has broader options. What must be elaborated in a prolonged dialogue with de Gaulle—and with other Europeans—is a framework for a U.S. partnership with the new Europe, not with France alone. Important as de Gaulle may be in the European configuration, it would be as dangerous to focus too much on his role as it would be to think he can be ignored.

Relations with the General will never be easy. The French President carries old scars and suspicions from his wartime experience with Britain and the United States. His new attachment to Europe is as nationalistic as his continued attachment to France. Had it not been for de Gaulle's veto, it is likely that Britain would be in the Common Market now. Without a doubt, de Gaulle was and remains an obstacle to real federal union in Europe, to an integrated defense in NATO, and to a partnership of mutual confidence with the United States. But an obstacle is not the same as an immovable roadblock. We must not be misled by the understandable temptation to blame all the current difficulties on de Gaulle's obstruction. We must not overlook what the

United States and its friends in Europe failed to do in the past—and need to do in the future—to organize the West, whether or not de Gaulle is in office.

In my opinion, for example, de Gaulle for a time was prepared to accept British entry into the Common Market. Prior to November 1962, a French veto was politically impossible in any case, for it would have brought down de Gaulle's government and precipitated new elections in France under highly unfavorable circumstances. The veto became possible as a result of Britain's dilatory tactics, a surprise political upset in France, and disarray among the Five—particularly, the defection of Adenauer. Errors by Britain, the United States, and their friends in Europe contributed to that disarray and provided de Gaulle with added incentives, plus a pretext, for his destructive "Non!" in January 1963. At the end, a last-minute opportunity at Nassau to reverse de Gaulle's decision was missed by the United States and Britain.

Britain contributed to its own exclusion from the Common Market by its earlier resistance to economic, then political union of the Six and its later insistence on clinging to Commonwealth preferences, its EFTA allies, its special relationship with the United States, and its unique agricultural system.

The United States came late to its Grand Design and, prior to de Gaulle's January 1963 press conference, saw no need to act vigorously to implement it. Whether everything should have been hinged on British entry into the Common Market can be argued. But it certainly was unwise to leave the development of America's relations with a uniting Europe so completely and so long in the hands of the negotiators of another country.

What was chiefly lacking in Washington, prior to January 1963, was something de Gaulle once described as "that organic whole of continuous plans, matured decisions and measures carried to their conclusion, which we call a policy"—a policy to bring the Grand Design about. No lesson of the 1963 crisis was more important than that.

The Road Ahead

The setback to Atlantic partnership in January 1963 forced some hard thinking on both sides of the ocean. The results have not been unhopeful. Nor do prospects for the future warrant pessimism, despite the new conflict with de Gaulle over the projected Atlantic nuclear force that began building up in November 1964.

For one thing, disarray among the Common Market Five is largely a thing of the past. As early as the spring of 1963, the debate in the West German Bundestag on the Franco-German Treaty showed Adenauer isolated even while he was still Chancellor. Government and opposition parties united on a preamble that ruled out key Gaullist policies. It assured German backing for federal union in Europe, integration in NATO, liberal trade programs, and partnership with the United States. Since then, Adenauer's departure from office has deprived de Gaulle of his only important ally, despite the out-of-office efforts of the Adenauer-Strauss faction to advance the Gaullist view.

Looking a bit ahead, the Third Stage of the Common Market in January 1966 will bring qualified majority voting on agriculture, tariffs, and other subjects. It will deprive France of its veto in these fields. At about the same time, Presidential elections in France may begin to unfreeze the French political situation. The Gaullist UNR will need allies by then, if by some chance de Gaulle does not run; they will need them a year later, in any case, for Parliamentary elections. Concessions in foreign policy may result; the only possible allies are firm advocates of European federal union and Atlantic partnership. All favor an integrated, multilateral European deterrent—or an Atlantic deterrent without a U.S. veto—rather than a French national nuclear force. De Gaulle's own Prime Minister believes a European deterrent will be an ultimate necessity—and that it must be based on a Franco-British, not a Franco-German core. His Defense and Foreign Ministers already have paid lip service publicly to the European-deterrent idea.

The most hopeful signs since January 1963 have been those indicating that Washington finally was beginning to shape a policy for the West and was seeking ways to implement it. Whether or not it devised the best tactics at the start is a matter of lesser importance. Tactics always can change.

The direction American policy must continue to take was set forth clearly and unmistakably in Kennedy's Paulskirche speech in Frankfurt on June 25, 1963.

"We look forward," he said, "to a Europe united and strong . . . a world power capable of meeting world problems as a full and equal partner . . . a fully cohesive Europe that can protect us all against fragmentation of our alliance. With only such a Europe can we have a full give-and-take between equals, an equal sharing of responsibility and an equal level of sacrifice . . . the choice of the paths to the unity of Europe is a choice Europeans must take. But . . . you should know that this new European greatness will not be an object of fear, but a source of strength, for the United States of America."

Atlantic partnership, the President said, is "the future of the West. . . . It will be achieved by concrete steps to solve the problems that face us all: military, economic, and political. Partnership is not a posture but a process." He called for "common industrial and agricultural policies across the Atlantic . . . to give new impetus to growth." He proposed commodity-stabilization agreements and Atlantic monetary reform: "The great free nations of the world must take control of our monetary problems if these problems are not to take control of us."

The President hinted that the American veto need not be permanent in the proposed NATO multilateral nuclear force. "As Europe moves toward unity," he said, "its role and responsibility, here as elsewhere, would and must increase accordingly."

In negotiations with Russia, he said, "we will not bargain one nation's interest against another." And while speaking of a "sharing of power" with Europe, he restated the American military commitment to the old world in these terms: "The United States will risk its cities to defend your freedom because we need your freedom to protect ours."

This dramatic Kennedy speech was drafted in consultation with Jean Monnet, who came to Washington for the purpose. From it, as from the whole context of the Kennedy trip to Germany, there emerged clearly the revised Kennedy strategy that President Johnson now is pursuing in Europe. That strategy leaves the door open for a dialogue with de Gaulle. But it concentrates on "shaping the inevitable" for the French President. It is a strategy based on two fundamentals.

First, there has been the effort to restore a relationship of confidence with West Germany, an effort that Kennedy launched in June 1963 and that Johnson effectively continued in his December 1963 and June 1964 meetings with Chancellor Erhard. That effort has taken many forms. Close consultation with Bonn on East-West negotiations has replaced the unilateral American talks with Moscow that aroused deep suspicions in 1961-62. Reunification of Germany, largely ignored in U.S. statements in 1961-62, was again highlighted after January 1963 as a Western objective. An increased voice in the West's nuclear strategy was offered West Germany and other NATO allies through the project for an Atlantic nuclear force. In addition, German officers—along with British, French, and Italian officers—are participating in target planning at NATO's Supreme Headquarters near Paris and at the U.S. Strategic Air Command in Omaha. Finally, renewed assurances have been given on the American commitment to Germany's defense, including the use of nuclear weapons, if needed, and the continued presence of six American divisions. The last has been the essential foundation for all the rest. For nothing thrusts Germans more rapidly toward a Gaullist view of the world—or toward thoughts of a deal of their own with Russia—than fear of American "disengagement" from Europe.

Taken as a whole, this new policy toward Bonn has been aimed neither at a "special relationship" with Germany nor at blocking Franco-German reconciliation. Its objective has been to encourage West Germans to seek their future in an integrated European Community that includes France, yet follows a liberal trade policy and maintains close ties with the United States.

The second and more important element in the Kennedy-Johnson strategy has been a series of concrete programs for joint U.S.-European action on critical problems within the West and around the world. These projects, designed to link the two North Atlantic continents more closely as Europe unites, have included: (a) the plan for an Atlantic multilateral nuclear force, an attempt to meet Europe's desire for a nuclear role while avoiding proliferation of national deterrents to West Germany and other countries; (b) Atlantic monetary cooperation and plans for reform now being studied by the ten-nation Paris Group; (c) the proposal for world agricultural agreements to be negotiated during the Kennedy Round in Geneva; (d) the Kennedy Round itself, which will seek substantial tariff reductions on both shores of the Atlantic; (e) efforts to find new ways to help the new nations finance their development; and (f) the November 1964 Johnson proposal for closer policy coordination with Europe through more frequent, perhaps bimonthly, meetings of NATO Ministers or Deputy Ministers.

President Johnson made this strategy his own as soon as he took office. In his first address to the Congress on November 27, 1963, he dedicated himself to the new "American dream" of "partnership across the Atlantic." Three weeks later, in a message to NATO, he pledged "an ever-closer collaboration between a united Europe and the United States in dealing with all the great and burdensome tasks of building and defending a community of free nations." That pledge, he said, reflected America's awareness "that its security can be assured, its interests and values can be furthered only by a close partnership with Europe in common tasks . . . [in] defense . . . in monetary affairs, in aid to the developing areas, and in trade."

These Johnson views were not hastily acquired. Long before, in numerous speeches as Vice President, he had spelled out his commitment to this objective in greater detail. Many of these speeches were based on drafts prepared in the White House or State Department. But the phrasing showed that Johnson frequently was willing to go beyond established policy to meet some of the most difficult issues head on. Some of these speeches tell more about Johnson's receptiveness to change than his more cautious remarks during the long interregnum that preceded the November 1964 elections.

Just twelve days before becoming President, Johnson in Brussels described the multilateral nuclear force (MLF) as only "a first step" toward "a greater European voice in nuclear matters." He went well beyond Kennedy's remarks about a greater future "role and responsibility" for Europe in the MLF. Johnson made it clear that the American veto would become negotiable and he hinted that the MLF could be converted into a European deterrent, if that was what a united Europe later wanted. "Evolution of this missile fleet toward *European control,* as Europe marches toward unity, is by no means excluded," he said.

During the same trip to the Low Countries, Johnson addressed himself to the knottiest economic problem of Atlantic partnership—agriculture. In a November 7 speech in Amsterdam, he went beyond Kennedy's call for "common agricultural policies across the Atlantic." He indicated agreement with the European view that, to organize the West's agriculture coherently, it would be necessary to coordinate the internal farm programs of the United States and Europe. "If the negotiations involve, as they may, questions of domestic agricultural policy," Johnson said, "we are equally prepared to discuss our domestic policies."

These views reflected a philosophy Johnson had outlined long before, most clearly in a Paris speech on April 16, 1961. That speech foreshadowed Kennedy's Grand Design. It went even further, for it spoke not only of common policies, but of "common institutions" in the Atlantic area. Said Johnson:

> No single nation has enough influence and power to maintain this spacious environment of freedom. The coalition of the peoples and nations of Western Europe and North America is indispensable to this end. . . .
>
> To the United States it is of prime importance to maintain and strengthen the coalition, both for its cohesion and power within the Atlantic area and its capacity for constructive action outside that area. If that cohesion and capacity are to be enhanced, vigorous measures will be required in the political, military and economic fields. . . .
>
> Progress toward an integrated European community will help to enhance that capacity and thus to strengthen the Atlantic Community. . . . The essentially national and loosely coordinated efforts of the past will no longer suffice.
>
> Our end goal . . . should be a true Atlantic Community in which *common institutions will increasingly be developed* to meet common problems. . . .
>
> In progressing toward such a community we can regain the sense of forward movement and imaginative thinking which has characterized the Alliance in its most creative periods.

The challenge that faces the Johnson of 1965 is precisely the one defined by the Johnson of 1961. Its essence, as Dean Acheson put it, is "to get the Atlantic Community moving again." That can best be done by joint European-American action on concrete programs in the economic and military fields. Such programs will get nowhere through "the essentially national and loosely coordinated" methods employed in the past. New, *ad hoc* institutions are needed to bring the United States, the Common Market, and Britain together for joint decisions and measures to implement them. Such institutions will achieve nothing if they are merely a cloak for American dominance, or if they lack genuine decision-making power. Europeans will assume the burdens of responsibility only to the degree that the exercise of power is shared. It is this element in American proposals for Atlantic partnership that will be scrutinized most closely in Europe. This would be so in any circumstances; but it is even more the case at a time when de Gaulle is active in spreading to others his own mistrust of U.S. intentions. Sincere American proposals will need to be explained and defended repeatedly to survive the pinpricks of Gaullist suspicion. Any false currency will be quickly exposed.

If, for example, the United States is ever to satisfy the desire of Europeans for a meaningful voice in nuclear defense, it will have to go considerably further than it did in 1963-64 in the discussions of an Atlantic nuclear force that, as projected, would be subject—at least initially—to an American veto. The United States ultimately will have to accept some variant of the proposal, made by Britain and West Germany as well as France, for a small allied political-strategic "directorate" that could participate in contingency planning and crisis management—giving major allies, in effect, a "seat" on the U.S. National Security Council.

If economic expansion is not to be hobbled by monetary instability, the Common Market and Britain must be won to a joint effort with the United States. Atlantic monetary cooperation is essential not only to protect the dollar and to head off the world "liquidity" problem of the future, but to lay a sound basis for intensified Atlantic cooperation across the whole spectrum of economic problems facing the West. The chief reform needed is one that gives the moneys of the Common Market countries a major reserve-currency role, thus lightening the load on the dollar and the pound. Achieving this will require some sacrifice of American monetary dominance and an increased voice for Europe in managing the currency of the West.

If development of the new nations is to be financed adequately, Europe's cooperation must be enlisted for a new approach. Grants and loans are pushing up against budget ceilings in all the donor countries. The need now is for trade to supplement aid by helping the world's poor nations finance their own industrialization out of increased export earnings. The Common Market is the world's biggest importer. Its cooperation is essential if, for example, world commodity prices are to be stabilized at a level that provides the raw-materials-exporting countries with a fair return on their labor. Only the United States and Europe, working together as the world's chief importers and raw-materials consumers, can accomplish this. The Common Market countries, including France, have expressed support for the idea, just as did the Kennedy Administration. The time has come for

President Johnson to fit these words to action. Successful action will require moving in the direction of joint U.S.-European boards with limited but real powers to work out price, output and trade arrangements with the producing countries. Only in this way can we avoid a class war between rich and poor nations which, in this century could prove just as disastrous as was the failure of Europe's Governments in the last century to come to grips in time with their own domestic class conflicts.

If the "Kennedy Round" of tariff and trade liberalization is to be successful in the agricultural field, it must go far beyond the policies epitomized by Secretary Freeman's "chicken war" and his futile drive to maintain U.S. farm exports to Europe at past levels. The U.S. effort in Geneva in 1965 will have to focus on the attempt that will be made, starting with grain, to solve the surplus problem through world agreements—a proposal that France originated and still supports. Effective agreements would require readiness by the United States and other countries to accept some degree of international control over farm prices, subsidies, production management, exports, and surplus disposal. If the main importing and exporting countries—the United States, the Common Market, Britain and the Commonwealth—can create joint decision-making machinery for these purposes, Atlantic partnership would begin to mean something. And the piling up of surplus stocks, while most of the world goes hungry, could be ended.

Joint enterprises of this kind can create a durable U.S.-European partnership only if power, sovereignty, and burdens are shared. And, in fact, there is no real alternative. Whatever may be thought by some of the Goldwater faction in America and some of the Gaullist faction in Europe, neither contingent any longer can "go it alone" in the world.

The cold war can be eased by persistent negotiation, as the test ban accord has shown. But the challenge of the East—whether primarily Russian, Chinese, or Sino-Soviet—is sure to continue. That challenge hinges on faith in the inevitability of a Communist world and determination to bring that Communist world about. There will be no stable peace until that faith and that determination are shaken. They can be shaken only by Western unity. It must be demonstrated that the non-Communist world can solve its political, military, economic, and social problems, that the United States and a uniting Europe are moving to construct a society that is as dynamic as it is viable.

Neither the United States nor Europe can solve the West's critical problems alone. The Common Market, despite its current difficulties, makes it possible for the United States and a revived Europe, which ultimately must include Britain, to undertake a joint approach. The uniting of Europe thus continues to be in the American interest even if it involves, as it must, some discrimination against American trade and the creation of another major center of economic, political—and, ultimately perhaps, military—power in the West, requiring major adjustments in American policy-making processes. The United States must remain in the future, as in the past, the catalyst in bringing about Europe's unity. At the same time, common U.S.-European programs must be shaped and given institutional form without awaiting the entry of Britain into the Common Market. If an Atlantic partnership gradually is to be constructed, Washington must take the initiative. In doing so, it will have to face the fact that partnership, by definition, can be achieved only if power is shared.

It is no longer possible to preach supranational principles to Europe and to practice national decision-making in the United States. The day is past when Washington can urge European nations to integrate, yet insist on complete freedom of action for itself. A "ferment of change" has been introduced into the world by the resurgence of Europe and the new method devised there to unite nations for common action. It may be a long time before Americans are prepared to go as far as Europeans in sharing sovereignty, but the first steps must now be taken on a problem-by-problem basis to adapt the European method to the Atlantic basin.

In nuclear matters, NATO strategy, arms control, monetary affairs, agriculture, aid to the developing nations, and in other fields, American initiatives can spur the concept of joint U.S.-European efforts. But the key to success lies in a progressive sharing of decision-making power along with the financial burdens of free-world responsibility.

As Europeans are won to such proposals, de Gaulle either will go along or face isolation, something he dislikes intensely. In either case, the way will have been prepared for the Atlantic partnership that must follow—and might even precede—de Gaulle's departure from the public scene.

NOTES ON CONTRIBUTORS

MAURICE ALLAIS is Professor of Economics at the Ecole Nationale Supérieure des Mines and at the Institut de Statistique de l'Université de Paris. He is also Research Director at the Centre National de la Recherche Scientifique. Author of the prize-winning *Traité D'Economie Pure* (1952) and *Evaluation des Perspectives Economiques de la Recherche Minière sur des Grands Espaces—Application au Sahara Algérien* (1957), his more recent publications include: *L'Europe Unie, Route de la Prosperité* (1960), *Les Aspects Essentiels de la Politique de l'Energie* and *Le Tiers-Monde au Carrefour—Centralisation Autoritaire ou Planification Concurrentielle* (1962).

GEORGE W. BALL, Under Secretary of State since 1961, and a distinguished lawyer by profession, has served in the past as Associate General Counsel to the Lend-Lease Administration and later the Foreign Economic Association (1942-44); Director of the U.S. Strategic Bombing Survey, London (1944-45); General Counsel to the French Supply Council, Washington, D.C. (1945-46); and Under Secretary of State for Economic Affairs (1961).

ANDRÉ BEAUFRE, Général, French Army (Retired), is Director of the Institut Français d'Etudes Stratégiques, Paris. Formerly Deputy Chief of Staff at SHAPE for Logistics and Administration, he was Chief of the French delegation to the NATO Standing Group, 1960-61. He is the author of *Introduction à la Stratégie* (2nd ed., 1964) and *Dissuasion et Stratégie* (1964).

KURT BIRRENBACH is a Member of the Foreign Affairs Committee of the Bundestag of the German Federal Republic and Chairman of the August Thyssen Hütte Aktiengesellschaft, Duisburg-Hamborn and of the Thyssen Aktiengesellschaft für Beteiligungen, Düsseldorf. An active supporter of European integration and Atlantic unity, he is chairman of the Policy Committee of the Atlantic Institute, Paris; Vice-President of the Europe-Union, Bonn; and a member of the Committee for the United States of Europe. He is author of *The Future of the Atlantic Community* (1963).

KARL BRANDT is Director of the Food Research Institute and Professor of Economic Policy, Stanford University. A former member of the President's Council of Economic Advisors (1958-61), he is the author of *The Reconstruction of World Agriculture* (1945), a co-author of *Management of Agriculture and Food in German-Occupied and Other Areas of Fortress Europe: A Study in Military Government* (1953); and a contributor to *National Security: Political, Military, and Economic Strategies in the Decade Ahead* (1963).

HENRY W. BRIEFS, co-editor of the present volume, is Associate Professor of Economics, Director of the Graduate Program in Public Policy Economics, and Research Principal at The Center for Strategic Studies, Georgetown University. Formerly Senior Staff Economist of the Council of Economic Advisors, he is author of *Three Views of Method in Economics* (1960), *Pricing Power and "Administrative" Inflation* (1962), and a contributor to *National Security: Political, Military, and Economic Strategies in the Decade Ahead* (1963).

HENDRIK BRUGMANS is Rector of the College of Europe, Bruges, Belgium. A pre-war member of the Belgian Parliament and then active in the wartime resistance movement, he was an early supporter of the postwar movement for European unity and is presently President of the Comité Fédéral de l'Action Européene Fédéraliste. He is the author of *Historie de l'Europe,* Vol. I: *Les Origines de la Civilisation européenne* (1958); *Vol. II: L'Europe prend le large* (1961), and co-author of *Le Fédéralisme contemporain: Critères, institutions, perspectives.*

W. RANDOLPH BURGESS is Vice Chairman of the Atlantic Treaty Association and Chairman of the Per Jacobsson Foundation. A former Under Secretary of the Treasury, he was U.S. Ambassador to NATO and U.S. Representative to the Organization for European Economic Cooperation, 1957-1961. In 1960, he was Chairman of the "Groupe de Quatre" whose planning for a reorganized OEEC led to the Organization for European Cooperation and Development. He is the author of *Reserve Banks and the Money Market* (1927; rev. eds., 1936, 1946): editor of *Reserve Policy in the Speeches and Writings of Benjamin Strong* (1930); and co-author of *Our National Debt* (1950).

KARL H. CERNY, co-editor of the present volume, is Associate Professor of Government, and Research Principal at The Center for Strategic Studies, Georgetown University. During 1958-59 he was Fulbright Professor of Political Science at the University of Nijmegen, The Netherlands. He has contributed to *Soviet Total War* (1956) and to *America* magazine and is currently working on a text in comparative government.

MILORAD DRACHKOVITCH is a Senior Staff Member of the Hoover Institution on War, Revolution, and Peace, and Lecturer in the Department of Political Science, Stanford University. He is the author of *Les Socialismes Français et Allemand et le Problème de la Guerre, 1870-1914* (1953), *De Karl Marx à Leon Blum: La Crise de la Social-Démocratie* (1954), and *United States Aid to Yugoslavia and Poland: Analysis of a Controversy* (1963). Presently he is engaged in a joint project on the history of the Third International.

JOHN W. HOLMES is President of the Canadian Institute of International Affairs. Formerly he was a member of the directing staff of the National Defense College, Kingston, Ontario (1951-53) and Assistant Under Secretary of State for External Affairs (1953-60). In recent years he has contributed to *Foreign Affairs* and other scholarly journals.

HENRY A. KISSINGER is Professor of Government, faculty member of the Center for International Affairs, and Director of the Defense Studies Program, Harvard University. He is also Director of the Harvard International Seminar. He is the author of *A World Restored: Castlereaugh, Metternich, and the Restoration of Peace, 1812-1822* (1957), *Nuclear Weapons and Foreign Policy* (1957), and *The Necessity for Choice: Prospects of American Foreign Policy* (1961).

ROBERT KLEIMAN is presently a member of the Editorial Board of *The New York Times*. A correspondent in Europe for more than fifteen years, he served as Paris Bureau Chief of the Columbia Broadcasting System and previously as Western European Editor and Paris Bureau Chief of *U.S. News & World Report*. He is the author of *Atlantic Crisis: American Diplomacy Confronts a Resurgent Europe* (1964).

KLAUS KNORR is Professor of Economics and Director of The Center of International Studies, Princeton University. He is the author of *British Colonial Theories* (1944), *The War Potential of Nations* (1956), *NATO and American Security* (1959), and co-editor of *The International System* (1961) and *Limited Strategic War* (1962).

LAWRENCE B. KRAUSE is a Senior Staff member, The Brookings Institution. A former consultant to the State Department and Special U.S. Representative for Trade Negotiations, he is the co-author of Report on the *New England Textile Industry, 1952* (1953), *The United States Balance of Payments in 1968* (1963) and editor of *The Common Market: Progress and Controversy* (1964).

JAMES E. MOORE, General, U.S. Army (Retired), is presently a consultant to the Research Analysis Corporation. A former Chief of Staff, SHAPE (1952-1963), he served as Deputy Chief of Staff for Military Operations, High Commissioner of the Ryukyu Islands, and Commandant of the Army War College.

HANS J. MORGENTHAU is Albert A. Michelson Distinguished Service Professor of Political Science and Modern History and Director of the Center for the Study of American Foreign and Military Policy, University of Chicago. A consultant to the Department of State and Department of Defense, he is the author of *Scientific Man vs. Power Politics* (1946), Politics Among Nations (1948, 1954, 1960), *In Defense of the National Interest* (1951), *Dilemmas of Politics* (1958), *The Purpose of American Politics* (1960), and *Politics in the 20th Century* (1962).

PHILIP E. MOSELY is Professor of International Relations and Director of the European Institute, Columbia University. He is also Associate Dean of the Faculty of International Affairs in charge of research. A former officer of the United States Department of State and Director of Studies at the Council on Foreign Relations, New York, he is the author of *Russian Diplomacy and the Opening of the Eastern Question in 1838 and 1839* (1934) and *The Kremlin and World Politics* (1960), and editor of *The Soviet Union, 1922-1962: A Foreign Affairs Reader* (1963).

STEFAN T. POSSONY is Director of the International Political Studies Program at the Hoover Institution on War, Revolution, and Peace, and is a Research Associate at the Foreign Policy Research Institute. Formerly Special Advisor to the United States Air Force, he is the author of *Tomorrow's War* (1938), *Strategic Air Power* (1949), *A Century of Conflict: Communist Techniques of World Revolution, 1848-1950* (1953), *Lenin, the Compulsive Revolutionary* (1964), and co-author of *The Geography of Intellect* (1963).

FRIEDRICH RUGE, Vice-Admiral, Federal German Navy (Retired), is presently at the University of Tübingen. Former Chief of the German Navy, he is the author of *Entscheidung im Pazifik* (1951), *Der Seekrieg 1939-1945* (1954), *Seemacht und Sicherheit* (1955), *Rommel und die Invasion* (1959), and *Politik, Militär, Bündnis* (1963).

SIR JOHN COTESWORTH SLESSOR is Marshal of the Royal Air Force and Vice President, Institute for Strategic Studies, London. A former Commandant of the Imperial Defense College and Chief of the Air Staff, he is the author of *Air Power and Armies* (1936), *Strategy for the West* (1954), *The Central Blue* (1956), *The Great Deterrent* (1957), and *What Price Co-existence?* (1962).

ROBERT STRAUSZ-HUPÉ is Professor of Political Science and Director of the Foreign Policy Research Institute, University of Pennsylvania. Executive Editor of *Orbis,* he is the author of *Geopolitics* (1940), *Balance of Tomorrow* (1945), *Zone of Indifference* (1952), and co-author of *Protracted Conflict* (1958), *Forward Strategy for America* (1961), and *Building the Atlantic World* (1963).

PIERRE URI is Director of Studies, Atlantic Institute, Paris, and chairman of the Experts' Group on Long Term Development in the European Economic Community. Formerly Economic Director of the European Coal and Steel Community, he is the author of Report of the French Delegation on the Treaty of Paris Instituting the Coal and Steel Community (1951), Report of the Inter-Governmental Committee on the Common Market and Euratom (1956), Report on the Economic Situation of the European Community Countries (1958), *Dialogue des Continents* (1963), and *Partnership for Progress: A Program for Transatlantic Action* (1963).

STANISLAW WASOWSKI is Associate Professor of Economics, Georgetown University. Since October 1964 he has been on leave of absence to serve as economist in the Economic and Political Studies Division, Institute for Defense Analyses. He is the author of *The Impact of the Common Market on the American Economy* (1962) and has in preparation *International Commodity Arrangements: The Long Term Aspect* (to be published in 1965).

INDEX

— A —

Abshire, David, ix
Acheson, Dean, 17, 63, 431-32, 437, 457
Action Committee for a United States of Europe, 435, 438
Adenauer, Konrad, 146, 186, 431, 446-47, 450, 453-54
Advisory Committee on Economics to the Committee on International Economic Policy, 340
Africa, 44, 87, 125, 142, 301, 333, 361-62, 383, 389, 399, 406, 422; East, 395; West, 395
Afro-American bloc, 301
Agricultural production, 71, 180, 311, 313, 324; policy, 314, 323-24, 338-42, 349, 353, 355, 445; subsidies, 313, 341-42, 347, 354
Alaska, 295
Albania, 410, 418, 422, 484
Alexeyev, A., 418
Algeria, 139, 142, 293, 366, 368, 377, 391, 395
Allais, Maurice, 43, 66, 73, 76-79, 106, 111, 114, 116, 120, 359, 361, 365, 367-68, 463
Allen, Richard V., ix
Alliances, classical, 11-12, 24, 126, 128, 131, 368-69
Alphand, Hervé, 448-49
Amsterdam, Holland, 457
Arab League, 137
Arkansas, 367
Arms control (*See* disarmament, Nuclear Test Ban Treaty)
Aron, Raymond, 392
Asia, 29, 44, 87, 142-43, 261, 301, 361-62, 389, 399, 406, 422
Associated Press, 18
Atlantic Community (union, world), 51, 68, 114, 131-32, 290, 292, 294. 300-02, 310, 322-25, 331-32, 346-47, 359-60, 368-69, 371-81, 383-86, 405, 407, 436, 443, 457, 460; Atlantic federation, 51, 107, 111, 295, 297, 397; Atlantic partnership, xi-xiii, 9, 12, 30, 35, 45, 51, 67, 100, 111, 114-19, 122, 129, 133, 143, 158-59, 179-83, 186, 197, 319, 346, 349, 355, 395, 397-98, 403, 433-38, 441, 453-54, 456-60
Atlantic Convention of NATO countries (Paris, January 8-20, 1962), 359
Atlantic Institute (Paris), 402
Atlantic Parliamentary Assembly, 384
Atom bomb, 449
Atomic Energy Act, 171, 192, 200, 447
Atomic Energy Commission, 449
Australia, 111, 294, 301, 303, 341
Austria, 266, 307-08, 333

— B —

Balance of payments, 7, 66, 77, 315, 317, 335, 337, 343, 355, 382; U.S., 74, 279, 315-18, 336-37, 382-83, 432
Balance of power (balance of terror), 26, 126, 136, 150, 156, 220, 227, 388
Balkan federation, 411
Ball, George, W. 44-45, 47-48, 50, 53-54, 58, 100, 106, 283, 442, 461
Bamboo Curtain, 387, 398
Barnett, Ross, 390
Baruch plan, 200, 202
Basic Values of the Atlantic Community, 393
Baumgartner, Wilfred, 440
Bay of Pigs, 292
Beaufre, André, 37-39, 43-45, 48, 62, 107, 207, 215, 461
Belgium, 83, 142, 189, 241, 306, 316, 377
Belgrade, Yugoslavia, 402, 424
Beloff, Max, 306
Benelux, 179, 333, 424-25
Berger, Wolfgang, 417
Berlin, Germany, 24, 41, 52, 86, 89, 108, 125, 171, 178, 195, 205, 223, 248, 284, 292, 329, 377, 388-89, 392, 406-07, 446-47
Berliner, Joseph, 412
Bieri, Ernest, 393
Birrenbach, Kurt, 26, 271, 462
Bismarck, Otto von, 11

Blum, Leon, 394
Board of Economic Warfare, 8, 96
Bonaparte, Napoleon, 11
Bonn, Germany, 234, 298, 446-48, 450-51, 455
Bowie, Robert R., 284
Brandt, Karl, 66, 69, 72, 80, 90, 93, 118, 120, 327, 341-42, 462
Brazzaville Conference (1942), 391
Briefs, Henry W., 3-10, 65, 77, 82, 462
British nuclear policy, 204-05, 309-10; foreign policy, 294
Brookings Institution, 352
Brown, J. F., 419
Brugmans, Hendrik, 51, 57-58, 80, 83, 85, 89, 93, 106-07, 112, 116, 120, 387, 393, 462
Brussels, Belgium, 286, 288, 310, 338, 456
Brzezinski, Zbigniew, 421, 423, 428
Bucharest, Rumania, 420
Budapest, Hungary, 424
Bulgaria, 411-13, 415, 417, 419, 426
Bundy, McGeorge, 283, 437
"Burden sharing" in Western alliance, 18, 158; aid, 58, 317, 438; defense, 307; nuclear technology, 443-44; weapons production, 58, 331-32
Burgess, W. Randolph, 25, 44-45, 47-48, 73, 82, 177, 462
Burke, Arleigh, 168
Byelorussia, 136
Byrnes, Robert F., 412

— C —

Cairo, Egypt, 295
California, 367
Canada, 96, 104, 108, 111, 120-21, 185, 293, 296, 301, 316, 325, 328-29, 333, 341, 346, 349, 381, 440
Captive nations (*See* East European satellites)
Carnegie Endowment for International Peace, 340
Castro, Fidel, 299, 394
Castroism, 293
Center for Strategic Studies, vii, 85
Central Region, 173-76
Cerny, Karl H., 3-10, 23, 30, 37, 44, 99, 106, 463
Chamberlain, Neville, 424
Chatham House, 388
"Chicken war," 313-14, 459
China, Communist, 28, 85, 89, 112, 119, 125, 203, 246, 253, 261-62, 290, 293, 303-04, 343, 361, 363, 366, 395-96, 398, 414-15, 418, 422, 429-30, 448, 451, 459
China, Nationalist, 304
Chou En-lai, 293
Churchill, Winston S., 204, 242, 250
Christian Democratic Party (Germany), 446
Civil War, U.S., 121
Clemenceau, George, 13
Cominform, 411
Comintern, 422
Committee on Foreign Relations, 327
Commodity agreements, 72, 308, 340, 342
Common Agricultural Policy, 314
Common Market (*See* European Economic Community)
Common Market Treaty, 375
Commonwealth, 109, 294, 308-09, 348, 359
Communist bloc, 8, 82-85, 116, 138, 140, 275, 285, 297, 318, 329, 388, 402, 405-30
Communist strengths, 360, 389-90
Communist weaknesses, 365-66, 389-90
Comparative advantage, 341
Concord, 322
Conference on Trade and Development, 341
Congo, 103, 116, 178, 286, 292, 294, 317, 366, 377
Connecticut, 367
Conservative Party (Great Britain), 63, 155, 310, 446, 451
Constantinople, 386
Consultation, 5-6, 9, 16-17, 19, 48-49, 52, 55-56, 59, 94, 107, 116-17, 193-94, 197, 220, 230, 276, 278, 281, 287, 302, 419
Consumer Report, 325
Conventional forces, 27-28, 35, 41-42, 55, 61, 91, 102, 150, 169, 171-74, 176, 203-04, 208, 211, 218-19, 306, 328, 437
Coppock, John O., 324
Corn Laws, 323-24

Council of Ministers, 295
Council of Mutual Economic Aid, 1949 (COMECON), 86, 119, 411, 415-16, 418, 420, 424
Couve de Murville, Maurice, 407, 425, 448
Cuba, 24, 85, 92-93, 96, 111, 125, 155, 171, 196, 208, 211-12, 244-45, 247, 250, 286, 290, 292, 303, 317, 366, 377, 389, 392-94, 398, 422
Cuban Crisis, x, 29, 102, 260, 297-99, 369
Cultural exchange, 329, 377, 384-85, 400
Current Digest of the Soviet Press, 416
Cyprus, 3, 4, 106, 109, 116, 125, 142, 195, 291, 294, 304, 366, 368, 378
Czechoslovakia, 137, 244, 343, 412-13, 415, 417, 419-20, 426

— D —

DM, 325
Dakar, French West Africa, 301
Daladier, Edouard, 137
Danube—Black Sea Canal Project, 412
Davis, Joseph, 340
Decision-making, 51, 58, 60, 68, 112, 132, 181, 188, 235, 255, 284, 293, 441, 460
Declaration of the Atlantic Convention of 100 Citizens of NATO (Paris, January 20, 1962), 384
Declaration of Independence, 346
Delaware, 367
Delhi, India, 301
Denmark, 307
Department of Agriculture, 341
Department of Commerce, 333
Department of State, 342, 456
Détente, 53, 104, 143, 388, 408
Deterrence (*See* nuclear deterrence)
Devaluation, 76, 334, 337, 348, 382
Developing areas (*See* underdeveloped areas, Third World)
Dewhurst, J. Frederic, 324
Dia, Mamadou, 362
Dillon, Douglas, 438
Dillon Round, 313
Dimitrov, 411
Disarmament, 156, 195, 245 (*See also* Nuclear Test Ban Treaty)
Djilas, Milovan, 414, 427
Dougherty, James E., 406
Drachkovitch, Milorad, 83, 85, 393, 405, 410, 463
Dulles, John Foster, 104, 275

— E —

East European satellites, 48, 84, 87, 94, 96, 361, 388, 399, 405-30
East Germany, 92-93, 97, 116, 139, 317, 410, 413, 415, 417, 420, 448, 457-58
East-West nonaggression treaty, 424
East-West trade, 8, 65, 82, 86, 88, 313-14, 318, 329, 339, 341-42
Economic and Social Council of the U.N., 340
Economic growth, 67, 302, 304-05, 307-08, 310, 317, 336-37, 355, 364-65
Economic integration, Atlantic, 84, 302, 346, 373; East European, 374-76, 413, 416-20; West European, 34, 265, 303-11, 398, 422, 455
Economic protectionism, 65, 120, 302, 313, 321, 323-25, 341-42, 347, 353-54
The Economist, 129, 131, 325
Eden, Sir Anthony, 184, 241, 293
Eisenhower, Dwight D., vi, 105, 184, 186, 190, 245, 435, 437, 439, 450
Elbe River, 405, 409
Erhard, Chancellor Ludwig, 97, 375, 445-46, 455
Escalation, 62, 150
European Coal and Steel Community (ECSC), 84, 306, 313, 375, 378
European Congress at the Hague, 179, 376
European Defense Community, 118, 180, 306, 397
European defense policy constraints, 158
European defense expenditures, 185, 191, 332, 345, 379
European Economic Community (EEC,), 67, 70, 72, 83-84, 86, 112-13, 117-18, 120, 144, 178, 182, 283, 288, 295, 305-14, 318, 323-25, 336-37, 341-42, 346-55, 369, 373-76, 381-84, 386, 395, 400, 407, 410, 421-24, 431-46, 450-54, 457-60

European Free Trade Association (EFTA), 68, 308-09, 311, 325, 333, 336, 341, 382, 453
European nuclear forces (deterrent), 217, 264, 284, 435, 446, 450-51, 454
European Parliamentarianism, 403
European political unification, vii, 27, 29, 34, 39-40, 45, 47, 53, 64, 87, 110, 210, 283, 285, 306-08, 346-47, 370, 434, 443-44, 450-51
Exchange rates, 66, 315, 334-35, 337, 353, 382

— F —

Far East, v, 430
Der Faschismus in seiner Epoche, 392
Federalism, European, 107, 179-80, 396, 402, 434, 445-46, 451-52
Finland, 309
Finletter, Thomas K., 62
Firestone Company, 394
First Socialist International, 328
First-strike force, 36, 218, 221, 281
Fiske, John, 179
Florida, 295
Floyd, David, 414
Foch, Marshal, 13, 49
Food Research Institute, 340
Force de frappe (*force de dissuasion*), 152-53, 166, 203, 246, 248, 252, 448, 450
Foreign Assistance Act, 339
Foreign investment, 316-17, 335, 343-44
Formosa, 388
Forsyth, Murray, 403
France, 3, 6, 13, 26, 30-34, 39-41, 45, 54, 66, 69, 104, 125, 128-29, 131, 136-37, 142, 144, 146, 149, 151-55, 157, 159-60, 162, 164, 166, 169-71, 178, 187, 203, 205, 208-09, 225, 240, 243, 251, 262, 268, 273, 285-86, 292-93, 297, 301, 306-07, 310, 312-13, 316, 322-23, 333-34, 346, 356, 365-66, 360-70, 377, 394, 398, 407-09, 422-23, 425, 433-34, 443, 446-55, 458
Franco, General, 85, 426
Franco-German Treaty, 450, 453
Frankfurt, Germany, 454
Free enterprise, 313, 331, 338, 356
Free trade, 71-72, 78, 311, 341-43, 366, 373, 382, 441-42; agricultural commodities, 72, 308
Free Trade Area Plan of London, 441-42
Freeman, Orville, 459
French Affairs, 408
French National Assembly, 407
French nuclear policy, 38, 43, 205, 447-51, 454; foreign policy, 292, 300, 307, 425-28, 451-54
French revolution, 389
Friedman, Milton, 382
Friendship Pipeline, 420
Fulbright, J. William, 290

— G —

Gaillard, Pierre, 186
Galati Steel Works, 419
Gamarnikow, Michael, 418
de Gara, John P., 400
de Gasperi, Alcide, 125
de Gaulle, Charles, 24, 26, 30-31, 39, 43, 50, 53, 60, 62-63, 82, 100, 108-09, 127, 132-33, 141-42, 151, 155, 158, 178, 180, 183-84, 189, 192, 209, 219-20, 247-48, 259, 267, 292, 307, 309-11, 315, 347, 369-70, 391, 398, 401, 407-09, 423-25, 428, 431-37, 445-53, 458, 460
Gaullism, 292, 395
General Agreement on Tariffs and Trade (GATT), 67, 311-12, 314, 337, 343
General Electric, 322
Geneva, 7, 67-70, 72, 206, 295, 322, 337, 340, 383-84, 456, 459
Geneva truces, 293
German nuclear policy, 205
German reunification, 93, 139, 306, 409, 448, 455
Germany, 26, 32, 33, 42, 64, 69, 104, 134, 138-39, 154
Gheorghiu-Dej, Gheorghe, 418
Giffin, S. F., 429
Gold, price of, 66, 76; reserves, 76, 315, 335-36, 382, 434
Goldman, Marshall I., 417
Goldwater, Barry, 459
Gomulka, Wladislaw, 414, 426

Great Britain, (*See also* United Kingdom, London), 6, 13, 31-34, 37, 39-40, 54, 61, 63, 70, 74, 103, 125, 128, 131, 141, 146, 149, 152, 154, 157, 159, 164, 166, 170-71, 180, 196, 200, 203-05, 208-09, 221, 240, 243, 251, 267-68, 273, 284-85, 288, 293-94, 297, 301, 307-10, 313, 322-23, 325, 340-41, 346-48, 350, 354-64, 366, 369-70, 376, 383, 394-95, 398, 406, 408, 431-47, 450-53, 457-60
Great Depression, 316, 340
Greece, 54, 125, 141, 178, 195, 201, 226, 333
Griffith, William, 422
Group of Ten, 316
Grove, David L., 336
Growth rate (*See* economic growth)
Guerrilla warfare, 328
Gumpel, Werner, 420

— H —

"Haddock," Operation, 243, 248
Hallstein, Walter, 319, 436, 443
Hamilton, Alexander, 50
Havana, 295
Herter, Christian, 384
Hickenlooper Amendment, 339
Hinterhoff, Eugene, 406
Hitler, Adolf, 140, 433
Hoffer, Eric, 429
Holland, 442
Holmes, John W., 82, 106-07, 110-11, 114, 120-21, 289, 463
Holzman, Franklyn D., 420
Hoxha, Enver, 422
Hungary, 411-15, 417, 419-20
Hungarian revolt, 366-67, 399, 414
Hyannisport, Massachusetts, 448
Hydrogen bomb, 447, 449

— I —

Iceland, 141, 333
Independent nuclear deterrents (*See* national nuclear deterrents)
India, 348, 362-63, 396
Indochina, 293, 392
Indonesia, 395
Indrapura Valley, 392
Infant industry argument, 79
Inflation, 7, 66, 69, 73, 119, 316-17, 334-35, 353, 355, 382
Institutional reforms, NATO, 106, 280, 375-76, 384
Intercontinental Ballistic Missiles (ICBM), 166, 168, 328
Interdiction, 251
International Access Authority to Berlin, 407
International Bank for Reconstruction and Development, 75, 82, 343
International Bank of Economic Cooperation, 420
International commodity agreements (*See* commodity agreements)
International Labor Office, 340
International liquidity, 7, 74-76, 316, 337, 382, 441, 458
International Monetary Fund, 75, 82, 95, 315-16, 324, 337, 339-40
International Tariff Organization, 340-41
Ireland, 294
Iron Curtain, 387, 398, 425
Isolationism, 101, 131-32, 154, 302, 356
Italy, 54, 69, 100, 137, 149, 159, 166, 188-89, 211, 306, 316, 333, 346, 356, 370, 422, 425
Izvestia, 423

— J —

Jamaica, 301
Japan, 89, 112, 136, 140, 301, 303, 316, 349, 356
Jaster, Robert S., 418
Jerusalem, 393
Johnson, Lyndon B., vii, 18, 105, 390, 445, 447, 449, 455-57, 459
Joint Economic Committee of U.S. Congress, 14, 313, 382
de Jouvenel, Bertrand, 388, 396

— K —

Kasai, 389
Kawalkowski, Alexander, 409-10
Keith BBC lectures (1957), 420
Kennan, George F., 420-21, 427-28
Kennedy, John F., vi, 26, 59, 63-64, 105, 132, 144, 157, 182, 190, 205, 230, 281, 283, 311, 346, 393-94, 406, 424, 431-32, 435-37, 439-40, 443-45, 447-50, 454-57

Kennedy Round (*See* tariff negotiations)
Keynes, John M., 77, 346
Khrushchev, Nikita, 84, 86, 88, 95, 128, 206, 244-45, 260, 292, 329, 388-89, 400-02, 410, 412-16, 418-19, 422-24, 428, 446
Kissinger, Henry A., 26-28, 38, 43, 54, 100, 102, 168, 284, 405, 407, 463
Kleiman, Robert, 62-64, 431, 463
Knorr, Klaus, 23, 30-32, 35, 37, 58, 81-82, 89, 91, 93, 103, 149, 464
Kohn, Hans, 388, 393
Koran, 393
Korea, 168, 178, 201, 213, 295, 392
Korean War, 274, 339
Kostolany, André, 392
Krause, Lawrence B., 65-66, 73, 94, 303, 307, 314, 319, 321, 464
Kremlin (*See also* Moscow, USSR), v, 84, 93, 127, 199, 247, 261, 292, 388, 409, 418, 424-26, 428
Kutt, Aleksander, 420

— L —

Labor Party (Great Britain), 63, 155, 446
Latin America, 27, 44, 69, 108, 111, 292, 301, 334, 341, 399
Lebanon, 194, 317
Lemnitzer, Lyman L., 164, 167
Lenin, V. I., 138, 329, 400, 416
Leninism, 388, 428
Lerner, Max, 297-98
Liberation of Soviet satellites, 388, 406, 410
Lindsay, Kenneth, 403
Linebarger, Paul, 104-05
Lisbon, Portugal, 42, 50, 293
Lisbon Conference (1952), 345
Little Rock, Arkansas, 390
London (*See also* Great Britain), 294, 340, 444, 447
Lorimer, 365
Low Countries, 33, 457
Luxemburg, 113, 306

— M —

Machines Bull, 322
McCarthy, Mary Catherine, ix
McMahon Act, 53, 200-02, 209
Macmillan, Harold, 59, 186, 310, 435, 451
McNamara, Robert, 437
McNamara Doctrine, 192, 275
Maginot Line, 391, 398
Malaysia, 341
Malenkov, Georgi, 413
Manchester, England, 390
Mao Tse-tung, 105, 261, 329, 389
Marshall Plan, 105, 202, 219, 305, 382, 411, 430, 434, 440,
Martinique, 450
Marx, Karl, 329
Marxism, 300, 385, 388
Matsu, 194
May, Alan, 200-01
Mendershausen, H., 420
Michelin Company, 394
Miller, William Lee, 298
Mirage Planes, 171, 203, 322, 448
Mississippi, 367
Le Monde, 424
Mongolia, 415
Monnet, Jean, 145, 155, 210, 253-54, 283, 307, 435-36, 438-40, 343, 345-46, 355
Moore, James E., 40-42, 61, 161, 464
Morgenthau, Hans J., 24-26, 28, 44-45, 50, 88, 95, 115, 125, 464
Morocco, 139
Moscow, (*See also* Kremlin, U.S.S.R.), 41, 97, 105, 387-88, 402, 412, 415-16, 419-20, 424, 436, 448
Mosely, Philip E., 30-31, 37-38, 44, 97, 257, 464
Moslems, 368
Most favored nations principle, 311, 313, 321, 355, 383, 422; conditional, 325
Moulin, Leo, 393
Mozambique, 106, 291
Multilateral nuclear force (MLF), vi, 4-7, 15-16, 44-48, 50-51, 53-54, 56, 58, 61, 64, 103, 130, 145-46, 156, 159, 167-68, 189-91, 210, 246, 249-52, 254, 256-57, 263, 283-84, 296, 407, 437, 445, 455-56
Multinational nuclear force, 6, 54, 59-60, 209, 239, 249
Myrdal, Gunnar, 411

— N —

Nagy, Imre, 412-13, 427
Napoleon, 11
Nassau, 240, 249, 286, 310, 431, 437, 447, 453
Nationalism, 147, 306-07, 318, 330, 378, 392, 394-95, 397, 401, 426, 433
National Assembly of Hungary, 413
National Bureau of Economic Research, 365
National nuclear deterrents, 5-6, 23-25, 28, 38-40, 45, 48, 53-54, 132, 134, 166-67, 170, 204-05, 240, 243, 246, 250, 256, 258, 291, 435, 437, 447, 450, 454, 456
Nazism, 240, 392, 399, 424
Netherlands, 142, 189, 241, 306, 314, 316
Nehru, Jawaharlal, 396
New Economic Policy (NEP), 329
New York Times, 131, 426
New Zealand, 341
Nichols, Patrick, 121
Nolte, Ernst, 392
Norstad, Lauris, 52, 63, 170, 213, 436
North Atlantic Treaty (1949), 327, 378; Article I, 368, Article II, 345
NATO Ministerial Council, 437
NATO Parliamentarians' Conference, 300
North Korea, 415
North Vietnam, 415
Norway, 108, 141, 155, 293, 307
Nuclear control, 28, 45, 47, 60, 101, 106, 192, 200, 210, 220, 228, 234, 253-54, 282, 370; strategy, 45, 49, 52, 116, 140, 156, 161, 171, 199, 203, 217, 256, 283, 328, 398
Nuclear deterrence, 14-15, 29, 31-34, 40, 46, 104, 127, 131, 155, 176, 201, 204, 247, 298, 332, 391, 397, 433, 457
Nuclear pre-programming, 55, 233-34
Nuclear proliferation, 6, 14-15, 23, 26, 37-39, 45, 48, 50, 54, 57, 130-31, 134, 141, 156, 167, 228, 250, 269, 370, 435, 456
Nuclear technology, 29, 40, 43, 54-55, 153, 202, 213, 217, 228, 269
Nuclear Test Ban Treaty (*See also* disarmament), 101, 115, 146, 447, 449, 459
Nuclear trigger problem, 27-28, 39, 57, 127, 145, 170, 228, 230, 236, 268
Nuremberg trials, 367

— O —

O'Brien, William V., 28
Oder-Neisse frontier, 409
Omaha, Nebraska, 211, 455
Organization of American States (OAS), 137, 244, 299
Organization for European Economic Cooperation (OEEC) 288, 308, 317, 333, 345, 411, 438-39
Organization for Economic Cooperation and Development (OECD), 82, 91, 95, 112, 114, 119-20, 181, 288, 300-01, 317, 333, 337, 345, 438-41
Oregon, 295
Oslo, Norway, 293
Ostrava, Czechoslovakia, 413
Ottawa, Canada, 167, 191-92, 249, 255, 283-84
Oxford English Dictionary, 298

— P —

Pakistan, 348
Pan Africanism, 395
Panama, 109, 155
Pan American, 292
Paris, France, 62, 105, 194, 234, 298, 333, 395, 448-52, 455, 457
"Paris Club," 440-41, 456
Parliamentary assemblies, 193, 376, 403
Parliament of the European Community, 403
Partnership for Progress, 324
Paulskirche, 454
Peaceful coexistence, 329, 388, 423
Pearson, Lester, 11
Peking, China, 105, 138, 158, 286, 293, 387-88, 402, 414, 419, 448
Pericles, 11, 100
Philadelphia, Pennsylvania, 144, 288, 346, 432, 436
Pilsen, Czechoslovakia, 413
Plenary Session of Communist Party of CPSU, 416
Poland, 92, 343, 409, 412-15, 417, 420, 424, 426

Polaris, 310, 424, 431, 445, 447
Politique Etrangère, 409
Polycentrism, 92, 101, 288
Population growth, 78, 338, 362, 364-65; projections, 78, 338, 362-64
Portugal, 125, 139, 141-42, 226, 309, 333
Possony, Stefan T., 28, 31, 34, 36, 40-41, 54, 57, 60, 90, 114, 225, 464
Potsdam, 408
Prague, Czechoslovakia, 405, 424, 426
Pravda, 419
Prebisch, Paul, 341
Pure Theory of Politics, 388
Pyrenees, 263

— Q —

Quemoy, 194

— R —

Radford, Arthur, 60-61, 275
Rakosi regime, 399, 413
Ramerie, Louis, 419
Rapaki, Adam, 423; plan, 423-24
Rapallo, 428
Reciprocal Trade Agreements Act, 432
Reporter, 424
Reuss, Henry, 442
Roosa, Robert V., 337, 441
Rostow, Walt, W. 431
Rougemont, Denis de, 393
Ruge, Friedrich, 35, 42, 199, 465
Rumania, 89, 411-15, 417-19
Rusk, Dean, 62
Russell, Bertrand, 364

— S —

San Francisco, California, 429
Sanctions (*See* trade embargo)
Sarnoff, David, 364
Scandinavia, 178, 294, 309, 333
Schroeder, Gerhard, 446
Schuman, Robert, 145
Schwartz, Harry, 414
Scotland, 265, 295
Second-strike force, 36, 230
Shell Oil Company, 394
"Shield" forces, 28, 174, 206, 250, 437
Shub, Anatole, 426
Shulman, Marshall D., 421
Sicily, 295
Sino-Soviet bloc (*See* Communist bloc)
Sixth Congress of the Communist Party of Yugoslavia, 412
Skybolt, 309
Slessor, Sir John Cotesworth, 35-40, 43, 95, 117-18, 120, 239, 465
Sofia, Bulgaria, 424, 426
South Africa, 76, 303, 368
South America, 361
Southeast Asia, 27, 60, 116, 290
Southeast Asia Treaty Organization (SEATO), 137, 253
Sovereignty, 27, 29, 51, 55, 67, 103, 110-12, 114, 135, 137, 144-45, 161, 179, 181, 184, 262, 265-66, 268, 271-72, 288, 307-08, 330, 360, 370-71, 377-79, 396, 402, 416, 418-19, 438, 441, 459-60
Soviet strategy, military, 207; political, 406 (*See also* Kremlin, Moscow, U.S.S.R.)
Spaak, Paul-Henri, 195-96, 423-25, 427, 445
Spain, 85, 221, 263, 426
Stalin, Josef, 3, 127-28, 329, 360, 388-89, 406, 410-12, 414, 418, 426
Stewart, Alistair, 121
Stillman, Edmund O., 413
Stockholm, Sweden, 308
Stolte, Stefan C., 418, 420
Strategic Air Command (SAC) 64, 255, 437, 450, 455
Strausz-Hupé, Robert, 29-30, 53-54, 94, 96, 100, 103-04, 115, 120, 122, 135, 465
Streit, Clarence, 120, 383
Suez, 116, 127-29, 139, 178, 267, 286, 292, 297, 307, 366-67
Supranationalism, 51, 84, 117, 159, 180, 183, 185, 214, 297, 396, 416, 418-19, 460; institutions, 8-10, 86, 111, 115, 182, 377, 396, 403
Supreme Allied Command Europe (SACEUR), 16, 42, 46, 61, 64, 164-65, 167-69, 173-75, 188, 192, 203, 206, 250, 278, 280
Supreme Headquarters Allied Powers Europe (SHAPE), 47, 64, 163, 165, 167, 185, 191, 211, 252-53, 274, 280
Sweden, 266, 295, 303, 307, 316

Switzerland, 76, 121, 175, 208, 211, 295, 303, 307-08, 316, 333, 381, 440

— T —

Tactical nuclear weapons, 60-61, 121, 140, 150, 181, 189, 206, 277
Tariff negotiations, 7, 30, 65, 67, 70-73, 311-14, 318, 325, 348-49, 352, 375, 432, 445, 450, 456, 459
Taylor, Edmond, 423-24
Thermidor, 389
Third force, 100, 293, 307, 378, 435-36
Third World (*See also* underdeveloped areas), 7, 65, 77, 81, 216, 219, 378, 380-81, 384-85, 388, 391, 395
"Three Wise Men" report (1956), 286, 345
Times of London, 431
Tirana, Albania, 424
Tito, Marshal (Josip Broz), 411-14, 422
Togliatti, Palmiro, 422
Toma, Valentin, 419
Trade Act (1958), 442
Trade Agreements Legislation, 311
Trade expansion (*See also* East-West trade, Third World), 70, 72, 94, 109-10, 339; reciprocal liberalization, 78-79, 321, 325, 349-52, 373, 374-76, 382, 384, 442, 445; nonreciprocal liberalization, 79; strategic restrictions, 349, 383; embargo, 85, 94, 382
Trade Expansion Act (1962), 70, 180, 288, 311-12, 348-49, 351, 432, 441-42, 444
Trade Relations between the Common Market and the Eastern Bloc, 400
Treaty of Rome, 120, 179-80, 306, 308, 33, 376, 383
Triffin, Robert, 315
Truman, Harry S., 62, 200
Turkey, 54, 100, 111, 125, 139, 141, 166, 188, 195, 201, 226, 295, 333
Turks, 386
Tuthill, John 439
Twentieth Congress of the CPSU, 413
Two-key system, 47, 60

— U —

Ukraine, 136
Underdeveloped areas (*See also* Third World), 7, 68, 70, 78-81, 119, 317-18, 337-41, 343, 355, 361-64, 384, 389-90, 458-60
Unemployment, 7, 242, 315-17, 335-36
Unilever, 394
UNR, 454
United Fruit Company, 394
United Kingdom (*See also* Great Britain), 159, 162, 171, 180, 188, 192, 194-95, 316, 333, 346, 381
United Nations, 68-69, 295, 329, 341, 374
United Nations Charter, 367
UN Conference on Trade and Aid, 317-18, 322
UN National Security Council, 458
US Air Force, 437
US Armed Forces, 437
US Army, 437
US Congress, 311, 313, 327 439, 442, 456
US News & World Report, 400, 425, 439
USSR (*See also* Kremlin, Moscow), 13, 24, 32, 34, 37, 39, 53, 58-59, 76-77, 84, 86-96, 103-04, 115, 119, 125-31, 138, 143, 150, 153-54, 169, 171, 177, 187, 190, 195, 201, 205-06, 211-15, 226-27, 245, 247, 266-68, 275, 298, 303, 306, 317, 327, 337-40, 343, 360-61, 365, 383, 385, 394-95, 398-99, 406-30, 434-35, 446-47, 455, 459
Upanishad, 393
Uri, Pierre, 33, 36, 69, 73, 76, 78, 120-21, 322, 324, 345, 465
Uruguay, 301

— V —

V-bombers, 209, 447
Vienna, Austria, 295, 440
Vietnam, 103, 112, 293, 366, 389, 451
Volkswagen, 323

— W —

War planning, 28-29, 62
Warsaw, 424
Warsaw Pact, 4, 87, 101, 137, 199, 202, 213, 407, 410, 429
Wasowski, Stanislaw, 321, 465
Weimar Republic, 69
Western European Union (WEU) 213, 279-80, 310
West Germany, 31, 41, 48, 125, 131, 136, 144, 146, 151, 155, 159, 170-71, 173-74, 184-85, 187, 189, 205-

07, 210-11, 225, 252, 254-55, 268, 283, 292, 306, 314, 316-17, 333-34, 346, 356, 370, 375, 377, 406-08, 423, 425, 434, 442, 445-48, 450, 452, 455, 457
West German Bundestag, 453
West Irian, 395
Which? 325
Winston, Victor, 415
Wisconsin, 442
World Marxist Review, 416
World War I, 13, 28, 36, 110, 151, 287, 335, 375, 385
World War II, 17, 32, 36, 49, 69, 72, 110, 140, 151, 175, 287, 306, 335, 340, 367, 408, 433
Wszelaki, Jan, 411

— Y —

Yalta, 87, 408-10, 423, 425, 448
Yates, P. Lamartine, 324
Yugoslavia, 89, 343, 410, 422, 426

— Z —

Zanzibar, 389
Zauberman, Alfred, 415, 418, 422
Zollverein, 144

This book was designed and lithographed by Graphic Arts Press, Inc., Washington, D. C., in April, 1965. The paper was specially made for this publication. The typeface in the book is Times Roman.